For *la Patria*

For *la Patria*

Politics and the Armed Forces in Latin America

Brian Loveman

A Scholarly Resources Inc. Imprint
Wilmington, Delaware

First published 1999
Printed and bound in the United States of America

Scholarly Resources Inc.
104 Greenhill Avenue
Wilmington, DE 19805-1897

Cover
Photos from *Ejército de Chile: Testimonio y proyección de una vocación* (Santiago: Departamento Comunicacional del Ejército de Chile, 1997), pp. 44 (back cover) and 61 (front cover). Reproduced courtesy of the Departamento Comunicacional del Ejército de Chile.

Library of Congress Cataloging-in-Publication Data

Loveman, Brian.
For la Patria : politics and the armed forces in Latin America / Brian Loveman.
p. cm. — (Latin American silhouettes)
Includes bibliographical references and index.
ISBN 0-8420-2772-6 (alk. paper). — ISBN 0-8420-2773-4 (pbk. : alk. paper)
1. Civil-military relations—Latin America. 2. Latin America—Armed Forces—Political activity. 3. Patriotism—Latin America. 4. Latin America—Politics and government—1830–1948. 5. Latin America—Politics and government—1948– . I. Title. II. Series.
JL956.C58L68 1998
322′.5′098—dc21 98-7793
CIP

♾ The paper used in this publication meets the minimum requirements of the American National Standard for permanence of paper for printed library materials, Z39.48, 1984.

For Sharon and la patria chica

About the Author

Brian Loveman is professor of political science at San Diego State University. He has written extensively on civil-military relations in Latin America, Latin American politics, and inter-American relations. His book *Chile: The Legacy of Hispanic Capitalism* (2d ed., 1988) is the most widely read history of Chile in English and his *Constitution of Tyranny: Regimes of Exception in Spanish America* (1993) received the Hubert Herring Prize for best work on Latin America in 1995. Two co-edited volumes with Thomas M. Davies, Jr., have been widely adopted as texts in universities in the United States: *The Politics of Antipolitics: The Military in Latin America* (3d ed., 1997), and *Che Guevara, Guerrilla Warfare* (3d ed., 1998). Professor Loveman is currently working on a two-volume history of political conflict and the politics of reconciliation in Chile with Chilean psychologist Elizabeth Lira. He is married to Sharon Loveman and has five children.

Acknowledgments

It is impossible to teach about Latin American politics without focusing on the armed forces. More than twenty years ago my dear friend and colleague, Thomas M. Davies, Jr., asked me to join him in researching and writing about Latin American military institutions. We edited two books together on military topics, both now in their third editions, and have shared years of conversation, banter, and seminars. While I have written *For la Patria*, Tom's inspiration, wit, and intensity are in every chapter.

Generous colleagues have read all or part of the manuscript and made numerous suggestions for improvements. I usually took their advice but now cannot properly cite their particular contributions. They include Carlos Acuña, Felipe Agüero, Charles Andrain, William Beezley, Mark Burkholder, Paul Drake, Judith Ewell, J. Samuel Fitch, Gonzalo Palacios, Iván Jaksić, Lyman Johnson, Elizabeth Lira, Mara Loveman, John Martz, Patrice McSherry, Tommie Sue Montgomery, Deborah Norden, Frederick Nunn, Antonio Palá, David Scott Palmer, David Pion-Berlin, Marcial Antonio Riquelme, Frank Safford, Lars Schoultz, and Augusto Varas. In addition to reading various drafts of the manuscript and providing valuable suggestions, Elizabeth Lira generously assisted in collecting photographs and other material reproduced in the book. She has also been an inspiration at every stage of thinking about and writing this book. At Scholarly Resources, Richard Hopper, Carolyn Travers, Ann M. Aydelotte, Sharon L. Beck, and Linda Pote Musumeci have been consistently encouraging and patient. This is the third book on which I have been privileged to have their help.

Students at San Diego State University in undergraduate courses on political change in Latin America and in seminars on the military have "tested" the manuscript and helped me to improve it for classroom use. To them I am indebted for their patience with rough drafts. Special mention must go to Major Douglas Keepper and Captain Joe Lontus (U.S. Army) for their comments as students of civil-military relations and also as informal consultants regarding the manuscript. Thomas Reichart, a talented future historian of Latin America, carefully assisted in preparing the bibliography and editing the notes.

Contents

Introduction: Armed Forces, Militarylore, and *la Patria,* **xi**

1 The Iberian Military Tradition: From the Kingdoms of *las Españas* to *la Patria,* **1**

2 Inventing *la Patria*: Wars, *Caudillismo,* and Politics, 1810–1885, **27**

3 Foreign Military Missions and *la Patria,* **63**

4 Variations on Patriotic Themes: *La Patria* and the Armed Forces from the Great Depression to the Cold War, **101**

5 *La Patria* and the Cold War: From Pearl Harbor to the Bay of Pigs, **139**

6 *La Patria* and the Cold War: From the Bay of Pigs to the Gulf of Fonseca, **165**

7 *La Patria,* Regional Security, and "Democracy," **195**

8 *La Patria,* the Armed Forces, and Human Rights, **227**

9 *La Patria* and *Perestroika*: Toward the Twenty-first Century, **253**

Glossary, **287**

Bibliography, **291**

Index, **323**

Introduction: Armed Forces, Militarylore, and *la Patria*

> When *la patria* is threatened, everything is licit, except allowing it to perish.
>
> —José de San Martín

> Necessity recognizes no laws.
>
> —Simón Bolívar

> First we'll kill all the subversives. Then we'll kill the collaborators, then the sympathizers, then the undecided. And finally, we'll kill the indifferent.
>
> —General Ibérico Saint-Jean, Argentina, 1977

Defending *la patria* (the nation, or fatherland) against internal and external threats is the historical mission claimed by Latin American armed forces. This mission, according to the region's militarylore, is inherent in human nature and in the nature of modern nation-states.[1] The threats facing *la patria* and the identity of its enemies may change, but the armed forces' basic role—national defense and security—is immutable. Ask Argentine General Aníbal Ulises Laiño, who wrote in 1996:

> From their origins nation-states have had to confront a vast range of conflicts, both interstate and intrastate. Conflict is inherent in human nature, and this persists everywhere on the planet, despite the ideas of idealistic theorists. . . .
>
> The need for armed forces results from the very existence of the State. There are armed forces because there are sovereignty, territory, life, decisions, plans, resources, etc., to preserve, and it is through its military instruments that a State exercises its monopoly on legitimate violence, to meet whatever challenge might threaten its character as a sovereign political entity.[2]

General Laiño's words reflect the accumulated wisdom and shared perceptions of generations of military officers.[3] Such words, and the military credo they express, have justified a pervasive military influence in Latin American politics since the early nineteenth century. But how did General Laiño and most of his fellow officers come to share this definition of the armed forces' central role in politics and of a world in which *la patria* is perpetually menaced by threats to sovereignty and security? Why does *la patria* eternally confront "potentially critical situations" against which it must be defended by the armed forces? This book attempts to answer these questions and to relate the political consequences of actions based on the premises of Latin American militarylore and of the military version of patriotism.

As a political referent, Latin America includes Brazil, Haiti, and the Spanish-speaking republics south of the Río Grande. These republics share certain historical, cultural, and institutional attributes, but there also exists tremendous diversity among them. There is no real "Latin America." The term was popularized in the midnineteenth century as a result of French cultural and political influences.[4] None of the nations of Latin America was part of the Roman Empire, none has Latin as its official language, and most of the region's nations have predominantly non-European populations. The diversity of Latin America necessarily makes interpretation of the political role of the armed forces a constant balancing between regional generalizations and analyses of national histories. Case studies and comparative analysis as well as awareness of national idiosyncrasies and of subregional and regional commonalities are necessary to understand the political role of Latin American military institutions.

Latin American civil-military relations and the role of the armed forces in politics, like those of all modern nation-states, are framed by constitutional and legal norms specifying the formal relationships between the armed forces and the rest of society. In practice, they are also the result of expectations, attitudes, values, and actions evolved over centuries—integral aspects of national political cultures. In Spanish America and Brazil these include the military tradition of Iberia (and therefore many Roman legal and institutional traditions) as well as the legacy of Spanish and Portuguese colonialism into the nineteenth century.[5] The region also shares the basic features of modern military institutions and the premises of civil-military relations that developed simultaneously with the rise of the modern nation-state in Europe. Until the 1930s the major foreign influences on the Latin American armed forces came from Europe, especially Spain, France, and Germany, with some British impact on certain navies. During and after World War II, U.S. military doctrine, arms, equipment, and presence greatly increased as military missions covered Latin America and its army personnel trained in U.S. facilities. Thus, Latin American military institutions have blended local histories with a complex composite heritage of imported martial law, codes, doctrine, technology, and militarylore from medieval and imperial Spain, nationalistic nineteenth-century Europe, and the post-1930s United States. Military institutions in each Latin American nation blend local and imported influences, thus developing a distinctive pattern of civil-military relations.

Notwithstanding these distinct national modes of civil-military relations, all of the imported European and U.S. militarylore and constitutional traditions postulate civilian control over the military's institutions and its accountability to legally constituted governments. But the meaning of "civilian control" differs among political systems, and the institutional arrangements devised to establish this control vary significantly. Despite extensive global variety in political ideologies and regimes, no twentieth-century political system has formally vested sovereign authority in military institutions. The underlying political premise is always that the armed forces are instruments of sovereign authorities, not themselves the reservoirs of sovereignty.

Since 1945, however, military *juntas* have governed many nations. In most other nation-states the armed forces have exercised considerable political influence. Implementing the norm of military subordination to legally constituted governments as practice has been the exception rather than the rule in much of the world. Even where military subordination is taken for granted, as in the United States and most of Western Europe, periodic incidents of contention or even apparent insubordination put policymakers on notice that the meaning of "civilian control" is not always unambiguous. In Latin America, military leaders and institutions have exercised great influence in politics since the end of World War II.

The relationships and overlapping roles among military institutions, civilian government policymakers, and the rest of society are the core issue of civil-military relations and a central challenge to the creation and maintenance of democratic polities in Latin America as well as elsewhere. These relationships involve dynamic interactions among various groups, conditioned by domestic and global circumstances. The armed forces are both part of society and apart from it. They evolve with society and with government institutions, sometimes taking leading roles in politics and policymaking and at other times taking less visible, more subordinate roles. In some policy areas, such as defense planning and intelligence, foreign relations, certain types of scientific research, disaster relief, and civil defense, military institutions routinely and legitimately exercise significant influence. Their participation in policymaking and implementation is expected. And this list of routine and legitimate areas varies considerably from country to country and over time within countries.

The notion that the "final say" in decision making rests with the legally constituted government does not preclude participation by military institutions in many areas of policymaking beyond narrowly construed "military" missions. Indeed, constitutions, legislation, and evolved practice may assign to the armed forces, both implicitly and explicitly, authority and responsibility for many tasks. Constitutions and laws may also assign to them several political guardianship functions: upholding the constitution, maintaining law and order, and the overall tutelage of the nation's sovereignty. This has been the common practice in Latin America since independence.

Four key questions regarding civil-military relations may be asked: Who decides, and through what procedures, what the armed forces' functions will be? When and how are their missions carried out? What is the relative autonomy of the armed forces (or, conversely, the extent of civilian oversight and supervision) on professional and institutional matters such as military education, career systems, promotions, retirements, budget expenditures, deployments, and tactics? And what occurs when there are disagreements between and among military and civilian officials on interpretations of the military's constitutional role, legal authority, and participation in policymaking and implementation? Often these issues are summarized as "subordination" to civilian authority versus varying degrees of military autonomy, co-government, or even "insubordination" and predominance over civilian government officials. But this characterization of civil-military relations is overly simplistic, except in clear clashes of will and direct confrontations over policy or the survival of incumbent governments. Usually there is little public debate on these questions; routine, inertia, and lack of controversy prevail except when scandals, socioeconomic crises, and political polarization bring civil-military relations to the forefront of popular concern. Military officers invariably recognize publicly their subordination to civilian officials, except when civilians are perceived to have exceeded their authority or put at risk national values, interests, and security that the armed forces are sworn to defend or when civilian factions urge the armed forces to resolve conflicts that the civilian political system has failed to settle. The military acts when the judgment is made that governments have put *la patria* at risk. By the time this judgment is made public, the military coup-makers commonly have the support of some key civilian groups, or even of a majority of the civilian population, although this support may not be sustained after the incumbent government is ousted.

Who decides that *la patria* is threatened—the nature of the threat, the proper remedial action, and on what basis—is crucial. Whether weak or strong, preconditions and predispositions for irregular military intervention (rather than routine influence), coups, and governance exist almost everywhere.[6] They are usually overridden by political, institutional, cultural, and professional inhibitions. Yet sometimes, more frequently in some countries than in others, the inhibitors fail and military rule, whether brief or prolonged, ensues. In most of Latin America the premise that elements within the armed forces may decide that threats to *la patria* exist, and that the threats warrant military intervention to contain or eradicate them, is an integral part of militarylore. It is also a premise shared by many civilian groups, based on constitutional and legal norms and historical experience. The armed forces' role as "guardians" in a system of "protected democracy" is thus part of Latin American political culture and is not restricted to the military subculture and militarylore. This premise is more embedded in the political culture and experience of some Latin American nations than others, but almost nowhere entirely absent.

The character of civil-military relations, and the relative strength and influence of military institutions in politics and policymaking, depends greatly on the development of civilian political institutions and the commitment of most groups in society to a shared political vision.[7] When civilian political institutions are weak, when underlying consensus on the legitimacy of political institutions is absent or fragile, and when nations are polarized along ideological, ethnic, religious, and cultural lines, military institutions tend to play a more direct role and to exercise broader policymaking prerogatives.[8] Routine military influence and participation in policymaking, whatever the degree of autonomy in professional matters, are not inconsistent with military subordination to civilian authority and to constitutional government. Lack of expertise and even disinterest often limit the effectiveness of civilian policymakers regarding national defense, security, and related matters. Indeed, elected civilian officials in most democratic regimes regularly consult with military advisers on security and defense policies, legitimating their decisions (especially controversial decisions) by referring to the fact that they are based on such consultation with the military "experts."

Civil-military crises may occur when officers question publicly government definitions of the national interest and security policy, but even such political insubordination does not necessarily imply challenges to the legitimacy of civilian government authority. Policy differences rarely, by themselves, provoke military coups. Even such coups and direct rule by military governments are not the equivalent of asserting that sovereignty is (or ought to be) vested in military institutions and that military domination over society is legitimate as a permanent political formula. These coups usually occur as a result of complex processes that culminate when endemic socioeconomic and political tensions are compounded by "triggering" events ranging from economic crises and extreme political polarization to public drunkenness on the part of the nation's president or the breakdown of law and order. Direct, overt threats of intervention and coups invariably question the legitimacy of the incumbent government's authority, the manner of its exercise (asserting, for example, unconstitutional or illegal behavior by the president and other government officials), and sometimes of the political regime itself. Whatever the triggering event, leaders of military coups and their civilian allies usually justify their apparent breach of discipline and subordination to civilian authority as responses to government illegitimacy and inefficacy that imperil *la patria*, not as claims that the armed forces have permanently assumed the role of sovereign. In any case, military rule must be distinguished from rule by a particular military officer who comes to power through a coup and then personalizes an authoritarian dictatorship. The distinction may be more or less subtle, but there are important differences between rule by military institutions via *juntas* that make public policy, with more or less equal collaboration in defense ministries and public administration, and the governments of such figures as Juan Perón in Argentina, Gustavo Rojas Pinilla in Colombia, or the Caribbean dictators of the 1930s to 1950s, such as Rafael Trujillo in the Dominican Republic and Fulgencio Batista in Cuba.

An expanded policy role for the military or direct intervention may be justified, by both military and civilian leaders, as temporarily necessary to confront crises, or for sundry other reasons, but not as a permanent substitute for the exercise of popular sovereignty. Thus, *junta* members almost always mention elections, in the however distant future, to restore "democracy," even as they assume political power. Permanent martial rule is rarely, if ever, desired or proposed by military or civilian elites even in cases of extreme political crisis. Military leaders do not conceive of their institutions as appropriate instruments for permanent governance of society. They have, however, often found constitutional, legal, and situational rationales for temporary military rule and political "salvation" of nations that they perceive menaced by external and internal threats. Temporary military rule is justified by "necessity," by the armed forces' role as guardians of the nation's destiny, by their historical identity with the nation in its creation and formation, and by their undeclinable mission (*misión indeclinable*) as the ultimate bastion of their nation's sovereignty. *La patria*, its "way of life," its sovereignty, and its destiny are the armed forces' special mission.[9]

Recurrent military intervention and institutionalized political guardianship, of course, impede the development of strong, independent legislative and judicial institutions, of effective political parties and electoral systems, of autonomous local and regional voluntary associations, and of free and critical mass media. They undermine the evolution of a civilian political culture that effectively immunizes the body politic against the militarization of politics and of a military subculture that shares the commitment to principled subordination to civilian authority.

Endemic invocation and ostentatious practice of military guardianship are both a cause and the result of weak governments and weak civil societies. Contrarily, the evolution of strong political institutions and of deeply embedded social norms proscribing overt military intervention and insubordination increases the disposition of military officers to obey civilian officials. It also decreases their disposition to openly contest government decisions.[10] Over time, strong civilian institutions and effective government encourage transmission of norms in military schools and academies that emphasize narrower boundaries for "proper" military influence and action in public affairs. But military subordination to incumbent governments is never unconditional; unconstitutional, illegal, or otherwise illegitimate government behavior raises the issue of obedience versus insubordination. Political, cultural, institutional, and conjunctural thresholds for overt insubordination may vary greatly, but no system of civil-military relations is entirely immune from rupture.

Implementing the norm of military subordination to civilian authority takes time, effective political and military leadership, constitutional and legal underpinnings, military education systems, and *fortuna*. Even then, subordination is never absolute or irreversible. Areas of political and institutional contestation always remain; they may be exacerbated by domestic and international conflicts.[11]

In much of Latin America, military participation in politics, policymaking, and a host of nonmilitary functions is expected. The constitutional and statutory definitions of the armed forces' missions, a lack of underlying consensus on the legitimacy of political institutions, weak civilian governments and political party systems, and the historical weight of iterated military intervention have made the armed forces key political actors. In some countries, such as Argentina, Bolivia, Peru, Ecuador, El Salvador, Honduras, and Guatemala, they have dominated politics and government for much of the twentieth century. In others, such as Chile, Brazil, and Uruguay, they have intervened directly at critical moments to reshape their nation's histories.

This "monumental fact" of Latin American politics does not make future coups and military governments inevitable, but it certainly makes unlikely a quick, easy end to extensive military influence in politics. Civilian politicians, political parties, interest groups, and the general population all recognize this fact. With significant variation from country to country, they seek alliances with, and reassurances from, military leaders to achieve their own ends. Moreover, they implicitly accept military review and prior veto of certain policies, thus reinforcing the historical and constitutional role of the armed forces as guardians of national destiny.

Civil-military relations occur not just between "civilians" and "the military" but also among competing civilian interests and military elites divided over policy and their nation's future. Civilians call on the military for expertise, legitimacy, and power to support their own interests; military factions seek civilian allies for their own institutional and policy objectives. Sometimes civilian groups and movements push the military to bare their sabers, or threaten to bare them, as part of an escalating political bargaining process. Sometimes civilians virtually plead for military coups, with the expectation that after "saving" *la patria* the armed forces will allow the "outs" to replace the deposed government. At other times such civil-military alliances lead to military governments but rarely without some civilian participation. These governments typically use civilian officials and advisers and often come to power with substantial social support. Thus, the military coups in Brazil (1964), Peru (1968), Chile (1973), Uruguay (1973), and Argentina (1976) were initially acclaimed by many civilians, although human rights violations and other unpopular policies later lost support for the new regimes.

Despite this complexity, there is general consensus among military elites that defending their nation against external and internal enemies is their primordial historical mission—a mission legitimated by tradition, by historical myths, and by professional education for officers in military schools and academies. It is also stated explicitly in constitutions, statutes, and military codes.[12] Uruguayan Colonel Sergio H. Caubarrere put the matter simply in 1996, proclaiming that "the military profession develops within a constitutional and legal frame that defines its mission and demarcates the cultural norms that governs its conduct. In Uruguayan law the fundamental mission of the armed forces is to defend the Republic's honor, independence, peace, territorial integrity, constitution, and laws. . . . they should also support and take as their task whatever development plans are assigned by political authorities."[13]

Defending *la patria* requires the construction of deterrent capabilities to dissuade potential enemies and aggressors as well as intelligence operations to ferret out emergent, existing, and clandestine threats. When necessary it requires the use of violence to repress or destroy those who threaten the nation's sovereignty, interests, values, or security. Those who so threaten *la patria* are defined as enemies, either foreign or domestic. They may be other nation-states, nonstate actors such as international political movements (for example, communism), terrorists, drug cartels, or domestic supporters of menacing ideologies or demands. Culturally subversive art, movies, and music, heretical ideas, and disrespectful behavior such as flag burning may also be viewed as potential threats to *la patria* requiring military surveillance and suppression. This search for what General Laiño labels "potentially critical situations" mimics and updates the restored Spanish Inquisition's war against heresy, immorality, and other subversions of the colonial sociopolitical order (the Bourbon imperial *patria*) in the late eighteenth and early nineteenth centuries.

But what is *la patria*? To this question there are many answers. It is a fusion of territorial, racial, ethnic, cultural, and political myths whose conservation and defense demand the ultimate loyalty and sacrifice. An "imagined community,"[14] *la patria* is also "a living soul, a spiritual principle . . . a moral consciousness [defined by] the common possession of a rich heritage of memories."[15] *La patria*, as nation, originated in sixteenth-century England and took on diverse meanings (sovereign people, sovereign nation-state) with political regimes such as absolute monarchies, constitutional monarchies, and liberal-republican polities.[16] According to Anthony Smith, a nation is "a named community of history and culture, possessing a unified territory, economy, mass education, and common legal rights. . . . the nation is not a once-and-for-all,

all-or-nothing concept; . . . historical nations are ongoing processes, sometimes slow in their formation, at other times faster, often jagged and discontinuous, as some features emerge or are created, while others lag."[17]

The nation is an imagined, invented, deliberately constructed, and also, in part, "natural" core of networks of loyalties and associations that permit some degree of political identity and unity. After the outbreak of the French Revolution in 1789, wars and inspired political leadership forged some nations into nation-states; in the nineteenth century these became the basic components in international politics. When military officers referred to *la patria* they usually meant the nation-state, with associated (if disputed) territorial, cultural, and historical identities. Sometimes *la patria* was a "fatherland," other times a "motherland" (*madre-patria*), and still other times a biological metaphor for a precious mystical organism that required compliance from its human components. Whatever the particular version of nation, when organized as a nation-state it claimed the ultimate loyalty of its citizens/subjects.[18]

By the time Argentines fought for independence from Spain, the great Creole patriot (and former Spanish military officer) José de San Martín proclaimed that "in the name of *la patria*, all is licit." Similarly, for Latin American military officers at the end of the twentieth century, nationalism and patriotism meant "love for *la patria*, devotion to its soil and all its traditions, and a permanent preoccupation for its defense and integrity. Conserving *la patria* (its frontiers) is a fundamental task of the Armed Forces and maintaining its internal equilibrium (order and security) is the first priority, since *la patria* is an entity of destiny that begins in the home and the school and projects itself to society."[19] Indeed, *la patria* is an "entity of destiny," sacred, eternal, and transcendent. Yet revolutions, whether slow and imperceptible or quick and violent, transform societies and their cherished constructed identities. Nation-states come and go, their configuration changes, their destiny is redefined. Since 1789 overt revolutionary movements have typically been instigated in the name of "the people" of a nation— a *patria* to be cleansed of evil and oppression, resurrected, (re)united, and made glorious. Whether to conserve by resisting violently the present's transgressions of the eternal *patria*, or to transform by violently overturning the present's violation of the *patria*'s essence, coups d'état,[20] rebellions, and revolutions are precipitated by calls to right previous wrongs, to impose justice, dignity, honor, and patriotic virtue, and sometimes to construct a new nation (*patria nueva*). *La patria* survives, its destiny and transcendence assured through reaffirmation of nationality and patriotism, even when in practice this means their redefinition.

Thus, *la patria* is both eternal and ever changing. This seeming contradiction and the ongoing conflict over its territorial, ethnic, linguistic, cultural, and institutional identity frame its domestic politics and shape its international relations. Military officers, as guardians of the mythically eternal, are virtually secular priests of *la patria*. They are inevitably biased arbiters of the legitimacy of efforts to alter its normative and institutional identity. This role makes officers key actors in politics, although they claim to be above politics—that is, partisan politics.

What more difficult mission is there than being "above politics" while conserving the essential values and interests of an eternal nation inevitably subject to internal and external pressures for change? What more political mission is there than protecting (in part by redefining) the permanent and transcendental national interests of dynamic, complex, variegated, and permeable social organisms called *la patria*? As the military collaborates in defining *la patria* and its transcendental interests, it engages in redefining the current meaning of the nation's past, of patriotism, and national interests. And its sacred temples, the military schools and academies, instill an updated patriotic-antipolitical credo in the new officer generations in the quest to protect and conserve *la patria*.

Writing in 1916, Mexico's foremost archaeologist, Manuel Gamio, noted that his country, lacking a common language, a common character, a homogeneous race, and a shared history, did not yet form a true nation.[21] The Indian communities comprised hundreds of *patrias chicas* that did not participate in national life. If this was true of Mexico, what of Guatemala, El Salvador, Honduras, Bolivia, Ecuador, and Peru? And Brazil and Cuba, with recently freed slaves? Or Chile, Argentina, Colombia, and Venezuela, with their vast rural *casta* and mestizo populations, illiterate, impoverished, and unconnected with modern notions of nation and nation-state? Gamio referred to *pequeñas patrias* (little nations)—the Aztec, Maya-Kiché, and Inca, among others, who might have come to form a "great indigenous *patria*," as occurred in China and Japan, had it not been for Christopher Columbus and the Europeans who followed.[22] He claimed that the grand aim of the 1910 Mexican Revolution was to create a "powerful *patria* and a coherent defined nationality."[23]

Where in Latin America did such a *patria* exist? How could the armed forces embody and defend a *patria* still unforged? With Indian majorities in much of South America and Afro-American majorities or significant minorities in Brazil and much of Central America and the Caribbean, how could a European notion of nation and the even more recent, or rediscovered, political invention, the republic, serve as the ultimate object of loyalty and identity? Gamio saw in the Mexican Revolution a chance to create a new nation "in which Indian and European could be forged together on the miraculous anvil of the *patria nueva*, a blend of iron and bronze. There is the iron. . . . There the bronze. . . . Strike, brothers! (¡*Batid, hermanos*!)"[24]

Generations of rebels, revolutionaries, loyalists, military coup-makers, and *juntas* shared this dream of a "new *patria*" from the 1820s. For the first hundred years after independence, however, with few exceptions, there did not exist in Latin America what Gamio called the "inherent characteristics of a defined and integrated nationality, nor a single feeling of, or consensual concept of, what was *la patria*." There existed instead many *pequeñas patrias* and local nationalisms.[25] No matter. The post-independence constitutions affirmed the existence of nations and nation-states. At first, large federations and confederations, doomed by geography, poor communication and transportation systems, and political rivalries, emerged in Central America and northern South America. The Bolivarian dream was smashed; there would be no grandiose Spanish-American republics to counterbalance the threat of U.S. hemispheric hegemony. Those for whom *la patria* meant *nuestra América*—that is, Hispano-America—would have to settle for European definitions of nationalism and nation-states in the forging of Ibero-American *patrias*.[26] Uruguayan essayist and philosopher José Enrique Rodó's nostalgic Hispanicism and anti-Anglo abstractions of the early twentieth century had long been superseded by regional wars, invented nationalisms, and more territorially delimited, if mythical, *patrias* by the time he published his short essay, "El concepto de la patria" (1906), in which he wrote: "*Patria* is, for Hispanic Americans, Spanish America. Within the meaning of *patria* also is included the no less natural and indestructible feeling of belonging to a province, a region, or locality [*comarca*]; and provinces, regions, or localities of that great common *patria* are the nations in which it has been politically divided. . . . the dream of Bolívar is still a dream."[27]

Regional disintegration, war, boundary disputes, political intrigue, and *fortuna* left Latin America as a region of Spanish-speaking republics, Brazil, and Haiti. By the beginning of the twentieth century, with Cuba's separation from Spain and Panama's from Colombia, the term *patria* generally referred (for political elites and Spanish- or Portuguese-speaking "nationals") to these territorial states, despite the persistence of more poetic, romantic, and abstract usages. Rodó's own literary and spiritual resurrection of the grander Hispanic American *patria*, was itself partly a philosophical response to U.S. interventions in Cuba and Panama. Thus, he called on Spanish America "to maintain the continuity of its history and the fundamental originality of its race, beyond the conventional frontiers that divide it in nations . . . including Panama, which an international policy of usurpation and plunder has torn from its [Latin America's] mangled entrails."[28]

Everywhere armed forces (but rarely national armies) played a central role in creating and defining these territorial states. They also lamented, with civilian nationalists, the lack of real nations for want of common racial, linguistic, and cultural foundations. Particularly in the late nineteenth and early twentieth centuries, they sought to forge such nations (as they imagined had been done in England, France, Germany, Italy, and Japan) even as they assumed a more permanent role as guardians of *la patria*'s territory, security, internal order, government, and cultural symbols. Creating modern, professional armed forces, often with the assistance of contracted European officers or full-scale military missions, coincided with redefinitions of citizenship, patriotism, and *la patria*. In part, the crusade for obligatory military service that swept Latin America in the early twentieth century responded to the dream that Indians, peasants, and former slaves—the majority of the region's peoples—could be made into citizens, genuine members of *la patria*'s family. In this mission, the barracks would be the school of patriotism and citizenship, the armed forces the soldier-technocrats engineering an integrated nation.

As guardians of national sovereignty and security, the Latin American armed forces did not "intervene" in politics. They became, in effect, a fourth branch of government or better, a supragovernmental tutelary elite carrying out both the quasi-religious role of secular priests and the constitutional and statutory roles assigned to them when Spanish American colonies and Brazil gained their independence. Their participation and influence in politics had clear historical, constitutional, and legal foundations. They also claimed an historically legitimated supraconstitutional authority to guard vigilantly the survival of the state (*velar por la supervivencia del estado*), a mythic-foundational connection to *la patria*. In this sense, they retain a residual duty in the name of the nation and its fictionally integrated peoples that obligates them to prevent governments of the moment, elected or not, from sacrificing the invented and engineered nation's supposed permanent interests to short-term political and economic exigencies.

According to this view, the armed forces preceded, and then created, *la patria* in glorious struggles for independence, defended it against internal and foreign enemies, and became the reservoir of nationalism and patriotism. They form the spinal column of the nation; they are the nation-in-arms. These ideas, in their particular national versions, are shared by military officers and taught to their troops from the Río Grande to the Straits of Magellan. Some civilians may find them exaggerated, corny, unsophisticated, cynical, or self-serving. For the officers, and for some civilians, they are self-evident truths, part of a glorious martial heritage that began with the seven-hundred-year reconquest of Spain from the Moors (711 A.D.–1492) and continued with fifteenth- and sixteenth-century Spanish and Portuguese conquests in the Western Hemisphere and the creation of global empires that endured until the 1820s.[29]

These truths are inspired partly by the military traditions and values of Iberian imperialism, partly by Papal sanction for conquest and subordination of infidels and Indians, partly by the legacy of the military's role in nineteenth-century nation-building, and also by the imported lessons of European (mainly German and French) military professionalism. They are matters of faith and doctrine, legitimizing and sanctifying military institutions. They make even symbolic attacks on the armed forces a threat to nationality and national security.

To understand the self-concept and political role of the Spanish American and Brazilian militaries in the twentieth century requires reconstructing the ideological, doctrinal, legal, and mythic contributions of Iberian colonialism and nineteenth-century militarism to the foundations of modern military institutions. Latin American military professionals premise their values, beliefs, careers, nationalist sentiments, and institutional identities on real, imagined, and invented histories of glory and sacrifice. For these officers the past lives in the present, legitimates and obligates current action, motivates salvation of the eternally reborn *patria*'s future from temptations and threats of all sort. These sentiments are aptly captured by El Salvador's Lieutenant Colonel Mariano Castro Morán, writing in the early 1980s: "In the process of creating nationality, in all epochs of the history of peoples, the ultimate and decisive stage is the formation of national armies, or, in modern times, the institutionalization of national armed forces. . . . Here in El Salvador, the National Army was created in the dawn of the Republic. . . . In effect, the history of our country in the nineteenth century is nothing more than the history of our men in uniform who created and reformed laws and institutions in the fields of culture and liberal, democratic humanism."[30] Born with the nation, the armed forces must be strong for the nation to be strong, ever alert for the nation to avert internal and external threats. Preventing governments from forgetting, neglecting, or attacking the permanent national interests is the armed forces' moral and legal duty as "the carnal, concrete, living expression of *la patria*, whose mission is the defense of unity, of integrity, and of honor, as well as of everything essential and permanent in the country."[31]

Executing this mission requires constant planning, training, modernization of forces and weapons, and development of operational and intelligence capabilities to detect potential and actual dangers, or what Argentina's General Laiño calls *situaciones potencialmente críticas* (SPOCs).[32] When discovered, such threats must be eliminated. Of course, this mission also depends on the current definition of *la patria*'s "eternal" destiny and its national interests.[33] The armed forces' roles as custodians of this destiny, presumedly above politics, and as its protectors against the excesses, opportunism, and corruption of politicians make them quintessentially political! As political arbiters, the symbol and embodiment of patriotism, and national totems, the armed forces strongly influence the content of an acceptable definition of *la patria*'s immediate interests—that is, the present's (re)definition of its eternal values and security.[34]

Basic to this recurrent definition of the nation's eternal values and interests is the notion of sovereignty. The nation-state is not realized without "sovereignty." Problematically, sovereignty is essentially an impossible dream and juridical fiction of international relations—even more so for economically, politically, and militarily weak nations. Even approximating the virtually absolute and exclusive exercise of authority over a demarcated territory and population (that is, sovereignty) was an illusion for most Latin American countries in the nineteenth century and has become explicitly more problematical at the end of the twentieth. Yet in accord with this delusionary, if powerful, concept, the Latin American military (like others around the world) seeks to ensure that the state may exercise, without restriction, full sovereignty over its inhabitants, territory, and fundamental principles, permitting it to attain its historical aspirations. If the armed forces see political and social conflict threatening the nation, they must use the force they judge appropriate to eliminate the threat. Their mission "transcends governments, groups, and persons, responding only to the permanent interests of the nation, where the principle of National Security predominates over all others."[35]

In short, the armed forces identify themselves as the ultimate custodians of patriotism, nationalism, and the nation itself. They are the nation's permanent guardians—and its saviors when required. In the words of Peru's General and former President Francisco Morales Bermúdez, "in a democratic system . . . the participation of the armed forces in [resolving] the great issues is necessary because they form part of the national being (*ser nacional*)."[36] Similarly, retired Honduran General Walter López Reyes wrote in 1993 that "military institutions would defend the country from any attempt to destroy the permanent and transcendent values of *hondureñidad*."[37]

According to this part of the military ethos and militarylore, no policies or measures adopted by transitory governments, either constitutional or de facto, can be allowed to subvert the nation's permanent interests and security. Neglecting the armed forces' resource requirements, offending their honor, attacking their prerogatives or authority—indeed, any weakening of the military institutions—might constitute a threat to *la patria*. The armed forces must respond to perceived internal and external threats to national security, whether these are strictly military, socioeconomic, or even psychological, to fulfill their historical and constitutional mission.

The military's current definition and understanding of its historical, constitutional, and statutory missions, frames and defines their role in Latin American politics. At the same time, the military must reconcile these missions with the language borrowed from the French revolutionaries after 1789 and inserted into most nineteenth-century constitutions that define the armed forces as "nondeliberative" and subordinate to civilian authority. Most nineteenth-century Latin American constitutions contained phrases such as the following: "La fuerza pública es esencialmente obediente. Ningún cuerpo armado puede deliberar" (Chile, 1833, Art. 157); "La fuerza armada es esencialmente obediente; en ningún caso puede deliberar, y está en todo sujeta a los reglamentos y ordenanzas militares, en lo relativo al servicio" (Bolivia, 1880, Art. 129). This language was borrowed from the French Constitution of 1791 (Title IV, Art. 12): "The armed forces are essentially obedient, no armed force may deliberate." This French restriction on the military—the armed forces were not to enact laws, policies, and regulations for society (*delibérer*) but rather to act (*agir*) subject to civil authority—became boilerplate in Spanish America after independence. Such language has been preserved in most twentieth-century Latin American constitutions.

But "essentially obedient" and "not deliberating" must be balanced against constitutional language charging the armed forces with other missions: maintaining internal order, defending the constitution and the republican form of government, and providing for internal and external security. According to military perceptions and militarylore, these constitutional missions may require the armed forces to protect *la patria* and its institutions against incumbent governments, internal security threats, and external dangers. Under this interpretation, military political action is not "deliberation" nor does it violate the principle of "essential obedience." Encapsulating these views, Argentine General Leopoldo Fortunato Galtieri explained the patriotic action of that nation's armed forces in the battle against subversion and terrorism from 1975 to 1980:

> Five years ago, on February 9, 1975, the Argentine Army had to go to the mountains of Tucumán in order to halt and destroy a threat that jeopardized the very existence of *la patria* . . . representatives of foreign doctrines, based on a religion with neither God nor priests, whose goal was destruction for destruction's sake, tried to install here in Argentina . . . a regime that blasphemed . . . freedom, the family, private property, and the nationality of mankind.
>
> It was necessary for the Argentine Army and the other armed security and police forces to come together to eradicate that scourge and to reestablish order and security, engaging with the people in an undeclared war. Since 1810, the armed forces of *la patria* have always been able to explain all their actions: . . . they must participate [in politics] in order to safeguard our most important interests.[38]

General Galtieri's words express essential elements of a Latin American regional military value system: commitment to patriotism and dedication to conserving national traditions, honor, and sovereignty, as the military institutions and the Latin American nations' particular political cultures define them.

They also reflect the belief that the armed forces are crusaders when necessary, unwilling to see their vision of national interests and security sacrificed to the expediency and pragmatism of politicians or to the shifting currents of political fashion and opportunism (*politiquería*).

Dedicating their lives and institutions to *la patria* necessarily, if regrettably, involves the armed forces in politics. In their view, politics is dirty business, corrupting, compromising, and confusing. It threatens the integrity of military institutions when civilians control the government—and even more so when the military is "forced" to take direct political control to overcome the ineptitude of incumbents, restore order, fight subversion, and defend the nation's fundamental institutions.

The armed forces must be constantly alert. With civilians in control, there is always the risk of partisan politics intruding into military education, doctrine, promotions, careers, and even troop deployments. According to this view, civilian politicians are sometimes naive, sometimes subversive, usually opportunistic, and never entirely to be trusted. They rarely understand defense and security policy, let alone the permanent interests of the nation. According to the military credo, that is the essential nature of politicians, just as the reverse is the essence of the officer.

However, when the armed forces displace civilians by making policy, staffing the public administration, and attempting to govern, their normal hierarchy and discipline are menaced by the realities of day-to-day politics and governance. Officers and soldiers are diverted from strictly military missions, thereby affecting preparedness, training, morale, and institutional self-perception and threatening their purity and institutional insulation. Barracks and military academies are profaned by politics. The soldier-priest's natural organic role as society's apolitical guardian is threatened—all due to the failures of civilians to properly manage the affairs of state.

While Latin American officers share a common credo, distrust of civilians, and military profession, there are important differences among the region's military institutions as well as significant political, ideological, and philosophical cleavages within each country's armed forces. Just as there is great diversity in the size, ethnicity, cultures, economies, and political systems of the Latin American nations, significant variations exist in the evolution of military institutions and their participation in politics. Latin America means the enormity of Brazil and the tiny territory of El Salvador, the relative cultural and ethnic homogeneity of Uruguay, and the multilingual, multicultural Andean nations, Guatemala, and the Caribbean. Military institutions reflect imperfectly but recognizably the societies that raise them, pay for them, task them, and glorify and vilify them. Like the societies of which they are a part, they are also influenced by global and regional conflicts, the international economy, technological innovations, and foreign models. The historical and institutional differences among Latin American armed forces as well as their similarities must be explored to understand their political role.

Neither for the region nor for the individual nations are civil-military relations and the armed forces' political roles static. Societies change, even if values, attitudes, institutions, and behavior persist long after "revolutions" supposedly have transformed them. (Despite adopting "liberal" constitutions, most of Latin America retained colonial legal codes and administrative practices long after independence). Armed forces change too, although they tend to be more conservative in many respects than most institutions. (Most Spanish American armies retained the essentials of Spanish colonial regulations and military codes at least until the late nineteenth century, and often nearly to the end of the twentieth.)

As Latin American societies developed and differentiated, the armed forces did the same. The effects of some common external influences, disparate experiences with defeat and victory in war, deployment in civil disorders, patterns of national political development, and absorption of foreign doctrines, technology, and organizational models created unique national identities for military institutions. Officers and institutions were afforded greater prestige in some nations, for example, in Chile and Peru, than in others, such as Colombia, Bolivia, Nicaragua, and Costa Rica. Distinctive socioeconomic and political responses by their countries to the opportunities and constraints meted out by the international economy, and by international conflicts, also influenced individual Latin American military establishments. Despite this variety, the armed forces remain key actors in Latin American politics from Mexico to Chile. The historical evolution of their political role from colonial times to the end of the twentieth century is the subject of the chapters that follow.

Notes

1. By "militarylore" is meant both the formal, self-conscious discourse in military histories, curriculum, and doctrine and the traditional, popularized versions of military knowledge and orientations such as rituals and attachment to patriotic symbols and myths. This meaning is in accord with the older use of the term "lore" to refer to learning or the whole body of knowledge. Certain aspects of militarylore are shared globally; other aspects are idiosyncratic to particular nations. See Frederick M. Nunn, *The Time of the Generals: Latin American Professional Militarism in World Perspective* (Lincoln: University of Nebraska Press, 1992): xi, passim.

2. General de División Aníbal Ulises Laiño, "Desafíos al estado nación," *Military Review*, Hispano-American edition (July–August 1996): 46–48.

3. For a look at the meaning of the end of the Cold War for Latin American military institutions and militarylore see Brig. Gen. Carlos Molina Johnson, "Conflicto y cooperación: Un enfoque conceptual," *Military Review*, Hispano-American edition (January–February 1997): 30–41.

4. Arturo Ardao, *Génesis de la idea y el nombre de América Latina* (Caracas: Centro de Estudios Rómulo Gallegos, 1980).

5. See William Glade, *The Latin American Economies: A Study of Their Institutional Evolution* (New York: Van Nostrand, 1969).

6. "Explanations" for military coups d'état usually refer to "predisposing factors" and "triggering factors," making the coups the result of complex cumulative processes. See Mauricio Solaún and Michael A. Quinn, *Sinners and Heretics: The Politics of Military Intervention in Latin America* (Urbana: University of Illinois Press, 1973).

7. Claude E. Welch and Arthur K. Smith suggest four "summary variables" influencing the propensity for military coups: the extent and nature of political participation of the populace; the strength of civilian institutions; military strength; and the nature of military institutional boundaries (shared attitudes and values of the military regarding their social and political roles). *Military Role and Rule* (Belmont, CA: Duxbury Press, 1974): 34–42.

8. See Gino Germani and Kalman Silvert, "Politics, Social Structure and Military Intervention in Latin America," *European Journal of Sociology* 2 (1961): 62–81.

9. This is true to some extent of modern armed forces worldwide, not only in Latin America. See Bengt Abrahamsson, *Military Professionalization and Political Power* (Beverly Hills, CA: Sage Publications, 1972): 80.

10. For a discussion of these issues regarding the Argentine case after 1984 see Ernesto López, *Ni la ceniza ni la gloria: Actores, sistema político y cuestión militar en los años de Alfonsín* (Buenos Aires: Universidad Nacional de Quilmes, 1994).

11. The classic formulation on civilian control of the military through "subjective" and "objective" measures is Samuel Huntington, *The Soldier and the State* (Cambridge, MA: Harvard University Press, 1957). Huntington's views have been both applauded and severely criticized but remain the starting point for most academic discussions of civil-military relations.

12. Frederick Nunn calls this tradition "professional militarism" based on a willingness and propensity "to provide solutions for national (and sometimes international) problems." *The Time of the Generals*, xi.

13. As part of this mission, Colonel Caubarrere lists subsidiary tasks from "preserving national values" to "contributing to maintenance of world peace," maintaining public order and essential services, engaging in geographic research, conserving the environment, and fighting drug trafficking. Col. Sergio H. Caubarrere, "La cultura militar en el siglo XXI," *Military Review*, Hispano-American edition (July–August 1996): 54–63.

14. Benedict Anderson, *Imagined Communities: Reflections on the Origin and Spread of Nationalism* (London: Verso, 1983).

15. Ernest Renan, *The Poetry of the Celtic Races and Other Studies* (London: W. Scott, 1896): 61–83, cited in D. A. Brading, "Nationalism and State-Building in Latin American History," in Eduardo Posada-Carbó, ed., *Wars, Parties and Nationalism: Essays on the Politics and Society of Nineteenth-Century Latin America* (London: Institute of Latin American Studies, 1995): 89–90.

16. For an intriguing discussion and comparative study of the origins of modern nationalism see Liah Greenfeld, *Nationalism: Five Roads to Modernity* (Cambridge, MA: Harvard University Press, 1992), esp. the Introduction.

17. Anthony D. Smith, "The Origins of Nations," in Geoff Eley and Ronald Grigor Suny, eds., *Becoming National: A Reader* (New York: Oxford University Press, 1996): 106–8.

18. See Talcott Parsons, "Certain Primary Sources and Patterns of Aggression in the Social Structure of the Western World," in Talcott Parsons, ed., *Essays in Sociological Theory* (New York: Free Press, 1954): 298–322.

19. Juan M. Gallardo Miranda and Edmundo O'Kuinghttons Ocampo, "Doctrina militar en el acontecer político de Sudamérica," *Military Review*, Spanish edition (November–December 1992): 8.

20. In Latin America and Spain the term *pronunciamiento* is often used to indicate that the coup-makers have a legitimate motive for ousting the government, perhaps based on constitutional and statutory obligations to uphold the rule of law or prevent usurpation of authority, perhaps based on the threat to national interests or to immediate social, economic, and political crises. In this sense, coups may be perceived by their makers as legitimate, even obligatory, despite their apparent violation of requirements for usual government succession.

21. Manuel Gamio, *Forjando patria*, 2d ed. (México: Editorial Porrua, 1960): 6–8, 12, 183.

22. Ibid.: 5.

23. Cited in Brading, in Posada-Carbó (1995): 103.

24. Gamio (1960): 6.

25. Ibid.: 7.

26. While, for clarity, an effort has been made to conform to the conventional use of Spanish America to refer to Spanish-speaking republics in the Western Hemisphere, Ibero-America to include Brazil, and Latin America to include Haiti, these terms have not been used consistently for the last four hundred years and are packed with latent political connotations. Use of the concept of *patria* inevitably triggers terminological debate as part of the underlying political conflict.

27. José Enrique Rodó, "El concepto de la patria," *Almanaque Ilustrado del Uruguay* (1906), in idem, *Obras completas*, 2d ed. (Madrid: Aguilar, 1967): 1184.

28. José Enrique Rodó, "Sobre América Latina," *Cartas y Caretas* (August 25, 1906), in idem, *Obras completas* (1967): 1185.

29. On the role of the reconquest in shaping Spanish society and military institutions there is a vast literature. Américo Castro's assertion that "the reconquest was a loom on which the history of Spain was warped" is widely cited, as is Claudio Sánchez-Albornoz's affirmation: "I consider the Reconquest the key to the history of Spain." See John A. Crow, *Spain: The Root and the Flower*, 3d ed., expanded and updated (Berkeley: University of California Press, 1985).

30. Mariano Castro Morán (Lt. Col.), *Función política del ejército salvadoreño en el presente siglo* (El Salvador: UCA Editores, 1984): 24.

31. *El Soldado* (January–February 1984), cited in Carina Perelli, "The Military's Perception of Threat in the Southern Cone of South America," in Louis W. Goodman et al., eds., *The Military and Democracy* (Lexington, MA: Lexington Books, 1990): 97.

32. "[Any] potentially critical situation [*situación potencialmente crítica*, or SPOC] . . . might require military action to prevent, dissuade, or confront threats to the vital interests of the nation. [SPOCs] may be psychological-cultural, political, religious, economic, and military that affect, or might affect, the nation-state." Laiño (1996): 46–48.

33. This is related to, but a less time-bound notion than, the traditional Hispanic focus on the "common good" (*bien común*) as the main criterion for policymakers and sovereigns. What constitutes the common good may change with time, of course, but not so, at least philosophically,

the "eternal" destiny of *la patria*. See Richard M. Morse, "The Heritage of Latin America," in Howard Wiarda, ed., *Politics and Social Change in Latin America: The Distinct Tradition* (Amherst: University of Massachusetts Press, 1974): 25–69; and Glen Dealy, "The Tradition of Monistic Democracy in Latin America," in Wiarda, ed. (1974): 71–103.

34. The use of the term "totem" here is meant to imply both the emblematic and reverential aspect of the totem among North American Indian peoples, and the fear that it inspires should it choose, when offended or defied, to punish the perpetrators and restore the proper hierarchy and behavior within society.

35. Gallardo and O'Kuinghttons Ocampo (1992): 3–15.

36. Francisco Morales Bermúdez, "Reflexiones sobre la política nacional," *Defensa Nacional, Revista del Centro de Altos Estudios Militares* 2(2) (1982): 44.

37. "Comentario al estudio 'Fuerza policial y fuerza armada en Honduras' " (Presented at a research conference, "Between Public Security and National Security: The Police and Civil-Military Relations in Latin America," sponsored by the Latin American and Caribbean Center, Florida International University, Woodrow Wilson Center, Washington, DC, October 21–22, 1993).

38. Translated and reprinted from *Clarín* (Buenos Aires), February 10, 1980. The full speech is reprinted in Brian Loveman and Thomas M. Davies, Jr., eds., *The Politics of Antipolitics: The Military in Latin America*, 2d ed. (Lincoln: University of Nebraska Press, 1989): 201–4.

1

The Iberian Military Tradition

From the Kingdoms of *las Españas* to *la Patria*

> Every subject or free citizen of America has the obligation to defend his *patria* and serve the king.
>
> —"Reglamento para las milicias," Cuba, 1769[1]

Over seven hundred years of intermittent struggle to recapture the Iberian kingdoms from North African conquerors, the so-called *reconquista* (711 A.D.–1492), gave military institutions and exploits special importance in Spanish history. The *reconquista*, or reconquest, was simultaneously and contradictorily religious war (between factions of Christians and Muslim Moors), dynastic war, civil war, family feuds, territorial and economic battles, ethnic and cultural conflicts, and local and regional political disputes. This on-again, off-again crusade engendered anomalous alliances, temporary truces, and illusory pacifications. It also engendered the beginnings of Spanish military-lore, the foundational national myths of Catholic Spain, and institutions for conquest and imperial administration. From the *reconquista* emerged also a warrior-priest tradition that fused military conquest, religious and cultural subordination of the conquered, and political authoritarianism.

For their holy victories over the Moor invaders (and their Christian allies), soldiers in Spain were rewarded with booty, land, tax exemptions, special legal status (*fueros*), and royal privileges. Contracts between the Crown and leaders of military expeditions offered favors (*mercedes*) for military service. In some cases these favors included official positions, such as that of *adelantado*, that conferred military and government authority over conquered territory. This tradition of religious-cultural warfare, rewards for conquest, military privileges, and fusion of military and government authority came with the *conquistadores* to the new world that Spain called *las Indias*.

Retrospectively, the *reconquista* as national myth was transformed into a glorious crusade without pause against the Moor interlopers. The final victory at Granada, in the same year that Columbus first sailed to the Caribbean, was followed shortly afterward by a Spanish internal crusade to convert or expel Moors and Jews and by military expeditions to North Africa. In 1502 a royal decree (*pragmática*) ordered the expulsion of all unconverted adult Moors. Although not rigorously enforced, it identified Spain with Catholicism and with policies of cultural and religious intolerance.

For more than three centuries after Columbus's first voyage, Iberian military glories and defeats, institutional innovations and defects, legal codes, and patterns of civil-military relations were imprinted on Spanish and Portuguese colonies. To the traditions, heroic myths, crusading zeal, and political institutions of the *reconquista* were added "nation-building" on the Iberian Peninsula and three centuries of colonial rule in *las Indias*. Spanish armies fought against the Protestant Reformation in Europe and engaged in countless dynastic wars. Meanwhile, the Holy Inquisition waged war in Spain against heretics, witches, adulterers, and political subversives. Sword and cross crusaded for religious, cultural, and political orthodoxy.

By the time of Spanish American and Brazilian independence movements in the early nineteenth century, complex patterns of civil-military relations that involved the military routinely in politics and public administration were taken for granted as natural elements in Iberian and colonial government. Likewise, persecution of dissidents, censorship of books, art, music, and cultural events, and special prisons for heretics, Jews, and political enemies were established practices. Military personnel joined with Church officials in enforcing these policies. Army officers were both agents of internal political control and instruments for the defense of Spain and its colonies against other European powers and pirates. These basic premises and practices of Iberian civil-military relations—as well as military codes, fusion of civil and military territorial administration, military *fueros*, use of the armed forces in law-enforcement (police) functions, and jurisdiction of military courts over civilians in cases related to public order and national security— long persisted after independence. Spanish America's armed forces inherited from the mother country its military law and regulations as well as concepts of honor, discipline, religious fervor, abnegation, and patriotism. They also inherited a tradition of brutality, intolerance, privilege, corruption, and relative autonomy from civilian government officials. These elements of civil-military relations endured to varying degrees and with differential impacts in twentieth-century Latin America. An abbreviated retrospective on this colonial legacy is thus the unavoidable starting point for understanding the present-day political role of the Latin American armed forces.

Iberia before 1700

In 1492 there was no Spain. Instead, there existed *las Españas*, multiple kingdoms, or *patrias chicas*, held loosely together for the next two centuries by Habsburg dynastic rulers and the political myths of Christendom.[2] Force of arms in civil wars had made possible the marriage in 1469 of Ferdinand and Isabella and thus the dynastic union of Aragón and Castile, two of Iberia's five principal medieval divisions (the others were Portugal, Navarre, and Granada). Military conflicts and institutions continued to influence significantly state- and nation-making in Iberia and the Iberian colonies for the next four centuries.

Columbus's first voyage to *las Indias*, much of which came to be called America or "the Americas," coincided with the fall of Granada, the last Muslim stronghold. Restoration of Christian hegemony in Iberia was followed by the persecution of Jews, Muslims, gypsies, and other infidels. It also inspired an evangelical crusade that encompassed much of North America, the Caribbean, South America, and the Philippines.[3] Sword and cross purged ancient Indian civilizations, destroying their written histories, cultural artifacts, temples, cities, and armies. From the outset, military conquest was also ideological, religious, and cultural. In Habsburg Spain, religious, cultural, and ethnic conflicts were barely distinguished from more narrowly political dissent. Achieving submission to dynastic and religious norms through force of arms, evangelism, and bureaucratic rule was the prime objective of official orthodoxy and Spanish imperial policies. The *conquistadores* in *las Indias* meshed politics and religion, officially tolerating neither political nor cultural dissent.

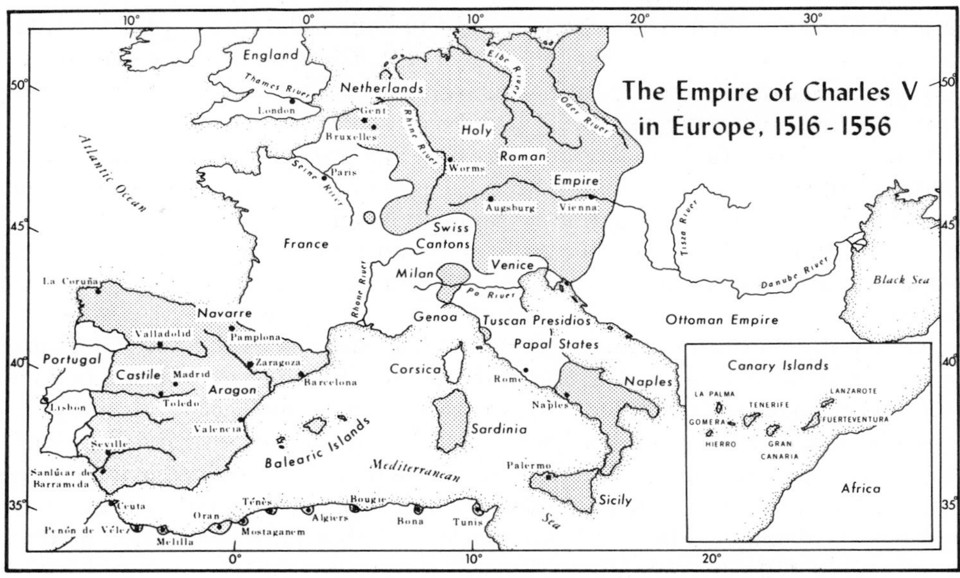

Map 1–1. The Empire of Charles V in Europe, 1516–1556. From Cathryn L. Lombardi and John V. Lombardi, with Lynn Stoner, *Latin American History, A Teaching Atlas*, published for the Conference on Latin American History by the University of Wisconsin Press, 1983, p. 10. Reprinted by permission of the University of Wisconsin Press

In the decades after 1517, the year when Martin Luther posted his theses protesting papal indulgences, the Habsburgs became a leading force in the Counter-Reformation, crusaders in the Catholic cause against Protestantism in Europe. During the next two centuries, Spain was almost always at war, preparing for war, or recovering from war. The Iberian rulers' armies fought in North Africa, the Mediterranean, the Low Countries (Belgium, Holland), and Italy, while their navies were engaged in the Atlantic and the Caribbean. They fought against the Turks, Algerians, Moroccans, French, English, Germans, Dutch, and other Europeans. Spanish kings sent expeditions against pirates in North Africa, the Atlantic, and the Caribbean and defended Iberia's coasts against North African and European raiders. They fought native peoples in the Americas from the Southwest in the present-day United States to Patagonia and Tierra del Fuego: Apache, Comanche, Pueblo, Navajo, Chichimec, Aztec, Maya, Inca, Araucanian, and many others. Through the Inquisition, police, and army, they also battled internal enemies of the faith, the Crown, and the empire: Jews,

Moors, Protestants, ethnic separatists, traitors, and subversives (*infidentes, facciosos, sediciosos*, and other categories of "enemies").[4]

As elsewhere in Europe in the sixteenth century and afterward, armies in Spain made war but were also responsible for external defense, internal security, public order, and law enforcement. Neat distinctions between police and military functions did not exist, although local police and militia customarily attended to most law-and-order issues. Whatever the particular division of labor among the police, the militia, local volunteers, and the army, military force ultimately determined who ruled. It also made tax collections possible.

These traditional internal missions of the armed forces became more critical during the reign of Carlos II, the last Spanish Habsburg, and still more important as the French Bourbons sought to consolidate their position after the War of the Spanish Succession (1701–1713). The new dynasty confronted the resurgence of local conflicts and insurgencies. After 1713 the armed forces, both in Spain and in the colonies, played a critical role in upholding Bourbon rule and implementing royal policy. The Bourbon monarchs thus bequeathed a tradition of military participation in politics and administration, and a legal foundation for such participation, to Spanish America. To understand this fusion of military and government tasks in nation-building and public administration requires a brief review of the transition from Habsburg to Bourbon rule in Spain.

The pathetic Carlos II (reigned 1665–1700), the last of the Spanish Habsburgs, inherited the throne at four years of age. His mother, Mariana of Austria, served as regent and ruled with an aristocratic *junta de gobierno* until 1675, when he reached fourteen. Carlos's reign "lasted another twenty-five years, during which he was always ailing, often close to death, and increasingly neurotic in his behaviour."[5] In 1677 this boy-king was challenged by the charismatic bastard son of Felipe IV, Don Juan José of Austria, who invaded Madrid from Aragón with an army of 15,000.

This army had been fighting the French in Catalonia. It now became the instrument for altering the central government at Madrid. This was, in a sense, the first *pronunciamiento*, the term for the commonplace Spanish military coup of the nineteenth century (and the term preferred by Latin American military officers to characterize their salvational ousters of civilian governments to defend *la patria* in the twentieth). Like its nineteenth- and twentieth-century analogues, this movement had a "program," formalized in the 1676 *documento de la grandeza*: good government, removal of "evil" ministers and their followers in the bureaucracy, and an end to the "disorder" attributed to the machinations of Mariana.[6] The *pronunciamiento*'s demands would be echoed by Spanish and Latin American military coup-makers for the next three centuries.

The rebels succeeded in forcing the king to remove his principal adviser, Prime Minister Fernando Valenzuela, and to banish the queen mother to Toledo in a virtual coup d'état supported by the nobility and regional interests opposed to central authority. Like many later military coups, this movement claimed significant civilian support, mobilized diverse social groups against the incumbent government's policies and personalities, and made the army the political arbiter of the moment. While the army was the key element of power, it acted with important support from civilian elites and social groups.

Don Juan José made himself the effective ruler of Spain, a *caudillo* who ruled in the king's name, just as later coup-makers would rule in the name of national interests and constitutions supposedly violated by ousted governments. But this was only possible with substantial social and political support from Carlos's adversaries.

Juan José of Austria had triumphed with regional support from Aragón and Catalonia and from an army diverted from external war. He took power commanding an army allied with aristocratic political factions, but he lacked the authority to actually depose the king. It was a coup in which powerful domestic interests and the army temporarily controlled the court without destroying it. They "saved" the monarchy and Spain from supposed internal threats, incompetence, disloyalty, and policy drift. The *pronunciamiento* was a precedent for Spanish civil-military coalitions and, later, for Spanish American civil-military coups.

While Juan José vigorously repressed opponents and strictly monitored the king, he could not overcome the financial and diplomatic crises facing the government. Spanish armies lost pitifully to French forces in wars in the Low Countries, Catalonia, and Sicily. Army and Church support for the prime minister eroded. In 1679, Louis XIV of France offered his niece, Marie Louise of Orléans, as Carlos's queen, and Juan José of Austria "was only saved from political disaster by his death on 17 September 1679."[7]

Carlos turned his government over to aristocratic ministers, beginning with a former president of the Council of the Indies, the agency responsible for overseeing the colonial empire. In the following years, Louis XIV's scheme for controlling the Spanish succession failed to produce an heir. France repeatedly nibbled at Spain's European territories in incessant, if minor, wars. The last Spanish Habsburg presided over the erosion of his kingdom's military power. By 1691 a decree for general conscription in Spain declared that the country had "insufficient ships and troops for its defence . . . and in most towns one can hardly find a musket, arquebus [matchlock gun], or pike."[8]

In his last anguished years, Carlos II, still without an heir, did nothing to repair the internal decomposition of the government or to reverse the decline in Spanish defense capabilities. He finally wrote his will in October 1700, and died on November 1, leaving his Spanish dominions to Louis XIV's grandson, Philip of Anjou. This decision precipitated more than a decade of warfare between the French Bourbons and the allies of the Austrian Habsburgs, who also sought the throne—and Spain's colonial empire. The war was fought over a country that "resembled a corpse, picked at by noble parasites and foreign marauders,"[9] a "decentralized, devertebrated, ataxic Spain."[10]

The War of the Spanish Succession

As the war began, Carlos II had left his successor "almost without land forces and navies, and a frontier almost without fortresses. . . . what army existed consisted of mercenary regiments, almost always German, Italian, and also Dutch."[11] The nobility, Church, and provinces regained many privileges and reasserted political and economic autonomy that the earlier Habsburgs had struggled to curtail. Many positions in the bureaucracy were purchased from the Crown. Army officers likewise obtained commissions through purchase or patronage. In the army this system impeded creation of a professional officer corps and fostered pervasive corruption, including phantom regiments. Officers enriched themselves by overstating the size of their forces to feast on bloated budgets. This tradition of paper regiments and falsified muster rolls would be a common feature of Spanish American armies into the twentieth century.

Despite the bedraggled state of the armed forces, defense expenditures were paramount in the royal budget. Inefficiency, corruption, and incompetence turned New World treasure into inflation and misery for the largely peasant population without providing effective internal security or external defense. The century ended with bread riots in Madrid (1699) and Valladolid (1700) and with Spain unable to maintain internal order, defend its borders, or protect its empire. Such was the Spain that became the spoils of the War of the Spanish Succession.

For the next thirteen years European contenders fought for control of the throne. Pitting Philip of Anjou, now Felipe V (reigned 1700–1746), against the Austrian Habsburg Carlos VI, this war allied Britain, Portugal, the Austrian Habsburgs, and some Belgians and Italians against Louis XIV and his supporters. The Archduke Charles, son of Leopold I of Austria, was crowned king of Spain in Vienna in 1703; in his name the allies sought to wrest the peninsula away from Felipe V. Involving numerous and complex dynastic and territorial issues in Europe along with the Spanish succession, this war reflected the absolutist, patrimonial, and pre-national character of European politics at the beginning of the eighteenth century.

In practice, the French took control of the war effort in Spain from 1702 until 1712, disdaining the decadent local nobility and appalled by the inadequacy of the military. But the War of the Spanish Succession was also a global conflict. The European powers consciously made war to control colonial territory and resources, particularly Spain's Mexican and South American silver and agrarian commodities. And they made war in the colonial theaters: the Mississippi Valley, Canada, the Caribbean, and South America. Louis XIV made clear the colonial focus in a 1709 letter to his ambassador in Madrid: "The main object of the present war is the Indies trade and the wealth it produces."[12] Control over the resources, commerce, and strategic bases of the Spanish empire could tip the economic and military balance on the continent. After 1700, war in Europe routinely meant colonial ("global") wars.

Civil War, Internal Order, and the Militarization of Politics

The War of the Spanish Succession was also a civil war in Spain. Many Aragonese supported the Habsburgs, most Castilians the Bourbons, but everywhere historical antagonisms and religious, ethnic, regional, and local rivalries complicated any clear, permanent definitions of political alliances in Spain. Some nobles in Castile and other provinces defected to the Habsburg claimant as a matter of dynastic loyalty, while others did so when the Austrian-dominated alliance seemed victorious. At stake was not only the balance of power in Europe but also the redistribution of wealth, influence, and power in the Iberian Peninsula. Though confounded by dynastic claims, the notion of *las Españas* often prevailed over that of *España,* and loyalty to *la patria chica* over identification with *la patria española.*

During the war, the Habsburgs twice occupied Madrid (1706, 1710). Nobles, clergy, burghers, merchants, and military units opportunistically changed sides. Shifting alliances and family intrigues, war and peace treaties, and renewed war and concessions of territory eventually confirmed the new Bourbon dynasty in Spain. The Treaties of Utrecht (1713) and Rastadt-Baden (1714) marked the official European settlement of the Spanish succession. The Bourbons took Spain; Spain lost realms throughout Europe; and the British obtained important commercial concessions in the Americas, including the *asiento,* or right to provision Spanish America with African slaves.[13]

The Bourbon victory in Castile was resisted in Aragón and elsewhere. Barcelona only surrendered to the king in 1714 after a lengthy, bloody siege, while armed resistance to the Bourbons ended in Mallorca the next year. Felipe V sought to apply Castilian law and authority in Aragón, effectively merging it with Castile and ending the reign of local *fueros* and custom that had defined its relative autonomy since before the rule of Isabella. In some provinces, Bourbon militarization of internal administration and repression of Habsburg supporters spawned political banditry and guerrilla warfare. Adopting the imperial eagle (the Habsburg emblem), some of the Bourbons' opponents therefore called themselves *aguiluchos.* A revival of these provincial and local movements within Spain periodically occurred when the forces of Felipe V and Carlos VI again squared off in European conflicts during the next decades.

During and after the War of the Spanish Succession, Felipe V attempted to strengthen the armed forces. He likewise sought to tighten up and centralize public administration. In 1704 the king imposed selective conscription. Chosen by lot, conscripts served for three years. Nobles were exempt, as were those from certain other social groups (*estamentos*) and from certain provinces. The introduction of conscription, however, was the beginning of a citizen-based standing army, an incipient national army that identified with *España* rather than one or another of *las Españas.*

"Nation-building" and Militarization of Provincial Administration

At war's end the king redesigned the country's internal administration, replacing the old viceroyalties with provincial captaincies-general. First introduced in Aragón, Valencia, Mallorca, and Asturias from 1715 to 1717, this system finally prevailed throughout Spain (except for Navarre) by 1790. The captain-general, symbol of the transition from "kingdom" with local law and custom to province ruled by Castilian authority, became the most important administrative officer. Usually he was president of the *audiencia,* the highest provincial civil and criminal court, head of the provincial *consejo de guerra,* and commander of troops stationed in the province.

This fusion of administrative, judicial, and martial authority made military officers "the superior authorities of the entire administrative system and the ordinary justice system."[14] It responded to the king's belief that "in order to effectively legislate, enforce the laws, and implement judicial decisions, the existence of a permanent army was necessary, not only for external defense but within the kingdom. . . . This explains the position achieved by the military in Spanish territorial organization in the eighteenth century."[15] Although the administrative reforms were resisted, applied unevenly, and even aborted in certain provinces, they gradually took hold from 1717 until Felipe V's death in 1746. He abolished the old provincial constitutions and conciliar government and made military officers the most important agents of public administration. Militarization of internal administration was an essential tool for forging an overarching Spanish *patria* from the collection of kingdoms and viceregal jurisdictions inherited from medieval and Habsburg times. In the same vein, Felipe promulgated a law in February 1714 abolishing the naval squadrons of the individual kingdoms and establishing the *armada real*. Gradual centralization and professionalization of the navy resulted: in 1717 an intendant general was created, in 1726 the minister of the navy was given his own department, and in 1737 an admiralty was established on the British model.[16]

These reforms from 1714 to the 1740s did not overcome the financial constraints and corruption that had plagued the military, but they did reflect the intensified Bourbon concern with consolidating centralized political control over the provinces—and the central role of the military in achieving this objective. In the words of Spanish historian José Ramón Alonso, "the army was converted into the foundation of Felipe V's monarchy, a military monarchy from its origin, with an army almost always in action from the New World to Milan. Without the constant support of the Army, Spain might have been dismembered, as England desired until 1715."[17] In addition, in 1734 the king established a system of "disciplined militia" in Castile, a sort of home-defense force to which were conceded many of the traditional military *fueros*. The Crown standardized militia organization, equipment, and uniforms. This militia further engaged numerous Castilians in military training and accustomed them to its discipline. Moreover, militarization of civilians was accompanied by militarization of politics. By the 1730s the Army had grown tremendously; officers served in key government positions, as ambassadors, and as the king's principal advisers. Defense ministers directed Spain's foreign policy—indeed, managed much of Spanish public policy.

Faced with the basic challenge of alignment with one of Europe's two superpowers, France or England, Spain had to choose between buildups of land forces to defend itself against France, or naval forces to resist the British in the Mediterranean and the Western Hemisphere. To the 1760s both these choices were made alternately, implying a naval construction program and large expenditures on the army. In 1751 military expenditures accounted for 77 percent of the budget; in 1760 they were 60 percent.[18] Just as politics, the public administration, and policymaking were militarized, so was the budget.

So, too, was colonial administration. Almost all of the viceroys in Río de la Plata, Peru, Mexico, and New Granada were military officers. When New Granada was elevated to the status of viceroyalty in 1739, for example, the king appointed as the first viceroy Lieutenant General Sebastián de Eslava (who would become minister of war in the mid-1750s).[19] Military officers also served as captains-general in Chile, and as governors in Cuba and the Philippines.

The trend was extended and intensified in the 1760s and 1770s due to problems of internal order in Spain, the humiliating if temporary loss of Havana and Manila to the British in the Seven Years War (1756–1763), and several serious local rebellions in the colonies. The *Ordenanza de Intendentes del Río de la Plata* (1782) and that of New Spain (Mexico, 1786) further emphasized the fusion of military and civilian authority, giving viceroys, intendants, and other *comandantes general* "total authority." The 1803 *Ordenanza de Intendentes* reconfirmed this concentration of power (except in Venezuela), recognizing the viceroys, captains-general, and *audiencia* presidents' "full and superior authority, consistent with their high rank."[20]

The Spanish Military and Internal Order after 1766

Political disorder and urban protests from the 1760s onward, and Spain's reaction to the beginnings of the French Revolution in 1789, provoked military reforms that further militarized internal politics and administration. Riots broke out in Madrid in 1766. The rioters were protesting the policies of the Marqués de Squillace, Carlos III's economic adviser, who had loosened price controls on grain, raised taxes, and carried out other "enlightened" reforms. They also protested the forbiddance of wearing capes and broad-brimmed hats that might conceal weapons, a measure adopted as part of policies such as improved street lighting that were designed to reduce crime in Madrid.

The rioters destroyed the Marqués's house, marched on the royal palace, insulted the soldiers, and killed ten of the king's Walloon guards. The riots spread to Cuenca, Zaragoza, Salamanca, Extremadura, and Andalucía. Historian Laura Rodríguez suggests that the riots were to some extent orchestrated by the Church and aristocracy, who opposed Carlos III's reforms in an extension of the struggle to retain privileges and immunities against the Bourbons' centralizing tendencies.[21] The king fled to his country palace at Aranjuez. To end the violence he dismissed his adviser and sent him to Italy, granted amnesties to the rioters, and intervened to control grain and bread prices. After peace was restored, however, Carlos III revoked the amnesties. Blaming the Jesuits for the riots, he ejected them from Spain and Spanish America in 1767. The king also sought to prevent a repeat performance through new legislation to restrict public protests and suppress opponents and by strengthening the military's role in maintaining law and order.

In July 1767 the province of Castile became the captaincy-general of New Castile, presided over by the president of the Council of Castile, the Conde de Aranda. Having fused civil and military authority, the king made Madrid a military department and stationed 15,000 troops in the capital and its environs. Alonso calls these events, with some exaggeration, "the first direct intervention of the military in Spanish life . . . creating something similar to an authentic dictatorship established by royal order."[22] The military had previously played an important role in Spanish life, but this militarization of Madrid's administration and the repressive measures that followed made clear both the perceived threat to royal authority and the Bourbons' military response to socioeconomic and political protests.

Aranda subjected opponents to trials in ad hoc tribunals and ordered secret executions and the "disappearance" (*desaparición*) of enemies. He established a temporary police state, harshly enforcing existing criminal legislation and promulgating new decrees aimed at curtailing opposition to the regime. These decrees regarding public order, Aranda's use of the military to suppress dissent, and the brutal treatment of political opponents would be models for nineteenth- and twentieth-century counterrevolutionary regimes. To guarantee military support, the government augmented military budgets and granted officers and troops salary increases. New militia charged with fighting contraband, suppressing banditry, and maintaining "internal peace" were created in Castile.

In 1768, Carlos III implemented reformed regulations (*reales ordenanzas*) that extended military jurisdiction over civilians for crimes committed during the riots. They also gave military administrators the authority to approve or prohibit public meetings, and to take "preventive measures" when the king requested them. When a disturbance occurred, the regulations transferred to military jurisdiction any territory for approximately five leagues from the garrison's base. Military forces were also assigned routine police functions and service as bailiffs in civil and criminal courts. All cases of treason, subversion, and sedition were also transferred to military jurisdiction.

In these repressive measures can be found the legal and pragmatic foundations of the overlapping police and military functions so common in twentieth-century Latin America. The Bourbon reforms made Spanish (and then Spanish American) armed forces responsible for political intelligence operations, conserving internal order, assuring or restoring political stability, and suppressing political dissent as an integral part of their mission. These extensive political functions of the military would be reaffirmed in Spanish American constitutions and military codes in the early nineteenth century after independence. Even much of the language in the 1768 *ordenanzas* and subsequent late eighteenth-century decrees regarding the role of the military in internal security survived almost verbatim in parts of Latin America during the nineteenth century and even to the end of the twentieth. Provisions in the 1768 *ordenanzas* requiring "due obedience" to orders and to military regulations ("*del exacto cumplimiento de las órdenes particulares que tuviere, y de las generales que explica la Ordenanza*") were incorporated almost verbatim into many Latin American military codes in the nineteenth century, remained in effect for much of the twentieth century, and were used as a defense against accusations of human rights' abuses as late as the 1990s. These regulations are reproduced here, with the relevant phrases highlighted, to illustrate the longevity of both the spirit and wording of military law and doctrine in Spanish America.

> *Spain, 1768, Article 9*
>
> Todo oficial en su puesto será responsable de la vigilancia de su Tropa en él; *del exacto cumplimiento de las órdenes particulares que tuviere, y de las generales que explica la Ordenanza*, como de tomar, en todos los accidentes y ocurrencias que no le estén prevenidas, el partido correspondiente a su situación, caso, y objeto, debiendo en los lances dudosos elegir el más digno de su espíritu y honor.

Chile, 1839, 1860, Ordenanza para el Regímen, Disciplina, Subordinación i Servicio de los Ejércitos de la República, Titulo XXXII (9)

Todo Oficial en su puesto será responsable de la vigilancia de su tropa en *el exacto cumplimiento de las órdenes particulares que tuviere, i de las generales que explica la Ordenanza,* como de tomar en todos los accidentes y ocurrencias que no le estén prevenidas, el partido correspondiente a su situación, caso i objeto, debiendo en los lances dudosos elegir el más digno de su espíritu i honor.

Argentina, 1969, Reglamento del Servicio Interno

El que comandare una tropa será responsable de la vigilancia de ella, *del exacto cumplimiento de las órdenes particulares que tuviere y de las disposiciones contenidas en las leyes y reglamentos,* como de tomar, en todos los accidentes y ocurrencias que no estén previstos, el partido correspondiente a su situación, caso y objeto, debiendo en los lances dudosos eligir él que considere más digno de su espíritu y honor.

Peru, 1975, Reglamento General del Servicio Interno

Todo oficial es responsable de la vigilancia de su tropa, *del exacto cumplimiento de las órdenes particulares que tuviere y de las prescripciones reglamentarias,* así como de tomar en todos los accidentes y ocurrencias que no estén prevenidos, la actitud correspondiente a su situación, caso y objeto, debiendo en los trances dudosos elegir el más digno de su espíritu y honor.[23]

The longevity of these provisions in military codes and the spirit that pervaded them could not be foreseen in 1768. But the legacy of the 1766 riots and the subsequent royal decrees profoundly, if not always consciously, influenced civil-military relations in Latin America. These military regulations and the internal security measures taken by the king and Aranda created the legal and policy foundations for managing political dissidence and protests in Spain and independent Spanish America.

Further militarization of internal politics and administration was added in the early 1770s. Army units were ordered to clear towns of vagrants and to impress them into military service. Resistance to this or to other troop action would be considered an attack on the king's sovereignty, punishable by execution, regardless of *fuero* (that is, applicable to ecclesiastics, aristocrats, and other privileged groups as well as to plebes and peasants). Carlos III intended to prevent or suppress further popular tumult and aristocratic conspiracies.

To this end, on April 17, 1774, the king issued a *pragmática* that outlawed placing or distributing unapproved posters in public places.[24] Those knowing of such posters and subversive writings (*papeles sediciosos*) and failing to report them to the local authorities were considered accomplices to the crime. If an order were issued to disperse during a public protest or meeting, any group of ten or more were considered guilty of criminal organizing. The *pragmática* also allowed the closing of bars, churches, and other places where people might congregate—virtually a lock-down of the town. If people refused to retire to their homes, troops were authorized to use whatever force was necessary to impose order. This precedent for the military's repression of dissidents and for the use of whatever force was necessary to control civil disturbances would be emulated regularly after independence in Spanish America.

Carlos III would continue to expand military jurisdiction and implement new policies against vagrants, gypsies, miscreants, bandits, dissidents, and adversaries in the next decade.[25] From 1774 to 1779 the government created three new militia to fight highwaymen, vagrants, and evildoers (*salteadores, vagos, malhechores*). In 1781 regular army troops were stationed in Andalucía and Extremadura to fight contraband and banditry, with orders to act "as if they were in a state of war." Control of all prisons was transferred in 1782–83 to the captains-general, including military jurisdiction for crimes committed by prisoners. Thus, with the exception of the Madrid *presidio*, the military controlled almost the entire Spanish prison system by the end of 1783. In the same year, all persons apprehended for banditry were placed under military jurisdiction. Upon arrest, bandits were to be whipped, and those using firearms to resist arrest were to be executed.

Banditry had become a crime against public order, to be suppressed by applying methods of military justice. So had horse theft. A Royal Instruction in 1784 consolidated much of the anti-banditry, anti-vagrancy, and anti-gypsy legislation, allowing impressment of such undesirables into military service. It also obligated the captains-general to compile lists and information concerning bandits in their jurisdictions, and to share such information across jurisdictions, an internal intelligence function that, if taken literally, required a permanent political espionage system.

Deliberate confusion between "bandits" and political adversaries became the rule in Spain and Spanish America. It was no accident that in the twentieth century, Pancho Villa in Mexico, Augusto César Sandino in Nicaragua, and other revolutionary leaders would be characterized as "bandits." Internal surveillance of "suspicious" persons, possible "subversives," and "bandits" became commonplace. Subsequent reliance on Spanish law and practice gave Latin American governments and military officers firm legal foundations for monitoring civilians and for preventive detention, or even summary execution, of "bandits" and others who "disturbed public order."

By the early 1780s the military reforms had consolidated the role of captains-general as the most important administrative officials in Spain. They also established the armed forces' permanent role in maintaining internal order, fighting subversion and banditry, and suppressing popular protest. When Carlos III died in 1788, the military held key positions in Spanish politics and administration, in the judicial system, and in the daily lives of the urban and rural populations. In 1800 the newly created post of "second chief" or deputy commander "put an end to all hesitation and doubts as to who should perform the complex of military duties and civil functions inherent in the office of captain general in the event of the incumbent's absence or of an interim appointee."[26] By 1805 army officers presided over every territorial tribunal in Spain.

The Bourbons' notion of enlightened despotism sought to forge a Spain from *las Españas*; "King and *Patria*" replaced the Habsburgs' motto of "God and King." Military reforms, militarization of politics, and repression of internal enemies were foundations of this emergent modern nationalism. These elements of the Bourbons' Spanish nationalism were gradually transferred to the American colonies. When independence came, they were integrated into the political foundations of the new Spanish American *patrias*.[27] So, too, were many features of Spain's colonial armies.

War, Military Reforms, and Colonial Militia

When the Bourbons ascended to the Spanish throne, France and Britain had long since successfully settled in North America (in Canada and the present-day Eastern United States), some Caribbean outposts had been lost (for example, Jamaica in 1655), and pirates, smugglers, loggers, and merchants had established a presence in Central America and the Caribbean. Spanish hegemony in the Americas was finished. But, with ups and downs, and variations from colony to colony, the colonial system still produced a surplus for the Crown. Much of this output was used to finance war. Like the Habsburgs, the Spanish Bourbons permanently involved themselves in European wars, alternately identifying their interests with a "family compact" (with the French Bourbons), England, and other transitory European alliances.

In the eighteenth century, European wars were also American wars. Indeed, sometimes peace in Europe did not include territories "beyond the [Tordesillas] line"—that is, in the colonies. Naval and land forces in Bourbon Spanish America repeatedly faced armed harassment, temporary invasions, and even occupation of key towns by Spain's European adversaries. These eighteenth-century wars more than once required Spain to devise new defense policies, reorganize home and colonial armies, and redefine civil-military relations.

From 1713 to 1810, Spain periodically made efforts to rebuild its navy and buttress colonial defenses. Security relied primarily on fixed fortifications (for example, at Havana, Vera Cruz, Campeche, Cartagena, Callao) garrisoned by small detachments of Spanish regulars (the *fijos*, or fixed battalions) and supported by local militia. During wartime, Spanish defense doctrine anticipated reinforcing these garrisons with regular army troops sent from Spain. The first *fijo* garrison was established in 1719 at Havana, the most important defense installation in the colonies and the point of departure for the treasure ships back to the mother country. According to regulations, only 20 percent of the enlisted men at Havana might be non-Iberian. This rule was also applied when the system was extended to Cartagena in 1736, Santo Domingo in 1738, Vera Cruz in 1740, and Panama and San Juan, Puerto Rico, in 1741.[28] According to the dominant strategic doctrine, intelligence on British, Dutch, or other expeditions leaving Europe to raid the Americas would permit timely reinforcement—if tropical diseases failed to decimate the enemy during extended sieges.[29]

During the War of Jenkins' Ear (1739–1748), Cartagena came under siege by British Admiral Edward Vernon's fleet of some 140 warships with an army of over 11,000.[30] In 1741 the tiny Spanish garrison and six ships figured to suffer a quick defeat. Instead, the British were unable to breach the walls of the castle of San Felipe de Barajas, despite bloody frontal assaults by waves of soldiers. Disease and discord between Vernon and the British army commander did the rest. The admiral failed to take Cartagena and lost still more troops to disease on the voyage back to Jamaica. In the same year, Vernon's forces also harassed Havana, blockading the port for two months and marauding in eastern Cuba after landing at Guantánamo Bay. Guerrilla tactics eventually discouraged the British, who withdrew.[31] A subsequent ill-planned attack on Porto Bello, Panama, also resulted in their defeat. Overall, the British lost more than 10,000 soldiers of a force originally estimated at 14,000.

The victories at Cartagena and elsewhere in the Caribbean from 1740 to 1742 reinforced the credibility of Spain's colonial defense doctrine, although Cartagena and Havana could easily have been lost if the British navy and army commanders had bickered less and taken advantage of their opportunities. In response to wars in the 1740s, Ferdinand VI (reigned 1746–1759), advised by the Marqués de Ensenada, ordered a naval construction program, strengthening of the army, and attention to colonial fortifications. In 1751 the navy had fewer than 30 warships; England had 250.[32] Ensenada proposed an increase to 60 warships, achieved by the 1760s, and financed in part from increased colonial revenues during the temporary peace. Despite the naval buildup, the overall defense strategy conceded naval superiority to Spain's adversaries. It resulted eventually in the temporary loss of Havana and Manila to the British (1762–1763), recurrent attacks on various ports and towns, and the gradual disappearance of even the illusion of effective Spanish control by the end of the 1750s.

Carlos III (reigned 1759–1788), Ferdinand's brother, came to Spain from Naples in 1759. The Seven Years War had begun three years earlier, with the British advancing against the French in Canada, the Caribbean, and Europe. Committing himself to a third "family compact" in 1761, Carlos III threw Spain's lot in with the French. In January 1762 the British declared war. Havana fell in August, in a replay of the 1741 Cartagena battle but with a different outcome.[33] The loss of Havana prompted rethinking of colonial defenses. Despite fears that arming the colonials might be dangerous, even encouraging them to revolt, Spanish financial and military weakness made this the lesser evil in light of the British threat. In 1763 the Conde de Ricla, a battle-experienced career officer, proposed the creation of a disciplined colonial militia in Cuba, a system that would then be extended to the rest of the colonies. Named Captain-General of Cuba after the Seven Years War, he began implementing the military and other administrative reforms in the mid-1760s.

As part of the reforms, regulations were drawn up in 1764 and eventually published in 1769. After considerable debate, members of the colonial militia were granted a broader *fuero militar*, in both civil and military cases, than their counterparts in Spain. For officers and sergeants, these cases even included ones in which they were the plaintiff, not the defendant (the so-called active *fuero*, not just the passive *fuero*). They were also extended immunities from various royal and municipal taxes and other privileges (*preeminencias*).[34] These reforms were extended to Mexico, with the appointment of Lieutenant General Juan de Villalba y Angulo as *comandante general* and *inspector general* of the army of New Spain in 1764, and gradually in the 1770s to Peru, New Granada, and elsewhere in the colonies.[35]

The *fueros militares* were enticements for militia and army service. They were often abused, making members of the armed forces not accountable for civil and criminal transgressions and immune from the usual judicial processes. Lyle McAlister recounts the story of Fulano Miliciano (militiaman "John Smith"), who opened a barbershop at his house despite the local barbers' guild regulation stating that shops had to be at least four blocks apart. When his neighbor, who already had a shop, complained to local authorities, Fulano sought relief from a military court. His commanding officer ruled that he could use his house however he wished.[36] Clearly a minor episode, this special status and legal treatment for military personnel would have enduring influence in Spanish America and extended into realms much more important than the barber trade. In practice it often implied impunity for military personnel who abused their authority or mistreated civilians.

American-born Spaniards (*criollos*, or Creoles) came to dominate the militia officer corps and even, in some colonies, the regular army garrisons. *Criollo* officers constituted 33 percent of these ranks in 1760, and 60 percent in 1800. At the end of the eighteenth century in Mexico, for example, *criollos* held over 60 percent of commissioned officers' positions in the regular regiments and more than 50 percent in the militia.[37] More than 90 percent of the troops were colonials in Buenos Aires.[38] In Chile, where permanent warfare against the Araucanian Indians had led Spain to station regular garrisons there since 1603, more than 50 percent of the officers and noncommissioned officers were *criollos* in the 1790s. Most troops were also American-born.[39]

Overall, colonials comprised over 80 percent of the Army's troops in the colonies between 1780 and 1800. Many had been "recruited" from prison, from among vagrants, and from those condemned to military service for real or imagined crimes.[40] This figure contrasted markedly with the Bourbons' efforts to reduce the *criollo* role in the *audiencias*, royal bureaucracy, and even higher-level Church positions after the 1750s. Thus, as the Bourbons attempted to reassert Spanish administrative and fiscal control over colonies that had attained a certain de facto autonomy and sense of *patria chica*—that is, a nascent local pride, if not nationalism—their colonial military reforms created armies and militia predominantly officered and garrisoned by colonials. These armies and militia were increasingly financed by intracolonial revenue transfers (*situados*) from Mexico to the Caribbean, Florida, and Louisiana, and from Peru to Chile and elsewhere in South America.[41] The military would become, in these senses, the first "national" institution in Spanish America, visible symbols of *la patria*, despite the Crown's belated post-1780s efforts to mitigate this dangerous trend.

In the 1770s and into the 1780s, Spain continued the military reforms and naval reconstruction program. By Carlos III's death in 1788 the warship fleet had grown to 150 vessels.[42] Spain and France at this time helped to separate the American colonies from Britain by offering financial and military support to the North American revolutionaries. In particular, the French fleet off North America's East Coast, and Spanish regiments in Louisiana and Florida, some drawn from Cuba and Mexico, harassed the British and assisted the nascent United States in its struggle for independence.

Shortly thereafter, revolution spread to France. In 1793, when radicals guillotined the Bourbon monarch, Louis XVI, for "threatening the security of the state"—that is, the new liberal state of the French Republic—Spain briefly joined Britain in war against the revolutionary government. The war against France ended in September 1795; before the end of 1796, Spain had again aligned with France by the Treaty of San Ildefonso and resumed hostilities against Britain. It then faced British revenge. Admiral Horatio Nelson blockaded Cádiz (1797), virtually choking off imports from America and exports to Mexico and South America. At the same time, Spain suffered a naval defeat at Cape St. Vincent and, in America, the loss of Trinidad.

As the war continued, Spain became simply an appendage of Napoleon's anti-British policies. In 1804, the year in which he was crowned Emperor of the French, British vessels seized a treasure shipment from Buenos Aires and Callao. The next year at Trafalgar the Spanish fleet was destroyed by its nemesis, Admiral Nelson. In 1806, British troops invaded the Río de la Plata but were defeated by colonial militia when Spanish regulars fled Buenos Aires. This colonial victory inspired local pride and incipient *criollo* nationalism but did not help Spain. No Spanish ships reached Havana and, on the eve of Napoleon's occupation of Portugal and Spain in 1807, no treasure reached the mother country from the colonies. Thus, forty years of massive expenditures on naval construction and military reorganization were for naught. In the colonies, the worst of Spain's military tradition—the corruption, mismanagement, arbitrary treatment of civilians, special privileges and legal jurisdiction for military officers, lack of professionalism and military preparedness—was the bequest of its imperialism. In addition, colonial silver financed Spain's lost cause, siphoning resources from internal development, particularly during the Seven Years War, the war against Great Britain (1779–1783), and the war against the French Convention (1793–1795).[43]

Napoleon's invasion of the Iberian Peninsula during 1807 and 1808 and the outbreak of Spanish American independence movements in 1810 presaged years more of warfare. The Napoleonic Wars and Spanish American independence sealed the imperial coffin, but allowed the military tradition of the past to shape Spanish America's future from the empire's tomb. By 1825, England, France, the United States, Holland, and even Russia had better access to Spanish American resources and trade than did Spain. More than three centuries of empire in the Western Hemisphere left Spain a domestic legacy of mythical glory and past splendors, a present of defeat, delegitimation of the absolutist monarchy, and political instability. The Bourbon response to the challenges of eighteenth-century political instability, international relations, and colonial defense strategy (including upgrading the colonial militia) had enhanced the political and administrative roles of the armed forces. This legacy was an important one for independent Spanish America.

Colonial Tax Protests, Rebellions, and Counterinsurgency

Even as the Bourbons sought to consolidate control of Spain and defend the overseas empire against European adversaries, their fiscal, military, and administrative reforms were resisted in the colonies as well as on the Iberian Peninsula. Policies intended to raise Crown revenue, increase exports, strengthen the military, modernize the bureaucracy, and reduce corruption, contraband, smuggling, and tax evasion threatened entrenched interests in the colonies.

Even more important, they squeezed ever tighter the poor, nonwhite, and Indian peoples working in mines, urban peripheries, and the countryside who produced the wealth that supported the imperial system.

Occasional tax protests, rural uprisings, and local revolts against unpopular administrators occurred before the consolidation of Bourbon rule. In the late seventeenth and early eighteenth centuries, for example, the regional movements in the Mexican Sierra Zapoteca in Oaxaca or the 1712 Tzeltal insurrection in Chiapas, and many more localized rebellions, tested Spanish authorities. Often violent, such outbursts seriously concerned the Crown but failed to spread.[44] In the 1720s and 1730s a so-called *comunero* movement in Paraguay saw *criollos* attempt to eject the Jesuits and gain control over the colony. Uprisings in Venezuela in the 1740s and 1750s against the monopoly concessionaire that controlled the cacao trade and colonial commerce, the Caracas Company, also challenged royal authority. The small regular army regiments usually contained such localized violence easily, never requiring significant reinforcement and never truly finding themselves overwhelmed.

The post-1750 reforms angered different colonials for a variety of reasons. The Crown ended the sale of *audiencia* positions (*oidores*) and that of *corregidores* (for example, Peru had been divided into fifty *corregimientos*, or provinces), systematically replacing *criollos* with *peninsulares*. According to historian John Lynch, "Other sectors of the bureaucracy were recolonized by Spaniards. A growing number of senior financial officials, and even some minor ones, were appointed from the peninsula, 'one of ours,' as the Spanish used to say. . . . The object of the new policy was to de-Americanize the government of America, and in this it was successful."[45]

Creation of new administrative units—the viceroyalty of Río de la Plata (1776), the captaincy-general of Venezuela (1777) and Chile (1778)—and replacement of the *corregidores* and lesser officials with intendants had as their intention reassertion of royal control. The de-Americanization of public administration offended *criollos*, but the reforms were not intended to offend; they were simply to raise revenue and regain control of the imperial bureaucracy. They were meant to extract from the colonies the income and resources needed to pay for mounting defense expenditures and leave a surplus for the Crown. In this they proved relatively successful.

Increasing the yield of royal income generated also a harvest of violence and revolt. Beginning with tax protests in Quito in 1765, a series of local and regional rebellions demanded military responses into the 1780s. The Quito uprising, originating in higher sales taxes, fiscal reforms, and the operation of a royal monopoly on a popular alcoholic beverage (*aguardiente*), began as a riot and turned into the first major revolt against the Bourbon reforms in the colonies. It affected elites, *castas*, and Indians. From Quito it later spread to Ibarra, Otavalo, and Cuenca. Given that regular regiments were quite small (the royal army of Peru had fewer than 2,000 men, New Granada about 3,500, Mexico about 6,000), suppressing such violence necessarily drew on the colonial militia, dominated by the *criollo* elite.[46] In Quito popular protests eventually evoked fear among *criollos* as well as *peninsulares* that they could turn into race wars or provoke uprisings by Indians in the hinterland. After quelling the violence in

Quito through negotiation, the authorities transferred control of the city to the military commander, who created a new Spanish-dominated garrison to maintain order.[47]

There followed numerous minor rebellions in the Peruvian Andes in the 1770s, in Oaxaca, Mexico (1772), in northwestern Venezuela, and in Arequipa, Cuzco, La Paz, Cochabamba, and Socorro (in New Granada) in the early 1780s. Historian Scarlett O'Phelan Godoy lists over eighty such occurrences in Peru and Bolivia from 1765 to 1783.[48] Fear of popular protest, Indian revolts, and *criollo* resistance to royal authority all made necessary military preparation as well as military participation in internal administration.

The culmination of these revolts was a series of bloody rebellions in Peru and Bolivia from 1780 to 1783, associated with the Túpac Amaru uprising (1780–81), although they persisted for several years after José Gabriel Túpac Amaru's grisly death. Inspector General José Antonio de Areche had arrived in Peru in 1777, armed by the king with "extraordinary powers." He began to implement fiscal and administrative reforms: new taxes on non-Indian people to support expansion of the colonial militia, and a new "census" of potential tribute payers, which seemed to threaten non-Indians with taxes or even labor obligations that had previously applied only to Indians. Areche's initiatives caused protests in towns and the countryside, eventually provoking the bloodiest revolt in Spanish colonial history.

José Gabriel Condorcanqui, a *mestizo* who claimed descent from the last Inca, sought relief from certain of Areche's reforms, requesting exemption from the Potosí labor draft. Failing in these efforts, he returned from Lima to Tinta province, took the name Túpac Amaru II, and became legendary in his fight and death. The Túpac Amaru revolt began when José Gabriel proclaimed his loyalty to Carlos III, celebrated the king's birthday with the hated Cuzco *corregidor*, and then ordered him executed in the public plaza. In 1780, Túpac Amaru defeated a force of 600 Spaniards at Sangara, burned the church in which they took shelter, and killed those attempting to escape.[49]

The war had begun in earnest. Military repression of the uprising drew troops from Buenos Aires, Upper Peru (Bolivia), and Peru. By the time it was quelled by an army over 17,000 strong (more than the regular garrison strength in Mexico, Peru, and New Granada combined), there were thousands dead and rising fears of widespread race war. Túpac Amaru's defeat and capture was followed by exemplary punishment:

> José Gabriel was then brought to the center of the plaza. There the executioner cut out his tongue and threw him on the ground face down. He tied his hands and feet with four cords, fastened these to the girths of four horses, which four mestizos then drove in four different directions. Either the horses were weak or the Inca unusually strong, for he was not immediately torn to pieces, but remained suspended in mid-air, spider-like, for some time while the horses strained to pull him apart. The hard-hearted *visitador*, who witnessed the execution from the Jesuit College, finally ordered the Inca's head cut off. At the same time he arrested the corregidor of Cuzco and another official for not providing suitable horses. The Inca's body was dismembered, as were the bodies of his wife, son, and uncle. Only the heads were removed from the bodies of the remaining victims. . . .

> The trunks of the mutilated bodies of the Inca and his wife were taken to the height of Picchu. There they were thrown into a bonfire and reduced to ashes, which were scattered into the air and cast into the Huatanay River. . . .
>
> Later, on different days, many of the other rebels were tortured and executed. Among them was Puma Inca, cacique of Quiquijana and Túpac Amaru's chief justice, who was broken to pieces by swords.[50]

The fiercest struggles followed Túpac Amaru's death. Still rebelling against evil administrators, particularly the *corregidores* and tax and customs' collectors, in the name of Carlos III, Túpac Amaru's generals terrorized Spanish towns, torturing and killing in brutal reaction to Spanish repression. Túpac Amaru's program had promised freedom for slaves who joined his army, protection for *mestizos* and other non-Indians against their inclusion in the labor obligation applied to Indians (especially the dreaded *mita* at Potosí), relief from taxation (the *alcabala*), and relief from exaggerated labor obligations (tribute paid by communal *caciques* and the *mitayos* at Potosí) in the mines. It also called for an end to certain royal monopolies and administrative corruption.

Mestizos, blacks, and *castas* joined in the revolt, which in practice became a series of local and regional uprisings with different provocations but all related somehow to the Bourbon reforms meant to extract new resources from the colonies. In some cases, *criollos* also became insurgents, and Indian *caciques* and their forces fought on both sides of the conflict. The various elements of the revolutionary program appealed to a multi-ethnic, multi-class clientele, but eventually the potential for race war solidified *criollo* and *mestizo* support against the rebellion.

Blood flowed through the highland valleys of Peru and Bolivia until 1783, when the revolt lost momentum and the region was cruelly pacified. The efforts to draw highland Quito and even New Granadan regions into the revolt greatly concerned royal officials, who suppressed outbreaks in Socorro (north of Bogotá) and even in Venezuela during these years. Spanish commanders routinely ordered torture, hanging, and quartering of prisoners. Lesser punishments included deportation to African *presidios*, whipping women rebels through the streets, and publicly shaving women's hair and eyebrows. After pacification, many amnesties granted to Indians and *mestizos* as a tactic for pacification were nullified. Systematic persecution and executions purged even leaders who had agreed to peace with Spanish officials. Indeed, the viceroy tried to wipe out the whole Inca family. Even persons connected by marriage did not escape. Francisco Tadeo Díaz de Medina reported: "Neither the King nor the state thought it fitting that a seed or branch of that family should remain, or the commotion and impression that the wicked name of Túpac Amaru caused among the natives."[51]

Despite its vigorous suppression, the revolt induced reforms: abolition of the commodity *repartimiento* (monopolies by the *corregidores* and forced sale of commodities to "their" Indians), establishment of a new *audiencia* at Cuzco (1787), and an end to the *corregimiento* system. It also left a legacy of fear, racial hatred, and strengthening of the Spanish military garrisons and *criollo* militia—for example, *cuerpos de patricios* in Peru, Upper Peru (later Bolivia), and the Río de la Plata. In 1784, Peru was divided into seven intendancies, with an additional two created in Chile under the command of Viceroy Teodoro de Croix, former general of the Frontier Provinces of New Spain. The new viceroy had had experience fighting Indians on the northern Hispanic frontier; his instructions included making the colonial militia a more effective military force.[52] The manner of repression of the 1780s revolts served as a clear warning to subversives and Indian rebels. The social and racial cleavages that underlay the uprisings, the fear of race war and social revolution, and the brutality of Spanish officials, armies, and colonial militia in suppressing the rebellions were all precedents for insurgency and counterinsurgency in independent Spanish America. "Dirty wars" against "subversives" in twentieth-century Latin America would not surpass in violence and counterviolence the state terrorism under late Bourbon colonialism.

The Túpac Amaru revolt was complex, widespread, and devastating. It allowed diverse types of protests against Spanish policies and permitted discontent to surface from most sectors of society. In the decade that followed, and particularly after the outbreak of revolution in France, the intendants in Spanish America reported more frequently back to Spain on disaffection, civil disturbances, and conspiracies in the colonies.[53] Ultimately, the French Revolution and Napoleon's invasion of Spain and Portugal would turn discontent into a struggle for independence. Even after independence, the memory of the eighteenth-century rebellions would be a symbolic referent for the internal order missions of the armies of the new Spanish American republics. Fear of race war and slave revolts lurked below the surface in much of Spanish America and in Brazil. The armed forces would have the duty of preventing or suppressing such movements as an unwritten part of their historical mission and a vivid ingredient in national militarylore.

Military Reforms in Brazil

After 1750 important fiscal and military reforms also came to Portugal and Brazil. During the tenure of Sebastião João de Carvalho e Melo (1750–1777), the principal adviser to João I, who became the Marqués de Pombal in 1770, analogues to the Spanish Bourbon reforms were devised to centralize authority and enhance royal revenues. Brazil was administered by a governor-general and provincial captains-general. Its vast territory, poor communications, and fragmented economy made reform even more difficult than in Spanish America. The captaincies, the largest administrative jurisdictions, were divided into *comarcas* and these further into *termos, freguesias* (parishes), and *bairros* (suburbs). Each captaincy, depending on its importance, was headed by a viceroy, captain-general, captain-major, or merely governor. This officer had supreme military authority over the territory and also was in charge of general administration.[54] Moreover, each captaincy had the regular army units (*tropa de linha*), militia, and *corpos de ordenanças* (territorial units). The first of these were usually Portuguese-officered and -garrisoned, with reinforcements recruited locally. Officially, only whites were eligible for service. The militia and territorial troops were poorly organized, badly equipped, and barely trained auxiliaries, but officership offered status and noble rank to upper-class Brazilians (*mazombos*).

The *ordenanças* were only for local exigencies, and the militia moved about the country to support regular forces when required. They remained organized in the old *terços* rather than the reformed regiments on the French model until after independence. With little real military importance in defending frontiers or in international conflicts, the territorial units became instead the primary law-enforcement agents in the Brazilian hinterland. They also administered justice and sometimes collected taxes and supervised public works projects. With officers from the largest landowners and slavocracy, the *ordenanças* linked local elites to the colonial administration, creating an official base of authority for the "colonels" (*capitães-mor*) who came to dominate rural Brazil. In the eighteenth century, with variations among regions, the militia became more important than the *ordenanças*, but military rank, prerogatives (*foros*), and political and economic power had fused in the Brazilian colony.

Pombal eliminated the remaining private hereditary captaincies and unified the two realms of Brazil: Maranhão and Brazil. He encouraged sugarcane, cotton, and other agrarian production and the importation of thousands of additional slaves. By 1800 nearly one-third of Brazil's three million people were slaves. Pombal also expelled the Jesuits in 1759, eight years before Spain did the same in the Iberian Peninsula and its colonies, and ordered an attack in 1776 on the Colônia do Sacramento across the river from Buenos Aires in modern-day Uruguay. Ultimately, war between the forces commanded by the first Spanish viceroy of Río de la Plata, Pedro de Cevallos, and Portuguese units shaped the eventual peace treaty. In 1777 the Treaty of San Ildefonso would return Santa Catarina and coastal Rio Grande to Brazil but leave the Spaniards with Colônia.[55] As Spain and France allied with the North American rebels against England in 1776, Pombal joined sides with the British, thus closing Portugal's ports to ships from England's rebellious colonies.

Pombal's reforms, like those of post-1760 Bourbon Spain, sought to increase royal revenues and political control, reduce tax evasion and corruption, and improve colonial defenses. He repressed political opponents harshly, established a board of censors to discourage public discussion, and jailed his adversaries.[56] To Brazil he sent nobles and high-ranking military officers to govern the captaincies; moved the capital from Bahia, Portugal's main shipyard, to Rio de Janeiro (1763); and reinforced army and militia strength in the south. Defense of the southern frontier in military actions (1762–63, 1767–68) and increased military expenditures indicated the importance of Brazilian territory and revenue to the Portuguese Crown.

In contrast to the Bourbon reforms in Spanish America, however, the Pombaline reforms did not seriously discriminate against Brazilian-born subjects. Important positions in the royal bureaucracy and the expanding militia went to Brazilians. Only minor rebellions and conspiracies marred the late eighteenth century. These focused on opposition to Portuguese commercial and industrial policy that discriminated against Brazil, and to new taxes or the more determined collection of previous levies, such as the royal *quinto* in the mining areas. The most serious, the 1798 Minas Gerais revolt and that in Bahia, quelled immediately in 1795, never approached the scale of the Andean and Mexican uprisings faced by the Spanish. Other conspiracies (Rio de Janeiro, 1794; Pernambuco, 1801) were easily suppressed. While discontent existed in Brazil, a large slave population, a vast decentralized economy and administration, and reliance on local militia and British oversight distinguished Portuguese Brazil from Spanish America. Both at home and in the colonies, international conflicts, political disorders, and rebellion in the late eighteenth century gave more importance to military institutions in Spain than in Portugal and Brazil.

The French Revolution and Nascent *Patrias* in the Americas

The crisis of Bourbon Spain and the Portuguese monarchy in the last decades of the eighteenth and first decades of the nineteenth centuries coincided with the first modern European revolution and the rise of true national armies. Indeed, the modern idea of "nation-state," in contrast to the patrimonial monarchical state, coincided with the French Revolution, the Spanish resistance to the French invasion (1808–1814), and the creation of independent Latin American polities. Each of these depended on spilling blood to affirm, reaffirm, or establish sovereignty. After 1789, "nation" (*patria*) no longer simply meant people with common origins. Now it referred to a politically defined territory and sovereignty—the nation-state. In the words of the eminent Spanish historian Manuel Espadas Burgos, only after 1789 did "nation [signify] a specific territory with well-defined boundaries, homogeneity of race, language or culture, as well as a *general sovereign will*, i.e., a manifest desire to form a *state*, which on occasion coalesced with the idea of a *people*, in the sense of a community capable of developing a will for self-determination. The new concept of nation took root in the French Revolution, immediately spread throughout Europe, and leap-frogged across the Atlantic."[57]

This meaning of nation merged the challenge to absolute monarchy and the idea of popular sovereignty. The new concept of nation eliminated patrimonial absolutism and divine right monarchy; sovereignty passed from the Crown to "the people." This version of nation was both authoritarian and revolutionary. For its implementation it depended on military power for external defense and for consolidating internal authority. The Spanish American armed forces' historical links to the development of Spanish nationalism, and then their central role in the independence struggles that created new nations in the former colonies, made them identify their institutions with the *patria* as independent nation-state. The "national" army predated the modern *patria*, won it, created it, defended it, and became its guardian.

At first, Spain attempted to insulate itself from the French Revolution. Carlos IV's principal adviser, the Conde de Floridablanca, ordered all nonresidents to leave Madrid and directed that "all prints, papers, printed matter, manuscripts, boxes, fans, and any other object alluding to the events in France [be sent] from the custom ports directly to the secretary of state."[58] The Inquisition was revived to ferret out subversive literature and revolutionaries, while troop strength increased along the Pyrenees frontier. Secret police monitored sympathizers of revolution. Meanwhile, poor harvests, food shortages, and rising prices in 1788 brought riots to New Castile and Barcelona, and tax protests followed in 1790–91 in Galicia. Rapid salary increases for troops and repressive legislation quelled the violence, again emphasizing the importance of the military to royal control. In Alhama in December 1789, Spanish troops, apparently for the first time, were used to supervise local elections, putting down a minor tumult that resulted in the death of one soldier.

Carlos IV again enhanced military responsibilities in December 1790, assigning jurisdiction to anti-banditry forces over the contraband tobacco trade, and several new anti-banditry units were formed in the Basque provinces and along the Portuguese frontier. A new decree in 1793 characterized bandits as "disturbers of public tranquility," subject to the jurisdiction of courts-martial (*consejos de guerra*).[59] It also ordered troops to take "those measures and provisions considered appropriate (*conveniente*) to preserve the public peace." This same vague language would later appear in Latin American constitutions and national security legislation, giving license to suppress those persons perceived to be threatening internal security. In the same year the *consejos de guerra* were made permanent institutions in a decree directed at sedition, tumult, and protests by military personnel over wages and rations. In 1797, troops were ordered to assist in urban night-time patrols, a further militarization of police functions.

Spain went to war against revolutionary France after Louis XVI's execution. Its officers, however, and especially the highest-ranked captains-general, were trained in provincial politics and administration, not in warfare that required interprovincial logistics, communications, and organization. Thus, in April 1794 the French pushed the Spaniards back over the Pyrenees and seized a chunk of Catalonia. The Peace of Basle in the following year returned all lost territory to Spain, but the Caribbean island of Santo Domingo was ceded to France. From 1796 to 1807, Spain again allied with France, but it was always concerned about the spread of revolutionary activities to the homeland.

After 1799, with Napoleon's rise to power, the Spanish military, commanded by the royal favorite Manuel Godoy, again went to war. The War of the Oranges sent 60,000 men to Portugal. Militarily weak, Portugal surrendered after only three weeks despite the Spanish Army's pitiful performance in mobilization, logistics, and combat—and despite the fact that numerous Spanish generals had refused to participate in the campaign. Efforts at further military reforms followed, from 1801 to 1806, without great impact. The Spanish brass resisted creation of a general staff, on the French model, and continued to insist on an army raised from provincial recruitment and organization. While the reforms did not improve the military's fighting capability, it did further increase the judicial authority of captains-general, particularly in the colonies. In 1806 the captains-general were given authority to review the decisions of civilian courts in times of war.[60]

Godoy staffed the officer corps with his partisans while impressing masses of vagrants, criminals, and unfortunate peasants into the regiments. In short, the military functioned usually as the provincial fiefdom of favored captains-general; it functioned poorly as a military force. It had extensive experience at repressing bandits, persecuting political dissidents, and putting down riots and protests. It lacked any general staff, cohesive national officer corps, coherent military doctrine, logistics system, or integrated combat capabilities. It was a politicized army, in which condemned peasants, criminals, vagrants, and former bandits were ordered about by incompetent officers.

When Napoleon invaded Spain to consolidate the Continental System and exclude Britain from Europe, Spanish irregulars fought a "war of independence" (1808–1814) against the French. This was Spain's first essentially *national* war. In resisting Napoleon, the *junta suprema* of Seville proclaimed: "The defense of the fatherland and the king, of laws, and religion, of the rights of all men—crushed and violated in unparalleled fashion by Napoleon, Emperor of the French, and by the troops he has sent to Spain—has forced the entire nation to take up arms and to choose a government of its own."[61] In exhorting armed resistance to the French, assemblies throughout Spain followed with proclamations that *la patria* was in danger. This rhetoric would be emulated frequently, indeed ritually, in Spain and Latin America for the next century. When *la patria* was in danger, the armed forces had to fulfill their messianic mission. Medieval Iberian military mystique merged with the new nationalism to make the armed forces the guardians and saviors of their nations.

French troops in Spain and a French king, Joseph Bonaparte, Napoleon's brother, on the throne in Madrid created a political crisis and provoked massive popular resistance and guerrilla warfare. The crisis in Spain precipitated independence movements in Spanish America. It also brought forth Spain's first modern constitution, the Cádiz Constitution (1812), the rise of liberalism, and a military coup in 1820 against the restored Bourbon monarch, Ferdinand VII, led by military officers proclaiming liberal principles and seeking to avoid another expedition to reconquer the American colonies. In all this, the key actors were the armed forces—royal regiments, militia, guerrillas, Spanish American revolutionaries, and royal officers who, by changing uniforms and loyalties, became legendary patriots in Spanish America.

Notes

1. "Reglamento para las milicias de infantería y caballería de la isla de Cuba," in Richard Konetzke, ed., *Colección de documentos para la historia de la formación social de Hispanoamérica, 1493–1810*, 3 vols. (Madrid: Consejo Superior de Investigaciones Científicas, 1962), 3:351.

2. For a classic description of the 1469–1716 period see J. H. Elliott, *Imperial Spain, 1469–1716* (New York: New American Library, 1963, 1977).

3. Bailey W. Diffie and George D. Winius, *Foundations of the Portuguese Empire, 1415–1580* (Minneapolis: University of Minnesota Press, 1977), esp. Chapter 2.

4. Fear of the Inquisition, its torture chambers, and its seemingly unrestricted power pervaded colonial life, much as secret police and clandestine "dirty wars" would create a climate of fear in parts of Latin America from the 1960s to the 1990s. The political and cultural reach of the Inquisition, as well as the nature of colonial society, is portrayed brilliantly in Marcos Aguinis's novel, *La gesta del marrano* (Barcelona: Editorial Planeta Argentina, 1993).

5. John Lynch, *The Hispanic World in Crisis and Change, 1598–1700* (Oxford: Blackwell, 1992): 367.

6. Ibid.: 369.

7. Ibid.: 374.

8. Cited in ibid.: 380.

9. Ibid.: 383.

10. I. A. A. Thompson, *War and Government in Habsburg Spain, 1560–1620* (London: Athlone Press, 1976): 287.

11. José Ramón Alonso, *Historia política del ejército español* (Madrid: Editora Nacional, 1974): 21.

12. Cited in Henry Kamen, *The War of Succession in Spain, 1700–1715* (Bloomington: Indiana University Press, 1969): 135.

13. Pere Molas Ribalta, "The Early Bourbons and the Military," in Rafael Bañon Martínez and Thomas M. Barker, eds., *Armed Forces and Society in Spain Past and Present* (New York: Columbia University Press, 1988): 51–80.

14. W. N. Hargreaves-Mawdsley, *Eighteenth-Century Spain, 1700–1788: A Political Diplomatic and Institutional History* (London: Macmillan, 1979): 10.
15. Alfonso García-Gallo, *Los orígenes españoles de las instituciones americanas* (Madrid: Rivadeneyra, 1966).
16. John Lynch, *Bourbon Spain, 1700–1808* (London: Basil Blackwell, 1989): 127.
17. Alonso (1974): 30
18. Ibid.: 36.
19. Allan J. Kuethe, *Cuba, 1753–1815: Crown, Military, and Society* (Knoxville: University of Tennessee Press, 1986): 8.
20. Alfonso García-Gallo, *Los orígenes de la administración territorial de las Indias* (Madrid: Rivadeneyra, 1944): 982.
21. Laura Rodríguez, "The Spanish Riots of 1766," *Past and Present* 59 (1973): 117–46.
22. Alonso (1974): 54.
23. Cited in Ministerio de Defensa Nacional, El Salvador, *Doctrina militar y relaciones ejército/sociedad* (San Salvador: ONUSAL, 1994): 130–31.
24. Printed in full in *Novísima recopiliación de leyes de los reynos de las Indias*, 5:338–41.
25. See Heidi Ly Beirich, "The Birth of Spanish Militarism: The Bourbon Military Reforms (1766–1808)" (Master's thesis, Department of Political Science, San Diego State University, 1994): 74.
26. Molas Ribalta (1988): 58.
27. Richard Konetzke, *América Latina, II, La época colonial* (Madrid: Siglo XXI Editores, 1976): 144–52 (Vol. 22 in the Historia Universal Siglo Veintiuno).
28. Lynch (1989): 342.
29. For a discussion of changing Spanish military doctrine and policy in the eighteenth century see Juan Batista, *La estrategia española en América durante el siglo de las luces* (Madrid: Editorial Mapfre, 1992).
30. See Reed Browning, *The War of the Austrian Succession* (New York: St. Martin's Press, 1993).
31. Kuethe (1986): 9–12. For a British view see Richard Harding, *Amphibious Warfare in the Eighteenth Century: The British Expeditions to the West Indies, 1740–1742* (Suffolk, Eng.: Royal Historical Society, Boydell Press, 1991).
32. Lynch (1989): 175–78.
33. Kuethe (1986): 15–22.
34. Ibid.: 45–49.
35. See Christon I. Archer, *The Army in Bourbon Mexico, 1760–1810* (Albuquerque: University of New Mexico Press, 1977); Lyle N. McAlister, *The "Fuero Militar" in New Spain, 1764–1800* (Gainesville: University of Florida Press, 1957); John R. Fisher, Allan J. Kuethe, and Anthony McFarlane, eds., *Reform and Insurrection in Bourbon New Granada and Peru* (Baton Rouge: Louisiana State University Press, 1990); Leon Campbell, *The Military and Society in Colonial Peru, 1750–1810* (Philadelphia: American Philosophical Society, 1978); Santiago Gerardo Suárez, *Las fuerzas armadas venezolanas en la colonia* (Caracas: Biblioteca de la Academia Nacional de la Historia, 1979); and Juan Marchena Fernández, *La institución militar en Cartagena de Indias, 1700–1810* (Seville: Escuela de Estudios Hispanoamericanos, 1982).
36. McAlister (1957): 58.
37. Michael C. Meyer and William L. Sherman, *The Course of Mexican History*, 3d ed. (New York: Oxford University Press, 1987): 275.
38. For a detailed study of Spanish military policy and deployments in the colonies in the decades before independence see Julio Albi, *La defensa de las Indias (1764–1799)* (Madrid: ICI, Ediciones Cultura Hispánica, 1987); and Juan Marchena Fernández, *Oficiales y soldados en el ejército de América* (Seville: Escuela de Estudios Hispanoamericanos, 1983).
39. See Sergio Vergara Quiroz, *Historia social del ejército de Chile*, 2 vols. (Santiago: Universidad de Chile, 1993).
40. Lynch (1989): 343.
41. See Carlos Marichal and Matilde Souto Mantecón, "Silver and Situados: New Spain and the Financing of the Spanish Empire in the Caribbean in the Eighteenth Century," *Hispanic American Historical Review* 74, no. 4 (November 1994): 587–613.
42. Molas Ribalta (1988): 72.
43. Marichal and Souto Mantecón (1994): 590.
44. See William B. Taylor, "Patterns and Variety in Mexican Village Uprisings," in John E. Kicza, ed., *The Indian in Latin American History: Resistance, Resilience, and Acculturation* (Wilmington, DE: Scholarly Resources, 1993): 109–40.
45. Lynch (1989): 339.
46. Juan Marchena Fernández, "The Social World of the Military in Peru and New Granada," in Fisher et al., eds. (1990): 60–61.
47. Anthony McFarlane, "The Rebellion of the *Barrios*," in Fisher et al., eds. (1990): 197–254.
48. See Scarlett O'Phelan Godoy, *Un siglo de rebeliones anticoloniales, Perú y Bolivia, 1700–1783* (Cusco, Peru: Centro de Estudios Rurales Andinos Bartolomé de las Casas, 1988).

49. Henry Dobyns and Paul L. Doughty, *Peru, A Cultural History* (New York: Oxford University Press, 1976): 134–35.

50. Lillian Estelle Fisher, *The Last Inca Revolt, 1780–1783* (Norman: University of Oklahoma Press, 1966): 236–37.

51. Ibid.: 379.

52. Dobyns and Doughty (1976): 136–37.

53. John Lynch, *Spanish Colonial Administration: The Intendant System in the Viceroyalty of the Río de la Plata* (London: Athlone Press, 1958): 264–67.

54. Caio Prado, Jr., *The Colonial Background of Modern Brazil*, trans. Suzette Macedo (Berkeley: University of California Press, 1969): 358–59.

55. Mark A. Burkholder and Lyman L. Johnson, *Colonial Latin America* (New York: Oxford University Press, 1990): 254–55.

56. Peggy K. Liss, *Atlantic Empires: The Network of Trade and Revolution, 1713–1826* (Baltimore: Johns Hopkins University Press, 1983): 60–61.

57. Manuel Espadas Burgos, "The Spanish Army during the Crisis of the Old Regime," in Bañon Martínez and Barker, eds. (1988): 85.

58. Cited in John D. Bergamini, *The Spanish Bourbons: The History of a Tenacious Dynasty* (New York: G. P. Putnam's Sons, 1974): 115.

59. *Novísima recopiliación de leyes de los reynos de las Indias*, 5:376.

60. Félix Colón de Larriátegui, *Juzgados militares de España y sus Indias*, 5 vols. (Paris: C. Farcy, 1828), 3:147.

61. Cited in Espadas Burgos (1988): 87.

2

Inventing *la Patria*

Wars, *Caudillismo*, and Politics, 1810–1885

> The tyrants of my country have taken it from me, and I now have not even a *patria* for which to sacrifice myself.
>
> —Simón Bolívar

> Make me a colonel. I'll do the rest.
>
> —Felipe Santiago Salaverry, Peru, 1835

Just as the development of European nation-states in the centuries after 1492 resulted in part from warmaking and the rise of modern armies, so too in Latin America did new states emerge from independence wars between 1810 and 1826. These were not "nation-states," for no nations existed. They lacked clear territorial demarcation and their peoples did not share a single cultural and historical past—except perhaps the glorious (for *conquistadores*) and painful (for the conquered, the enslaved, and their offspring) legacy of conquest and colonialism. Creole patriotism, the Spanish American elite's growing self-identity and hostility to Spanish rule, usually excluded native peoples and Afro-Americans.[1] There was no cherished *patria*, no post-French Revolution liberal *patria*, only *patrias chicas* to defend against Simón Bolívar and other liberators' dreams of continental unity.[2] Not until the late nineteenth century did the modern configuration of territorial nation-states become firmly imprinted.

Wars, rebellions, and pervasive violence dominated Latin American politics almost to the end of the nineteenth century. Besides killing and immiserating, war challenges the fiscal and administrative capacity of governments, dislocates economies, and destroys infrastructure. It also mobilizes resources, encourages technological innovation, generates new economic opportunities, and changes societies. War alters boundaries—territorial, social, and psychological—and both centralizes and fragments political authority. Sometimes it creates (or consolidates) nations; other times it mutilates or destroys them. It gives soldiers the right to dispose of lives and property, and the opportunity to do so without the right. If war and civil strife become permanent, the habits of war become the habits of society, shaping attitudes and expectations, subverting respect for political principles and civility, and cheapening human life. This was what war did in much of Latin America.

Latin America consisted of ports and poorly connected towns and villages amid vast contested hinterlands. It was a patchwork of local and regional fiefdoms separated by rugged mountains, gigantic river systems, deserts, plains, jungles, and the irregular armies of hundreds of ex-patriot officers, landowners, and political bosses. Personalist, factional, regional, religious, racial, and ideological conflicts made it virtually impossible to consolidate and legitimate governments in the new countries. Such varied conflicts make it even more difficult to generalize regarding nation-building in the region without drawing the ire of historians rightfully concerned with national and regional particularities. Nevertheless, some common patterns emerged.

Reestablishing political order after separation from Spain and Portugal was a monumental challenge made more difficult because of disagreement on boundaries and because of the lack of consensus on basic political principles, on whether the new states should be monarchies or republics, and on whether they should be organized on centralist, federal, or confederal models. Controversies over the Church's role in the independent states exacerbated political conflicts. Spain, France, Italy, and Germany also experienced considerable internal strife and international wars in struggling to create and consolidate nation-states, but three centuries of colonialism, miscegenation, cultural syncretism, and politically imposed racial stratification distinguished nation-building in Spanish America and Brazil from nineteenth-century Europe. Wars against hostile Indians in Mexico, Río de la Plata, and Chile, *criollo* fears of race war, and the lingering slavery issue also temporarily impeded national consolidation and complicated policy debates—as in the United States. These conflicts, worsened by wartime destruction, weak economies, and vulnerability to foreign intervention, contributed to the militarization of Latin American politics. They made "generals," "colonels," and garrisons paramount for more than one-half century after independence.

Great variations existed in the character, degree, and duration of post-independence Latin American militarism. In Mexico and to some extent Peru, former royalist military officers dominated post-independence governments. In northern South America and Chile this was less so, although independence war heroes such as José Antonio Páez (Venezuela), Andrés Santa Cruz (Bolivia and Peru), Juan José Flores (Ecuador), and sundry generals and colonels dominated politics almost to midcentury. In Central America, independence came virtually without war, although civil-military *caudillos* created the new nations that fragmented from the failed Central American Federation (1824–1838).

Latin Americans fought wars to determine national boundaries, to create large confederal nations—Central America (1824–1838), Gran Colombia (1821–1830), Peru-Colombia (1828–1830), Río de la Plata (1817–1860), Peru-Bolivia (1836–1841)—and then to carve smaller countries from them. In the case of Uruguay, a new country emerged from war between Brazil and Río de la Plata mediated by England (1825–1828). These were essentially wars of political consolidation (see Table 2–2) that determined both the boundaries of new states and the composition of "national" governments. Wars against European invaders and against other Latin American states further determined territorial boundaries and yielded a small pantheon of military heroes.

Whatever the circumstances, these wars simultaneously involved nation-building, territorial disputes, internal ideological and political conflicts, personalist and factional strife, and naked struggles over political power and government revenues. They were always more complex than pithy retrospective summaries indicate. Commonly, however, the wars sprang from a lack of political consensus and a failure to consolidate new nation-states within the larger Spanish colonial jurisdictions. They were fought by armies of peasants, ranch hands, vagrants, artisans, and workers led mainly by officers without

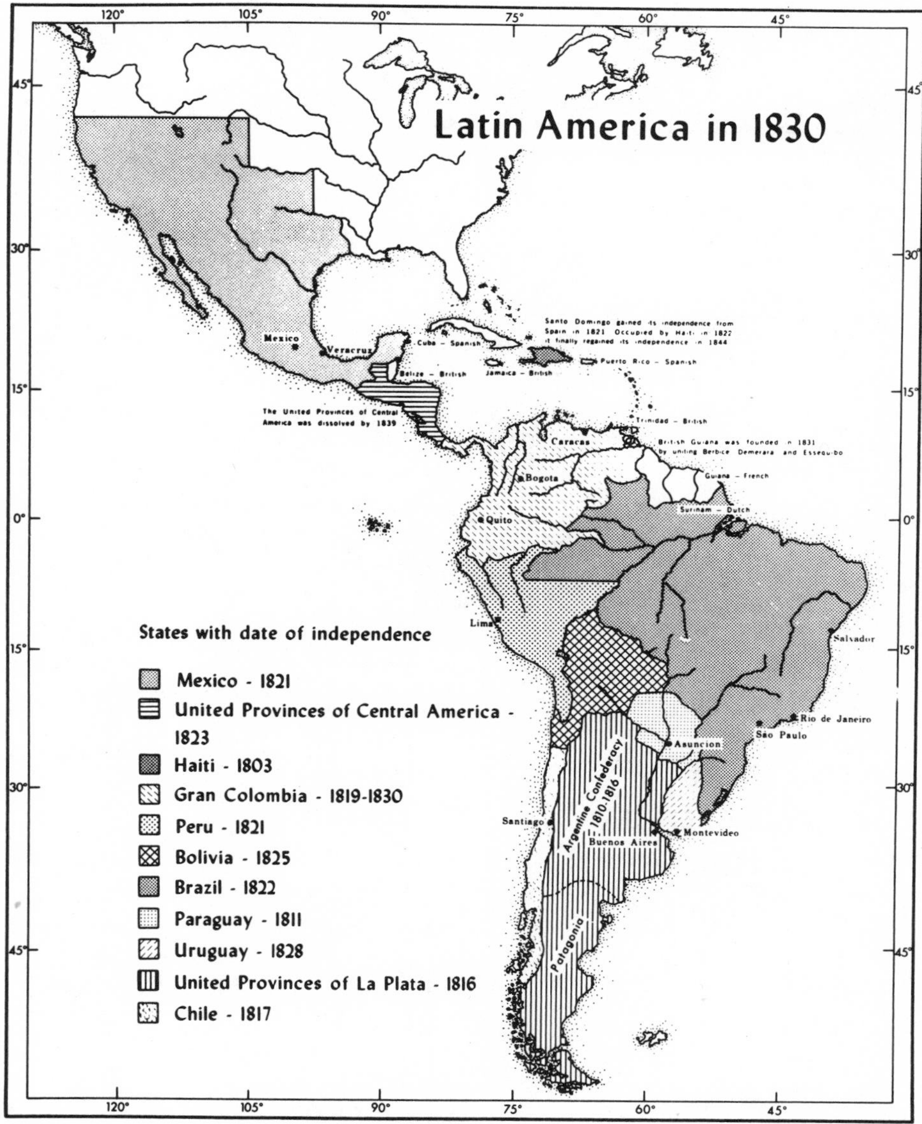

Map 2–1. Latin America in 1830. From Cathryn L. Lombardi and John V. Lombardi, with Lynn Stoner, *Latin American History, A Teaching Atlas*, published for the Conference on Latin American History by the University of Wisconsin Press, 1983, p. 49. Reprinted by permission of the University of Wisconsin Press

any formal military training. These armies were pre-modern and pre-professional. They lacked officers educated in military academies with common doctrines, strategic and tactical orientation, and career systems. They were not organized under an operational general staff, did virtually no planning for diverse military threats, carried out few military exercises, and were unprepared for sustained combat. Equipped with muskets, bayonets, small arms, knives, machetes, swords, lances, and the occasional artillery pieces, these armies killed and maimed at close range, typically hand to hand, without dis-

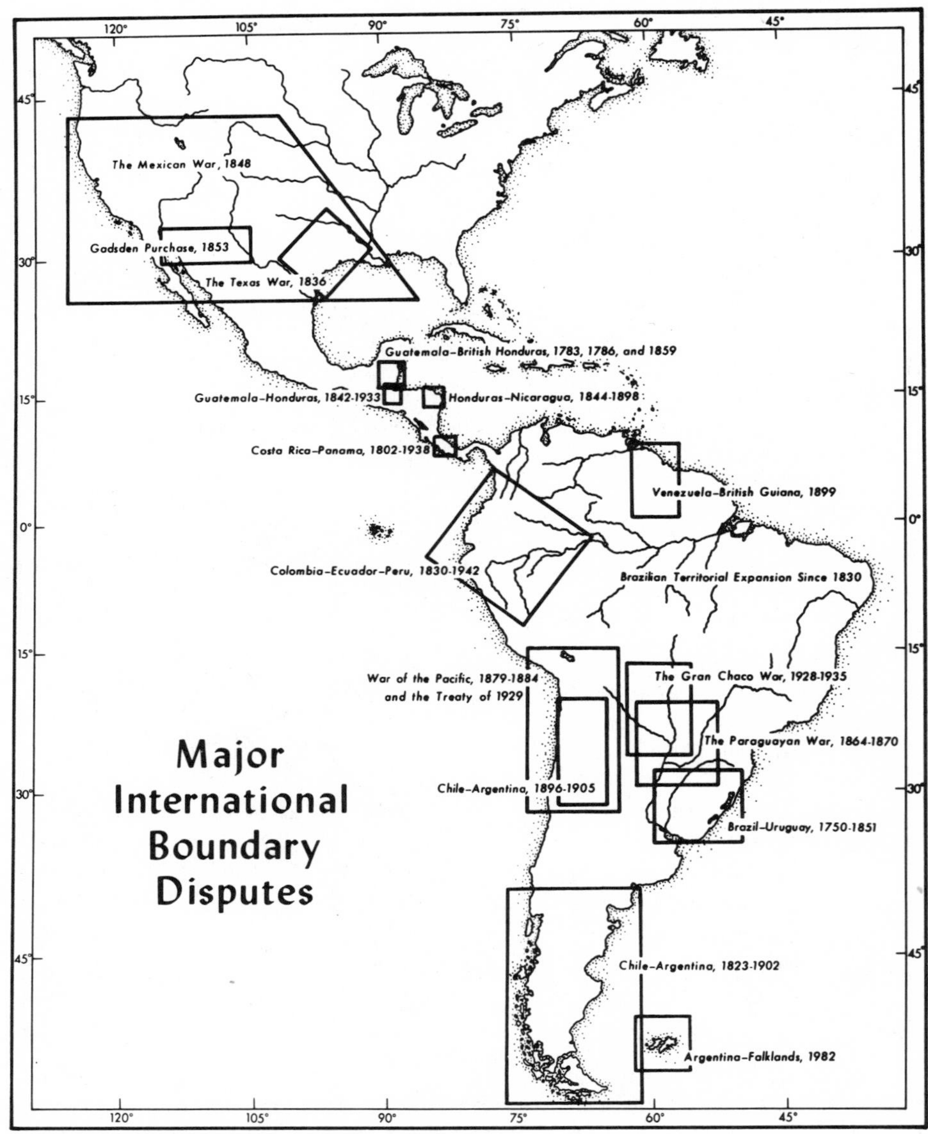

Map 2–2. Major International Boundary Disputes. From Cathryn L. Lombardi and John V. Lombardi, with Lynn Stoner, *Latin American History, A Teaching Atlas*, published for the Conference on Latin American History by the University of Wisconsin Press, 1983, p. 52. Reprinted by permission of the University of Wisconsin Press

cipline or practiced maneuvers. They not infrequently finished battles, if they could, with massacres.

Yet these armies fought in the name of *la patria,* and their victories and defeats became part of the martial mythology of the Latin American armed forces. Whatever the immediate "causes" of war, at stake was the meaning of *la patria,* its territory, historical myths, military heroes, and fundamental values. Would *la patria* be liberal or conservative, Catholic or pluralistic, centralist, federal, or confederal? Would the myths eulogize or demonize the Iberian conquest, glorify or despise the native peoples, sanctify hierarchy and racial stratification with pseudo-science or proclaim the virtue of "equality"? Would *la patria* be conceived as an organism, with a brain (government) and a central nervous system, subject to injury, infection, and cancer that would require political cures? Or as a patriarchal family in which miscreant children were disciplined? Or as a homeland (*madre-patria*) that would nurture diversity and tolerate pluralism in the "national family"?

New *patrias* had to be constructed, defended, and governed. Elite and European versions sometimes blended and sometimes collided with regional, local, and peasant objectives and visions of collective identity. Ultimately, "Peru," "Bolivia," "Chile," "Uruguay," "Mexico," and other nations emerged from hundreds of local, regional, and international conflicts in which peasants fought for land, Indian peoples for communal integrity, slaves and former slaves for liberation and opportunity, *caudillos* for wealth and power, and intellectuals for "civilization"—all in the name of some *patria* or other.[3]

At first, *patria* referred to multiple and overlapping territories and identities: "Spanish America," a province, a geographical region, an administrative center, or even a particular hacienda (the extreme version of *patria chica*), not to an abstract nation united by culture, language, or common history. In the Río de la Plata region the term *patria* referred to a person's native province, not to an Argentine, Paraguayan, or Uruguayan nation: "What does the *patria* mean to you? The fatherland for the *correntino* is Corrientes; for the *cordobés*, Córdoba; for the *tucumano*, Tucumán; for the *porteño*, Buenos Aires; for the gaucho, the *pago* [locality] where he was born. Everyone fights for his own corner, and the larger national interests are an 'incomprehensible abstraction.' "[4]

As in most of Spanish America, in the Río de la Plata region no nation-state existed until after midcentury. Powerful landowners and warlords ruled vast territories in a countryside populated by small guerrilla bands, bandits, cattle rustlers, itinerant ranch hands, and vagabonds. Even when frontiers were better defined toward the end of the nineteenth century, integrated nations failed to develop within defined boundaries. For many Indian people and racially heterogenous *castas* in the countryside and towns, fighting for *la patria* did not mean the nation but "freedom," as during the independence wars.[5]

In most of Latin America, alternative, overlapping versions of *la patria* coexisted. This dilemma made armies the immediate arbiters of political debate. The vote of the bayonets was difficult to resist, but its victory over political argument and elections hindered political consensus while further embedding authoritarian and violent political practices and "solutions." Still, different histories implied development of distinctive military institutions from nation to nation.

The Independence Wars and the First Generation of Military *Caudillos*

The independence wars brought carnage to Venezuela, quasi-race wars to Upper Peru (Bolivia), and royalist counterinsurgency campaigns to Mexico. In contrast, the struggle in Peru was relatively brief, with José de San Martín's combined Argentine-Chilean expedition invading by sea, and Simón Bolívar's armies from northern South America defeating the royalists. Estimates on the Mexican independence war dead range from 250,000 to 500,000 (some 5 to 10 percent of the population), and Venezuela suffered, proportionately, even more. Extensive economic destruction occurred in northern South America and Mexico alike. On the contrary, few died in Central American independence struggles. There, the infrastructure, such as it was, survived until the onset of later wars.

From Napoleon's invasion of the Iberian Peninsula in 1807–1808 to the 1820 military coup that prevented Ferdinand VII from sending reinforcements to his beleaguered forces in the Western Hemisphere, events in Spain influenced the fate of the Latin American independence movements. Spain managed to restore military and political control over the colonies from 1814 to 1817 except in the Río de la Plata provinces.[6] The reconquests that occurred in Chile and northern South America were vicious, with armies on both sides committing atrocities in the name of *la patria*. Bolívar declared "war to the death" against the Spaniards in 1813; various Spanish officers reciprocated, mercilessly torturing and massacring defeated rebels and civilians in the following years.

From 1810 to 1815, Spain never lost control in Peru, Mexico, Central America, Cuba, or Puerto Rico, but it suffered military setbacks in Río de la Plata, Chile, and northern South America. General Pablo Morillo's expeditionary force reestablished Spanish authority in Venezuela (1815) and Colombia (1816), and General Mariano Osorio temporarily reconquered Chile with reinforcements from Peru (1814–1817). Thereafter, rebels gradually defeated Spanish and loyalist armies in South America. Only to Venezuela and Colombia could Spain send a significant army, estimated at 10,000 troops, to reconquer its rebellious colonies. This force was fewer than the 15,000 troops that Portugal sent to Brazil after 1815, some of whom captured Montevideo in 1817, "to recover [for the Portuguese king] what in other times he possessed with a just title dating from the conquest, and which the crown of Castile wrested from him by violence."[7]

Despite Spanish invasions of northwestern Argentina (Salta) and battles in Chile from 1817 to 1821, the Río de la Plata provinces and Chile had gained their independence by 1818. After 1820, Spain lacked the military resources and political resolve to regain control. Internal strife and Colonel Rafael Riego's use of the army intended for colonial reconquest to instead reimpose the 1812 Constitution ended Spain's military prospects against the independence forces. Mexican independence came in 1821 as a reaction against the Spanish liberals who had offended the Church and decreed elimination of the military *fueros*. Peru did not fall until 1824, still not reinforced from Europe; Upper Peru (Bolivia) and some outposts on the Pacific coast, including Callao, held out until 1826. Spain retained Cuba and Puerto Rico. It did not recognize the independence of any of its former colonies until relations were established with Mexico in 1836, three years after Fernando VII's death.

Strikingly, almost all the best known "liberators" of the colonies emerged from Spain's royal army and colonial militia (although some, such as Antonio José de Sucre and Felipe Santiago Salaverry, were too young to have served in Spanish ranks when the independence movements began). Venezuelans and Colombians played key roles in the liberation and early politics of Ecuador, Peru, and Bolivia. And for the next several decades the presidents, would-be presidents, and political and military leaders came disproportionately from the generation of independence war officers, many of whom had fought on both sides before independence was won. Military chieftains from the independence wars became a sort of natural elite in the decades after separation from Spain.

In Mexico and Peru, where royal authority and armies persisted longest, former royalist officers played a particularly important role in the first half of the nineteenth century. In Mexico, of the 118 generals and colonels listed in 1840, 81 had started their careers in the royalist army (and only 12 had served in the insurgent armies).[8] In Peru and Bolivia, key military figures and presidents such as Andrés Santa Cruz and Agustín Gamarra served with the royalist forces until the 1820s, some even after San Martín's liberating army invaded the viceroyalty from Chile. While this situation did not hold everywhere, and many "military" leaders were appointed on the battlefields and by presidential decree, Table 2–1 indicates the Spanish military background of selected "liberators," well-known *caudillos*, and early national heroes.

The independence wars changed Spanish America in important ways: mobilizing the underclasses, upsetting traditional social lines, redistributing landed estates and urban property, routinizing brutality, diffusing weapons among the population, and making the leaders of armies the source of short-term political authority through the delegation of emergency powers and "extraordinary authority" (*facultades extraordinarias*). The wars produced the *caudillos* who would dominate vast areas of Latin America in the nineteenth century. They also set important precedents for the role of military forces in the region's international wars and internal conflicts during the next chaotic half-century.

First, both royalists and rebels relied extensively for cannon fodder on free blacks, slaves (who were promised freedom), *casta* peasants, ranch hands, cattle rustlers, bandits, vagabonds, and Indians. War also provided an opportunity for social mobility as mulattos, *mestizos*, and Indians served as officers. In Venezuela, Tomás Boves led the racially mixed, royalist, *llanero* guerrilla cavalry against Bolívar's forces and became the rebels' "most terrible enemy" before a lance ended his time on Earth. On the rebel side, General Manuel Piar, a *pardo*, carried on the fight against the royalists in the east after a defeated Bolívar temporarily quit the country (1814–15) and fled to Jamaica and Haiti.

Piar's concern for race, perhaps even beyond his concern for independence, led him to challenge Bolívar's authority in 1817. Bolívar condemned him to death as a conspirator and rebel, fearing that racial antagonisms would threaten the independence struggle and, not incidentally, Bolívar's own star. In contrast, "General" Páez, a hardened plainsman who came to terms with Bolívar

Table 2–1. Selected Spanish American "Liberators" in Spain's Army and Militia

Liberator	*Background*
José Artigas (Uruguay)	Officer in the *Blandenques* anti-banditry unit stationed at Colonia, 1797–1818; fought against Portuguese; exiled in Paraguay after 1820.
Simón Bolívar (Northern South America, Peru, Bolivia)	Most important independence leader in northern South America; served in militia of the Valleys of Aragua; royal commission as militia ensign, 1798.
José Miguel Carrera (Chile)	Spanish army officer; fought in Spain, 1808–11; Chilean dictator in early independence movement.
Ramón Castilla (Peru)	Cadet in Spanish army in Chile; taken prisoner at Battle of Chacabuco; escaped and returned to Peru in 1818; promoted to *alférez;* joined San Martín's army in Peru; fought at Ayacucho against Spaniards.
Juan José Flores (Venezuela, Ecuador)	Soldier in Morillo's Spanish army; switched sides after capture by rebels; Ecuador's first president (1830–34) and key political leader until midnineteenth century.
Agustín Gamarra (Peru)	Officer in Spanish army until 1821; Peru's president (1829–33, 1839–41) and military *caudillo;* died at Battle of Ingavi in 1841 against Bolivians while seeking to merge Bolivia, or part of it, into Peru.
Martín Güemes (Argentina, Salta)	Entered Spanish army at age fourteen; in Salta 1799–1805, then in Buenos Aires fighting against British invasion in 1806; went over to independence movement in 1810; killed in 1821.
Agustín de Iturbide (Mexico)	High-ranking royalist officer until 1821; directed counterinsurgency campaign against rebels until going over to independence movement and becoming "emperor" of Mexico.
José de la Mar (Peru)	Spanish officer; fought against French; brigadier in 1814; joined rebels after fall of Callao, 1821; as Peru's president (1827–29), led Peruvian anti-Bolivarian faction in war against Colombia (1828–30); exiled to Costa Rica after being deposed by coup.

Antonio López de Santa Anna (Mexico)	Royalist army commander and subaltern of Iturbide; overturned Iturbide's "empire"; many-term president of Mexico.
Francisco de Miranda (Venezuela)	Captain in infantry company in 1772; fought in North Africa; served in Cuba, Florida (against British in Spanish army supporting U.S. independence movement), and the Bahamas; left service in 1783, accused of spying for British and contraband trade.
José María Obando (Colombia)	Royalist guerrilla leader; switched sides and became *caudillo* in southwestern provinces; president of Colombia (1853).
Joaquín Prieto Vial (Chile)	Lieutenant in Spanish cavalry in Chile, 1805; Chilean president, 1831–41.
José de la Riva-Agüero (Peru)	Short service with Spanish army before 1809; briefly Peruvian president after independence.
Bernardino Rivadavia (Argentina)	Colonial militia; fought against British in 1806–07 invasion; leading unitarist in Buenos Aires and "Argentine" president; ousted during war against Brazil (1827) by federalist *caudillos*; sent into exile.
José de San Martín (Argentina, Chile, Peru)	Served in Spanish army from 1789–1811 in Spain, France, Portugal, and North Africa; "supreme protector" of Peru (1822).
Andrés Santa Cruz (Bolivia, Peru)	Officer in Spanish army until 1820 when captured at Battle of Cerro de Pasco; briefly interim president of Peru (1827) and founder of Peru-Bolivia Federation (1836–39); plotted return to Bolivia from exile and creation of monarchy in South America.

but never became subordinate, raised a patriot *llanero* force in Apure. He commanded the same sort of mixed-race irregular cavalry in the name of independence that Boves used against Bolívar. These *llaneros*, like those under Boves, fought out of loyalty to their leaders, for plunder, and for freedom of their plains from government control. They became the most important political currency in Venezuela, eventually helping to make Páez the nation's first president and its most important politico-military *caudillo* for the next two decades.

Aware of the volatility of the race question, Bolívar attempted to convince the troops that his revolution gave them what Piar pretended: "Have not our armies broken the chains of the slaves? Has not the odious distinction between classes and colours been abolished forever? Have I not ordered national property to be distributed among you? Are you not equal, free, independent, happy and respected?"[9] The answer, in Venezuela as in most of Latin America, was *no!* But the army did offer more opportunities than elsewhere. While the wars lasted, mobility seemed possible and equality plausible. In most of the region, however, slavery endured much beyond independence, and racial discrimination persisted unabated. *Criollos* incorporated successful military *caudillos* into the landowning classes, making these new *latifundistas* less interested in social reform than in consolidating their position in the old social hierarchy. Examples abound. Páez the *llanero* became a great Venezuelan cattle baron and conservative president. Flores, a Venezuelan upstart, married into the Quito aristocracy, served as independent Ecuador's first president, and later favored monarchy.

Indians, the recipients of unkept promises by both loyalists and patriots, also served both sides in the independence wars. The *cacique* Pumacahua, for example, who had fought against Túpac Amaru in the 1780s, joined rebel forces in Peru and Upper Peru. At La Paz the Spanish garrison was slaughtered; in Arequipa the intendant and other prisoners were shot. By mid-1815, however, the Spanish reconquest was complete and the leading rebels, including Pumacahua, were executed. In contrast, at Ayacucho in 1824, Indians fought on the royalist side in the losing cause against Sucre's Venezuelan-Ecuadorian polychromatic army. Indian, black, and *casta* troops bled for both sides, with their own objectives and dreams, but were never able to wrest permanent social and economic gains from either one.

Even in the most important campaigns, armies rarely exceeded 8,000 men, and, more typically, "battles" involved 500 to 2,000 combatants. Some 500 to 1,500 slaves, free blacks, and Indians made up an army. The "armada" of seven warships and less than twenty transports that carried San Martín's liberating expedition to Peru, for example, brought an army of 4,500, and Bolívar's combined Peruvian, Colombian, Venezuelan, and Chilean force that liberated Peru reached 8,000. The soldiers were always darker-skinned than most of their officers, the *criollo* elites, the Spanish loyalists, and the British, other European, and sometimes U.S. mercenaries.

The character of warfare and of military service promoted disrespect for traditional social lines, allowed upward mobility for selected war heroes and troops, and offered widespread redistribution of land and wealth. Spanish commanders and royal officials confiscated *haciendas*, cattle, horses, and provisions from supporters of the independence movements; rebels did the same against loyalists. Both sides abused, tortured, and executed prisoners—military and civilian, men, women, and children. They confiscated property to finance their campaigns and to stuff their own pockets. Descriptions of savagery, repression, and abuse by loyalists and patriots abound. In 1810 in Upper Peru (Bolivia), the liberating army "initiated a rule of terror which soon alerted even the patriots. Royal officials were shot, Spaniards penalized, . . . the auxiliary army was on the rampage, terrorizing anyone who stood in its way."[10] In Venezuela in 1814–15, "the counterrevolution imposed itself as a violent reconquest. Many patriots were punished; some were executed . . . rebels were defined widely enough to include leaders, supporters, passive followers, and emigrants.

. . . In 1815 over three hundred haciendas were taken from creole rebels."[11] To the west, in Colombia in 1815, "Morillo landed his expedition at Santa Marta in July 1815. Cartagena maintained a suicidal resistance to a siege which lasted a hundred days, and was finally occupied on 6 December; the town was dead, its streets littered with corpses, and the few patriots still alive were butchered by the loyalists."[12]

These practices affected *criollo* and Spanish elites alike, temporarily upsetting the clear hierarchical socio-racial lines that separated the white peak of colonial society from the colored masses at the bottom. Although *criollos* sought to reestablish traditional social domination in the decades after independence, the armed forces, more than any other institution, permitted political and economic mobility for some who had been excluded by the colonial order. *Caudillo* presidents, generals, colonels, and garrison commanders used their military power to offset their lack of social status and to acquire economic resources. The old *criollo* elite's disdain for these new officers underlay a festering civil-military tension that survived into the twentieth century. In the decades after independence the "race question" and the "Indian question" gave the armed forces an often unspoken *razón de ser* (reason for being): to defend towns, cities, haciendas, and "civilization" itself against the ever-present threat of slave and Indian uprisings, wars by hostile tribes (especially in Argentina, Chile, and Mexico), and disorder by the urban *castas*. Loss of the political legitimacy and "social peace" imposed by Spain made post-independence political leaders and economic elites much more dependent on the armed forces for maintaining internal order than had been the colonial regime.

A second important change resulting from the independence wars was the widespread diffusion of weapons, militias, guerrilla bands, and military jurisdiction. Vast territories were subjected to martial law for decades. Military commanders, under emergency decrees or self-conferred authority, peremptorily disposed of property and lives. The military's jurisdiction over civilians, and its immunity from civil authority and courts, established a self-perpetuating culture of arrogance and domination legitimated by appeals to defend *la patria*, God, liberty, and independence (or monarchism, in the case of loyalists) against their enemies. Military orders were law; there existed no legal counterbalance, judicial remedy, or accountability when abuses occurred. Impunity prevailed, became the norm, and buttressed the armed forces' role in post-colonial society. This jurisdiction included regular armies, regional militias, and local *caudillo* bands commanded by landowners and so-called colonels.

In largely agrarian societies with the population concentrated in and around huge landed estates, politics, law enforcement, and political authority outside the cities and towns depended on armed force. National politics, to the extent that such existed, depended on controlling, balancing, and co-opting the dispersed military bands within the country. Inability to establish political order and effective law enforcement, widespread banditry, racial and social antagonisms, conflicts over land and water, and widespread corruption reinforced the importance and pervasiveness of the military role. And desertion, mutinies, scavenging, and brigandage were common in armies composed of forcibly recruited peasants, former slaves, vagrants, ranch hands, and town dwellers: "Most of the Colombian cavalry . . . was originally mounted on horses seized from private owners. Such exactions . . . could at least be justified by reasons of military necessity. . . . There were always some exactions, on the other hand, that can be classed as simple robbery for the benefit of individual officers and men. . . . Indeed a very high proportion of the crimes of violence committed during the decade of Gran Colombia [1821–1830] were cases involving the military."[13]

The new states were left with "virtual armies of occupation, whose function was principally the welfare of their own members."[14] Like many of the new Spanish American nations, Gran Colombia spent from 50 to 75 percent of its budget to finance the armed forces even as the nation sank further into debt. With Spain unreconciled to the loss of its colonies, a persuasive rationale existed to maintain national armies and militia. Into the 1840s, Spain plotted a return to northern South America and actually reestablished colonial rule in the Dominican Republic from 1861 to 1865. It also seized Peru's Chincha Islands, the source of guano, its main export; occupied Callao in 1864; and in 1866 bombarded Chile's main port, Valparaíso.[15] Recurrent foreign intervention and regional and civil wars reinforced the habits of military preponderance acquired from 1810 to 1826.

Related to the diffusion of weapons, militia, irregular armies, and banditry was a third feature of the independence wars that gave a predominant political role to the military: early Spanish American political charters and constitutions fused civil and military authority in powerful, virtually dictatorial executives. Constitutions typically gave these executives extraordinary powers to meet emergencies, assure internal security, and respond to external threats. These constitutional regimes of exception permitted suspension of civil liberties and rights, allowed confiscation of property, and inspired general contempt for due process and the rule of law. They initiated the Spanish American tradition of constitutional dictatorship. Typical examples of such legitimation of dictatorship were the 1814 *Reglamento para el Gobierno Provisorio* for Chile that gave the "supreme director" "full and unrestricted authority" (*facultades amplísimas e ilimitadas*), and the 1821 Constitution for Gran Colombia that vested in the chief executive "those extraordinary powers deemed indispensable."[16] This Gran Colombian charter authorized that "in times of internal commotion and armed conflict endangering the security of the Republic," the president take "whatever extraordinary measures, not within the normal sphere of his authority, that the case may require." Similarly, San Martín made himself "supreme protector" of Peru, explaining: "On my arrival at Pisco, I announced, that, owing to the imperative circumstances, I found myself invested with the Supreme Authority, and that I was responsible to the Country for the exercise of it: Circumstances have not changed, because Peru still has internal Enemies to combat; and it is consequently necessary that the political and military command should continue in my person."[17]

With president-generals on the battlefield and their regional and local commanders exercising war powers, policymaking, administration, and execution came frequently from the saddle rather than from the congress and bureaucracy. Flores, for example, exercised "supreme military and civil authority" in Quito from 1825 to 1830 while heading an occupation army. When the independence wars were won, the cattle-baron "colonels" and "generals" who emerged from the rebel armies were rewarded with land grants for their service to *la patria*. They continued making policy and administering their version of justice. These were the *caudillos*, the men on horseback with irregular armies who dominated Latin America for much of the nineteenth century.

Caudillismo meant "the rule by any kind of pre-eminent leader who derived authority more by an ability, through force of character and patronage, to command the loyalty of a substantial band of armed followers, than from adherence to the rule of law or the constitution."[18] *Caudillos* "used violence or the threat of violence for political ends—whether as a professional officer commanding regular army units, or as a militia officer or civilian on horseback leading militia or irregular forces into battle, or (more broadly) as an essentially civilian leader who engaged in violent repression."[19] These *caudillos* proudly displayed military rank; most were not professional soldiers. Nineteenth-century Latin America was dominated by *caudillos*, violence, and the military, but not by professional armed forces. The beginnings of truly professional armies, with officers sharing common doctrines, knowledge, skills, and esprit de corps acquired in war academies and technical schools, would not appear until after the mid-1870s.

The *caudillos* inherited both the loyalist and Bolivarian tradition of "war to the death" against adversaries, always fighting in the name of liberty and some "ism" (republicanism, unitarism, federalism) and against evil enemies (unitarists, federalists, liberals, godless subversives, Catholic fanatics, Freemasons, and other targets of opportunity). Juan Manuel de Rosas, for example, the most famous of Argentina's conservative, pro-clerical, and federalist *caudillos* who dominated Buenos Aires and the interior from 1829 to 1852, ruled with "extraordinary powers." He had his portrait placed on church pulpits, outlawed the opposition press and "political writings," and used a secret police (the *mazorca*) to murder and intimidate opponents under the banner (which appeared on public documents), "Death to the Savage Unitarians." Rosas assembled a more or less permanent army camped outside of Buenos Aires that became the ultimate basis of his power.[20] To the north, Colombia's liberal president, Francisco de Paula Santander (1832–1837), who had opposed Bolívar's dictatorial style, implacably repressed "traitors" who conspired against his government. Thus, a plot in 1833 by a purged general, José Sardá, resulted in "his being tracked down by loyal officers who were admitted to his hideaway on the pretense of wanting to join his movement—and instead shot him in cold blood. . . . Santander's enemies raised a hue and cry over the unnecessary cruelty used, but Santander refused to reprimand his subordinates. By that time seventeen others had already been shot in the main square of Bogotá, as Santander (who rejected the court's recommendation of clemency in seven of the cases) watched through an office window."[21]

Repression could be ordered in the name of any convenient "ism," any cause, any high-sounding principle. Always, the *caudillo* in power (and his opponents) justified the quest for power, patronage, and personal aggrandizement and the need to kill, repress, exile, and confiscate property from their adversaries with defense of *la patria*, and with the particular political slogans of the moment (some might say ideology, such as liberalism and conservatism, but this seems too exaggerated a claim for most early nineteenth-century *caudillos*). Whatever the cause, lances, bayonets, swords, the gallows, firing squads, prisons, and exile were the main political instruments.

Those exiled sometimes provided vivid descriptions of *caudillo* heavy-handedness. Future Argentine president Domingo Sarmiento published *Facundo* (1845) from exile in Chile. It was a passionate attack on *caudillo* barbarism and the politics of terror that became a classic interpretation of politics and culture in the first half of the nineteenth century: "Let us not deceive ourselves: terror is a means of government which produces greater results than patriotism and fervor."[22] Of course, years later as governor of the province of San Juan, Sarmiento, the liberal champion of civilization against *caudillo* barbarism, justified this politics of terror in fighting banditry and rebels. When his militia captured, killed, and displayed on a pole the head of Angel V. Peñaloza, the *caudillo* from La Rioja, Sarmiento wrote to President Bartolomé Mitre: "If we had not cut off the head of that inveterate scoundrel and placed it on display, the mob would not have quieted down in six months."[23]

Applying emergency powers and military ordinances against political opponents, "subversives," and bandits became routine—indeed, the most ubiquitous feature in nineteenth-century Spanish American politics. The independence wars and their constitutions thus provided the legal rationale for presidentialism and dictatorship as well as for the preeminent role of the armed forces in politics. They also nurtured an infant militarism that gradually came to pervade Latin America, even when presidents such as Santander in Colombia opposed large standing armies and military political involvement.

A fourth legacy of the independence wars assured another important role for the region's armed forces: border wars and defense against periodic military interventions by European nations. Spain's colonial territories had been poorly demarcated, and administrative jurisdictions had been frequently reconfigured. The principle of *uti possidetis* (right to possession) provided that "republican governments are being founded within the limits of the former viceroyalties, captaincies general, or presidencies."[24] But which limits, and where were they? And what of smaller jurisdictions, such as Quito and Charcas? And what of disputed jurisdictions such as those across the river from Buenos Aires (the *banda oriental*) that would later become Uruguay? These questions fueled decades of conflict, border disputes, all-out wars, intervention by *caudillos* supporting their allies across "international" frontiers, and therefore the need for military forces to defend territorial and jurisdictional claims.

International wars could not be distinguished entirely from internal wars and disputes among rival *caudillos*, particularly in Central America, Peru, Ecuador, Colombia, and the Río de la Plata region until the 1860s. Unsettled claims of the independence wars encouraged militarization of Latin American politics, and foreign military intervention made it unavoidable. Battles between contending *caudillos* within "nations" made border disputes elements of internal political conflict and international war. Before the dissolution of Gran Colombia and Bolívar's death (1830), for example, battles between his allies and anti-Bolivarians made civil wars and separatist struggles inseparable from Bolívar's personal project to consolidate "the basis of the social compact, which ought to form of this world a nation of republics."[25]

No "nation of republics" emerged, but fighting the independence wars and the post-independence conflicts was expensive. A fifth legacy was the high cost of financing the military campaigns, the debt accumulated, the excessive expense of maintaining armies and paying pensions to retired officers, the emergence of war as a source of business opportunity for the favored, and the accumulation of grievances by uncompensated and defrauded veterans. Internal and foreign loans partly financed the destruction and butchery. Nonpayment of the debts accumulated in independence wars and post-independence disorder motivated conflicts among the new Spanish American nations and also invited foreign intervention. European powers sent military expeditions to defend their nationals, force payment of private and public debts, avenge supposed diplomatic slights, and enforce their commercial and territorial claims. Occasionally, they were also invited by Latin American factions to support their cause against internal rivals, thus provoking military responses by "nationalists" and would-be presidents. *La patria* rarely lacked external military threats—from Europe, other Latin American nations, and the United States.

In all of these conflicts, the post-independence *caudillos* and their small irregular cavalry bands found opportunities to wield knives, machetes, and lances to defend *la patria*, the constitution, and other sacred causes—and to profit from their service if they won the battle. Wars, big and small, meant opportunity for gaining land, booty, and social mobility. For many Latin Americans this was the only chance, or the best one, for bettering their lot. Although war offered soldiers opportunities for social mobility and economic rewards, from the time of the independence wars governments frequently failed to keep their promises to veterans. Abolition of slavery, land grants, pensions, patronage, and other enticements for wartime service eluded retired soldiers. Worse still, presidents and *caudillos* purged the ranks of opponents and rewarded their personal followers, making "politics" an enemy of the wounded, betrayed, and cashiered. Páez, for example, had persuaded Bolívar to promise bonuses ranging from 500 pesos for common soldiers to 25,000 pesos for a *general en jefe.* While Páez and Santander benefited handsomely, acquiring large confiscated estates, many soldiers and officers received little, if any, of the promised benefits. Festering resentment produced political malcontents, bandits, and opposing armies. Corruption, speculation in the vouchers (*vales*) for land and currency sometimes distributed to veterans, and outright fraud further lowered government credibility. Although some veterans in all the nations received recompense for their patriotic service (and some generals fabulous rewards in land and money), the mass of veterans had the unreliability and venality of government proved to them most painfully. Political influence was usually needed to obtain promised patronage, promotions, and pensions. Political "outs" could count on nothing. How could military officers not be involved in politics?

Sixth, conflicts arose over the constitutional, political, and professional status of the military in the new nations. Debates of varying intensity in each nation took place on the perpetuation or elimination of military *fueros*, on the extent of military jurisdiction over civilians, on the propriety and desirability of suffrage for officers and common soldiers, and on the merits of militia versus standing regular armies. Military budgets strained impoverished, indebted governments, and efforts to demobilize and shrink the independence armies threatened social peace when soldiers returned to the countryside and towns without land, jobs, or prospects.

Political supporters, including officers, could be rewarded from the public coffers and promoted at presidential whim (although sometimes legislative approval was required). Political opponents, including officers, could be stripped of command, demoted, cashiered from service, and exiled, their property confiscated and their families persecuted. The stakes for political losers were high and the risks substantial enough to make control of violence literally worth everything. Each shift in government potentially threatened catastrophe or proffered a windfall. Until this situation changed, the loyalty and effectiveness of both regular armies and irregular bands would make the difference between presidents and corpses, between opulence and poverty, between tranquility and exile, between life and death. Officers could lose and win their commands, be promoted and stationed in the capital, or sent to the provinces and penury as the result of political fate. With politics so crucial to their personal and professional lives, and so volatile, "liberty, equality and fraternity gave way to infantry, cavalry, and artillery, as the republics bled themselves in constant warfare."[26]

Appointments of generals and colonels by presidents and ranking officers multiplied, thus derailing efforts to limit military expenditures and to professionalize the officer corps. Indeed, prior to the 1870s, or even the end of the century when European missions were contracted to develop more professional military organizations, armies in Central America and elsewhere "were the *caudillos'* personal militia, composed of ill-disciplined and low-paid rabble who enjoyed privilege and prestige of a sort, but also evoked universal disdain and fear."[27]

Discipline in these armies was brutal; beatings, whippings of from one hundred to five hundred lashes, and other savage punishments were common. Such treatment was passed on to miscreants, bandits, and enemies with whom the troops came into contact. Soldiers who were not ranch hands on the *caudillos'* personal estates were frequently "recruited," as noted earlier, from the ranks of slaves, as punishment for vagrancy, or directly from the prisons. Military duty was itself a punishment for many crimes; serving *la patria* was often not voluntary. Illustrative were the crocodile tears shed by Uruguay's Colonel León Palleja in 1853: "I deplore as anyone the terrible necessity of corporal punishment prescribed by our military laws. But take a look at the people in our army: they are composed for the most part of indolent African slaves accustomed to brute force; only in that way will they clean themselves and comply with the duties of a soldier, and [others] even worse, recruited from the jails. And it is desired to eliminate [whippings]? First, reform the personnel in the Army and get rid of these criminals."[28] This phenomenon was "not exclusive to Uruguay, but was more or less common . . . to all of Latin America in the decades after the definitive expulsion of the Spaniards."[29]

With no requirement that officers had to obtain professional training at military academies and with virtually no specialized schools (later called *escuelas de clase*, or *escuelas de suboficiales*) for noncommissioned officers, the military was inherently politicized, both as a resource of ambitious political leaders and in the dependence of officers on political circumstances for career advancement. Both of these factors irritated the small corps of military careerists who aspired to more patriotic and autonomous professional roles. This system of patronage made armies political instruments and politicians dependent on military intervention in politics—all justified by the reverent and ritual invocation of *la patria*.

"International" Wars and Internal Conflicts in the Early Nineteenth Century

Spanish America and Brazil went without pause from independence wars to a series of post-independence territorial and boundary disputes (see Map 2–1), wars with European nations, and civil wars. The confusion of these conflicts allowed all sides to claim patriotic inspiration as they killed, confiscated property, despoiled the countryside, sought to erect personalist fiefdoms, and endeavored to define the territorial boundaries of the new nations and the type of political systems that would govern Latin America. Roughly, such wars fell into four main overlapping categories: 1) transnational wars of political consolidation (those that determined the political existence and territory of nascent republics, including secession wars) (Table 2–2); 2) international wars (those between existing countries over other than boundary issues and territory, which nonetheless might involve transfer of territory from losers to victors) (Table 2–3); 3) wars against European military intervention, including Spanish efforts to restore imperial authority (Table 2–4); and 4) civil wars.

A table listing civil wars and rebellions in nineteenth-century Latin America, even if such a list could be accurately compiled (and this is not likely), would require an additional volume. Historian David Bushnell, for example, lists eleven "national level rebellions" in nineteenth-century Colombia. He adds: "Indeed, what was a civil war? . . . And should one—could one—count all the outbreaks whose immediate aim was to overthrow only regional authorities?"[30] Dana Munro comments on Bolivia that after the overthrow of Sucre (1827–28), "nearly every change of government had been the result of a mutiny in the army, and every officer of the higher ranks had come to regard himself as a potential dictator."[31] Peru's most insightful historian, Jorge Basadre, counts thirteen military uprisings in Bolivia from June to October 1840,[32] and "Mexico had sixteen presidents and thirty-three provisional national leaders, a total of forty-nine administrations in thirty-three years."[33] Not even Brazil escaped post-independence political violence:

> The regency had already suffered from a rash of rebellions . . . in Maranhão (1831–32), Bahia (1832–1835), Minas Gerais (1833), and Mato Grosso (1834). The *Cabanagem* revolt in Pará began in January 1835 and continued until 1837, leaving the province in ruins. . . . it degenerated into a senseless orgy of murder and pillage. Later in 1835 the most serious revolt of all began—the Farroupilha, or War of the Ragamuffins, in Rio Grande do Sul. The *farrapos*, so-called because of the fringed leather they wore on the cattle ranges, were influenced by some of the separatist currents in the Río de la Plata region, for Rio Grande do Sul bordered on Uruguay, and neither side paid much attention to international boundaries.[34]

Table 2–2. Transnational Wars of Political Consolidation and Secession, 1825–1870

Wars	*Motivations/Outcomes*
Mexican Empire/Central America (1823)	Vicente Filísola sent by Emperor Iturbide to conquer El Salvador and incorporate it into the empire; fighting erupts in Nicaragua, Costa Rica; Central America declares independence, July 1823; Chiapas remains with Mexico.
Brazil/Buenos Aires (1825–28)	Creates independent Uruguay; Brazilian and Provincias Unidas (Argentine) "guarantee" of independence until 1835.
Colombia-Peru (1828–30) (also Bolivia, "Ecuador")	No real settlement of outstanding boundary issues; dissolution of Gran Colombia, creation of Ecuador, 1830.
Peru-Bolivia Confederation/Chile, Río de la Plata provinces (1836–39)	Dissolution of Peru-Bolivia Confederation; consolidation of conservative regime in Chile; renewed civil wars in Peru and Bolivia; Rosas defeats rivals in Río de la Plata.
Provincias Unidas/Uruguay (1838–51) Known in Uruguay as "La Guerra Grande"	Coincides with French blockade (1838–40); partly Fructuoso Rivera versus Rosas, partly battle over territory, partly Rosas's refusal to recognize Uruguayan independence, partly continuation of civil wars—Rosas versus Anti-Rosistas (1838–51).
Dissolution of Central American Confederation (1838–65)	Intermittent war between Conservatives led by Rafael Carrera in Guatemala (1839–65) and Liberals; Liberal Francisco Morazán attempts to restore federation, 1842; defeated and executed.
Panama/New Granada (1840–41)	Panama declares its independence; remains autonomous for two years.
Peru/Bolivia (1841)	Peruvian *caudillo* Agustín Gamarra invades Bolivia; defeated by Gen. José Ballivián. An extension of the Peru-Bolivia Confederation war, with Gamarra seeking to incorporate part or all of Bolivia under Peruvian control. Gamarra killed in battle at Ingavi. War confirms Bolivian independence.
Brazil, Uruguay, Río de la Plata factions against Rosas in Buenos Aires (1851)	Argentine *caudillo* Justo José de Urquiza with internal allies and support from Brazilian emperor, Uruguayan factions, and exiled unitarists. In part a continuation of the "Guerra Grande."
Guatemala/El Salvador (1863)	Carrera invades El Salvador and replaces Gerardo Barrios with Conservative Francisco Dueñas.
Guatemala, Honduras/ El Salvador (1871)	Dueñas defeated and Field Marshal Santiago González made president.

Table 2–3. Western Hemisphere International Wars, 1826–1885

Wars	*Motivations/Outcomes*
Chile/Peru-Bolivia Confederation (1836–39)	Chile and Rosas defeat Provincias Unidas, Andrés Santa Cruz; Peru and Bolivia separated; war between Peruvian and Bolivian *caudillos* continues until 1841.
United States/Mexico (1845–48)	Extension of Texas independence war (1836) and U.S. intent to annex territory. Simultaneous internal federalist-centralist wars in Mexico. Country loses vast northern territory; Mexico City occupied.
War of the Triple Alliance, Paraguayan War (1864–70)	Paraguay devastated by Brazilian, Argentine, and Uruguayan armies. War begins, in part, as Paraguayan protest against Brazilian meddling in Uruguayan politics and Paraguayan invasion across Argentine territory to defend political allies. Also involves long-standing border and territorial disputes between Argentina-Paraguay, Paraguay-Brazil. Paraguay loses disputed territories after military defeat.
War of the Pacific (1879–84)	Chilean defense of economic interests and treaty rights against Bolivian government; "secret treaty" brings Peru into war; Bolivia loses its seacoast and Peru its southernmost province.
Guatemala (now under Liberal rule of Gen. Justo Rufino Barrios) (1876–85)	Periodic interventions in Central American states; failed effort to restore federation under Guatemalan tutelage; Barrios killed in battle in El Salvador, 1885.

Rebel military officers deposed presidents, closed congresses, called constitutional conventions, overthrew emperors (in Mexico and Brazil), and fought one another. Armed force was the political instrument of choice; *golpes de cuartel* (barracks uprisings) and general civil wars caused frequent changes of government. These struggles could be short and bloodless, but they could also be protracted and messy, as in many of the Argentine and Uruguayan "internal" wars from the 1830s until after the Paraguayan War (1864–1870).

All four types of armed conflict sometimes involved European intervention, meddling across frontiers by rival *caudillos* supporting their allies in neighboring nations, and *caudillos* in exile joining with invading armies to overthrow their enemies at home. The conflicts involved contention over the very definition of "national" and international matters in addition to disputes over internal policies (Church versus state, federalism versus centralism, tariffs, taxation, Indian lands). They were also struggles over power, patronage, and the national purse, but these cannot be dismissed simply as unprincipled combat among military *caudillos*, although sometimes such was the case. Some *caudillos* "expressed a realistic sense of nationalism which defined the nation in terms

Table 2–4. Major Foreign Interventions, 1826–1885

Wars	*Motivations/Outcomes*
Spain in Mexico (1829)	Spanish king sends expedition as retribution for law expelling Spaniards; Spanish invade at Tampico, defeated by yellow fever and General Santa Anna.
Britain takes Malvinas Islands (renamed Falklands) (1833)	Argentina still claims these islands; most recent war to recover them in 1982.
France in Río de la Plata (1838–40)	French blockade Buenos Aires to protect commercial interests; withdraw after two years, agree to arbitration.
France in Mexico (1838)	The "Pastry War"; brief incursion to support claims of French citizens.
France and Britain in Río de la Plata (1840–45)	French and British blockade La Plata to protect nationals, defend commerce, support Rosas's Uruguayan and Argentine enemies. Military base created on an island and in Uruguay. Rosas prevails; British and French withdraw (1847–48).
Britain in Central America (1843–50)	British government assumes Mosquitia protectorate (1843); British occupy San Juan del Norte, rename it Greytown (1848–50); British occupy Tigre Island in Gulf of Fonseca (1849).
United States/Nicaragua (1854)	U.S. Navy bombards Greytown.
Filibuster Expedition (1855–60)	William Walker arrives in Nicaragua; assists Liberals, becomes president in 1856; after ouster, Walker mounts new expeditions; captured and executed in 1860.
Spain in Dominican Republic (1861–65)	Spain reimposes colonial rule at request of Dominican president, who becomes captain-general; withdraws after U.S. Civil War and internal resistance make colony indefensible.
Britain in Central America (1862)	Belize settlement becomes British colony of British Honduras.
France, Spain, Britain in Mexico (1862)	Europeans intervene to protect nationals in Mexico; Spanish and British withdraw; French establish an "empire" under Maximilian until 1867.
Spain/Peru, Chile, Ecuador, Bolivia (1865–66)	Spanish naval squadron takes Chincha Islands, Peru's main source of foreign exchange (from guano deposits); formal declarations of war from Peru, Chile, Ecuador, Bolivia. Spain attacks Valparaíso, Callao, and Ecuadorian ports; hostilities

	formally suspended in 1871. Spain and Peru sign peace treaty in 1879.
Britain in Central America (1894–95)	Last intervention on Mosquitia coast. U.S. mediation ends British blockade of Corinto, Nicaragua.
United States/Spain (1898–1902) Spanish-American War	United States intervenes in Cuban inde pendence movement; defeats Spain, occupies Cuba and Puerto Rico.

of immediate interests. They responded effectively to external threat, either of neighbors or of foreign powers. And in defending the resources of their country against outsiders, they were forced to apply a distinction between natives and foreigners."[35] Rosas in Buenos Aires and the Blanco faction *caudillos* in Uruguay (beginning with José Antonio Lavalleja, and then Manuel Oribe) were identified with a nationalist, rural-nativist, anti-European, and anti-cosmopolitan spirit that became an integral part of Argentine and Uruguayan nationalism. Peruvian, Bolivian, and Chilean *caudillos* in the wars from 1836 to 1841 also fought to create and master new *patrias*; Santa Cruz, Gamarra, José Ballivián, and Manuel Bulnes all served as generals, presidents, and icons of national histories constructed later. These early nineteenth-century wars made armies—often only key garrisons—political arbiters. Civilians of all parties, factions, and opinions were dependent on military force to achieve personal and political objectives. They encouraged military intervention on their own behalf.

Two illustrative cases of early nineteenth-century transnational wars of political consolidation are the conflict that created an independent Uruguay (1825–1828) and that of the Peru-Bolivia Confederation against Chile and Rosas's Río de la Plata confederation (1836–1839). In each one, national territory and boundaries were at stake, as was the very existence of a nation-state. These core issues were complicated by internal political and ideological conflicts, personal feuds, regionalism, and cross-national *caudillo* alliances. In the Uruguayan case, wars were waged almost continuously from the 1830s to the end of the War of the Triple Alliance in 1870. Almost all of the wars were international as well as internal, involving "surrogate foreign forces and alien armies."[36] Intriguingly, the endemic Uruguayan guerrilla wars were called *patriadas* (wars for *la patria*); they were "such a common occurrence that guerrilla warfare was perceived in the rural areas as a 'natural' feature of political life." This was also true in Bolivia and Peru, and even in Chile, if somewhat less so after the mid-1830s.[37]

Even a bare-bones description of these nineteenth-century wars into the 1860s requires mention of the *caudillos* who fought for power and patronage within the territories not yet consolidated as nation-states. Their names clutter the story of nation-building and are tedious for readers; without them the wars make no sense, but the wars were not merely personal conflicts without complex cultural, racial, economic, national, and international motives. And in these wars former colonies gradually became internationally recognized nation-states. Latin American *patrias* emerged from the bloodshed and strife of the first half of the nineteenth century.

Later Nineteenth-Century Wars

By the 1860s the rough shapes of Latin American nation-states had been carved out, although territorial disputes, dreams of reunifying fragmented colonial jurisdictions, and transnational political meddling persisted. Two regional conflicts in the last part of the century, the War of the Triple Alliance against Paraguay and the Chilean defeat of Peru and Bolivia in the War of the Pacific, again readjusted boundaries but confirmed the essentials of the evolved South American nation-state system. In Central America the defeat in 1885 of Guatemala's Justo Rufino Barrios in his efforts to reunify the isthmus solidified the autonomous existence of Costa Rica, Nicaragua, Honduras, El Salvador, and Guatemala.

These later wars were more clearly international conflicts, and their devastating outcomes for the losers (and the winners' fears of revenge) pushed Latin Americans toward more modern, professional armed forces after the 1880s. Brutally demonstrating the cost of unpreparedness, military weakness, and poor political leadership, these wars further politicized the armed forces and created demands for military and economic modernization, European military missions, and reform of national politics.

The War of the Triple Alliance, 1864–1870

In many ways the Paraguayan War was similar to previous transnational *caudillo* intermeddling and an extension of the Brazilian-Argentine tutelage and intervention in Uruguay from the time of the 1825–1828 war that created that country. It also involved long-standing territorial conflicts between Paraguay and its two larger neighbors. From the 1840s, Paraguay, Buenos Aires, and Brazil had sparred over control of the rivers of the Río de la Plata system. The French-British military interventions (1838–1840; 1845–1850), Rosas's periodic efforts to blockade Montevideo, and Paraguay's autarchic development and security policies adversely affected regional commerce and politics. Unresolved bilateral conflicts between Brazil and Paraguay over river access, including Paraguayan incursions into Brazil, and between Paraguay and Rosas's confederation, such as military penetration of Corrientes province (in support of local *caudillos* against Rosas), simmered until the early 1860s.

In 1863 the former Uruguayan president and leader of the Colorado party, General Venancio Flores, returned from Argentina to challenge the Blanco party government at Montevideo. He was joined by volunteers from Corrientes and Entre Ríos provinces and assisted by the Brazilian government. Brazil and Argentina supported the Colorados for different reasons: Flores had helped President Mitre defeat his rival, General Urquiza, in 1852; and the Brazilians had been repeatedly offended by the Blanco government, which they suspected of fomenting rebellion in the Rio Grande region. In short, transnational *caudillo* politics confounded the development of nationalism and independent foreign policies. It also provoked wars against governments that meddled in the internal politics of neighbors.

As the Uruguayan political conflict intensified in 1864, the Paraguayan dictator, Carlos Solano López, offered to mediate but clearly favored the Blanco

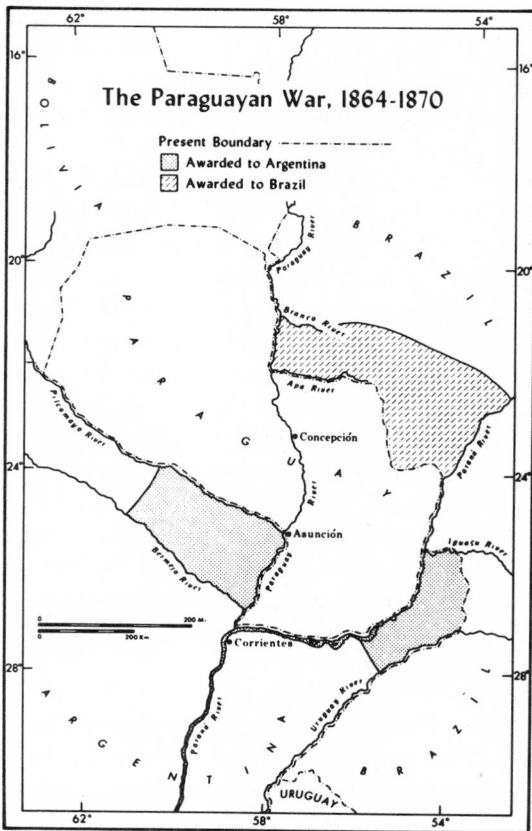

Map 2–3. The Paraguayan War, 1864–1870. From Cathryn L. Lombardi and John V. Lombardi, with Lynn Stoner, *Latin American History, A Teaching Atlas*, published for the Conference on Latin American History by the University of Wisconsin Press, 1983, p. 59. Reprinted by permission of the University of Wisconsin Press

party. He also desired to reaffirm Paraguay's territorial claims against Brazil and Argentina and, most of all, had an overblown notion that he could be the Napoleon of South America. Though unprofessional and poorly equipped, Paraguay had the largest army in the region. Brazil invaded Uruguay in the same year; Paraguay responded by capturing a Brazilian merchant ship on the Paraguay River and by invading Matto Grosso with 3,000 soldiers. Besieged and blockaded, Montevideo fell to the Brazilians in February 1865. General Flores was made provisional governor, supported by the occupation army.

Both Brazil and Paraguay then requested permission to transit Argentine territory to pursue the war. President Mitre rejected both requests, seeking to keep Argentina out of the war. Solano López ignored the directive and sent troops across Corrientes, massing forces south of the Paraná River. Paraguay seized several small armed Argentine vessels, having previously declared war on Argentina. On May 1, 1865, Argentina entered into a secret treaty (the Triple Alliance) with Brazil and the Flores government in Uruguay. Initially, Mitre was given command of the alliance's land forces; eventually, Brazil's armies bore the brunt of the fighting.

The war lasted five years, in part due to the allies' lack of military preparedness and professionalism, Argentina's continued internal strife, and the war of positions permitted by the terrain to Solano López. Fortifications on the region's rivers gave the Paraguayans a great advantage and required amphibious operations that made costly the eventual victory. The Brazilian Navy, the largest in South America in the 1860s, destroyed Paraguay's tiny fleet at the war's only important naval battle, at Riachuelo on June 11, 1865. From that time, the Paraná River served Brazil as a main supply line for its troops and allowed Argentine agricultural, livestock, and artisan industries to prosper as purveyors of Army necessities.

Argentina could never deploy more than half its army to Paraguay. Indian wars and internal rebellions (by one estimate, 117 uprisings of one sort or another from 1862 to June 1868) caused more casualties than Argentina suffered in Paraguay to mid-1868. Uruguay's General Flores led 1,500 men into Paraguay. Having taken heavy casualties in early battles, the Uruguayan army's presence faded. Indeed, after 1866 it was virtually nonexistent. (Flores was assassinated in Montevideo in February 1868.)

The allies' lack of effective joint commands and military coordination, periodic shortages of food and supplies, the terrible medical corps deployed on all sides, yellow fever, cholera, and more than occasional mutinies among Argentine and Brazilian troops also delayed the war's end. Finally, Brazil's Marshal Luís Caxias occupied Asunción and declared victory in 1869. There remained only the operatic conclusion: the wounded, disheveled Paraguayan dictator lanced to death at Cerro Corá in March 1870, reputedly leaving as his last words, " I die with my *patria*" (or, by some accounts, "I die for my *patria*").

Paraguay was not dead, but it was horribly mutilated. It had lost half of its prewar population of 400,000. A major problem in Asunción was finding enough wagons to remove bodies for burial. Brazil maintained an army in Paraguay until 1876; a republican constitution (1870), the country's first, was inspired by Brazilian and Argentine "suggestions." Brazilian and Argentine meddling on behalf of one or another Paraguayan faction continued into the twentieth century.[38] Despite these calamities, the war reinforced Paraguay's nationalistic pride, glorified its military heroes, and set the country apart from its neighbors. In this sense, it confirmed nationhood, a *patria* for which Solano López claimed to have given his life. For thirty-five years after the war, with brief interludes, military officers controlled the presidency. Heroes of the war, these officers formed a faction of the Colorado party that dominated Paraguay into the 1990s.

In Argentina the war exacerbated internal strife, but eventually it gave the republic most of the disputed territory held by Paraguay and contributed to the consolidation of the Argentine Republic as a nation. Mitre lamented: "If half of Corrientes had not betrayed the national cause, arming itself to support the enemy; if Entre Ríos had not twice rebelled; if almost all the contingents had not rebelled at the time of fulfilling their duty, who can doubt that the war would have concluded sooner?"[39] Argentina spent half as much again on suppressing internal enemies—the die-hard federalists and *caudillos*—as on the war against Paraguay. Internal strife also diverted over half the army. To combat internal resistance, Mitre ordered opposition newspapers closed and sent critics into exile. Less ferocious than Chile's Diego Portales, Mitre nevertheless used the war to dispose of internal political enemies. The eventual victory assisted Mitre's successor, Domingo Sarmiento, in strengthening the national (federal) government, much as had occurred in Santiago after Chile's defeat of the Peru-Bolivia Confederation.

Ironically, Mitre's rival, General Urquiza, had managed not only to keep himself out of the cross fire but also to accumulate great wealth from the wartime demand for meat, leather, and horses. Brazil's General Osorio purchased some thirty thousand horses from the Entre Ríos *caudillo*, keeping Urquiza's cavalry from turning on Mitre while further enriching the country's most important regional *caudillo*. Mitre's supporters also did well with war contracts. After Paraguay's defeat, the victorious army suppressed the remaining "great *caudillos*" such as Ricardo López Jordán in Entre Ríos (who murdered Urquiza and his two sons in 1870).[40]

After 1870 the Argentine national (federal) army would gradually become the country's most important political resource, as an Argentine nation gradually replaced the conglomeration of *republiquetas* that had existed since the 1820s. The Paraguayan War had given new credence to the idea of "Argentina." Symbolic references to "such terms as 'the constitution,' 'national honor,' and 'the nation's dignity' had come to hold new meaning for the troops who had fought through the genuine international struggle with Paraguay."[41] A concern for military preparedness, modernization, and professionalization would also become evident from the obvious limitations of Argentina's armed forces in 1865.

In Uruguay the war left the Colorado party in power until midtwentieth century. International meddling in the country's internal politics had been the immediate cause of the war. Flores's assassination in 1868 had snuffed out the original personalist motives, ending the career of the *caudillo* supported by Argentina and Brazil at the war's commencement. But Brazilian and Argentine meddling in Uruguayan factional politics persisted well into the twentieth century.

The war assumed national geopolitical meaning for Brazil, Uruguay, Argentina, and Paraguay. In effect, the postcolonial dispute between Brazil and Buenos Aires (Argentina) over the *banda oriental* remained at a stalemate. Uruguay survived as an independent buffer between South America's two largest countries, with military presidents succeeding one another until the 1890s. Paraguay was prostrate, a politically feeble entity to be manipulated by pretenders to hegemony. The total dead of all the participating armies numbered "at least 350,000—a figure more than twice the population of Buenos Aires in 1864, and about equal both to the population of Uruguay and to the estimated population of Rio de Janeiro in that year."[42]

For Brazil the war had profound and long-term consequences. By war's end the army, led by professional white officers from the Escola Militar at Rio de Janeiro, had grown to over 50,000. Mobilization of a large, predominantly black and mulatto army made the slavery question (Brazil still had almost two million slaves in 1870) more pressing and called attention to the country's archaic social and political system. Slaves earned their freedom for wartime service, and some provinces offered veterans monetary bonuses and land grants. In the northeast, veterans bought small farmsteads, but many veterans were cut loose from the army without significant pensions or rewards. Most refused to return to the status quo ante, although this meant joining the growing urban work force, becoming migrant workers, vagrants, or bandits. In 1871 the Lei do Ventre Livre (Law of the Free Womb) freed the children of slaves, thus anticipating abolition in 1888.

Before the war, the Brazilian military had received second-class treatment, despite its importance in suppressing regional rebellions and its key role in defeating Rosas, in alliance with Entre Ríos *caudillo* Urquiza, in 1852. During the war, Brazil acquired ironclad ships, modern artillery, and state-of-the art repeating rifles from Europe and the United States. It also created an engineering corps that proved decisive in constructing an eleven-kilometer road through the Chaco that permitted Marshal Caxias to outflank Solano López in the Lomas

Valentinas campaign in 1868.[43] As in Europe and the United States, engineers and artillery officers were at the forefront of military modernization. Brazil's military victory over Paraguay raised the generals to national attention and created a new national pride in the army. A "new militant, independent social and political force had arisen within the empire."[44]

The war also "left its mark in a distrust of politicians who would declare war without providing adequate means or force to fight it with, and who would ignore and deprecate the victors, the wounded, the widowed, the orphans. Officers came to believe that only they were concerned about Brazil's defense."[45] As Argentina and Chile contracted for European missions in the 1880s and 1890s, Brazil's officers would take political matters into their own hands by overturning the monarchy and creating the Brazilian Republic (1889). Brazil's army would create a new *patria* and a new political order. Like their South American counterparts they would be the midwives of their nations and republican institutions.

For all the participants, the Paraguayan War meant an accelerated move toward national politics, a national army, and an expanded military influence in government. It also meant important socioeconomic, demographic, and political transformations. Political and diplomatic conflict had led to war, and war to political change and militarization of politics. Thus, the era of the *caudillos* was ending, and that of stronger Latin American nation-states and national armies was commencing.

The War of the Pacific, 1879–1884

The last major nineteenth-century regional war once again engaged Chile against Peru and Bolivia. And, once again, *caudillo* politics in Bolivia and Peru complicated what seemed an international conflict. Like many of the nineteenth-century wars, the conflict between Chile, Peru, and Bolivia originated partly in unsettled boundary disputes. Its origins, however, did not significantly involve transnational support for *caudillos* and political factions. The War of the Pacific, more than any other nineteenth-century war in Latin America, was one of sovereign states (if not integrated nation-states) fighting over national security and economic interests.

Bolivia's weak presence in the coastal desert and Chile's development of nitrate, guano, and mineral enterprises between 23 and 25 degrees south set the stage for conflict from the 1840s to 1860s. In 1866, Mariano Melgarejo (1864–1871), the president and infamous *caudillo,* agreed on a treaty with Chile that fixed the northern Chilean boundary at 24 degrees south, with the proviso that Chileans and Bolivians could exploit mineral deposits in a sort of "joint sovereignty" in the disputed territory. The two countries would share the tax revenues. This treaty was as good as Melgarejo's word; when he was overthrown, his successors repudiated the bombastic drunkard's agreements. Negotiations reopened. In 1874 a new treaty reaffirmed the 24 degree-south boundary with Bolivia, dropped Chilean pretensions of joint sovereignty in the disputed territory, imposed a tax of ten centavos per metric quintal (100 kg.) on nitrate shipments to Bolivia's benefit, and prohibited Bolivia from increasing this tax for twenty-five years.

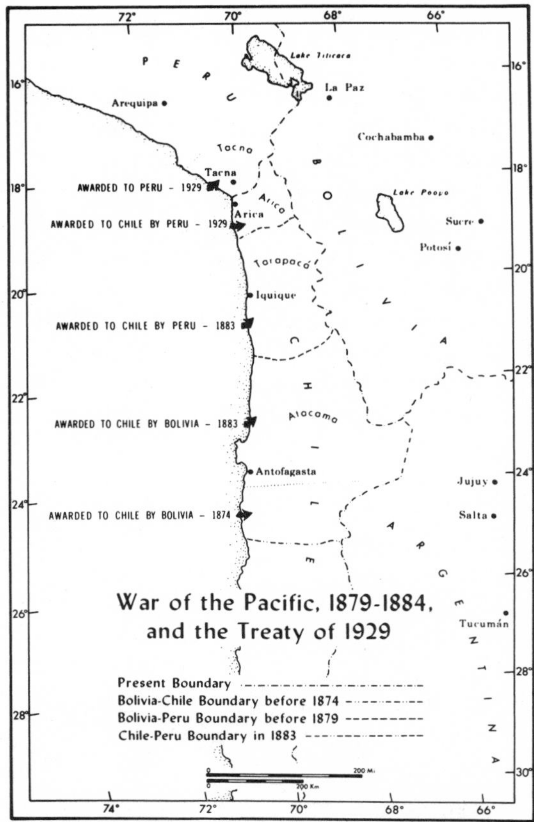

Map 2–4. War of the Pacific, 1870–1884, and the Treaty of 1929. From Cathryn L. Lombardi and John V. Lombardi, with Lynn Stoner, *Latin American History, A Teaching Atlas*, published for the Conference on Latin American History by the University of Wisconsin Press, 1983, p. 56. Reprinted by permission of the University of Wisconsin Press

Peru, meanwhile, entered into a secret alliance with Bolivia in 1873 that provided for mutual guarantees of support against aggression by third parties. Peru, with its heavy dependence on nitrate and guano exports, was experiencing an economic crisis that pushed it to nationalize nitrate properties. It was heavily indebted to foreign bondholders. Any change in the nitrate industry, whether from Bolivian or Chilean initiative, concerned Peru.

In 1878 the Bolivian president, General Hilarión Daza, ordered a ten-centavo surcharge on nitrate exports by the Compañia de Salitres y Ferrocarriles, a Chilean-British firm that dominated the nitrate sector in Antofagasta. (Of the port's 8,000 inhabitants, 75 percent were Chilean.) This order clearly violated the 1874 treaty, and the company refused to comply. The Bolivian government notified the company that its assets would be auctioned to pay the back taxes; the port captain suspended nitrate exports, leaving 2,000 workers unemployed. In response to Chilean protests, Bolivia revoked the nitrate concession, putting the company out of business, and then rescinded the tax. After arbitration failed, Chile sent a military expedition to Antofagasta and took control of the city. Chilean forces occupied Caracoles (a silver mining center) and Salar del Carmen and sent a warship to the small port at Cobija to protect Chilean interests. Bolivia declared war. Peru attempted first to mediate and then joined Bolivia in accord with the secret treaty as Chile then declared war on both Peru and Bolivia in April 1879.

None of the belligerents was prepared. Chile's army, mostly stationed on the southern Indian frontier, numbered perhaps 2,500; it had no supply or medical system, lacked authority to conscript soldiers, and had no training in modern warfare. The national guard, supposedly a nationwide reserve, was more a political instrument for controlling elections and maintaining public order than a military organization. Chile's navy consisted of six ships, only two of which the director of arsenals even considered seaworthy. Having closed the Naval Academy and School for Mariners in 1876 and sold off ships as an economy measure, the Chilean government had to hire foreigners to man its miniature armada.

Peruvian and Bolivian forces, although they greatly outnumbered the Chileans, suffered from the effects of over a half-century of *caudillismo* and internal strife. Peru, like Chile, had a small fleet, largely manned by foreigners, described by contemporaries as "the offscouring of the foreign merchant and naval services." Peru's army, and even more so Bolivia's, was not equipped to fight a modern war. Moreover, Bolivia faced immense geographical barriers in deploying troops to the Pacific coast, one of the reasons that this territory had been settled and developed mostly by Chileans. Following a series of naval skirmishes, Chile controlled the sea-lanes while its armies, augmented by forced drafts of peasants, miners, and urban riffraff, occupied most of the Bolivian desert. When Chile occupied Pisagua and Iquique, political disorders ousted the presidents in both Peru and Bolivia.

Figure 2–1. Chilean troops kill Peruvian wounded during the War of the Pacific. *El repase* by Ramón Muñiz (1888). Original in the Museo Histórico Militar del Perú, Callao

After U.S. and British mediators failed to settle the conflict, Chile sent an army of 25,000 to Lima, crushed Peruvian defenders in mid-January 1881, and occupied the capital. The war was essentially won, but no official peace was achieved for two more years. Chileans looted Lima and took literary, art, and other treasures back to Santiago, thus ensuring more than a century of bitter recollections and demands for revenge. Peruvian guerrillas resisted in the Andean sierra into 1883, but the Chileans levied taxes on the local population to support their occupation army, imposed new port duties in Callao, and encouraged increased nitrate production in the conquered territories.

Figure 2–2. Andrés Cáceres, Peruvian military hero in the War of the Pacific and leader of guerrilla resistance against the Chilean occupation.

Figure 2–3. Chilean Colonel Alejandro Gorostiaga. According to Peruvians, he was "a miserable bastard" who ordered prisoners executed on their knees and shot in the back in the Battle of Huamachuco during the War of the Pacific. Rubén Vargas Ugarte, a Peruvian historian, says of Gorostiaga: "There are crimes that time doesn't erase and that can't be forgotten." Original in the Archivo Courret, Lima

Chile imposed harsh terms on Peru in the Treaty of Ancón (October 1883), signed by a Peruvian president approved by Chile. The loser country ceded Tarapacá province and accepted a ten-year Chilean administration of Tacna and Arica, to be followed by a plebiscite to decide the ultimate fate of these provinces. No plebiscite was ever held. Bolivia agreed to an armistice in March 1884, but no peace treaty was signed for twenty years. That nine of the fourteen articles in the treaty referred to guano and nitrates justified the conflict's nickname: "the Fertilizer War."

The War of the Pacific enlarged Chilean territory by more than one-third, stimulated agricultural, industrial, and shipping activity, and pulled the country out of the prewar economic stagnation that had threatened its political stability. More factories were founded from 1880 to 1889 than had existed in Chile beforehand. The war added leaders such as General Manuel Baquedano and Captain Arturo Prat to the pantheon of military heroes and reinforced the prevailing belief in the nation's racial and cultural superiority over Bolivia and Peru. Rapid victory also made available a large army of over 40,000, armed with repeating rifles and capable of subjugating the native people of Araucania. Simultaneous campaigns by Argentine troops and completion of the southern railway integrated the southern frontier into the Chilean nation.

The defeat of the Araucanians ended the most important pre-1879 rationale for a standing army. The Indian frontier had provided a genuine military mission since independence. Acquisition of the nitrate territory and lingering border disputes with Argentina gave the postwar military a new mission. Threat of Peruvian and Bolivian revanchism made military preparedness and professionalization urgent. In 1885, Chile contracted a Prussian military mission to direct the modernization of the armed forces. The use of foreign missions to modernize the armed forces would be emulated in Argentina, Peru, Bolivia, and later the nations of northern South America.

The War of the Pacific thus proved to be a turning point in Chilean political and economic development and in civil-military relations. By 1890 one-half of the government's ordinary income derived from the nitrate fields taken from Peru and Bolivia. A modern army was required to defend the war's booty and the expanded *patria*. During the war, despite its eventual victory, Chile's military establishment endured bitter criticism in the congress and the press. The lack of strategic plans, poor tactics, and needless loss of life evidenced a backward army and unprofessional leadership. A War Office report suggested that 2,000 to 3,000 Chilean lives could have been saved had General Baquedano flanked Lima's defenses instead of adopting "sledge hammer" tactics; and that without civilian insistence on creation of supply and medical corps, the military would have botched things even further. Officers resented these attacks by civilian politicians that "introduced into the military encampment the plague of politics, demoralization, discord and internecine war."[46] Although officers detested civilian intrusion in war planning and strategy, they availed themselves of congressional and executive supporters to counter charges of incompetence. The war politicized the military and militarized politics.

Figure 2–4. "Peru Defeated But Not Humiliated" (1881). Allegorical engraving after the Chilean occupation of Lima. Original in the Biblioteca Nacional, Lima

For Peru and Bolivia the war's wounds healed slowly, if at all. Bolivia lost its access to the Pacific, making it South America's second land-locked nation. It also lost a promising source of income in the nitrate fields and the desert's copper and silver mines, and the military lost what credibility remained. General Daza joined Melgarejo in the pantheon of anti-heroes who populate the nation's history books. His successor, General Narciso Campero, who had been trained at the French military academy at St. Cyr, was routed at Tacna in May

Figure 2–5. Burying the dead after the Chilean victory in the Battle of Tacna. From Ejército de Chile, *Academia de Guerra, 1886–1986* (Santiago: Ejército de Chile, 1986), 67. Courtesy of the Chilean Army

1880 but nevertheless became a hero for his resistance against Chile and for his role in establishing stronger civilian institutions after the war.

Loss of coastal access and the desert territories did not affect Bolivia's core. The war was fought in Peru; Chileans saw no advantage, and many obstacles, to an expeditionary force crossing the desert and scaling the high Andes. If Bolivia wished to maintain a state of hostilities, or later an armistice without a peace treaty, these barriers might provide a reason for military preparedness but not for invasion. Ironically, however, its loss in the War of the Pacific facilitated evolution of a two-party system of Conservatives and Liberals (the latter led by General Eliodoro Camacho, another hero in Bolivia's defeat) and eventual civilian control of government (not without electoral violence and occasional coups). Mining magnates replaced garrison commanders as presidents from the 1880s until the 1930s; constitutional regimes of exception employed by military and civilian leaders against political adversaries left the armed forces as arbiters of disputes among civilian factions. It also raised the issue of military professionalization, as it did in Peru.

Peru's loss in the War of the Pacific unleashed vituperative military assaults on civilian politicians and the country's oligarchy. Most Peruvians blamed political instability and civilian bungling for the disaster (for example, the president had gone to Europe in December 1879 to obtain a loan; a late 1879 coup made Nicolás Piérola president; troops were issued the wrong ammunition for their weapons; and "Piérola demonstrated that it takes more than putting on a military uniform and Prussian boots to become a general").[47] Military occupation, looting, and denigration could neither be forgiven nor forgotten. Chile's ransacking of Peru's national library stood as testimony to the invaders' barbarism. (Historian Jorge Basadre recounts that of over fifty thousand volumes the Chileans left fewer than one thousand, although he does not reveal how they chose which ones to leave.)

When the Treaty of Ancón was signed in 1883, three Peruvians claimed the presidency. Chile recognized "General" and *hacendado* Miguel Iglesias, who attempted to govern the country after the occupation forces withdrew. Shortly after the Chileans left, partisans of General Andrés Cáceres, leader of the guerrilla resistance, organized the Constitutionalist party. Their platform was simple: restoration of the 1860 Constitution and replacement of Iglesias with Cáceres. As in Bolivia, a war hero would direct Peru's destiny in the years after 1883. Two coup attempts and numerous casualties later, Iglesias left the country. An unopposed General Cáceres won the 1886 presidential "elections" and dominated Peru as president and president-maker from 1886 to 1895. "Ever impressed with the example of virtue, self-sacrifice and patriotism which he and his followers of the *sierra* had set while so many civilian politicians were conducting themselves shamefully, he remained stubbornly convinced that only the soldiers who had rescued their country's dignity during the War of the Pacific deserved the privilege of governing it in peacetime."[48] According to this view, Peru's defeat was the fault of incompetent, venal politicians who betrayed *la patria* and the armed forces.

In March 1895, Piérola, a war-time civilian president, led troops and irregulars (*montoneros*) against Cáceres: "Between two and three thousand bodies lay on the streets of Lima. An additional eight thousand men had died in the provinces in the course of the fighting that had preceded the final assault on Lima."[49] The incompetent, if valiant, Piérola overturned Cáceres's dictatorship with the support of military factions and then sought to professionalize the military. He contracted a French military mission in 1898 (to counter the Prussian mission in Chile) and also adopted a universal conscription law to replace kidnapping Indians, vagrants, drunks, and criminals to fill the army's ranks.

The War of the Pacific bequeathed to Peru another generation of militarism. With the nitrate fields lost and foreign bondholders demanding repayment, the government eventually sold off the railways and put the country's financial and communication systems in the hands of foreign investors. However, with the War of the Pacific, and then Piérola's coup in 1895, the age of the old *caudillos* vanished, as it did in Chile and Bolivia. Peruvian officers, now called to save *la patria* by civilians, would hear "the people's clamor" (*clamor del pueblo*) for *la patria*'s defense in the new French-influenced Chorrillos Military School rather than in isolated towns and barracks. As in Chile and Bolivia, the War of the Pacific encouraged modernization, professionalization, and increased foreign influence in the Peruvian armed forces. It also further politicized the Peruvian military.

The Legacy

The wars and political violence of the nineteenth century left Latin America with a deserved reputation as chaotic, violent, and authoritarian. Armies became political arbiters, patriotic guardians of their nations' institutions and sovereign interests. The armed forces mediated civilians' conflicts, often at their request, and substituted themselves for civilian governments when such governments could not contain political conflict, disorder, and social polarization. In most of the region it was now expected, as in nineteenth-century Spain, that the armed forces execute this mission for *la patria*. Military self-perception and evolving militarylore identified the armed forces as their nations' guardians and saviors. It also demonized politics and denigrated politicians for their meddling in military affairs and their lack of patriotism.

After 1885 traditional *caudillo* warfare declined as national states were consolidated and integration into the international economy provided resources for military modernization. Heavy artillery, repeating rifles and machine guns, rail transportation, steamships, the telegraph, and improved roads slowly decimated the regional *caciques* and *caudillos* who would not be bought by national dictators. Mexico's General Porfirio Díaz ruled with *pan o palo* (bread or the club), and Argentina's General Julio Roca in 1879 conquered "the wilderness" in an extermination campaign against the hostile Indian tribes. Consolidating Argentine nationhood with Buenos Aires as the national capital, General Roca, as president (1880–1886), promoted railroads, economic growth, and military modernization. Standing armies in the provinces were outlawed. Returning to the presidency in 1898, he founded the Superior War College and contracted a German mission "to provide military leadership capable of countering Chile's recent gains."[50]

The regional *caudillos* all over Latin America now faced the implacable (and expensive) military instruments of national governments. The nineteenth-century wars created *patrias*, militarized politics, and gradually centralized political authority. Consolidating and centralizing national governments both depended on and buttressed the armed forces' political role. As the military institutions embarked on modernization and professionalization, they became still more politicized, more disdainful of civilian political parties and factions, more nationalistic, and more dependent on foreign doctrine, methods, and weapons. These contradictions underlay the transformation of the Latin American militaries and their increasing institutional involvement in politics in the first four decades of the twentieth century.

Notes

1. The complexity and variation in the forging of multi-ethnic, multiclass, and transregional notions of *patria* in Spanish America and Brazil from the 1770s onward and "the elite's appropriation of nationalism . . . and [their attempt] to exclude or marginalise the majority" are treated in Brian R. Hamnett, "Process and Pattern: A Reexamination of the Ibero-American Independence Movements, 1808–1826," *Journal of Latin American Studies* 29, part 2 (May 1997): 279–328.

2. For the intellectual origins and development of Creole patriotism see D. A. Brading, *The First America: The Spanish Monarchy, Creole Patriots, and the Liberal State, 1492–1867* (Cambridge, Eng.: Cambridge University Press, 1991). Brading notes that it was an exiled Jesuit, Juan Pablo Viscardo y Guzmán (*Carta dirigida a los Españoles Americanos*, 1799), who first exhorted Creoles to revolt against the Crown, and that only in Mexico, with the cult of the Virgin of Guadalupe, was there a truly national foundation for nationalism: *mexicanidad*.

3. See Florencia E. Mallon, *Peasant and Nation: The Making of Post-Colonial Mexico and Peru* (Berkeley: University of California Press, 1995).

4. Esteban Echeverría, *Dogma socialista* (La Plata: Universidad Nacional de la Plata, 1940): 112, 126–27, cited in John Lynch, *Caudillos in Spanish America, 1800–1850* (New York: Oxford University Press, 1992): 136.

5. Lynch (1992): 141.

6. See E. Christiansen, *The Origins of Military Power in Spain, 1800–1854* (London: Oxford University Press, 1967); and Stanley Payne, *Politics and the Military in Modern Spain* (Stanford, CA: Stanford University Press, 1977).

7. General Carlos Frederico Lecor, cited in Charles Edward Chapman, *Republican Hispanic America: A History* (New York: Macmillan, 1948): 55–56; A. Curtis Wilgus, ed., *South American Dictators* (New York: Russell and Russell, 1937): 52.

8. John Lynch, *The Spanish American Revolutions, 1808–1826* (New York: W. W. Norton, 1973; 2d ed., 1986): 330.

9. Cited in Lynch (1973): 211.

10. Ibid.: 120.

11. Ibid.: 208.

12. Ibid.: 241.

13. David Bushnell, *The Santander Regime in Gran Colombia* (Newark, DE: University of Delaware Press, 1954): 255–56.

14. Lynch (1973): 343, citing John J. Johnson, *The Military and Society in Latin America* (Stanford, CA: Stanford University Press, 1964): 32–35.

15. See William C. Davis, *The Last Conquistadors: The Spanish Intervention in Peru and Chile, 1863–1866* (Athens: University of Georgia Press, 1950).

16. For a comparative description of these constitutional dictatorships see Brian Loveman, *The Constitution of Tyranny: Regimes of Exception in Spanish America* (Pittsburgh, PA: University of Pittsburgh Press, 1993).

17. Cited in Wilgus, ed. (1937): 228.

18. Guy P. C. Thomson, "Nineteenth-Century Latin American Caudillismo," in David G. LaFrance and Errol D. Jones, eds., *Latin American Military History: An Annotated Bibliography* (New York: Garland, 1992): 105.

19. Frank Safford, "Politics, Ideology, and Society in Post-Independence Spanish America," in Leslie Bethell, ed., *Cambridge History of Latin America*, vol. 3 (London: Cambridge University Press, 1985–86): 347–421.

20. Lynch (1992): 206.

21. David Bushnell, *The Making of Modern Colombia: A Nation in Spite of Itself* (Berkeley: University of California Press, 1993): 87.

22. Domingo Faustino Sarmiento, *Facundo*, foreword by Alberto Palcos (La Plata: Universidad Nacional de la Plata, 1938): 179.

23. Cited in Lynch (1992): 416; after José S. Campobassi, *Sarmiento y su epoca*, 2 vols. (Buenos Aires: Editorial Losada, 1975). For more on Sarmiento see Tulio Halperín Donghi, Iván Jaksić, Gwen Kirkpatrick, and Francine Masiello, eds., *Sarmiento: Author of a Nation* (Berkeley: University of California Press, 1994).

24. Letter from Bolívar to Sucre in 1825 regarding the possible creation of a new country in Bolivia. Cited in William Spence Robertson, *The Rise of the Spanish-American Republics* (New York: D. Appleton and Co., 1918): 286–87. "Presidencies" referred to the audiencias, the highest courts for a particular jurisdiction, created within each viceroyalty as the empire evolved: Nueva España (Mexico)-Santo Domingo (1511); Mexico (1527); Guatemala (1543); Guadalajara (1548); Perú-Panamá (1538); Lima (1543); Santa Fe de Bogotá (1548); La Plata de los Charcas (1559); Quito (1563); Chile (1563–1573, definitively 1606); Buenos Aires (1661–1672, definitively 1776); Caracas (1786); Cuzco (1787). See Konetzke (1976): 123.

25. Cited in Lynch (1973): 252–53.

26. Johnson (1964): 37.

27. Ralph Lee Woodward, *Central America: A Nation Divided*, 2d ed. (New York: Oxford University Press, 1985): 169.

28. Cited in Carlos Bañales Guimaraens, "Las fuerzas armadas en la crisis uruguaya," in Virgilio Rafael Beltrán, ed., *El papel político y social de las fuerzas armadas en América Latina* (Caracas: Monte Avila Editores, 1970): 293.

29. Bañales Guimaraens (1970): 294.

30. David Bushnell, "Politics and Violence in Nineteenth-Century Colombia," in Charles Bergquist, Ricardo Peñaranda, and Gonzalo Sánchez, eds., *Violence in Colombia* (Wilmington, DE: Scholarly Resources, 1992): 12–13.

31. Dana Munro, *The Latin American Republics, A History*, 3d ed. (New York: Appleton-Century Crofts, 1960): 269.

32. Jorge Basadre, *Chile, Peru, y Bolivia independientes* (Buenos Aires: Salvat Editores, 1948): 192.

33. Donald F. Stevens, *Origins of Instability in Early Republican Mexico* (Durham, NC: Duke University Press, 1991): 59.

34. Donald E. Worcester, *Brazil: From Colony to World Power* (New York: Charles Scribner's Sons, 1973): 92, 94.

35. Lynch (1992): 148.

36. Fernando López-Alves, "Wars and the Formation of Political Parties in Uruguay, 1810–1851," in Eduardo Posada-Carbó, ed., *Wars, Parties and Nationalism: Essays on the Politics and Society of Nineteenth-Century Latin America* (London: Institute of Latin American Studies, 1995): 7.

37. López-Alves (1995): 7–8.

38. See Loveman (1993): 309–12 for a summary of Brazilian and Argentine intervention in Paraguayan politics.

39. Cited in Félix Best, *Historia de las guerras argentinas,* 2 vols. (Buenos Aires: Peuser, 1960), 2:308.

40. David Rock, *Argentina, 1516–1982: From the Spanish Colonization to the Falklands War* (Berkeley: University of California Press, 1985): 128.

41. Charles J. Kolinski, *Independence or Death! The Story of the Paraguayan War* (Gainesville: University of Florida Press, 1965): 192.

42. Ibid.: xiii.

43. Ibid.: 51–62.

44. Ibid.: 196–97.

45. Frank D. McCann, Jr., "Origins of the 'New Professionalism' of the Brazilian Military," in Brian Loveman and Thomas M. Davies, Jr., eds., *The Politics of Antipolitics: The Military in Latin America,* 3d ed. (Wilmington, DE: Scholarly Resources, 1997): 44.

46. William Sater, *Chile and the War of the Pacific* (Lincoln: University of Nebraska Press, 1986): 55.

47. Carlos Miró Quesada, *Autopsía de los partidos políticos* (1961), cited in Frederick Pike, *The Modern History of Peru* (New York: Praeger, 1969): 146.

48. Pike (1969): 158.

49. Ibid.

50. Loveman (1993): 289.

3

Foreign Military Missions and *la Patria*

> The twelve years in which General Clément and Colonel Dogny presided over the Military School as its directors marked the "golden age" of our Army. Only military ideas were heard in its classrooms. Political interests dared not intrude on its grounds. . . . the Chorrillos School was a temple of military science.
>
> —General Pedro Pablo Martínez, Peru, 1935

Foreign military advisers and mercenaries played an important role in Latin American independence wars, both on land and at sea. British naval officers and continental mercenaries fought against the Spaniards and trained rebel armies in northern South America, Chile, and Argentina. A "British Legion" composed of English and Irish mercenaries served with Bolívar; San Martín employed Lord Cochrane to command the navy that liberated Peru, and the Peruvian navy hired another English commander, Martin Guise.[1] Other foreign officers also served in most Latin American countries during the first half of the nineteenth century, but not as representatives of their homelands or as part of official military missions invited through diplomatic channels. Such isolated efforts made little systematic doctrinal or organizational impact on the armed forces.

Beginning in El Salvador in the 1860s and Guatemala in the early 1870s, Spanish American governments contracted individual European officers and then military missions to modernize and professionalize their military institutions. These foreign missions supervised reforms of military law and regulations; established, staffed, and reformed military schools and academies; introduced new curricula and strategic and tactical doctrines; and implemented routine drill and maneuvers. They also encouraged arms and equipment purchases, usually from their home countries. By the early 1900s, Latin American officers and soldiers wore uniforms, bore arms, marched, and drilled in Spanish, French, and German style. They shared the Europeans' militarylore and published their views in the new professional military magazines.

The impact of foreign missions depended on both national and international influences. Geography and geopolitics, natural resources, demographic, ethnic, and linguistic variability, socioeconomic circumstances, wars with neighboring countries, and the character of national political systems all made their impact on civil-military relations. But everywhere the foreign missions imparted nationalistic, antipolitical, and quasi-religious military doctrines that imbued the armed forces—both armies and navies—with a "special" relationship to, and responsibility for, *la patria*.[2]

Military professionalization and modernization meant forming an elite corps of academy-educated officers and a new career system. These initiatives divided the officer corps into the old guard who had won their rank in battle or from political patronage and a new group of academy graduates—engineers, cartographers, weapons' experts, geopoliticians, strategists, medical doctors, and professors. The new military elite, echoing their Spanish, German, and French tutors, equated progress with economic development and technological advance in transportation, communications, and science. They advocated economic development, industrialization, political order, and "nation-building": *forjando patria*. They also learned the importance of "professional" versus "political" criteria in the career system and duty assignments. But this focus on insulating military professionals from partisan politics as a keystone of the "new military" was usually unattainable in practice, creating an ongoing source of dissension within the armed forces and of tension between the armed forces, civilian governments, and domestic political groups. The foreign missions' sermons on the necessity of technical and economic modernization as foundations for professionalization and for national security were well received, but they left unanswered the question of what to do when Latin American governments and political leaders failed to take the lead in these developmental tasks.

The importance of modern weapons, railroads, improved communications, and economic growth for internal political purposes was obvious. From the 1870s to the end of the century, Krupp cannons, Mauser rifles, machine guns, and the extension of telegraph, road, and rail networks together with increased government revenues from export enclaves virtually ended regional *caudillismo*. Symbolically, as Uruguayan military presidents gradually imposed political order, an 1876 decree forbade private ownership of the Remington rifle. In Argentina, where "the Winchester rifle helped to close the Argentine frontier, and with the rifle came barbed wire, windmills, and railroads,"[3] General Julio Roca's program of "conservative liberalism" adopted the slogan, "Peace and Administration." According to José Luis Romero, "Peace, to Roca, meant not only severe repression of all revolutionary attempts like those . . . in 1874 and in 1880, but also the determined elimination of any fair and open struggle for power which might be considered dangerous for a country in the process of being transformed."[4] General Roca brought a German military mission to Argentina in 1899 to catch up with the modernization occurring under the direction of German officers in Chile since the mid-1880s. In neighboring Brazil, the flag of the new republic created by army officers in 1889 bore the motto *ordem e progresso* (order and progress), and Mexico's President Porfirio Díaz's policy advisers were known as *científicos* (scientists). Díaz encouraged study by Mexican officers in German military academies and imported German weapons and regulations.

Technology without doctrine, military education, and training could not professionalize armies as Latin American leaders desired. Just as "civilization" and "progress" meant copying European cultural trends and importing technology, so did professionalization mean emulating European military institutions. In theory, such professionalization would upgrade the army's capabilities for defending *la patria* while eliminating military participation in politics. In practice, it tended to increase military political involvement as the officers became more conscious of the socioeconomic and political defects of their nations and more convinced of their own special talents for nation-building.

In Guatemala, for example, Spanish officers helped create the Escuela Politécnica in 1873. For the next three decades, Spanish, French, Polish, British, and U.S. officers imported training manuals, formed specialized engineering, artillery, and telegraphy schools, and encouraged purchases of artillery, machine guns, and rifles. After World War I, French missions further "professionalized" Guatemalan army education, doctrine, and organization, even creating a tiny air force.

From the 1870s the Escuela Politécnica educated a small officer cadre that became a technocratic and political elite with a fervent nationalist ethos. This ethos was reflected in the words of President (General) José María Orellana, the first Politécnica graduate to be "elected" president of Guatemala. Speaking to the cadets in 1924, Orellana sermonized: "[The Politécnica] converts a man and transforms a citizen into a priest of a supreme cult to *la patria*, whose symbol is the flag, and whose gospel is the constitution."[5] In 1925 the president added: " 'All for the Army' is exactly the same as saying 'All for *la Patria*.' "[6] He did not mention that the constitutional gospel had been modified frequently to permit dictatorial *continuismo*; that its *garantías* had been suspended even more often; that the officers had served the will of Manuel Estrada Cabrera (1898–1920), one of the region's most repressive dictators; that his minister of war, General Jorge Ubico, viciously repressed worker and political party opposition in the 1920s; that Orellana used troops as scabs in 1923 to break a strike against the United Fruit Company, a U.S. corporation that controlled Guatemala's transportation, communications, and export infrastructure; that the patriotism and nationalism of the high-ranking officers did not prevent their own enrichment and collaboration with U.S. corporate investors.[7] He also failed to mention that the many Indian groups who accounted for 65 to 70 percent of the population could neither read nor understand the constitutional gospel nor identified themselves with the general's concept of *patria*. The Politécnica's "priests of *la patria*" knew their mission, but the flesh was weak.

Foreign missions and imported ideologies contributed to the creation of a mythic military self-image and ritual language professing nationalism and love of *patria*. (No matter that the top generals and presidents had collaborated in expanding the influence of the foreign fruit companies that dominated the economy and used the army to contain Indians' and workers' demands for dignity and a piece of the economic action.) It also made military education, abroad and in Guatemalan academies, an important criterion for promotion and career advancement. Academy graduates gradually donned the mantle of political as well as military leadership. Their training indirectly revealed that civilians lacked the technical capabilities, strategic orientation, and patriotic abnegation necessary to drag Guatemala into the modern world. Officers mapped the country, directed construction of roads, bridges, and public works, and eventually dominated internal administration.[8] Like their counterparts in most of the region, they also maintained internal order, repressed political opposition, and intimidated the nascent labor movement. In these respects the foreign missions reinforced militarylore and relegitimated functions inherited from the *reconquista*, Bourbon armies, and the heroic independence war era. European military missions and doctrines reaffirmed for the Guatemalans (and other Latin American armed forces) their role as "warrior-priests" and guardians of national destiny. They came accompanied with professional norms, technical and vocational education programs, and commitments to "progress" and "modernization" that linked the military's traditional internal and defense missions to the current challenges of "nation-building," economic development, and political order.

In 1931, General Ubico became Guatemala's president. Ubico's family, businesses, education, and military career connected the landed oligarchy to the military. He epitomized the opportunities for new officers: *jefe político* of Alta Verapaz (1907–1909) and Retalhuleu (1911–1919), minister of war (1921–1923), presidential candidate (1926), politician, landowner, favorite of the U.S. Embassy in Guatemala. He eliminated pretenses of an independent legislature, purged the judiciary, and ran the country in the personalist fashion of an owner of a large rural estate, or *finca*. A military *finquero* with a country as his domain—except that he was forced to accede to the "needs" of the United Fruit Company and U.S. diplomacy—Ubico was genuinely committed to fostering economic growth, reducing corruption, and making public administration more efficient. He invested in road building and public works. Above all else, political order took precedence to make the other objectives possible. And order became the army's principal mission. In a break with the army's ties to Spain and France, Ubico invited a U.S. military officer to direct the Politécnica, the first such appointment.

In the 1936 Ley Constitutiva del Ejército, all Guatemalan males from age fifteen to fifty who were morally, physically, and mentally apt for military service were made members of the army, whether or not on active duty (Article 7). Thus, in practice, they could be mobilized at election time and instructed for whom to vote. They could also be used on public works projects and in the suppression of strikes and political protests. Article 3 formalized the army's "civilizing mission": "The principle of civic education is instituted in military corps; they must aim to overcome illiteracy among the troops and to mold them as citizens." Guatemala's constitution made military service compulsory; the barracks were the schools of citizenship and nationalism. Only in that way could the mass of Indians become real Guatemalans. And only in that way could there be a real *patria*. Unlike Mexican archaeologist Manuel Gamio's dream that revolution would create a Mexican nation, in Guatemala this goal would be carried out by the army.

General Ubico militarized the country's public administration, appointing generals as governors in each department. He bound Guatemala together with networks of officers, garrisons, and barracks. The army became a truly national force with a recognizable high command, career ladder (if still marred by cronyism and patronage), and military-political presence in regional commands and garrisons in the highlands, jungles, and on the coasts. Politécnica graduates would be Guatemala's political masters for most of the twentieth century.

Fifty years of military professionalization in Guatemala, although it was not as extensive as that accomplished by foreign missions in Chile, Argentina, or Peru, did reequip, reorganize, and reorient the army. It brought important changes in officer training, values, career systems, and corporate identity. What it did not mean was depoliticizing the armed forces; indeed, it meant the opposite. By and large, the professional soldiers did not covet political authority, but they did assume that they would participate in making policy and administering the nation. They shared with the small civilian technocratic elite and rising professional classes a desire for "order and progress," which meant, as in Spain, Germany, and France, containing the threats from leftist movements and organized labor. They desired psychological and material inclusion in the civilized (that is, European) world and, particularly, respect from their military counterparts in other countries. For themselves, they aspired to institutional autonomy, stable professional careers, increased budgets, modern equipment, and proper status in the emergent *patria*.

In most of Central America, even less military modernization and professionalization occurred before the 1930s than in Guatemala. Elsewhere in Latin America, it mimicked imperfectly, and in miniature, that of the United States, Europe, Japan, Russia, and Turkey. Latin American armed forces imported military hardware, training manuals, doctrine, martial music, uniforms, spiked helmets, and even mustache styles and monocles. In South America and Mexico, European military and police missions imparted the newest fads and fashions of wholesale death and technified armies.

Military professionalization and modernization via foreign missions, however, was typically incomplete and idiosyncratic. Bolivia, for example, contracted three Prussian officers to direct the Escuela de Guerra and the Colegio Militar in 1901 and also purchased German rifles and French and German artillery from 1900 to 1907. French officers were contracted between 1907 and 1910, followed by a German mission from 1911 to 1914. Prussian influence dominated beginning in 1911, but most of the German officers returned to Europe during World War I. Afterward, the German mission's director, Colonel Hans Kundt, became head of the Bolivian General Staff, then minister of war. He Prussianized instruction in the military schools and, typically, had German military legislation and manuals translated into Spanish. Bolivia imported German weapons and its soldiers were taught to goose-step. The army was partially professionalized and thoroughly politicized, becoming an instrument of the Republican party. Kundt assured the predominance of his political patrons. According to U.S. diplomat Jesse S. Cottrell, writing to the State Department:

> During the six years he has been here as Chief of Staff, General Kundt has served the Liberal party one year and the Republican party five. He had only limited authority during his year's tenure with the Liberals and it is a recognized fact that had he been in complete control of the Army in 1920, the coup d'état which placed the Republicans in control of the Government would never have been accomplished. No sooner had the Republicans come into power than they gave General Kundt absolute authority and control of the Army with orders to keep the Republican party in power. . . . He gradually dropped from the Army all officers and soldiers of Liberal ideas.[9]

Kundt returned later to Europe but was eventually recontracted to command the Bolivian army against the Paraguayans in the Chaco War (1932–1935).

As in Guatemala and Bolivia, the nature, extent, and impact of European-directed military modernization throughout the region depended on local socioeconomic and political conditions. Like political leaders in Germany and Italy, late nineteenth-century Latin American elites engaged in creating nations, nationalism, and national governments through war and economic integration. The armed forces could hardly fail to occupy center stage. As Argentina's Lieutenant Colonel A. Maligne wrote in 1911, a decade after German officers began to mentor the country's army, "the army is the nation. It is the external armor that guarantees the cohesive operation of its parts and preserves it from shocks and falls."[10] For better or worse, in most of Latin America the army (or army and national police) was the only truly national government institution, the "spinal columns" of these skeletal nation-states. Military officers and soldiers were the principal, if not sole, manifestation of the state in rural regions and even in provincial capitals until post offices, schools, telegraph and railroad stations, and other government agencies later appeared. Soldiers assumed numerous functions, including law enforcement, as they had since the eighteenth-century Bourbon reforms in Spain and colonial Spanish America. While the Church and its control over the rituals of birth, baptism, marriage, and death reached more deeply into everyday life, military institutions appeared as symbols and representatives of the emergent nation-state.

The armed forces became not only the primary symbols of the nation but also self-consciously the creators, agents, and guardians of national values. Paradoxically, with the influence of the foreign military missions these "national values" were partially imported. The French and German concepts of "nations in arms," and the idea that the barracks was the "school of nationalism," spread throughout Latin America. Colmar von der Goltz's notion in *Das Volk in Waffen* (1883), that the army was the binding agent of citizenry and state, was widely disseminated and popularized. It reappeared in numerous Latin American versions, beginning appropriately in Chile where a German mission thoroughly imbued post-War of the Pacific officers with a new professional ethos that made "the barracks the school of the people." According to General Juan de Dios Vial, "the soldiers in the barracks are the nation in arms, they are the force, and naturally in this force resides true sovereignty."[11] Chilean Colonel Ernesto Medina Franzani's *El problema militar de Chile* (1912) emphasized that the mission of modern military institutions was "to maintain national integrity, 'political, territorial, administrative, and governmental, to respond to, and to solve, international situations and problems, [and] to intervene [that is, participate in the solution of] those problems that, directly or indirectly, affect the interests and the future of the republic.' "[12] How could this broad definition of the military mission be compatible with the constitutional provision for its subordination to legally elected governments and to the constituted authorities of the state? If governments failed to adequately respond to problems that "affect[ed] the interests and the future of the republic," what should be done by the military guardians of nation and state? These questions framed civil-military relations in Latin America until the end of the twentieth century.

Whatever the precise influence of the European missions (and in some cases of their Latin American surrogates, particularly the Chileans, who took their own military missions to Ecuador, Colombia, Venezuela, and El Salvador and invited officers from other countries in the region to study in the Santiago War Academy), it invariably involved officers in politics. And, when fused with Iberian and Latin American military traditions, these European missions resulted in highly politicized armed forces that lamented their nations' technological, social, and economic backwardness. Officers recognized that military modernization and professionalization, as imparted by their European tutors, required economic development and effective government. In their own governments and politicians they saw only failure to meet these challenges. Indeed, they came to believe and proclaim that the civilian politicians' corruption, incompetence, and lack of patriotism impeded national development and put *la patria* at risk. But this shared perception did not provide the officers with a common alternative program for national development. In Argentina, Bolivia, Brazil, Peru, and Chile, for example, officers trained by Prussian and French missions identified with different political ideologies, allied with diverse civilian parties and movements, and vied with one another for control of governments and the privilege to define the "road to modernity" for their nations. The missions politicized the officers by directing their attention to the relationship between political, economic, and military modernization. But they did not prevent ideological, personalist, and generational factionalism within the armed forces from the early twentieth century into the 1950s.

World War I taught emphatically the critical relationship between economic modernization and national security. Military officers saw the contrast between economic and industrial mobilization in Europe and the United States and the pathetic incapacity of Latin American economies to meet the minimum needs of their citizens, let alone of military preparedness. From this recognition, the basic geopolitical and defense concepts later associated with Cold War national security doctrine (NSD) insinuated themselves into militarylore and curricula by the 1920s. Some Latin American officers advocated more active government development policies, government-directed industrialization schemes, and national economic planning—with a prominent role for the armed forces.[13] Such was the thrust of Argentine Colonel Luis Vicat's 1926 article, "Industrial Development as a Military Mission":

> True national defense is a vast and complex matter. It may be defined by saying that *it involves all those activities and all those measures necessary to assure the tranquility, prosperity, and independence of a country as well as rapid victory in the case of conflict*.
>
> No matter how well trained, the armed forces are useless if in the moment of action weapons lack ammunition, resupply is not possible, troops cannot be transported . . . or if they lack fuel. . . .
>
> We must look to the future and foresee its dangers, trying to provision ourselves [from domestic industries] in every sense.[14]

As Latin American military leaders became more attuned to European professional norms and expectations, they more vociferously and vigorously denounced inept, short-sighted civilian politicians who shamelessly fought like pigs over slop in the public trough while failing to create political stability or promote economic development. Like their German and French tutors, Chilean, Argentine, Peruvian, and other Latin American officers were galled by political meddling in military affairs, promotions, and even strategic decision making. They detested the nefarious impact of politics on their *patria*'s security and also the politicians' inability, and even unwillingness, to understand the true meaning of patriotism. If national defense involved all activities affecting national tranquility, could the armed forces allow civilian politicians to threaten national security? This question would be answered repeatedly in the negative in the years after 1930, and even more emphatically after 1964.

The foreign military missions taught that politics corrupted society and corroded the arteries of *la patria*. Only authoritarian government allied with the professional military could purge *la patria*, save it from the slow death imposed by politicians, and then strengthen it, as Chancellor Otto von Bismarck had done in Germany or, in the 1920s, as dictator Primo de Rivera did in Spain. Unfortunately, however, politics also corroded the military institutions, further exasperating officers who believed in the professional, apolitical mission taught, if not always practiced, by their foreign tutors.

Professionalization via foreign military missions thus further politicized the armed forces from the late nineteenth century until the late 1930s, encouraging demands for autonomy from civilian oversight and increased participation and influence in national life. Officers were taught, and came to believe, that they possessed virtues, expertise, and patriotic values that mere civilians could never attain. They separated themselves from civilians morally, intellectually, socially, and eventually physically, in military neighborhoods. Their daughters and sons intermarried with great frequency. With variations from country to country, they came to form a virtual subculture. Although they were never entirely isolated from civilian elites, the self-concept of the professionalized officer corps made clear distinctions between the supposed virtue, valor, and honor of the military and the moral weakness of the civilians, particularly the politicians. The officers were patriotic and principled, the politicians were opportunistic and pragmatic. But these officers' ties to foreign missions, doctrines, ideologies, and technology made their nationalism and patriotism schizophrenic. They both adulated and resented foreign influences. And, of course, the foreign governments that sent these missions to Latin America had their own policy objectives, whether limited to encouraging weapons exports and protecting foreign firms or to cultivating more extensive political influence in the host countries.

For Europeans and Americans, military missions and training Latin American officers meant commercial lucre as well as political influence. Teaching doctrine and technical skills usually implied language training and some cultural adaptation. Latin American officers made friendships with Spanish, Italian, French, and German officers that sometimes lasted a lifetime, as would later occur with U.S. officers, with both political and economic consequences. The push for military modernization brought competition from European and U.S. weapons' firms for Latin American markets. While the Germans and French dominated in South America, Spain also influenced military and police forces in Central America and Peru. British influence was strongest among the Latin American navies. The United States established constabularies in Cuba, Haiti, the Dominican Republic, Panama, and Nicaragua, following military interventions and occupations beginning with the 1898 Spanish-American War and continuing until the marines withdrew from Nicaragua in 1933.

The U.S.-created constabularies lacked the military traditions of the French- and German-tutored armies in South America. In part this lack resulted from the U.S. focus on police-like functions, on the U.S. military's lack of geopolitical doctrine to match the Germans and French, the overt racism manifested toward Central American and Caribbean peoples by U.S. military officers and soldiers, and because the United States did not take seriously the external defense mission for Caribbean and Central American armed forces. The constabularies created under these conditions invariably became the corrupt instruments of dictators, the foundations for tyranny: Rafael Trujillo in the Dominican Republic; Anastasio Somoza and his sons in Nicaragua; Gerardo Machado and, later, Fulgencio Batista in Cuba. These constabularies never achieved the professional levels or military capabilities of Chilean, Argentine, or Peruvian armed forces. They operated almost as military gangsters, keeping order, controlling gambling, prostitution, and other rackets, and extorting resources from the citizenry in the name of "law and order" and a superficial patriotic fervor. Illustrative was the Cuban case of the late 1920s and early 1930s described by Louis A. Pérez, Jr.:

> The frequent and prolonged suspension of constitutional guarantees, abrogating civil rights, facilitated government use of the armed institution. Military supervisors displaced civilian political administrators; army personnel replaced provincial governors and municipal *alcaldes* (mayors) throughout the island. . . . The creation of a national militia in 1932 subjected the island's national, judicial, and secret police agencies to army jurisdiction. . . . Virtually every government agency passed under some form of military jurisdiction or review.[15]

Contrary to Washington's proclaimed policy, the armed forces in Cuba and other small countries where the United States created constabularies from the early twentieth century into the late 1920s did not become "a nonpartisan armed force patterned along the line of the military forces of the United States, with modifications to suit local conditions."[16] Rather, they passed into the hands of personalist authoritarian presidents as instruments for patrimonial rule. Like the military institutions created by European foreign missions (with the difference that they were created as a result of military invasion rather than by contract with a sovereign government), they became the new foundations of the twentieth-century's Central American and Caribbean armed forces in Latin America. But unlike the armies mentored by the Europeans, the U.S.-created Central American and Caribbean armies and constabularies lacked the historical roots and nineteenth-century glories of Chilean, Argentine, and Peruvian armed forces. Their claims to be reservoirs of national destiny were less credible, their moralizing discourse denouncing politicians less convincing. Their performance made them detested by much of the civilian population, and their repressive operations reinforced nationalistic, anti-United States sentiments in the Caribbean Basin.

Such weaknesses were not limited to the constabularies. The semi-national, semi-personalist, yet increasingly academy-trained officer corps that Chilean advisers helped to create for Venezuelan dictator Juan Vicente Gómez (1908–1935) also suffered from corruption and a lack of legitimacy, although it sought to overcome its poor reputation by harking back to the glorious exploits of Bolívar and Páez in the wars of independence. As Gómez alienated more and more of Venezuela's national resources to U.S. investors and the army repressed his opponents, it became more difficult to sustain the nationalist myths. Similar contradictions between the armed forces' hyperbolic nationalism and their government's actual policies also affected Argentina, Ecuador, Bolivia, and Colombia, leading to cleavages within the armed forces—and even to the formation of secret officer societies (*logias*)—to foment more nationalistic policies. Some of these *logias* favored more corporatist, even fascist, approaches to politics; by the 1930s such sentiments prevailed in much of Latin America.

In the early twentieth century, however, military and civilian elites in most of the region recognized the dangers of external dependence, particularly in the areas of national finance and defense. They disdained or, at best, pitied the Caribbean and Central American satrapy-nations such as the Dominican Republic, Haiti, and Nicaragua, with their small U.S.-created constabularies and economies dominated by U.S. customs' receiverships. Nationalists and pragmatists urged caution in mechanically copying foreign military models; they warned against foreign influence via military missions and sought to overcome technological dependence. They advocated the creation of national armaments factories and heavy industries. Well before World War I, various Latin American nations sought at least partial autonomy through local production under the foreign licensing of gunpowder, ammunition, pistols, rifles, machine guns, and even cannons.

Isolation from European suppliers during World War I as well as the limited willingness of the United States to replace French and German sources further encouraged military planners to establish domestic armaments and related industries. In practice, such industries were controlled by military institutions. The trench-warfare butchery of World War I taught brutally not only the killing power of modern weapons but also the industrial foundations of modern warfare. Neither the Germans nor the French had prepared for a long war; after 1919 no War Ministry could ignore the relationship between society, economy, political unity, and warfare. Plans for a "total war" imposed the need for permanent defense planning with enlarged economic roles for government. It also gave ever more importance to professional, technologically advanced, permanent standing armies and economies to support them. No modern nation could be without such forces; their role in politics and society in peacetime became a permanent issue in Europe, Asia, the United States, and Latin America, as did their manner of officering and soldier recruitment. Of course, armies in Latin America seldom exceeded 50,000 men, unlike the massive German and French standing armies (almost 500,000 in the 1890s) and the millions mobilized in European and U.S. armies in World War I. The Mexican army, on paper at least, was 30,000 at the outbreak of the revolution in 1910; that of Chile, under Prussian tutelage, between 10,000 and 15,000; of Argentina, 20,000 to 25,000; of Colombia, 5,300; of Peru, 7,000; and in Brazil the federal army numbered 40,000 to 50,000. Central American constabularies and armies in most of South America rarely reached 5,000 effectives in peacetime, although Guatemalan military sources claim to have mobilized over 40,000 troops in the brief war against El Salvador and Honduras in 1906.[17]

Modern armies required professional officers and a cadre of experienced noncommissioned officers (NCOs) with common doctrine and military expertise. Professionalization entailed replacing status-based recruitment of amateur officers and uneducated, often press-gang troops with achievement-recruited, permanently uniformed, and well-trained officers and conscript and volunteer soldiers. This replacement was accompanied by the creation of mass armies, standardization of equipment, and organization of central staffs and specialized military corps, such as supply, medical, engineering, and a variety of combat branches. Professionalization required trained soldiers with specialized skills, committed to national values.[18] The vagrants, prisoners, drunks, and unlucky peasants of the pre-1880s era would be replaced with citizens selected under obligatory military service legislation adopted throughout the region from the end of the nineteenth century (see Table 3–1).

Table 3–1. Adoption of Obligatory Military Service Laws in Selected Latin American Countries

Country	*Year*
Argentina	1901
Bolivia	1907
Brazil	1908, 1916 (implemented)
Chile	1900
Colombia	1896
Ecuador	1902, 1905
Paraguay	1916
Peru	1898, 1901, 1912
Uruguay	Heavily debated in first decades of twentieth century; none adopted

Troops were conscripted. Recruitment and advancement within the officer corps gradually came to depend, at least in theory, on merit and performance rather than on direct appointment and promotion by presidential whim or political influence (so-called appointments *a dedazo*). By the 1920s and 1930s, or even earlier in some countries, the social composition of the officer corps became predominantly middle class and disproportionately provincial, rather then from national capitals. And like their European mentors, the newly professionalizing Latin American armies would teach not only military skills but also literacy, citizenship, and patriotism. These changes in military education required inventing new meanings for *patria* and patriotism as well as new racial and national myths to emulate the various German, French, and other European ethnic-nation and citizen-nation mystiques: the Chilean "warrior race" (Araucanians and Spaniards), the heroic Paraguayans (Guaraní and Spaniards), and all the other glorious new soldier-citizens. The armed forces would be the primary instrument for nation-building and defense by creating citizens as well as making them soldiers.

Writing in the recently established Peruvian *Boletín del Ministerio de Guerra y Marina* in 1910, a decade after a French military mission undertook the task of professionalizing Peru's army, J. C. Guerrero urged: "Let us educate the Indian, . . . and we will have citizens; once we have citizens we will have a nation."[19] Chilean Captain Tobías Barros in *Vigilia de armas* (1920) graphically depicted the sorry state of his country's underclasses, the civilizing mission of the armed forces, and the growing disdain for the civilian elite that evaded its patriotic duty:

> Three-fourths of the recruits are illiterate, poor peasants from the countryside and workers; their spiritual nature is not much different from that of a young child. . . . it is common for the peasant recruit to be unaware of the existence, and therefore, the use of undergarments, except an undershirt, . . . we even have to show them how to put on their socks and other intimate pieces of clothing . . . under the seeming air of indifference and passivity the [peasant recruit] also has a native astuteness and malice difficult to measure. This malice of the peasant is inherited from the Indian and can give us problems. [On the other hand] this is 90 percent of our recruits. The rich, with honorable exceptions, believe that the obligatory service law, noble in principle, well thought out and democratic in its objective, was not meant to apply to them. . . . [each lieutenant] should become a good educator of citizens, of soldiers, without doubt the most noble and important . . . mission of an officer.[20]

And in Venezuela, where General Juan Vicente Gómez contracted Chilean Colonel Samuel McGill to direct the military academy and modernize the army, similar initiatives were introduced. An Escuela de Clases was created in 1912 to educate NCOs, and the army introduced literacy classes in most garrisons. The government constructed new barracks and training centers throughout the country and purchased modern rifles and artillery from Germany. Soldiers were trained as mechanics, tailors, saddlemakers, and in other trades with the idea that the army could be more or less self-sufficient except for imported weapons, and that such skills would be useful after military service. As in Chile, Peru, and Argentina, official military publications appeared. In Venezuela, the *Boletín Militar*, created in 1910, "published articles on the role of the armed forces in protecting national sovereignty and upholding the laws, military morals, obedience, and discipline, . . . and norms for better recruitment and treatment of the soldiers."[21] There were calls for improvement in the garrisons' food, described in 1908 as "so atrocious, . . . that looking at it is enough to extinguish any appetite," and in sanitary conditions, since "the soldiers slept on the floor covered with spittle."[22] Modernizing and professionalizing such armies meant drastic changes in barracks, living conditions, supply, training, and military customs.

Gradually, the norm prevailed that officers must be educated in military schools with common values, technical skills, and professional standards. Regulations specified the minimum time in rank necessary for promotion, tests in academic subjects, and systematic evaluations for advancement. Mexico experienced this process later and less completely than Chile, Argentina, and Peru, but by 1892 some 30 percent of its officer corps had graduated from the newly reformed military academy; eight years later this figure had almost doubled.[23] Friendships and loyalties forged by classmates in the academies would serve as the basis for factions within the military institutions and even, in some instances, be the main influence in military careers.

Not infrequently the new professional norms took hold incompletely and were tampered with by politicians. Applied inconsistently, departures from the new professional standards generated resentment. As cadres of academy-educated officers emerged, political interference in the armed forces for partisan and ideological purposes pitted civilian politicians against a new generation of military elites. It also divided armies between the pre-academy, higher-ranking officers and the new military technocrats. Their careers threatened by the new professionalism, the old political officers sometimes joined with civilian allies to oppose the "denationalizing" effects of foreign military advisers.

Civilians in Europe and Latin America, whether royalists, conservatives, Social Democrats, or liberals, wished to win over the armed forces to their own vision of *la patria* and their immediate political aims. For their part, the armed forces, partly as self-protection and partly as a gradually evolved institutional ethos, wished to place themselves outside of immediate political disputes and above politics. Their mission would be to protect *la patria*'s permanent interests and values, to prevent politicians, even kings, from sacrificing the "transcendent" for short-term political gain. This did not mean that military officers withdrew from policymaking circles or public administration; rather, they expected politicians to refrain from interfering in professional military affairs. Professionalization implied more military autonomy in strictly "military matters," not less military involvement in politics. The professional officers theoretically eschewed partisanship and electoral politics, but they increased their interest in matters of state, economic development, and national security.

In practice, civilians and military officers violated the norms of the professional creed, which often led to violent divisions within the armed forces as politicians sought to gain military adherents for a variety of causes and officers took advantage of political connections to advance their careers. These contradictions between the new professional norms and political reality were a permanent source of tension. The conflict over the extent of military autonomy from political oversight and the role of the new professional officers took different forms in Spain, France, Germany, Italy, and even Britain. Everywhere, it affected civil-military affairs. In Latin America it incubated contempt by officers for civilian politics and for the superficial formal democracies that struggled for survival from the 1880s until the wave of military coups in the 1920s and 1930s (see Table 3–2).

Table 3–2. Illegal Government Succession with Military Participation, 1924–1937

Country	*Year(s)*
Argentina	1930
Bolivia	1930, 1934, 1936, 1937
Brazil	1930, 1937
Chile	1924, 1925, 1927; 1931–32 (various)
Cuba	1933
Ecuador	1925, 1931, 1935, 1937
El Salvador	1931
Guatemala	1931
Panama	1931
Paraguay	1936, 1937
Peru	1930, 1931, 1933, 1936
Uruguay	1933
Venezuela	1936

Political in-fighting in the armed forces corroded discipline and lowered morale. Yet these same officers often turned to civilians, or joined them in political conspiracies, to achieve their own ends—and the civilians returned the favor. The politics of military professionalization further politicized the armed forces in the name of removing them from politics.

By the early 1900s armies in much of Latin America were emulating not only French and German war academies, military texts, and drill but also codes, martial law, compulsory military service laws, and even railroad load plans for mobilization. Field Marshal Helmuth von Moltke's model schemes for the use of railroads in Prussia's wars against Austria and France from the 1850s to 1870s, and the parallel French military railroad plans, reached even Mexico's barely modernized army. In 1894, President Díaz decreed detailed regulations for the military use of the nation's expanding rail system. Updated periodically to the outbreak of the 1910 revolution, these regulations provided a bureaucratic snapshot of armies ranging from the United States, Europe, Japan, and Turkey to Latin America that were moving from horse-and-buggy technology to that of railroads, armored cars, tanks, and airplanes:

> **Shipment of Livestock**
> After saddles are loaded behind the livestock, sergeants and corporals will close the doors of the boxcars (*furgones*) . . . spreading straw or grass on the floors of the cars, and if possible dirt or sand over the ramps from the loading dock or ground.
>
> Care should be taken to post a soldier on each side of the ramps to prevent horses from leaving them.
>
> At the order of the squadron captain, the first soldier on the right of each unit will march in the direction of the car door and open it; the rest will follow maintaining the three-meter spacing stipulated in the maneuver regulations, taking care that their horses lower their heads to enter the car.
>
> Once the first horse has entered, it will be taken to the right, placing it against the longitudinal wall opposite the entrance, with its head turned toward the middle of the car. This first soldier will remain as guard for the horses.
>
> The second soldier will lead in his horse and place it next to the last, and continue thusly until the loading of the number of horses that fit into the car is completed, in accordance with the table that is found at the end of this *reglamento*.[24]

Similar regulations covered the loading of troops, saddles, all sorts of supplies, and even the amount of personal baggage that officers and soldiers could take along when using the trains in peacetime and war. Mexico and its army had formally entered the age of technology and bureaucratization, even if its society, like that in much of Latin America, remained in many respects archaic.

Preparing for modern warfare also meant important economic and social changes. By the end of the nineteenth century the largest industries in Europe were manufacturers of armaments.[25] To survive, these firms needed markets beyond their own fickle governments. In turn, European nation-states depended for their survival and security on technical and economic developments to compete with adversaries on the continent and in the colonial empires that fed both their urban populations and machines. From the end of the Franco-Prussian War until World War I, the Europeans refrained from large wars on home territory but expanded their garrisons and empires. Colonial wars in

Africa and Asia, the Boer War in South Africa (1899–1902), and the Russo-Japanese War (1904–1906) hinted at the devastation to come in Europe after 1914. The armaments industry followed wars and military missions around the globe, seeking support for their sales. These missions sold weapons, doctrine, and, sotto voce, political ideology.

Figure 3–1. Loading the Federal cavalry horses during the Mexican Revolution. Photograph by Agustín Víctor Casasola. From Fondo de Cultura Económica, *Jefes, héroes y caudillos* (Mexico: Fondo de Cultura Económica, 1986, 1990), 72.

With important variations within Latin America, the years from 1880 to the 1920s brought waves of immigrants, foreign investment, booming if cyclically vulnerable export economies, a stapled-on veneer of modernity, incipient industrialization, and rapid urbanization. Working-class organizations and political parties also appeared as radical ideologies crossed the Atlantic and indigenous nationalist movements emerged. As in Europe, this traffic meant the rise of class conflict and social violence. In Latin America the armed forces became the main bulwark of the state against the tide of labor unrest, just as they had in Germany and France. They also resented this role. Instead, they favored the reform of archaic social and labor systems and in some countries, such as Chile, Brazil, Bolivia, and Ecuador, promoted social legislation, public enterprise, and economic nationalism in the 1920s and 1930s.

Lessons learned from foreign military missions were not strictly military. Armies in Prussia, France, Spain, Italy, and Russia engaged not only in preparations for external defense (and offense) but also in internal missions to defend the social order against revolutionary doctrines and movements. The French army defeated by Prussia in 1870–71, for example, repressed the Paris Commune in 1871. Three days after Emperor Louis-Napoleon's humiliating defeat at Sedan a revolt in Paris deposed him and its leaders declared a republic. Besieged, republican Paris held out bravely against the Prussians. When the army and government withdrew to Versailles, the "Reds" (*fédérés*) proclaimed the Commune. It lasted seventy-two days until, under pressure of the peace terms imposed by Bismarck, the French army invaded Paris at the end of May and the Commune was "put down in an appalling bloodbath, with the estimated slaughter of over 20,000 Communards."[26] Thus, "one immediate legacy of the nightmare of the Franco-Prussian War and the Commune was to persuade France's political leaders that henceforth the Army would have to be treated with the utmost tender loving care."[27]

The French army had both a renewed external mission, to reconquer the lost territories and avenge German barbarism, and an internal one, to maintain order against "socialist" and anarchist subversion. By 1906 the General Confederation of Labor had decided that "in every strike the Army is for the employers" and denounced its recurrent participation in strike-breaking.[28] The army that emerged in the post-1871 decades, and the Ecole Supérieure de Guerre created in 1875, would be a model for many Latin American soldiers, and French military missions and doctrine would exert influence in much of Spanish America, especially in Peru, Guatemala, and Brazil. Latin Americans learned their lessons from a highly political, politicized, professional, and modern army that quelled riots, broke strikes, and from 1871 until 1914 fueled political debate more frequently than it fought external enemies. Unlike the presumed coincidence of military professionalism and apoliticism in the United States, the French army was never removed from politics, outside political debate, or uninvolved in political affairs. This status would also apply to most Latin American armies until the end of the twentieth century.

The same was true for the victors in the Franco-Prussian War. The Prussians had even more influence than the French in Spanish America, first in Chile, Argentina, and Bolivia, and then, through Chilean influence, in Central America and northern South America. From the late 1850s, inspired by von Moltke, the Prussian army became the envy of Europe. Von Moltke pioneered the use of rail transport to mobilize armies, war gaming, strategic planning, and management of industrial resources in war. Determined to unify Germany, he viewed war with France as inevitable and military preparedness as a moral and political obligation. Von Moltke despised political meddling in military affairs and believed that "war had become too serious a matter for soldiers to be able to tolerate the interference of civilians. . . . [His] theoretical writings on the subject gave authoritative backing to the army's inborn distrust of politicians and diplomatists, and served to widen the gap between the army and the civilians."[29]

The development of these attitudes coincided with Bismarck's protectionist industrialization policies, the rise of a German proletariat, and of a Social Democratic party demanding social and political reform. With William II still convinced of the divine right of kings, the army, which took a personal oath to his person, had as its role "to preserve the established order, to uphold the authority of the Kaiser against any demands for democratization."[30] Like its French counterpart, the German army would have a critical internal mission in protecting the state against the challenges of class conflict, leftist parties and movements, and "politics." It successfully insulated itself from parliamentary oversight and control, cooperated with the *Kriegerverein* organizations that supported monarchy and patriotism, and identified Social Democracy as the internal enemy. In the late 1890s local army commanders often chaired these organizations "for the meeting of all patriots against the revolutionary efforts of the Social Democrats, and for the salvation of our people and our beloved Fatherland."[31] German unification and nationalism was a combined military-cultural mission. The army conquered and guarded German territory; intellectuals invented a Germanic cultural nationality.

Bismarck's Germany enacted the first comprehensive social welfare and labor protection legislation, modeled on that adopted by the Krupp armaments factory, the first industrial concern to provide its own workers' protection and insurance scheme. Thus, Europe's leading munitions firm and innovative producer of naval steel plate pioneered in modern social reforms. When these failed to pacify workers, however, the army offered an alternative mode of pacification.

In Latin America, likewise, military officers sometimes promoted social legislation and a tutelary role for the state to ameliorate worker-employer conflicts. In the 1920s and 1930s, Chilean, Ecuadorian, Bolivian, Peruvian, and Brazilian officers took the initiative in implementing labor codes and industrial relations systems after toppling civilian governments. Military professionals favored an active role for government (and themselves) in economic modernization and improvement of workers' conditions. They opposed antinationalist, socialist, and Marxist ideologies and movements that incited workers to indiscipline, crime, and violence. Officers, in this sense, were neither traditional rightists nor leftists but, rather, nationalists and sometimes populists. The new generations of officers were not, in the long run, reliable instruments for simply maintaining the status quo ante. They identified with "progress" and "modernization," not with the old order and reaction, as they developed a corporate identity and sense of mission.

Frequently, professional officers made nationalism and military tutelage of national politics synonymous. At the same time, like their Prussian and French mentors, they detested internationalist and disruptive (and therefore antipatriotic) ideologies and movements, such as anarchism, socialism, and pacifism. In this sense, they had more in common with conservative nationalists than with Social Democrats and progressive Catholics influenced by the post-1890s Church social doctrine. On the other hand, they gradually distanced themselves from the old aristocracy and landed oligarchy in their quest for modernization. This quest helps to explain the apparently leftist sentiments of the nationalist, populist military movements of the 1920s and 1930s such as those in Mexico, Argentina, Peru, Ecuador, Chile, Bolivia, and Brazil.

When reform legislation failed to avert sharper conflicts, however, and when workers' movements and radical parties identified with internationalist doctrines, the armed forces drew the line with machine guns and steel, as had German and French soldiers before them. Systematic campaigns to repress working-class ideology and the spread of Social Democracy in Germany before World War I made the army the kaiser's political instrument; it also sought to protect the officer corps' own vision of imperial Germany. After 1896 no soldier was allowed to attend any meeting without an officer's permission, or to sing any revolutionary or Social Democratic song, or to possess or distribute Social Democratic literature. Soldiers were also ordered to denounce any comrades suspected of dealing with Social Democrats.[32] It was no coincidence that the Prussians' star pupils in Latin America, men such as Chile's Carlos Ibáñez and Argentina's José Uriburu (see Chapter 4), combated radical labor and political parties and came to power in the 1920s and 1930s as coup leaders denouncing "politics."

Overviews of the foreign military missions in Chile, Peru, and Brazil from the 1880s to the 1930s illustrate variations in impact of military professionalization as European doctrines and practices were absorbed through different Latin American social and political filters. But such an overview also reveals a common pattern of increased military commitment to overcoming the defects of civilian governments, political parties, and social reaction through authoritarian, antipolitical, and nationalist policies. European missions politicized their Latin American students, educating generations of future antipoliticians. The missions not only reinforced the armed forces' moralizing lore and public discourse but also provided irresistible opportunities for personal lucre and institutionalized corruption in arms purchases and sales, military contracting, public works, and militarization of public enterprises and regulatory agencies. These contradictory influences of the foreign missions varied in their particular impacts from country to country; everywhere they further politicized the armed forces.

The Prussian Missions in Chile

In Chile, in the aftermath of victory in the War of the Pacific, military leaders and civilians recognized the inadequacies in army training, organization, preparedness, and equipment before 1879. They also feared Peruvian and Bolivian *revanchismo* and the recurrent border disputes with Argentina. Blessed with the flood of nitrate revenues from the recently acquired northern provinces, Chile could afford to invest in defending its conquests. Preliminary discussions concerning the possibility of bringing a Prussian mission to Chile took place in Berlin in the early 1880s. At the suggestion of officers who had studied the needs of the Chilean army and its errors in the recent war, President Domingo Santa María contracted a military mission from Germany, to be headed by Captain Emil Körner. The latter had worked with several Chilean officers, including Colonel Emilio Sotomayor, war hero and director of the Escuela Militar, which had been established in 1863. In September 1886 a new Academia de Guerra was created and in May 1887, the Escuela de Clases; in the same year the curriculum at the Escuela Militar was completely restructured. The *Revista Militar de Chile* first appeared in February 1885.

Santa María's successor, José Manuel Balmaceda, allocated significant resources to the military modernization program, coincident with large public investments in education, public works, communications, and transport. He also provoked the bitter animosity of congressional opponents with his arbitrary and authoritarian style. In 1891 the political and constitutional crisis led to civil war. The navy supported the congress, with most of the army remaining loyal to Balmaceda. Körner, however, along with some of his protégés and anti-Balmacedista officers, joined the congressional opposition. He organized an army in northern Chile and collaborated in the military defeat of Balmaceda's forces. Balmaceda had used the army to suppress strikes in the north the year before, and some resented its role as enforcer for the foreign nitrate conglomerates, although most officers remained loyal to the president. This division within the army proved tragic; thousands died in the brief civil war.

The congressional victory and purge of loyalist officers gave Körner free rein to completely reorganize the army, mocking any pretense of apolitical armed forces. Balmaceda had clearly been a constitutional president with legal authority over the army. The congressional opposition and military officers who won the civil war used force to overthrow a president to resolve a presidential-legislative stalemate that had escalated into a constitutional crisis. Military force and foreign technology determined the outcome of intraelite political conflict. The victors executed some of Balmaceda's officer-supporters; many others had their careers temporarily derailed or permanently destroyed. Despite the kaiser's reprimand for taking sides in Chile's internal conflict, Körner was promoted to brigadier general by the new Chilean government. (Later the kaiser pardoned Körner and decorated him with the Order of the Crown.) He gained the nickname: the Chilean von Moltke.[33]

Beginning in 1892, the Chilean government named Körner head of a commission to create a new army. A spate of initiatives followed: reorganizing the Ministry of War and General Staff; creating health, veterinary, and supply branches; importing new weapons (100,000 Mauser rifles in 1892, Krupp artillery, and more); and establishing munitions and gunpowder factories (1894). The army was reorganized from top to bottom, including the creation of an archive in 1903, various specialized officer and NCO schools, and even railroad and telegraph battalions (1909, 1910). Körner retired in 1910, the same year that officers established the Club Militar—later a locale for military political conspiracies and social gatherings.

The German mission's work continued with periodic restaffing and purchases of weapons until 1914.[34] It transformed the Chilean army from its educational and career system to uniforms, customs, manners, and weapons. Numerous Chilean officers studied in Germany and served in the latter's armed forces. The officers molded by the mission took the Prussian model to Central America and northern South America, including Colombia, Venezuela, Ecuador, and El Salvador. Latin American officers also came to Chile's Escuela Militar. Paraguay, for example, sent small contingents of officers from the late 1890s, including General Eugenio Alejandro Garay, an almost mythical figure in Paraguayan militarylore, revered for his bravery and intelligence in the Chaco War against Bolivia (see Chapter 4).[35] Nowhere did European military missions more thoroughly penetrate a Latin American army than Chile, and nowhere did a supposedly apolitical professional army become more imbued with doctrine that made its officers contemptuous of civilian politics and politicians.

The purges and trials after the civil war and the subsequent amnesties set precedents within the army for blaming the inefficacy and betrayal of civilian politicians for the nation's ills. From the 1890s until 1924, governments used the army to suppress strikes in ports, mines, and cities and to maintain order during elections (and sometimes to intimidate opposition voters and tamper with ballot boxes). Politicians courted individual officers but at the same time ignored their professional and institutional aspirations. The young officers, trained in the German tradition embedded in the military academies, came to despise the quasi-parliamentary political system that dominated Chile from 1891 to 1924.

The politicians failed to adequately provide for military salaries and modernization, interfered in the promotions process, and neglected pressing social issues affecting the country. In 1907 junior officers formed the Liga Militar to lobby for improved conditions and benefits for the army. Four years later its leaders broached the possibility of a military coup with Gonzalo Bulnes Pinto, the son, grandson, and nephew of Chilean presidents. Bulnes Pinto eventually distanced himself from the coup talk, but not before Liga members had publicly expressed opinions on government corruption, public education, crime, economic policy, and the need for more resources for the armed forces. An abortive military movement in 1915 aimed to empower "a strong government able to end the political anarchy preventing the progress of the nation"; and in 1919 another conspiracy among high-ranking officers "to avoid political chaos" and end "the dangers of communism" fizzled, although politicians from all the parties took it seriously.[36]

World War I accelerated the pace and intensity of socioeconomic change and, at war's end, brought a demagogic and charismatic Arturo Alessandri to the presidency. Like Balmaceda, Alessandri faced hostility and obstructionism from the congressional opposition. Ministerial changes, delays in budget and tax bills, and failure to authorize the garrison to stay in Santiago (required by the constitution) exacerbated the economic crisis and the tide of labor protest. Only forty days after taking office, notwithstanding his proclaimed commitment to social justice and reform, Alessandri ordered troops to put down a strike at the San Gregorio nitrate plant; a brutal massacre added new martyrs to the labor movement's struggle.

Alessandri's use of the police and army to maintain order during congressional elections in 1924 angered the opposition and delegitimated the outcome. The president had sent numerous reform proposals to the congress, including social security, unionization, collective bargaining, and strike laws, but it refused to act. The political stalemate persisted into mid-1924 when, on September 4, some four hundred lieutenants and captains met at the Club Militar "to strengthen the unity and comradeship among elements of the army in these difficult times." The officers attacked the war minister, who was ejected from the meeting. Alessandri, dropping the formality of dealing with the military through the war minister, agreed to meet directly with an army delegation. Although some controversy exists concerning this meeting, Alessandri apparently asked the officers to present a list of projects to the congress the next day, "promising" that if it did not act he would "close the session, convoke a constitutional convention, and, with the army's support, proceed to make a 'new Chile.' "[37]

Major Carlos Ibáñez then orchestrated the creation of a military junta (*junta militar y naval*) to coordinate the armed forces' political activity. No generals were included; all thirty-five members from colonel to lieutenant were staff officers and former students of the War Academy. They commanded key artillery, cavalry, engineer, and infantry units, or served as instructors and administrators in army schools. As Frederick Nunn notes, many had received training in Germany; some had served in Chilean army missions to Colombia and El Salvador. The three most influential *junteros*—Lieutenant Colonel Bartolomé Blanche Espejo, Major Ibáñez, and later Major Marmaduke Grove—as well as others had been classmates at the War Academy.[38]

On September 5 the *junta* met again at the Club Militar. General Luis Altamirano, now heading the Alessandri cabinet, also symbolically assumed *junta* leadership. Generals and many colonels wished to control this junior officers' movement; they also held more conservative, in some cases pre-German mission, views on the military and society. Army General Juan Pablo Bennett and Navy Admiral Francisco Neff occupied the war and finance ministries, giving the cabinet a decidedly military face. But political factionalism in the navy and army brought fears of repetition of the 1891 tragedy. Private negotiations avoided clashes between the armed forces and prevented battles among army units; general officers were able to reestablish discipline among the ranks.

Officers delivered their list to President Alessandri, wanting action on the budget, social security and income tax laws, labor legislation, reformed pension and public employee salary measures, and new promotion schedules for the armed forces. Under pressure, the congress passed all the laws contained in the military petition, including legislation for new retirement and promotion standards, salary increases, armaments acquisition, and augmentation of the army's size. *Junta* leaders announced, despite this congressional surrender, that it would not disband "until convinced that their mission was completed,"[39] which proved unacceptable to Alessandri, who was unwilling to share formal power with the *junteros*. He resigned (then was persuaded to take an authorized "leave of absence" instead) and left for Italy via the trans-Andean railway to Argentina. A provisional government consisting of Generals Altamirano and Bennett and Admiral Neff dissolved the congress and announced that a return to normalcy would occur as soon as possible. The military *junta* movement, however, feared rightly that the new government was more concerned with reestablishing order than with political reform.

Behind the scenes, divisions within the army and among officer generations made consolidation of a true military *junta* government impossible. Antagonism between army and navy *junteros* further complicated the situation. As the political situation in Santiago degenerated, Ibáñez decided on a coup d'état. He toppled the conservative military *junta* on January 23, 1925, then cabled Alessandri in Italy requesting that he reassume the presidency. Alessandri demanded in exchange a return to civilian rule, creation of a constituent assembly to consider constitutional reform, and return of the armed forces to their barracks. Negotiations between navy and army factions prevented further armed conflict. Alessandri resumed his presidential duties in March. He returned to Chile, "a prisoner of war cloaked in the garb of a Roman triumphant."[40] Ibáñez became war minister, cranked up the weapons acquisition program, reassigned loyal officers to key commands, and retired dissidents. Once again, politics made and broke officers' careers.

Alessandri's term had nearly six months remaining. Upon his return, at Ibáñez's insistence, he neglected to reconvene the congress. He oversaw the work of a constituent assembly; in August a national plebiscite, with less than 50 percent of the electorate voting, approved the 1925 Constitution that would endure until a military coup in 1973. Months earlier, in June, soldiers had machine-gunned striking workers at La Coruña and destroyed their living quarters with field artillery. Under state-of-siege authority in Antofagasta and Tarapacá, the military applied martial law to "agitators" and "Communist revolutionaries." In July, despite presidential orders to the contrary, Ibáñez ordered police to use force in Iquique against demonstrators waving red flags.

Ibáñez became a presidential candidate to succeed Alessandri in September 1925. When he published a letter to the president explaining his unwillingness to resign his position as minister of war (as was customary for ministers who chose to run for elective office), Alessandri resigned the presidency for the second time, citing "military pressure." Ibáñez almost immediately withdrew his candidacy, but Alessandri's resignation stuck. The traditional political parties agreed on a compromise candidate: Emiliano Figueroa Larraín. Unable to cope with the political situation after his election, Figueroa resigned in May 1927, after first requesting a leave of absence. Ibáñez then had himself elected president in a carefully controlled election in which he obtained more than 220,000 votes of the slightly more than 230,000 cast.

Ibáñez's "election" was the culmination in the rise of the Prussian-trained officers to political prominence and also highlighted their growing role as arbiter in the country's social conflicts. Emulating the anti-labor role of its Prussian mentors, from 1911 to 1920 the Chilean army had intervened in almost three hundred strikes.[41] By the early 1920s, Chile's leading young officers demanded reforms to resolve the "social question" and cleanse the body politic. Ibáñez's patriotic rhetoric in February 1927 embodied the political lessons and ritual condemnations of "politics" disseminated in the new military academies. It also blared out the message of anticommunism, political intolerance, and identification of opposition with treason that would characterize Chilean military antipolitics in the remainder of the twentieth century:

> The final hour—the hour for settling accounts has arrived. The malevolent propaganda of a few professional politicians and the disunifying propaganda of an audacious few who oppose all authority is not acceptable. It is necessary to apply cauterization from top to bottom. . . . This action has developed thanks to the treasonous actions of a number of professional politicians who think the Country cannot exist and progress without their concourse. . . .
>
> I am sure that our sister the Navy supports the wishes of the Army. The two constitute the bulwark of Chile, not only in the case of external conflict but also in moments of internal gangrene. There are times when the Armed Forces must be the saviours of the people. The question stated thus, I tranquilly await developments and have faith that the sensible and patriotic portion of our country will cooperate with my work and will comprehend the motives that guide my deeds, and which are inspired by the old motto: "*La Patria* before all things."[42]

Ibáñez ruled Chile until 1931, decreed its first labor code, and encouraged foreign investment, public works, and industrialization. He reorganized the na-

Figure 3–2. Carlos Ibáñez del Campo, Academia de Guerra (1912–1914), president of Chile (1927–1931, 1952–1958). From Ejército de Chile, *Academia de Guerra, 1886–1986* (Santiago: Ejército de Chile, 1986), 108. Courtesy of the Chilean Army

tional police force as the Carabineros de Chile. They helped him to repress the leftist labor movement and establish public order until the crisis of the Great Depression led to his ouster. His portrait still adorns the Carabinero Historical Museum in Santiago as Chile turns toward the twenty-first century.

Above all, Ibáñez disliked politicians, a view shared with other authoritarian modernizers from Mexico and Guatemala to Argentina. For him, *haciendo patria* meant overcoming the corroding influence of partisan politics. This antipolitical sentiment was shared by most officers, especially the German-trained academy graduates. The need for "political housekeeping," or, as Ibáñez often said, for a surgeon to heal the body politic and save *la patria*, inspired the army's 1927–1931 "honorable mission."[43]

Between 1924 and 1932 the officer corps precipitated constitutional and legal reforms that transformed the old political order. From the perspective of Chilean officers, there would have been no 1925 Constitution, nor the 1931 labor code, nor the Carabineros, nor the reconstituted party system, nor the 1931–32 decree legislation that expanded the role of the state and encouraged industrialization without the salvational mission of 1924. Not until 1973 would the armed forces again be needed to fulfill this patriotic duty, but Ibáñez's role in "cleansing" and restructuring Chilean politics and the lessons of the Prussian missions remained sources of pride for Chilean officers.

The French Missions in Peru

French military missions in Peru had some political effects similar to those of the Germans in Chile, mediated by the unique political and socioeconomic circumstances of post-War of the Pacific Peru. Like the Peruvians, the French had been defeated in a major war (1870–71) and faced the task of political and military reconstruction. The French engaged in a massive arms buildup to recover the lost Alsace-Lorraine territories. This effort paralleled the Peruvian obsession with retaking the provinces conquered by Chile in the War of the Pacific. By the 1890s the French military had regained its prestige at home, had extensive colonial experience in Africa and Asia, and was imbued with its own version of the "civilizing mission." In Africa it incorporated non-Europeans into local armies, a task thought comparable to the Peruvian need to incorporate the Indian population into "national" life. Since in 1900 over 90 percent of

Peruvians were illiterate and therefore disenfranchised, programs to make the barracks into schools of citizenship and literacy, and to "make Indians into Peruvians," seemed a prerequisite for creating a modern nation.

Like their Prussian counterparts in Chile and Argentina, the French in Peru promoted obligatory military service, pushed weapons purchases, directed the formation of specialized army corps (medical, veterinary, supply, engineering), oversaw the installation of munitions and weapons factories (1908–1912), and reorganized officer education. Peru also contracted a French naval mission (1905–1912)—the first Latin American country to do so.[44] This mission reorganized the navy, and Commander Paul de Marguerye was named director of the Naval Academy. The naval mission supervised the acquisition of warships and submarines.

French officers directed reform of the Chorrillos Military School and created a Superior War College (Escuela Superior de Guerra, or ESG). The ESG offered its first courses in 1904; from 1914, Peruvian graduates intermittently served as directors. Military engineers and cartographers produced the only modern maps in Peru. As in Guatemala and Chile, the new officer corps emerged as a technocratic and political elite. Twenty-five years after he had directed the reopening of Chorrillos, General Paul Clément wrote: "The Escuela Militar de Chorrillos is not just an institute where that virile vocation of national defense is imparted, but a sanctuary in which we profess a fervent cult of honor, the highest moral attribute of the perfect soldier."[45] By 1930, 27 percent of officers ranking colonel or higher had graduated from the ESG. Officers graduating in the 1904–1914 period were imbued with a sense of patriotic mission and were convinced that the army was the reservoir of talent whose skills should be applied to the tasks of development—much as the French colonial officer in Africa.

The French missions encouraged reforms in military law and administration, including a new code (Código de Justicia Militar, 1898) that extended the jurisdiction of military courts over civilians, assigning cases involving damage to railroads, telegraph installations, and bridges to military tribunals. It also broadened the authority of the military over "bandits" and "seditionists."[46] These legal foundations for repressing political opponents, censoring the mass media, and restricting civil liberties and rights survived with modifications throughout most of the twentieth century. French officers sought also to instill in their Peruvian students the "true" meaning of military professionalism and the "civilizing mission" that it conveyed. Peru needed to be unified: geographically, economically, politically and culturally. The armed forces were "patriotic priests" called on to carry out the mission of *forjando patria*. This mission required the transformation of the army and of Peru itself.

Partisan conflict, subversion of military discipline, and factionalism within the army undermined French efforts to create apolitical, professional armed forces in Peru. Civilian political bickering and the recurrent coup attempts and provincial uprisings first brought the new professionals to the political circus's center ring in 1914. Allied with civilian elites and congressional leaders who feared the populist rhetoric and authoritarian style of President Guillermo Billinghurst, the French mission's star pupil, Colonel Oscar Benavides, chief of

Figure 3–3. Military officers, Cuzco, Peru, 1910. *Reflejos de medio siglo. Imagenes fotográficas andinas, 1900–1950* (Santiago: LOM Ediciones, 1994), photo no. 9. Courtesy of LOM Ediciones

Figure 3–4. Military parade, Cuzco, Peru, 1920. *Reflejos de medio siglo. Imagenes fotográficas andinas, 1900–1950* (Santiago: LOM Ediciones, 1994), photo no. 6. Courtesy of LOM Ediciones

the General Staff and hero of a 1911 skirmish between Peruvian and Colombian troops in the Putumayo region, organized a coup. The 1914 coup joined civilian elites with army professionals to curb Billinghurst's demagoguery and prevent him from dissolving the congress, arming workers, and cutting the military budget, as he had threatened. It was justified much as congressional rebels had defended their movement against Chile's President Balmaceda in 1891: defense of the constitutional order against presidential Caesarism. The army commander, José Urdanivia Ginés, declared: "The Army will insist that the Constitution and laws be respected." He also referred to defending the authority of the congress and assuring Peru's territorial integrity. Years later, Urdanivia claimed that Billinghurst had planned to renew diplomatic contacts with Chile and settle the Tacna-Arica plebiscite issue lingering since 1884. Inasmuch as Billinghurst was a millionaire with economic interests in the territory that Chile had occupied, the military action not only defended the constitution but also the territorial demands of *la patria*.[47]

While the French officers did not participate directly in the 1914 coup as the Prussians had in Chile in 1891, they did influence the outcome. Billinghurst apparently wished to arm a worker militia to defend his government against the coming coup. He decreed that control of the artillery, and particularly the Santa Catalina facility that stored weapons, would pass from the General Staff to the war minister. General Marcel Desvoyes, head of the French mission, threatened to cancel the mission's contract if the president insisted on this "technically flawed" decision. The artillery was nevertheless put directly under the orders of the minister of war, a political appointee. Desvoyes's action was clearly out of line. In effect, he had taken sides in the conflict between the minister of war and the coup leaders. Of the sixteen officers directing the coup, seven were graduates of the new Escuela Militar; of the eight ranking major or higher, four had graduated from the ESG and three had studied in France. Thus, in 1914, Peru experienced the first coup of the "new professionals."

Benavides and the Peruvian officers turned power directly back to civilians after a brief interim government (1914–15). The army still lacked institutional cohesion and commitment to directly govern the country. It remained, to a great extent, a conglomeration of garrisons dedicated to policing the rural hinterland and suppressing social disorder. In the same year as the Benavides coup, the army massacred hundreds of Indians led by a former major calling himself Rumi Maqui (Hand of Stone), who had organized a rebellion with a messianic call to reestablish the Inca empire of Tahuantinsuyo. *Haciendo patria* in Peru still begged the questions of which *patria*, whose *patria*, and what sort of *patria*.

Neither the civilian political elite nor the officers could agree on answers to these questions. Meanwhile, the congress promoted the officers who had ousted Billinghurst, in violation of the law regulating military careers (Ley de Situación Militar) that defined the professional career system, the backbone of the French professionalizing scheme. Colonel Benavides became a brigadier general. From 1916 to 1919 military salaries rose dramatically. Politics clearly mattered in the modern army, a lesson that would not be lost on Peruvian officers.

In 1919 former president (1908–1912) Augusto B. Leguía was again elected president, but congressional conspiracies threatened his confirmation. Leguía orchestrated a coup (July 4, 1919) to guarantee himself the presidency. He was supported by War of the Pacific hero and former president Andrés Cáceres and, more important, by the police in the palace guard who betrayed the incumbent, President José Pardo (1915–1919).[48] Leguía announced that he "not only came to liquidate the old state of affairs, . . . but also to detain the advance of Communism which, because it is premature among us, would produce dreadful consequences."[49]

The Leguía coup initially divided the officers, but it did not produce a decided defense of the Pardo government. Leguía began, in the Peruvian tradition, by dissolving the congress, calling for a constitutional convention, and imposing a new constitution. The 1920 Constitution was amended several times, allowing Leguía to rule as constitutional president-dictator for eleven years, the so-called *oncenio*. He presided over a booming economy, spectacular expansion of the government bureaucracy, glitzy public works programs, and a significant military buildup. Hoping to create a modern navy, he contracted a U.S. naval mission, made the navy minister independent of the minister of war, opened a naval Escuela Superior de Guerra, and purchased four submarines. Leguía also founded two air force schools and the Guardia Civil, a national police force with ranks, privileges, and equipment equal to or better than that of the army. Placed under the authority of the Ministry of Interior and Police, the Guardia became a presidential counterpoise to the army. For the Guardia Civil, Leguía contracted a Spanish Guardia Civil mission, as Ibáñez had contracted Italians to train the Chilean *carabineros*. He retained ties with the French for the army. The Peruvian armed forces thus had heterogeneous foreign influences after 1919 and experienced internal as well as interservice conflicts. These conflicts would later result in bizarre alliances among navy, army, air force, and Guardia Civil units in the numerous uprisings and coups from 1920 until World War II.

Leguía proclaimed his intent to create a *patria nueva* uncorrupted by the traditional political parties—a Peruvian version of antipolitics. He called for army cooperation (promoting officers for their help, retiring and reassigning those who missed the political bus) but paid close attention to all the armed forces. Blatant favoritism and corruption introduced by the *oncenio* divided them. Several important military and civil-military uprisings from 1919 to 1930 tested the government: in Iquitos, 1921 (with behind-the-scenes involvement of Benavides); Cuzco, 1922; and Cutervo, 1924. To the Guardia Civil, however, went the new machine guns and the mission of guarding the presidential palace. And in 1925, Leguía let lapse the French mission, which had virtually disappeared during World War I and then returned at war's end. When the United States refused to replace the French, he brought a group of German officers under General Wilhelm Faupel, who had previously served in Argentina. This mission lasted only until 1929, when Leguía responded to army complaints and requested Faupel's resignation.[50]

As long as the economy remained relatively strong, Leguía held power much like Ibáñez had in Chile from 1927 to 1931. With the New York stock market crash in 1929, animosity within the army, and the rise of new militant political movements on the left (such as the Alianza Popular Revolucionaria Americana, or APRA, in 1924, and the Communists), Leguía was practically without allies. Peru confronted labor unrest, the challenge of Aprismo, economic crisis, and political instability—a formula for military salvation.

Leguía had subverted the French-inspired professional career ladder with political appointments and corruption. The army was desperately factionalized. Discipline eroded, and resentment mounted over political meddling in its internal affairs. While the weakness of Peru's parties and government institutions made the armed forces political arbiters, their own lack of cohesiveness prevented a unified response to the political morass, thus condemning Peru to a decade of recurrent coups, coup attempts, and political violence. In August 1930, Lieutenant Colonel Luis M. Sánchez Cerro, hero of the 1914 coup against Billinghurst, led a military uprising that precipitated virtual civil war.

Military and civilian factions contested for power. As leader of the *junta*, Sánchez Cerro purged and reassigned officers of doubtful loyalty, placing confidants in key positions. Army uprisings in Lima, Arequipa, and other garrisons, headed by General Pedro Pablo Martínez, ultimately convinced Sánchez Cerro to resign, but not before further confrontations took place among the armed forces and within the army. Sánchez Cerro went to Europe "commissioned to study possible arms purchases."[51] According to Daniel Masterson, "the Sánchez Cerro rebellion [of 1930] confirmed that after more than three decades of professional progress, corporate unity still eluded the armed forces."[52] After the 1930 coup and Sánchez Cerro's resignation, no central authority could control Peru. Military discipline was destroyed by frequent attempted coups and uprisings. Seeking a political solution, the *junta* in 1931 agreed to elections, which pitted Sánchez Cerro against APRA's leader, the demagogic Haya de la Torre. When APRA lost the elections, the Apristas organized a "general insurrection" that failed, the first of their many efforts to take power through popular uprisings. As Víctor Villanueva aptly wrote, "The army fulfilled what it believed to be its duty, but the country was bathed in blood. This was the cruelest tyranny Peru has suffered, at least in the present century."[53]

Sánchez Cerro joined forces with the political right and the army high command to defeat the Aprista-initiated civil strife. The Aprista offensive culminated on July 7, 1932, with an attack on the Trujillo garrison. After taking the garrison, the Apristas murdered sixty officers and enlisted personnel. In reprisal the army massacred civilians whose bruised shoulders or irritated fingers indicated their armed participation in the uprising. Estimates of the dead range from 1,000 to 6,000. This brutal confrontation between the army and Peru's most important reformist political party colored army-APRA relations and Peruvian politics into the 1970s.

On April 30, 1933, an Aprista assassin killed Sánchez Cerro as he left the San Beatriz racetrack; the president was reviewing 25,000 troops preparing for war with Colombia—a brief war that Peru lost, further demoralizing the armed forces. The congress selected General Benavides, the 1914 coup-maker against President Billinghurst and the most illustrious pupil of the French military mission, to complete Sánchez Cerro's presidential term. This decision directly violated the recently adopted 1933 Constitution's ban on electing active-duty officers as president. Benavides settled the conflict with Colombia and ended the civil strife. He finished the Sánchez Cerro term, then voided the presidential election results in 1936, dissolved the congress, and added three years to his own term. He governed as dictator until 1939, bringing German officers to Peru in 1937, an Italian air force and police training mission, and reinstating the U.S. naval mission canceled by Sánchez Cerro. Despite his attention to the training and equipment needs of the armed forces, the thoroughly politicized Peruvian military continued to suffer internal conspiracies and, now, penetration by APRA militants who sought to subvert the military institutions.

By World War II, foreign missions had influenced the Peruvian military for almost half a century. Officers now came from the academies. They shared professional expertise and doctrine, fought in small external wars, and sought to maintain internal order. They were the country's most important political force, politicized by the missions, by the politicians, and by Peruvian circumstances from 1895 to 1939. They saw themselves as the bearers of a "civilizing mission" and as the ultimate bulwark of Peruvian national values, much like their French tutors. They also recognized that both the old *patria* and new *patria* had a long way to go before an authentic Peruvian nation could emerge. They saw politics and politicians as the enemy barring the road to this dream, yet they remained themselves ideologically divided and irremediably factionalized. Some favored corporatist, quasi-fascist regimes, others more democratic alternatives, and still others any sort of authoritarian system that would overcome the malevolent influence of politicians and politics (*politiquería*).

After more than four decades of professionalization and modernization, foreign military missions had not been able to take the Peruvian armed forces out of politics or politics out of the armed forces. Indeed, they had just the opposite effect. Officers primarily blamed civilians for this outcome: Leguía's dictatorship, the threat of Aprismo, the Communists, the irresponsible oligarchy, the venal politicians, the incoherent political parties, and the imported "internationalist ideologies" that afflicted the nation. In contrast, the armed forces claimed that they sought to overcome these obstacles, to create and sustain a modern, progressive, prosperous Peru—for all Peruvians.

General Benavides's last will and testament, executed in Lima on November 30, 1935, eloquently said it all—and like Chile's Ibáñez, Benavides had learned well the tenets of military patriotism:

> I declare that I have dedicated all my life to the service of my *patria* with the greatest abnegation and honesty, that I always sought her aggrandizement and prestige, and that it is a great stamp of pride for me to bequeath to my children a name without stain. I declare, again, that at no time in my life have I aspired to be President of the Republic and that my only ambition was to be always a good soldier of my *patria*. Only unexpected circumstances, against my will . . . have carried me twice to exercise the Supreme command of the Republic to save the country from anarchy and chaos. . . . In sum, I have the happy satisfaction given by my conscience that tells me that I have done whatever has been possible for the good and grandeur of *la patria*.[54]

The Foreign Missions in Brazil

Like Benavides and his Peruvian comrades, Brazilian officers also learned lessons on *la patria* from a French mission, although it arrived later to Brazil's national army than to Peru's. Brazilian military professionalization had proceeded more slowly and less successfully than in Chile and Argentina, to the consternation of officers who feared Argentine "adventurism" and noticed the defenseless "internal frontiers" of the Amazon Basin. Border disputes with Bolivia, regional uprisings, and recurrent military conspiracies begged for a program of military reform. For the first time in twenty years, the army carried out field maneuvers in 1905, and from 1906 to 1908 sent a handful of officers to Germany for further training. Hermes da Fonseca, Brazil's leading military Germanophile, convinced the foreign minister of the need for German-trained officers "to direct a renovation of the armed forces," but partisan political conflicts and the influence of those favoring a French mission prevented fulfillment of the dream.[55]

Brazil's first direct presidential election in 1910 brought da Fonseca to power. He used federal troops to impose allies in several state governorships and attempted to accelerate army modernization by sending new contingents of officers to Germany. The president also contracted for new warships for the navy. He failed, however, to convince the congress, the most powerful states, and the partisan opposition to allow the army to follow the examples of Peru, Chile, and Argentina. No foreign military mission came to train Brazil's federal army before World War I.

Lacking a European mission, officers returning from German military schools nevertheless formed a cadre of professionalized officers, an "internal mission" that spread the gospel of reform and modernization. In 1913 they began publication of *A Defesa Nacional*, whose editorial board included Lieutenant Bertholdo Klinger and Lieutenant Leitão de Carvalho, later to be important decision makers in Brazilian army politics. They denounced civilian entrapment of the army in politics and claimed that it "was the only truly organized force in the midst of an amorphous mass of ferment."[56] Klinger wrote that the army needed to be equipped for its "conservative and stabilizing function," and "prepared to correct internal troubles so common in the tumultuous life of societies in formation."[57]

Da Fonseca's efforts to make Brazil a nation-state rather than a collection of fiefdoms controlled by regional political machines fared no better than the proposal to bring a German military mission. National government institutions penetrated only shallowly in many regions, and the state militia counterbalanced the federal army. Militia forces in São Paulo had received modern machine guns and other armaments in the 1890s and played a key role in assuring President Floriano Peixoto's position against the naval revolt and federalist rebellions of 1893–1894. In many regions, state militia continued to be more important than federal garrisons. The national (federal) army had no real General Staff, reserve system, or modern financial administration until the end of World War I.

Brazil finally contracted a foreign army mission in 1919, calling on the French victors in the war, instead of the Germans, to the distress of Klinger and his brethren trained in the Prussian tradition. Headed by General Maurice Gamelin, the French mission assigned officers and civilian instructors to the Escola de Estado Maior at Praia Vermelha, the Escola Militar, and the Escola de Aperfeiçoamento, but they received no command positions. They were also barred from certain military schools, a nod to those officers and civilians who still resisted foreign influences. The French discarded the old German manuals and pressed hard to sell French armaments to replace the German infantry weapons and artillery that were standard in the army. As in Peru, the French found Brazilian troops to be poorly educated (over two-thirds illiterate), badly fed, and poorly disciplined. French doctrine still emphasized the importance of making soldiers into citizens and the officer corps into a "priesthood" of patriotic abnegation.

The French geopolitical doctrines and their emphasis on professionalism rapidly influenced a small cadre of officers, raising political issues and focusing attention on the socioeconomic defects in Brazilian society. The mission convinced Brazilian officers of the relationship between internal security, national defense, and economic development. This theme would inspire a more fully elaborated national security doctrine in the 1950s and provide a rationale for military government after 1964. The French mission also taught Brazilians the "proper" role of officers and the nefarious influence of politicians. Unfortunately, as in Peru, the French neglected to adapt strategic and tactical principles to local circumstances and resources. Their Brazilian students dreamed of an idealized European army and a modern Brazilian nation. Like their Argentine, Chilean, Peruvian, and Guatemalan counterparts, these dreams pushed them into political action.

In 1922 disputes over presidential succession brought da Fonseca back to center stage, now as president of the Clube Militar. He and his military colleagues denounced political corruption (although they neglected any mention of pervasive corruption within the army), lack of attention to military needs, and the inept, repressive regime of President Artur da Silva Bernardes.[58] Junior officers (the *tenentes*) took up the cry; Brazil's twentieth-century cadre of military nationalist reformers would be born in revolt against civilian politics in 1922, three years after the French arrived. An alleged affront to the armed forces by Bernardes precipitated a revolt at Rio's Copacabana Fort; sixteen young officers were killed when they refused to surrender to government forces.[59]

After da Fonseca's death in 1923, the mantle of military modernization and disdain for politicians and parliaments passed to a generation of younger officers who shared with their colleagues across South America a new vision. These *tenentes*, contemporaries of the 1924 Chilean *juntistas*, revolted again in 1924. When suppressed, they began a trek across the country, fighting diverse opponents and proclaiming their message of modernization for a "new Brazil." The Prestes Column, named after Luis Carlos Prestes, one of the rebel officers who later became the leader of the Communist party, marched over fifteen thousand miles and engaged in over fifty battles and skirmishes before going into exile in Bolivia in 1927.[60] This heroic feat became legendary; state police, armies of thugs organized by landowners, and the federal army failed to destroy or capture Prestes's forces.

Meanwhile, incipient industrialization, the formation of working-class organizations and populist political parties, and social conflicts accentuated the regime's lack of legitimacy and credibility. More officers came to believe that "the Army, and only the Army, was the organized force which could be placed at the service of democratic ideals and popular demands, against the interests of the bosses and oligarchies."[61] Both the German- and French-trained officers were embittered by Brazil's inefficient, corrupt, and fragmented administration, and by the inability of political parties to provide effective representation and leadership. Many admired and came to favor Spanish, Portuguese, and Italian authoritarian models to transform Brazil into a real *patria*, a corporatist antiliberal nation.

The country's politicians exacerbated military discontent by neglect of the armed forces, blatant avarice, political corruption, and electoral fraud. They routinely governed under states of siege and other constitutional and statutory regimes of exception, curtailing freedom of the press and civil liberties and rights. Official government candidates for president typically won elections with overwhelming victories secured from the "electoral herds" rounded up by the rural political bosses known as "colonels." This system of *coronelismo* delivered the presidency in 1926 to Washington Luis Pereira de Sousa, governor of São Paulo state. With the Communist party outlawed and civil liberties suspended, the official results were 688,000 to a mere 1,116 for the opposition.[62]

Four years later, the government again prevented a fair election. Contesting the outcome, the opposition candidate, Getúlio Vargas, supported by *tenentes* returned from exile and stars of the French mission, such as Colonel Pedro Aurélio de Góes Monteiro (who fought against the Prestes Column) and the *tenente* Juarez Távora (who broke with Prestes for his radical politics), launched a successful revolt. The victorious rebels imposed a military *junta*, followed by Vargas's appointment as "chief of the provisional government." Army and navy commanders again "found themselves cast in a position which was to become increasingly familiar in subsequent Brazilian history: the role of final arbiter in domestic politics."[63]

The economic collapse after 1929, with coffee prices plummeting and the international debt unpayable, gave special urgency to the 1930 presidential succession. Charges of fraud, the assassination of the opposition vice-presidential candidate, and virtual civil war precipitated the uprising that brought Vargas to power. Underlying these developments was the increased visibility and prominence, as in Argentina, Chile, and Peru, of the European-trained officers and their commitment to transform Brazil and its armed forces. Vargas promised "national reconstruction," a war on corruption, amnesty for those involved in the 1920s revolts, a program of economic modernization and industrialization, and constitutional reform. This nationalist redemptive crusade, like the policies of Ibáñez in Chile and Benavides in Peru, greatly appealed to many of *la patria*'s guardians. Though divided ideologically, the *tenentes* and Vargas's other military supporters shared a dislike for politicians, civilian government, and the congress. And they shared a dream for a new Brazil, led into the battle for modernization by the armed forces.

Vargas was a charismatic politician with military and militia experience. He favored a new order in Brazil much as other authoritarian leaders in the 1930s had elsewhere in Latin America and Europe. Klinger, who as a young lieutenant trained in Germany had written in *A Defesa Nacional*'s first issue (1913), emerged as chief of staff of the so-called Movimento Pacificador that ousted President Pereira de Sousa and installed Vargas. President Vargas abolished the congress, attacked leftist political groups, and suppressed civil liberties and rights. After defeating a Communist revolt in November 1935 and consolidating his control over the army, he moved Brazil toward a more centralized and authoritarian political system. Less bloody than El Salvador's 1932 *matanza*, the Brazilian response to revolt in 1935 nevertheless cost many lives and seriously affected air force, army, and navy units. Brief as was the Communist-led revolt of 1935, it was to leave a legacy of anticommunism on the part of most of the officer corps that would still be highly operative well beyond 1964. Indeed, the anniversary commemorations would be favorite occasions for impassioned oratory against the menace of leftist subversion even in the late 1980s.[64]

Vargas amended the 1934 Constitution to expand presidential authority under regimes of exception, imposed a more severe national security law, and obtained power to dismiss subversive military personnel. In January 1936 the formation of the National Commission for the Repression of Communism was announced; earlier in the month, police captured Harry Berger (a.k.a. Arthur Ewert), a Comintern official, with his wife and numerous Communist party documents. Prestes was also taken prisoner two months later, after the American Communist Victor Allan Baron was tortured until he revealed the ex-*tenente*'s hiding place. Berger claimed that he and his wife "had been forced to watch each other's sufferings; they had been burned with cigar butts and electrodes, and Elisa had been stripped, dragged across the floor by her hair and breasts, and raped repeatedly." (The prison warden denied the accusations and called Berger a "low type of social extraction."[65])

To enforce the new national security law, the Vargas government in 1936 created the National Security Tribunal (Tribunal de Segurança Nacional, or TSN). It judged alleged acts of "treason" until 1945. Addressing Brazilians in May 1936, Vargas appealed to their nationalism and patriotism in the crusade against communism: "The destructive activities of Russian communism are varied and multifaceted. . . . The struggle against our internal enemies . . . must be hard, dedicated and relentless."[66] In Brazil, as in Chile, Guatemala, Peru, and Argentina, fierce repression of "internal enemies" in the name of national security and *la patria* much preceded the Cold War and the Cuban revolution. Professional officers influenced by foreign military doctrines led the anti-Communist crusade with their civilian allies.

Playing on the divisions within the armed forces, skillfully manipulating traditional regionalism, and gaining the support of conservatives and nationalists, Vargas established a corporate-populist regime in 1937, the so-called Estado Nôvo. The "new state" endured until the end of World War II. Former *tenentes* and future presidents such as Eduardo Gomes, Humberto de Alencar Castelo Branco, and Artur da Costa e Silva joined in Vargas's modernizing, nationalist crusade. Acting as Vargas's chief of staff, Góes Monteiro proclaimed that the armed forces were "the only national organizations and so ought to develop their own policies, their own politics. . . . the army was an 'essentially political instrument,' whose 'collective conscience' should produce a 'politics *of* the army' to avoid 'politics *in* the army.' " According to Góes Monteiro, the army's sole objective was "the greatness of the common *patria*."[67]

The model for Brazil's corporatist order was the fascism of Portugal's Oliveira Salazar and also the authoritarian constitutions of Italy and Poland. To implement the new model, Vargas sought to reduce the authority of the states. He imposed federal "interveners," often military officers, on state governments and allowed the regional army commands to absorb the state militia.[68] This move was a direct attack on the traditional political system, which, while it did not entirely succeed, moved Brazil toward a more centralized regime.

From the mid-1930s until 1945 the armed forces participated actively in Vargas's massive industrialization and public works projects, extending their influence and power into the states, federal government, and the economy. The army expanded from 50,000 to 93,000 during the 1930s, finally outnumbering the state militia in Rio Grande do Sul, Rio de Janeiro, Paraná, Pará, and Mato Grosso, if still not those in São Paulo and Minas Gerais. Robert Levine's study of the Vargas regime concluded: "Of the legacies of the first (1930–45) Vargas administration, two can be considered the most lasting: the consolidation of the power of the federal armed forces, and the transformation of the federal government into a vehicle for national integration."[69] Other legacies were pervasive military influence in public enterprises, regulatory institutions, censorship, secret police operations, and growing corruption within the armed forces.[70]

Thus, in Brazil as elsewhere in Latin America, European military missions had contradictory long-term political as well as professional and technical impacts. As in Guatemala, Chile, Argentina, and Peru, the missions and officer education in Europe imparted new doctrines, geopolitical strategic concepts, "traditions," corporate identity, and technological modernization to the Brazilian armed forces. They also further politicized Brazil's young officers, making them self-conscious political elites in the decades after 1920. The missions came from the most highly professionalized, modern armed forces in Europe, but they were armed forces with highly politicized, anti-civilian, anti-socialist, and fervently nationalistic doctrines. They had a commitment to economic development, to the application of scientific and technological advances to society and the armed forces, and to overcoming social anachronisms such as inefficient manorial-like agricultural systems (and liberal "democracy," if it got in the way of order and progress). Such political commitments made the "new professionals" unreliable allies for the old order in Italy, France, and Germany as well as in Latin America. From the late nineteenth century, these European military establishments became the inspiration, models, tutors, and agents of military professionalization in Latin America. Their influence varied in timing, quality, and degree, but they conveyed various versions of military nationalism, developmentalism, antisocialism, and antipolitics. They emphasized the special relationship of the armed forces to society and to the nation-state.

An Overview

Modernization and professionalization in Latin America via foreign missions imbued military institutions with highly politicized militarylore. Everywhere this lore recounted the urgency of "rescuing" *la patria* from the politicians' incompetence, naiveté, corruption, and lack of patriotism. The foreign missions introduced the sort of geopolitical thought on internal development and external ideological enemies that would generate more aggressive national security doctrines after World War II—the basis for extended periods of military rule in much of the hemisphere. They molded officers and instilled the belief that "the word PATRIA encapsulates . . . our family, our companions, our possessions, our memories, our history, our lives, in short, everything we have and everything we are."[71] The missions injected the armed forces with a near-religious zeal and professional mysticism: "the officer's profession must be a priesthood (*sacerdocio*) [of the *patria*]."[72] To the Iberian warrior-priest tradition, the legacies of Bourbon military institutions, and the multiple missions of nineteenth-century nation-building, the European mentors added a heavy dose of geopolitics, romantic military nationalism, and a visceral contempt for civilian politicians, legislatures, and their offspring: corrupt, ineffective, "liberal democracy." For Latin American officers and their civilian allies, "democracy" without adjectives ("authoritarian democracy," "protected democracy," "integral democracy," "selective democracy," etc.) became an obstacle to *forjando patria* rather than a desirable political future.

The foreign military missions, however, were superimposed on particular Latin American realities; the discourse of patriotism and nationalist virtue, the commitment to "development," the war against "politics"—whether in Peru, Guatemala, Brazil, or elsewhere—justified military tutelage and salvational "intervention" without preventing corruption of government institutions and of the armed forces themselves. In Brazil, for example, "the contradiction between military corruption and the Brazilian Army's claim to be the moral guardian of the nation has long been at the heart of Brazilian politics."[73] This dilemma was shared throughout most of the the region. The *sacerdocio de la patria* was often abused, the professional mission perverted. European-tutored military institutions and U.S.-supported constabularies in the Caribbean and Central America were more "modern" but hardly less politicized as Latin America entered the Great Depression of the 1930s.

Notes

1. Efraín Cobas, *Fuerza armada, misiones militares y dependencia en el Perú* (Lima: Editorial Horizonte, 1982): 19.

2. Robert L. Scheina, *Latin America: A Naval History, 1810–1987* (Annapolis, MD: U.S. Naval Institute Press, 1987): 294–96, lists nine revolts against Latin American presidents from 1890 to 1943 in which navies played some role: Argentina, 1890, 1893, 1930, 1943; Brazil, 1891, 1893; Chile, 1891; Mexico, 1924; Paraguay, 1941. To this should be added the navy mutiny in Chile in 1931.

3. Thomas F. McGann, "Introduction," in José Luis Romero, *A History of Argentine Political Thought*, trans. Thomas F. McGann (Stanford, CA: Stanford University Press, 1963): xiii.

4. Romero (1963): 185–86.

5. Cited in Col. Enrique Ruiz García, ed., *Historial de la Escuela Politécnica* (Guatemala: Editorial del Ejército, 1973): 183. Orellana graduated from the Politécnica in 1890 and was president from 1921 to 1926.

6. Ruiz García, ed. (1973): 184.

7. For a detailed account of the influence of U.S. business interests in Guatemala from the late nineteenth century to 1944 see Paul J. Dosal, *Doing Business with the Dictators: A Political History of United Fruit in Guatemala, 1899–1944* (Wilmington, DE: Scholarly Resources, 1993).

8. Paul J. Dosal, *Power in Transition: The Rise of Guatemala's Industrial Oligarchy, 1871–1994* (Westport, CT: Praeger, 1995): 79.

9. U.S. Department of State, Serial Files on Bolivia, 1910–1929. Records relating to the internal affairs of Bolivia, National Archives, 824.20/31. Letter from Jesse S. Cottrell, June 1, 1925.

10. A. Maligne, "El ejército en octubre 1910," *Revista de Derecho, Historia y Letras* (Buenos Aires) (March 1911): 397, cited in Alain Rouquié, *El estado militar en América Latina* (México: Siglo Veintiuno Editores, 1984): 129.

11. Cited in Patricio Quiroga and Carlos Maldonado, *El prusianismo en las fuerzas armadas chilenas* (Santiago: Ediciones Documentas, 1988): 100.

12. Cited in Frederick M. Nunn, *Yesterday's Soldiers: European Military Professionalism in South America, 1890–1940* (Lincoln: University of Nebraska Press, 1983): 138–39. Nunn's work is the most important comparative study of the impact of European military missions in Latin America, and I have relied on it extensively in this chapter.

13. For illustrative material see José A. Yelpo, *Ejército, política, proyecto alternativo: 1920–1943* (Buenos Aires: Guardia Nacional, 1987).

14. Col. Luis Vicat, "El desarrollo industrial como empresa militar," in Juan Cozeneuve et al., eds., *Ejército y revolución industrial* (Buenos Aires: Jorge Alvarez Editor, 1964): 25, 45. Emphasis added.

15. Louis A. Pérez, Jr., *Army Politics in Cuba, 1898–1958* (Pittsburgh: University of Pittsburgh Press, 1976): 64.

16. NAVMC 2890, *Small Wars Manual* (1940): SWM 12-4, 2.

17. In the 1906 war, Chilean officers fought alongside their Salvadoran pupils against the Guatemalans.

18. Abrahamsson, (1972): 151–53.

19. "La educación e instrucción de la raza indígena en las escuelas civiles de tropa," *Boletín del Ministerio de Guerra y Marina* (June 1910): 666–68; cited in Nunn (1983): 141.

20. Tobías Barros (Capt.), *Vigilia de armas* (Santiago, Chile: 1920; reissued by the Estado Mayor del Ejército in 1973 after the coup and again in 1988).

21. Angel Ziems, *El gomecismo y la formación del ejército nacional* (Caracas: Editorial Ateneo de Caracas, 1979): 113–14.

22. Cited in Ziems (1979): 134.

23. W. S. Ackroyd, "Descendants of the Revolution: Civil-Military Relations in Mexico" (Ph.D. diss., University of Arizona, 1988): 71.

24. México, Secretaría de Guerra y Marina, *Reglamento de transportes militares por ferrocarril* (México: Talleres del Departamento de Estado Mayor, 1910): 34–35.

25. Bruce D. Porter, *War and the Rise of the State: The Military Foundations of Modern Politics* (New York: Free Press, 1994): 153–55.

26. Alistair Horne, *The French Army and Politics, 1870–1970* (London: Macmillan, 1984): 13.

27. Horne (1984): 14.

28. Cited in ibid.: 27.

29. Martin Kitchen, *The German Officer Corps, 1890–1914* (Oxford, Eng.: Clarendon Press, 1968): xx.

30. Ibid.: xxviii.

31. Paul Westphal, *Das deutsche Kriegervereinswesen*, cited in ibid.: 134.

32. Kitchen (1968): 151–53.

33. Quiroga and Maldonado (1988): 62–63.

34. Carlos Molina Johnson, *Chile: Los militares y la política* (Santiago: Editorial Andrés Bello, 1989): 84–86.

35. Col. Luis Vittone, *Las fuerzas armadas paraguayas en sus distintas épocas* (Asunción: Editorial El Gráfico, 1969): 257–59.

36. Brian Loveman, *Chile: The Legacy of Hispanic Capitalism*, 2d ed. (New York: Oxford University Press, 1988): 211–12.

37. Frederick M. Nunn, *Chilean Politics, 1920–1931: The Honorable Mission of the Armed Forces* (Albuquerque: University of New Mexico Press, 1970): 56.

38. Ibid.: 58.

39. Ibid.: 64.

40. Ricardo Donoso, *Alessandri, agitador y demoledor*, 2 vols. (México: Fondo de Cultura Económica, 1952): 1:404, citing Carlos Acuña.

41. Alain Joxe, *Las fuerzas armadas en el sistema político de Chile* (Santiago: Editorial Universitaria, 1970): 53; Molina Johnson (1989): 93.

42. *El Mercurio* (Santiago), February 9, 1927, reprinted and translated in Nunn (1970): 182–84.

43. Nunn (1970).
44. Chile then contracted a British naval mission in 1911, which helped found the Naval War College. The mission ended in 1914 with the outbreak of World War I. See Scheina (1987): 127–42.
45. Cited in Nunn (1983): 120.
46. Víctor Villanueva, *Ejército peruano: Del caudillaje anárquico al militarismo reformista* (Lima: Editorial Juan Mejía Baca, 1973): 138.
47. Villanueva (1973): 147–51.
48. Gen. Felipe de la Barra, *Objetivo: Palacio del Gobierno* (Lima: Editorial Juan Mejía Baca, 1967): 136–48.
49. Cited in Pike (1969): 217.
50. Daniel M. Masterson, *Militarism and Politics in Latin America: Peru from Sánchez Cerro to Sendero Luminoso* (Westport, CT: Greenwood Press, 1991): 33.
51. Villanueva (1973): 203.
52. Masterson (1991): 34.
53. Villanueva (1973): 212.
54. Cited in de la Barra (1967): 171.
55. Nunn (1983): 132–33.
56. Cited in ibid.: 135.
57. Cited in Frank McCann, Jr., "Origins of the 'New Professionalism' of the Brazilian Military," in Brian Loveman and Thomas M. Davies, Jr., eds., *The Politics of Antipolitics: The Military in Latin America*, 2d ed. (Lincoln: University of Nebraska Press, 1989): 65.
58. On the pervasive corruption within the Brazilian army from the 1920s to 1954, and the "enduring paradox" between this corruption and the army's self-definition as national savior and its attacks on civilian corruption, see Shawn C. Smallman, "Shady Business: Corruption in the Brazilian Army before 1954," *Latin American Research Review* 32(3) (1997): 39–62.
59. Robert M. Levine, *The Vargas Regime: The Critical Years* (New York: Columbia University Press, 1970): 2.
60. Ronald Schneider, *"Order and Progress": A Political History of Brazil* (Boulder, CO: Westview Press, 1991): 104.
61. Glauco Carneiro, *O revolucionário Siqueira Campos* (Rio de Janeiro: Gráfica Record Editora, 1966): 2:104–5. Cited in Schneider (1991): 111.
62. Schneider (1991): 109.
63. Thomas E. Skidmore, *Politics of Brazil, 1930–1964: An Experiment in Democracy* (New York: Oxford University Press, 1967): 6–7.
64. Schneider (1991): 134.
65. Cited in Levine (1970): 127.
66. Cited in ibid.: 137.
67. Cited in McCann in Loveman and Davies, eds. (1989): 65.
68. Federal intervention in state government to deal with "emergency" conditions was common in Argentina, Mexico, and other Spanish American federal systems as well as in Brazil.
69. Levine (1970): 170.
70. Smallman (1997): 44–47.
71. Manuel Rodríguez Solís (Col.), comp., *Deontología militar: Tratado de los deberes militares* (Guatemala: Ministerio de la Defensa Nacional, 1964): "Culto a la Patria," pp. 72–79.
72. Cited in Nunn (1983): 197.
73. Smallman (1997): 58.

4

Variations on Patriotic Themes

La Patria and the Armed Forces from the Great Depression to the Cold War

> When the nation, as a result of bad rulers, is put into a situation where there are no constitutional solutions, [the military] has a duty to fulfill: to put the nation in order.
>
> —General Arturo Rawson, Argentina, 1943

The 1930s global depression ravaged Latin America. Skyrocketing unemployment, mass migrations, labor conflicts, political protests, and violence afflicted the region. Governments toppled and extremist movements mushroomed. Between 1930 and 1935, fifteen of twenty Latin American countries experienced military or civilian-military coups (see Table 4–1). While some officers and civilians flirted with local variations of corporatism and fascism, European geopolitical doctrines also spread among Latin American officers.[1] Most of these officers preferred nationalist, authoritarian responses to the social unrest and economic crisis. In common they rejected both liberal democracy and Marxism. Spain's General Primo de Rivera and then Francisco Franco, Italy's Benito Mussolini, and even German Nazism were admired and emulated in efforts to provide harmony, order, and unity against the challenges of modernizing capitalism's social dislocations. Military support for such approaches, however, did not indicate monolithic support for fascism. And even when the 1930s crisis brought direct military rule, it revealed numerous ideological currents, personal cliques, and generational cleavages within the armed forces as they faced institutional and political challenges. While the military emphasized unity and patriotic sacrifice for *la patria*, the exercise of government responsibilities exacerbated internal conflicts and interservice rivalries.

Officers favoring corporatist models resurrected organic versions of *la patria*, depicting it as a metaphoric "body" defending itself against external and internal "political infections" such as Marxism, socialism, or local populist movements—for example, APRA in Peru, the MNR in Bolivia, and Acción Democrática in Venezuela. These infections threatened *la patria*'s health or very survival. They needed to be "treated" and eradicated. In other cases, such as Nicaragua, the Dominican Republic, Honduras, and Paraguay, nationalist rhetoric barely disguised personalist patrimonial dictatorship based on, but not directed by, military institutions. There, too, authoritarian anticommunism was part of patriotism, but often it was less important than control over smuggling,

Table 4–1. Establishment of Depression Dictatorships, 1930s

Country	*Regime*
Argentina	Gen. José Uriburu (1930–32) Gen. Agustín P. Justo "elected" president (1932–38)
Bolivia	Self-coup and "elections" with oversight by military *junta* (1930); army "arrests" President Daniel Salamanca (1934); Cols. David Toro, Germán Busch; "military socialism" (1936–39)
Brazil	Military *junta*, then regime of Getúlio Vargas with army support (1930–45)
Chile	"Socialist republic" (1932)
Cuba	Fulgencio Batista; "sergeants' coup" (1933)
Dominican Republic	Gen. Rafael Trujillo (1930–38; 1942–52)
Ecuador	Nineteen presidents from 1931 to 1948; none complete term; 1932, four-day civil war, Quito garrison drives congress from capital, provincial regiments restore congress; coup in 1935, army imposes Federico Páez (1935–37); coup by Minister of Defense Gen. Alberto Enríquez (1937–38)
El Salvador	Gen. Maximiliano Hernández Martínez (1931–44)
Guatemala	Gen. Jorge Ubico (1931–44)
Honduras	Gen. Tiburcio Carías Andino (1932–47)
Nicaragua	Gen. Anastasio Somoza (1936–56)
Paraguay	Col. Rafael Franco (1936) Gen. José Félix Estigarribia (1937–40)
Peru	Col. Luis Sánchez Cerro (1931–33) Gen. Oscar Benavides (1933–39)
Uruguay	President Gabriel Terra (self-coup) (1933–38)
Venezuela	Gen. Eleazar López Contreras (1935–41)

gambling, prostitution, government contracts, and public enterprises. The most ghastly version of depression-era anti-Communist patriotism occurred in the 1932 Salvadoran army's massacre of thousands of peasants and Indians who joined in an uprising partly instigated by El Salvador's weak Communist party.[2]

To combat the political infections and the economic crisis, Latin American governments turned to economic nationalism to insulate *la patria*, to the extent possible, from the depression, and to political nationalism to rally the population to *la patria*'s defense. These policies implied increased government intervention in the economy, protectionist trade regimes, subsidies for domestic producers, and incentives for industrialization. They also meant more rigorous surveillance, intimidation, and repression of opposition political movements, labor organizations, and the mass media. Most military officers agreed with European and local intellectuals who preached the need for energetic leadership to rescue nations from moral and spiritual degeneration. Everywhere, politicians and politics were blamed for the crisis. So, too, were liberalism and social democracy, political systems that allegedly allowed *la patria*'s enemies to poison and corrupt its spirit.

All the region's armed forces faced labor and peasant agitation and strikes, the seemingly never-ending pox of elections and electoral violence, and the meddling of politicians in military affairs. More than ever, maintaining internal stability meant repressing both organized and spontaneous popular movements. Whether "military socialists" as in Bolivia, conservative modernizers as in Paraguay, or frankly repressive agents of patrimonial dictatorships as in Nicaragua and the Dominican Republic, Latin American armed forces deployed against internal enemies, arresting, abusing, and sometimes killing their own citizens. Somehow, patriotism and defending *la patria* required excluding certain compatriots from participation in political life.

Yet the armed forces did not limit their self-concept and missions to repression. Their notion of patriotism and responses to the 1930s crisis included a desire to jump-start their nations' social and economic development. They energetically supported public works programs, investment in industry and public enterprise, government control of natural resources, the creation of military and heavy industries, and improved educational opportunities. They pushed hard for new roads, communications systems, and subsidies for economic sectors flagellated by the depression. Exemplary were the funding of public housing and low-cost popular restaurants during General Oscar Benavides's administration in Peru (1936–1939) and Getúlio Vargas's Estado Nôvo in Brazil (1937–1945). They also encouraged constitutional and legislative reforms such as labor and social security legislation (see Tables 4–2 and 4–3).

No simple snapshot does justice to the diversity of political views, influence, contributions, and institutional evolution of the Latin American armed forces from 1930 to the mid-1950s. Governments and the armed forces confronted the common dilemmas of economic crisis, political protest, urban unrest, labor and peasant organizing, and then the impacts of World War II and the beginnings of the Cold War. They did so through the filters of unique histories and systems of civil-military relations. In some cases, officers took the lead in promoting social and economic reforms. Military populism and support for economic modernization usually went hand in hand with authoritarian political experiments and rejection of pluralist-liberal democracy. In other cases, the armed forces remained tied, if not uniformly or uncompromisingly, to the old order, the rural landowners, the export economy, and the traditional political parties. Rarely, however, did these ties make them reflexive, compliant instruments of a "ruling class."

Table 4–2. Military "Modernizers" and New Labor Laws, 1930–1955*

Country	*Legislation*
Argentina	1943–46 Peronista reforms; 1949 Constitution
Bolivia	1939 Labor Code
Brazil	1931–34 social legislation; 1934 Constitution; 1937 Constitution
Chile	1924 "social laws" incorporated into 1931 Labor Code
Ecuador	1937–38 minimum wage law; Labor Code
Paraguay	1937 labor laws
Peru	1936 Social Security Law
Venezuela	1936 Labor Code

*Labor codes, labor laws, social security laws, and the creation of labor ministries under military governments supported by civil-military coalitions.

Table 4–3. Military "Modernizers" and New Constitutions, 1925–1950*

Country	*Leadership/Year of Constitution*
Argentina	Gen. Juan Perón (1949)
Bolivia	Cols. David Toro, Germán Busch (1938)
Brazil	Getúlio Vargas/military support (1937)
Chile	Military *junta*/Arturo Alessandri (1925)
Cuba	Fulgencio Batista (1940)
Dominican Republic	Rafael Trujillo (1934; 1942)
Ecuador	Military *junta*, 1925 (1929; 1945)
El Salvador	Lt. Col. Oscar Osorio (1950)
Guatemala	Civil-military coalition ousts Jorge Ubico (1945)
Paraguay	Marshal José Félix Estigarribia (1940)
Peru	Col. Luis Sánchez Cerro (1933)
Uruguay	President Gabriel Terra (self-coup, with military acquiescence) (1934)
Venezuela	Death of Juan Vicente Gómez (1936); two military presidents (1945, 1947)

*New constitutions adopted under military presidents or during regimes constituted by civil-military coalitions.

Regional wars also influenced civil-military relations. From 1932 to 1935, Paraguay and Bolivia engaged in a terrible slaughter over the Chaco region (see Map 4–1); in 1933, Peru and Colombia fought a brief war over Leticia; and from 1940 to 1942, Peru and Ecuador fought over the Zarumilla-Marañón, renewing boundary issues pending since an 1829 treaty that had imperfectly established national frontiers after dissolution of the Gran Colombia confederation.[3] The Chaco War cost thousands of lives, while the other two conflicts were smaller in scale and quickly settled. Bolivia and Ecuador lost territory; Peru lost territory to Colombia but gained it from Ecuador. These wars relegitimated the need for military preparedness, standing armies, modernization, and external defense missions. Wartime mobilization not only armed and radicalized Indian *campesinos* (peasant farmers), miners, and urban workers but also accelerated the demand to transform archaic rural social and land-tenure systems. Both officers and soldiers, ill-equipped, poorly trained, and victimized by political incompetence, resolved to improve their countries' economic capabilities, reform society, and cleanse corrupt governmental systems. The wars, like the nineteenth-century Paraguayan War and the War of the Pacific, brought to national leadership military heroes who blamed civilian politicians for poor defense planning, incompetence, corruption, and lack of economic development.

The distinctive Bolivian and Paraguayan experiences during and after the Chaco War and the stories of civil-military relations in Argentina, Chile, and El Salvador partially reveal the national idiosyncracies and common themes in regional civil-military relations from the 1930s to the beginnings of the Cold War.[4] The abbreviated national stories that follow caution against overgeneralization in characterizing the political role of the region's armed forces and reaffirm the importance of militarylore (in its national versions) and antipolitical attitudes in framing military discourse and involvement in government and politics. At the same time, these individual histories make clear that the past does not determine, even when it shapes, military responses to emergent political conditions and that factional cleavages within the armed forces are as important in understanding civil-military relations as interactions between military and civilian groups and institutions. Shifts in international relations and the global economy, technological innovation, evolving socioeconomic circumstances, emergent social movements, ascendant ideologies, politico-institutional change, and the quality of civilian and military political leadership form part of the complex web of contingencies that influence the armed forces' role in national politics. The five stories that follow illustrate this complexity and reveal some important regional patterns into the 1950s.[5]

The Chaco War: Motives and Political Consequences in Bolivia and Paraguay

Bolivia

Poor, geographically fragmented, and economically overdependent on tin exports, Bolivia approached the 1930s depression politically polarized but still under elected civilian governments. Despite its reputation for *caudillo* rule, elected civilians had presided in the country since the 1880s. But Bolivian politics in the 1920s featured the rise of radical student, labor, and political movements that challenged the dominance of the rural landlords, mine owners, industrialists, and financial interests. The first socialist parties, founded in the early 1920s, and the Federation of University Students of Bolivia (FUB), founded in 1928, called for revolutionary transformations of *la patria*. Policy debates concerning foreign investments in petroleum fueled nationalist flames, both from the political right and the growing leftist movements, and were complicated by long-standing territorial disputes with Paraguay over parts of the Chaco region.

Meanwhile, the majority of the population, the Indian peoples, lived in the countryside.[6] Episodic struggles by Indians to better their lot in the rural highlands sent police and the army to quell rebellions, invariably leaving many dead and more resentful. From the early 1920s into the 1930s the armed forces repressed social unrest in the countryside and the mines. Among the more notable episodes, military units killed hundreds of Indians in a massive uprising in Jesús de Machaca in the Lake Titicaca district in 1921; crushed the Uncía mine strike in 1923, indiscriminately killing workers and their families; and again deployed troops against Indian peasants at Chayanta in Potosí in 1927.

As political unrest and violence mounted, Bolivia's most important export declined in price. The tin companies attempted voluntary production cutbacks to no avail. Malaya, Nigeria, and Indonesia, the world's other major tin producers, failed to follow suit. Finally, departing from their previous glorification of private enterprise and market forces, the tin magnates called for government intervention. In 1931, in cooperation with tin's colonial masters, the Netherlands and Britain, the International Tin Control Scheme went into effect. Widespread unemployment resulted in Bolivia as prices dropped from over U.S. $900 per ton in 1927 to U.S. $385 per ton in 1932.

President Hernán Siles, responding to the crisis, sought special congressional extension of his term and named an interim military *junta* to oversee his "reelection." Students rioted, a "Marxist" rebellion in the frontier town of Villazón urged a peasant-worker uprising, and an army rebellion with the participation of cadets from the Escuela Militar ended Siles's effort at *continuismo*.[7] The oligarchy rallied to form an all-party coalition, choosing Daniel Salamanca, an old-style liberal, as their candidate. The government faced labor conflicts, fiscal crisis, and political opposition from left and right. In late July 1931 it announced that it would default on the external debt.

A turn to international affairs seemed one way to divert attention from the internal difficulties. Salamanca proposed a major shift in policy toward the disputed Gran Chaco, an almost uninhabited region of over 100,000 square miles of grazing land, terrible desert, and jungles west of the Paraguay River. Dominated by mosquitos, ants, parched land, and seasonal floods, the Chaco was a nightmare for living and more so for fighting. Yet, with the region landlocked since its defeat in the War of the Pacific, Bolivia's civilian and military leaders aspired to access to the Atlantic through the Paraguay-Paraná river system.

The president sent small army units into territory claimed by Paraguay. Despite the economic crisis, he next announced an increase in military expenditures and his intention to suppress union activism. Alluding to a Communist menace, he proposed a Social Defense Law that gave him emergency powers (*facultades extraordinarias*) to confront the threats to internal order. In the tradition of Bolivian (and most Spanish American) constitutions, such extraordinary presidential powers meant constitutional dictatorship implemented by police and military forces. Untraditionally, protests resulted in congressional refusal to grant the president the requested extraordinary authority.

Frustrated by his political adversaries, Salamanca looked to the Chaco. He sent military colonization units into contested areas and expanded exploration of unmapped and unsettled regions. In May and June 1932 minor skirmishes between Bolivian and Paraguayan army forces escalated into war. Salamanca advised his countrymen that Paraguayan troops had occupied a Bolivian outpost but failed to mention that it was a fort that Bolivians had taken from Paraguay in May. He ordered a general mobilization and declared a state of siege.

The Bolivian army initially resisted Salamanca's orders, despite the perception that it was better equipped and armed than the Paraguayans. A desert and jungle war for Indian conscripts from the Andean highlands seemed unpromising. Only after the General Staff elicited a written acknowledgment of the president's full responsibility for a "suicidal" war, against the national interest, did it agree to carry out Salamanca's decision.[8] Under state-of-siege authority, labor leaders and leftist politicians were jailed, or conscripted, as Bolivia mobilized for all-out war. Paraguayan leaders still believed that generalized war was unlikely, but Bolivia seized three more forts thought critical for Paraguayan defense. Salamanca then ordered a halt to the advance.

While Bolivian generals and civilian leaders debated the next move, Paraguay decided on their behalf, encircling the Bolivian troops and forcing their surrender. From this beginning, "the war quickly deteriorated into a corrupt, bloody, and bottomless defeat and disaster for Bolivia."[9] By December 1932 internal opposition and military setbacks forced Salamanca to resort to external assistance. From Europe he recalled General Hans Kundt, the German officer originally sent to direct professionalization of Bolivia's armed forces before World War I. Kundt was asked to head the war effort. His tactics proved reckless and unsparing of Bolivian blood. Paraguayans held their forts against ghastly frontal attacks into machine guns and artillery; they also pushed forward to take Bolivian territory. Both armies suffered from thirst (especially the Bolivians), hunger, and poor treatment of wounded and prisoners. Guaraní, Quechua, and Aymara Indians, underprovisioned and barely trained, died in the name of mythical *patrias*: Paraguay and Bolivia.

General Enrique Peñaranda and Colonel David Toro took charge of the Bolivian war effort, temporarily stemming Kundt's losses, until Paraguay's Marshal José Félix Estigarribia broke through their defenses and headed toward the Andean foothills. Now the Paraguayans were within striking distance of known Bolivian oil deposits; and the war, later reinterpreted as a struggle between Standard Oil (Bolivia) and Royal Dutch Shell (Paraguay), genuinely smelled of petroleum. Salamanca completed his botched and tragic contribution to nationalism by attempting to relieve Peñaranda and also to impose his own protégé, Franz Tamayo, as the next president. When the president arrived at army headquarters at Villa Montes, he was arrested and deposed. The military turned the government over to Vice President José Luis Tejada Sorzano.

Bolivia was now fighting close to its supply lines and defending its own territory. Major Germán Busch assumed command of the southern theater, defeated the Paraguayans at Villa Montes, and then pushed them out of Tarija and Santa Cruz—none of which Paraguay had claimed before the war. Busch's victories meant that at war's end Bolivia and its army would also have war heroes to reward and glories to recall. By 1935 both sides were exhausted and ready for peace. With international support a peace conference was held in Buenos Aires in May and a treaty signed in June 1935. Formal ratification came in 1938.

The war left thousands of casualties on both sides and precipitated a new era for Bolivia and Paraguay. The military deposition of Salamanca had ended an unbroken string of civilian presidents since 1880. From 1936 to 1939 the heroes Toro and Busch, despite their differences, implemented "military socialism," canceling Standard Oil's petroleum concession, adopting a new "social" constitution (1938), and emulating the 1920s military reformism in Chile, Ecuador, and Mexico regarding labor legislation, social security laws, and public enterprise. In particular, creation in 1937 of the national petroleum company, Yacimientos Petrolíferos Fiscales de Bolivia (YPFB), anticipated Lázaro Cardenas's expropriation of U.S. oil interests in Mexico and the deepening of its social revolution. By the 1950s these military initiatives would lead to a public enterprise system that accounted for almost one-half of Bolivia's gross national product.

The era of military socialism (1936–1939) decreased the size of the army and increased its budget. The officer "generation of the Chaco" became a leading force in Bolivian politics. In 1939, Busch decided on dictatorship, followed by decree laws on public morality, reform of public administration, and a labor code nicknamed the Código Busch. He became even more of a hero to leftists and nationalists as well as to military and civilian antipoliticians. When he committed suicide in August 1939, he ensured his historical veneration but left Bolivia leaderless on the eve of World War II. Nonetheless, it was the Chaco-generation officer cohort that had set in motion state-directed modernization and challenged the rural landlords and tin barons. The military's new version of patriotism, of *haciendo patria*, incorporated the heroics of the Chaco War, the nation's rescue from civilian adventurism, the nationalization of oil reserves, and the beginnings of developmentalist economic policies. The labor code and social legislation also were now part of the legacy of "military socialism"—much like the military-imposed "social laws" in Chile in 1924 and reform legislation in Ecuador. General Carlos Quintanilla, Busch's army commander, like most of the older upper-rank officers, did not share the martyr's radicalism and was willing to return power to an elected government. He called for elections under the 1938 Constitution, supported the candidacy of General Peñaranda, and exiled key leftist officers who threatened to gain ascendancy. Peñaranda's victory against José Antonio Arze, a Marxist-nationalist who had opposed the Chaco War from exile, marked the formal entry of fascist, Marxist, and corporate-nationalist forces into Bolivian electoral politics. It presaged

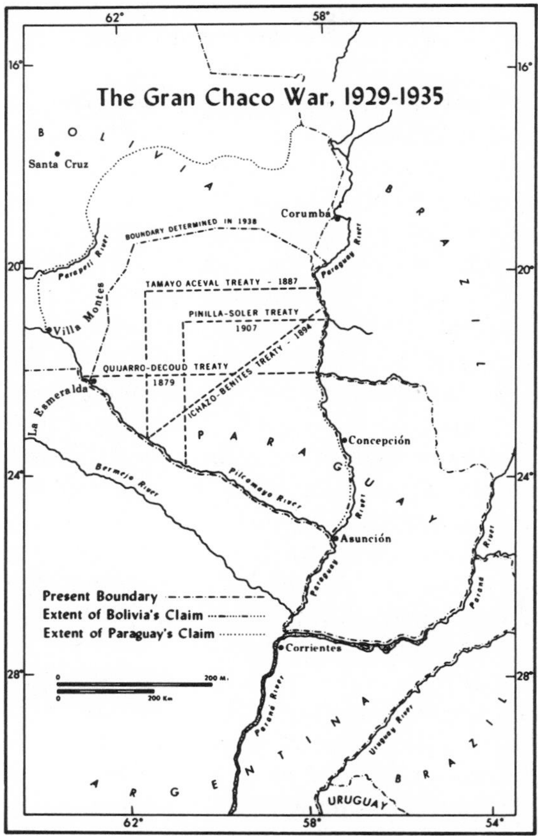

Map 4–1. The Gran Chaco War, 1929–1935. From Cathryn L. Lombardi and John V. Lombardi, with Lynn Stoner, *Latin American History, A Teaching Atlas*, published for the Conference on Latin American History by the University of Wisconsin Press, 1983, p. 59. Courtesy of the University of Wisconsin Press

the rise of political movements demanding further radicalization, agrarian reform, and the nationalization of the tin mines.

From 1940 to 1943, Peñaranda faced increasing worker militancy. In 1942 troops slaughtered hundreds of workers and family members at Catavi, a landmark event in the country's political and labor history. Labor strife and factional jockeying for control of the government divided political opinions and loyalties among army ranks. Officers also disagreed over Bolivia's alignment in World War II. Moreover, U.S. efforts to control the prices of tin and tungsten exacerbated pro-Axis opposition to Peñaranda.

Two new political groups emerging from the Chaco War gradually gained importance. Within military ranks a semi-secret officer society (*logia*) that had originated among junior officers in the prisoner-of-war camps during the conflict represented the most nationalist, anti-imperialist, anti-liberal, and arguably fascist tendencies. Taking the name Razón de Patria (RADEPA), its members sought to create a new Bolivia free from the machinations of venal politicians and the old parties that had sent the army ill-prepared to the Chaco. Among civilians, the Movimiento Nacionalista Revolucionario (MNR), led by Víctor Paz Estenssoro, initially espoused overtly fascist, anti-Semitic, and nationalist ideology. The MNR sought recruits within the military, labor organizations, and petty bourgeoisie. In 1943, RADEPA and the MNR allied in a coup against Peñaranda and installed a *junta* headed by RADEPA leader Major Gualberto Villarroel. Paz Estenssoro served as Villarroel's finance minister, making the radical officers and MNR co-responsible for the "new Bolivia."[10] Eventually forced by circumstances (the impending Allied victory in Europe) to shed its fascist leanings, the Villarroel government encouraged the development of miners' unions and hinted at nationalizing the tin mines. It also organized the first national Indian Congress in La Paz in May 1945, decreed (without implementing) an end to labor service tenantry in the rural *latifundias*, and promised expanded educational services in the Indian communities. Thus, the Villarroel-MNR alliance attacked the three most important nonmilitary foundations of power: the tin barons, the rural landlords, and traditional political parties.

While the Villarroel government combined nationalism and populism, it treated its opponents harshly. According to Herbert Klein, "the Villarroel regime would prove to be one of the most vicious in national history. When the PIR [Left Revolutionary Party] took a major portion of the votes in the constitutional convention elections of 1944, the government simply assassinated its leaders and jailed its followers."[11] The United States, alleging concern over the government's pro-Axis tendencies and also its links with the Argentine military government that refused to break relations with the Axis powers, initially refused diplomatic recognition. After World War II, internal opposition to the Villarroel government gained strength. In March 1946 a protest march escalated into revolt. Killing the president and dragging his body to the central plaza in La Paz, a mob hung his corpse from a lamppost. Villarroel's cadaver, like Busch's suicide, became a symbol of military patriotism, the two men becoming emblematic martyrs for *la patria*—victims of the conspiracy and treachery of imperialists, oligarchs, foreign investors, tin barons, and corrupt politicians. When the MNR returned to power with the 1952 revolution, the lamppost that had supported Villarroel's corpse became a national shrine, watched over by an honor guard.

Despite their nationalist and anti-political party inclinations, most senior officers rejected Busch's policies and Villarroel's methods. They preferred normalization of politics, a return to a semblance of formal democracy. Still, they were proud of the armed forces' defense of *la patria* at war, the recovery of territory conquered by Paraguay, and the social and economic reforms introduced from 1936 until 1945. There remained, however, the contradictory military role in repressing Indian miners and peasants, their suppression with considerable bloodshed in 1949 of a MNR-led revolt that lasted more than two months, and the 1950 artillery and air attack on factory workers in La Paz. Gradually the MNR became for most army officers an enemy, like APRA for the Peruvian army and the Peronistas for many Argentine officers. An all-out confrontation brewing between the MNR and the army would soon produce surprising results.

In May 1951, Paz Estenssoro ran as the MNR presidential candidate from exile. When he won, the army intervened at the behest of the outgoing president, who resigned in favor of a caretaker military *junta*. The General Staff appointed General Hugo Ballivián as president; he quickly annulled the elections and labeled the MNR, previously characterized as fascist, Communist. Civil war ensued. Miner and *campesino* militia and then the national police (*carabineros*) joined the MNR. The army—divided, poorly prepared for a massive upheaval, and surprised by the intensity and momentum of the uprising—was defeated.

In 1952 revolutionary groups that had emerged from the Chaco War and the era of "military socialism" unleashed one of the few major social revolutions in twentieth-century Latin America. The new regime enfranchised illiterates, nationalized the tin mines, and supported agrarian reform. It temporarily closed the military college, purged the officer corps, and reduced the army to a skeletal force while relying on miner and peasant militia. The radicalism and nationalism of the Chaco-generation officers had led, indirectly, to the army's virtual destruction and, gradually, to its reincarnation under the MNR governments, as a Cold War political force in Bolivian politics.

To a great extent, the foundations and inspiration of this revolution emanated from the armed forces. Their militarylore now included another tale: they had begun the creation of a new *patria* after civilians, in particular President Salamanca, jeopardized national security for political expediency. They had saved most, if not all, of Bolivia's territory and reconstituted its political system in the 1938 Constitution; they provided a labor code, social security legislation, and nationalized the country's oil; and they began construction of a network of public enterprises. Most important, they had rescued *la patria* from civilian betrayal and incompetence and had linked nationalism and patriotism to the political role of the armed forces in modern Bolivia. Then politics and politicians again betrayed the army. The chameleon-like MNR and its leaders first destroyed the army and then wavered and waffled from 1952 to 1964 as *la patria* confronted the Cold War era. In 1964 the reconstituted armed forces would rise from the ashes to renew their salvational mission. Such was the version of Bolivian militarylore that justified the 1964 coup. Listen to General Alfredo Ovando Candía:

> At the end of the Chaco War [in 1935] the new generation was confronted with the necessity of transforming the traditional society. Today we find ourselves obligated to resume that uncompleted task and rectify the errors of those who made a mockery of the Bolivian people's longing for liberation. . . . the problems of the past were aggravated by the presence of inept and venal politicians, conspirators for the possession of power. Masters of the art of destruction, they turned out to be incapable of establishing the foundations of the Second Republic called for by the Bolivian Revolution. . . . the armed forces of Bolivia embody the national and democratic essence. This fact allows us to comprehend the need for profound change. . . .
>
> Honorable Gentlemen, I must solemnly state before you that the armed forces took power in 1964 to make the Bolivian Revolution a reality and to establish the foundations of the Second Republic.[12]

This version of Bolivian history became the public discourse of military nationalists. Politicians betrayed *la patria,* leaving it vulnerable to its enemies. The armed forces then came to the rescue, recovered lost territory, and initiated political reform. Military nationalists attempted to wrest the country's resources away from international oil companies and tin magnates, defend *la patria* from U.S. hegemony, incorporate workers into the political system, and begin agrarian reforms and state-directed industrialization. In this mission they met fierce resistance from international and domestic enemies, thus leaving the "military socialists" and 1940s nationalists as martyrs. Politicians—so-called revolutionaries—again betrayed the country after 1952. And after twelve years, resurrected military institutions again assumed the challenge of a salvational-developmental mission and also of defense against a different international enemy with domestic surrogates: Che Guevara and the spread of the Cuban Revolution to Bolivia. With this militarylore, the Bolivian armed forces, though still factionalized and only partially professionalized, returned to politics in the 1960s (see Chapter 6).

Paraguay

Pre-Chaco War Paraguay was a backward rural country about the size of California, with a population of less than one million—about one-third that of Bolivia. It had not yet fully recovered from the War of the Triple Alliance (1864–1870), in which it lost most of its male population. Guaraní and Spanish made Paraguay a bilingual country, with *mestizos* and *criollos* using both to some extent. The country had few industries, poor infrastructure, and displayed little evidence of the populist political movements and labor organizations that appeared in most of Latin America in the late nineteenth and early twentieth centuries. No parallels existed to the radical mine workers and nascent Marxist and nationalist political groups that had sprouted in Bolivia.

In 1932, Paraguay's army was small, stretched for resources, and hardly prepared for a three-year war. It had no coordinated high command in peacetime and lacked even a truck fleet capable of transporting a 5,000-man army.[13] Serious efforts at military professionalization began later than elsewhere in South America. Paraguayan officers went first to Chilean military schools; then French, German, and Argentine military missions were contracted. A new Escuela Militar was created in 1915, the Escuela de Aviación Militar in 1923, and the Escuela Superior de Guerra only in 1931.

Despite a long history of *caudillismo* and militarism, civilian governments had ruled Paraguay since 1924; in 1928 for the first time two candidates disputed the presidency in an open election.[14] Civilian presidents left military matters to the small officer corps, although failed coup attempts in the early 1920s occasionally jolted those who believed that military *juntas* had been relegated to the past. Border clashes between Bolivian and Paraguayan forces produced momentary politico-military crises, including a 1928 incident mediated by the League of Nations. Neither civilian nor military leaders expected that Bolivian provocations in 1932 would lead to full-scale war. When Bolivia seemed to leave the Paraguayans no choice, they responded resourcefully and skillfully. Marshal Estigarribia and his cohorts outmaneuvered the German, Hans Kundt, and his Bolivian successors. They were frustrated when Paraguay's supply lines grew too long, but not before its armies occupied significant amounts of Bolivian territory.

According to Paraguayan officers, the army had won on the battlefield despite civilian neglect and myopia. The Bolivian invaders had been repulsed and territory gained. In 1935, however, the settlement accepted (imposed!) in mediation and the League of Nations' intervention betrayed the armed forces' sacrifices. Full of their own heroism, intent on modernizing their backward nation, and disgusted with the old liberal politicians, they declared themselves the agents of Paraguayan national development and liberation. War hero Colonel Rafael Franco overthrew President Eusebio Ayala before his term ended in February 1936. A military *junta* declared: "Paraguayans! Your soldiers in arms swear to you that we shall fulfill our mission: the Nation will return to [the greatness] of its historical past in the Río de la Plata, [to] freedom of its territory, and [to the] grandeur of its future."[15]

Franco proclaimed the need for agrarian reform (and land grants to war veterans), distribution of food to the poor, and reorganization of the nation on the model of Nazi Germany—at least to the extent of subordination of capital and labor to the common good of *la patria*. This Paraguayan version of Bolivian "military socialism" lasted for six months; old-line politicians and more conservative officers, allied with those outraged by Franco's jailing of Estigarribia, ousted him in 1937. In his place they installed the president of the University of Asunción. Two more rebellions failed in the next six months. In 1939 presidential elections gave Paraguayans one choice: Marshal José Félix Estigarribia, offered by the Azules. The Partido Colorado boycotted the election.

Estigarribia exemplified the professional officer (military education in France, a real war hero, dignified, and self-confident). He offered Paraguay a "nationalist revolution." Faced with significant internal opposition, and caught between those who wished to return to prewar politics and the Chaco veterans, new politicos, and students who demanded intensified modernization, Estigarribia "requested" that the congress disband to give him carte blanche "to fight anarchy." With this demand he made himself dictator with extraordinary powers, packed a constitutional convention with his delegates, and held a plebiscite for approval. Five weeks after the plebiscite ratified the 1940 Constitution, Estigarribia and his wife died in an airplane crash.

The cabinet designated War Minister Higinio Morínigo interim president; he decided on no new elections until 1943. The interim president established a police state, jailed and killed opponents, opened detention camps in the Chaco for political adversaries and "Communists," outlawed the Febreristas and other political parties, censored or shut down the media, and announced that he would "orient, once and for all, the Paraguayan revolution." Morínigo promoted what he called "selective democracy." To ensure that this orientation would proceed on schedule, the 1943 elections offered Paraguayans one choice: General Morínigo.[16]

In the meantime, supporters of former presidents Franco (the Febreristas, so-called because the Franco coup had occurred in February 1936) and Estigarribia were exiled, imprisoned, and subjected to police and military surveillance. As the Morínigo government moved to the right, the Febreristas and others offered more populist alternatives, insisting on the need for labor legislation, agrarian reform, and income redistribution. As in Bolivia, this insistence left the military ideologically divided and factionalized. The rise of small student and labor movements also challenged the government, which repressed, jailed, brutalized, and murdered political opponents.

In response to efforts to organize a general strike in 1945, Morínigo decreed all unions "dissolved." He allied with the reactionary Partido Colorado, thus alienating some of his military associates. Until 1944, officers with fascist and Nazi sympathies received preferential treatment; after 1945 the president diplomatically removed them from key positions. Army officers swore loyalty to the president, proclaiming that "the system of liberal individualism has been the principal cause of political anarchy, economic misery, and material backwardness of the nation." They added that professional politicians had to be repressed to prevent any threat to the stability of the Nuevo Orden Nacionalista Revolucionario (New Nationalist Revolutionary Order).[17]

Twenty-seven separate rebellions, many including garrisoned military units and factions, sought to oust Morínigo from 1940 to 1947. The last of these, nearly a civil war from February to August 1947, brought Partido Colorado peasant militia allied with parts of the army against other units that favored Morínigo's ouster. The rebels, led by Franco and allying Febreristas, liberals, and Communists, were defeated in fierce fighting. With the government's victory, the Partido Colorado and its army allies completed their conquest. Gradually the government had become synonymous with the Partido Colorado, and the party had colonized the military. Those unwilling to accept this outcome could now be purged.

Where Peru's APRA had failed, and Bolivia's MNR had been victorious (by virtually destroying the army after 1952), the Partido Colorado had taken a different route. When Morínigo intimated that he would not stand for reelection in 1948 (and was then deposed), the presidential succession depended on internal party wrangling, a fraudulent election, and then several coups from June to August 1949 that left Morínigo's foreign minister, Federico Chaves, as president. Chaves governed the country under a state of siege. In 1953 the army formally swore loyalty to the Partido Colorado. On May 5, 1954, General Alfredo Stroessner ousted Chaves, called "elections" with one candidate (yes, General Stroessner), and ruled Paraguay until 1989.

The victorious army of 1936 was divided by ideological and personalist cliques, battered by political infighting and civil strife, and then transformed into a repressive political machine. Officers became the sycophantic concessionaires and managers of illicit businesses such as cattle rustling, smuggling, prostitution, gambling, and, later, the drug trade. Paraguay's patriots became partisan (by obligation) politicized gangsters and enforcers. With the Cold War, anticommunism was added to the justifications for repressing political adversaries, and U.S. military and intelligence agencies found Paraguay a useful base for regional intelligence gathering and covert operations. If ever there was defeat in victory for Latin American armed forces, the degeneration of professionalism suffered by the post-Chaco generation of Paraguayan officers was its epitome.

For nationalist officers the legacy of Franco's brief "military socialism" (and fascism) and the spirit of Estigarribia remain distant reminders of martial glories and political possibilities. Uniquely in Latin America, prior to the 1959 Cuban Revolution, the Paraguayan armed forces allowed formal politicization of their institutions, in their alliance with the Partido Colorado. After 1954, General Stroessner gradually made the army the foundation for military "sultanship." Officers' careers depended on the whim of the president, but loyalty brought professional and economic opportunities. Positions throughout the government, public concessions and government contracts, and control over graft and the vice industries were implicit rungs on the ladder to successful military careers. In collaboration with the Partido Colorado, the armed forces administered Stroessner's patrimonial domain. With the exception, perhaps, of the 1980s narco-impresarios' penetration of the Bolivian armed forces and the unflattering comparison with Nicaragua's Guardia under Somoza and Cuba's army-mafia under Batista (1953–1959), the Paraguayan armed forces were the most systematically corrupt in Latin America. After 1939 they sacrificed little for their *patria*, although they continued to proclaim themselves its guardians.

Civil-Military Relations in Argentina

In 1930, Argentine society, politics, and military institutions differed dramatically from those in Bolivia and Paraguay. Rapid growth in the late nineteenth century made Argentine society prosperous, vibrant, and fluid. With socioeconomic change came the development of middle-class political parties, working-class organizations influenced by anarchism, socialism, and Marxism, and rapid urbanization. Large-scale immigration, mostly from Italy and Spain, transformed the ethnic and cultural character of the country. In 1914 nearly one-third of the population was foreign born.[18] Buenos Aires became a cosmopolitan capital city, the Paris of South America, and Argentines prided themselves on their European orientation.

As in Chile, a Prussian military mission had directed modernization and professionalization of the Argentine army. The 1901 universal military service law gradually expanded and ethnically diversified the army. Legislation made officer careers formally dependent on professional education, codified promotion procedures, and established internal officer panels that determined status and assignments. After 1905 only Colegio Militar graduates could obtain regular commissions, and promotion to major required passing a special examination. Promotion to colonel and general required legislative approval, but military recommendations usually ensured rubber-stamp action by the senate. A school for noncommissioned officers (Escuela de Clases, established in 1908, renamed Escuela de Suboficiales in 1916) operated at the Campo de Mayo garrison and became especially powerful. Scholarships to these military schools and active efforts to promote loyalty and literacy in the barracks made the armed forces truly national institutions. Between 1917 and 1928, fourteen of thirty-five officers promoted to brigadier general were second-generation Argentines. The "melting pot" character of the officer corps was also evident in the Círculo Militar, the social and sometimes political club that included most active-duty and retired officers.

By the 1920s, Argentina, like Chile, had an essentially professional officer corps. But despite prohibitions on political activism, some officers identified with reformist movements. In particular, the Radical party (Unión Cívica Radical), founded in 1891 and headed by Hipólito Yrigoyen, attracted some officers favoring modernization and the end of the traditional oligarchy's political domination through electoral fraud. The Radical party incited uprisings from the early 1890s and challenged the disguised presidential dictatorship established by General Julio Roca in the 1880s. From the late 1890s the Radicals battled for reform, sometimes overtly and other times clandestinely, by abstaining from voting, organizing workers, plotting coups, and seeking to proselytize among the armed forces. A failed rebellion in 1905 included junior officers who, in the 1920s, would be rewarded by President Yrigoyen with pensions and promotions, although they had been cashiered for their part in the uprising. Radicalism became the country's most important middle-class movement, crusading for electoral reform, labor legislation, and national regeneration. Eventually successful in wresting universal male suffrage from enlightened oligarchs in the Conservative party (1912), the Radicals elected Yrigoyen president in 1916. The reformed election law tasked the armed forces with supervising elections to ensure their probity, thus making the military into guarantors of political rectitude, as would occur in Chile after 1941.

Yrigoyen governed from 1916 to 1922, using the constitutional device of "intervention" in the provinces to gain Radical party seats in the congress and to control provincial administration. Intervention allowed federal authorities to replace, temporarily, provincial authorities "to guarantee the republican form of government" and to combat "sedition" (Article 6). This constitutional clause diluted Argentine federalism and allowed presidents to use the army to impose their will and their party's candidates on the provinces. As in the past, favored officers became identified with the president's political manipulations and, in Yrigoyen's case, with his progressive reforms in labor legislation and the universities as well as the creation of a national oil company (Yacimientos Petrolíferos Fiscales, or YPF). Indeed, General Enrique Mosconi, a leading military exponent of industrialization, headed the YPF from 1922 to 1930. Yrigoyen adopted contradictory policies toward the army, favoring increased salaries, pensions, and benefits but rejecting and delaying major expenditures on military installations, armaments, and maneuvers. His personal attention to personnel matters angered officers intent on maintaining professional norms and autonomy.[19]

Conservative opposition to Yrigoyen focused on electoral irregularities, abuses in the provincial "interventions" (used previously by the Conservatives to ensure their own predominance), and the surge of labor agitation that brought bloodshed to the streets. In 1919 a labor dispute escalated into the so-called *semana trágica*, a week of bloody clashes with mob violence and vigilante response. Military officers found that soldiers and noncommissioned officers in at least two garrisons had been forming "soviets" (just two years after the Russian Revolution); this discovery resulted in purges and punishment, and in the formation of a secret lodge, the Logia General San Martín. The Logia demanded more attention to the professional needs of the army, respect for military regulations, and a crackdown on subversives and leftists. Although the Logia represented few officers, its nationalist, statist, and anti-Marxist orientations would be influential in the coming decades.

Yrigoyen's administration (1916–1922) did much to intensify factionalization both in the armed forces and the Radical party. While most of the high-ranking officers had undergone German training, their diverse philosophical and political orientations reflected imperfectly the major political cleavages of Argentine society: middle-class, social democratic, statist nationalism (favoring the Radical party's program, if with some reservations); corporatist nationalism (admirers of Spain's General Primo de Rivera and Italy's Benito Mussolini); "liberals" (identified with Conservative party civilians and the agrarian economy); and a small number of "socialists." Within the army, these factions had visible leaders. As generals in the late 1920s they would, with civilian allies, contest for control of Argentina: General Luis Dellepiane, Yrigoyen's ally; General José Uriburu, the Prussians' militantly antisocialist star pupil, who favored a more "organic" approach to government and had supported Argentine neutrality in World War I; and General Agustín Justo, socially and politically identified with the old landed and commercial oligarchy. The years added more factions—personal, ideological, and professional—

that further contradicted the supposed internal cohesion and hierarchical norms espoused officially by all officers.

As elsewhere in Latin America, advanced technical education and professionalization of the career system via European missions did not mean ideological and political unity for the Argentine armed forces. Although they shared the romantic nationalism and vanguardist views of their mentors, officers differed on the ways to guarantee *la patria*'s destiny. Identification with different political and ideological alternatives, the vicissitudes of coups and counter-coups, and factional wrangling determined their career prospects. The wrong political choice sometimes forced retirement and, especially after 1930, even resulted in incarceration, torture, exile, or death.[20]

Yrigoyen's successor, Marcelo T. Alvear (1922–1928), chose General Justo, director of the Colegio Militar, as his defense minister. Justo gained congressional approval for large-scale military appropriations, directed the first major maneuvers in a decade, and encouraged the development of a military-controlled domestic arms industry. But personalist and factional struggles continued, culminating indecorously in 1929 in a duel between Justo and Dellepiane after the latter accused the War Ministry of irregularities in military construction projects. Uriburu, Inspector General of the Army, served as referee and halted the duel after both men were wounded.[21] No more primitive evidence could exist of the personalization of military factions and the extent to which the army was permeated by, and reflected, cleavages in civilian society. This pattern would endure and become more complex during the next three decades.

In 1928 the prospect of Yrigoyen's reelection sparked coup rumors. Justo and other officers proclaimed their loyalty to the Argentine constitution and to normality. Reelected to the presidency, and more self-righteous than ever, Yrigoyen renewed aggressively the politicization of the army promotion process and insisted on massive pay raises over the objection of his defense minister, General Dellepiane. At the same time, he suspended orders for armaments contracted by his predecessor, which both embarrassed and angered the army and navy. The Justo and Uriburu factions, despite their leaders' retirements, plotted a coup. Dellepiane warned the president, then resigned four days before the first of many twentieth-century Argentine military coups.[22]

The September 6, 1930, coup was a turning point in the country's history. Uriburu's temporary dictatorship proposed replacing liberal democracy with an authoritarian centralized government coordinating society for the "common good"—much like Italian and Spanish fascism. He intended to eliminate "the reign of demagoguery" and suppress the existing political parties, but he welcomed the collaboration of conservative intellectuals, civilian technocrats, and "independent" patriots. Uriburu formed an antipolitical regime (that is, antipartisan, anti-political party, anti-liberal) but not strictly a military government.[23] His military adherents and civilian supporters, however, were unable to win over the majority of the officer corps or civilian elites to the program of economic nationalism, political authoritarianism, and state terrorism.

Uriburu ruled under a state of siege, then martial law. Civilian and military opponents were arrested, beaten, and tortured. Officers suspected of sympathy for the ousted Radical party and President Yrigoyen were purged. The government invited paramilitary groups, such as the Legión Cívica Argentina, to barracks to prepare themselves to defend "public order." Despite the economic crisis, Uriburu reinstated the War Ministry contracts suspended by Yrigoyen, increased army conscription, and doubled enrollments in the Colegio Militar.[24] In the name of eliminating "politics" (that is, partisan and party politics) from the armed forces, Uriburu thoroughly politicized the army. His "aide, Juan Bautista Molina, was charged with classifying each officer on the basis of political inclinations and with rewarding or punishing accordingly. For those who cooperated with the Uriburu movement, life was to be a bed of roses. Promotions, expensive junkets to Europe and the United States, new cars, double salaries for fulfilling civilian and military posts at the same time . . . in a secret decree dated November 25, 1930, the Uriburu regime offered to pay all proven debts of Argentine army officers. The army was now knee-deep in politics and rent with bitter discord."[25] Personal patronage, clientalism, and political purges within the armed forces would be emulated by military and civilian presidents in the 1930s and 1940s and then taken to extremes by Juan Domingo Perón after 1951. While officers blamed civilians for politicizing the armed forces, military clientalism and factionalism made a mockery of the career system.

Believing that Argentines were grateful for his rescue of *la patria,* Uriburu mistakenly allowed provincial elections in Buenos Aires in April 1931. To his chagrin, the Radicals won. Several failed military rebellions followed. Recognizing that he had not gained control over the army, that the Radicals were resurgent, and that a definitive break with the Conservative party threatened—and also suffering from terminal cancer—Uriburu allowed supporters of General Justo to take charge of the Ministry of Interior, which meant control of the elections. Thus, "elected" president in November 1931, Justo ruled Argentina in alliance with Conservative and independent politicians until 1938. His government created an elaborate system of federal agencies to subsidize key sectors of the agrarian economy, implemented an impressive public works program, and encouraged military and civilian industry. These policies, intended to buffer the traditional export sector from the depression and promote economic recovery, provided the institutional foundations for later government-directed industrialization schemes. In the 1950s, Perón would convert the price control and marketing agencies created in the 1930s into instruments for extracting resources from the rural economy, controlling international trade to finance his two five-year economic plans, and funding his largesse to the army and organized labor. Justo and the old-line Conservatives and liberals inadvertently paved the way for Peronismo.

Officers associated with the Alvear faction of Radicalism plotted Justo's overthrow after Yrigoyen's death in 1933. Conservative nationalist officers, particularly from the Uriburu faction, opposed his liberalism and the "return to the past." Justo established an internal political espionage network for surveillance of army dissidents, quietly purged opponents, released political prisoners, and ended the state of siege. He wished to give Argentina the appearance of normality and return the army to the barracks—although he depended on loyal officers and the Logia to buttress his government.

Justo used electoral fraud and military control of the provinces in 1938 to secure a moderate civilian successor, Roberto Ortiz. Unwilling to be Justo's puppet, Ortiz supervised honest elections in Buenos Aires and the provinces and genuinely sought to restore democratic forms. His political efforts were hampered by illness. The press bashed him for scandals involving the Ministry of War's purchase of land near the Campo de Mayo for an inflated price (the Palomar land scandal). Competing military factions, some favoring the Allies and others the Axis powers in World War II, buffeted the president with requests for appointments and influence in key political and military posts. Under increasing pressure from the United States and Britain, Ortiz allowed the German military advisers' contracts to expire, an action that offended Germanophiles. These issues further deepened the personalist, generational, professional, and ideological divisions within the Argentine armed forces.

Ortiz's disability forced him to take leave; his vice president, Ramón Castillo, assumed the presidency. Castillo governed until 1943 (as acting president until 1942, and president after Ortiz resigned) amid political intrigue and military conspiracies. Essentially pro-Axis, but needing Justo's support, he adopted a policy of neutrality while returning to fraudulent elections to ensure internal support. From 1941 to 1943, Castillo cultivated nationalist, anti-Radical party, and antidemocratic officers to gain some independence from retired General Justo's tutelage. He appointed Colonel Manuel Savio, an outspoken antidemocratic nationalist, as the director of the newly created General Directorate of Military Factories, proclaimed a nationwide state of siege (shortly after the Japanese attack on Pearl Harbor), and canceled a public meeting in homage to President Franklin Roosevelt.[26] He then named a new commander of the Federal Capital Police, General Domingo Martínez, known for his nationalist, pro-German views.

These initiatives troubled the Justo faction and other army officers while encouraging the nationalist-fascist groups. The United States decided, after the 1942 Rio Conference and creation of the Inter-American Defense Board (see Chapter 5), to exclude Argentina from military assistance while providing Brazil and Uruguay with Lend-Lease equipment. When Brazil entered the war on the Allied side in 1942, the Argentine government explored the possibility of obtaining German and Italian war matériel ranging from submarines and aircraft to antiaircraft batteries. In the meantime, Justo was preparing the way for another presidential campaign and a reversal of Castillo's policies. Death in January 1943 prevented his bid to return to the presidency.

Castillo then announced his chosen successor: the sugar plantation magnate and Conservative politician, Senator Robustiano Patrón Costas. He had helped Castillo secure the vice presidency and orchestrated the legislative extension of the state of siege. President Castillo began an informal campaign of dinner invitations and requests for support for his candidate, but only the army could make Patrón Costas president through rigged elections. He held no appeal for the nationalists, was detested by the Justo and Radical sympathizers, and disdained by the professional officers. His candidacy was a nonstarter for the armed forces.

In March 1943 nationalist anti-Communist officers, ranking from captain to colonel, organized a secret military lodge. (Its acronym, GOU, has been variously interpreted as Gobierno, Orden, Unidad; Grupo de Oficiales Unidos; Grupo Obra de Unificación; or Grupo Orgánico Unificado.) The GOU claimed that its only interest was "the welfare of the Army and *la Patria*."[27] And it opposed Patrón Costas's election. The war minister, General Pedro Ramírez, was aware of the GOU's plotting but did nothing to deter it; indeed, later discussions concerning the possible alliance of the GOU and the Radical party to elect Ramírez took place in May 1943. Again, army factions and cliques within political parties plotted a coup.

Civilian politicians from all groups courted the military's support, encouraged its conspiracies, and unintentionally legitimated its tutelary role in Argentine politics. In great contrast to events in Chile during these years, where the civilian political system recovered its strength in part by refraining from calls for military tutelage and by respecting the career and promotion system, Argentine political leaders virtually invited military arbitration and intervention. The polarization and internal factionalism of Argentine civilian parties, the overtly fraudulent elections, and the lack of public respect for the congress, provincial legislatures, and public administration left to the military the "salvation" of *la patria*.

Events since the late 1920s, however, had also profoundly factionalized the military. It was not clear whether weak civilian institutions and political crises provoked military coups or whether iterated military coups, internal conflicts, and plotting kept civilian institutions from developing the strength, respectability, and coherence necessary to create a consensual political order. Whichever caused which, Argentina was stuck with both—a polarized, discredited political system and a factionalized politicized army. After 1930 the country experienced periodic coups, restoration of civilian government, and more coups: Uriburu's coup in 1930; succession by Justo, with fraudulent elections held in 1932 and 1938; coups in 1943 and 1944; Peronismo from 1946 to 1955; several failed coups from 1951 to 1955; and Perón's ouster in 1955.

Argentine politics was more cynical and tragic than any tango. Some military officers sincerely believed that their intervention could substitute efficiency for pathetic civilian bungling, probity for corruption, patriotism for opportunism. Yet with each intervention the armed forces became more political, more corrupt, more partisan, and less professional. And almost always, they intervened at the urging or plea of civilians, sometimes on their own, often in alliance, but never without significant civilian support. In this sense, after 1930, Argentina never experienced a strictly military coup, even when officer rhetoric condemned politicians and temporarily banned them from the halls of government. In the words of José Luis de Imaz, "resort to the armed forces as a source of legitimacy [became] a tacit rule of the political game in Argentina. This is an aspect of political life of which nobody expressly approves, but from which all the political groups have profited at least once. All will publicly deny this rule, but in private Argentine politicians cannot ignore that, at one time or another during this quarter century [1930s to 1960s], they have all knocked on the doors of the garrisons."[28]

When Castillo sought to remove General Ramírez as war minister, an improvised coup on June 4, 1943, ousted the lame-duck president. At first, Brigadier General Arturo Rawson, chief of cavalry, emerged as leader of the ideologically diverse group of officers that toppled President Castillo. The group had no common links except frustration with Castillo, dislike for Patrón Costas, and a desire to establish a military government to clean up the mess that they blamed on civilians. The Castillo government had "defrauded the hopes of Argentines by adopting as a system venality, fraud, peculation and corruption."[29] According to General Rawson, "When the Nation, as a result of bad rulers, is put into a situation where there are no constitutional solutions, [the military] has a duty to fulfill: to put the Nation in order."[30]

Except for Rawson and Ramírez, this coup had been organized by junior officers, lieutenant colonels, and colonels. Gradually, the GOU influence became more evident; among its members was Colonel Perón. After making several incredibly inadvisable decisions on key cabinet positions, Rawson, under pressure, resigned as president of the *junta* and was replaced by General Ramírez. The latter selected his cabinet in consultations with the GOU. General Edelmiro Farrell was named war minister and Colonel Perón, his subaltern, headed the War Ministry's secretariat; other GOU officers took command of troops in the capital and at the Campo de Mayo. Within the *junta*, however, the old ideological and personalist factions resurfaced, as did differences over Argentine sympathies toward the Allies and the Axis powers. Meanwhile, Perón attempted to reinvent the June 4 coup with the claim that the GOU had been its true inspiration and initiator.

Ramírez was unable to contain the GOU's influence or its insistence on maintaining neutrality in the war in Europe as "a symbol of national sovereignty." By October 1943 he had incorporated additional right-wing nationalists into the cabinet, and the government's pronouncements recalled those of Uriburu's interim dictatorship. On December 31, 1943, a decree dissolved all political parties and further curtailed civil liberties and rights. The government announced:

> The people wish tranquility and justice. The political aspect should be characterized by an eminently Argentine orientation. No politician—whatever his affiliation—shall be summoned to collaborate with the government. . . . The political parties are not important now. All inhabitants should be directed in the same manner, with the sole exception of those who seek to disturb the government's actions. These shall be treated like enemies of the fatherland. The Communists and Communist sympathizers are enemies of the fatherland and as such should be eradicated from the country.[31]

Military conspiracies continued within the Ramírez government, with various factions seeking advantage. Ramírez's surprise decision to break off relations with the Axis, apparently attempting to soften the impact of documents implicating him and others in schemes to purchase German arms, precipitated a new crisis. Under pressure from Farrell, Perón, and anti-*junta* professionals, Ramírez gave way to Farrell, who held on for two years and slowly increased Perón's responsibilities to include the Labor and War Ministries.

With the end of World War II and the Allies' victory, elections seemed prudent to confirm Argentina's place in the emerging inter-American system and the newly formed United Nations. (Close to war's end, Argentina finally declared war against Germany, hoping thereby to prevent its exclusion from the United Nations and the Organization of American States.) As interim war minister, Perón had positioned himself well to gain officer support, as he had earlier cultivated support among workers with his populist policies as minister of labor. He decreed reduced time in rank necessary for promotion and increased army size and opportunities in the higher ranks. A new nationalist and populist alliance was in the making, one that would dominate Argentina in varying forms from 1946 until 1955. Perón, the charismatic officer-politician, assured his officer brethren that "we soldiers should remain . . . impervious to the sinful insinuations of the politicians whether from one side or another."[32]

Before Perón could aspire to the presidency, liberal officers and supporters of the Allies had to be purged (April 1945). Perón's enemies retained enough influence to have him removed from the ministry and imprisoned, only to see massive popular protests and key army supporters gain his release and return him to the limelight. Once again, the army anti-Peronists faced purges (October 1945), and this time navy and air force garrisons were also affected. Perón next formed a new political party, the Partido Laborista, and prepared for presidential elections scheduled for February 1946. U.S. Ambassador Spruille Braden's denunciations of Perón as a fascist provided ammunition for electoral posters that queried: "¿Braden o Perón?" Argentine nationalists, workers, and patriotic army officers answered "¡Perón!" in honest elections supervised by the army. The Peronists also won two-thirds of the seats in the chamber of deputies and all but two seats in the senate.

Perón announced the creation of a "new Argentina," just as the Bolivian and Paraguayan military leaders proclaimed their *patrias nuevas* in the 1930s and 1940s. A new Argentina would mean a new constitution in 1949, a radically populist and developmentalist economic program, and an interventionist state. It also meant a charismatic and personalist authoritarian regime that first bribed, flattered, and glorified, then politicized, purged, and undermined the armed forces' professionalism. But according to Perón, the new Argentina would be an "organized community" in which the armed forces would serve as the "vertebral column sustaining the whole organism, forming part of the national unity, not an inert part, but like a live organ, integrated with all and integrated by the rest."[33]

Perón attempted to forge a revolutionary, and ultimately unmanageable, coalition between organized labor and the armed forces. With pragmatic manipulation he offered the armed forces salaries comparable to those in the United States, control over a growing sector of public enterprises and military industries, and prestige and opportunities for corruption that exceeded anyone's expectations. Military enterprises eventually gave great economic autonomy to selected officers and, more generally, to military institutions. To the workers he offered higher salaries, participation in government, and tantalizing demagoguery—in short, respect, economic welfare, and power but also "bread and circuses" (*pan y circos*). He attempted to balance these two props of his regime, using carrots and sticks, as long as the currency reserves accumulated from selling war supplies to the Allies held out and until inflation, recession, corruption, and the costs of populist economic policies finally forced restraints on public largesse.

From 1946 until 1950, Perón was largely successful, although he made many enemies within the army and other armed services. An unsuccessful coup attempt in 1951, followed by the predictable purges and Perón's effort to make all officers loyal to the Peronist (now called Justicialista) program, presaged the coming regime breakdown. Interservice rivalries, particularly the navy's dislike of Perón, and increasing dissension within the army tempted him to arm workers. During the next three years the national labor confederation (CGT) and Peronist leaders threatened to form workers' militias as economic conditions deteriorated. Most army officers opposed creation of such militias. To this worry, Perón added an ill-advised political campaign against the Catholic Church and support for a divorce law, measures that both alienated Catholic nationalist officers and moved the Church hierarchy into overt opposition.

Still, Perón retained the loyalty of many officers and noncoms. He also counted on the adulation of the poor, the *descamisados* (literally, the shirtless ones). But Perón's efforts to imbue training and curricula at the military academies with Justicialista doctrine (defined as a vague "third path" between materialistic Marxism and capitalism) and to personalize the armed forces' loyalty departed from the norms of the German-inspired lore of military professionalism. Such initiatives reminded officers of Latin American praetorian armies rather than their idealized view of Argentina's beloved professional institutions. Although it is difficult to capture the full complexity of the divisions within and among Argentina's armed forces and the parallel divisions in civil society in the early 1950s, Marvin Goldwert's succinct summary of the situation in 1951 indicates the severity of political polarization:

> the army officer-corps was once again divided roughly into three groups. About 40 percent of the corps was staunchly Peronist, bound to the regime by personal and professional gains. About 20 percent of the corps was skeptical of the regime if not opposed to it, and this group was growing. The failure of Perón to deliver a powerful, united industrial state had obviously taken its toll. The remaining 40 percent was passive, cautious, and neutral, seeking to avoid a civil war at all costs. The air force was deemed to be weakening also in its loyalty to the Perón regime, and the liberal nationalist navy had never really been in the camp at all.[34]

If the armed forces were Argentina's "vertebral column," then the national organism had a painful, multiply fractured backbone.

After the failed 1951 coup, Perón's torturers interrogated a civilian conspirator and uncovered a plot to assassinate the president that involved over one hundred officers (mostly retired or purged between 1945 and 1951) belonging to a secret lodge called the Logia Sol de Mayo. Radical party politicians were also implicated. Perón responded by expanding the secret police, gendarmerie, and federal and provincial police forces. He imposed political filters for key command positions and squirreled spies into army units.

Conspiracies, failed coups, and intensified social and political tensions resulted from 1952 to 1954. A final straw for nationalist officers was Perón's backsliding on the issue of foreign investment in Argentina's oil industry, a last-gasp attempt to buoy the regime with external support and desperately needed foreign capital. In June 1955 a failed coup by navy and air force units lacked the necessary army support. By September, army dissidents, including retired generals, joined with navy and air force units to overthrow Perón, but not without significant armed conflict, exchanges of artillery fire, and casualties among army units. In the end, an admiral threatened to bombard Buenos Aires after blockading the port city. Thus, the navy tipped the balance against Perón in the intra- and interservice conflict.

Some of the victorious rebels favored drastic repression of all Peronists, but there was hardly one high-ranking officer who had not colluded in some way in the Peronist experiment. Others wished to gradually erase Perón's influence in the army. Still others remained loyal to Perón, as did many noncommissioned officers and recruits. His supporters continued to dominate the labor movement and, until 1984, never lost a national election in which they were allowed to participate. Perón's ouster left the armed forces bloodied, divided, and responsible again for reconstituting *la patria*. Anti-Peronism excluded the Argentine majority from electing a president and legislators for most of the next thirty years. National "unity" that excluded the majority of voters was hardly a recipe for reconciliation or political pacification.

Perón, the professional soldier turned populist demagogue and reformer, had intensely politicized the armed forces and Argentine society. He attacked the old order and political parties, whether leftist or rightist; transformed and then destroyed the economy; mobilized a militant working-class movement; and hoped to rule with the armed forces and labor. Always pragmatic and ideologically vague, Perón, and his version of nationalist populism, left the armed forces irretrievably fragmented, ultimately spilling their own blood in fratricidal civil war.

With Perón's ouster in 1955, the Argentine armed forces joined willingly in the hemispheric battle against socialism and communism—on this enemy of *la patria*, army factions had agreed since before World War I. Until 1973 they repeatedly intervened in politics to prevent the return of Perón and to limit the influence of his followers. In this attempt, they were finally unsuccessful, but Perón's return in 1974 and his death shortly thereafter coincided with the armed forces' most horrifying intervention ever in national politics, followed by their devastating defeat in a war over the Malvinas Islands against Britain in 1982 (see Chapter 7).

Like APRA in Peru and the MNR in Bolivia, Peronismo had both enemies and supporters within the Argentine military. For most of the period after 1955, however, Peronismo became the military's bête noire, a populist threat to *la patria* against which the armed forces needed to maintain constant vigilance. Peronism had emerged from both the army and society; it left the armed forces as divided and conflictive as Argentina itself. Neither civilians nor military officers could agree on a political regime or policies for their country. Lack of political consensus, the weakness of political parties and the party system, and society's inability to absorb the demands of emerging social groups in the 1940s invited military intervention. Military modernizers, initially predominantly antiliberal nationalists, took charge of Argentina and jerry-built an unsustainable alliance: factions within the armed forces, workers and middle-class groups favoring state-directed industrialization, and industrialists.

Perón accepted the "invitation" to fill the political vacuum left by the political parties and civil society. He decreed a radical program to benefit workers and salaried employees: new pension laws, labor courts, the "statute of Perón," regulations concerning apprenticeship of minors and on domestic service workers, laws on paid vacations and a separate New Year's bonus, job protection regulations prohibiting arbitrary dismissals, rent freezes, and then the 1949 Constitution with its charter on the "Rights of Workers." He converted the Secretariat of Labor (basically a labor ministry) into an advocate for workers and an instrument for government control of organized labor. In 1948 real wages were almost 40 percent higher than in 1943.[35]

Perón's populism not only squandered the resources necessary to make economic modernization successful, but politicization of the armed forces and repression of the opposition also alienated many of his military comrades. His more favorable treatment of foreign investors and less nationalistic attitude toward Argentina's oil resources after 1952 lost him the support of nationalists. Conflict with the Catholic Church tipped the scales against him, both within civil society and among army traditionalists. The September 16, 1955, coup was led by General Eduardo Lonardi, whose "Liberator Revolution" closed the congress and sent Perón into exile. More liberal factions in the army ousted Lonardi in November, bringing General Pedro Aramburu to the presidency. Officers in the divided armed forces agreed on their political-guardian role, but not on the objectives of their political mission.

After 1955, in the midst of the Cold War, army factions and civilians alternated in power, making efforts to exclude or limit Peronist influence. But they never achieved a consensual vision of *la patria*, nor did they eradicate the Peronist movement. For the next forty years, Peronismo polarized Argentina, factionalized the armed forces, and framed national politics. Argentines still debated and fought over what they meant by *haciendo patria* and how best to defend its "eternal" values after Perón's death in 1974—and endured a vicious "dirty war" between "subversives" and military "saviors" from 1976 to 1983. Just as Peruvian civil-military relations could not be understood after the 1930s without reference to Aprismo, and Bolivian civil-miliary relations without reference to the Chaco War officer generation and the MNR, in Argentina the influence of Peronismo permeated the armed forces, their relations with civil society, and their role in politics.

Civil-Military Relations in Chile

Events in Chile from 1930 to the mid-1950s tell a very different story from those in Argentina. Chile shared with most Latin American countries the trauma of world depression; the stress of radical labor and political movements; the challenge of socioeconomic modernization, urbanization, and industrialization; the expanded role of the state and creation of public enterprises; and the beginnings of the Cold War. Yet despite several abortive coups and the rhetoric of small groups of nationalist, antidemocratic officers and civilians, no successful military coup occurred after 1932 until 1973. Chile was the only Latin American country with no irregular change in government during this period.

From the 1930s to the 1950s, military and civil-military cliques with fanciful patriotic acronyms (Grupo de Oficiales Seleccionados, or GOS, 1941–42; Acción Anticomunista Chilena, or ACHA, 1948; Por una Mañana Auspiciosa, or PUMA, 1951; Línea Recta, 1955) raised the specter of military politicization and even, in the latter case, a sort of Peronist-inspired loyalty oath to President

Carlos Ibáñez, who returned as elected president in 1952. In all these cases, however, most officers rejected repoliticization and stayed loyal to constitutional norms, partly to protect their careers and institutions, partly because their military institutions had inculcated as official doctrine a constitutionalist, nondeliberative role for the armed forces, and partly due to the strengthening of civilian political institutions, especially the party system and the congress. Reciprocally, the political parties, economic interest groups, and the civilian coalition governments generally refrained from involvement in internal military affairs. Both civilian restraint and formal military participation in many government programs and public enterprises deterred ruptures in civil-military relations and enhanced military professionalism.

The story of the Chilean armed forces is illuminating. It offers considerable insight into the importance of civilian political institutions, movements, and parties in defining the armed forces' political role, and to the risks of episodes of unconstrained political mobilization, as occurred in Argentina, Peru, Bolivia, and Guatemala in the 1930–1955 period. It also exemplifies the importance of dedicated, professional military leadership in keeping the armed forces out of partisan politics.

The apparent political reclusion of Chilean officers from 1932 into the 1960s, notwithstanding the episodic coup plots and grumbling, owed much initially to the leadership of General Oscar Novoa Fuentes, President Arturo Alessandri's army commander from 1933 to 1938. Novoa accepted his command on the condition that the army's internal autonomy would be respected; that assignment, promotion, and retirement decisions would be made according to professional norms; and that he would have unrestricted authority to deal with plotters of whatever ideological persuasion. Alessandri agreed. Novoa used the armed forces against striking workers, Communists, and political protests at government request. He also used troops to keep the railroads running in 1936 when strikes threatened to interrupt service, and again in internal political intelligence missions. But Novoa also operationalized the developmental and subsidiary missions of the army by deploying them in public works and in response to natural disasters. He attempted to avoid partisan commitments and deftly retired or reassigned would-be military conspirators. Military role expansion occurred gradually and was accepted appreciatively by the government and the citizenry. Meanwhile, civilians essentially stayed out of military affairs. Novoa's successor ably responded to the catastrophic 1939 earthquake, making Chileans grateful for the military's efficiency and compassion.

Novoa informed officers of his intentions via circulars and enforced the reestablished professional norms, thus making possible, but not inevitable, the restoration of civilian political leadership and military obedience.[36] He accomplished this goal despite army resentment over the existence of—indeed, government support for—a "republican militia" from 1932 to 1936. The militia opposed military participation in politics and superficially emulated the Portalian militia of the nineteenth century in guaranteeing the constitutional order. Led by representatives of the traditional political parties (Conservatives, Liberals, and Radicals), rural landowners, industrialists, and retired military officers, and encouraged by the right-wing press, the militia had its own schools and barracks nationwide.

Novoa skillfully managed potential conflicts between the army and the militia until 1936. By then, the militia was losing civilian support, and civilian government had been solidly reestablished. With the Radical party's move toward the left and the creation of a popular front in 1936, the militia also suffered internal divisions and defections. Before dissolving in 1936, however, it had outnumbered, if not outgunned, the army.[37] In common with the armed forces, the militia was militantly anti-Communist. Its best-known members later joined nationalist cliques that threatened the liberal constitutional order, but in the 1932–1936 interlude it played a significant role in consolidating civilian government and precluding new military interventions.

The other side of the coin of Novoa's leadership was civilian reconstitution of the political system, limits placed on populist initiatives, and Chile's firm anti-Communist internal policies, which discouraged military political interventions. From 1931, when the Communists were blamed for a naval mutiny that was overcome with air force bombs and civil-military mobilization, civilian governments, even the Popular Front (1938–1941), limited rural and urban political mobilization with laws, administrative decrees, police, and, occasionally, the armed forces. Anticommunism was reinforced after 1946 with the armed forces' participation in the Rio Pact (1947), and the benefits of arms transfers and military educational opportunities in the United States.

Anticommunism was combined with a political system that prevented radical political reform. Chile's election system, until 1958, guaranteed landowners (thus the Conservative and Liberal parties, and some Radical party candidates in the southern provinces) control over rural votes. This setup gave veto power over fundamental political and constitutional change (requiring two-thirds votes in the senate) to powerful economic elites and political minorities. Unlike in Argentina, where Conservatives essentially lost control of political initiative in the 1940s to the military, and then to Peronism, Chile avoided an extensive state-directed, top-down policy revolution until after the 1958 electoral reform that unlocked the rural vote and deprived the political right of veto power in the congress. Also unlike Argentina, Chile's party politicians generally refrained from knocking on the doors of the barracks to resolve political disputes and from politicizing military promotions and duty assignments.

In a sense, political immobilism, albeit with substantial revolutionary and counterrevolutionary rhetoric, left the armed forces willingly on the sidelines except when governments requested assistance in maintaining stability and enforcing the law. The national police (*carabineros*) dealt with most problems of public order. The armed forces controlled elections, according to the 1941 election law, and were proud of their consistency in maintaining electoral decorum. Since Chile incorporated women and illiterate voters later than Argentina, and presidential manipulation of elections was greatly reduced, all factions and parties could be represented in the congress (with the exception of the Communists' exclusion from 1948 to 1958) and in presidential coalitions, in contrast to the one-party or *junta* governments that prevailed in Bolivia, Paraguay, Argentina, El Salvador, and Guatemala.

The precise mechanisms for creating this unique Chilean political "arrangement" have been detailed elsewhere.[38] Most important, however, the multiparty presidential system successfully constrained full-on political mobilization through political rather than military means, except on rare occasions, and supported a truly professional officer career system that was generally unmarred by political purges, party proselytizing, and military deprofessionalization. The Chilean armed forces were often neglected, underfunded, even deprecated, but their institutions and professional careers progressively gained more autonomy and insulation from civilian political meddling. In 1956, for example, the army promotions board (*junta de calificaciones*) and courts-martial weeded out overly "politicized" officers.[39]

From 1936 to 1958 military institutions were increasingly assigned formal government responsibilities and participation. These roles ranged from virtual commercial independence authorized in 1936 for military industrial production in the Fábricas y Maestranzas del Ejército (FAMAE, created in 1924) to official participation in the National Economic Council, the National Telecommunications Council, the National Meteorological Council (1946), the Civil Aeronautics Board, and the Merchant Marine School (1948). As the public sector expanded, the armed forces were unobtrusively invited to assist in internal development, a seemingly logical and innocuous recognition of their role in national development.[40] Modified national security laws also expanded the armed forces' functions in maintaining internal order and their jurisdiction over civilians.[41]

Presidential succession and government changes in Chile after 1932 meant retirements and high-level policy appointments that affected some officers, but rarely any threat of widespread intrusion into the armed forces' internal affairs. Both civilians and officers had learned the lessons of the 1920s and early 1930s. This "political learning" contributed immensely to the armed forces' willingness to remain in the background, in contrast to officers elsewhere in Latin America. Underlying the arrangement was military and civilian consensus on the desirability of constitutional government as well as a commitment to constrain political mobilization and, when necessary, to repress the Communist party and its labor, student, and community adjuncts. These elements of Chilean political culture developed slowly, and not without contradictions. Nevertheless, taken together, they restrained overt military intrusion into most spheres of policymaking, except where invited by civilian leaders. In exchange they increased insulation of the military career system from political meddling.

Anticommunism was a key element in Chilean civil-military relations. In 1941, Brigadier General Jorge Berguño Meneses, at the request of President Aguirre Cerda, oversaw an extensive investigation into labor conditions in the coal mines. This report, disseminated in the national press and debated in the congress, found that the Communists were "acting against patriotic values and against their principal guarantors, the armed forces. . . . one of the most important aspects of international Marxism is the destruction of national values in those countries it wishes to conquer, for which it is necessary to undermine the foundations of the armed forces that sustain them."[42] In response, the army recommended strengthening internal security legislation and undertook a "campaign of *chilenidad*," which was adopted also by the navy and air force. This campaign was directed at all the citizenry, not just the armed forces, and reached the schools, mass media, and even popular *fiestas* attended by military bands.

Figure 4–1. General Jorge Berguño Meneses, who investigated Communist activities in the Coal Zone, 1941. From Estado Mayor General del Ejército, *Historia del Ejército de Chile*, vol. 9 (Santiago: Ejército de Chile, 1985), 55. Courtesy of the Chilean Army

In the same year, the new election law assigned supervision of elections to the armed forces. Implemented in the municipal and congressional elections in 1941 and in the 1942 presidential elections, the law made the military *jefes de plaza* directly responsible for preventing electoral fraud and violence. No more emblematic symbol of the armed forces' identification with the constitutional system could have been imagined than their presence at every polling place.

Presidential elections in 1946 featured an unlikely coalition headed by the Radical party's Gabriel González Videla. The Radicals had dominated presidential coalitions since 1938, and González Videla's coalition included the Communist party (represented in the congress since the 1920s) and the right-wing Liberals. Like many Chilean electoral coalitions since the nineteenth century, it was not sustainable as a governing coalition. Communist party influence in the new government greatly concerned military authorities, landowners, and industrialists. It also worried competing socialist labor movements and factions of the Socialist and Radical parties.

When the Communists mobilized workers and peasants between 1946 and 1948 in a wave of strikes in the countryside, the factories, and the coal mines, the congress granted the government *facultades extraordinarias* to take repressive measures (Law 8837, 1947). González Videla's anti-Communist initiatives had broad support, including the major faction within the Socialist party, competitor with the Communists for control of the labor movement. It was also assisted by U.S. financing of non-Communist labor organizations, and the United States sent emergency coal shipments and guarantees of further support if necessary. With this reinforcement, the government sent police and troops to the mines, the factories, and the countryside to demobilize union organization and strikes; outlawed the Communists; decreed the Law for the Permanent Defense of Democracy (1948); and opened detention centers (labeled concentration camps in Chile). Military officers assigned to these camps learned some of their updated anticommunism in the United States (beginning in 1946, in Fort Leavenworth, Fort Knox, Fort Sill, Fort Benning, and Fort Belvoir) and also firsthand. The General Staff instituted internal security measures to monitor Communist activities and efforts to proselytize among military personnel; the armed forces broke strikes in the coal mines and arrested Communists throughout the country.

According to the General Staff's official army history, written during the 1973–1989 military regime, "The army reacted energetically against these subversive threats, behind which was the hand of international communism, that threatened our national essence (*chilenidad*)."[43] Remembering his part in the repression of the Communists and his duty at the Pisagua detention center, then-captain Augusto Pinochet Ugarte recounts:

> My infantry unit was ordered to go to the Humberstone nitrate works and arrest a number of communists who were well known to us, a list of them having been prepared by the Investigations Department. I remembered how on several occasions many of these people had shown their arrogance [toward] the army. The operation was completed quickly and the people arrested very soon filled the military trucks. . . . Then we began the transfer of prisoners to Pisagua. . . . In January 1948, I was designated Chief of Military Forces in Pisagua. . . . The mission was an unwelcome one, for I had been accepted at the War College and was about to return to Santiago to join my wife, who was expecting our third child. . . . Several times I caught the communist leaders teaching veritable Chairs of Marxism, but they denied it, claiming that they were teaching their comrades to write to their relatives. . . . The Pisagua camp was turning into a true Marxist-Leninist university. . . .
>
> Another event that I find among my notes, which I remember for the implications it might have had in the future, was the arrival of a group of congressmen on a visit to the *relegados* [exiles], among whom I was told was the socialist senator Salvador Allende. . . . I told them that there was no permit from the Iquique authority to pass. As they insisted that they would pass, permit or no permit, I had them advised that if they did they would be fired on, on the road.[44]

Pinochet, like his military comrades, learned anticommunism as part of patriotism. To defend *la patria* meant to monitor and, when necessary, repress radical and Marxist subversion. It also meant, however, in the tradition of General Novoa and those who followed, compliance with orders from civilian authorities and a constitutionalist armed forces—as long as civilians respected military professional autonomy and maintained political stability.

To a great extent, the limited intervention of the Chilean armed forces in politics from the mid-1930s until the late 1960s resulted from the civilian construction of an exclusionary, nonmobilizational formal democracy that impeded radical reforms. Chilean "democracy" had special characteristics that made political competition among diverse ideological groups rhetorically incendiary but institutionally conservative. This political concoction made military careers more secure and politics less cataclysmic than in Peru, Bolivia, Paraguay, and Argentina. It made General Novoa's constitutionalist vision functional for career officers. When these conditions later disappeared with electoral reforms in 1958, political polarization in the 1960s, and the election of Salvador Allende in 1970 (with the promise of a "Chilean road to socialism"), the armed forces were called back to political duty by the civilian opposition to the Unidad Popular coalition in defense of the constitutional order that President Allende allegedly violated from 1970 to 1973. As in 1924, September would bring regime change via military *pronunciamiento* in 1973.

Civil-Military Relations in El Salvador

In 1930, El Salvador was still predominantly agrarian, dependent on coffee exports, and without any significant industry. Unlike Chile and Argentina, it had a very small middle class, important ethnic and cultural differences between the elite and the masses, and virtually no history of meaningful electoral politics and reformist experiments before the late 1920s. A modern political party system barely existed in a society ruled by a family-based landed oligarchy, the coffee barons, and their clients.

Chilean officers brought Prussian military ideology and methods to El Salvador's army in the first decade of the twentieth century. Spanish military missions also exerted some influence, as they had in Guatemala. But in El Salvador, like Guatemala, military professionalization at best was limited to a select group of academy-educated officers. The country had a small garrison-deployed army, an overabundance of senior officers promoted during the brief 1906–07 war against Guatemala, no reserve corps, and no regularized promotion system until 1913. And "it was not uncommon as late as 1920 to find regimental commanders sufficiently influential to dictate selection of their staffs or to move their officer corps with them when they were transferred to another regiment."[45] Provincial commanders ran rural fiefdoms more like nineteenth-century *caudillos* than post-World War I professional officers. In this respect, Salvadoran officers exercised authority much like that of their Guatemalan counterparts under General Jorge Ubico.

As in Brazil, Chile, and Argentina, the 1920s brought generational conflicts between senior and junior officers to El Salvador. A cadet insurrection in 1922 resulted in the closing of the Escuela Politécnica. In 1927 a new Escuela Militar was established and reforms introduced in army regulations and the career system, and by 1930 the first lieutenants had graduated under the new regime. These institutional changes coincided with President Pío Romero Bosque's liberalization of politics. After 1927 he lifted the state of siege (in place the past four years) and allowed more freedom of the press. The president also instituted labor legislation and regulations for mediating labor conflicts. Calls for agrarian reform and an end to semi-feudal labor conditions for peasants concerned estate owners. In short, El Salvador was experiencing a late, miniature version of the pressures for reform shared in much of Latin America in the 1920s.

A failed coup in 1927 indicated opposition to these reformist measures, particularly the army reforms, by senior officers who allied with the civilian oligarchy. The officers also objected to the president's son's appointment as minister of war. Divisions within the army as well as junior officer support for reform derailed the coup; the ringleaders were executed (some condemned to death in absentia) after trial by a *consejo de guerra*. The president finished his term without further significant military conspiracies, but increasing political mobilization and the upcoming elections greatly concerned the nation's political elite and military leadership.

Salvadoran politics were highly personalistic, family-based, and oligarchic. Unlike in Chile, Colombia, or even Argentina, no effective political party and electoral systems emerged in the nineteenth century. Parties had little mass constituency or stable organization. Not until 1931 did the first "clean" elections take place, and even then no modern national political parties competed. The elected president, Arturo Araujo, came to office on a reformist program, promising land reform, support for labor legislation, elimination of taxes, and other populist measures. His proposals were doomed by the Great Depression and the dramatic fall in the price of coffee, the country's main source of foreign exchange. Convinced of the need to reduce military expenditures and army personnel, the president made one blunder after another, from failing to pay military salaries to ordering officers to withdraw from medical and engineering programs in the national university. Officers went without pay for months. Worse still, from the army and landowners' perspective, Araujo neglected the spread of Communist propaganda and organization in the countryside and towns, although he finally decreed suspension of civil liberties and rights (*garantías*) in July 1931.

The depression, labor agitation, army discontent, landowners' fears, and hysterical media attention to the Communist threat resulted in the obvious. On December 2, 1931, the army deposed Araujo and replaced him with the vice president, General Maximiliano Hernández Martínez. This unscheduled government succession strained relations with the United States, which refused to recognize the new regime, citing the 1923 Treaty of Washington that prohibited recognition of Central American governments coming to power through coups. Hernández Martínez persisted and eventually obtained U.S. recognition (1934), in part by demonstrating his terrifying anti-Communist credentials and in part because the Roosevelt administration had realistically accommodated its policy to his staying power. Recognition by Costa Rica in 1934 smoothed the way for the United States to follow without losing face regarding the 1923 Treaty.

From 1931 to 1932 propaganda by El Salvador's nascent Communist party included calls for soldiers to disobey their officers and "kill the chiefs and officers. Place yourselves under the orders of the Comrade Soldiers who have been named Red Comrades by this Central Committee."[46] Barracks revolts followed, as did a popular uprising that the government met with fierce repression. Declaring a state of siege, the Hernández Martínez government executed the Communist leaders, including Agustín Farabundo Martí (for whom the 1970s revolutionary movement in El Salvador would be named) and brutally murdered thousands of Indians and peasants, shoveling their corpses into mass graves across the country. This massacre, called La Matanza, is the political and psychological benchmark for modern Salvadoran history, the symbol of the army and oligarchy's violent anticommunism, racism, and determination to maintain their privileges.

The 1932 massacre was provoked by images of "Indian" hordes attacking "white" towns and shops, of a vicious race war and Communist coup thwarted only by the army's effectiveness in carrying out its sacred duty. These images have survived for decades, although the insurrectionists killed and injured few civilians, police, and army personnel. In contrast, the dictator's vengeance left no doubt about the victors in this "war":

> Around Izalco a roundup of suspects began. As most of the rebels, except the leaders, were difficult to identify, arbitrary classifications were set up. All those found carrying machetes were guilty. All those of a strongly Indian cast of features, or who dressed in a scruffy, *campesino* costume, were considered guilty. To facilitate the roundup, all those who had *not* taken part in the uprising were invited to present themselves at the *comandancia* to receive clearance papers. When they arrived they were examined and those with the above-mentioned characteristics seized. Tied by the thumbs to those before and behind them, in the customary Salvadoran manner, groups of fifty were led to the back wall of the church of Asunción in Izalco and against that massive wall were cut down by firing squads. In the plaza in front of the *comandancia*, other selected victims were made to dig a mass grave and were then shot. . . .
>
> The roadways were littered with bodies in many areas, the drainage ditches along the side serving as expeditious burial places. In some cases burial was too shallow or nonexistent and the "pigs and buzzards ate for a while.". . . How many died at any particular place is difficult to say.[47]

The government also applied martial law in the towns and cities, summarily executed Communist voters and sympathizers, and killed others as personal vendettas masqueraded as anti-Communist pogroms.

The total number of dead has been estimated at 10,000 to 30,000. As with all such atrocities, no accurate accounting is possible. La Matanza began the reign of Hernández Martínez, which lasted until 1944. Importing German and Italian military instructors and equipment, overtly sympathetic to the Axis cause, and outlawing favorable mention of the Allies in the press (until it was obvious that the tide of war had turned and the United States had come to account for over 90 percent of Salvadoran trade), his political party, Pro-Patria, provided a civilian facade and supplementary militia for a personalist military regime.

Hernández Martínez periodically dressed his dictatorship in the garb of elections and constitutional reforms. In August 1934 he transferred the presidency to his minister of war, General Andrés Ignacio Menéndez, while he campaigned for reelection. (Menéndez appointed candidate Hernández Martínez as Minister of War in the interim.) A stacked convention adopted a new constitution in 1938 and named the general to serve the first term under the new charter. Implemented in 1939, the constitution eliminated municipal and university autonomy. It also precipitated ministerial resignations and the first hint of serious dissidence in the army. Undersecretary of War Colonel José Ascencio Menéndez resigned and went into exile.

Such "succession constitutions" and legislative window dressing for dictatorship were common devices in nineteenth-century Latin America. Hernández Martínez had ample precedent for this sort of legalistic chicanery, if not for his esoteric theosophy that gained him the nickname "El Brujo" (The Warlock). Like Leguía in Peru and Ibáñez in Chile, he built new police forces to counterbalance the army; and like his Latin American counterparts and his European fascist idols, he created a militia from the Pro-Patria party in 1941. In the early 1940s he sought to create a one-party (his party) state: Pro-Patria.

Despite his eccentricities, Hernández Martínez governed with recognizable authoritarian methods. His army remained essentially loyal, patrimonial, personalistic, and only partially professional. But like its Argentine, Bolivian, Peruvian, and Paraguayan counterparts, factionalization undermined its mythical hierarchical unity. Its main tasks were to maintain internal order, ensure labor discipline and the sanctity of private property, and fight communism. Hernández Martínez used the grisly memory of the 1932 uprising to control the country, attempting few populist or reformist initiatives until near the end of the dictatorship. He did, however, preside over a moderate expansion of the Salvadoran government bureaucracy and the creation of public agencies to confront the depression: the Central Reserve Bank, the Mortgage Bank (Banco Hipotecario), the National Coffee Company, the Cotton Cooperative, and rural credit institutions. In the words of a well-known Salvadoran military author, "Maximiliano Hernández Martínez, along with Jorge Ubico [Guatemala], Anastasio Somoza [Nicaragua], Tiburcio Carías Andino [Honduras], governed Central America; Hitler, Mussolini, and Franco provided these pocket dictators with the international examples."[48]

In 1944 the general adopted another constitution in a self-coup to perpetuate his rule. Army dissidents now joined civilians in opposition. Led by officers from the first graduating classes of the Escuela Militar (founded in 1927), allied with civilian professional, business, and labor organizations, a failed coup attempt in April resulted in trials by *consejos de guerra* for civilians and officers. Executions of ringleaders followed. Ironically, a group of the army's new professionals could now claim a central role in fighting the dictatorship. The "new military" was anti-Hernández Martínez. Like the Bolivian "military socialists," the Brazilian *tenentes*, the Chilean 1924 saber-rattlers, and the Guatemalan colonels who overthrew General Ubico in 1944, they offered the blood of their martyrs in the struggle for modernization, development, and "democracy."

Student protests and a strike (*huelga de brazos caidos*) in 1944 brought the country to a standstill; Hernández Martínez responded with a populist tirade promising, without any credibility, profound social reforms. He even brought hundreds of peasants armed with machetes to the capital, and quartered them in military barracks to frighten oligarchs and urban middle-class opponents.[49] Opposition leaders vowed that no one would work until the dictator stepped down, despite maintenance of the state of siege. When the American son of a rich landowner was killed by police, his funeral served as a massive demonstration against the president; the U.S. ambassador advised him that the party was over. Hernández Martínez turned the government over to Andrés Ignacio Menéndez, his reliable stand-in as provisional president, and retired to an agricultural estate in Honduras. Soon thereafter, a ranch foreman hacked him to death with a machete.[50]

General Menéndez, provisional president from May to October 1944, received extraordinary powers from the constitutional assembly and scheduled congressional and presidential elections (in January and July, respectively). During a brief "liberalized" interlude the 1886 liberal constitution was reinstated. The leading civilian candidate, Arturo Romero, campaigned on a vague populist platform recalling that of Araujo; the landowners and old-line generals remembered 1932. Labor and pro-Romero publications offended the army, raising the specter of so-called Communist threats to *la patria* and military institutions. The rhetoric of the electoral campaign frightened landowners and provoked the ire of officers. An attack on army barracks by an unruly crowd in October precipitated army action. The brief "political opening" ended with a coup by Colonel Osmín Aguirre y Salinas, leader of the 1931 coup and the 1932 repression. The interim president willingly resigned at the request of the officer corps' "military legislature" (an assembly of officers); and Hernández Martínez's congress, still functioning as a rubber stamp, "legalized" the coup by naming Aguirre y Salinas interim president.

Romero went to Costa Rica; Aguirre y Salinas became provisional president (October 1944–February 1945), and General Salvador Castaneda Castro won the presidential election. In July the army published a manifesto asking the Salvadoran people "to have full confidence in the Army, which is the safeguard of republican institutions and support for constitutional guarantees, guided by no other desire than the authentic greatness of our *Patria*."[51] Romero then led an 800-man invasion from Guatemala to bring democracy to El Salvador. Army troops turned the invaders back. General Castaneda governed the country under a state of siege for the next four years. He enjoyed the presidency and sought to play the *continuismo* game in 1948. Reformist officers, now intent on military and political modernization, ousted Castaneda for his "unconstitutional behavior," and Major, then Lieutenant Colonel, Oscar Osorio emerged as their new paladin. He was made interim president of the *junta* and then "elected" president (1948–49; 1950–1956). Osorio promulgated a new constitution in 1950 that brought El Salvador current with labor legislation, promises of agrarian reform, and social concerns. He also invented a new political party, the Partido Revolucionario de Unificación Democrático (PRUD), modeled on Mexico's Institutional Revolutionary Party (PRI), with the innovation that the army would control the governing party.

Osorio introduced military-supported modernization and industrialization in a vague nationalist and developmentalist program. The landowners' terror of "communism" (meaning any mention of land reform and peasant organization) and the U.S. fear of international communism's advances in neighboring Guatemala (1944–1954) elicited ambiguous internal and external support for Osorio's military reformism. Populism and repression, reform and maintenance of the rural social system, and nationalism and collaboration with the United States alternately and simultaneously characterized military rule in El Salvador from 1950 to 1957.

In 1957, Osorio delivered the presidency to his chosen successor, Lieutenant Colonel José María Lemus, the minister of interior, thereby continuing military rule in Central America's smallest nation. Salvadoran military populism and calls for modernization had a familiar ring: "The army exists . . . not to enthrone tyrannies . . . [but] to observe the sacred institutional postulates of fulfilling the law and of being the guardian of the national sovereignty. . . . The army is the main bulwark in the defense of the popular rights which were so valiantly fought for in the 1948 revolution. . . . There is now an ideological [that is, democratic] identification between the army and the people."[52]

In the 1950 elections the people chose between two colonels; in 1956 four of five candidates were colonels.[53] There was no civilian president in El

Salvador from 1931 to 1962. The weakness of civilian parties, the lack of effective legislative and judicial institutions, and the particular legacy of La Matanza in 1932 made the military the most important political institution in the country into the 1970s.

A New Era

Shortly after the 1944 coup that ousted General Hernández Martínez, Guatemala's General Jorge Ubico was also removed from power by popular demonstrations and military insubordination. In many ways, the end of Ubico's regime resembled the demise of El Salvador's El Brujo. In contrast to the Salvadoran military's restoration of order and control over civilian reformers and revolutionaries, events in Guatemala ushered in a new era for Latin America, the United States, and the Latin American armed forces. But the region's armed forces would continue to be plagued by incomplete professionalization and factionalism. Conflicts between the image of the idealized warrior-priest (*sacerdocio de la patria*) heralded by militarylore and the realities of institutional and political strife in their nations frustrated military officers.

To this contrast would be added, after 1945, the impact of their inclusion as subordinate allies of the United States in the Cold War and the subsequent post-1959 battle against the influence of the Cuban Revolution. The visceral anticommunism of the past would blend with U.S. Cold War anticommunism to create an inter-American security system that included more sophisticated, systematically repressive, and regionally "coordinated" Latin American armed forces. This era began with the creation of the Inter-American Defense Board (1942), the signing of the Rio Treaty (1947), the founding of the Organization of American States (1948), and the beginning of the Cold War in Latin America. It brought new challenges, opportunities, and disappointments to the region's armed forces and new wrinkles in civil-military relations.

Notes

1. See Jack Child, "Geopolitical Thinking in Latin America," *Latin American Research Review* (Summer 1979): 89–111; and idem, *Geopolitics and Conflict in South America: Quarrels among Neighbors* (Stanford, CA: Hoover Institution/Praeger Publishers, 1985), esp. Chapter 2.

2. See Thomas P. Anderson, *Matanza: El Salvador's Communist Revolt of 1932* (Lincoln: University of Nebraska Press, 1971).

3. On this conflict see David H. Zook, Jr., *Zarumilla-Marañón: The Ecuador-Peru Dispute* (New York: Bookman Associates, 1964).

4. See Leslie Bethell and Ian Roxborough, eds., *Latin America between the Second World War and the Cold War, 1944–1948* (Cambridge, Eng.: Cambridge University Press, 1992).

5. The work of Robert Potash on Argentina (see Bibliography) is exemplary in this regard. He has carefully investigated and written the history of Argentine civil-military relations in a fashion not emulated by research on other Latin American countries.

6. For the best detailed history of Bolivia during this period see Herbert S. Klein, *Bolivia: The Evolution of a Multi-Ethnic Society* (New York: Oxford University Press, 1982). Klein's *Parties and Political Change in Bolivia, 1880–1952* (London: Cambridge University Press, 1969) is also superb. I have relied on Klein for the basic "story," footnoting only key data or direct citations.

7. Víctor Andrade, *My Missions for Revolutionary Bolivia, 1944–1962* (Pittsburgh: University of Pittsburgh Press, 1976): 5.

8. Klein (1982): 188.

9. Ibid.: 190.

10. Here, parallels exist with the Venezuelan coup in 1945, with Acción Democrática joining reformist officers to initiate agrarian reforms and incorporate organized labor into the political system from 1945 to 1948.

11. Klein (1982): 219.

12. "Justification of the Revolution of November, Speech by General Alfredo Ovando Candía, 1966," in Loveman and Davies, eds. (1989): 212–16.

13. Vittone (1969): 189.

14. Gustavo Gatti Cardozo, *El papel político de los militares en el Paraguay* (Asunción: Universidad Católica, Biblioteca de Estudios Paraguayos, 1990): 21.

15. Cited in ibid.: 22.

16. Austin F. MacDonald, *Latin American Politics and Government*, 2d ed. (New York: Thomas Y. Crowell, 1954): 517.

17. Cited in Gatti Cardozo (1990): 45.

18. Rock (1985): 166.

19. See Robert A. Potash, *The Army and Politics in Argentina, 1928–1945* (Stanford, CA: Stanford University Press, 1969). I have relied extensively on Potash's work, citing in notes only direct citations and paraphrasings.

20. José Luis de Imaz, *Los que Mandan* (Those Who Rule), trans. Carlos A. Astiz (Albany: State University of New York Press, 1970): 70.

21. Marvin Goldwert, *Democracy, Militarism, and Nationalism in Argentina, 1930–1966* (Austin: University of Texas Press, 1972): 15.

22. Potash (1969): 50–51.

23. Ibid.: Chapter 3 passim.

24. Goldwert (1972): 39–41.

25. Ibid.: 39–41.

26. Potash (1969): 165.

27. Ibid.: 186.

28. Imaz (1970): 88.

29. Cited in Potash (1969): 197.

30. *Ejército y Armada* 3(30) (June 1943): 46. Cited in Potash (1969): 202.

31. Confidential instructions from General Luís Perlinger, Minister of Interior, to provincial administrators, cited in Potash (1969): 226.

32. Cited in Potash (1969): 246.

33. Speech by Juan Domingo Perón, July 5, 1950, in *La Prensa*, July 6, 1950: 5–6. Cited in Goldwert (1972): 101.

34. Goldwert (1972): 111–12, citing Russell H. Fitzgibbon, "Argentina after Eva Perón," *Yale Review* 43 (Autumn 1952): 35–36.

35. Donald Hodges, *Argentina, 1943–1976: The National Revolution and Resistance* (Albuquerque: University of New Mexico Press, 1976): 16–19.

36. Frederick M. Nunn, *The Military in Chilean History: Essays on Civil-Military Relations, 1810–1973* (Albuquerque: University of New Mexico Press, 1976): 226–30.

37. For the organization and role of the republican militia see Carlos Maldonado Prieto, *La milicia republicana, Historia de un ejército civil en Chile, 1932–1936* (Santiago: World University Services, 1988).

38. See Loveman (1988): Chapter 8; Brian Loveman, *Struggle in the Countryside: Politics and Rural Labor in Chile, 1919–1973* (Bloomington: Indiana University Press, 1976).

39. Joxe (1970): 82.

40. For details and descriptions of the various laws that regulated this process see Hugo Frühling, Carlos Portales, and Augusto Varas, eds., *Estado y fuerzas armadas* (Santiago: Taller El Gráfico, 1982).

41. See Loveman (1993): Chapter 8.

42. "Informe Berguño," cited in *Historia del Ejército de Chile*, multiple volumes (Santiago: Estado Mayor del Ejército), 9 (1985): 44–45.

43. Ibid.: 50.

44. Augusto Pinochet Ugarte, *The Crucial Day* (Santiago: Editorial Renacimiento, 1982): 23–27.

45. Robert V. Elam, "The Military and Politics in El Salvador, 1927–45," in Brian Loveman and Thomas M. Davies, Jr., eds., *The Politics of Antipolitics: The Military in Latin America*, 2d ed. (Lincoln: University of Nebraska Press, 1989): 136.

46. Cited in Elam (1989): 142.

47. Anderson (1971): 131–32.

48. Castro Morán (1984): 162.

49. Elam (1989): 148.

50. James Dunkerley, *The Long War: Dictatorship and Revolution in El Salvador* (London: Junction Books, 1982): 34.

51. Romeo Fortín Magaña, "Inquietudes de un año memorable" (1944), cited in Castro Morán (1984): 184.

52. Lt. Col. José María Lemus, *Pueblo, ejército y doctrina revolucionaria* (San Salvador: Imprenta Nacional, 1952): 3–13, cited in Edwin Lieuwen, *Arms and Politics in Latin America*, rev. ed. (New York: Praeger, 1961): 95.

53. Edwin Lieuwen, *Arms and Politics in Latin America* (New York: Frederick A. Praeger, 1960): 95.

5

La Patria and the Cold War

From Pearl Harbor to the Bay of Pigs

> The Armed Forces of the Republic have decided to take charge of the government. The Armed Forces have acted thus because they are loyal to the supreme trust which historically has been bequeathed to them by the Liberator, Simón Bolívar, and by *la patria* itself. . . . All of this is in harmony with the teachings of Christ Our Lord, and of the Liberator Simón Bolívar.
>
> —General Gustavo Rojas Pinilla, Colombia, 1953[1]

World War II cut most Latin American trade, arms, and military ties with the Axis powers and established the United States definitively as the regional hegemon. For South American armed forces instilled with European traditions and doctrine, the sudden and widespread presence of U.S. military missions was both novel and alarming. Such was particularly the case for the militaries with long-standing ties to Germany, Spain, and Italy, but even for those with a historical connection to France and Britain (in the case of some navies), the switch to U.S. tutelage presented problems. In Central America and the Caribbean, the return and increased visibility of U.S. armed forces, ostensibly to defend sea-lanes and the Panama Canal, recalled the interventionist era before 1933.

Despite the frictions, by war's end the U.S. military virtually replaced European influence in the hemisphere, and the Latin American armed forces attempted to adjust their strategic and tactical doctrines, organization, equipment, and self-perception to the emerging bipolar international system. Their adjustment to the Cold War era implied merging over a century of conflicting military-political tradition and practice with the distinct, often incompatible, vision of the Pentagon's defense planners and officers. In particular, the historical political role of Latin American armed forces and their specific versions of patriotism and defense of *la patria* were alien to U.S. military professionals. Likewise, the region's armed forces could hardly be expected to accept blithely the barely disguised disdain with which some U.S. advisers viewed their institutions and, not infrequently, their ethnicity and culture.

From Poland to Chapultepec, 1939–1945

Though unable to obtain Argentine and Chilean declarations of war against Germany, Italy, and Japan until late in World War II, the United States gradually implemented a wartime regional security plan that suited its own strategic needs. Offering Latin American officers limited amounts of matériel as inducements, the United States obtained military bases, airfields, natural resources, intelligence networks, and growing political influence. During the war, U.S. officers engaged in highly autonomous diplomatic contacts with Latin American officers, often to the consternation of the latter's governments and the State Department.

Only Brazil sent large troop contingents to Europe (to Italy), and Mexico sent an air force unit to the Pacific. Nevertheless, U.S. diplomacy and military-to-military contacts created a loose inter-American security system that emphasized bilateral relations under cover of a multilateral hemispheric defense doctrine. Four days after Germany invaded Poland in 1939, the United States created a neutrality patrol to track and report on belligerent airborne and naval forces approaching its own and West Indies' coasts.[2] In October 1939 the Consultation of Foreign Ministers in the hemisphere adopted the Declaration of Panama, proclaiming a neutral zone from Canada to Cape Horn, extending three hundred miles from the Atlantic and to the Pacific. Collective security began with collective neutrality. It was violated by the British pursuit of the German pocket battleship *Graf Spee* into the Río de la Plata in December 1939, and frequently thereafter.

The U.S. Navy initiated patrols in a two-hundred-mile off-shore zone from the Grand Banks of Newfoundland into South American waters. The Roosevelt administration asked for port, airfield, and land base rights and other assistance from the Latin American republics. Argentina refused; to some extent all other countries agreed, with varying requests for arms, military training, and other reciprocal measures. (Nicaragua's General Anastasio Somoza, for example, eventually obtained financing for special road projects—the Rama Road—connecting his personal properties to the Pan-American Highway built ostensibly as a part of the war's national security programs.)

Military staff agreements, negotiated bilaterally with each country, obliged Latin Americans to request assistance from the United States if attacked; to take all possible measures to defend themselves; to cooperate in creating and operating an intelligence network to maintain continental security; to permit U.S. forces transit privileges en route to assist a neighbor; to provide aerial photographs or permit taking such photographs as required for U.S. operations; and to allow the United States to make engineering, medical, and signal surveys.[3] In March 1941, Congress passed the Lend-Lease Act, permitting arms transfers to Latin American nations, and stepped up its military mission and foreign officer-training programs. During the war, over 73 percent of Lend-Lease aid went to Brazil, with only small amounts to other regional republics. Even so, the lure of Lend-Lease aid and training opportunities enticed Latin American armed forces starved for new equipment and isolated from traditional suppliers.

In 1920 the United States had sent its first official mission to Latin America, a four-man group to Peru. A naval mission went to Brazil in 1922, a U.S. Navy and Marine Corps mission was dispatched to Nicaragua in 1926 to organize and train the National Guard, and a U.S. Army officer was named director of Guatemala's Escuela Politécnica in 1931. The United States had also organized, reorganized, and trained constabulary forces in the Dominican Republic, Haiti, Cuba, and Panama. President Franklin Roosevelt's Good Neighbor Policy, initiated in 1933, included a quiet effort to counter European military influence in Latin America. No new U.S. missions went to the region before 1938, although three navy officers were permitted to serve as instructors, under personal contracts, at Argentina's new Naval War College. In that year, mission agreements were negotiated with Peru, Argentina (army aviation), Haiti, and Colombia (army aviation). Between 1939 and the Japanese attack on Pearl Harbor in December 1941, eight additional agreements were signed. By war's end only Mexico, Cuba, Honduras, and Uruguay were without formal U.S. military missions, which largely displaced the German, French, Italian, Spanish, British, and other European ones.[4] These efforts marked the beginning of a quasi-monopolistic U.S. influence over Latin American armed forces and of its role as principal supplier of military equipment until the mid-1960s.

After the bombing of Pearl Harbor, the United States sought to commit the Latin American nations more completely to a formalized inter-American security system. At the same time, Roosevelt's defense planners quickly decided that, with few exceptions (most notably Brazil), the Latin American contribution to the war effort would include strategic resources, bases, local support units, and intelligence, but not combat troops.[5] Until the early 1930s, U.S. security policy toward the region had been unilateral; rarely did U.S. diplomats or military officers consult with Latin Americans on strategic planning or ask advice before armed interventions. Contingency plans for the region, the so-called Color Plans developed between 1919 and 1941 (Plan Green, for Mexico; Tan, Cuba; White, Panama and the Canal; Grey, Haiti, the Dominican Republic, Guatemala, and Nicaragua; Purple, Colombia, Venezuela, Ecuador, Peru, Brazil, Argentina, Chile, and Uruguay), were either academic staff exercises or unilateral intervention scenarios. None involved multilateral regional security concepts such as those proposed to confront World War II.[6]

The United States desired a hemispheric security doctrine to mask its essentially unilateral policies. Within a week of the attack on Pearl Harbor, nine Latin American states declared war on the Axis and four more broke relations. A symbolic security coordinating mechanism seemed advisable; thus was born the Inter-American Defense Board (IADB) at the 1942 Rio de Janeiro Meeting of Consultation. Created with the mission "to study and recommend" measures necessary for the defense of the continent, the IADB had no authority to enforce its recommendations and no operational or logistical functions. Jack Child, an expert on inter-American security issues, has suggested that the limited role assigned to the IADB was part of an "elegant and emasculating compromise" between Congress, the State Department, the War Department, and Latin American governments and diplomats regarding the creation of hemispheric security doctrine and institutions.[7]

The U.S. military clearly had little regard for their Latin American counterparts in the early 1940s, although the U.S. Ambassador to Venezuela proposed in 1943 the possibility of using Guaraní Indians from Paraguay as jungle fighters, and Indians from the highlands of Bolivia and Ecuador as high-altitude tail gunners in aircraft since they would not need oxygen.[8] At the State Department some officials wished to provide a symbol of inter-American solidarity; and the Latin American military, cut off from traditional sources of professional training and arms, wished to obtain some benefits from their countries' collaboration in the Allied war effort. So began the Inter-American Defense Board, which survived still with ambiguous functions into the 1990s. In the next two decades the IADB served as a clearinghouse for ideas, doctrine, and, informally, intelligence for the region's military officers. It also was the first step in the creation of an inter-American security system, what Child has called an "unequal alliance."[9]

By 1944 the eventual Allied victory seemed certain. U.S. defense planners began considering the prospects for postwar security collaboration with Latin America. At first, planning for postwar relations was premised on the Pentagon's desire to "standardize," meaning to convince the Latin American armed forces to use U.S. weapons, doctrine, and training, and to accept U.S. missions, to the exclusion of European influence. The Truman administration defined its major strategic objectives in Latin America as follows: 1) cooperating with the region's military to enhance defense of the hemisphere and the Panama Canal; 2) preserving peace in the hemisphere; 3) continuing the flow of strategic resources; 4) accessing air and naval bases; 5) establishing U.S. military missions in each republic; 6) standardizing Latin American military equipment with the United States as supplier; 7) training of the region's officer candidates in U.S. military schools; 8) avoiding unnecessary diversion of U.S. military resources to the hemisphere; and 9) continuing the special bilateral relationships with Brazil and Mexico.[10]

There was strong resistance in both Latin America and the United States to parts of this agenda. Latin American nationalists wanted no permanent bases on their territory, and Congress refused to approve President Harry Truman's proposed Inter-American Military Cooperation Act. Opponents in Congress listened to regional critics who objected to the costs of arms and the buttressing of dictatorships with U.S. military assistance. Latin Americans also objected to a Uruguayan proposal, supported by the United States, to create a multilateral inter-American military force to guarantee "democratic government" in the hemisphere.[11]

Postwar Hemispheric Security

U.S. interventionism before President Roosevelt's Good Neighbor Policy made the region's governments understandably cautious about creating a permanent instrument for hemispheric "guarantees of democracy." Notwithstanding the controversies, from 1945 to 1961 the United States and the Latin American nations developed a hemispheric security system based partly on the former's unilateralism, partly on consultation and collaboration, and partly in response to regional and international conflicts. Table 5–1 lists the benchmarks in the evolution of the inter-American security system discussed in the text.

Table 5–1. The Inter-American Security System and the Cold War, 1942–1963

Benchmark
Inter-American Defense Board (IADB) (1942)
Bilateral staff conferences (1944–45)
Chapultepec Conference; Act of Chapultepec (1945)
End of Lend-Lease (mid-1945)
Failure to pass Inter-American Military Cooperation Act (IAMCA) (1946–48)
Truman Doctrine ("Containment of Communism") 1947
Rio Conference; Inter-American Treaty of Reciprocal Assistance (Rio Treaty, given acronym of TIAR in Spanish) (1947)
Bogotá Conference; creation of Organization of American States (OAS) (1948)
Mutual Defense Assistance Act (1949)
NSC-68; formal adoption of "containment" doctrine (1950)
Korean War (1950–54)
Mutual Security Act (1951)
Mutual Defense Assistance Agreements (MDAAs) (1952–)
NSC-141; application of NSC-68 to Latin America (1952)
Eisenhower administration announces "rollback" policy (1952)
Military Assistance Program (MAP) (includes U.S. military missions, or MILGPS) in eighteen countries; military assistance specifically prohibited for internal security except in special circumstances (1952–61)
Caracas Conference and Caracas Declaration of Solidarity (U.S.-sponsored coup in Guatemala) (1954)
Cuban Revolution (1959)
Foreign Assistance Act; Internal Development and Security Act; funds for civic action and internal security; Alliance for Progress begins (1961)
Creation of Inter-American Defense College (Fort McNair, Washington, DC) (1962)
Creation of Central American Defense Council (CONDECA) (1963)

From 1945 to 1948 the major formal institutions of the inter-American system were designed in regional conferences: 1945 in Mexico City, 1947 in Rio de Janeiro, and 1948 in Bogotá. At the Mexico City (Chapultepec) Conference, Argentina was excluded since it had not cooperated in the war effort, an imposition of U.S. bipolar antagonism against its pro-Axis military governments.

This meeting, the Inter-American Conference on the Problems of War and Peace, preceded the scheduled 1945 San Francisco Conference in which the United Nations would be established. The United States sought to limit regional initiatives until after that conference, but it did agree to annual meetings of foreign ministers, quadrennial general conferences, and other measures to strengthen hemispheric solidarity, including instructing the Governing Board of the Pan-American Union to prepare a draft treaty for consideration at Bogotá in 1946.

The Latin Americans looked to the United States for postwar economic assistance; the latter shuttled the former to the sidelines as concerns for reconstruction in Europe took precedence. This conflict between Latin American and U.S. priorities would alternately simmer and boil from the 1950s to the 1990s. Inconsistently, but predictably, Washington preached socioeconomic reform and parsimony in military expenditures while also opposing socioeconomic reform and encouraging Latin American militarism.

In 1945 a central issue for the hemisphere was its relationship to the new United Nations' regional systems, a political and philosophical conflict between "regionalists" and "universalists." Article 51 of the UN Charter, treating regional organizations, was based on a compromise formulated by Senator Arthur Vandenberg in the subcommittee chaired by Colombia's Alberto Lleras Camargo. This compromise assured that "nothing in this Charter shall impair the inherent right of individual or collective self-defense if an armed attack occurs against a member of the United Nations, until the Security Council has taken the measures necessary to maintain international peace and security."[12] Latin Americans agreed to this phrasing with the understanding that an inter-American conference would devise a regional defense treaty, but U.S.-Argentine bilateral quarrels delayed the conference until 1947.

Argentina had finally declared war against the Axis on March 27, 1945, just past the deadline for participation in the 1945 San Francisco Conference. An inter-American system without Argentina was not plausible; the United States finally accepted the Argentine government's participation both to achieve the desired defense agreement and because the military's (and Juan Perón's) past Axis ties were less objectionable with the onset of the Cold War. On September 2, 1947, Latin American and U.S. representatives signed the Inter-American Treaty of Reciprocal Assistance, or Rio Treaty, as it came to be known. This treaty defined the security regime for the hemisphere and established procedures for its operation. It was the first treaty to be signed under Article 51 of the UN Charter, but it did not provide for a permanent collective security force or operational command. In this respect it differed from the North Atlantic Treaty Organization (NATO) and subsequent regional security systems created in the Cold War era.

Nine months later, at Bogotá, the Organization of American States (OAS) was created, giving formal treaty status and permanent organizational form to the loose collection of Pan-American Union resolutions and conferences. The OAS charter obliged the member nations to cooperate "for the common welfare and prosperity of the peoples of the continent" and to refrain from interventionism: "No state may use or encourage the use of coercive measures of an economic or political character in order to force the sovereign will of another state and obtain from it advantages of any kind." The OAS retained the IADB "to act as the organ of preparation and recommendation for the collective self-defense of the American continent against aggression." It did not assign any autonomous authority, forces, or budget to the IADB, leaving it for much of the next two decades as a shadow agency facilitating contacts among military officers, or, in the view of some more cynical observers, as a regional sounding board for coup-plotting and indoctrination of officers and enlisted personnel. Restricted to planning for continental defense, it theoretically was [and is] barred from concern with conflicts between and among OAS member states.

Postwar Political Liberalization and Reaction

Coincident with the framing of the postwar inter-American security system (1944–1948), a wave of political liberalization in Latin America ousted dictators, brought reformist parties and activist labor movements to the fore, and seemed to augur democratization. Politics, with the inevitable national variations, shifted to the left, became more populist, and frightened the old landed elite, the more traditional military officers, and the old-line liberal and conservative political parties. Military officers intent on modernizing their nations participated actively in politics, allying with reformist parties and popular movements to topple dictatorships in El Salvador (1944), Guatemala (1944), Ecuador (1944), Venezuela (1945), Brazil (1945), and Honduras (1947) and supporting socioeconomic change in much of Latin America. Paraguay and the Dominican Republic initially resisted the tide of liberalization, but they were not unaffected by it as the symbolic end to press censorship, elections (however tainted), and democratic rhetoric surfaced even in these authoritarian bastions. Military officers were in the forefront in the push for government intervention to stimulate industrialization, overcome economic and technological dependence, and modernize public communications and transportation systems. They also recognized the need for improved educational opportunities as well as the impediment to progress inherent in traditional landed estates in the countryside.

These "political openings" and economic initiatives almost everywhere included the legalization, or tolerance, of Communist parties, even their participation in government coalitions, as in Costa Rica and Chile, and of their nationalist-reformist competitors, such as APRA (Peru), MNR (Bolivia), AD (Venezuela), and Peronism (Argentina). Labor conflicts were widespread as postwar inflation and relaxation of wartime labor discipline provided propitious circumstances for seeking to redress inequities in income distribution. Calls for land reform from the Río Grande to Tierra del Fuego added to the intensity of popular mobilization.

By the end of 1946 in some countries (and by 1948 almost everywhere), the brief interlude of reform and political liberalization gave way to government repression of the Communists and leftist labor. Modernizing military officers sustained their support for economic nationalism but returned to their historical internal security roles in suppressing rural and urban social movements and to their traditional anticommunism. They recognized the contradiction between social and political mobilization and the need for order to encourage investment. They also recognized the dangers to their own institutions of insurgent movements and of the Marxist programs for the region.

The Rio Treaty, the formation of the OAS, and the IADB's informal coordination of Cold War anticommunism gradually relegitimated the Latin American military's self-perceptions. They had old-"new" enemies: the Communists. They had old-"new" missions: protecting *la patria* against external threats and internal subversion. The Cold War reconfirmed the central role of the armed forces in politics, eroded U.S. support for "democratization," and encouraged a new round of coups that reestablished order partly in the name of anticommunism, partly in the name of the danger of subversive populist movements: in Peru (1948), Venezuela (1948), Cuba (1952), Colombia (1953), Guatemala (failed coup in 1949; 1954), and Paraguay (1954). Each of these regimes implemented new repressive legislation, enhancing military and police authority and stifling political opposition.

In Peru, for example, General Manuel Odría, president of the military *junta* (until he orchestrated his election as constitutional president in June 1950), modified the penal code to punish "political terrorism" with the death penalty and adopted a draconian Internal Security Law. Odría offset the political repression with generous pay raises for the armed forces and populist programs benefiting especially the urban poor. The main target of Odría's wrath was APRA, but the legislation that permitted persecution of APRA also facilitated repression of other regime opponents.

In Venezuela the 1948 coup eventually brought Marcos Pérez Jiménez to power. He had graduated first in his class from the Maracay Military Academy and studied at the Peruvian Superior War College at Chorrillos in 1939. He detested the reformist Acción Democrática party (AD), just as his Peruvian comrades hated APRA. By 1953, Pérez Jiménez had a compliant constituent assembly adopt a new constitution and extend to him virtual dictatorial authority. Reformist and Communist political leaders, teachers, labor organizers, university students, and journalists were hunted down, incarcerated, put into concentration camps, or killed. Many Venezuelans fled into exile. Like Odría in Peru, Pérez Jiménez created new internal security forces, purged disloyal officers, and increased military salaries and perquisites to ensure the armed forces' support. These post-World War II military-led governments spent lavishly on public works, workers' housing, and other populist measures to gain political support; they contested the political clientele of reformist parties and the left, making "development" a military objective rather than an exclusive banner of civilian reformers and Marxists.

By 1954 thirteen of twenty Latin American republics had military-dominated governments. In other instances, coups were avoided or made unnecessary as the armed forces carried out their constitutional and statutory missions, including detaining and repressing Communists and other subversives outlawed by new anti-Marxist and internal security laws, such as anti-Communist legislation in Brazil (1948) and Chile (1947–48).[13] Nowhere, however, did political unity prevail within the armed forces, occasioning episodic coup-plotting and conspiracies with opposition parties and movements. Military governments did not mean monolithic military support for the postwar regimes or an end to factionalism within the armed forces.

In Peru, a naval uprising in 1948 supported by APRA precipitated a coup that led to an interim military government and then to a "constitutional" dictatorship with suspension of constitutional guarantees under General Odría. Emulating, to some extent, the Perón experiment in Argentina, Odría combined public works populism, increased military expenditures, and a U.S. naval mission to gain the armed forces' approval, until the bonanza of Korean War exports ended and public funds were exhausted. By 1955–56 military opponents allied with civilians intent on restoring civil liberties to obtain a "return to democracy." APRA's leader, Haya de la Torre, spent the years from 1950 to 1954 as an imprisoned guest in the Colombian Embassy, surrounded by a moat and machine guns. Odría approved the creation in 1950 of the Centro de Altos Estudios Militares (CAEM), in part as a duty station for troublesome colonels. To his chagrin, this new center of civil-military doctrine would adapt Aprista, socialist, and developmentalist themes to the military's guardianship and salvational roles, eventually becoming the most important source of Peruvian military doctrine. In the meantime, Odría, like Perón in Argentina, Pérez Jiménez in Venezuela, and Rojas Pinilla in Colombia, politicized the military, made personal loyalty a basic criterion for promotion, and left a factionalized armed forces on his departure in 1956 (though never as polarized as the armed forces under Perón in Argentina).

An even more byzantine variant of postwar liberalization followed by Cold War anticommunism occurred in Costa Rica, unexpectedly resulting in the dissolution of the army and its constitutional abolition. As in Chile, the Costa Rican Communists (Partido Vanguardia Popular, or PVP) participated in a presidential electoral coalition and exercised influence in the government in the postwar years. Much more moderate than the Chilean Communist party, the PVP still made U.S. policymakers and some Costa Rican landowners uneasy. When the coalition sought to sustain itself by manipulating the 1948 elections, the United States supported efforts by opposition leaders, including José "Pepe" Figueres, to forcibly oust the incumbent.

Civil war ensued, with the U.S.-supported opposition militarily buttressed by the so-called Caribbean Legion, a group of social democratic politicos and romantics sworn to oust the region's dictators, from Trujillo in the Dominican Republic to Somoza in Nicaragua. Organized after World War II in Cuba, it received support, arms, and financing from diverse sources including the Peruvian Apristas and Juan José Arevalo's government in Guatemala. Over 700 Legionaries (a larger force than Costa Rica's army) invaded Costa Rica to defend the apparent victory of the opposition presidential candidate, Otilio Olate. U.S. diplomats as well as military attachés and engineers, and even a former Royal Air Force intelligence officer, discreetly and ambiguously assisted the rebels despite the incumbent president's declarations of support for the OAS and the inter-American system.

The United States had already cut off military assistance to Costa Rica. Paradoxically, Nicaragua's Anastasio Somoza allowed former Costa Rican president Rafael Calderón to organize a rebel movement and invade Costa Rica from Nicaraguan territory, supplied Calderón from his country's military arsenals, and also used Nicaraguan troops to oppose Figueres's "Liberation Army." Somoza was not concerned with Calderón's previous electoral coalition with the Communists; he hoped to defeat Figueres and the troublesome Caribbean Legion that was sworn to overthrow dictatorships in the Caribbean and Central America, including his own. After the United States threatened to withhold recognition of his new government and made clear its aims, Somoza withdrew his forces.

Costa Rica's army of less than 500 soldiers, led by officers loyal to presidents and confirmed by politicians, had experienced little professionalization and lacked a tradition of doctrinal anticommunism. It was greatly outnumbered by the police. In practice, the government's military strength was divided among small units loyal to President Teodoro Picado, some Communist militia, and the police. Unable to coordinate these weak assets and obviously confronting a U.S.-backed "international" military movement, Picado resigned and signed a peace accord with the opposition on April 19, 1948, in Mexico City.

The new government, an interim *junta* headed by Figueres, outlawed the Communist party and then disarmed and dissolved the old army. This move gave great importance to the issue of the foreign soldiers—the Caribbean Legion—in Costa Rican politics and also raised the specter of the country permanently being used as a launching pad for conspiracies and liberation wars against Central American dictators. The United States favored stability in the Caribbean, particularly in the region near the Panama Canal, while Costa Rican nationalists objected to internationalizing any new armed forces.

Continued border incidents and support by Somoza for Costa Rican rebels led by Calderón resulted in the first invocation of the Rio Treaty by a signatory state. On December 11, 1948, the San José government denounced the invasion of its territory by "armed forces proceeding from Nicaragua" and requested convocation of a meeting of the Council of the Organization of American States "in order that it may be apprised of the situation . . . acting as Provisional Organ of Consultation because of the urgency of this case." The Council appointed the Inter-American Commission of Military Experts, consisting of five officers representing Brazil, Colombia, Mexico, Paraguay, and the United States, to investigate the conflicting allegations of Costa Rica and Nicaragua. After six months the two governments confirmed the Pact of Amity, with Costa Rica agreeing to disarm the Legion and prevent its territory from being used to invade Nicaragua, and the Nicaraguans agreeing to prevent anti-Liberación Nacional Costa Ricans from using its territory to attack Costa Rica. The San José government announced that the Legion would be disarmed and disbanded, although many of its members did not immediately leave Costa Rica.[14]

This Cold War version of Central America's traditional cross-border political intrigues had at least one unique result, apart from the first invocation of the Rio Treaty. In 1949 a new constitution adopted by Costa Rica's interim *junta* permanently abolished the army, making that country the only one in the world with such a constitutional prohibition. Figueres became a hero of Latin American antimilitarists; the U.S. military mission concerned itself with training the Costa Rican national security and police forces, which had, in any case, always outnumbered the army. The Truman administration achieved its anti-Communist objectives while Figueres and Olate continued with their social democratic political agenda. Recalling the events, Colonel Edgardo Cardona, the former minister of security, remarked: "The idea of eliminating the army did not have a philosophical foundation. The army, as it functioned, was not suited to the circumstances. An army in the barracks was useless, and it could not be maintained. It was necessary to create a well-disciplined Civil Guard with capable personnel. The chief of the American mission offered us assistance in organizing the new force."[15]

U.S. Regional Security Policies

The United States had initially favored the democratic movement in Latin America after World War II. By 1946 the use made of political liberalization by the region's Communist parties and by organized labor frightened Truman administration policymakers as well as Latin American elites. The United States was convinced that the Communist parties threatened democracy and, more important, that they were surrogates for Soviet penetration in the hemisphere. Resolution 32 of the Final Act of the Bogotá Conference, entitled "The Preservation and Defense of Democracy in America," identified the existence of legal Communist parties as an *external* threat, thus making them double targets of the region's armed forces as threats both to internal and external security. In this context, the constitutional abolition of Costa Rica's army was an idiosyncratic outcome of a civil war enmeshed in the beginnings of the Cold War and the creation of the inter-American security system. This Costa Rican innovation represented a grave threat to the Latin American armed forces, one whose emulation they were determined to prevent. Admittedly, it had occurred in a small country virtually without professional armed forces. Nevertheless, the small Costa Rican army's identification with a government "soft on communism," together with its lack of institutional doctrine, professional careerism, and close ties to the United States, had cost its very existence. This was not a lesson easy to forget.

The Cold War updated the Monroe Doctrine with anticommunism; communism was an "extra-hemispheric" ideology, just as monarchism had been in the nineteenth century and fascism more recently. It was an Old World (that is, European) political idea that had no place in the Western Hemisphere—the territory of free republics, constitutional government, and liberal democracy. Disagreeably, to prevent the spread of communism, it was sometimes necessary to support military coups against elected governments unable to resist Communist subversion—to wit, rapid diplomatic recognition for coup leaders Manuel Odría in Peru and Marcos Pérez Jiménez in Venezuela in 1948.

The old guard in Latin America, both civilian and military, was quick to catch on to the new U.S. regional policies, but it was understandably resentful that the United States failed to back up its anti-Communist postulates with effective economic and military assistance. Threatening the United States with the Communist bogeyman secured diplomatic recognition for governments of force (and even medals for some of Latin America's dictators, such as President Dwight Eisenhower's 1954 decoration of Odría and Pérez Jiménez with the Legion of Merit). However, needed economic aid, investment, and military assistance came slowly and reluctantly, especially before 1951. Latin American civilian and military leaders could not fail to notice the disregard with which they were treated by officials in Washington and diplomats in their capitals.

The United States offered the Latin American militaries, with the exception of Brazil and Mexico, only token assistance until 1949, the year in which Mao Tse-tung drove Chiang Kai-shek to Formosa and the free world "lost China." The 1949 Mutual Defense Assistance Act permitted Latin American nations to obtain arms in the United States on a reimbursable basis, thus severely limiting acquisitions. In the same year, President Truman authorized an ad hoc committee of State and Defense Department staff to prepare an assessment of the nation's foreign interests, of potential threats and responses. The subsequent *Report by the Secretaries of State and Defense on United States Objectives and Programs for National Security, April 7, 1950* was presented as a memorandum of the National Security Council and became known as NSC-68.[16] This memorandum identified a global Communist threat, a worldwide "assault on free institutions" that had to be met with increased military preparedness and a determination to contain communism by defending U.S. allies, particularly the front-line "forward-defense" nations on the periphery of the "free world."

Latin America was still a marginal concern in U.S. global geopolitics. Until 1951 the Latin Americans purchased light cruisers, training aircraft, arms, ammunition, and spare parts, but not often on bargain terms and not always the matériel they desired. They also bought ships, planes, arms, and equipment from Britain and Europe. These purchases ran counter to the declared objective of "standardization" and reflected the lack of coordination between the State Department, defense planners, presidential advisers, and Congress.

Latin American officers and governments were understandably frustrated by the gap between U.S. rhetoric and policy. The threat of Soviet communism to the Western Hemisphere seemed largely theoretical and rhetorical—useful as a pretext for repressing internal opposition and the small Communist and socialist movements that arose, but hardly an immediate external danger. In any case, Latin American armed forces possessed no deterrent capability against a major military power and little ability to defend themselves should such a threat materialize. With the partial exception of Brazil, Argentina, Chile, and Mexico, local military industries were unable even minimally to supply the armed forces in peacetime, let alone if faced by external aggression. Argentina had produced the Third World's first tank (the Nahúel) in 1943 and its first jet fighter (the IA-27 Pulquí I) in 1947, but it was still largely dependent on external suppliers.[17] In 1955 only Argentina had an army, on paper, of over 100,000; none of the region's armed forces had stand-alone logistical, transport, or combat capabilities for more than brief, minor skirmishes against an opposing army. For the most part, they were dependent constabularies and border defense forces whose elite officer corps studied some grand strategy and large doses of tactics.

They did not relish this role, nor did they fail to notice that their nations' economic underdevelopment and social atavisms condemned the armed forces to this dismal reality. Their nineteenth- and early twentieth-century lessons from Prussian, French, Spanish, Italian, and other European advisers had inculcated them with the importance of economic development as a foundation of military and political power. These lessons would be reinforced as the Cold War intensified and the socioeconomic foundations of subversion were made standard fare in the new General Staff schools and U.S. military institutions attended by Latin American armed forces personnel. To the mid-1950s, however, only Peru's CAEM and Brazil's Escola Superior de Guerra (ESG, 1949) elaborated sophisticated security doctrines that linked national economic development, geopolitics, and national defense to provide a rationale for increased military participation in national politics. Both the Peruvians and Brazilians drew lessons from the U.S. National War College (created in 1947) and the French internal security and counterinsurgency doctrines to formulate their own national security precepts. They also had recourse to the isolated theorizing by officers in military journals from Mexico to Argentina since the 1920s that posited the geopolitical and economic foundations of the armed forces' defense and security missions.

The outbreak of the Korean War jarred U.S. legislators and diplomats; Latin Americans could now use the war to remind their "partners" in the unequal alliance of their defense needs. Ironically, the 1951 Mutual Security Act that authorized military assistance to Latin America justified this assistance with the rationale of "hemispheric defense," prohibiting the use of equipment provided for internal security. In 1952 the Truman administration delineated its containment policy for Latin America in NSC-141, an elaboration on the NSC-68 document: "In Latin America we seek first and foremost an orderly political and economic development which will make the Latin American nations resistant to the internal growth of communism and to Soviet political warfare. . . . Secondly, we seek hemisphere solidarity in support of our world policy and the cooperation of the Latin American nations in safeguarding the hemisphere through individual and collective defense measures against external aggression and internal subversion."[18]

Recognition of the need to support "political order" and "economic development" would be the main intellectual foundations of U.S. policy toward Latin America in the early Cold War era, unaccompanied by sufficient economic assistance to make the policy credible. The massive commitment to reconstruction in Europe and Japan, and the Marshall Plan, were never approximated in Latin America, despite the latter's pleas for compensation for wartime collaboration, compassion for the region's desperate poverty, and the internal security consequences of retarded economic development.

On the military side, however, the United States took hesitant initiatives provoked by the Korean War. Beginning with Ecuador, it negotiated bilateral Mutual Defense Assistance Agreements (MDAAs) with Cuba, Colombia, Peru, Chile (1952); Brazil, the Dominican Republic, Uruguay (1953); Nicaragua, Honduras (1954); Guatemala, Haiti (1955); Bolivia (1958); El Salvador, Panama, Costa Rica (1962); and Argentina (1964). Debates on Capitol Hill resulted in inconsistent loosening and tightening of conditions for grant-aid, sales, and arms transfers from 1952 to 1959, as critics added clauses to certain MDAAs to emphasize the contention that military aid supported dictators. Grants of U.S. military aid to Latin America during these years totaled $317 million, accounting for 1.3 percent of MDAA funds spent worldwide and approximately 5 percent of the $1.4 billion spent annually by Latin American governments on the armed forces (see Table 5–2). Even in 1959 the Mutual Security Act required an annual presidential finding that "military assistance is necessary"; that military equipment and materials be furnished "only in furtherance of missions directly relating to the common defense of the Western Hemisphere which are found by the president to be important to the security of the United States"; and that "internal security requirements shall not, unless the President deems otherwise, be the basis for military assistance programs to American Republics."[19]

Table 5–2. U.S. Military Assistance to Latin America, 1950–1960

Country	*Total MAP*		*Per Capita*	
	(Millions of $)	*Rank*	*(1955 population)*	*Rank*
Argentina	0.07	16	0.003	18
Bolivia	0.44	14	0.14	14
Brazil	164.80	1	2.82	7
Chile	48.10	3	7.11	2
Colombia	30.60	4	2.37	8
Costa Rica	0.005	18	0.005	17
Cuba	[16.00] (end 1958)	—	[2.61]	—
Dominican Republic	8.00	8	3.17	6
Ecuador	18.70	7	5.07	4
El Salvador	0.02	17	0.009	16
Guatemala	1.10	12	0.34	11
Haiti	2.00	10	0.17	13
Honduras	0.82	13	0.49	10
Mexico	3.20	9	0.11	15
Nicaragua	1.40	11	1.12	9
Panama	0	19	0	19
Paraguay	0.36	15	0.23	12
Peru	50.90	2	5.42	3
Uruguay	24.00	5	9.18	1
Venezuela	21.60	6	3.74	5

Source: Department of Defense, Director of Military Assistance, *Military Assistance Programs—Programs and Deliveries, Fiscal Years, 1950–1961* (Washington, DC, 1961), after Charles Wolf, Jr., *United States Policy and the Third World: Problems and Analysis* (Boston: Little, Brown and Co., 1967): 102. MAP includes grant-aid, credit assistance, and deliveries from excess stocks.

Only Colombia sent troops to Korea: an infantry battalion and a frigate.[20] U.S. military planners preferred that Latin American troops maintain internal stability and ensure the flow of strategic resources. In any case, no Latin American armed forces could provide self-sustaining combat units to the UN command, and their piecemeal integration into UN forces was thought more trouble than benefit. The pretext of hemispheric defense, however, did allow the U.S. military and their Latin American counterparts to overcome the congressional opposition to military assistance prevalent since 1946. From 1951 to 1961 the Military Assistance Program (MAP) with military missions (MILGPS) expanded considerably; involved the training of thousands of Latin American officers and soldiers in the United States, the Panama Canal Zone, and in the host country; included extensive arms transfers and sales; and made possible professional junkets for officers to the United States. The U.S. Southern Command (SOUTHCOM) supervised these programs.

All military aid for Latin America during this period, except where specifically determined by presidential findings that internal security problems existed affecting U.S. security, was ostensibly for hemispheric defense. Of course, training, equipment, and arms and ammunition could not be closely monitored, and even if only used for hemispheric defense, their acquisition would have freed resources for purchase of equipment for internal security. U.S. policymakers seemed unaware of the constitutional and statutory missions of the Latin American armed forces and their historical participation in politics. The Latin Americans pretended, usually, not to notice the feigned (and unfeigned) naiveté of U.S. diplomats and officers. U.S. officers never entirely accepted the "political" role of the Latin American armed forces nor the apparent idiocy of U.S. diplomats regarding military and security policy. Latin American officers resented their U.S. counterparts' condescension and pig-headed notion that the only right way to do things was the "American way."

Despite these frictions, important officer-to-officer relationships and friendships linked the U.S. and Latin American military establishments in greater number and in a more personal manner than had ever occurred with the earlier European missions. These contacts were perhaps the most successful aspect of Washington's military assistance programs from the 1950s, which, before the Cuban Revolution, had primarily political objectives. The "hemispheric defense" rationale for this assistance never made military sense, but it always made possible some military-to-military contacts and political intelligence. For the Latin Americans it made available some equipment and professional perquisites, including training and junkets to the United States. Latin American officers never forgot their own regional geopolitical threat scenarios; the planes, ships, submarines, tanks, and other equipment obtained ostensibly for hemispheric defense were considered of deterrent and symbolic value in relation to potential conflicts with their neighbors. More often, especially in the 1950s and early 1960s, they were used in interservice and intraservice combat during coups—for example, in Argentina in 1955 (cavalry versus infantry), the army-air force confrontation in Ecuador in 1961, and the failed air force coup in Guatemala in November 1962.

In sum, the military assistance programs from 1952 to 1961 successfully linked the United States to the Latin American armed forces, but U.S. policies also created friction and resentment with their inconsistency, political fickleness, and evident cynicism concerning the real potential of those armed forces in contributing to hemispheric defense. (This situation changed after 1961, when Latin Americans were expected to fight communism against guerrilla forces inspired by the Cuban Revolution in combat rather than with rhetoric against leftist politicians and selective repression of political dissidents.)

During those ten years the MAPs also contributed to an increasing gap among the Latin American armed forces in technical, doctrinal, and combat professionalization. Increasingly, modern military forces required expensive aviation, naval, artillery, and armor elements, with their associated personnel and maintenance systems. Small, poor countries could not generally afford such luxuries nor, in most cases, did they need them for external defense. There were exceptions, of course; and most Latin American military planners persisted, not unrealistically, in preparing for military threat scenarios involving neighboring states. Conventional war planning was a real concern for Latin American military leaders, even if U.S. policymakers failed to take them seriously. Evidence for the plausibility of conventional threat scenarios included Peru's 1930s and 1940s conflicts with Ecuador and Colombia and historical antagonism toward Chile; Bolivia's desire to reclaim access to the Pacific and its 1930s war with Paraguay; episodic territorial and maritime disputes between Colombia and Venezuela; unresolved frontier issues between Chile and Argentina; Brazilian-Argentine competition for South American hegemony and Brazil's numerous boundary disputes with its neighbors; and Central America's unending, if brief, cross-border military clashes.

Latin American weapons acquisitions, whether through grant-aid or purchase, were monitored by neighbors; thus, the MAPs unintentionally contributed to a not-always-subtle regional arms race. To illustrate, when Brazil contracted for two light cruisers in 1951, Argentina requested similar equipment to keep pace, and Chile then followed. All three ended up with two cruisers, at considerable expense and ongoing maintenance obligations.[21] Military assistance programs also increased the disparity between the armed forces that developed credible external defense capabilities, such as Chile, Argentina, Brazil, and, to a lesser extent, Peru, Colombia, and Venezuela, and the armed forces that had symbolic armor units and small numbers of aircraft—useful for controlling capitals and regional towns during coups but useless as serious offensive or deterrent forces against opposing armies. This was even more the case for naval and air forces, the more expensive and highly technified services in the 1950s. Only Chile, Argentina, and Brazil had real, if limited, naval capabilities, and Peru could be added to this list when considering the region's air forces. Even these countries maintained forces largely composed of equipment that was generations behind NATO and Soviet-bloc front-line technology.

Although the Latin American armed forces lacked significant military capabilities by international standards, they had more than enough firepower to topple governments and repress subversive political movements. Thus, most governments in the 1950s, both civilian and military, sought to keep the officer corps content with economic, political, and professional inducements. In some countries, such as Venezuela, Cuba, and Colombia, these benefits reached extremes, with extravagant officers' clubs, lucrative public works contracts, appointments to government positions, and opportunities for self-enrichment. In Venezuela, Pérez Jiménez's ordnance chief made millions of dollars from parking meter and transportation contracts, and control of the lottery and race track made fortunes for numerous officers. Cuba's military leaders controlled organized vice, and in Colombia the Rojas Pinilla government was riddled with corruption. These illegal and questionable operations eroded military professionalism; contradicted the liturgy of probity, honor, abnegation, and patriotism taught in the military academies; injured the image and myth of the soldier as "patriot-priest"; and confounded military vocation and dedication to *la patria* with organized crime in the name of national defense. Such developments affected the region's armed forces differently, and not everywhere did profiteering and corruption replace commitment to national security. Chilean officers, for example, experienced role expansion and participation in diverse government programs without pervasive corruption; in the mid-1950s, President Ibáñez asked their understanding for his cuts in weapons acquisitions and limited budget allocations for military exercises. Overall, however, the Latin American armed forces experienced declining prestige and moral probity in the 1950s, even as they were called on to defend the hemisphere from the Soviet threat.

The Cold War Comes to Latin America: Guatemala, 1954

While the United States operated a halfhearted military assistance program in Latin America, it fought a war in Korea that resulted in a stalemate, the first war in which it emerged without a victory (although technically this was a UN peacekeeping mission, not a U.S. war). Korea frustrated U.S. leaders and public opinion. Communists were able to thwart Washington's policy, the U.S. nuclear monopoly had ended, and the Soviet Union and China were gaining in strength and prestige not only in Europe but also in parts of Latin America. In 1954, Vietnamese guerrillas, led by the Vietnamese Communist Party, defeated the French in seemingly another example of the advances of communism spearheaded by the Soviet global conspiracy. In the United States, a frenzy of anticommunism, led by Senator Joseph McCarthy, created a veritable witchhunt against those "soft on communism"; artists, writers, intellectuals, teachers, union leaders, and many others faced ostracism or worse as the cauldron of intolerance boiled over.

Guatemala became a target for this pent-up frustration and frenzied anticommunism. Since 1951 a reformist regime in that country, headed by Colonel Jacobo Arbenz, had allowed the Communists to increase their influence in the government and labor movement, and had implemented an agrarian reform that seriously affected the United Fruit Company. Arbenz was a career military officer who had participated in the ouster of Jorge Ubico in 1944, served as minister of defense to President Juan José Arévalo, and shared with many of his fellow officers a desire to modernize Guatemala and its armed forces. He found in Guatemala no strong party system, non-Communist labor unions, or other institutional props for modernization. In the army, he saw a divided, partly professionalized institution that favored economic nationalism and political integration but feared the growing influence of the Guatemalan Communists and the potential reaction of the United States.

The agrarian reform and peasant unionization agitated the Guatemalan countryside as never before, creating panic among the rural elite and raising the never-far-from-the-surface race and class conflicts that endemically afflicted Guatemala. The anti-Arbenz forces remembered longingly the Salvadoran massacre of 1932; supporters had hopes for fundamental reforms and modernization inspired in nationalism. With the political mobilization of peasants, workers, and leftist intellectuals on the ascent, Guatemalan elites and some officers were not adverse to a Cold War rationale (or any rationale) for suppressing the wave of social reform before it drowned the old order.

Arbenz's main rival in the army, Colonel Francisco Arana, had engaged in an abortive coup plot against President Arévalo and was assassinated in 1949. Arana had accused Arbenz of Communist ties. Many Guatemalans believed that both Arbenz and Arévalo had ordered the hit on Arana. In response to the murder, Colonel Carlos Castillo Armas led a failed coup attempt in 1950. Pardoned, he went into exile in Honduras. Arbenz, elected president in 1950, intensified the reform program and sought to combine political support from the Communists and progressive reformers with the nationalist modernizing tendencies in the army to transform the country.

President Eisenhower's administration had key policymakers with personal and economic ties to United Fruit. These men included Secretary of State John Foster Dulles and his brother, CIA Director Allen Dulles. Fervently anti-Communist, deeply religious, and committed to defending the hemisphere from Soviet penetration, the Dulles brothers—some believe influenced by their ties to United Fruit, others more by their dedicated anticommunism—plotted the overthrow of the Arbenz government. According to Foster Dulles, Communism was "not a theory, not a doctrine, but an aggressive, tough, political force, backed by great resources and serving the most ruthless empire of modern times."[22] (These words would be echoed in President Ronald Reagan's war against the Soviet "evil empire" in the 1980s.)

Foster Dulles tied the fight against communism to the Monroe Doctrine, which he called "the first and most fundamental of our foreign policies." In its original 1823 version, the Monroe Doctrine had stipulated that creation of new European colonies in the Western Hemisphere should not be tolerated and that European political systems (at that time monarchies) should not be transferred to the new republics of the hemisphere. This doctrine had been used and abused in so many ways from 1823 through World War II that many Latin Americans believed it was merely a cloak for whatever U.S. security and economic interests prevailed. In particular, the "big stick" update of the Monroe Doctrine contributed by President Theodore Roosevelt in the twentieth century's first decade had justified numerous armed interventions and instances of diplomatic bullying from 1907 until the 1930s. A less cynical view was that the United States genuinely meant to encourage the spread of democracy in the hemisphere and to protect it from European intrusion, but that interest groups in the United States and Latin America used the Monroe Doctrine and U.S. intervention to protect their investments, archaic social arrangements, and political privileges.

Whether Washington's intentions were benign or malevolent, in the 1950s the Monroe Doctrine merged with Cold War anticommunism and the doctrines of containment and rollback. President Eisenhower was convinced that "Moscow leads many misguided people to believe that they can count on Communist help to achieve and sustain nationalistic ambitions. . . . Actually, . . . the Communists are hoping to take advantage of the confusion resulting from destruction of existing relationships and in the difficulties and uncertainties of disrupted trade, security and understandings, to further the aims of world revolution and the Kremlin's domination of all people."[23] Eisenhower's perspective went well beyond any concern for U.S. investments in Guatemala, although the influence of the United Fruit Company in manipulating public opinion on events in Guatemala, including articles in major newspapers such as the *New York Times,* should not be underestimated. By 1953 the Eisenhower administration was committed to overthrowing the Arbenz government. The president's brother, Milton Eisenhower, had returned from a fact-finding mission to Latin America, and his report concluded: "Highly disciplined groups of Communists are busy, night and day, illegally or openly, in the American republics, as they are in every nation of the world. . . . One American nation has succumbed to Communist infiltration."[24]

The U.S. government concluded that communism had already established itself in Guatemala. That country would be the target for the first cannonade of the rollback version of the Monroe Doctrine in Latin America. To prepare the way, Secretary Dulles cajoled, threatened, and implored the governments of the region to adopt a clear position on communism in the hemisphere at the Caracas Conference in 1954. The Latin Americans hedged, reaffirming the principle of nonintervention but agreeing on the Caracas Declaration of Solidarity (over Guatemala's objection and with Mexico and Argentina abstaining). This document declared that communism, "by its antidemocratic nature and its interventionist tendency, is incompatible with the concept of American freedom." The Latin Americans agreed "to adopt within their respective territories the measures necessary to eradicate and prevent subversive activities."

The Caracas Declaration further proclaimed that "the domination or control of the political institutions of any American State by the international communist movement extending to this Hemisphere the political system of an extra continental power, would constitute a threat to the sovereignty and political independence of the American States, endangering the peace of America, and would call for a meeting of consultation to consider the adoption of appropriate action in accordance with existing treaties."[25] Latin Americans could not elect Communist governments or those viewed as an extension of international communism without provoking recourse to the updated Monroe Doctrine. The Rio Treaty, bilateral military assistance agreements, and even the right to self-defense could be invoked to counter Communist penetration in the hemisphere. Ironically, a parallel Declaration of Caracas adopted in the same conference reiterated "the inalienable right of each American State to choose freely its own institutions in the effective exercise of representative democracy, as a means of preserving its political sovereignty . . . without the intrusion of any form of totalitarianism."

In June 1954 the CIA executed Operation PBSUCCESS, using exiled Colonel Castillo Armas as the figure-head leader of a "liberating army" that invaded Guatemala from Honduras. The details concerning this operation have been recounted by various authors; in the event, the United States was able to neutralize the Guatemalan army through bribes to individual officers, threats of intervention, and inducements involving renewed military assistance and training opportunities that had been cut off during the Arbenz presidency.[26] Castillo Armas's ragged little force equipped by the CIA, a U.S. disinformation campaign, cooperation by Central American dictators (including Anastasio Somoza), and some bombs-for-effect in Guatemala City convinced Arbenz to leave the country. To the last, he resisted arming a workers' militia against the army or provoking civil war, as some supporters advocated. Repression of the

Communists followed; land was returned to landowners, and thousands of Indian peasants were killed. Shifting army factions would rule Guatemala from 1954 until the 1980s with only a brief civilian presidency from 1966 to 1969.

The Cold War had begun in earnest in Latin America. The rollback in Guatemala made clear the old-"new" prime mission for the Latin American armed forces: defending *la patria* against internal subversion, communism, and disorder. The Cold War brought convergence between the constitutional, statutory, and traditional roles of the region's armed forces and the U.S. bipolar military-security agenda for the 1950s. Just five years later, the Cold War would produce a real security threat to the United States and the hemisphere: the Cuban Revolution. It would also bring real war—insurgencies, guerrilla movements, and continental schemes for establishing socialism in Latin America.

From Arbenz to Fidel (and Che Guevara)

The ouster of Arbenz received vigorous support from the United States' closest friends in mid-1950s Latin America: military dictators in Cuba, the Dominican Republic, Peru, Nicaragua, El Salvador, and Venezuela. These dictators, with the exception of Odría in Peru, presided over armed forces and related security services that constituted patrimonial constabularies whose main functions were internal order and terrorizing political opposition. Garrison based, they operated as mafia-like enforcers dominating organized vice, smuggling, and racketeering. They also routinely extorted money from ordinary citizens. Associated as they were with the dictators and the corruption they represented, their level of professionalism was minimal; they enjoyed little prestige and elicited much fear.

The Cuban military, not the worst of the lot but certainly without professional merit, was commanded by a nepotistic clique headed by the Tabernillas family. Nepotism and corruption also extended to the national police. After the coup that brought him to power in 1952, Fulgencio Batista courted the armed forces with the same sort of public largesse used by Perón in Argentina and Pérez Jiménez in Venezuela: housing subsidies; technical education; special social security, health, and pension programs; and vast opportunities for off-the-books income. General Francisco Tabernillas, Batista's chief of staff, admonished the traditional political parties for having ignored the armed forces' needs or, as he put it, for ignoring the three other "parties": the yellow, blue, and white (army, police, and navy).[27] Batista thoroughly politicized the officer corps and excluded younger officers from promotions and choice assignments. The armed forces became, almost literally, a mafiacracy.[28]

Factional strife and a coup plot in 1956 by Colonel Ramón Barquín, who had represented Cuba in the Inter-American Defense System and served with U.S. intelligence, reflected discontent within the armed forces. A naval mutiny in 1957, eventually overcome by Batista's supporters, involved members of all the armed services and civilian political parties. Batista purged hundreds of officers from the armed forces (in 1955 the total army strength was estimated at 19,000), reinforced political criteria in posting and promotions, and further militarized the public administration. Army and navy officers controlled regional and local government, the custom houses, the Ministry of Labor, and other public services.

The Cuban army received new shipments of U.S. arms, Jeeps, and fighter planes (for which it had no pilots) as part of the Inter-American security system. Batista was a milder version of Caribbean dictator than his counterpart in the Dominican Republic, Rafael Trujillo, and even somewhat less objectionable than General Pérez Jiménez in Venezuela. Admittedly, he had not served in Korea, like General Rojas Pinilla who took control of Colombia in 1953, and he was less violently anti-Communist than General Odría in Peru and the consummate U.S. sycophant, Anastasio Somoza in Nicaragua. He fit, however, with his times and those of the hemisphere. Like his dictator colleagues, he faced occasional domestic conspiracies and even armed forces' discontent.

Unlike his counterparts, however, after 1956 Batista confronted a guerrilla movement in the Sierra Maestra Mountains led by a revolutionary lawyer named Fidel Castro, who was accompanied by an Argentine doctor, Ernesto "Che" Guevara, and a small band of fighters. Batista used Castro's movement to justify intensified repression, controlling the urban areas with brutal police-state tactics and torture of dissidents. He initially gave little military importance to Castro's rebels, who were able to defeat local rural guard units far from Havana. His army, however, was unprepared for counterinsurgency and mountain fighting. According to Louis Pérez, Jr., "the mold in which the American Military Defense Assistance Program (MDAP) cast the Cuban military . . . weakened the rural effectiveness of the army. Prepared to meet an illusory Soviet assault on the Western Hemisphere, the Cuban military institution may very well have conducted itself commendably against a Russian invasion of the island."[29]

Pérez's charitable assessment aside, the army lacked leadership, fighting morale, and a commitment to defeat the rebels. Castro announced that he was not at war against the armed forces but against the dictatorship, and he called on soldiers to desert. Benign treatment of prisoners encouraged defection, and Castro's ability to avoid large-unit engagements allowed him to achieve numerous small victories while mobilizing internal and international political support. In the end, the U.S. government deserted Batista (as did many Cuban soldiers) and imposed an arms embargo on the island that forced the dictator to flee on January 1, 1959. The defeat of the Cuban army by Castro's guerrillas embarked Latin America and the United States on an era of revolutionary and counterrevolutionary warfare that would change the region's armed forces' main concern to the threat of internal insurgency. They would be dedicated now not to an illusory Soviet invasion but to saving their *patrias* from the threat of international communism and its hemispheric instruments: Fidel Castro, Che Guevara, and the export of Cuba's revolution to other Latin American countries.

With rare exceptions, the Latin American armed forces were not prepared for this mission. If they were to achieve success, the United States would have to reinvent the Rio Treaty to focus on internal security missions. In both the Caracas Declaration of Solidarity and the ouster of Arbenz there were precedents for protecting the region against "extra-hemispheric doctrines" such as Marxism and communism and efforts to install Communist governments. This doctrinal and treaty-based rationale had to be implemented in effective economic and military measures if the threat of Cuban-inspired insurgencies was to be successfully confronted. Castro's purge of the Cuban military and his well-publicized, internationally broadcast executions of officers provided sufficient motivation for the Latin American armed forces to recognize in the Cuban Revolution a real threat not only to the United States but also to their own institutions and their own version of *la patria*.

Castro also sought to defend his *patria*, proclaiming as his slogan, *Patria o muerte, Venceremos*. His version of *la patria*, however—a socialist, Marxist-Leninist, internationalist, anti-imperialist concept—would be incompatible with the traditional nationalism, religiosity, and historical vision of the Latin American armed forces. His eventual identification of the Cuban Revolution with Soviet foreign policy and the construction of communism would directly challenge the Rio Treaty and the Cold War framework established since 1945. Thus, for different reasons, the Cuban Revolution posed the most fundamental challenge to U.S. foreign policy and to the Latin American armed forces since the nineteenth-century independence wars. The U.S. and Latin American response to the Cuban Revolution would dominate domestic and regional politics until the 1990s. It would also dramatically increase the political role of the Latin American armed forces.

The U.S. Response and the Latin American Military, 1959–1962[30]

The Cuban revolutionaries, even before Fidel's public announcement that the island would build a socialist society, proclaimed their commitment to collaborate in the destruction of dictatorship in the hemisphere. Cuba's so-called *foco* model—revolution sparked by small groups of guerrillas in the countryside—would be exported to Central America, the Caribbean, and South America. A later-day version of the Caribbean Legion, this time with Cuban-trained and -equipped guerrilla fighters, would light the fires of revolution in the hemisphere and overcome repressive dictatorships and the hegemony of U.S. imperialism. Guevara took charge of this romantic venture; the face of "Che" the "heroic Guerrilla" and slogans of the Cuban Revolution adorned walls, banners, and placards at universities and in mass demonstrations from the Caribbean to the Río de la Plata.

In 1960, Guevara published *Guerrilla Warfare*, a tedious compendium of practical prescriptions concerning the organization, supply, personal qualities, and operations of guerrilla bands. Theoretically it added little, if anything, to previous contributions by Clausewitz, Lenin, Stalin, Mao, and Vietnam's Vo Nguyen Giap. Its most important political contribution was to reject orthodox Marxism's patient wait for "objective conditions" to favor revolution and to insist that guerrilla *focos* could create "subjective conditions" that would make revolution possible. At first, Che limited the applicability of this theory to the "Caribbean dictatorships" most like Batista's in Cuba, such as Somoza's in Nicaragua and Trujillo's in the Dominican Republic. This restriction left few areas for *foco* operations, inasmuch as only six military-dominated regimes remained in Latin America in 1959: Paraguay, Guatemala, Nicaragua, El Salvador, Haiti, and the Dominican Republic. Fidel and Che's revolutionary aspirations stretched quickly to the "oligarchic dictatorships"—that is, the elected governments that they claimed sought to legitimate capitalist domination of Latin America's masses. Che's 1963 article, "Guerrilla Warfare: A Method," preached the need for *focos* to force the "unmasking" of the oligarchic dictatorships, following Fidel's observation that the Andes Mountains would be the Sierra Maestra of South America.[31]

Guevara was committed to socialist revolution through armed struggle directed by a revolutionary vanguard (a *foco* vanguard, but not necessarily a Communist party one). He believed that the revolution could only be achieved by destroying the prevailing repressive military-bureaucratic apparatus of Latin America's capitalist states. Translation: destroy the existing military and political institutions of the region; destroy the version of *patria* in place there and substitute a revolutionary socialist *patria*. The phrase *Patria o muerte*, borrowed from Cuba's nationalist independence leader and anti-imperialist, José Martí, referred to a different *patria* (in the same territory with citizens transformed into the "new socialist man") from that defended by Latin America's armed forces.

Cuban and Cuban-trained guerrilla fighters began an influx into mainland Latin America within months of Fidel's victory. Rumors of an invasion of Guatemala prompted President Eisenhower to order naval patrols into the Caribbean, and in March 1960 he approved a CIA plan to organize and equip an exile army to invade Cuba, or perhaps to replay the 1954 overthrow of Arbenz in Guatemala. Economic sanctions against the Havana government were met with reprisals, the nationalization of U.S. companies, and the signing of trade and other agreements with the Soviet Union. The Soviets offered military assistance and training of Cuban pilots in Czechoslovakia to fly Soviet MiG jets.

In April 1961 the United States botched an invasion with a Cuban exile force at the Bay of Pigs and embarrassed itself at the United Nations with transparent deceptions that denied culpability for the gross violation of international law and the island's sovereignty. After twenty months the United States ransomed over 1,100 prisoners taken at the Bay of Pigs for food and medicine. At the Inter-American Defense Board the Cuban delegates were first shunned, then denied classified information, and later barred. In October 1962, the same month that the IADB opened the Inter-American Defense College to provide ten-month courses and high-level contacts for elite Latin American lieutenant colonels and colonels (or their equivalent in navy, air force, or other security forces) from the Rio Pact countries, Washington and Moscow went to the nuclear brink when it was discovered that the Soviets were installing medium-range, nuclear-capable missiles in Cuba. After global tensions reached a peak with U.S. and Soviet vessels squared off to test the U.S "quarantine" of Cuba, the Soviets agreed to withdraw the missiles. In return, the United States promised in a secret memorandum that it would not invade Cuba. Castro lost face, as the Soviets agreed to remove the missiles without consultation, but gained immunity (lasting into the 1990s) from direct U.S. military intervention.

Newly elected President John F. Kennedy inherited both the Bay of Pigs invasion plan and the drastic change in inter-American relations implied by the Cuban Revolution and a real Soviet presence in the hemisphere. In January

1961, State Department officialdom declared that "the military arm of Mr. [Nikita] Khrushchev's . . . doctrine is clearly guerrilla warfare. . . . we have, indeed, begun to take the problem of guerrilla warfare seriously."[32] The State Department's Policy Planning Staff prepared a paper entitled "A New Concept for Hemispheric Defense and Development" (January 1961), concluding that the United States should phase out programs that unrealistically assign continental defense roles to Latin American armed forces and "to influence Latin American military leaders towards greater emphasis on maintaining intra-hemispheric peace and contributing to the internal development of their countries . . . in executing a concept of defense through development, with all [that] this entails."[33] What it entailed were significant and overt military role expansion, attention to economic development, civic action (development programs and "winning the hearts and minds" of civilians to keep them from supporting Communist guerrillas), and counterinsurgency to combat the guerrillas and their supporters militarily.

By September 1961, Congress passed the Internal Development and Security Act, changing the avowed purpose of military assistance to Latin America from hemispheric defense to internal defense and development. This new rationale was part of the Kennedy administration's reassessment of global military strategy and implementation of a so-called flexible response doctrine. However, the missile crisis agreement precluded direct U.S. invasion to eliminate the Castro government after 1962. The Kennedy administration's "flexible response" would therefore have to assume the existence of a hostile Soviet ally ninety miles from Florida, committed publicly to fomenting revolution in the hemisphere.

This challenge to U.S. foreign policy and the inter-American security system generated an expanded and refocused military assistance program and the Alliance for Progress with Latin American countries to halt the spread of subversion. As the Cold War reached the region, it heated up into prolonged, nasty, internal insurgency and counterinsurgency campaigns. Superpower conflict by proxy dominated regional politics and inter-American relations from 1961 until the early 1990s. These conflicts drastically modified the relations between the U.S. military and its Latin American counterparts, the military tasks and doctrine of the Latin American armed forces (and some U.S. forces covertly engaged in counterinsurgency campaigns), and the character of Latin American politics. By 1964 a tide of new military regimes swept over much of the region, bringing with it an old-"new" national security doctrine and old-"new" methods of repression. To save "democracy" and *la patria* from Soviet- and Cuban-inspired communism, and to ensure "national security," the post-World War II generation of Cold War officers mounted a draconian crusade against *la patria*'s enemies.

Notes

1. *El Tiempo* (Bogotá), June 15, 1953, cited in Samuel L. Baily, *Nationalism in Latin America* (New York: Alfred A. Knopf, 1971): 170–72.

2. Samuel Eliot Morison, *History of United States Naval Operations in World War II: The Battle of the Atlantic, September 1939–May 1943* (Boston: Little, Brown and Co., 1947), 1:14, cited in Raymond Estep, *United States Military Aid to Latin America* (Maxwell Air Force Base, AL: Aerospace Studies Institute, Air University, 1966): 6.

3. Estep (1966): 9–10.

4. Ibid.: 36–39.

5. Included in ibid., appendix B, are details on individual Latin American country cooperation with the U.S. World War II effort.

6. Jack Child, *Unequal Alliance: The Inter-American Military System, 1938–1978* (Boulder, CO: Westview Press, 1980): Chapter 2.

7. Ibid.: 42.

8. Ibid.: 46.

9. Ibid.

10. Memo for the Assistant Secretary of War, 10 January 1945, OPD 336 LA, Entry 418, Record Group 165, National Archives, cited in Child (1980): 73.

11. Cited in J. Lloyd Mecham, *A Survey of United States-Latin American Relations* (Boston: Houghton Mifflin Co., 1965): 173.

12. Cited in Mecham (1965): 163.

13. For detailed descriptions of the variations in the 1944–1949 experience see Bethell and Roxborough, eds. (1992).

14. For details on this conflict and the documents exchanged among the parties see *Applications of the Inter-American Treaty of Reciprocal Assistance, 1948–1956* (Washington, DC: Pan-American Union, 1957): 19–55. The Caribbean Legion also provoked other applications of the Rio Treaty in Haiti and the Dominican Republic in 1949 and 1950. With support from the Cuban and Guatemalan governments, the Legion or its "disbanded" supporters attempted to oust dictators in Haiti, the Dominican Republic, and Nicaragua. The Rio Treaty was invoked again by Costa Rica against Nicaragua in 1955 when Calderón's supporters invaded from Nicaragua and, in the same year, by Ecuador, claiming that Peru intended an armed aggression.

15. Cited in Mercedes Muñoz Guillén, *El estado y la abolición del ejército, 1914–1949* (San José: Editorial Porvenir, 1990): 159.

16. See "The World in a Funhouse Mirror," *NACLA Report* (November/December 1983): 2–34, for a succinct summary of U.S. Cold War policy.

17. José O. Maldifassi and Pier A. Abetti, *Defense Industries in Latin American Countries* (Westport, CT: Praeger, 1994): 17.

18. NSC-141 ("A Report to the National Security Council by the Secretaries of State and Defense and the Director for Mutual Security on Reexamination of United States Programs for National Security, 19 January 1953"), cited in Richard H. Immerman, *The CIA in Guatemala* (Austin: University of Texas Press, 1982): 11.

19. Mutual Security Act of 1959, cited in Estep (1966): 26–27.

20. Child (1980): 117.

21. Lieuwen (1960): 229.

22. Cited in Immerman (1982): 10.

23. Diary entry, 11 June 1949, Dwight D. Eisenhower, *Diaries*, cited in Immerman (1982): 16.

24. Cited in Immerman (1982): 18.

25. "Declaration of Solidarity for the Preservation of the Political Integrity of the American States against International Communist Intervention," Tenth Inter-American Conference, March 28, 1954, Caracas, Venezuela.

26. See Immerman (1982); Stephen Schlesinger and Stephen Kinzer, *Bitter Fruit: The Untold Story of the American Coup in Guatemala* (Garden City, NY: Doubleday, 1982); Ronald Schneider, *Communism in Guatemala* (New York: Octagon Books, reprint, 1979); and Piero Gleijeses, *Shattered Hope: The Guatemalan Revolution and the United States, 1944–1954* (Princeton: Princeton University Press, 1991).

27. Pérez (1976): 132.

28. Thomas P. Wickham-Crowley, *Guerrillas and Revolutionaries in Latin America* (Princeton: Princeton University Press, 1992), uses the term "mafiacracy" to refer to "patrimonial praetorian regimes." The term was particularly appropriate for Cuba in the 1950s with the government's direct connection to U.S. crime syndicates, gambling, prostitution, and abortion enterprises.

29. Pérez (1976): 155.

30. This section draws heavily on Brian Loveman and Thomas M. Davies, Jr., eds., "*Guerrilla Warfare*, Revolutionary Theory, and Revolutionary Movements in Latin America," in Brian Loveman and Thomas M. Davies, Jr., eds., *Che Guevara, Guerrilla Warfare*, 3d ed. (Wilmington, DE: Scholarly Resources, 1997): 3–37.

31. Che Guevara, "Guerrilla Warfare: A Method," in Loveman and Davies, eds. (1997): 148–62.

32. Walt W. Rostow, "Countering Guerrilla Attack," in Frank M. Osanka, ed., *Modern Guerrilla Warfare* (New York: Free Press of Glencoe, 1962): 464–71.

33. U.S. State Department, "A New Concept for Hemisphere Defense and Development," January 15, 1961, cited in Child (1980): 147–48.

6

La Patria and the Cold War

From the Bay of Pigs to the Gulf of Fonseca

> Our every action is a battle cry against imperialism, and a battle hymn for the people's unity against the great enemy of mankind: the United States of America.
>
> —Che Guevara, "Message to the Tricontinental," 1967

The threat of "more Cubas" turned President Kennedy's attention urgently to Latin America. His liberal idealism and anticommunism inspired the Alliance for Progress, which sought to promote social justice and economic growth and a simultaneous counterinsurgency war to combat Soviet-Cuban-inspired revolutionaries. The Alliance for Progress proposed political and economic reforms financed by billions of dollars in public and private investment. Over the next decade it largely failed to meet its objectives. Meanwhile, the counterinsurgency wars supported by U.S. assistance programs further militarized Latin American politics and brought new-style military governments to power: antipolitical national security regimes committed to long-term military rule. Twenty years after Fidel Castro defeated Fulgencio Batista and entered Havana, almost two-thirds of Latin Americans were living under military governments. Defending *la patria*'s "eternal values" required brutal counterinsurgency campaigns and resulted in thousands of people dead, tortured, "disappeared," and exiled.

Cuba and U.S. Latin American Policy

Officially recognizing that desperate poverty and injustice incubated social discontent, the United States promoted the Alliance for Progress "to bring a better life to all the people of the continent," and "to strengthen democratic institutions through application of the principle of self-determination by the people."[1] To convince a reluctant Congress to fund the Alliance, Kennedy warned that failure to meet the Cuban challenge risked "a grave danger that desperate people will turn to communism or other forms of tyranny as their only hope for change. Well-organized, skillful, and strongly financed forces are constantly urging them to take that course."[2]

Kennedy announced the Alliance for Progress in March 1961, only one month before he authorized the disastrous Bay of Pigs invasion intended to overthrow Castro with a CIA-trained and -equipped exile army. Castro's army and militia defeated the invasion force and humiliated the United States before world opinion.[3] Not only could an avowedly anti-U.S. regime survive ninety miles from Florida, but it also could resist the sort of U.S. intervention that had ousted the Guatemalan government in 1954. In 1962, however, Washington and Moscow nearly went to war over nuclear-capable missiles installed in Cuba. Without consulting Castro, the Soviets agreed to remove the missiles, making clear the limits of their commitment in the Caribbean and highlighting the connection between the Cuban Revolution and superpower global conflict. Castro's October 1962 setback was bittersweet. As part of the agreement ending the U.S.-Soviet missile crisis, the United States promised not to invade Cuba. This promise allowed a revolutionary socialist government to survive in the Americas as both a platform for Latin American insurgency and a military and political asset for the Soviets until the late 1980s.

The Alliance for Progress supposedly would inhibit "more Cubas" and limit the influence of revolutionary parties and movements. A play on the Spanish verb *parar* (to stop) gave Kennedy's new policy a different translation for Latin American revolutionaries: the Alliance Stops Progress (*la alianza para el progreso*). For this policy to be effective required military and law-enforcement measures against guerrilla bands and leftist political movements. Such military and police action implied dramatic changes in the operations of Latin American armed forces and in U.S. military assistance programs. It also required changes in doctrine to emphasize internal war and the dangers of international communism within the hemisphere. Small, poorly trained, technically outdated armies and constabularies had to be converted into effective counterinsurgency forces.

After 1961, with U.S. support, Latin American armies went to war against internal subversion and international communism. Some of these wars were brief and decisive; others lasted for decades. Insurgencies and civil wars ignited, flamed, were extinguished, reignited, and crossed frontiers.[4] To the early 1970s, the most important rural insurgencies operated in Guatemala, Nicaragua, Venezuela, Colombia, Peru, and Bolivia. Less successful ones were quickly suppressed in Uruguay and Argentina. Mexico also experienced limited guerrilla warfare, especially in the state of Guerrero where Lucio Cabañas led the Army of the Poor and Peasants' Brigade against Injustice until the army's counterinsurgency campaign mostly ended the threat in 1974 (although violence, banditry, and drug trafficking continued). A small rural guerrilla movement (Araguaia Guerrilla Force, or FOGUERA) inspired by the Brazilian Communist party and financed by the Albanian government also gave the Brazilian military some practical experience in counterinsurgency. According to Colonel Alvaro de Souza Pinheiro, "About three years after the start of the counterinsurgency campaign, and having collected a great number of important lessons learned for all levels of command, the most dangerous center of rural guerrillas in Brazil was eliminated. Furthermore, the Brazilian Armed Forces had established a sound basis for doctrine and operations in jungle and mountain environments."[5] Urban guerrillas added to the violence, most seriously in Venezuela, Brazil, Uruguay, and Argentina.[6] Defeated or pacified temporarily, these guerrilla movements reorganized, changed tactics, and repeatedly warred on Latin American governments.

With the exception of Colombia, where guerrilla movements, bandit gangs, and political armies had operated since the 1920s, the post-1961 insurgencies had no recent parallels in the region. Until his death in 1967 at the hands of U.S.-trained (and -accompanied) Bolivian special forces, most rural insurgencies were inspired by Che Guevara's (and Regis Debray's) *foco* theory. This method for revolution relied on small cadres of guerrilla fighters (*focos*) operating in the countryside and mountains who would eventually gather broad popular support and attain military victory. They attempted to create the conditions necessary to topple incumbent governments as supposedly had occurred in Cuba from 1956 to 1959.[7]

Foco theory challenged conventional Marxist insistence on the leading role of a vanguard party in making revolution and on not initiating revolutionary wars of national liberation where the objective conditions necessary for successful revolution were lacking. It also rejected the Maoist argument that guerrilla forces should necessarily be instruments of a revolutionary party—not autonomous agents of revolution. By the late 1960s most revolutionaries recognized the many political, strategic, and tactical limitations of the *foco* thesis. From this recognition emerged more sophisticated, less romantic, and more long-term strategies adapted from the Vietnam War experience. Summed up in the term "prolonged popular war," the post-1960s revolutionary movements combined diverse ideological and organizational strategies for revolution, made alliances with civilian political parties and religious, labor, and human rights organizations, and created political fronts. They also orchestrated international propaganda campaigns in the effort to influence U.S. public opinion. Despite these adjustments in theory and tactics, before 1979 no guerrilla army succeeded in emulating Castro's victory against Batista.[8]

Counterrevolutionary warfare changed the Latin American armed forces, their role in politics, and their relations with the United States. They suffered casualties and public criticism while asking themselves why insurgencies had arisen and why government leaders had been unable to devise political responses to the challenges of development. Returning to the lessons of French, German, Italian, and Spanish tutors, and to definitions of national security that encompassed technological and economic development, they concluded that failed political leadership had seeded *la patria* with the revolutionary weeds that they were now forced to pull out by the roots. To inhibit the weeds' spread, to sanitize *la patria,* required not only immediate military measures but also drastic political and institutional transformations. Eventually, they also concluded that given the weakness of government institutions and political parties, and the incompetence of civilian politicians, only military institutions could successfully direct such profound changes. A short experiment with an institutional military regime instead of the old-style personalist military coups occurred in Ecuador from 1963 to 1966 and was established as a regional trend after the 1964 Brazilian coup.[9]

Latin American armies prevented revolutionary movements from winning military victory or deposing incumbent governments until 1979, when the Sandinista National Liberation Front (FSLN) in Nicaragua ignited a popular insurrection that ousted the last dictator of the Somoza dynasty (see Chapter 7). The guerrillas and revolutionary movements did "succeed," however, in provoking a succession of coups, military governments, and massive human rights violations that made the 1960–1980 decades a nightmarish blur of guerrilla and terrorist attacks, counterrevolutionary repression, and militarization of politics.

Meanwhile, succeeding U.S. presidential administrations slightly changed the spin of Latin American policy and added ostensibly new doctrines (notably the Mann Doctrine in 1964 under President Lyndon Johnson and the Nixon Doctrine in 1969) to Kennedy's Alliance for Progress. Underlying the superficial policy changes was a consistent commitment to limiting Soviet and Cuban influence and halting revolutionary advances in the hemisphere. This commitment derived partly from the perception that guerrilla war in Latin America was an extension of the Vietnam War (and of Soviet policy favoring wars of national liberation in the Third World). Guevara's call on Latin Americans to "create a second or third Vietnam" and to defeat capitalism "in a world confrontation . . . in a long war . . . and a cruel war" confirmed Washington policymakers' views on the Cuban threat.[10] Table 6–1 lists major benchmarks in U.S. policy, Latin American counterinsurgency efforts, and the rise of the antipolitical military regimes after 1963.

Table 6–1. U.S. Policy and Militarization of Latin American Politics, 1963–1979

Benchmark	*Year(s)*	*U.S. President*
Central American Defense Council (CONDECA) created	1963	Kennedy
Ecuador coup	1963	Kennedy
Mann Doctrine	1964	Johnson
Brazil coup (military regime 1964–85)	1964	Johnson
Bolivia coup (military presidents 1964–82 with brief interlude)	1964	Johnson
Invasion of Dominican Republic	1965	Johnson
Argentina coup (Gen. Onganía)	1966	Johnson
Che Guevara killed in Bolivia	1967	Johnson
Peru coup (military regime 1968–80)	1968	Nixon
Panama coup (military regime 1968–81)	1968	Nixon
Rockefeller Report	1969	Nixon
Nixon Doctrine	1969	Nixon
Popular Unity government in Chile	1970–73	Nixon
Bolivia coup (Gen. Banzer ousts Gen. Torres)	1971	Nixon
Honduras coup (military regime 1972–82)	1972	Nixon
Ecuador coup (military regime 1972–78)	1972	Nixon
Chile coup (military regime 1973–90)	1973	Nixon
Uruguay coup (military regime 1973–84)	1973	Nixon
Declaration of Ayacucho	1974	Ford
Argentina coup (military regime 1976–83)	1976	Ford
Carter's new human rights policy	1977	Carter
Panama Canal Treaty; Nicaraguan revolution deposes Somoza	1979	Carter
El Salvador coup	1979	Carter

Even before the announcement of President Kennedy's new policies, the Inter-American Defense Board had approved Resolution XLVII in December

1960: "Contribution of the Armed Forces to the Economic and Social Development of the Nations." This resolution recommended that member nations consider using their armed forces in civic projects and suggested that U.S. bilateral assistance might be forthcoming for such efforts.[11] In part a response to the recommendations of President Dwight Eisenhower's Presidential Committee to Study the United States Military Assistance Program, headed by Major General William Draper (which was itself a response to Vice President Richard Nixon's disastrous 1958 Latin American tour), such a recommendation echoed geopolitical and security doctrines familiar to the region's officers.[12]

The new U.S. policies repeated the lessons of the European missions and reaffirmed the armed forces' internal security tasks. Generations of Brazilians, Peruvians, Chileans, and Argentines had heard the message regarding incorporating Indians and peasants into *la patria* and promoting economic development to ensure national security and external defense. In the early 1950s new or reorganized military command and staff schools, such as Brazil's National War College (ESG) and Peru's Center for Higher Military Studies (CAEM), emphasized the need to define national objectives, expand military participation in internal development and defense planning, and become more self-sufficient for weapons and military supplies.

Military officers had long ago identified weak political institutions and poor government performance as impediments to development and inducements to revolution. The failure of public policy and politicians to overcome these deficits in the first half of the twentieth century made *la patria* vulnerable, after 1959, to the Soviet-Cuban threat. U.S. policymakers had finally stumbled onto the obvious due to the Cold War and the Cuban Revolution, but it was old news to Latin American officers. Thus, writing about the "new" social role of the military institutions in 1957, Peruvian Captain Mario Lozada Uribe commented on the important work of Peru's army in road building, communications, and other civic action and then proposed using 30 percent of all armed forces' personnel in the following tasks: agricultural colonization in every military zone; organization and orientation of Indian communities for a better way of life; project studies and construction of roads, railroads, bridges, and communications systems, consistent with the strategic and logistic needs of the nation; creation of industries necessary for national defense; and oversight of civic and moral education, "since that imparted by the Ministry of Education is deficient and antipatriotic."[13] The Mexican army likewise engaged routinely in *labores sociales*, a broad range of civic action, public works, and service delivery missions, particularly in rural areas. Such "non-military" missions preceded the Cold War and the Cuban Revolution by decades (if not centuries) in Latin America.

U.S. policymakers and military advisers were generally ignorant of the Latin American armed forces' professional and institutional evolution. Likewise, they misunderstood the historical internal security mission, variations in national threat perception and military doctrine, and local political nuances. With missionary zeal these advisers sought to remake the Latin American militaries and deploy them as surrogates for U.S. forces in the regional war against communism. Usually biting their tongues, Latin American officers accepted training, weapons, equipment, and other resources to wage their own wars against subversion despite the arrogance, paternalism, and misconceptions of many U.S. personnel.

Even with U.S. training, ideological indoctrination, and new equipment, the Latin American armed forces retained their national idiosyncrasies and their own versions of patriotism. Accepting the counterinsurgency mission, they nevertheless resented Washington's impositions, badgering, and presumptions of superiority. While they respected the technological and professional expertise of U.S. military advisers, they were frustrated by the incomprehension and ignorance of U.S. policymakers, diplomats, and military personnel regarding local history, political circumstances, and sociocultural conditions. This frustration contributed to a love-hate relationship and mistrust between U.S. and Latin American military officers that mirrored diplomatic relations and public opinion in Latin America. It also meant that the region's military governments could maintain or establish relations with the Soviet Union, as in Argentina and Peru; proclaim nationalist agendas, such as renegotiating the Canal Treaty and eventually gaining sovereignty over the Panama Canal Zone (the Torrijos government); or nationalize major U.S. firms, as with the International Petroleum Corporation in Peru and the Gulf Oil concessions in Bolivia in the late 1960s.

Fighting against internal subversion and communism in an alliance of convenience with the United States did not necessarily mean abandoning national aspirations or forgetting historical geopolitical premises that guided military doctrine, deployment, and operations. Likewise, collaborative security and intelligence efforts against guerrilla and insurgent forces never entirely erased traditional threat scenarios and geopolitical premises. Peruvian military planners always looked north to Ecuador and south to Chile as well as inward to the guerrilla threat in the Andes. This viewpoint remained true into the 1990s, as the Peruvians sought to liquidate the military and political challenge of Sendero Luminoso while briefly engaging Ecuadorian troops in a 1995 border skirmish. Argentine military leaders, bent on destroying Communists and errant Peronists after 1976, almost provoked war against Chile in 1978 over longstanding territorial disputes. Similarly, efforts to coordinate the anti-Communist effort through the Central American Defense Council (CONDECA) created in 1963 failed to prevent the so-called Soccer War between El Salvador and Honduras in 1969.

For the United States, however, the most important concern was battling against Soviet "wars of national liberation" and preventing the spread of the Cuban Revolution. From 1961 to 1963 the Kennedy administration built a new counterinsurgency security structure, the army's Special Forces were substantially expanded, and a Special Action Force was installed in the Canal Zone at Fort Gulick, designated for special warfare missions in Latin America. The Southern Command in the Panama Canal Zone shifted its strategic emphasis to counterinsurgency.[14] Antiguerrilla advisory teams began instructing personnel, and groups of officers received jungle warfare training at Fort Gulick and the U.S. Army's Special Forces School at Fort Bragg, North Carolina.

Between 1961 and 1964 the School of the Americas in the Canal Zone (called the U.S. Army Caribbean School until 1963) trained over 16,000 Latin American personnel in counterinsurgency and civic action (with more than one-half from Central America). Military assistance funds for Latin America increased from $48 million in 1958 to almost $92 million in 1961; during the 1960s and 1970s sales of military equipment also surged, as grant-aid gradually declined. Central American and northern South American insurgencies after 1962 further loosened U.S. congressional purse strings to combat communism in the hemisphere, although the importance of military assistance to individual countries varied greatly. In Panama, for example, this assistance accounted for over 30 percent of that country's defense spending from 1964 to 1967 and was also significant in Bolivia (21.9 percent), Uruguay (18.0 percent), Paraguay (17.0 percent), and Ecuador (16.0 percent). In Venezuela, in contrast, despite active insurgencies, U.S. military assistance accounted for less than 1 percent of defense expenditures, and for less than 10 percent in Peru, Chile, El Salvador, the Dominican Republic, Argentina, and Brazil.

Most of the military assistance and sales programs emphasized vehicles for rough terrain, helicopters, communications and surveillance equipment, tactical aircraft, and antiguerrilla infantry weapons. During the 1960s and 1970s the overall effort was organized in various programs: Military Assistance Program (MAP), which included direct grants of arms and equipment; International Military Education and Training (IMET) to train foreign military personnel; Foreign Military Sales (FMS), including credit-assisted sales; Excess Defense Articles (EDA), which permitted transfer of surplus equipment and weapons; and Economic Support Fund (ESF, formerly Security Supporting Assistance Program) to provide cash subsidies and loans to governments facing immediate security threats.[15] In each recipient country a U.S. Military Assistance Advisory Group (MAAG) oversaw the security assistance program and also served informally as a political liaison with the host country's armed forces. The United States valued this channel to the Latin American military, although many more traditional U.S. military officers opposed the shift to an emphasis on unconventional warfare and disliked civic action programs. The Latin Americans used the MAAG group not only as a sounding board and message conduit but also as a way to send misinformation back to Washington policymakers.

The Kennedy administration also alerted police to the Communist threat and taught methods to combat it. To supplement the military programs, the Agency for International Development (AID) established the Inter-American Police Academy at the Canal Zone's Fort Davis in July 1962. Twelve special police-training programs focused on counterinsurgency and counterterrorism were set up in Latin American countries from 1962 to 1963. Police intelligence and operations were militarized and often commanded by military officers. Further, counterinsurgency themes dominated articles in military journals with such colorful titles as "MATA (Military Assistance Training Adviser) Army Conditioning Course Puts Cold Warriors on the Spot";[16] "Damn the Insurrectos"; "Counterinsurgency Courses Conducted Army Wide"; and "Counterinsurgency: Global Termite Control."[17] Such articles paralleled the State Department's Internal Defense and Development (IDAD) concept: "The U.S. should start the process of convincing the Latin American military—however long it may take—that their most patriotic role, and their true defense role, lies in executing a concept of defense through development, with all this entails."[18]

U.S. policymakers initially preferred to ally with legitimately elected governments, and to buttress them with expanded and more professional internal security forces to meet the threat of the Cuban-supported insurgencies. Between 1961 and 1964, however, eight military coups diminished this option and forced the Kennedy and Johnson administrations to reconsider their policy toward military governments (see Table 6–2).

Table 6–2. Latin American Military Coups, 1961–1964*

Country	*Date*
El Salvador	January 24, 1961
Ecuador	November 8, 1961
Argentina	March 29, 1962
Peru	July 18, 1962
Guatemala	March 31, 1963
Ecuador	July 11, 1963
Dominican Republic	September 25, 1963
Honduras	October 8, 1963
Brazil	March 31, 1964
Bolivia	November 4, 1964

*The proclaimed motivation for these coups varied greatly, but the threat of "more Cubas" was a backdrop to each of them.

Military Coups in the 1960s: New and Old Themes

Latin American military leaders, shaken by the Cuban revolutionaries' execution of over six hundred officers and destruction of the old armed forces, sensed the immediate danger for themselves and their institutions posed by weak civilian governments. As usual, they were divided by interservice and intraservice rivalries and by attachment to different political visions: reactionary praetorians defending personalist dictatorships; nationalists favoring a strong role for a modernizing state; moderates opposed to direct military intervention except temporarily, as a last resort, to "stabilize" the country (with ongoing internal security missions against Communists and subversives); liberal internationalists supporting a limited government role in the economy and a larger role for private investment, combined with severe repression of internal subversion; dedicated professionals wishing to evade political responsibilities and maintain the armed forces "above politics"; and an intense minority committed to long-term military rule.

Politically divided as they were, the armed forces nevertheless faced unavoidable military challenges. And they continued to perceive themselves as the ultimate reservoir of patriotism, the last bastion of defense in the war against internal and external enemies. Patriotism and nationalism united the armed forces against internationalist doctrines and subversive movements. The militaries (and police, which were frequently controlled by the minister of defense) could not wait for long-term socioeconomic change to eliminate the conditions that bred discontent. Their constitutional, statutory, professional, and historical missions demanded a military response to the "wars of national liberation" declared against them and *la patria* by revolutionary factions. The revolutionaries declared war on the existing order and on its military institutions. They called for their destruction, as in Cuba. Not only patriotism and constitutional missions but also the armed forces' corporate interests demanded suppression of Cuban-supported and -inspired insurgents—however U.S. policy veered.

The armed forces also feared that established reformist movements such as Aprismo (APRA) in Peru, Peronismo in Argentina, Acción Democrática in Venezuela, and Juan José Arévalo's Revolutionary party in Guatemala (although Arévalo was kept in exile) might radicalize their programs as they sought to compete with the appeal of Fidelismo. Even relatively moderate reformers such as Chilean, Salvadoran, and Venezuelan Christian Democrats and Argentine Radicals posed some threat to the armed forces. After all, supposedly middle-class reformers (like Castro, who had proclaimed himself committed to Cuba's 1940 Constitution and democracy when fighting against Batista in the Sierra Maestra), could "turn" after assuming government responsibilities.

Complicating this scenario, some officers identified with the goals of the nationalist reformist movements that their brother officers despised. Many military nationalists favored expropriation of foreign investments in key economic sectors, less reliance on U.S. military assistance, expansion of public enterprise and defense industries, and populist economic programs that mirrored in some ways the agrarian and social reforms proposed by socialists and social democrats. In rare cases, most notably in Guatemala, the guerrilla leadership included U.S.-trained officers who adopted revolutionary politics and joined the military struggle against the old order. Unmentioned, but unforgotten in military enclaves, was José Figueres and the Partido de Liberación Nacional's solution in Costa Rica: turning barracks into schoolhouses and eliminating the army (at least in name, since a paramilitary police force replaced it).

Most important, the response of the armed forces to guerrilla movements and political radicalism was conditioned by their own national circumstances. The Cold War and the Cuban Revolution were superimposed on the centuries of colonial rule and over one hundred years of unique national political development. By the time Latin American officers confronted the Cuban challenge, the armed forces' political role was everywhere a historical fact. Coups, with varying frequency from country to country, had become "something of the functional equivalent of elections in North America. Leaders are recruited and selected, alternative programs weighed, coalitions built, public opinion consulted, new governments formed, etc. . . . both the electoral and nonelectoral routes to power carry some (but not total) legitimacy."[19]

Understanding the reasons for military coups in the early 1960s requires not only reference to the Cuban Revolution, U.S. policies, and the Cold War but also to historical regional patterns and to immediate national circumstances. A study of military coups from the 1820s to the 1960s found that their incidence, despite periodicity and evident peaks (1820s, 1840s, 1850s, 1870s, 1910–1915, early 1930s, late 1940s, 1962–1964) had been relatively constant.[20] A positive statistical correlation existed between coup cycles and international economic fluctuations, with downturns in economic conditions associated with a slightly increased likelihood of coups. They also occurred, however, in economic good times, to prevent elections that threatened to impose an unacceptable president or to undo election outcomes viewed as unfavorable. They occurred when the armed forces' institutional interests were threatened, when conflicts could not be resolved by civilian political parties, and when military leaders perceived *la patria*'s "transcendental interests" threatened by government foreign and domestic policy—in short, for many reasons other than economic crisis. This pattern continued into the 1950s (the post-Korean War economic recession) and early 1960s. From 1935 to 1964 an average of two successful coups occurred per year in Latin America. The years from 1961 to 1964 were fairly typical in this sense, with the four coups in 1963 somewhat high in number but less than the six revolts involving military participation in 1944 and five in 1948.

Military governments and presidents had been common since the early nineteenth century; just as common were transitions back to civilian regimes. A political role for the armed forces was embedded in Latin American society, evidenced in humor, literature, and art and observable in daily life. Coup attempts and successful coups took place periodically, if less frequently than presidential elections (see Tables 6–3, 6–4). From 1920 to 1960 there occurred at least seventy-eight successful coups.[21]

Table 6–3. Latin American Presidential Elections by Decade, 1840–1986

Decade	*Number of Elections*
1841–1850	12
1851–1860	39
1861–1870	35
1871–1880	45
1881–1890	40
1891–1900	42
1901–1910	40
1911–1920	45
1921–1930	41
1931–1940	43
1941–1950	38
1951–1960	38
1961–1970	35*
1971–1980	14*
1981–1986	21*

Source: Enrique Ochoa, "The Rapid Expansion of Voter Participation in Latin American Presidential Elections, 1845–1986," in James W. Wilkie and David Lorey, eds., *Statistical Abstract of Latin America* 25 (Los Angeles: UCLA Latin American Center Publications, 1987): Table 3424, p. 904.

*Does not include Brazilian elections from 1964 to 1984 because presidents were chosen by the congress.

From 1920 to 1960 successful military coups had occurred in every Latin American country except Mexico and Uruguay. The people of Uruguay suffered irregular regime changes with police and military participation in 1933–34 and 1942, and unsuccessful coups threatened Mexico at least four times before 1940. Likewise, the constitutional foundations for regimes of exception, national security legislation, and statutory assignment to the armed forces of numerous nonmilitary functions were in place long before 1959. To illustrate, in the decade before the Cuban Revolution (1950–1960), there were over one hundred declarations or extensions of a state of siege in Latin America—and this was a period without external or internal war, with perhaps the exception of the massive social violence referred to as *la violencia* in Colombia from 1948 to 1953.[22]

Table 6–4. Successful Military Coups, 1920–1960

Country	*Number of Coups*
Argentina	7
Bolivia	9
Brazil	5
Chile	2
Colombia	2
Costa Rica	1
Cuba	4
Dominican Republic	4
Ecuador	9
El Salvador	6
Guatemala	6
Haiti	5
Honduras	2
Nicaragua	1
Paraguay	7
Peru	4
Venezuela	4

Source: After José Nun, "The Middle-Class Military Coup Revisited," in Abraham Lowenthal and J. Samuel Fitch, eds., *Armies and Politics in Latin America*, rev. ed. (New York: Holmes and Meier, 1986): 60.

For Latin America, the era of insurgency and counterinsurgency commencing in 1959 was a new version of old scenarios of political conflict, competing visions of national objectives and destinies, struggles against social injustice, and competition to control the reins of political power. The Cuban Revolution and the threat of national liberation movements served as a new rationale for the exercise of guardianship, tutelage, and salvation of *la patria*. The new rationale did not eliminate the old ones, whether socioeconomic, political, or institutional.

In many ways, despite the Cold War, the coups that toppled elected civilian presidents from 1961 until November 1964 (see Table 6–2) resembled previous military actions and originated in old political cleavages. They resulted from "hereditary hatreds" and historic patriotic missions, albeit complicated by the Cuban Revolution.[23] Anti-Peronism in Argentina, military-APRA conflicts in Peru, memories of former president Arévalo's reformism and the threat of his imminent reelection in Guatemala, renewed military reformism by the 1948 officer generation in El Salvador, Liberal-Nationalist struggles for power and government sinecures in Honduras, the fight of former Trujillo supporters and competing military factions against Juan Bosch in the Dominican Republic, and the effort to prevent Víctor Paz Estenssoro from succeeding himself and serving a third presidential term in Bolivia all might have led to coups without the Cuban Revolution.

The policy of the United States toward the early-1960s military coups was erratic. In some cases it attempted to prevent coups and even broke off diplomatic relations and cut off military assistance to express its displeasure, as in Honduras and the Dominican Republic in 1963. In Guatemala, however, it clearly sided with the anti-Arévalo forces, encouraging the preventive coup that denied him a return to the presidency. This seeming inconsistency in U.S. policy was congruent with the overall policy objectives for Latin America: prevent "more Cubas"; limit Soviet and Communist influence in the hemisphere; promote political stability; and encourage economic growth through private foreign investment, U.S. economic assistance, and development of Latin American capitalism.

The United States also proclaimed its support for democracy, but this support did not include, in accord with the 1954 Caracas Declaration, the right of Latin Americans to choose Communist or socialist governments. These were defined as extra-hemispheric ideological and political intrusions into the Americas, just as monarchism and fascism had been so defined in the past. The Alliance for Progress was intended to exclude these influences from Latin America in an updated expression of the Monroe Doctrine and the enduring U.S. foreign policy principle of strategic denial—that is, keeping European and other powers out of "our backyard."

As Brigadier General W. A. Enemark, director of the Western Hemisphere region, emphasized in testimony before the Senate Foreign Relations Committee, "if the Alliance for Progress is to have its chance, governments must have the effective force required to cope with subversion, prevent terrorism, and deal with outbreaks of violence before they reach unmanageable proportions."[24] By 1963, and especially after President Kennedy's assassination, the struggle between principled support for democracy versus support for anti-Communist authoritarian governments was won by the latter. The Cuban-supported insurgencies and the Indochinese specter tipped both U.S. leaders and Latin American civil-military elites toward predominantly military responses, subordinating the push for "democracy," civil liberties and rights, and political reform to the requirements of anticommunism and political stability. While this trend intensified under President Johnson, President Kennedy had reiterated his administration's commitment to defeating Communist guerrillas and preventing "more Cubas" just before his death. On November 18, 1963, he declared: "The American states must be ready to come to the aid of any government requesting aid to prevent a takeover aligned to the policies of foreign communism rather than to an internal desire for change. My own country is prepared to do this. We in this hemisphere must also use every resource at our command to prevent the establishment of another Cuba in this hemisphere."[25] Such language was an invitation for "any government" to identify internal opposition with the "policies of foreign communism."

By the end of 1963 the United States plainly gave priority to military counterinsurgency and was willing to accept alliances with a region of dictators who joined in the anti-Communist crusade. However, military assistance also bolstered reformist governments and political movements against guerrilla threats and leftist political challenges. Important examples were the U.S. Army, Navy, Air Force, and Special Forces team sent in 1963 to create a Venezuelan joint operations command to defeat the National Liberation Armed Forces (FALN) guerrillas and the smaller team that advised and better equipped the Chilean armed forces and police before the 1964 presidential election. U.S. military advisers found that the Venezuelan armed forces never held joint exercises and were encumbered by serious interservice rivalries, while in Chile there were also deficiencies in joint operations, and joint actions had not been coordinated with the police (*carabineros*).[26] In both cases U.S. military assistance had clear political objectives: to support elected governments, and to undermine leftist political movements (and do political intelligence on their strength) while improving the professional and technical capabilities of the armed forces. Thus, while the Kennedy and Johnson administrations would accept alliances with military regimes, this was not the preferred outcome of the counterinsurgency programs; indeed, the reverse was true if it could be achieved, as the Chilean, Venezuelan, and Colombian cases made clear.

In 1964 a lieutenant colonel at the U.S. Army War College rhapsodized on the counterinsurgency effort: "Counterinsurgency is by definition geared to military, political, economic and civic action. . . . The major problem before us is to learn to orchestrate the magnificent counterinsurgency resources we have into a single symphony and to persuade the governments we help to apply their energies and resources against the threats that confront them."[27] Such a symphony represented a convergence of U.S. doctrine with Latin American military geopolitical thought and aspirations since the 1920s, with French doctrine on combating revolutionary war derived from the Algerian and Vietnam experiences, and with the newer national security doctrines emerging from the CAEM in Peru and the ESG in Brazil.[28] To prevent "more Cubas" through the Alliance for Progress, counterinsurgency, and civic action meant increased attention to social and economic development, military preparedness, training, and operations, and a more overt political role for the armed forces. This more overt role was accompanied by further government investment in military-related and defense industries and an expanding management role for the region's armed forces in defense and non-defense-related enterprises.

Argentina, Brazil, Chile, and other South American countries created new weapons industries and expanded existing firms. Brazil (along with Israel) became a leading arms exporter outside NATO and the Soviet bloc. Argentine, Brazilian, and Chilean ordnance and infantry weapons reached Africa, the Middle East, and back to the United States and Europe.[29] Even the Central American states and Mexico developed some small-arms manufactures under license from European firms, along with diversifying suppliers, as a hedge against diplomatic and political bullying by the United States. In addition, by the late-1960s, European, Israeli, and Soviet-bloc suppliers eroded the U.S. quasi-monopoly on arms sales in Latin America, which contributed to a regional arms race amid the supposed unified effort against internal insurgencies. Between 1968 and 1972, for example, both France and the United Kingdom sold more military equipment to Latin America than did the United States, an unintended consequence of the wars against subversion.[30]

Ultimately, the Alliance for Progress had many unintended consequences. The counterinsurgency operations and the expanded political and economic roles of the armed forces further militarized politics, eroded civil liberties and rights, and weakened civilian institutions. Even where civilian governments formally survived, military officials, garrisons, patrols, and courts became de facto governments in rural hinterlands and in regional towns and cities (for example, in Colombia, Venezuela, and Honduras). While the United States had employed contradictory rhetoric and policies in responding to Latin American military coups from 1961 to 1964, President Johnson and his principal advisers on the region decided that military governments were preferable to either "more Cubas" or to nationalist, populist disorder. In February 1965, following the 1964 coups in Brazil and Bolivia, Assistant Secretary of State for Latin American Affairs Thomas Mann submitted a memorandum to the House Subcommittee on Inter-American Affairs entitled "Current United States Policy in Latin America." The memorandum stated:

> The United States is playing a decisive role in the successful defense of this hemisphere against Communist aggression and subversion. Both on our own, and in close cooperation with other American governments, we have contributed in large measure to the defeats inflicted on the Cubans, Chinese, and Soviet Communists in their efforts to expand their rule and influence throughout Latin America. . . . It is our hope and intention that, with adequate defense against totalitarian intervention, Latin America will achieve further significant progress on the path of modern democracy.[31]

Figure 6–1. "Platform for Democracy?" by Roy B. Justus, *Minneapolis Star*, 1963. Courtesy of the *Star Tribune*, Minneapolis

Less than two months later, Mann counseled Johnson to invade the Dominican Republic to prevent a supposed Communist takeover, making clear both the administration's ineptitude and priorities. The Mann Doctrine made explicit what Latin American officers already understood: between authoritarian anticommunism and populist democracy that swerved too far to the political left, or seemed to adversely affect U.S. interests, the United States would choose the former. Democracy could wait.

Events in the Dominican Republic illustrated the complexity and hypocrisy of this policy. After supporting Rafael Trujillo's dictatorship from 1930 to 1961, collaborating in his assassination in 1961, and supporting his protégé, Joaquín Balaguer, the United States found Juan Bosch's reformist Partido Revolucionario Dominicano (PRD) a threat to inter-American security in 1965. The United States invaded the country to prevent "more Cubas" and ensured that reformist officers supporting Bosch were defeated.[32] Washington policymakers then propped up the twelve-year presidential regime of Balaguer (1966–1978). Corrupt elections and Balaguer's personal charisma allowed civilian government instead of direct military rule. Yet like the military regimes elsewhere after 1964, the Dominican armed forces colonized the public administration, became the main government presence in the countryside (reminiscent of the military role in eighteenth-century Bourbon Spain), and repressed dissidents in the name of anticommunism. Political assassinations, "disappearances," and torture were routine tools of Dominican "democracy."

Figure 6–2. "The Express Will Be a Trifle Late" by Roy B. Justus, *Minneapolis Star*, 1963. Courtesy of the *Star Tribune*, Minneapolis

As for the armed forces, they remained highly politicized and corrupt, with their loyalty to Balaguer purchased through sinecures, graft, and personal ties. U.S. military assistance and efforts to professionalize the military institutions barely dented the tradition of patronage that determined promotions and duty assignments. According to G. Pope Atkins, an expert on the Dominican military: "By the end of the Balaguer regime, high-ranking military men, with few exceptions, possessed important commercial interests and had investments in all economic sectors. With few professional incentives or motivations, personal interests were paramount and led to corruption down to the lowest officer level."[33] Still, the Dominican Republic was a "democracy," anti-Communist and anti-Fidelista—the main concern of U.S. regional security policy. Where this could not be achieved with sham democracies, the Mann Doctrine allowed for other methods.

Insurgency, Counterinsurgency, and *la Patria*

Between 1962 and the early 1970s sundry rural guerrilla movements and urban revolutionaries declared war on capitalist society and its political institutions. They proclaimed their commitment to some version of socialism; attacked police, military units, and economic targets (for example, by "expropriating" funds from banks); sabotaged communications, transport, and production facilities; and kidnapped businessmen and diplomats for ransom and for show. U.S. diplomats were frequent targets; in 1968, Guatemalan revolutionaries killed the U.S. Ambassador. They did so in the name of revolution, believing in the historical inevitability (with a little help from the guerrillas) of the victory of socialism.

Cuba and its Latin American emulators identified the United States as the principal buttress of the old order and, therefore, as their main enemy. They disdainfully labeled the Latin American armed forces as puppets and hired killers of the imperialists. Failure by the revolutionaries to understand the ferocious nationalism and institutional pride of the region's armed forces, even when they were also militarily inept and riddled with corruption, as in parts of South America and much of the Caribbean and Central America, fueled the cruel wars of extermination from the early 1960s into the 1980s.

Revolutionaries could not declare war on the existing order and its armed forces without provoking counterrevolutionary warfare, with or without U.S. assistance. Once war had been declared—by the revolutionaries—the military had constitutional and statutory missions to fulfill. Where there was doubt regarding the military's mission, civilian governments ordered the armed forces into combat against the insurgents. Whatever the real strength of the insurgent movements, their rhetoric was combative and deeply offended the region's armed forces. And their bullets, dynamite, sabotage, kidnappings, and assassinations were alarming. Their violent actions were criminal and their methods military. For Latin American governments and the armed forces, these revolutionary challenges made credible the need for counterrevolutionary legislation, suspension of civil liberties and rights, and persecution of suspected terrorists. Emulation of the Cuban guerrilla road to revolution by Latin American leftists invited repression.

The political right, though skeptical of the Alliance for Progress and opposed to new taxes, social welfare programs, liberalized labor legislation, agrarian reforms, and more "democracy," welcomed police and military repression of revolutionaries and their sympathizers. Mindful of past inconsistencies and unilateral changes in U.S. foreign policy, old-line conservatives and moderates nevertheless joined in a pragmatic alliance with social reformers that relied on U.S. and domestic counterinsurgency programs to prevent the spread of socialism.

Military assistance to Latin America from the early 1960s until the early 1980s experienced many shifts in target countries, types and quality of resources provided, and rationale. Active insurgencies brought military assistance, stepped-up civic action projects, and economic aid. U.S. foreign policy mimicked a fire brigade—respond to the alarm, snuff out the flames, and then proceed to the next brushfire. In some instances, such as in Guatemala (1966–1969), Colombia (mid-1960s), Venezuela (1961–1965), and Bolivia (1967), U.S. military assistance probably tipped the balance against guerrilla movements. In other instances, guerrillas would have been defeated without this assistance, and Latin American armed forces obtained weapons and training elsewhere.

Washington's domestic politics significantly influenced security policy toward particular countries, making the United States an unreliable partner for the Latin American military. When Cold War sentiments and fierce anticommunism predominated, moral and legal rationales for aid (for example, concern with human rights violations) played a minimal role. In contrast, during the administration of President Jimmy Carter (1977–1981), Latin American armed forces faced aid cutoffs and public sanction from Washington. Voices in the U.S. Congress protested support for military regimes and, from the early 1960s into the 1980s, repeated legislative hearings highlighted repression and human rights abuses that embarrassed Latin American governments, the Pentagon, and the foreign policy establishment. For Latin American officers, public discussion of security issues and overwhelming evidence of U.S. political schizophrenia merely confirmed that the regional hegemon was a capricious ally, that saving *la patria* ultimately rested on their shoulders. They believed that the fate of their nations and their transcendental national interests could not be safely left to the whim of U.S. public opinion and the zigzags of U.S. foreign policy.

Whether the overall impact of this military assistance was to encourage coups, support dictatorships, and intensify repression, or had sometimes positive effects in consolidating reformist regimes and further professionalizing the region's armed forces, is still debated. In practice, military assistance programs varied so widely in application and impact in different countries at different times from 1961 until the early 1980s that unqualified generalizations are inevitably misleading. Nevertheless, certain common results of U.S. assistance, the Latin American counterinsurgency and civic action campaigns, and the militarization of politics are identifiable.

First, new national security legislation and other laws expanded the authority, jurisdiction, and the internal missions of the armed forces. In addition to public order and law enforcement, including anti-drug and narcotics missions, control of labor protests, strikes, peasant land seizures, and crowd control at political demonstrations, military personnel were tasked with numerous civic action and development functions. These functions ranged from road building, communications, and transport to health services, forestry (firefighting, reforestation), irrigation, literacy training, youth athletics (giving away sports equipment, such as soccer balls), natural disaster relief efforts, and delivery of commodities (food, clothing, sewing machines, agricultural implements) as part of government programs to alleviate poverty. Military officers and institutions also participated in various public enterprises, thus developing some budgetary autonomy.

Such programs had existed in the past, but the 1960s and 1970s saw a dramatic expansion of civic action as an explicit response to insurgency and political unrest. It was viewed as preventive medicine against the disease of communism as well as a way to collect political intelligence. Program emphases and details differed greatly from country to country, but the overall trend of deploying armed forces personnel in civic action missions spread across the region, cutting into training time and affecting combat readiness. It also annoyed many officers who disliked diluting military professionalism with nonmilitary tasks. Soldiers dug latrines, vaccinated children, built schools, delivered potable water, built and improved roads, installed phone and telegraph lines, and provided martial music for fiestas. This more visible presence and expanded mission occurred even in

Figure 6–3. "Fighting Against Poverty" by Guillo in *El humor es más fuerte, 1973–1991* (Santiago: Ediciones del Ornitorrinco, 1990), 71. Courtesy of Guillermo Bastias

Mexico, where minor guerrilla movements in the early 1960s and the student demonstrations that resulted in the tragic massacre at Tlatelolco in 1968 induced President Luis Echeverría to use the armed forces in efforts to restore the populist mystique of the 1910 Revolution.[34]

Second, most Latin American armed forces expanded to confront the subversive threat. At different times and to different extents, they sometimes expanded, then downsized, then again increased in size. Such patterns are not obvious without scrutinizing force levels year by year, and they are difficult to explain except by reference to the changing internal and external security threats faced by each country (see Table 6–5).

Third, despite some significant temporary increases in force levels, the number of military personnel remained fairly constant in relation to the total population (with some notable exceptions, such as in Cuba, Nicaragua, Mexico, and Paraguay). Since they had traditional internal order and law-enforcement functions and the data include militarized police such as the Chilean and Bolivian *carabineros*, population increases normally would have been accompanied by some expansion in military force levels. (Table 6–5 provides five-year snapshots of this expansion but does not depict the annual ups-and-downs in force levels in some countries.)

Fourth, compared with other regions of the world (except Africa), Latin American armed forces were, on average, fewer in relation to total population (between 3.95 and 4.27 per 1,000, 1963–1973) and were budgeted less as a percentage of Gross National Product (from 1.32 to 2.03 percent, 1963–1973). They also accounted for a smaller percentage of total central government expenditures for the region (from 9 to 11.5 percent, 1971–1980).[35] This was true despite significant updating of equipment and increases in the numbers of officers and other personnel exposed to U.S. training of all sorts, from command and intelligence schools to infantry basic training in counterinsurgency warfare.

Fifth, between 1950 and 1978 the United States provided some sort of training for more than 81,000 Latin American military personnel; in the peak year of 1962 this figure reached 9,000, but it averaged 3,000–4,000 from 1964 to 1976. Training took place at military facilities in the United States and in the host country, and especially in the Panama Canal Zone at the Army School of the Americas, the Inter-American Air Force Academy, the Navy Small Craft Instruction and Technical Team, and the Inter-American Telecommunications Network School.[36] Until the late 1970s military instruction was laced with ideological content, especially anticommunism, even in technical courses on vehicle repair, communications, and weapons maintenance.

Sixth, armed forces with little combat experience received hard lessons in internal warfare that gave immediacy to improving military training and urgency to upgrading planning, logistics, and operational capabilities. These wars also drew officers' attention more concretely to the economic and infrastructural deficiencies affecting national security and the political limitations on their war-making capabilities. Recognition of these deficiencies tended to encourage increased military interest in economic and political reform and to promote measures to improve communications, transportation, and public services and the strengthening of government institutions. All these concerns were reflected in a spate of articles in Latin American military professional journals

Table 6–5. Latin American Armed Forces Personnel, 1959–1980*

Country	*1960*	*1965*	*1970*	*1975*	*1980*
Argentina	122.5	155	140	160	160
	6.92	*5.79*	*6.3*	*5.8*	
Bolivia	11.0	16	17	17	24
	3.87	*3.65*	*4.3*	*4.5*	
Brazil	214.0	320	375	455	455
	3.88	*3.96*	*4.2*	*3.7*	
Chile	35.7	70	70	110	115
	8.47	*7.71*	*10.8*	*10.5*	
Colombia	22.0	50	45	50	65
	2.67	*2.05*	*2.1*	*2.6*	
Costa Rica		2	2	2	4
	1.34	*1.15*	*1.0*	*1.7*	
Cuba	110	140	120	375	375
	13.97	*16.41*	*12.9*	*39.1*	
Dominican Republic	17.4	17	17	18	23
	4.65	*4.02*	*3.6*	*4.0*	
Ecuador	13.3	14	16	20	35
	2.72	*2.63*	*2.9*	*4.4*	
El Salvador	6.7	4	8	8	8
	1.36	*2.63*	*2.0*	*1.7*	
Guatemala	8.0	10	13	13	15
	2.18	*2.51*	*2.1*	*2.1*	
Haiti	4.4	15	12	6	7
	3.70	*2.65*	*1.2*	*1.2*	
Honduras	4.2	5	6	12	12
	2.19	*2.22*	*3.8*	*3.2*	
Mexico	52.5	65	80	95	110
	1.52	*1.58*	*1.6*	*1.6*	
Nicaragua	4.1	6	6	5	50
	3.62	*3.11*	*2.3*	*20.0*	
Panama	3.4	4	5	8	11
	3.25	*3.49*	*4.7*	*5.8*	
Paraguay	5.7	20	20	15	15
	10.05	*8.86*	*5.4*	*4.7*	
Peru	43.5	70	80	95	150
	6.03	*5.93*	*6.1*	*8.5*	
Uruguay	13	13	18	25	29
	4.78	*6.23*	*8.9*	*10.0*	
Venezuela	22.3	50	45	55	58
	5.42	*4.18*	*4.3*	*3.4*	

Source: U.S. Arms Control and Disarmament Agency, *World Military Expenditures and Arms Trade, 1963–1973,* and *1971–1980;* John Duncan Powell, "Military Assistance and Militarism in Latin America," *Western Political Quarterly* (June 1965): 382–92.
*Thousands, including militarized police forces, and *per 1,000 population.*

that mirrored the parallel surge of attention in U.S. journals to unconventional warfare, civic action, and the relationship between political development and successful counterinsurgency.

Seventh, increasing military preoccupation with the relationship between socioeconomic change and national security in the context of counterinsurgency wars enhanced the role of military intelligence. As the political character of prolonged internal warfare placed a premium on surveillance of, and operations against, civilian opponents of incumbent governments as well as guerrilla combatants, military intelligence units gradually gained more autonomy and influence. This growing autonomy of intelligence operations seriously concerned other officers; it violated traditional organizational norms and hierarchical relationships. Moreover, it also promoted divisions between the "political" military and the "professional" military that undermined institutional solidarity.

Eighth, military control and oversight of public policy gradually increased. By the mid-1970s military institutions were permanently concerned with defining "national objectives" and the strategies for their attainment; the distinction between politics and national security policy blurred. Almost any policy issue might have some national security implication, therefore requiring military scrutiny. This broadening of the concept of "security" made military institutions responsible for political and economic outcomes as well as vulnerable to increased corruption. Financial manipulation, money laundering, weapons smuggling, contamination by drug cartels, concessions for foreign investors, and even the illegal exploitation of natural resources that they controlled (as in Guatemala, Honduras, Panama, Bolivia, and Ecuador) eroded the image and integrity of the armed forces.

And ninth, fighting insurgencies and subversives institutionalized repression, which was then justified by patriotism, national security, and a broader defense of the "Western Christian way of life." Human rights abuses were so widely denounced, so clearly documented, and so terrible and gruesome that the armed forces made themselves easy targets for international human rights watchdog organizations. They became, in the words of a former defense minister in Central America, "international pariahs."

The Logic of War versus the Logic of Politics

Latin American insurgents inspired by the Cuban Revolution expected this militarization of politics and the increased repression. Propaganda against government abuses served their cause. As moderate groups were discredited and conflict further polarized politics, peaceful reform was less likely. Following Che Guevara's precepts, the guerrilla armies and related political movements sought "to unmask oligarchic dictatorships" by forcing governments and armed forces to adopt increasingly harsh and indiscriminate measures, thereby alienating the civilian population. For the armed forces, the guerrillas' attacks on army installations, police stations, private businesses, public transportation, power lines, and key economic facilities demanded military and police repression. Failure to respond to such unlawful and damaging acts would further erode government authority and credibility. Clearly, *la patria* and its institutions were targets directly menaced by insurgencies.

The logic and moral imperatives of war replaced those of politics, thus inevitably enhancing the role of the armed forces in policymaking and administration. Unlike law enforcement, which is focused on crimes by individual human actors, war is made on "enemies" and "targets." Sledgehammer tactics and the logic of war prevail: kill or be killed, destroy the enemy to attain victory. The logic of war replaces the niceties of civil liberties and due process. War substitutes coercion and killing for negotiation and compromise. War makes killing righteous; it is a strategic and tactical method to attain political and military objectives. And, in the words of South American independence hero José de San Martín, "when *la patria* is threatened, everything is licit, except allowing it to perish."

Escalation of this perverse interaction between revolutionary movements and the armed forces led to the creation of notoriously repressive governments. State terrorism became a routine weapon in the campaign to defend *la patria* against Marxist ideological penetration, revolutionary violence, and guerrilla armies. Routine and systematic torture of political prisoners and suspected subversives brutalized the armed forces, the guerrillas, and the civilian population. Massacres in rural villages and mass executions of prisoners became commonplace. Fear pervaded daily life; atrocities replaced political dialogue. The particular scripts for this drama had their local twists, many of which are detailed in the histories, personal testimonies, and mass media of the period. From the 1964 Brazilian coup until 1990, when Patricio Aylwin became Chile's first civilian president since 1973, the logic of war prevailed over that of politics throughout most of Latin America.

La patria's enemies, the insurgent politico-military movements, proclaimed Maoist, Trotskyist, Marxist-Leninist, and Fidelista ideals. For the armed forces, these philosophical nuances meant little, except that the left was divided: all were enemies. Internal and external threats to security merged as "exotic imported ideologies" (communism) challenged "Western Christian civilization." This stylized characterization of the conflicts reflected the Cold War frame for the Latin American graphic: a war between antagonistic cultures, worldviews, and ways of life transferred from its bipolar global version to the Caribbean, Central America, the Andes, the Amazon Basin, and the Southern Cone. Compromise seemed impossible. Military victory in the classic sense—destroying the enemy—seemed the only acceptable solution.

On both sides of the ideological and political trenches liberal democracy was dismissed as obsolete. Truly nationalist reform movements refusing to identify either with international socialism or the Western bloc were viewed by the revolutionaries as stalking horses for the United States and capitalism and by the counterrevolutionaries as dangerous dupes of international communism. Military officers confronted excruciating social, ideological, and political polarization within their societies. This polarization frequently divided the officer corps as well, thereby threatening their own institutions.

It was in this context that military leaders in much of Latin America, allied with civilian groups intent on repressing revolutionary movements and restoring economic and political order, eventually decided to replace civilian governments with military regimes. The new governments, some "populist" and others "rightist," were ostensibly committed to development, national security, and anticommunism. In other cases, most notably in Colombia and Venezuela, civilian governments remained in power but increased the political and operational autonomy of the armed forces. This power was legitimized by imposing constitutional regimes of exception, such as states of siege, and by implementing drastic new national security legislation. The era of insurgency and counterinsurgency also affected Cuba, where the armed forces grew in number, received Soviet technical support and equipment, and prepared for an eventual U.S. attack despite the promise not to invade after the 1962 missile crisis. And in Mexico, with the Institutional Revolutionary Party (PRI) still in control, the armed forces nevertheless shared a Mexican version of national security doctrine, counterinsurgency, and civic action. The influence of the antipolitical military regimes spread throughout the region—as a threat of things to come or as models of possible solutions to the problems of "subversion" and underdevelopment.

Military Antipolitics: Brazil and Beyond, 1964 and Afterward

Underlying variations in military assistance and Alliance for Progress programs was the commitment to prevent "more Cubas." By 1964, when Brazil's President João Goulart flirted with China, Cuba, and "nonalignment" while decreeing agrarian and social reforms at home, the United States unambiguously favored, encouraged, and even assisted the coup that toppled his government and installed a military president. Led by army officers trained in the 1920s by the French missions and with experience in World War II's Brazilian Expeditionary Force in Italy (FEB, the so-called Febianos), this coup was an important benchmark in Latin American military politics. Professional officers decided to put an end to populist demagoguery, repress revolutionary movements, and achieve Brazil's manifest destiny through direct military rule. Similar decisions were made elsewhere in the hemisphere from 1964 to 1973 (see Table 6–6).

Table 6–6. Antipolitical Military Regimes, 1964–1990*

Country	*Years*
Ecuador	1963–1966; 1972–1978
Guatemala	1963–1985
Brazil	1964–1985
Bolivia	1964–1970; 1971–1982
Argentina	1966–1973; 1976–1983
Peru	1968–1980
Panama	1968–1981
Honduras	1972–1982
Chile	1973–1990
Uruguay	1973–1984
El Salvador	1948–1984**

*In some cases, dating the beginning of these regimes is difficult inasmuch as military governments succeeded one another with changes in policies and personalities but maintained, overall, an antipolitical outlook and national security rationale for direct military rule. Sometimes brief civilian interludes seemed to interrupt military domination (for example, in Guatemala from 1966 to 1969, and Panama after General Omar Torrijos's death in 1981).

** El Salvador was dominated by military regimes from 1948 onward. It may be more appropriate to date the last episode from 1979, although the developmental focus and antipolitical themes of the *junta* headed by Major Oscar Osorio in 1948 anticipated a "Peruvianist" (or populist) version of antipolitics.

Brazil's 1964 coup responded both to immediate political circumstances and to the growing influence of national security doctrine among the armed forces' leadership. For the United States it was a victory in the regional war against communism that was openly and enthusiastically applauded. Brazilian national security doctrine (NSD)—part geopolitics, part frustrated hegemony over South America, and part dreams of national greatness and development—went back at least to the nation-building struggles from 1889 to the 1930s, to the French military missions from 1919 to 1939, and to Getúlio Vargas's Estado Novo. It had intellectual origins in Colonel Mario Travassos's *Projeção continental do Brasil* (1935) and in the historical concern regarding Argentine expansionism and the key role of Brazil's vulnerable and unoccupied hinterland if it was to attain its manifest destiny in South America.

Brazil's best-known NSD advocate, General Golbery do Couto e Silva (*Planejamento estratégico*, 1955; *Aspectos geopolíticos do Brasil*, 1957; *Geopolítica do Brasil*, 2d ed., 1967), became a trusted and influential participant and adviser in the military governments after 1964. Golbery had declared in 1955, thinking more of World War II and the recent Korean conflict than of a possible insurgency, that "the area of politics is permeated . . . by adverse pressures, creating a form of universalization of the factors of security, enlarging the area of politics of national security to a point where it almost absorbs all national activities."[37] Adapted to the Cuban threat and the 1964 Brazilian crisis, the Brazilian NSD provided a rationale for military rule. Similar adaptations in Peru, Argentina, Bolivia, and elsewhere elicited remarkably comparable justifications for the coups and installations of military regimes from 1964 to 1973. What they all shared, without exception, was a geopolitical foundation, a dream of national development, an antipolitical message, hatred for Marxism, and a disdain for traditional liberal democracy.[38]

Despite some important differences in the initial conditions that provoked a military coup, in economic and foreign policies and in political style these regimes focused first on a salvational role against populist, subversive, and Marxist threats and then on efforts to construct new political systems based on broader military participation in policymaking and administration. Thus, "the Brazilian military most feared chaos and communism"; and for the Peruvians, "elimination of the latent state of subversion now became the primary objective of military action."[39] In Brazil, Peru, and elsewhere the military rulers also adopted more explicit constitutional and statutory foundations for military guardianship. Constitutional amendments, decrees, and new legislation reaffirmed historical and constitutional missions (for example, the "moderating power" of the Brazilian military, or the "historical mission" of the Argentine armed forces). These initiatives also meant rejecting as outdated and inimical to national development the exclusion of military elites from direct participation in policymaking.

The coups that created antipolitical military regimes typically toppled reformist presidents (or prevented the election of populist ones) in highly polarized circumstances. They were not incited by an imminent victory of guerrilla armies, although the threat of civil war and the existence of insurgency, economic crisis, and political turmoil contributed to the decision to depose the incumbent governments in most cases. With varying degrees of fervor, coupmakers joined the anti-Communist crusade. They were supported by broad sectors of civilians responding to the political and economic crises afflicting their nations. In most cases, some civilians expected the military to rescue them from chaos, the threat of communism, and civil strife—as had become so common in Latin America. Indeed, in an interview in Spain one year after the 1973 coup in Chile, former president Eduardo Frei declared:

> Allende had no scruples about destroying the country to install a Leninist program and annihilate all opposition. . . . The world ignores [the fact] that the Chilean Marxists had arms hidden in thousands of places. . . . The military has saved Chile. . . . The military was called on by the nation and complied with its legal duty, since the legislature and judiciary, the congress, and the supreme court had publicly denounced that Allende's presidency and his regime did not respect the Constitution nor the laws of the legislature, nor the "statute of guarantees" signed by Allende, nor court orders. . . . Allende came to install communism through violence, not democratically. . . . when a people has been so weakened and harassed (*acosado*) that it cannot rebel . . . then the Army substitutes its arms and does the work.[40]

Conservative and moderate newspapers, business organizations, landowners, and even trade unions called on the military to save *la patria* in accord with the historical mission that civilians and military officers reflexively assigned to the armed forces. Opposition politicians, like Frei, unable to detain the populist or revolutionary wave with nonmilitary political instruments, called on the armed forces to conserve their version of *la patria*. While this was a rare event in Chile and Uruguay, and therefore more dramatic, it was a more common practice in Argentina, Peru, Bolivia, and even Brazil. Frei's language could not reaffirm more directly or more clearly the presumptions of militarylore and the expectations of much of civil society: the armed forces must perform their legal and historical mission to save *la patria*.

The newly installed military regimes blended national security doctrines based on old geopolitical concepts, French and U.S. counterinsurgency and civic action doctrines, and Latin American developmental nationalism. Such developmentalism could be rightist or leftist, statist or liberal, populist or demobilizational and exclusionary. Above all, the military regimes from 1964 to 1979, whether considered rightist (Brazil, Argentina, Chile, and Uruguay), or leftist (Peru, Panama, and Ecuador), drew on the historical identification of the armed forces with *la patria* and blamed civilian politicians, parties, and "politics" for the regional dilemmas of the 1960s and 1970s. They proclaimed a "new beginning," "national renovation," or "revolution."

Despite their revolutionary claims, the military regimes were greatly concerned with legitimacy, with form and procedures, and with constitutional, statutory, and administrative legality. Thus, the Brazilians initially retained the 1946 Constitution, the Argentines that of 1853, and the Uruguayans tampered little with their constitutional charter. In Ecuador, the military leaders of 1972 reinstated the 1945 Constitution. Subsequently, hundreds, even thousands, of institutional, administrative, and legal reforms were decreed (or, as in Brazil, extruded from a reorganized legislature). In several cases, new constitutions were adopted to consecrate the changes imposed by the military governments: in El Salvador, 1962; Guatemala, 1965, 1983; Brazil, 1967; Bolivia, 1967; Panama, 1972; Ecuador, 1979; Peru, 1979; and Chile, 1980. The military regimes' concern with a facade of legitimacy even led the Chilean *junta* to maintain in operation the judicial system, particularly the conservative supreme court, which gave its backhanded seal of approval to the new order with perfunctory consideration and rejection of appeals for writs of habeas corpus and injunctions to stop government abuses.

Whatever the particular economic models and policies adopted, the post-1964 military governments shared an antipolitical vision: political parties were banned, or their activities seriously curtailed; legislatures were closed "temporarily," or purged of undesirable politicians; selected labor organizations were outlawed, or their activities restricted; media censorship prevented public criticism, and opposition journalists were persecuted, jailed, and killed, while media favoring the regime were subsidized; universities were purged of subversives, professors lost their jobs, and student organizations were suppressed; and decree laws, "institutional acts," and "constitutional acts" replaced and modified existing laws.

The military governments attacked "politics" as the source of corruption and weakness of *la patria*. Rather than venal politicians and inept legislatures, national security councils, *juntas*, and their civil-military technocratic administrative teams took charge of defining national objectives. They redesigned government institutions and made policy by decree, short-circuiting the inefficient, antiquated, and despised institutions of liberal democracy. Military intelligence operations gained great autonomy; military *juntas* and presidents declared their commitments to national regeneration. They claimed that they did so to promote development and guarantee security, to defend *la patria* from international communism, and to overcome the underdevelopment of the past.

The coups were justified by reference to the armed forces' historical mission, their constitutional duties, the immediate crisis facing the country, and a promise of political and economic transformation. Even so, the new regimes were never exclusively military. They drew on the support and talents of civilian economists and technocrats, media specialists, bankers, and diplomats. Right-wing paramilitary patriots, such as the Patria y Libertad in Chile and the Argentine Triple A (Argentine Anticommunist Alliance), shared intelligence and "dirty war" functions (interrogation, kidnapping, torture, extralegal executions) with specialized military units. Paramilitary groups also operated in the more militarized civilian regimes, such as Colombia, and even in Mexico, with groups like the Halcones.

Torture, murder, and the exile of opponents took place everywhere, but much more so in Argentina, Guatemala, Chile, and Uruguay than in Peru (before 1980), Ecuador, and Honduras. Differences in the extent of repression made popular the labels *dictadura* and *dictablanda* (hard and soft dictatorships) to distinguish the more ferocious regimes from those that gave more latitude to opposition. In part, this difference corresponded to the initial strength of the revolutionary and populist left and the threat of internal resistance. Thus, the Ecuadorians and Hondurans faced almost no effective insurgencies, and the political parties constituted a weak opposition. In contrast, the Argentine, Brazilian, Chilean, and Uruguayan militaries seized power to destroy credible leftist movements, armed insurgents, or populist governments.

These military regimes were not easily labeled on a traditional "left" to "right" spectrum. They could as easily decree agrarian reforms (Peru, Ecuador, Honduras,[41] El Salvador, and Brazil) or take nationalist initiatives regarding natural resources and public enterprises (Brazil, Peru, Ecuador, and Bolivia) as become champions of neoliberal models (Chile, Uruguay, and, to a lesser extent, Argentina). The core of military antipolitics that dominated much of Latin America from 1964 into the 1980s was not any particular economic model or even a pro-U.S. foreign policy (the Peruvians sent home the U.S. military mission; the Panamanians pressed the Canal issue; the Ecuadorians and Peruvians fought over territorial infringement by U.S. fishing boats; the Argentines had good economic relations with the Soviet Union, and the Chilean *junta* with China; and the Brazilians and Argentines pursued defense, weapons development and export, and economic strategies inimical to U.S. interests). Rather, it was the commitment to long-term military rule to excise the rot of civilian politics and promote national development.[42] In some cases, such as in Chile, Uruguay, Argentina, Guatemala, and El Salvador, "surgically removing the cancer of Marxism" was a central feature of the military regimes. In other cases, such as in Ecuador, Panama, Honduras, Bolivia, and Peru (until the early 1980s), domestic leftist forces represented only minor threats, and military governments focused principally on antipolitical and developmental themes.

There was a striking similarity in the language justifying the antipolitical coups after 1964. Whether Brazilian technocrats, Peruvian "populists," Argentine anti-Peronists, or Ecuadorian reformists, the generals and colonels shared an antipolitical vision. The pervasiveness of national security doctrines as rationales for military regimes made popular the label "national security states" to describe these governments after 1964, and the term "new professionalism" to describe the armed forces' supposedly new orientations and role expansion.[43] José Comblin's frequently cited *The Church and the National Security State* (1979) was influential in labeling the diverse military regimes' orientation as "national security ideology": "I call it the national security ideology because it is the ideology of the national security system, the new political system of today."[44]

Despite these generic appellations, and the importance of national security as a rationale for military rule, the particular features of military regimes from Brazil to Guatemala after 1964 depended more on the armed forces' evolved political role, attitudes, dispositions, and the local circumstances that precipitated coups than on a single dominant national security doctrine. Thus, labor conflict, inflation, economic decline, political crisis, troop insubordination, and a "turn to the left" by President Goulart in Brazil provoked a coup in 1964; impeding MNR leader Paz Estenssoro from continuing in the presidency after 1964 motivated the Bolivian *golpe*; and the recent counterinsurgency experience, the International Petroleum Company conflict, and preventing an APRA victory in the upcoming presidential elections influenced the 1968 *pronunciamiento* in Peru.

Likewise, there was little new in their developmentalist and patriotic proclamations except a willingness to accept publicly the need for long-term military rule to attain development and to combat internal subversion. The willingness to assume a long-term institutional responsibility for national development as part of the national security mission was a fundamental change from previous caretaker and moderating roles for the armed forces. In the past, the armed forces effected "veto coups" to halt undesired government initiatives, or intervened to reestablish law and order and to correct temporary political and economic disequilibria. Now they asserted a combined vanguard and messianic role in directly guiding *la patria's* destiny. Recognition of the importance of this departure was made clear in the proclamations that justified the post-1964 coups as revolutionary initiatives rather than traditional restorations of the old order: Brazil, 1964—"What has occurred is an authentic revolution";[45] Argentina, 1966—"We feel as never before the essence of *la patria* overflowing our spirits. . . . The armed forces have begun the revolutionary process";[46] Bolivia, 1966—"The armed forces took power in 1964 to make the Bolivian Revolution a reality and to establish the foundations of the Second Republic";[47] Peru, 1968—"Upon assuming power in Peru, the armed forces want to make known to the Peruvian people the underlying causes for their far-reaching and historic decision, a decision which marks the beginning of the definitive emancipation of our *patria*."[48]

Responding to the bombastic rhetoric and military operations of Cuban-inspired revolutionary movements throughout the hemisphere, the military antipoliticians took charge. The Brazilian coup and the invasion of the Dominican Republic ushered in the era of antipolitical national security regimes. Parallel to these developments, the U.S. military assistance programs encouraged the creation of larger Latin American military forces, more heavily ideological training for officers and troops, and improved operational capabilities. These trends drastically affected military organization and operations and sent thousands of soldiers into combat. If civil libertarians and liberals objected that no "real war" existed to justify the repressive measures taken to combat the revolutionaries, then the revolutionaries themselves had declared that the war would be fought until final victory or death: *Patria o muerte. Venceremos*!

Special Cuban military schools, financed in part by the Soviet Union and Eastern European governments, trained Latin Americans as guerrilla fighters and political revolutionaries, supplied them clandestinely, and sent them to the Caribbean and to Central and South America to make revolution. Between 1962 and 1968 the romantic *foquista* movements faced the reality of U.S. and Latin American resolve. Invariably they suffered deprivation and military setbacks, although their political impact outlasted their temporary military defeat.

Che Guevara's death in Bolivia in 1967 at the hands of U.S.-trained Bolivian Special Forces and the publication of the Rockefeller Report in the United States in 1969 (affirming the positive role to be played by the "new" modernizing military officers in promoting economic development and fighting communism) confirmed the bittersweet success of counterinsurgency strategies against the guerrilla *focos* and the risks of expanded military roles in government:

> a new type of military man is coming to the fore and often becoming a major force for constructive social change in the American republics. Motivated by increasing impatience with corruption, inefficiency, and a stagnant political order, the new military man is prepared to adapt his authoritarian tradition to the goals of social and economic progress. This new role by the military, however, is not free from perils and dilemmas. There is always the risk that the authoritarian style will result in repression. The temptation to expand measures for security or discipline or efficiency to the point of curtailing

> individual liberties, beyond what is required for the restoration of order and social progress, is not easy to resist.[49]

As Nelson Rockefeller anticipated, the guerrillas' defeat was accomplished in much of the region at the price of the ascent of the repressive antipolitical military governments, extensive use of state terrorism, and curtailed civil liberties and rights. The 1969 Nixon Doctrine deemphasized direct U.S. intrusion in exchange for strengthened Third World powers' assuming greater responsibility for maintaining regional stability. Originating in the U.S. Vietnam experience, the Nixon Doctrine meant increased military sales and stronger support for the Latin American armed forces. President Nixon and Henry Kissinger's enthusiastic response to the Chilean and Uruguayan coups in 1973 were signs of the times.[50] The temporary emphasis on human rights as a condition for U.S. military and other assistance during the Carter administration gave way again to the concern for preventing "more Cubas" with the 1979 victory of the Sandinistas in Nicaragua (see Chapter 7).

The 1964 Brazilian coup and the military-civil regime that dominated the country until the mid-1980s had set the stage. The drama of antipolitics unfolded more or less tragically in unique national scenarios for the next twenty-five years. Monographs, diaries of torture victims, reports by international human rights organizations, national security updates by military and civilian bureaucracies, mass media journalism, and novels and short stories all relate multiple versions of the impact of insurgency, counterinsurgency, and military antipolitics between 1964 and the 1980s throughout the region. No reader of Ariel Dorfman's *Widows* (1983), Víctor Montejo's *Testimony, Death of a Guatemalan Village* (1987), or Omar Rivabella's *Requiem for a Woman's Soul* (1986), among many accounts of the era, could miss the pain, trauma, and unhealed wounds inflicted by insurgency and counterinsurgency after 1959. Whatever the particulars, by 1980 Latin America bore the marks of guerrilla wars, terrorism, and state terrorism. Military antipolitics also affected those countries where civilian governments survived. As a result, military guardianship had been more thoroughly institutionalized and leftist populism and Marxism defeated in most of South America.

Guerrilla defeats in South America did not deter renewed revolutionary fervor in Central America and the Caribbean, including the emergence of a pro-Cuba regime in Grenada. The 1979 Sandinista victory in Nicaragua, just before Ronald Reagan was elected president, reset the stage for a new drama: a decade of civil war in Central America, economic recession and a debt crisis afflicting most of Latin America, and the gradual extrication of the South American armed forces from direct military rule. In these years the "road to peace" and the return to civilian government was neither easy nor uniform. It challenged the ingenuity and courage of civilians and military officers alike. It also demanded rethinking and reformulating national interests, national values, and military missions. In most cases it produced sanitized "protected democracies" that enshrined military guardianship while restoring a modicum of open political debate. In others (for example, Colombia, Peru, Guatemala, Nicaragua, and El Salvador), continued internal wars prevented the return of "normal" civilian government for most of the 1980s.

Notes

1. "Declaration of Punta del Este," 1961, Charter of the Alliance for Progress signed by all OAS members, except Cuba, August 5, 1961, reprinted in *Inter-American Relations, A Collection of Documents, Legislation, Descriptions of Inter-American Organizations, and Other Material Pertaining to Inter-American Affairs*, 93d Cong., 1st sess., printed for the use of the Committee on Foreign Affairs, November 1973: 210–12.

2. Address to Congress, March 14, 1961, cited in Melvin Gurtov, *The United States against the Third World* (New York: Praeger, 1974): 89.

3. For a well-written account of the Bay of Pigs invasion see Peter Wyden, *Bay of Pigs: The Untold Story* (New York: Simon and Schuster, 1979).

4. See Willard F. Barber and C. Neale Ronning, *Internal Security and Military Power: Counter-insurgency and Civic Action in Latin America* (Columbus: Ohio State University Press, 1966).

5. Col. Alvaro de Souza Pinheiro, "Guerrilla in the Brazilian Amazon," Foreign Military Studies Office, Fort Leavenworth, Kansas, July 1995: 12.

6. See Donald C. Hodges and Abraham Guillén, *Revaloración de la guerrilla urbana* (México: Ediciones El Caballito, 1977).

7. Regis Debray, *Revolution in the Revolution?* (New York: Grove Press, 1967).

8. For a theoretical treatment of these guerrilla movements see Wickham-Crowley (1992).

9. The 1963 Ecuadorian *junta* adopted tax reforms, agrarian reforms, and identified both with the legacy of the 1925 military modernizers and the themes of the Alliance for Progress. See Anita Isaacs, *Military Rule and Transition in Ecuador* (Pittsburgh: University of Pittsburgh Press, 1993): 1–3.

10. Ernesto "Che" Guevara, "Message to the Tricontinental," Pamphlet published in English by the Executive Secretariat of the Organization of the Solidarity of the Peoples of Africa, Asia, and Latin America, Havana, April 16, 1967, reprinted in Brian Loveman and Thomas M. Davies, Jr., eds., *Che Guevara, Guerrilla Warfare* (Wilmington, DE: Scholarly Resources, 1997): 164–76.

11. Cited in Child (1980): 156–57.

12. See W. Michael Weis, *Cold Warriors and Coups d'Etat: Brazilian-American Relations, 1945–1964* (Albuquerque: University of New Mexico Press, 1993): 114–15.

13. Captain Mario Lozada Uribe, *Hacia un Perú mejor. El nuevo rol de los institutos armados y fuerzas auxiliares* (Lima: Imprenta LUX, 1957): 22–23.

14. The Southern Command, or SOUTHCOM, traced its origins to the first U.S. Marines in Panama from 1903 to 1914. In 1917, after replacement by army units, the Panama command became the Panama Canal Department of the U.S. Army. A name change in 1941 made this the Caribbean Command, and in 1963 it became SOUTHCOM. See Lars Schoultz, *National Security and United States Policy toward Latin America* (Princeton: Princeton University Press, 1987): 166, n.16.

15. See Michael T. Klare and Cynthia Arnson, *Supplying Repression: U.S. Support for Authoritarian Regimes Abroad* (Washington, DC: Institute for Policy Study, 1981): Chapter 3.

16. MATA—you kill, it kills, he kills, she kills, kill! in Spanish—was a less than subtle acronym.

17. For an overview of U.S. domestic reaction to the military assistance programs see Ernest Graves and Steven Hildreth, *U.S. Security Assistance: The Political Process* (Lexington, MA: Lexington Books, 1985).

18. U.S. Department of State, "A New Concept for Hemispheric Defense and Development," January 15, 1961: 1, 3, cited in Jack Child, "U.S. Policies toward Insurgencies in Latin America," in George Fauriol, ed., *Latin American Insurgencies* (Washington, DC: National Defense University, 1985): 133.

19. Howard Wiarda, *Critical Elections and Critical Coups: State, Society and the Military in the Process of Latin American Development* (Athens: Ohio University Center for International Studies, 1979): 39.

20. Warren Dean, "Latin American *Golpes* and Economic Fluctuations, 1823–1966," *Social Science Quarterly* 51 (June 1970): 70–80.

21. I say "at least" because some of these irregular changes in government involved more than one "event," and in other instances changes in government might be labeled coups although they passed as other sorts of government change. See Joseph F. Loftus, *Latin American Defense Expenditures, 1938–1965* (Santa Monica, CA: Rand Corporation, 1968); and Solaún and Quinn (1973): 213–16.

22. On *la violencia* in Colombia see Gonzalo Sánchez, "La Violencia in Colombia: New Research, New Questions," *Hispanic American Historical Review* 65(4) 1985: 789–807.

23. The term "hereditary hatreds" is taken from Robert Dix, *Colombia: The Political Dimensions of Change* (New Haven: Yale University Press, 1967): 211.

24. U.S. Congress, Hearings before the Committee on Foreign Affairs, House of Representatives, 87th Cong., Foreign Assistance Act of 1962, Parts I–VI and Index, 268.

25. U.S. Department of State Bulletin, December 9, 1963: 903, cited in Gurtov (1974): 110.

26. Col. Immanuel J. Klette, "U.S. Assistance to Venezuela and Chile in Combatting Insurgency, 1963–1964—Two Cases," *Conflict* 3(4) (1982): 227–44.

27. Jonathan F. Ladd (Lt. Col.), "Some Reflections on Counterinsurgency," *Military Review* (October 1964): 76, 78, cited in Alfred Stepan, *The Military in Politics: Changing Patterns in Brazil* (Princeton: Princeton University Press, 1971): 127.

28. The influence of French doctrine in Argentina and Uruguay is treated in Carina Perelli, "From Counterrevolutionary Warfare to Political Awakening: The Uruguayan and Argentine Armed Forces in the Seventies," *Armed Forces and Society* 20(1) (1993): 25–49.

29. On the Brazilian and Argentine arms industries see Ralph Sander, *Arms Industries: New Suppliers and Regional Security* (Washington, DC: National Defense University, 1990).

30. Glenn Alton Casey, "A Methodological Approach for Analyzing South American Arms Acquisition Behavior and U.S. Policy" (Master's thesis, Naval Post-Graduate School, Montgomery, California, 1974).

31. U.S. Congress, House Committee on Foreign Affairs, *Communism in Latin America: Hearings before the Subcommittee on Inter-American Affairs*, 89th Cong., 1st sess., February 9, 1965 (Washington, DC: Government Printing Office, 1965): 119, cited in Don L. Etchison, *The United States and Militarism in Central America* (New York: Praeger, 1975): 77.

32. For a detailed account of the U.S. intervention and the performance of the Inter-American Peace Force see Bruce Palmer (Gen., USA), *Intervention in the Caribbean: The Dominican Crisis of 1965* (Lexington: University Press of Kentucky, 1989).

33. G. Pope Atkins, *Arms and Politics in the Dominican Republic* (Boulder, CO: Westview Press, 1981): 52.

34. See Guillermo Boils, *Los militares y la política en México, 1915–1974* (México: Ediciones El Caballito, 1975).

35. U.S. Arms Control and Disarmament Agency, Washington, DC, *World Military Expenditures and Arms Trade* (1963–1973; 1971–1980).

36. Lars Schoultz, *Human Rights and United States Policy toward Latin America* (Princeton: Princeton University Press, 1981): 230–31.

37. Golbery do Couto e Silva (Gen.), *Planejamento estratégico* (Rio de Janeiro: Biblioteca do Exército, 1955): 38–39, cited in Alfred Stepan, "The New Professionalism of Internal Warfare and Military Role Expansion," in Alfred Stepan, ed., *Authoritarian Brazil: Origins, Policies, and the Future* (New Haven: Yale University Press, 1973): 56.

38. These national security doctrines also contained variations in theme and emphasis. See David Pion-Berlin, "Latin American National Security Doctrines: Hard and Soft-Line Themes," *Armed Forces and Society* 15 (Spring 1989): 411–29.

39. Luigi R. Einaudi and Alfred C. Stepan, *Latin American Institutional Development: Changing Military Perspectives in Peru and Brazil* (Santa Monica, CA: Rand Corporation, April 1971), for the Office of External Research, U.S. Department of State, R-586-DOS: 27, 86.

40. Cited in Molina Johnson (1989): 180–81.

41. The little-studied impact of Honduran military populism and agrarian reform is treated in Rachel Sieder, "Honduras: The Politics of Exception and Military Reformism (1972–1978)," *Journal of Latin American Studies* 27(1) (February 1995): 99–127.

42. Loveman and Davies, eds. (1997).

43. Stepan (1973): 47–65.

44. José Comblin, *The Church and the National Security State* (Maryknoll, NY: Orbis Books, 1979): 65.

45. Institutional Act 1, reprinted and translated in E. Bradford Burns, *A History of Brazil* (New York: Columbia University Press, 1970): 390–93.

46. Speech by Gen. Juan Carlos Onganía, 1966, cited in Loveman and Davies, eds. (1978): 175.

47. Speech by Alfredo Ovando Candía, 1966, cited in Loveman and Davies, eds. (1978): 181–85.

48. "Manifiesto of the Revolutionary Government of Peru," 1968, cited in Loveman and Davies, eds. (1978): 208–10.

49. Nelson A. Rockefeller, *The Rockefeller Report on the Americas: The Official Report of a United States Presidential Mission for the Western Hemisphere* (Chicago: Quadrangle Books, 1969).

50. Graves and Hildreth (1985): 22–23.

7

La Patria, Regional Security, and "Democracy"*

> To conserve *la patria* . . . is a fundamental task of the armed forces. *La patria* is truly an entity of destiny that begins in each household and school, then projects itself to society. . . . To assure the existence of *la patria* requires patriotic action not only against external threats but also to solve the economic, political, and social problems of the Nation.
>
> —Lt. Col. Juan M. Gallardo Miranda, Lt. Col. Edmundo A. O'Kuinghttons Ocampo, Chile, 1992[1]

In July 1979 a popular insurrection toppled the Somoza dynasty in Nicaragua. For the first time since 1959 revolutionary armed forces militarily defeated a Latin American dictatorship—perhaps the only one remaining that even approximated the Batista regime ousted by Fidel Castro in Cuba. The Sandinista National Liberation Front (FSLN) that spearheaded the Nicaraguan revolution openly identified with the Cuban Revolution and was committed to an anti-imperialist foreign policy. The Sandinista victory ended the era of "no more Cubas."

In the view of U.S. policymakers and Latin American military leaders, the Sandinistas were part of international communism's escalating offensive against "Western Christian values." This attack threatened to spread north to the Mexican border and directly menace regional and U.S. security. Guerrilla military successes in the early 1980s, particularly in El Salvador, gave credibility to this perception. In 1982 and 1983 revolutionary armies wreaked havoc on the Salvadoran economy, destroying bridges, electrical installations, and even 70 percent of Illopango Air Base. By early 1983, Reagan administration policymakers publicly recognized the fragility of the Salvadoran government; massive increases in military assistance to El Salvador and U.S. military operations in neighboring Honduras underscored the successes of the guerrillas.[2]

In Peru, the Sendero Luminoso revolutionary movement blasted spectacularly onto the scene in the early 1980s. Sendero rejected conventional Marxist and Soviet visions but nevertheless proclaimed itself a revolutionary Communist option for Peru and the hemisphere. Faced with a fast-deteriorating situation, the Lima government declared a state of siege in Ayacucho and sent in

*Parts of this chapter are based on the author's " 'Protected Democracies' and Military Guardianship: Political Transitions in Latin America, 1978–1993," *Journal of Inter-American Studies and World Affairs* 36(2) (Summer 1994): 105–89, included here by permission of the journal's editor.

2,000 regular army soldiers and paratroopers. Deploying light planes and helicopter gunships, the army's counterguerrilla operations seriously damaged Sendero but also resulted in hundreds of casualties among the peasants caught in the conflict. Thousands more would die before the 1980s ended.[3]

Chronic guerrilla insurgencies, rightist paramilitary groups, death squads, and drug-mafia violence also bled other nations. In Colombia a multifaceted "dirty war" mimicked the state terrorism of military regimes elsewhere.[4] Guerrillas and army counterinsurgency operations devastated Guatemala, with Indian villagers often the victims of brutal scorched-earth tactics. Small-scale armed resistance to military governments in Brazil, Uruguay, and Argentina also continued, with a declining but still significant toll of victims.

For the Latin American armed forces, there was no doubt that "Western Civilization" and their *patrias* were in danger. This view was reinforced by the punishing economic recession and debt crisis that savaged the region, bringing negative growth rates and downwardly spiraling living standards for millions of Latin Americans. According to the Economic Commission for Latin America: "Between 1980 and 1990 [poverty] worsened as a result of the crisis and the adjustment policies, wiping out most of the progress in poverty reduction achieved during the 1960s and 1970s. . . . estimates place the number of poor at the beginning of this decade, depending on the definition of poverty, somewhere between 130 and 196 million. . . . Recession and adjustment in the 1980s also increased income inequality in most of the region."[5] The debt crisis spread quickly after Mexico's 1982 announcement that it could not meet its obligations, thus undermining the Latin American economies and inflicting economic misery across the region.

To overcome the crisis, Latin American governments, both civilian and military, gradually accepted varying versions of the structural adjustment programs peddled and imposed by the International Monetary Fund, the World Bank, and the U.S. Treasury. These programs meant restrictive monetary policy, trade liberalization, reductions in fiscal deficits, cutting social welfare programs and subsidies to the poor for housing, transportation, and other public programs—and then "shrinking the state" and privatizing many public enterprises.[6]

The structural adjustment programs contributed to redefinition of the role and character of the Latin American governments. By the early 1990s neoliberalism had replaced or transformed statist and interventionist models, but this radical transformation occurred with differing intensity and timing from country to country. Everywhere, neoliberal policies brought unemployment and social conflicts in the short term. Supermarket riots, street demonstrations, strikes, and violent crime tested police and the armed forces most severely in the Dominican Republic, Argentina, Bolivia, Brazil, and Venezuela, but no nation entirely escaped the wave of protests and public disorder induced by the new economic policies.

The economic adjustment programs forced budget cuts on the armed forces in some countries and were accompanied by loss of prestige and bitter attacks from civilian sectors. In some instances (Ecuador, Argentina, Guatemala, and Venezuela, for example), factionalism resurfaced. Interservice rivalries, mutinies over internal matters, and coup attempts marred the 1984–1990 period. In other countries such as Chile, Colombia, Mexico, and Brazil, the armed forces

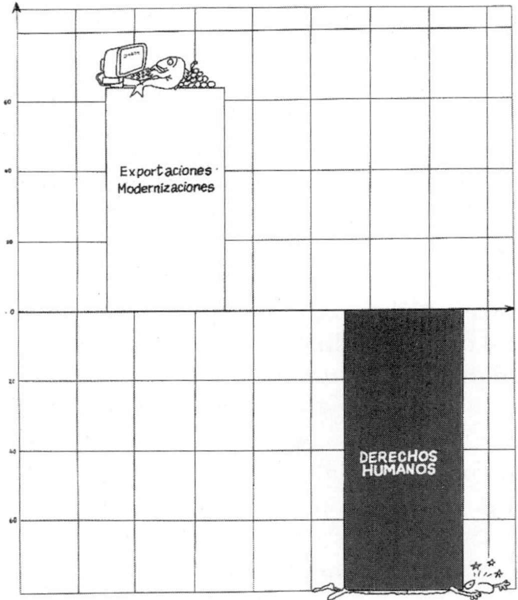

Figure 7–1. "Statistical Trends: Exports and Modernization on the Increase, Respect for Human Rights Going Down" by Guillo in *El humor es más fuerte, 1973–1991* (Santiago: Ediciones del Ornitorrinco, 1990), 74. Courtesy of Guillermo Bastias

limited the impacts of the economic and political crises on their institutions, retaining a relatively unified front against political revanchism and even squeezing additional funds from hardpressed governments for upgrading weaponry, communications, and transport material. Then, suddenly, the end of the 1980s brought an end to the Cold War. Still suffering the pains of the debt crisis and economic restructuring, the Latin American armed forces saw the fundamental framework for inter-American relations and the international rationale for their salvational missions disappear—but not before the Cold War's last battles badly scarred the region's economies, polities, and armed forces. Viewed retrospectively, the 1980s left the Latin American armed forces in the most vulnerable circumstances in their history. Ironically, this outcome was a result of their victories over the political left and of their collaboration with the United States in the battle against the Soviets' "evil empire."

U.S. Regional Security Policy in the 1980s

In 1980 the Committee of Santa Fe, a conservative advisory group to the Republican party, declared that World War III was under way and that "the Americas are under attack."[7] It pointed to the revolutionary regime in Nicaragua and to a renewed Soviet activism in Latin America and the Third World. Cuba, with Soviet support, trained guerrilla fighters and fomented revolution in the Caribbean, it increased its support for guerrilla armies and revolutionaries in El Salvador, Guatemala, Colombia, Chile, and elsewhere. It also deployed troops to Africa to support Marxist and nationalist regimes and to assist national liberation movements. Cuban and Soviet "soldier-internationalism" provoked new conflicts with former colonial powers and the United States. In December 1981 the State Department circulated a research report that detailed Cuba's "new drive to support armed insurgency" in various countries, and it concluded: "In a region whose primary needs are for economic development and social equity, and greater democracy, Cuba is compounding existing problems by encouraging armed insurrection." The report noted that in contrast with the 1960s, "instead of throwing up obstacles [since 1978], the Soviet Union has generally backed the Cuban efforts . . . to favor insurrectionary violence."[8]

This assessment of Soviet and Cuban activities, adopted by President Ronald Reagan when he took office in 1981, led to a hardening and further militarization of U.S. foreign policy. The Third World and Latin America would serve as battlegrounds in the war between the "free world" and the "evil empire."[9] To counter the Sandinista threat and the new Soviet-Cuban initiatives in the hemisphere, President Reagan preached moral and military resolve. He repeatedly declared that the battle against the Soviet Union's "evil empire" and its Latin American surrogates had to be won in the Americas to defend freedom globally: "The national security of all the Americas is at stake in Central America. If we cannot defend ourselves there, we cannot expect to prevail elsewhere. Our credibility would collapse, our alliances would crumble and the safety of our homeland would be put at jeopardy."[10]

In 1983, Reagan created the National Bipartisan Commission on Central America (also called the Kissinger Commission, for its chairman, Henry Kissinger). Its report, while recognizing the social and economic sources of discontent and also the human rights abuses connected with the counterinsurgency campaigns, emphasized the Soviet-Cuban threat and the military requirements for halting the Communist aggression in Central America:

> Cuban support was a particularly important factor in the Sandinista triumph. It was Castro who unified the three Nicaraguan guerrilla factions and provided the weapons, supplies, and advisers that enabled the Cuban-oriented *comandantes* to establish themselves as the dominant group in the revolution.
>
> Cuban and now also Nicaraguan support was subsequently critical in building the fighting forces of the Farabundo Martí Liberation Front in El Salvador, in maintaining them in the field, and in forcing them to unite in a combined effort in spite of deep-seated distrust among the guerrilla factions. . . . The evidence reveals that arms flowed into El Salvador from Nicaragua in preparation for the Salvadoran guerrillas' unsuccessful "final offensive" of January 1981. . . .
>
> None of the five Central American states is free of war or the threat of war. As the conflicts intensify, and as Nicaragua builds an armed force with firepower vastly greater than anything ever seen before in Central America, the threat of militarization hangs over the region.[11]

The Commission concluded that "the use of Nicaragua as a base for Soviet and Cuban efforts to penetrate the rest of the Central American isthmus, with El Salvador the target of first opportunity, gives the conflict there a major strategic dimension. The direct involvement of aggressive external forces makes it a challenge to the system of hemispheric security, and, quite specifically, to the security interests of the United States. This is a challenge to which the United States must respond."[12] The Sandinistas repeatedly proclaimed their solidarity with the Salvadoran guerrillas and their admiration for the Cuban Revolution. They insisted that the Nicaraguan revolution "goes beyond our borders," in the spirit of "revolutionary internationalism." This attitude made the Kissinger Commission's findings more than credible.

President Reagan also supported the creation of the National Endowment for Democracy, a quasi-private organization sustained largely with government funds. This organization was to promote democracy in Latin America and around the globe—that is, to renew the political war against socialism and

Soviet foreign policy by supporting elections and democratization. The democratization policy accompanied rather than replaced continued counterinsurgency efforts. It was a less idealistic return to the Alliance for Progress's themes of democracy and development to undercut the appeals of socialism and revolution. The United States would discourage new military coups but would not necessarily abandon its military allies still in power—until transition to civilian government seemed safe. Washington favored elected civilian governments that could provide a modicum of legitimacy for the fight against insurgencies. This policy encouraged "transition" to "democracy" while simultaneously intensifying the military operations against revolutionary movements.

Meanwhile, civil wars, guerrilla movements, and counterinsurgency campaigns bloodied South and Central America, while antigovernment violence was used to justify repression in Argentina, Uruguay, Chile, and Brazil until mid-decade. Troop numbers and military operations increased dramatically in the affected nations and also in neighboring countries drawn indirectly into the conflicts, such as Costa Rica, where the number of paramilitary police greatly increased, and Honduras, which served as a base for anti-Sandinista guerrillas (see Tables 7–1, 7–2). For reasons unconnected to the Central American wars and the Cold War, Ecuador, Mexico, and Venezuela also augmented their armed forces significantly. (In contrast, notable force reductions occurred in Argentina, Brazil, and Chile after 1984.)

These conflicts left a terrible toll of death, mutilation, and devastation. According to one detailed account on Central America, "a fair but conservative estimate would be 160,000 people killed and two million displaced during the decade; it is the scale not the precision that impresses."[13] Lasting into the 1990s, these wars involved numerous army sweeps into the countryside and villages as well as across international borders. They also sent refugees into Costa Rica, Mexico, and the United States.

At mid-decade, President Reagan enunciated the so-called Reagan Doctrine—a pledge of U.S. support for "freedom fighters" from Afghanistan to Nicaragua. As an important State Department official from 1983 to 1986 put it, "The United States was dramatically reengaged on the ground in the hardscrabble geopolitical contest with the Soviets on several continents."[14] The nation would fight the Soviets worldwide with suppport for anti-Communist guerrillas, much as the Soviets supported wars of national liberation. This pledge was a belated and unexpected return to "rollback" instead of "containment." In Central America it meant equipping, training, and directly, if covertly, assisting attacks by so-called *contras* on Nicaraguan military and economic targets.

The Reagan administration's ideological and military response to the Soviet doctrine regarding national liberation movements (and the United States' belated payback for the Soviet role in its humiliation in Vietnam with deadly military support for the Afghanistan resistance fighters) proved successful beyond the wildest dreams of U.S. policymakers. The Afghanistan war, accumulated economic woes, ethnic strife, erosion of the political legitimacy of the Communist party, *glasnost*, *perestroika*, and many other factors obvious only in retrospect overwhelmed the Soviet Union. By decade's end, *perestroika* shattered Communist party dominance and led shortly afterward to the Soviet

Union's demise and its fragmentation into a confederation of independent and sometimes warring republics. The Soviet Union's collapse between 1989 and 1992 crimped Cuba's economic and military lifeline. With Cuba's decline, and the Sandinistas' electoral defeat in 1990, the Salvadoran and Guatemalan revolutionary movements lost critical political and military support. More important, the credibility of "revolution" (meaning socialist revolution) evaporated.

Unexpectedly, the Cold War was ending. The shocking aftermath was resurgent nationalism, civil wars, territorial fragmentation, and the formation of new states. New maps and new nations confused policymakers and military planners. Ethnic bloodletting, secessionist movements, and unfamiliar borders

Table 7–1. Hemispheric Security and Military Conflict, 1979–1992

Events and Operations	*Year(s)*
Sandinista victory in Nicaragua; military buildup	1979–81
Committee of Santa Fe Report	1980
Archbishop Romero murdered in El Salvador	1980
Sendero Luminoso launches armed offensive	1980–82
Guerrillas' unsuccessful "final offensive" in El Salvador	1981
CIA director meets with Argentine military leaders to work out plan for training anti-Sandinista Nicaraguans (*contras*)	1981
Creation of UNRG (Guatemalan National Revolutionary Unity)	1982
Argentina versus England; Malvinas/Falklands War	1982
United States invades Grenada	1983
Contadora process begins (foreign ministers of Mexico, Venezuela, Colombia, Panama)	1983
Joint U.S.-Honduran military exercises on Nicaraguan border	1984
Kissinger Bipartisan Committee Report	1984
Public uproar over U.S. mining of Nicaraguan harbors	1984
José Napoleón Duarte elected president of El Salvador	1984
Sandinistas win elections in Nicaragua	1984
Stepped-up guerrilla offensive in Colombia; "Battle of the Palacio de Justicia"; army versus M-19	1985
OAS calls on U.S. to cease interference in Panamanian internal affairs	1987
Colombia-Venezuela skirmish in Gulf of Venezuela	1987
Esquipulas II, Guatemala (Central American presidents sign document calling for regional pacification) (Aug.)	1987
Cuba agrees to withdraw troops from Angola	1988
Honduras requests that UN provide border peacekeeping force (Oct.)	1988
Augusto Pinochet defeated in Chilean plebiscite	1988
Daniel Ortega agrees to negotiate with *contras* in accord with Arias's plan, but war continues	1988
Thirtieth anniversary of Cuban Revolution (Jan.)	1989
Committee of Santa Fe Report II	1989
UN Security Council votes to deploy 625-man ONUCA force to Central America (Nov.); staffed by Spain, West Germany, Canada	1989
FMLN offensive in El Salvador (Nov.)	1989
Panama National Assembly declares war on U.S.; U.S. invades Panama to oust Manuel Noriega (Dec.); OAS censures invasion	1989
Sandinista electoral defeat; government announces plan to cut army by 50 percent (June)	1990
Political accord to end war in El Salvador	1992

meant a comprehensive revamping of strategic concepts and military deployments. What was the objective of, or need for, NATO without a Soviet threat? With the division of Czechoslovakia, requests by Hungary, the Czech Republic, and Poland to join the NATO Pact, gruesome civil wars and ethnic conflict in a dismembered Yugoslavia, and failed military coups in the Soviet Union, the post-World War II international system and security regimes blew apart.

Table 7–2. Latin American Armed Forces Personnel, 1980–1990*

Country	*1980*	*1985*	*1990*
Argentina	160	129	85
	5.8	*4.2*	*2.6*
Bolivia	24	28	30
	4.5	*4.5*	*4.3*
Brazil	455	496	295
	3.7	*3.6*	*2.0*
Chile	115	124	95
	10.5	*10.3*	*7.2*
Colombia	65	66	110
	2.6	*2.2*	*3.3*
Costa Rica	4	8	8
		3.0	*2.6*
Cuba	375	297	297
	39.1	*29.4*	*27.9*
Dominican Republic	23	22	21
	4.0	*3.4*	*2.9*
Ecuador	35	43	53
	4.4	*4.9*	*5.4*
El Salvador	8	48	55
	1.7	*10.0*	*10.4*
Guatemala	15	43	43
	2.1	*5.1*	*4.5*
Haiti	7	6	8
	1.2	*1.1*	*1.3*
Honduras	12	21	18
	3.2	*5.0*	*3.8*
Mexico	110	140	175
	1.6	*1.8*	*2.1*
Nicaragua	50	74	28
	20.0	*23.5*	*7.7*
Panama	11	12	12
	5.8	*5.5*	*4.5*
Paraguay	15	14	16
	4.7	*3.5*	*3.4*
Peru	150	128	125
	8.5	*6.5*	*5.7*
Uruguay	29	30	25
	10.0	*10.0*	*8.0*
Venezuela	58	71	75
	3.4	*4.3*	*4.0*

Source: U.S. Arms Control and Disarmament Agency, *World Military Expenditures and Arms Transfers, 1971–1980,* and *1993–1994* (Washington, DC: 1983, 1995).
*Thousands, and *per 1,000 population.*

What, then, were the implications of the end of the bipolar Cold War system for U.S. national security and defense doctrine in the Western Hemisphere and for the armed forces in Latin America? What would become of the Rio Pact, the half-century crusade against international communism, and Communist-dominated internal subversion? How would the Latin American armed forces redefine their basic internal security doctrine and missions, adjust relations with civilian political and economic groups, and guarantee the integrity of their institutions in a rapidly changing international environment? Would the end of the Cold War make any difference in Colombia, Peru, and Guatemala's endemic guerrilla wars and the battle against drug-lord armies? Would it affect traditional border and regional issues that had led Colombia, Venezuela, Chile, Ecuador, and Peru to emphasize force and equipment modernization, at great expense, in the last half of the 1980s?

U.S. Policy and the Latin American Military in the 1980s

Local circumstances largely determined the extent to which the armed forces were scathed by the 1980s politico-economic crises, whether they had directly ruled their countries or whether, as in Colombia, Venezuela, and Mexico, they had collaborated with civilian governments in counterinsurgency and antidrug campaigns while avoiding institutional responsibility for the deteriorating political systems. Despite significant variations in the degree of control exercised by the armed forces over public policy at the beginning of the 1980s, the militaries that had ruled directly gradually withdrew, thus permitting transitions to elected civilian governments. In relinquishing this direct control, they sought through pacts with civilian parties, constitutional reforms, new legislation, and last-minute decrees before leaving power to limit damage to their institutions. Further, they sought to maintain political and economic leverage after civilian government was restored.

Military withdrawal from direct rule did not mean abject subordination to elected governments. The armed forces attempted to reassume their historical guardianship of *la patria* and made efforts to retain prerogatives assumed under military rule: defense of the constitutional and statutory missions that sanctioned broad military participation in the polity; the expanded influence and autonomy of military intelligence services; limitations on congressional oversight of military budgets, operations, professional education, and formulation of doctrine; control over promotions and duty assignments; maintenance of military jurisdiction over civilians for crimes involving national security; and a broad internal "developmental" mission.[15] In some cases, notably Argentina and Brazil, civilian governments enacted constitutional and legal reforms that more clearly limited the instances in which the armed forces might properly intervene in internal security matters, but in others, such as Chile and Ecuador, no such restrictions were achieved. To the extent that democracy means thorough control by elected civilian policymakers over military institutions and defense policy, and acceptance by the armed forces of their subordination to civilian institutions such as the legislature, courts, and the elected president, the transitions to elected government in Latin America in the 1980s did not entirely meet this criterion.[16]

Where the armed forces had not ruled directly, they nevertheless could not avoid altogether the institutional consequences of the economic crises and the changes in the global political system. Indeed, the armed forces in Venezuela, Colombia, Mexico, Nicaragua, and Cuba were affected as dramatically by global and regional developments, for different reasons, as the militaries in Brazil, Uruguay, and Chile. Increasing militarization of the narcotics-trafficking organizations, particularly in Colombia, Peru, Bolivia, and Mexico, and a surge in regional terrorism and of violent crimes concerned all the region's military and security forces. Colombia and Mexico were deploying new, more mobile special forces units at the end of the decade, and various armed forces were acquiring more sophisticated aircraft, small naval vessels, antiaircraft weapons, and equipment for low-intensity conflict. The armed forces became more technified, professional, and, at least for select units, more militarily proficient—but not less politicized.

Despite the dramatic and unexpected conclusion to the 1980s that startled the region's armed forces, Cold War rhetoric and the superpower struggle for influence in the Third World and Latin America had dominated most of the decade. As late as 1989 the Committee of Santa Fe reiterated its anti-Soviet discourse and called for renewed vigilance against the Soviet Union and Cuba in the Western Hemisphere. President Reagan relied extensively on the recommendations of the 1980 Committee of Santa Fe Report until 1985, particularly regarding increased military support for El Salvador, applying harsher economic and military pressure on the Sandinista government in Nicaragua, creating Radio Martí to target Cuban and Caribbean listeners, tightening the economic noose on the Cuban economy, proclaiming a "Caribbean Basin initiative" to counter Communist influence in the "American Mediterranean," and promoting a neoliberal economic agenda in the hemisphere to overcome "statism."

All five authors of "A New Inter-American Policy for the Eighties" (1980) served the Reagan administration in Latin America. In 1989 the Council for Inter-American Security published *Santa Fe II: A Strategy for Latin America in the Nineties*. Four of the authors of the 1980 report proclaimed at decade's end: "The Americas are still under attack. We warned of this danger in 1980. The attack is manifested in communist subversion, terrorism and narcotics trafficking. . . . This subversive-terrorist threat has grown, *not* diminished, in the past decade. Nicaragua and Cuba, the Soviet client states in the hemisphere, have become involved in the drug trade and have moved into cooperative and possibly dominant relationships with the drug mafias of Colombia."[17]

The tone of this declaration reflected accurately the mood among conservative U.S. policymakers and intelligence agencies in 1989. No official statements predicted an abrupt end to the Cold War in Latin America, the defeat of the Sandinistas in the upcoming 1990 elections, the total eclipse of the political influence of Cuban socialism, and, still less, the end of the Soviet Union. Some guerrilla movements in Latin America likewise retained their bellicose and utopian commitments to socialism through armed struggle. In Colombia in 1989, for example, the National Liberation Army (ELN) declared: "With the revolution that we impel we aim at the transformation of unjust structures existing in the country, realizing National Liberation and the construction of socialism, that is to say, to destroy the bourgeois State and to construct a State based on the exercise of democracy of the people dominated by the working class."[18] The Cold War rhetoric and premises that had shaped inter-American relations and Latin American politics for decades pervaded the 1980s, even on the unexpected brink of a new international order.

Three years later the Santa Fe II report read like ancient history and the ELN's declaration sounded like rhetoric from another age (although they continued to fight into the late 1990s, along with the FARC and other guerrilla forces in Colombia). There was no Soviet Union; Cuba was hard-pressed to feed itself and fuel its limited industrial plant. The divided Sandinistas were an opposition political party after electoral defeat in 1990. Yet only ten years earlier the ascendant Sandinista revolution had diverted and virtually monopolized U.S. attention in Latin America, thus shaping a decade of low-intensity warfare doctrine and practice and reinforcing the anti-Communist orientation of the armed forces.

War and Transitions to Civilian Government

In the view of the Latin American armed forces, the 1980s economic crisis and the gradual switch to civilian government beginning in Ecuador in 1979 offered new opportunities to their political enemies. The armed forces publicly interpreted accusations of human rights abuses as a convenient and cynical cover for international communism and its local allies (see Chapter 8). Their mission—to destroy, or at the least dissuade, such enemies—was also unmistakable. Throughout the 1980s they continued the crusade initiated against "exotic ideologies" and godless Communists in the 1920s and 1930s and intensified after World War II and the Cuban Revolution.

This Latin American military discourse was reinforced in the 1980s by U.S. policy, official proclamations, and covert operations at the same time that the Dr. Jekyll-and-Mr. Hyde-like U.S. policymakers called for democratization and respect for human rights. Until 1990, U.S. Latin America policy publicly treated the Nicaraguan revolution as a battlefront in the "third world war." In Central America, the enemy was "Sandinista totalitarianism," another instrument of international communism. The methods used to combat the Sandinistas included the full gamut of psychological, economic, and military operations—some legal, many in violation of international and U.S. law. Support for the *contras* (nicknamed the "freedom fighters"), organized and financed by the Reagan administration in the early 1980s with Argentine military advisers, made the United States the instigator and perpetrator by proxy of covert war against a sovereign state, even after opponents in Congress had attempted to curtail this policy.

The United States used Honduras and Costa Rica for clandestine air bases, covert intelligence operations, and military attacks against Nicaragua. Ongoing "exercises," beginning in 1983, included training Honduran troops, creating a U.S. command center at Comayagua, permanently stationing thousands of U.S. military personnel, equipment, and helicopters in the country, and constructing military airfields. Operation Big Pine II (1983) and related activities also permitted assistance to the anti-Sandinista guerrilla forces that attacked Nicaraguan targets from Honduran sanctuaries. These sanctuaries represented a permanent military threat for the Sandinistas as well as the prospect of an invasion, whether U.S.-backed or directly by U.S. forces.

Official military assistance in dollars to Central America skyrocketed from less than $10 million in 1980 to almost $300 million in 1984, the bulk to El Salvador and Honduras. (Assistance declined to "only" $131 million in 1989.)[19] The United States also encouraged Argentine, Israeli, and other foreign military assistance for the *contras* and for special operations in El Salvador and Guatemala. Reagan administration policies, a reaction to the undeniable Cuban and Nicaraguan support for guerrilla and revolutionary movements in Central America and elsewhere, unintentionally pushed Central America to the brink of regional war. Independent diplomatic action by the Contadora Group (Mexico, Venezuela, Colombia, and Panama) and by Costa Rican President Oscar Arias (for which he eventually received the Nobel Peace Prize) helped to prevent this outcome, but only after hundreds of thousands of casualties and widespread destruction. Meanwhile, the United States repeatedly declared its support for democratization (that is, elections) and applauded the inauguration of civilian presidents in Ecuador, Peru, Honduras, Bolivia, Argentina, El Salvador, and Uruguay.

These U.S. policies and practices alternately and simultaneously pleased, confused, and angered the Latin American militaries. Support for the British in the 1982 war provoked by the Argentine invasion of the Malvinas/Falkland Islands, over which Argentina had long claimed sovereignty, mocked the Monroe Doctrine and the Rio Treaty while elating some opponents of the military regime that had governed since 1976. And while abandoning the principles of hemispheric solidarity, even most opponents of the military regime were angered by the U.S. support for a NATO ally. In Honduras, officers and military institutions benefited from the "commissions" in money and matériel exacted for that country's use as a staging area for attacks on Nicaragua. They resented, however, the disrespectful quips characterizing their *patria* as the "U.S.S. *Honduras*," the disdain for Honduran sovereignty, and the lack of sensitivity to their internal political problems. Likewise, the salaries commanded by selected Guatemalan, Panamanian, Honduran, and Nicaraguan *contra* collaborators with U.S. intelligence agencies were appreciated, but they made recipients and others more cynical about Reagan administration proclamations seeking to appropriate the moral high ground and about U.S. demands for purges of officers accused of human rights violations—particularly when these officers headed special units and intelligence operations that the United States had financed and tutored. The arms embargo against Guatemala and resumption of good relations with the Brazilian military government, and with General Augusto Pinochet in Chile, all made clear the unprincipled, pragmatic, and self-interested fickleness of Washington's policy. The invasion of Panama in 1989 further outraged many officers in Latin America, both because it was a return to the unilateralism and interventionism reminiscent of the 1898–1930 period and because its target, General Manuel Noriega, had been a U.S. "asset" for years, even if he was brutal, corrupt, disloyal, and unreliable. Using U.S. troops to arrest Noriega while virtually destroying the Panama Defense Force was a terrible precedent for the Central American and Caribbean armed forces. It also angered nationalist officers in South America.

Clearly, U.S. military and diplomatic personnel knew about human rights violations in Spanish America and Brazil. They had cooperated with military officers and civilians guilty of such violations since the early 1960s. They had trained, equipped, encouraged, and participated in the war against guerrilla revolutionaries and their supporters, despite President Carter's brief human rights crusade in the late 1970s, and had also collaborated in countless covert operations. The U.S. invasion of Grenada in 1983, to oust a pro-Cuba government and deny the Soviet Union additional military platforms and choke points in the vulnerable Caribbean, reminded Nicaragua, and perhaps even Cuba, that direct military force was a feasible option to counter further Communist adventurism. More aggressive U.S. policies cheered some Latin American officers but disturbed others. Under President Reagan, clandestine operations were notorious—culminating, but not ending, with the Irangate scandal, illicit support for the *contras* operating in Honduras, Costa Rica, and Nicaragua, and the public debate over covert operations in Central America.

In the late 1980s and early 1990s, it appeared to Latin American officers that the United States wanted scapegoats to satisfy public opinion and the human rights organizations. The Bush administration again favored "democracy." But what did this mean for the Latin American military institutions and for U.S.-Latin American relations? Did the end of the Cold War imply bold reassertion of U.S. hegemony and disregard for the region's nationalism, national interests, and regional development? And did it mean, even worse, indifference, neglect, and even sacrifice of its erstwhile military allies to the realpolitik of the 1990s? These questions were left unanswered, for the United States had no explicit new foreign policy and security doctrine for the hemisphere until the mid-1990s (see Chapter 9).

In the 1980s the Latin American armed forces had first fought their battles in the "third world war," then retrenched, and reaffirmed their patriotism and commitment to their *patrias'* transcendental interests. They resisted trials for alleged human rights abuses and attacks on their professional integrity. In some cases they emerged relatively unscathed and with increased budgets and force levels. In others they lost prestige, resources, and political influence. Thus, the 1980s challenged the armed forces to once again conserve, defend, and reinvent *la patria* while preserving their institutions, historical role, and constitutional missions. They had to achieve this goal in the midst of economic crises, civil wars, insurgencies, internal divisions and interservice rivalries, and international reconfiguration. They were also confronted by erratic, confusing, and duplicitous U.S. policies, including pressure to "redemocratize" their nations and purge personnel identified as violators of human rights.

Transitions to "Democracy"?

The disparate impacts of the 1980s on the Latin American militaries make for no easy generalizations on the armed forces' professionalism, military capabilities, budgets, and political prerogatives by the early 1990s. With the exception of Chile, Haiti, and Paraguay, however, transitions to elected civilian governments occurred by 1989 (see Table 7–3). Everywhere, civilian governments and political leaders contested the military's traditional areas of professional autonomy and its political influence. Was this a new cycle of transitions from military to civilian regimes like those of the past? Or did the 1980s mark a truly new departure for Latin America and its armed forces?

Table 7–3. Transitions from Military to Civilian Governments, 1979–1993

Country	*Year*
Ecuador	1979
Peru	1980
Honduras	1982
Bolivia	1982
Argentina	1983
El Salvador	1984
Uruguay	1984
Brazil	1985
Guatemala	1986
Chile	1990
Paraguay	1993

The answer to these questions is both yes and no. The 1980s transitions featured much greater citizen participation and a deeper, more comprehensive move toward electoral democratization than ever before, as women, illiterates, and younger voters were included in the electorate (Tables 7–4, 7–5, 7–6). At the same time, there were immediate throwbacks to less democratic forms, to military saber rattling, and even to violent uprisings and coup attempts, particularly in Ecuador, Peru, Guatemala, Argentina, and, somewhat unexpectedly, in Venezuela (Table 7–7). As in the past, these coups and rebellions frequently involved military factions and intra-junta disputes. Between 1984 and 1998, however, no successful military coup took place in Spanish America or Brazil. Nonetheless, important constitutional, legal, and political impediments constrained the initiatives of civilian policymakers and subjected them to military oversight. These limits on elected officials belied a truly new departure for Latin American politics and its armed forces.

The existence of elected governments per se implies little about democracy. Elections may confer temporary, or even longer-term, legitimacy, or its veneer. They provide no other evidence of democracy or democratization. Napoleon Bonaparte's plebiscitary machinations, and those of dictators in Latin America since Argentine caudillo Juan Manuel de Rosas orchestrated a house-by-house verbal "yes-no" vote on his exercise of extraordinary powers in the early nineteenth century, demonstrate the importance of proper acknowledgment of "popular sovereignty" in the political creed that replaced monarchy.[20] Such electoral circuses, and more modern "demonstration elections," are essentially staged public relations devices: indispensable democratic sacraments administered by the high priests (domestic and/or foreign) of "transition."[21]

Table 7–4. Female Suffrage in Latin America, 1929–1965

Country	*Year First Enfranchised*	*Females First Vote in Presidential Election*
Argentina	1947	1951
Bolivia	1952	1956
Brazil	1932	1945
Chile	1949	1952
Colombia	1954	1958
Costa Rica	1949	1953
Cuba	1934[a]	1940
Dominican Republic	1942	(?)
Ecuador	1929[b]	1940
El Salvador	1939[c]	1950
Guatemala	1965[d]	1966
Honduras	1956[e]	1957
Mexico	1953	1958
Nicaragua	1955	1957
Panama	1946	1948
Paraguay	1961	1963
Peru	1955	1956
Uruguay	1932	1938
Venezuela	1947[f]	1947

Source: Mikael Boström, "Political Waves in Latin America, 1940–1988," *Nordic Journal of Latin American Studies* 19(1) (1989): 11, with addition of Cuba; also Dieter Nohlen, *Enciclopedia electoral latinoamericana y del caribe* (San José, Costa Rica: Instituto InterAmericano de Derechos Humanos, 1993).

[a]By decree of revolutionary government; not implemented when U.S. failure to recognize the government leads to its fall.

[b]*Facultativo* (voluntary) until 1967; voting mandatory for literate men.

[c]Vote is *facultativo*: age 25 if married, 30 if single. Men vote at 18, compulsory in 1886.

[d]Literate women enfranchised in 1945.

[e]Women have vote in 1954, but *facultativo* instead of mandatory.

[f]Vote in local elections in 1945.

Latin American leaders have resorted to these sacramental rituals since independence. In the early twentieth century, the United States was so firmly committed to political stabilization through elections in the Caribbean and Central America, and used the Marine Corps so frequently to supervise such elections, that it was made an official Marine mission until World War II. Indeed, Chapter XIV of the Corps's 1940 *Small Wars Manual* was called "Supervision of Elections." As the *Manual* suggests:

> The Government of the United States has supervised the presidential or congressional elections of neighboring republics on 12 different occasions. . . . The supervision of elections is perhaps the most effective peaceful means of exerting an impartial influence upon the turbulent affairs of sovereign states. Such supervision frequently plays a prominent role in the diplomatic endeavors that are so closely associated with small war activities. . . .
>
> It is well to consider the internal conditions that make the electoral supervision necessary. The electoral laws, the economic conditions, and the educational problems of the country concerned will often be found to be factors. The Electoral Mission can actually institute few permanent electoral reforms during the limited time that it is present in the country. It can, however, dem-

onstrate a method of conducting elections that may serve as a model to the citizens for future elections. A free, fair, and impartial election cannot be held in a country torn by civil strife. Before such an election can be held, the individual must be made to feel safe in his everyday life. The presence of United States military and naval forces is often necessary to furnish this guarantee.[22]

Table 7–5. Evolution of Voting Age and Literacy Requirements in Latin America

Country	*End of Literacy Requirements*	*Voting Age*	*Year*	*Mandatory or Not (1993)*
Argentina	1912	18	1863	yes[a]
Bolivia	1952	18[b]	1952	yes[c]
Brazil	1988	16	1988[d]	yes[e, f]
Chile	1970	18	1970	yes
Colombia	1936	18	1975	no
Costa Rica	1913	18	1971	yes
Cuba	1901	16	1976	yes
Dominican Republic	1865	18	1865[g]	yes
Ecuador	1978	18	1978	yes[e]
El Salvador	1883	18	1886[h]	yes
Guatemala	1945	18	1945	yes[e]
Honduras	1894	18	1924	yes[i]
Mexico	1857	18	1973	yes
Nicaragua	1893; 1948[j]	16	1984	no[k]
Panama	1904	18	1972	yes
Paraguay	1870	18	1870	yes
Peru	1979	18	1979	yes[e, a]
Uruguay	1918	18	1934	yes[i]
Venezuela	1946	18	1958[l]	yes

[a]Ages 18–70; optional if older.
[b]Changed in 1993 to 21.
[c]Vote rose from 120,000 in 1951 to 958,000 in 1956, first election after illiterates given vote.
[d]Optional for those ages 16–18.
[e]Optional for illiterates.
[f]Optional ages 16–18, over 70.
[g]1869–73: raised to 21; after 1873: again 18.
[h]1883: 21 or if married, any age; 1886: married or 18.
[i]Optional for women.
[j]Age increased to 21 for unmarried illiterates in 1939; 18 if married or literate in 1948.
[k]Registration mandatory, voting optional.
[l]First made 18 in 1946, raised to 21 from 1951 to 1958.

The *Small Wars Manual* further recognized that "in some countries, it is an established custom during electoral periods to arrest numerous citizens of the party not in power, for old offenses, for charges of minor infringement of law . . . and upon charges that have absolutely no foundation whatsoever," as such citizens are "automatically disenfranchised." Likewise, the *Manual* warned against the evils of government distribution of alcoholic beverages to voters, the use of public works projects to influence the vote, and government manipulation of the mass media.[23] Notwithstanding these laudable precautions, such supervised elections, or elections orchestrated by authoritarian regimes to buttress their position or provide a "soft landing" via extrication, rarely indicated that "democracy" had arrived (except in the eyes of some foreign observers) and never precluded future military coups or veto over government policy.

Table 7–6. Constitutional Suffrage Requirements in Latin America, 1993

Country	*Voting Age*	*Other Provisions*	*Constitutional Article(s)*
Argentina*			
Bolivia	21	18, if married	41
Brazil	18	mandatory until age 60; optional for illiterates and those age 16–18; active-duty conscripts may not vote	14
Chile	18	mandatory; active-duty military and police supervise elections	14 18
Colombia	18	active-duty military may not vote	40
Costa Rica	18	mandatory	95
Cuba	16	active-duty military may vote	132, 134
Dominican Republic	18	younger if ever married	13
El Salvador	18	mandatory	71-3
Guatemala	18	separate election law; active-duty military may not vote	147 248
Honduras	18	mandatory	36, 40
Mexico	18	mandatory	34
Nicaragua	16	registration mandatory	47
Panama	18	mandatory	125, 129
Paraguay	18	mandatory	118, 120, 152
Peru	18	mandatory until age 60	65
Uruguay	18	mandatory	74, 77, 80
Venezuela	18	mandatory	110

*The Argentine constitution in 1993 did not define suffrage requirements.

Even if elected governments, some competition, and expanded electorates were a weak indication of "democracy" (for example, an elected president, universal suffrage, the opposition obtaining at least 30 percent of the vote, with 20 percent of the population voting), in all of Latin America only Uruguay (with the exception of Venezuela from 1947 to 1948) met these criteria before 1950. By 1960 only seven countries (Argentina, Bolivia, Colombia, Costa Rica, Panama, Uruguay, and Venezuela) met these criteria, hardly a "wave" of democratization even by these low standards. From 1960 to 1984 the number of countries meeting the criteria never exceeded seven, although countries joined and fell from the list. In 1985, however, the number jumped to twelve, then to thirteen (1986–87), and back to twelve (1988).[24] In this sense there was a unique wave of electoral competition and participation in Latin America in the 1980s, even if it was not accompanied by more profound democratization of the political systems and national economies.[25]

Samuel Huntington's definition of "a twentieth-century system as democratic to the extent that its most powerful collective decision makers are selected through fair, honest, and periodic elections in which candidates freely compete for votes and in which virtually all the adult population is eligible to vote," is an important starting point for defining democracy, but only a starting point.[26] It neglects most of the crucial aspects of democracy, even the extent to which particular groups and parties are excluded from electoral competition and the media is chilled, so long as the candidates who do participate may "freely compete for votes" and most adults may cast ballots.[27] Also not mentioned is the fact that in most Latin American countries, voting (for those eligible) is compulsory, although the extent of enforcement and penalties for abstention vary considerably. This requirement means that it is often difficult to express dissatisfaction or simply avoid electoral participation through abstention. High turnouts impress foreign observers, and particularly the U.S. media, but the meaning of such turnouts is often lost on those who are unaware that abstention entails fines, prevents voters from obtaining government services, employment, or a passport—and sometimes much worse.

Even if elections and more inclusive suffrage are keys to democratization, Huntington's emphasis on "waves" of democratization would be somewhat misplaced. The number of presidential elections in Latin America (thirty-five to forty-five per decade) did not vary substantially from 1851 to 1990, with the exception of a precipitous drop from 1971 to 1980 (fourteen)—a return to the levels of 1841–1851. This dropoff roughly corresponds to the post-1964 era of antipolitical military regimes initiated with the Ecuadorian and Brazilian coups. In the five years from 1981 to 1986 the "wave" of presidential elections reached twenty-one, recuperating to traditional levels.[28]

The two most important formal limitations on electoral participation in Latin America, gender and literacy, were addressed gradually since the midnineteenth century, and particularly since World War II, but with no noticeable waves or cycles of voter incorporation unless 1946 to 1980 is viewed as a continuous wave. Likewise, enfranchisement of younger voters (age 16 to 18) is not entirely a recent phenomenon, although it has significantly increased the size of some electorates after the 1970s. By the early 1990s eighteen-year-olds voted everywhere except in Bolivia (unless married, then voting was permitted at 18). Sixteen-year-olds voted in Nicaragua and Cuba. In the Dominican Republic anyone who is, or has been, married obtained the suffrage, even if below the voting age of 18. Literacy requirements were abolished, although in some cases where voting was mandatory, it was optional (*facultativo*) for illiterates (Brazil, Ecuador) and for those over age 60 (Argentina, Brazil, Peru). One country enfranchised females in the 1920s, three in the 1930s, five in the 1940s, six in the 1950s, and two in the 1960s. In some cases female voting was optional, in contrast to mandatory voting for males. In other cases, the voting age for women varied from that of men, or even varied according to marital status. These discriminatory provisions generally disappeared by the 1990s.

By the end of the 1950s voters comprised 20 percent of the population in only seven Latin American countries, hardly a "wave" on this dimension of participation. However, greatly expanded electorates from the 1970s to the 1990s meant that the 1978–1990s transitions from military to civilian governments were associated with much more inclusionary eligibility rules and voter participation.[29] This was an important departure from the past for Latin American politics—but, to reiterate, not one that necessarily democratizes other aspects of the political systems. In particular, it does not guarantee that elected officials can generally make and conduct policy without military veto, either through preemptive intimidation or actual use of force, nor that the military subordinates its opinions and operations to the authority of elected officials regarding foreign, defense, military, and other policies. Without this, government succession by election rather than by coup is a sort of "low-intensity democracy" that followed the era of "low-intensity conflict" throughout the hemisphere.

More inclusionary voting rules, particularly before the 1990s, little affected the fundamental character of Latin American political systems; they were regimes founded on the notion of "protected democracy" and military guardianship. But significant variations existed in the extent to which military guardianship was overtly manifested and in the degree to which civilian leaders successfully (re)established civilian control over most areas of policymaking. By the early 1990s in Uruguay and Argentina, for example, the armed forces were clearly on the political defensive, while in Chile, Peru, and Ecuador they retained most of their political prerogatives. In El Salvador the 1992 peace accords led to purges of officers identified as human rights violators, changes in military doctrine, and considerable social ostracism; in Guatemala after the 1996 peace accords the impact of the human rights issue and the extent of real civilian control of the armed forces remained uncertain.

The transitions to civilian rule, except in Haiti, Chile, and Paraguay, took place before the official end of the Cold War. In no case did they result from the armed forces' military defeat by insurgents. The armed forces actually permitted transitions to civilian governments after negotiating acceptable terms and in some cases, such as Guatemala and El Salvador in the early 1980s, as part of the effort to relegitimize their counterinsurgency campaigns. They imposed conditions regarding the timing and framework for elections, permissible candidates, the limits of civilian policy initiatives in the post-transition period, and, usually, amnesties or de facto impunity for alleged human rights violations.[30] Underlying these transitions was a continued commitment to the military's guardianship role and, in most, to an explicit constitutional mission (the exceptions being Argentina and Uruguay, where the armed forces' mission had historically appeared in the military organic laws, military codes, and national security legislation rather than in the constitution). The armed forces also maintained significant degrees of professional and institutional autonomy. Of course, these efforts to constrain future government initiatives and policies were not foolproof, and in every case the armed forces faced some efforts to redefine or even reverse the transition accords after they turned over the government to civilians. Political maneuvering did not end with transition to civilian government, and in some instances the armed forces suffered important institutional and policy disappointments in the 1990s (see Chapter 9).

The armed forces and their civilian allies also insisted on institutional and political guarantees against a return to the populism and revolutionary rhetoric of the 1960s and 1970s. They wanted any "return to democracy" to be insulated from a resurgence of leftist parties and movements. Often this entailed "electoral engineering" with the redesign of voting districts and modification of laws regulating political parties and elections. Such "reforms" sought to guarantee overrepresentation and veto power in legislatures for groups and parties of the political right and center-right after military *juntas* and presidents left office. They also insisted on limits to the initiatives to be taken by civilian governments after military officers handed over the presidency and allowed a return to electoral politics. In short, they wanted elected civilian governments in order to restore their professional image, to reestablish internal discipline and traditional command hierarchy, to depoliticize their institutions, and to put a nonmilitary face on the body politic. They hoped to shed their image as international pariahs and their responsibilities for managing the economic crisis. But this was neither a commitment to deepening democracy nor to eschewing their tutelary mission.

In their view, the armed forces had demonstrated their indispensable political and military role from 1959 until the end of the Cold War. The restoration (or conservation) of democracy was made possible by their collaboration in the defeat of international communism and its local advocates. Democracy, always vulnerable to external and internal threats, made necessary their vigilance and protection against future (undefined) threats—domestic and foreign, military and political, international and subnational.

The Armed Forces and Protected Democracy

"Protected democracy," with the military institutions as the guarantors of the political and legal order and, implicitly, the adjudicators of their nations' common good, permanent interests, and national security requirements, has a long history in Latin America, as described in previous chapters.[31] It is a political model that sets vague formal limits on the scope of legal political activity and reform, and it is premised on the notion that people must be protected from themselves and from organizations that might subvert the existing political and social order. Such subversion, even when ostensibly legal, must be repressed. Groups with subversive aims might seek control of universities, labor organizations, the media, and even the legislature. Their actions potentially threaten "national values," the "permanent interests of the nation," and, in the Latin American version, "the Western Christian way of life." Thus, as in Plato's *Republic*, society requires guardians to defend these permanent values against internal and external enemies. In Latin America, the armed forces (and sometimes the police, who are often commanded by army officers and assigned formally to the Defense Ministry) have shouldered this historical mission, by constitutional and legislative prescription and also by self-assignment. To illustrate, a provision in Peru's 1856 Constitution obligated the armed forces to disobey the government if it violated the constitution or the laws. According to Víctor Villanueva, a former officer and leading authority on the Peruvian military, "This meant accepting, implicitly, that apart from the suffrage, sovereignty resided in the army rather than in the people. The latter had the right to elect governments and the army the duty of ousting them when it [the army] determined that they violated the constitution."[32]

More than a century after Peru's 1856 Constitution was promulgated, and two years before a coup that made him president of Argentina (1966–1970), Lieutentant General Juan Onganía reaffirmed this widely shared notion of military guardianship: "Obedience is due a government when its power is derived from the people. . . . It should therefore be clear that the duty of rendering such obedience will have ceased being an absolute requirement if there are abuses in the exercise of legal authority . . . when this is done as a result of exotic ideologies, or when there is a violent breakdown in the balance of independence of the branches of government, or when constitutional prerogatives are used in such a way that they completely cancel out the rights and freedoms of the citizens."[33] It is the duty of the armed forces, under these conditions, to "uphold the constitution" as "the last bulwark of nationality."[34] This was precisely the rationale for the Argentine coup in 1966 and for the Chilean coup in 1973. In the latter case, "the Armed Forces . . . intervened institutionally, . . . to depose an illegitimate government . . . assuming a role, in itself just and opportune, to achieve the salvation of the nation's traditions and its permanent values."[35]

Nowhere in Latin America from 1978 to the early 1990s—even in Argentina and Uruguay, where civilians made the most progress in reasserting their authority—did transition to elected civilian government eliminate the principal constitutional, juridical, and political foundations of protected democracy and, especially, the armed forces' self-perception as the reservoir of national values and as the "ultimate bastion" of *la patria*. In the words of Uruguayan President Julio María Sanguinetti, "trials for the military officers were incompatible with the climate of institutional stability and tranquility . . . if the military challenged the judiciary, we were faced with the [possibility] of a very dangerous institutional weakening [*degradación*] that, in the medium term, was going to result in institutional breakdown."[36] In Argentina, by 1990, new legislation and presidential pardons had undone the initial resolve to punish human rights abuses and to guarantee that such state terrorism would never occur again. In 1994, President Carlos Menem declared that "thanks to the armed forces, we triumphed in that dirty war that brought our community to the brink of dissolution."[37] And the chief of the Joint Chiefs "argued the traditional military position: the armed forces had eliminated a subversive attempt to conquer the country, and Argentines should put the past behind them."[38]

Despite the apparent subordination of the armed forces to civilian government, limits clearly existed if the military perceived that its institutional interests and prerogatives were threatened. The tension in Uruguayan civil-military relations stretched taut again in 1992, when the army refused presidential orders to confront striking police; and in June 1993, when the kidnapping of an important former DINA (Chilean secret police) agent implicated Uruguayan army intelligence and Chilean officers. In the last case, President Luis Alberto

Lacalle cut short a European trip and returned to Montevideo amid coup rumors. Lacalle "reassigned" the general heading army intelligence (Servicio de Información del Ejército). The Frente Amplio opposition leader, retired General Liber Seregni, commented that "this is a delicate problem, we must proceed carefully."[39] Uruguayans of all political groups recognized the danger of "pushing the military too far."

The Uruguayan and Argentine experiences illustrated dramatically that despite the different patterns of military extrication and transition to civilian government, important limitations on the transition and on key constitutional aspects of the subsequent political system were imposed by the military and its civilian allies. Human rights violations were rarely punished or were later pardoned. Thus, civilian governments either legitimated self-conferred amnesties or themselves amnestied human rights violators after taking office in the name of "consolidating the transition." In most nations, behind-the-scenes threats and bargaining sufficed to ensure restraint by civilian politicians and impunity for past violations. Summaries of the amnesty laws benefiting violators and of the limitations placed on elected governments after 1978 are presented in Tables 7–8 and 7–9.

But could democracy be consolidated on the basis of intimidation, threats of new coups, and pardoning massive and systematic torture and murder? Could impunity for the victimizers and the bitter resentment of the victims' families and the survivors of the torture chambers be foundations for democracy? Would "forgetting the past" and "moving forward," as the military and its political allies urged, really permit "social healing"? Or would it reinforce the tradition of impunity for official crimes, government nonaccountability, military autonomy, and popular cynicism that had impeded democratization in Latin America for so long?

Whatever the long-term answer to these questions, the immediate result of transition was a reaffirmation of certain antidemocratic, anti-civil libertarian institutions and practices. The military everywhere sought to reserve a residual "sovereignty," to sustain its virtually totemic status: feared and revered, quasi-sacred protectors of *la patria*. Civilian politicians looked over their shoulders, consulted with officers, feared offending them, and accepted the reality of military guardianship. On the other hand, failed coup attempts and mutinies revealed an underlying resistance to a return to military rule and also the persistent factionalism within the armed forces in Argentina, Bolivia, Venezuela, Ecuador, Brazil, Peru, and most of Central America (Table 7–7).

The protected democracies reborn from 1979 to 1993 generally maintained old penal codes and special legislation on the internal security of the state. They also incorporated many aspects of the national security doctrines[40] shared by the post-1964 antipolitical military regimes into the new constitutions, military law, and statutes covering internal security, terrorism, and public order.[41] They limited presidential and congressional control and oversight of military institutions, with concomitant increases in the armed forces' relative autonomy.[42] This autonomy included extensive domestic intelligence operations, with surveillance and electronic eavesdropping on politicians, labor leaders, and social activists as well as of the mass media. They also reaffirmed a long tradition of governance through constitutional regimes of exception.[43] While the political liberalization that occurred with transitions to elected governments was real and welcome, it did not dismantle the institutional foundations of protected democracy. The armed forces often remained unaccountable to civilian officials and immune from legal restraint. They had reaffirmed their role as

Table 7–7. Military Coup Attempts, Rebellions, and Uprisings, 1978–1993

Year(s)	*Country*	*Events*
1978	Honduras	Gen. Policarpio Paz García ousts Gen. Juan A. Melgar Castro
1978–80	Bolivia	Three failed coups; five presidents, none elected
1979	El Salvador	"Military Youth" progressive coup
1980	El Salvador	Progressives displaced within *junta*
1980	Bolivia	Gen. Luis García Meza proclaims his government has no fixed limits: "in this sense I am like General Pinochet"
1981	Bolivia	*Junta* ousts García Meza; headed by Gen. Celso Torrelio Villa
1981	Argentina	Gen. Galtieri deposes Gen. R. Viola
1982	Guatemala	Gen. E. Ríos Montt ousts Gen. B. Lucas García
1982	Bolivia	Gen. Guido Vildoso Calderón replaces Gen. Torrelio Villa
1983	Guatemala	Gen. Oscar H. Mejía Victores ousts Gen. Ríos Montt
1986	Ecuador	Rebellion led by Air Force Gen. Frank Vargas Pazzos
1987	Ecuador	President Febres Cordero kidnapped to obtain release of Vargas Pazzos; bloody confrontation between army and air force officers
1987	Argentina[a]	Holy Week rebellion; protest against trials for human rights violations
1988	Argentina	Monte Caseros uprising (Jan.)
1988	Brazil	Coup rumors (April); military confrontation with strikers at Volta Redonda and accusation by Gen. Tasso Villar de Aquino that strikers were prepared and directed by agents trained in Cuba and Nicaragua (Oct.)
1988	Guatemala	Abortive coup attempt in garrisons at Jutiapa and Retalhuleu
1988	Argentina	Villa Martelli uprising; Col. Seineldín uprising at Campo de Mayo (Dec.)
1989	Argentina	Attack by leftists on La Tablada garrison (Jan.); attackers defeated and several "disappeared"
1989	Guatemala	Defense Minister Gen. Héctor A. Gramajo suppresses coup attempt by retired officers, backed by air force units (May)
1989	Ecuador	Military threatens revolt if Abdalá Bucaram wins election; he loses
1989	Panama	Abortive coup by Maj. Moisés Giroldi; he is shot
1990	Argentina	*Carapintada* revolt suppressed; Operation Virgen de Lujan
1992	Venezuela	Two bloody revolts (Feb. and Nov.) and interservice conflicts; President C. Andrés Pérez barely escapes assassination attempt
1992	Peru	President Fujimori, with military support, closes congress; *autogolpe*; new constitution in 1993
1993	Guatemala	President Jorge Serrano failed "self-coup"; initial support from military factions

[a]For detailed analysis of the Argentine rebellions from 1987 to 1990 see Deborah L. Norden, *Military Rebellion in Argentina: Between Coups and Consolidation* (Lincoln: University of Nebraska Press, 1996).

Table 7–8. Amnesty Laws or Decrees for Human Rights Violations, 1978–1993[a]

Country	*Law or Decree*
Ecuador	None
Peru	None until 1995 (Law 26479). Covers military, police, and civilians accused of human rights violations from May 1980 until June 1995 (but in May 1993 military units took to streets to discourage congressional investigation of alleged human rights violations).[b]
Honduras	None
Bolivia	None (informal agreement between President Siles Suaso and military to separate from service officers associated with García Meza government).
Argentina	Military Amnesty Law 22924, 1983 (overturned by congress in December 1983); Law 23049 reforms military code but gives Supreme Military Council initial jurisdiction over human rights violations, subject to appeal in civilian courts; *punto final* Law 23492, 1986; Due Obedience Law 23521, 1987, after military mutinies. President Menem pardons high-ranking officers excluded from earlier laws, soldiers who revolted against President Alfonsín, and those convicted by court-martial after war with Great Britain in 1982, Decree 1002, 1989; 1990 pardons ex-*junta* commanders, ex-chiefs of federal police and others.[c]
El Salvador	Partial amnesty 1987, DL 805. Law of National Reconciliation, 1992, excludes those already convicted in jury trial and those "serious acts of violence whose impact on society requires, with greater urgency, public knowledge of the truth." General amnesty, March 1993.[d]
Uruguay	1984 Naval Pact; Ley de Caducidad, Law 15848, 1986, covers crimes before March 1985;[e] reaffirmed in 1989 plebiscite. Military commander instructs personnel not to appear before courts in human rights cases.
Brazil	1979 Amnesty Law 6683, covers crimes from 1961–79; informal agreement between high command, President Figueiredo, and civilian leaders, that if civilian were allowed to be president the 1979 amnesty would be respected; Constitutional Amendment 26, 1985.[f]
Guatemala	Agreement to no trials as part of 1985 transition; among sixteen decrees issued just prior to leaving office, military decrees amnesty for all those guilty of political or politically related crimes from March 1982 to January 1985.[g] Decree 8-86; congress declares amnesty for perpetrators of political crimes (June 1988).
Chile	1978 Amnesty Decree Law 2191 (only crimes before 1978, except assassination of Orlando Letelier in Washington, DC, in 1976); other cases pending. Supreme Court upholds 1978 amnesty decree in 1990.
Paraguay	None as part of transition

[a]See Tribunal Permanente de los Pueblos, *Proceso a la impunidad de crímenes de lesa humanidad en América Latina, 1989–1991* (Bogotá: N.p., 1991).

[b]See Ernesto de la Jara Basombrío, "El Gobierno de la Impunidad," *Ideele* 5 (59–60) (December 1993): 50–56.

[c]The *punto final* law (December 1986) was passed after investigation of human rights violations by the military government, indictment of hundreds of military personnel, and prosecution of *junta* members resulted in serious strains in civil-military relations. The "due obedience" legislation came after military rebellions (although ex-President Alfonsín denied the connection). Another uprising by the so-called *carapintadas* (commando units with painted faces) occurred in December 1988, and still another in December 1990. In 1989, President Menem pardoned most participants in the "dirty war," those convicted by courts-martial after the Malvinas/Falklands

War, and hundreds of officers and NCOs involved in the three rebellions against Alfonsín, followed in 1990 by pardons for the *junta* members and others excluded from earlier ones. Those who rebelled against the Menem government in early December 1990 were tried for insubordination but not for the more serious crime (in civilian courts) of rebellion. See Enrique I. Groisman, "La reconstrucción del Estado de Derecho en Argentina (1983–1989)," in Enrique I. Groisman, ed., *El derecho en la transición de la dictadura a la democracia: La experiencia en América Latina* (Buenos Aires: Centro Editor de América Latina, 1990): 40–53; and *Americas Watch*, "Truth and Partial Justice in Argentina, An Update," April 1991.

[d]See J. E. A., "Consideraciones sobre la Ley de Amnistía," *Estudios CentroAmericanos* (April–May 1993): 414–19; and International Commission of Jurists, *A Breach of Impunity: The Trial for the Murder of Jesuits in El Salvador* (New York: Fordham University Press, 1992).

[e]See "Texto de Acuerdo entre las Fuerzas Armadas y Políticos en el Que Se Acuerda el Nuevo Proceso Democrático," 1984; and "Ley de Caducidad de la Pretensión Punitiva del Estado por Delitos de Militares y Policías durante el Regimen de Facto," 1986.

[f]Alfred Stepan (1988): 59; Wilfred A. Bacchus, *Mission in Mufti: Brazil's Military Regimes, 1964–1985* (Westport, CT: Greenwood Press, 1990): 124–28.

[g]See *Derechos humanos en Centroamérica 1986, Situación en El Salvador, Guatemala y Nicaragua* (Guatemala: Instituto CentroAmericano de Estudios Políticos, INCEP, 1986).

Table 7–9. Military Limitations on Transitions to Elected Governments

Country	*Limitations*
Ecuador	Military monitors plebiscite on alternative constitutions; impedes participation of certain candidates in transition election, manipulates recount on first round of 1978 presidential election; assures respect for institutional prerogatives of armed forces and participation in naming defense minister.[a]
Peru	Participation in constituent assembly; pact with APRA on military prerogatives. (To confront terrorism, most of country was put under state of emergency, with military jurisdiction in military zones recurrently from 1982 to 1993.)
Honduras	Chief of armed forces selected by congress for five-year term from list proposed by Supreme Council of Armed Forces; can only be removed by two-thirds' congressional vote. All appointments made by armed forces chief (Arts. 277-282). Changed to three years (Decrees 188-85, 189-86). Numerous limitations on civilian control of armed forces in constitution and constitutive law of armed forces, including military budget oversight (Art. 293). All laws, decrees, decree-laws, regulations, orders, and other dispositions in effect at time of promulgation of new constitution remain valid, unless they conflict with constitution, are derogated or modified (Transitory Art. 376, 1982 Constitution).[b]
Bolivia	Transition by coup and negotiations between U.S. ambassador, military, party leaders, labor, and private sector. Elected president (1980) prevented by coup from taking office; U.S. refuses to recognize *junta*; new coup in 1981, more "reformist"; brings U.S. recognition; congress names same candidate (Siles Suazo) president, 1982. New coup attempt and kidnapping of president. U.S. ambassador telephones military leaders to express opposition to coup (led by special elite antidrug unit trained by U.S.). Siles released and thanks U.S. for its role in "restoring democracy." Military retains basic prerogatives; no trials for human rights violations, except prosecution of ex-president García Meza and forty-seven collaborators on various charges.[c]

Argentina	Military stays in power for one year after Islas Malvinas defeat; negotiates with Peronistas, but Radicals win presidency. Least successful case for military controlling transition, but gradual reassertion of military presence as civilian governments make concessions after mutinies and coup attempts, 1985–92.
El Salvador	Army retains most prerogatives; country under state of siege for most of 1984–93, involving broad military jurisdiction over civilians. Minimal civilian authority over military. Peace accord between government and FMLN in 1992 calls for civilian role in reforming military education through new Consejo Académico Cívico-Militar and in reviewing cases of officers accused of human rights abuses for their dismissal (*depuración*).[d]
Uruguay	Military vetoes candidacy of most popular presidential candidate; key opposition leaders in jail; obtains informal guarantees on prerogatives and temporary change in constitution for new regime of exception—"state of insurrection" (1984 Naval Club Pact);[e] Institutional Act 19, 1984. Army, navy, and air force commanders retain positions in transition; Lt. Gen. Hugo Medina becomes defense minister shortly after 1987 retirement. SIFA (Armed Forces Intelligence Service) continues surveillance of civilian politicians, activists, labor leaders, and media.[f]
Brazil	Military orchestrates transition. Maintains almost all prerogatives and relative service autonomy, no Defense Ministry permitted. Intelligence agencies (SNI) and National Security Council also retain much autonomy, despite later name changes and reorganization. Precludes direct elections for president and imposes state of emergency in Brasilia when congress votes on issue. Fail to entirely control transition election, but active participation in elaborating 1988 Constitution ensures broad constitutional mission, participation in policymaking affecting "national security" (e.g., labor and agrarian reform policy) and continued relative autonomy.[g]
Guatemala	Military creates Tribunal Supremo Electoral to control transition election, devises new election laws. Calls constituent assembly (1984) to adopt new constitution. Obtains confirmation of decrees of *junta* and guarantees against trials for human rights abuses. President Cerezo claims he has "30 percent of the power" (the army has the rest).[h]
Chile	Transition according to 1980 Constitution. Small concessions to opposition in 1989 reforms, but also implementation before President Aylwin takes office of *leyes de amarre* (group of laws that further limit authority of incoming government in many policy areas, including new organic laws for armed forces and national police just prior to transition). Electoral and political party laws prevent restoration of pre-1973 proportional representation system.[i]
Paraguay	Military coup by Gen. Andrés Rodríguez ousts Gen. Alfredo Stroessner (1989); Rodríguez wins presidency in manipulated election as candidate of official Colorado party with 74 percent of vote; military seeks to overcome factionalism in party, orchestrates constitutional convention in 1991; new constitution in 1992 allows military to retain most of previous prerogatives

(though prohibiting active duty personnel's participation in political parties); 1991 armed forces law stipulates "autonomy" of armed forces, congress cannot pass laws on military unless previously approved by president; preelection rumors that if Colorado candidate Carlos Wasmosy lost, armed forces would seize power. Various election irregularities.[j]

---

[a]The military also secured an allocation of petroleum revenues estimated at 23 percent of the total, named representatives to the boards of directors of the major state corporations (most created by the military), had a monopoly over air and sea transport, and became a major shareholder in a number of industries made by the Directorship of Army Industries. See David W. Schodt, *Ecuador, An Andean Enigma* (Boulder, CO: Westview Press, 1987): 138–39; Catherine M. Conaghan, *Restructuring Domination: Industrialists and the State in Ecuador* (Pittsburgh: University of Pittsburgh Press, 1988); Anita Isaacs, *Military Rule and Transition in Ecuador* (Pittsburgh: University of Pittsburgh Press, 1993); and John Martz, "The Military in Ecuador: Policies and Politics of Authoritarian Rule," Latin American Institute, University of New Mexico Occasional Papers Series, No. 3 (1988).

[b]See Ramiro Colindres O., *Análisis comparativo de las constituciones políticas de Honduras*, 4th ed. (Tegucigalpa: Graficentro Editores, 1988); and Leticia Salamón, *Política y militares en Honduras* (Tegucigalpa: Centro de Documentación de Honduras, 1992).

[c]"The Trial of Responsibilities: The García Meza Tejada Trial," *Americas Watch* 5(6) (September 10, 1993).

[d]See Knut Walter and Philip J. Williams, "The Military and Democratization in El Salvador," *Journal of Inter-American Studies and World Affairs* 35(1) (1993): 39–87. The authors note that in the 1980s the military "was successfully consolidating its presence in the state, expanding its network of control in the countryside, and maintaining its institutional autonomy" (p. 55). Also, that while the peace accords between the government and the FMLN "on paper, . . . go a long way in reducing the military's institutional prerogatives, . . . implementation of the reforms affecting the armed forces proved to be a difficult process" (p. 65). Moreover, "the accords fail to address adequately several important areas in which the military retains political influence [including] the military's administration of key state institutions [telecommunications (ANTEL), waterworks (ANDA), ports (CEPA), the General Directorate of Land Transport, the General Directorate of Statistics and Census, Customs, Civil Aeronautics, and the Postal Service]" (p. 67). For a more detailed discussion of the negotiation process see Gerardo Munck, "Beyond Electoralism in El Salvador: Conflict Resolution through Negotiated Compromise," *Third World Quarterly* 14(1) (1993): 75–93. Munck heavily emphasizes the critical influence of the United Nations and of U.S. military and civilian policymakers on the Salvadoran government and armed forces in ending the civil war in El Salvador.

[e]See "Texto de Acuerdo entre las Fuerzas Armadas y Políticos en Que Se Acuerda el Nuevo Proceso Democrático," in Juan Maestre Alfonso, *Constituciones y Leyes Políticos de América Latina, Filipinas y Guinea Ecuatorial*, II, *Los Regímenes de Seguridad Nacional*, I, *Chile, Uruguay* (Seville: Escuela de Estudios Hispano-Americanos de Sevilla, 1989): 483–86.

[f]For an overview of the major issues in civil-military relations in Uruguay from 1984 to 1990 see Juan Rial, *Las fuerzas armadas en los años 90, Una agenda de discusión* (Montevideo: PEITHO, 1990), esp. pp. 27–59; and Martin Weinstein, *Democracy at the Crossroads* (Boulder, CO: Westview Press, 1988).

[g]See Thomas E. Skidmore, *The Politics of Military Rule in Brazil, 1964–1985* (New York: Oxford University Press, 1988); Paul W. Zagorski, *Democracy vs. National Security: Civil-Military Relations in Latin America* (Boulder, CO: Lynne Rienner, 1992); and Wilfred A. Bacchus, *Mission in Mufti: Brazil's Military Regimes, 1964–1985* (Westport, CT: Greenwood Press, 1990).

[h]Susanne Jonas, *The Battle for Guatemala: Rebels, Death Squads, and U.S. Power* (Boulder, CO: Westview Press, 1991): 154–59.

[i]See Brian Loveman, "*Misión Cumplida*? Civil-Military Relations and the Chilean Political Transition," *Journal of Inter-American Studies and World Affairs* 33(3) (Fall 1991): 35–74.

[j]See Jan Knippers Black, "Almost Free, Almost Fair: Paraguay's Ambiguous Election," *NACLA Report on the Americas* 27(2) (September/October 1993): 26–28; and Marcial Antonio Riquelme, *Negotiating Democratic Corridors in Paraguay, The Report of the Latin American Studies Association Delegation to Observe the 1993 Paraguayan National Elections* (Pittsburgh: LASA, University of Pittsburgh Press, 1994).

guardians of *la patria*, as they defined it, with the defeat of international communism and the pacification (with the exceptions previously mentioned) of domestic insurgencies.

The Legacy

With rare exceptions, the armed forces achieved impunity from prosecution for human rights violations, and they continued to glorify their salvation of nations that they claimed were mortally threatened by subversion.[44] The military and civilian victors in the internal wars from 1959 until the early 1990s also won important, if incomplete, political victories.[45] They conditioned, controlled, and limited the extent of democratization in the hemisphere while installing themselves (with important variation and challenges from reformers from country to country) as the arbiters of national politics. In this role they were supported by the civilian parties and movements that remembered leftist and populist threats after the Cuban Revolution, and favored protected democracy. These victories were tempered by elections, civilian governments, and greater respect for civil liberties and rights in everyday life. They were further tempered by the armed forces' indisposition to assume responsibility for directly managing the socioeconomic morass bequeathed by the 1980s crisis and the challenge of a post-Cold War global economy. (Chile was an obvious exception, since the military turned the country back to civilians with a transformed and growing economy.)

With "democracy" virtually unchallenged ideologically, from the former Soviet Union to South Africa, the armed forces pragmatically pretended to swallow the cure-all democratic snake oil peddled by the Cold War's victors. The temporary lack of a credible internal subversive threat (again, with exceptions, such as in Peru, Guatemala, El Salvador, Colombia, and Nicaragua) also undermined the credibility of overt military pressure on elected governments as did the lack of verifiable claims of external linkages to the continuing internal insurgencies. These factors enabled civilian governments to chip away at military prerogatives, in some instances even leading to significant budget cuts, force reductions, privatization of military industries, and enhanced civilian control (and international monitoring) or elimination of pet projects such as the nuclear program in Brazil and Argentina's Condor missile.[46] Governments sought to eliminate informal and formal privileges, such as controlling appointments to defense ministries, maintaining secrecy regarding budgets, and even exercising exclusive control over the content of military education. Moreover, the armed forces faced the challenge of institutional retrenchment and mission redefinition with the end of the Cold War.[47] By the mid-1990s, the quasi-sacred status of compulsory military service was challenged, and even eliminated in Argentina and Honduras. In much of the region civil-military relations were in flux, evidenced by genuine contestation over, and questioning of, the historical and conjunctural role of the armed forces.

Despite these important changes in civil-military relations, and a generally more liberal political milieu, the philosophical, constitutional, and statutory foundations for "protected democracy" and military guardianship remained strong.[48] Protected democracy was never a model for permanent military rule but rather for military guardianship and tutelary regimes when the occasion arises. The idea of protected democracy legitimates regimes of exception, suspension of civil liberties and rights, and, when necessary, military rule as a response to political and economic crises. It presumes a permanent internal intelligence mission and operations, pervasive surveillance of persons and groups posing "potential threats" to *la patria*. Whether strictly military or collaborative civil-military agencies, such internal intelligence operations targeting political parties, mass media, labor organizations, and other such "threats" are inherently inimical to full-blown democracy. In Latin America after 1978 intelligence agencies borrowed heavily in ideology and personnel from the recent military regimes, both reinforcing the "fear of the past" and reaffirming the impunity of those charged with human rights violations in the 1970s and 1980s. In many countries of the region, officers associated with death squads and torture were routinely promoted, rising to command positions in the armed forces in the 1990s and some even serving in UN peacekeeping missions. Lingering fear of renewed repression, reinforced by constitutional and statutory constraints on the civilian governments, ongoing political intelligence operations, and overt and implied military saber rattling, blocked measures to dismantle the foundations of protected democracy. Civilian supporters of the defunct military regimes added their political influence (and votes in legislatures) to the effort to prevent a recurrence of populism by defending protected democracy and the military's historical role as political guardians.

As emphasized throughout this book, these generalizations must be tempered by more careful and extensive investigations of each case. The region-wide persistence of protected democracy allowed considerable variations from country to county in the 1990s in the extent of political competition and the enjoyment of civil liberties and rights. Protected democracy is designed to constrain conflict and limit policy initiatives through institutional legitimation of the premise that *la patria*'s "guardians" may be forced to intervene if "threats" (what Argentine General Laiño called "potentially critical situations") menace internal order, national security, and sovereignty. When threats are latent or conflict levels are low, protected democracy operates, in appearance, virtually as a formal liberal democracy. But its institutional foundations legalize constitutional dictatorship and regimes of exception whenever necessary, thereby "chilling" some types of political participation and cultural ex-

Figure 7–2. "National Security Is Like Love: There Is Never Enough of It" by Guillo in *El humor es más fuerte, 1973–1991* (Santiago: Ediciones del Ornitorrinco, 1990), 28. Courtesy of Guillermo Bastias

pression. What the limits are at any moment, and how they are culturally defined, vary from country to country. But protected democracy teaches and reinforces self-censorship, caution, and prudence, often evoking the sort of biting, macabre, coded, and encoded political humor so pervasive in Latin America.

In the 1980s and 1990s protected democracy recurrently evoked the danger of "returning to the past" (state terrorism and military governments) even as its civilian leaders applauded the extent of liberalization that had occurred. And liberalization had definitely occurred, much as it did regionally in the 1920s, the mid-1940s, and late 1950s.[49] But it was made possible in part by the defeat of the revolutionary political left, evisceration of the regional labor movement, imposition of neoliberal economic policies, the collapse of the Soviet Union and Eastern European socialist regimes (the end of the Cold War)—and the reaffirmation in Latin America of the constitutional and legal institutions of protected democracy and military guardianship that had evolved since the nineteenth century.[50] Whether political liberalization would permit gradual dismantling of the core institutions and discarding of the basic politico-cultural premises of protected democracy remained questionable.

No issue more reflected the tensions within Latin American protected democracies than the conflict over the alleged human rights abuses by the armed forces in their wars against subversion and the resistance of the armed forces to demands for trials to determine their culpability for actions taken to "save *la patria*." More than any other legacy, the open wounds and the collective trauma from the "dirty wars" against the revolutionary and terrorist threats after 1964 afflicted the region and its armed forces in the last decade of the twentieth century. To these wounds and the implications of the trauma for Latin American politics and the armed forces we turn in Chapter 8.

Notes

1. Gallardo Miranda and O'Kuinghttons Ocampo (1992): 3–15.
2. Loveman and Davies, eds. (1985): 412–14.
3. Ibid.: 321–23.
4. See Eduardo Pizarro, "Revolutionary Guerrilla Groups in Colombia," in Charles Bergquist, Ricardo Peñaranda, and Gonzalo Sánchez, eds., *Violence in Colombia* (Wilmington, DE: Scholarly Resources, 1992): 169–93; and Daniel Pecaut, "Guerrillas and Violence," in Bergquist et al. (1992): 217–39.
5. CEPAL, "The Fight against Poverty in the Hemisphere Agenda," *CEPAL News* 14(12) (December 1994): 1.
6. A good short synthesis of the debt crisis by Riordan Roett is "The Debt Crisis and Economic Development in Latin America," in Jonathan Hartlyn, Lars Schoultz, and Augusto Varas, eds., *The United States and Latin America in the 1990s* (Chapel Hill: University of North Carolina Press, 1992): 131–51.
7. Committee of Santa Fe, "A New Inter-American Policy for the Eighties," by Francis Bouchey, Roger Fontaine, David Jordan, Gordon Sumner, and Lewis Tambs (1980).
8. U.S. Department of State, Bureau of Public Affairs, "Cuba's Renewed Support for Violence in Latin America," Special Report No. 90, December 14, 1981.
9. See Peter W. Rodman, *More Precious than Peace: The Cold War and the Struggle for the Third World* (New York: Charles Scribner's Sons, 1994).
10. President Reagan before the Joint Session of Congress, April 1983.
11. *The Report of the President's National Bipartisan Commission on Central America*, foreword by Henry Kissinger (New York: MacMillan, 1984): 32–33.
12. Ibid.: 151.
13. James Dunkerley, *The Pacification of Central America: Political Change in the Isthmus, 1987–1993* (London: Verso, 1994): 3.
14. Rodman (1994): 259.

15. Alfred Stepan examines military contestation over many of these prerogatives, particularly in Brazil, in *Rethinking Military Politics: Brazil and the Southern Cone* (Princeton: Princeton University Press, 1988). Augusto Varas, ed., *La autonomía militar en América Latina* (Venezuela: Editorial Nueva Sociedad, 1988), provides a collection of articles comparing the relative autonomy of the armed forces and their efforts to retain their prerogatives in Argentina, Ecuador, Colombia, Peru, Venezuela, Brazil, Chile, Uruguay, Central America, Mexico, and the Dominican Republic.

16. The classic statement on civilian control of the military by Samuel Huntington refers to "subjective control" via military socialization, civic education, loyalty to constitutions, parties, and "the system"; and "objective control" via partial military autonomy in the professional sphere and limited military participation in other policy areas. See Samuel Huntington, *The Soldier and the State: The Theory and Politics of Civil-Military Relations* (New York: Vantage Books, 1964). Other theorists on civil-miliary relations propose different classification schemes but insist on the need for civilian control of the military as part of any definition of democracy. See, for example, Samuel Finer, *The Man on Horseback: The Role of the Military in Politics*, 2d ed. (Boulder, CO: Westview Press, 1988); Eric Nordlinger, *Soldiers in Politics: Military Coups and Governments* (Englewood Cliffs, NJ: Prentice-Hall, 1977); Claude E. Welch, ed., *Civilian Control of the Military: Theory and Cases from Developing Countries* (New York: SUNY Press, 1976); and Amos Perlmutter, *The Military and Politics in Modern Times* (New Haven: Yale University Press, 1977).

17. Committee of Santa Fe (1989): 1–2.

18. Unión Camilista-Ejército de Liberación Nacional, "Poder popular y nuevo gobierno," January 20, 1990, pp. 46, 48, cited in Mauricio García Durán, *De la Uribe a Tlaxcala, Procesos de Paz* (Bogotá: CINEP, 1992): 86.

19. See Dunkerley (1994): appendices 8 and 9: 145–46.

20. Juan Manuel de Rosas was made constitutional dictator in a plebiscite in Buenos Aires in 1835. Verbal votes given to an official who went house to house gave Rosas a 9,716-to-4 victory, thus ratifying his exercise of "the sum total of public authority." See Loveman (1993): 279.

21. See Edward S. Herman and Frank Brodhead, *Demonstration Elections* (Boston: South End Press, 1984); and Guy Hermet, Richard Rose, and Alain Rouquié, eds., *Elections without Choice* (New York: Wiley, 1978).

22. *United States Marine Corps Small Wars Manual* (Reprint of 1940 edition), NAVMC 2890, 1987.

23. Ibid.: Chapter 14: 5–9.

24. Mikael Boström, "Political Waves in Latin America, 1940–1988," *Nordic Journal of Latin American Studies* 19(1) (1989): 3–19.

25. See *Sistemas electorales y representación política en Latinoamérica*, 2 vols. (Madrid: Fundación Friedrich Ebert/ICI, 1986); and Rodolfo Cerda-Cruz, Juan Rial, and Daniel Zovatto, eds., *Elecciones y democracia en América Latina, 1988–1991* (San José: IIDH-CAPEL, 1992).

26. Samuel Huntington, *The Third Wave: Democratization in the Late Twentieth Century* (Norman: University of Oklahoma Press, 1991).

27. Ibid.: 5–9.

28. Enrique C. Ochoa, "The Rapid Expansion of Voter Participation in Latin America: Presidential Elections, 1845–1986," in James W. Wilkie and David Lorey, eds., *Statistical Abstract of Latin America* 25 (Los Angeles: UCLA Latin American Center Publications, 1987): 862–910 (Table 3423, p. 904).

29. Karen Remmer, *Military Rule in Latin America* (Boulder, CO: Westview Press, 1991): 52–53; Boström (1989): 13–15.

30. There were some important exceptions to the impunity achieved by most militaries in the region. In El Salvador, for example, officers were purged as part of the 1992 peace accords, and in other countries officers and police were tried for their abuses in particularly notorious cases or where international pressure was intense (for example, the conviction of former commanders of the Chilean intelligence service [DINA] for the assassination of Orlando Letelier in Washington, DC). Beyond legal impunity, officers sometimes suffered by public revelations in the press, from social ostracism, and from questions from their own family members and friends about their roles in "dirty wars." Generally, however, the military successfully avoided criminal prosecutions for the human rights violations of which they were accused.

31. On the basic constitutional and political dilemmas of protecting democracy through national security legislation and regimes of exception see Felipe González Morales, Jorge Mera Figueroa, and Juan Enrique Vargas Viancos, *Protección democrática de la seguridad del estado, Estados de excepción y derecho penal político* (Santiago: Programa de Derechos Humanos, Universidad Academia de Humanismo Cristiano, 1991); and Ignacio de Otto Pardo, *Defensa de la constitución y partidos políticos* (Madrid: Centro de Estudios Constitucionales, 1985).

32. Villanueva (1973): 66–67.

33. "The Government of the Armed Forces and the National Community," Address delivered by Lt. Gen. Juan Carlos Onganía at West Point, New York, August 6, 1964 (two years before the 1996 coup that made him president). Cited in Robert Potash, "Argentina," in Lyle N. McAlister, Anthony P. Maingot, and Robert A. Potash, eds., *The Military in Latin American Socio-Political Evo-*

lution: Four Case Studies (Washington, DC: Center for Research in Social Systems, 1970): 117. "Exotic ideologies" is a term that military officers and the political right used to describe leftist and Marxist ideas, indicating their "foreignness" and their incompatibility with "national values."

34. Lt. Gen. (ret.) Benjamín Rattenbach, *Sociología militar* (Buenos Aires: Libería Perlado, 1958): 128–29, cited in Potash (1970): 116–17.

35. Lt. Col. Carlos Molina Johnson, *Algunas de las razones del quiebre de la institucionalidad política* (Santiago: Estado Mayor del Ejército, 1987): 16–17. Molina Johnson notes that this "right of rebellion against illegitimate government is recognized by civilians as well as the military," citing former President Eduardo Frei's interview with the Spanish magazine *ABC* after the coup. Frei said, in part: "The military has saved Chile. . . . [they] were called on by the nation and they fulfilled their legal duty. . . . If a people has been so weakened and harassed (*acosado*) that it cannot rebel, . . . then the Army substitutes its arms and does its work" (91–92).

36. Cited in Gabriel Ramírez, *La cuestión militar, Democracia tutelada o democracia asociativa, el caso uruguayo* (Montevideo: Arca, 1989): 2:97. See also Julio María Sanguinetti, *El temor y la impaciencia, Ensayo sobre la transición democrática en América Latina* (Buenos Aires: Fondo de Cultura Económica, 1991).

37. See "Más elogios de Menem a militares y policías por ganar la 'guerra sucia,' " *Clarín* (November 4, 1994). For an account of military contestation of civilian government after transition see J. Patrice McSherry, *Incomplete Transition: Military Power and Democracy in Argentina* (New York: St. Martin's Press, 1997).

38. "El General Díaz contra las autocríticas: 'Debíamos haberlo olvidado,' " *Página/12*, May 5, 1995, cited in McSherry (1997): 265.

39. *El problema es muy delicado y hay que hilar muy fino*, cited in "Tensa situación en Uruguay por actuación de militares," *La Nación* (Santiago de Chile) (June 12, 1993): 8–9.

40. On the development of national security doctrines see Gen. Golbery do Couto e Silva, *Conjuntura política nacional: O poder executivo e geopolítica do Brasil* (Rio de Janeiro: Livaria José Olympio, 1981); Stepan (1973): 46–47; Genaro Arriagada Herrera and Manuel Antonio Garretón, "América Latina a la hora de las doctrinas de la seguridad nacional," in María Angélica Pérez, ed., *Las fuerzas armadas en la sociedad civil* (Santiago: CISEC, 1978), 144–229; Comblin (1979); George A. López, "National Security Ideology as an Impetus to State Violence and State Terror," in Michael Stohl and George A. López, eds., *Government Violence and Repression* (New York: Greenwood Press, 1986): 73–95; Pion-Berlin (1989): 411–29; and Francia Elena Díaz Cardona, *Fuerzas armadas, militarismo y constitución nacional en América Latina* (México: UNAM, 1988), esp. 119–38.

41. See, for example, Ecuador, *Ley de Seguridad Nacional, Actualizada a 4 junio de 1987*, in which the armed forces are designated the principal instruments in "guaranteeing the juridical order" and also called upon to "collaborate in the social and economic development of the country, and in other functions affecting National Security" (Articles 36–40). On the common themes of the military regimes after 1964 see Loveman and Davies, eds. (1997).

42. See Varas, ed. (1988).

43. Regimes of exception, such as state of siege, suspension of habeas corpus and civil liberties, granting broad decree powers to presidents, and subjecting civilians to military jurisdiction in times of "emergency," are not unique to Latin America. However, they are used much more routinely there than in Europe, where they originated, first in ancient Rome, and then in republican constitutions adopted after the French Revolution and the Spanish 1812 Constitution. See Loveman (1993).

44. A fierce, coherent, and legally based defense of the Argentine "dirty war" is Osiris G. Villegas, *Testimonio de un alegato* (Buenos Aires: Compañía Impresora Argentina, 1990).

45. See, for example, Servicio Paz y Justicia, *Uruguay, Nunca Más. Human Rights Violations, 1972–1985*, trans. Elizabeth Hampsten with an introduction by Lawrence Weschler (Philadelphia: Temple University Press, 1989); *Informe de la Comisión Nacional de Verdad y Reconciliación*, 3 vols. (Santiago: Ministerio Secretaría General de Gobierno, 1991); *Comisión Nacional sobre la Desaparición de Personas. Nunca Más: Informe de la Comisión Nacional sobre la Desaparición de Personas* (Buenos Aires: Eudeba, 1984).

46. See Scott D. Tolleson, "Civil-Military Relations in Brazil: The Myth of Tutelary Democracy," Paper delivered at the 1995 meeting of the Latin American Studies Association, Washington, DC, September 28–30, 1995.

47. As the U.S. military sought to redefine its mission in the post-Cold War years, many of the Latin American armed forces followed suit, more or less reluctantly, involving themselves in the new hemispheric security agenda: anti-narcotics operations, immigration control, international peacekeeping, "defending democracy," nation building, and even environmental protection. See the collection of articles in L. Erik Kjonnerod, ed., *Evolving U.S. Strategy for Latin America and the Caribbean* (Washington, DC: National Defense University Press, 1992).

48. For a comparative assessment of this process in Spain, Argentina, and Brazil see Jorge Zaverucha, "The Degree of Military Political Autonomy during the Spanish, Argentine, and Brazilian Transitions," *Journal of Latin American Studies* 25 (1993): 283–99. A more optimistic assessment of civilian contestation with the military to reduce its autonomy is Wendy Hunter,

"Politicians against Soldiers: Contesting the Military in Postauthoritarian Brazil," *Comparative Politics* 27(4) (July 1995): 425–43.

49. The number of governments headed by military officers declined from thirteen in 1954 to four in 1959 (Trujillo in the Dominican Republic, Stroessner in Paraguay, Idigoras Fuentes in Guatemala, and Lemus in El Salvador).

50. The debate over the extent of democratization that occurred in Latin America in the 1980s and 1990s sometimes takes the form of "is the glass half full or half empty?" Other times it reverts to definitional and semantic arguments over the meaning of "democracy." The point here is that there is a particular form of "democracy" that evolved in Latin America in the nineteenth century—protected democracy—accompanied by military guardianship and that this Latin American institutional pattern has been reaffirmed since 1979.

8

La Patria, the Armed Forces, and Human Rights*

> The armed forces, unlike all other instruments created and sustained by the State to serve the public interest, has a clearly defined mission. That mission is victory.
>
> —General Carlos Dellepiane, Peru, 1977[1]

The gradual transition from military to civilian governments in Latin America from 1978 to 1994 brought demands for trials and punishment of armed forces personnel accused of human rights violations. Demands for "justice" also arose in countries ostensibly ruled by civilians in the 1980s, such as Colombia, Peru, and Honduras, where the armed forces engaged in prolonged counterinsurgency and antiterrorist operations to protect national institutions and security. Under attack, military officers from Central America and the Caribbean to the Southern Cone sought to defend the dignity and honor of their institutions, reaffirm the salvational mission they had victoriously effected in the battle against international communism and internal subversion, and deny their personal criminal responsibility in particular cases of alleged human rights violations.

In some countries so-called truth commissions were created to investigate and report on these alleged violations.[2] In others, civilian governments indicted individual officers and prosecuted notorious offenders in the spotlight of the recently uncensored mass media.[3] Despite these efforts, political and legal bulwarks, immunities and amnesty decrees established during transition, lack of appropriate evidence, and threats both implicit and explicit against the new civilian governments generally impeded successful prosecution.[4]

These constraints on prosecution did not prevent widespread dissemination of detailed descriptions of abuse, torture, "disappearances," murder, and mass graves. International human rights organizations had routinely denounced these crimes for years; domestic human rights activists, political parties, church groups, and other regime opponents had done likewise and were frequently persecuted as a result.[5] The truth commissions in various countries added to

*An earlier version of this chapter was published in Brian Loveman and Thomas M. Davies, Jr., eds., *The Politics of Antipolitics: The Military in Latin America*, 3d ed. (Wilmington, DE: Scholarly Resources, 1997): 398–423.

the military's woes, investigating the alleged human rights abuses and publicizing the extent and ferocity of torture, murder, and repression of regime opponents.[6] Calls for punishment not only threatened individual officers but also besmirched the institutional integrity of the armed forces, threatened their role and relative autonomy in the new political systems, and questioned the legitimacy of the patriotic mission recently completed.

The armed forces rejected revisionist histories, such as those contained in the truth commissions' reports, that ignored the circumstances that had required their intervention (for example, in Brazil and Bolivia in 1964, Chile and Uruguay in 1973, Argentina in 1976). They reminded their compatriots of the international "war" of communism that threatened their nations' sovereign existence and of the internal subversion, terrorism, and impending civil wars that they successfully overcame. They also reminded their critics and accusers of the calls made by civilian legislators, party leaders, judges, and the business community for the military to save their nations from chaos and destruction.

With national variations, the armed forces elaborated a coherent historical, constitutional, legal, doctrinal, and political defense. This defense is important because it not only sought to legitimize "dirty wars" but also served as a more extensive moral, philosophical, ideological, and institutional rationale for "protected democracy." Centuries of militarylore reinforced by the post-1950s Cold War national security doctrines legitimated "total war" against *la patria*'s enemies. To understand the behavior of military officers, it is essential to take military values, doctrine, and political perceptions seriously—something not common for most civilians in Latin America (or elsewhere). Militarylore and doctrine shape and justify missions for these officers just as revolutionary ideology does for guerrillas, and religious and humanist values do for human rights organizations. Obviously, taking these values seriously does not require sharing them.

Figure 8–1. "Those with Impunity, the Victims, the Accomplices," a poster of the Agrupación de Familiares de Detenidos Desaparecidos, Chile, n.d. [1980s].

The moral, legal, and political foundations of the armed forces' defense against allegations of human rights abuses are described schematically in this chapter, using material from Argentina, Chile, and El Salvador to illustrate the main premises. The defense includes their version of nationality, sovereignty, nation-building, and their own historical and political missions and obligations. Despite national idiosyncrasies, characteristic internal social and political variations, and distinctive political histories, the Latin American armed forces shared historical conceptions, doctrines, constitutional missions, and claims of "residual sovereignty" (*últimas reservas morales*) in their respective nations when "permanent national interests" were threatened.[7] These common premises buttressed the armed forces' defense against the accusations and legitimated their current insistence on a continued role in national politics. Although these premises were under serious challenge in the 1980s and 1990s, they remained embedded in the structure of military doctrine and self-perception.[8]

The Historical Vision

The Latin American armed forces routinely trace their origins to Spain's colonial armies and militia. Institutional myths and official histories trace their martial glories to imperial Spain's Western Hemispheric conquests, settlements, and the defense of *las Indias* against other European powers and Indian resistance (described in Chapter 1). In some cases, the very creation of nationality and the "new race" is attributed to the army—an army that preceded the nation, eventually created it, and then defended the new nation against Spanish reconquest and other external and internal threats (see Chapter 2).[9] The armed forces were tasked with defending the new nations against external threats and maintaining internal security. These are the primordial purposes of the state, recognized as such by Thomas Aquinas, Machiavelli, Thomas Hobbes, Adam Smith, and almost every Latin American military officer since 1810. These officers base their mission on a presumed natural law: despite efforts to achieve peace there will always be war. This "law of war" imposes "the obligation to maintain a permanent army" charged with "the guardianship (*salvaguardia*) and defense of our liberty and independence."[10]

Figure 8–2. "Where Are They? The Government Must Answer," a poster of the detained and disappeared, Agrupación de Familiares de Detenidos Desaparecidos, Chile, 1987.

The formal source for this mission statement is taken from Article 274 of the French Constitution of the Year III (5 Fructidor [1795]): "The armed forces are instituted to defend the state against external enemies and to assure maintenance of internal order and compliance with the laws." This concept was included in Spain's 1812 Constitution and in later Latin American charters. But even without (and before) national constitutions, the armed forces regard themselves as the "concrete, living expression of *la patria*, whose mission is the defense of unity, integrity, and of honor, as well as of everything else essential and permanent in the country."[11] Religiously dedicated to patriotism and *la patria*, they are professional soldiers, but also a holy brotherhood, with barracks like monasteries. They have inherited the warrior-priest tradition

Figure 8–3. "Let's Build a South America without Disappeared," International Week Honoring the Disappeared, Agrupación de Familiares de Detenidos Desaparecidos, Chile, 1985.

Figure 8–4. Human rights protest march by the Grupo de Apoyo Mutuo (GAM), Guatemala, 1985.

of the Spanish *reconquista*, the Inquisition, and the conquest of a new world for God and king. In the late nineteenth and early twentieth centuries, modernization and professionalization of the armed forces coincided with nation-building and the "civilizing mission" that made citizens of Indians, former slaves, and illiterate peasants. The armed forces consolidated and integrated "eternal *patrias*" symbolized by the national anthem, flag, and coat of arms, and by the armed forces themselves (see Chapter 3). In a Guatemalan version of this regionally shared militarylore: "the visible representation of *la patria* is the **national flag**: these are the blessed colors that wherever they are displayed . . . with the coat of arms (*escudo*) of the Nation, an immaculate white at its center, represent our beloved *patria*. Their acoustic representation, to put it that way, is the *National Anthem*, whose beautiful notes bring joy and make our hearts flood with inexplicable emotion and happiness."[12] Thus, the armed forces have a historical mission: the defense and salvation of the nation's traditions and its permanent values.[13] They are the "last bulwark of nationality."[14] In this mission they find a fixed moral rationale for drastic defensive measures against *la patria*'s enemies: "Think always of *la patria* to defend it against whatever could cause pain to its children."[15]

This historical mission is iterated and reiterated in military publications, speeches, and rituals. A typical example is Colombian General Fernando Landazábal Reyes's 1993 reminder to his beloved (and politically besieged) comrades that "our armed forces are the ultimate supports (*sostenedores indeclinables*) of national integrity; and [they] must not forget that beyond the political interests of transitory governments (*gobiernos pasajeros*), in their hands is the historical responsibility for preserving it, without tarnishing its honor, in the plenitude of its sovereign splendor."[16] The location of "historical responsibility" for *la patria*'s defense and security in the hands of the armed forces is a basic premise shared by the Latin American military. This premise constitutes a sacred duty that cannot be subordinated to any transitory government—meaning, of course, to any government, since any government will be "transitory" relative to the life of *la patria*.

A corollary to this premise is that civilians generally lack the moral, spiritual, physical, and patriotic qualities of the true solider, making civilians ultimately unreliable guardians unable to protect *la patria*. Only the military can do this. Thus, "the barracks is the school of character and civic virtue, the forge that molds the ideals of *la patria . . . the crucible where men's purest and dearest thoughts are melded. . . . the army is a model of la patria* itself, in its hierarchical and ordered constitution."[17]

Civilians and political elites have accepted this historical vision often enough to give it credence and legitimacy. Colombia's President Julio César Turbay, for example, addressing the thirteenth Conference of Commanders of Latin American Armies in Bogotá in 1979, declared: "Naturally, in extreme cases, confronted with an ostensible political vacuum that leads toward generalized anarchy, the Armed Forces must (*se ven precisadas*) exercise power to reestablish the rule of authority."[18] As previously noted, Chile's former president Eduardo Frei Montalva, commenting on the 1973 military coup in that country, stated that "the military have saved Chile . . . they were called on by the nation and they fulfilled their legal duty. . . . If a people has been so weakened and harassed (*acosado*) that it cannot rebel, . . . then the Army substitutes its arms and does its work."[19] Most of Latin America, even those countries governed by popularly elected presidents with democratic values, expect the armed forces, "in crises," to exercise their "historical mission" to "save *la patria*."

The Constitutional Mission

The armed forces' historical mission is legally confirmed in a secular sacrament—the constitution. Latin American constitutions almost always define a broad obligation and authority for the military: external defense, internal security, upholding the laws, and protecting the constitution and national institutions. Variations in wording and mission evolved in the nineteenth century and changes occurred in the twentieth. Typically, however, the armed forces have constitutional status much like the congress, presidency, and judicial branch. This constitutional mission reinforces the armed forces' perceived historical role and legitimizes actions taken to protect, defend, and conserve *la patria*.[20]

Whatever the precise language, the military's constitutional mission requires exercising discretion in deciding when and how to protect *la patria* and its institutions. Evidently, this task is assigned to the military (and sometimes to the police) because it theoretically possesses the resources and power to achieve it. This custodial guardianship and protectorship role is the armed forces' specialized constitutional and political mission. "If the mission of the Army . . . is sustaining *la patria*'s independence, the integrity of its territory, and maintaining [internal] peace and respect for order and the legitimate institutions of the State, this imperative constitutes for those commanding troops an undeclinable obligation that must be achieved at all cost."[21] If politics and elections degenerate into "*politiquería*" and "promote disorder and endanger national honor and integrity," then in "fulfilling its patriotic duty the armed forces must reimpose order and legality (*fueros de la legalidad*)." The soldier must dedicate himself exclusively to "defense of *la patria* and the institutions that give it life."[22]

Through constitutional reforms and modification of military ordinances, efforts to erode this constitutional rationale for military review of civilian decisions have mounted in the late 1980s and 1990s. Combined with the "historical mission," however, this institutional foundation for military intervention remains viable, if dormant. It played a significant role in justifying the military *pronunciamientos* and the policies of the military regimes from 1964 to 1994 that stand accused of human rights violations.

Constitutional Regimes of Exception

As indicated earlier, Latin American constitutions typically allow suspension of civil liberties and rights to meet all manner of emergencies: natural disasters, threats to the constitutional order, insurgency, rebellion, and internal war. To the extent that human rights (including the right to life, liberty, due process, and "the rule of law") are interpreted as constitutional rights and liberties, these may disappear by presidential decree, legislative action, or, in certain circumstances, through decisions made by specialized governmental agencies such as the cabinet, by permanent congressional commissions, or even by the military high command. Frequently, the implementation of a regime of exception extends special authority to the armed forces and police, subjects civilians to military jurisdiction (laws, courts, and courts-martial), and even permits summary execution of "terrorists," "subversives," and "traitors."

One type of regime of exception is internal war, formalized in a variety of juridical modes such as "state of siege," "internal commotion," "state of assembly," and others. At war, the rules of war apply. The basic one is that the enemy may be killed. If political opponents become enemies in a war, either undeclared or declared, their annihilation is no longer a violation of human rights or even a common crime but rather a legitimate function of armies engaged in combat. Military intelligence agencies seek the whereabouts of the enemy; interrogating prisoners is one way to locate and destroy enemy resources and combatants. The distinction between interrogation, abuse, and torture may become blurred.

What in peace would be murder, in war becomes righteous, particularly if in doing so *la patria* and the national way of life are conserved. Declared regimes of exception that suspend civil rights and liberties, even without a declaration of war, enhance the military's (and police's) authority vis-à-vis citizens to carry out their mission. They also legitimize violence and withdraw the "normal" constitutional restraints on coercion. In other cases, the regime of exception itself constitutes, for legal purposes, a declaration that an internal state of war exists.

Regimes of exception are the result, in constitution-making, of a priori philosophical, moral, and political decisions that, at times, "human rights" must be subordinated to "protecting *la patria.*"[23] In the words of Argentine General Adcel Vilas, "The offensive against subversion presupposes in the first place freedom of action in all areas . . . *a series of special procedures*, an instantaneous response, *a persecution to the death.*"[24] Even before the 1976 coup, Argentina's elected government had declared a state of war against terrorism. The 1853 Constitution's state-of-siege provisions and related security legislation imposed a drastic regime of exception. (And eventually the government went far beyond pre-1976 legality and constitutionality in the antiterrorist war.) In Chile, in 1973, the military *junta* decreed a "state of siege in all the national territory," and in Decree Law No. 5 declared that the state of siege imposed implied a "state or time of war" for legal and judicial purposes, as established in the Military Code of Justice.[25]

Internal wars and regimes of exception change the rules; civil liberties and rights are suspended. Protection of human rights, as defined in international treaties or natural law, succumbs to the law of war and to the fundamental rights of all states to preserve their own existence. This right of states to preserve their existence does not unambiguously supersede international treaties on human rights. But the military's historical and constitutional missions are ratified in regimes of exception that recognize the existence of crisis, the need for special rules and drastic action, and the duty of the armed forces and police to protect *la patria* and its institutions against all internal and external threats. If national existence is truly at stake, can the armed forces subordinate their

Figure 8–5. Burning "subversive" books, 1973. *Memorias en blanco y negro. Imágenes fotográficas, 1970–1973* (Santiago: LOM Ediciones, 1993), photo 30. Courtesy of LOM Ediciones

primordial and undeclinable missions to international agreements signed by "transitory governments"?

National Security and Military Law

No Latin American country is without laws regarding the protection of internal security of the state, with provisions for media censorship, military ordinances, and a military justice code that potentially expands martial authority in times of crisis or even provides routine military jurisdiction over civilians. As indicated previously, there are great variations in the extent of the jurisdiction of military courts over civilians within Latin America; since the 1980s more countries have sought to reduce or eliminate this jurisdiction. However, the historical influence of this legislative and judicial "patriotic security blanket" reached its peak in the post-1964 regimes now under criticism for human rights violations. In many instances the security legislation and military jurisdiction over civilians provided clear legal bases for actions deemed retrospectively as regrettable or, less euphemistically, as human rights violations.

No detailed discussion of these laws and practices is possible in the present chapter. Excellent comparative and monographic summaries exist for some countries and less detailed versions for others.[26] Among the best studies of the evolution of the patriotic security blanket is Francisco Leal Buitrago's *El oficio de la guerra, La seguridad nacional en Colombia* (1994). After discussing the historical background, Leal describes the 1978 Colombian Estatuto de Seguridad, adopted under state of siege, "leading to outrageous, indiscriminate detentions and torture of [various persons] considered to be leftists." All these epi-

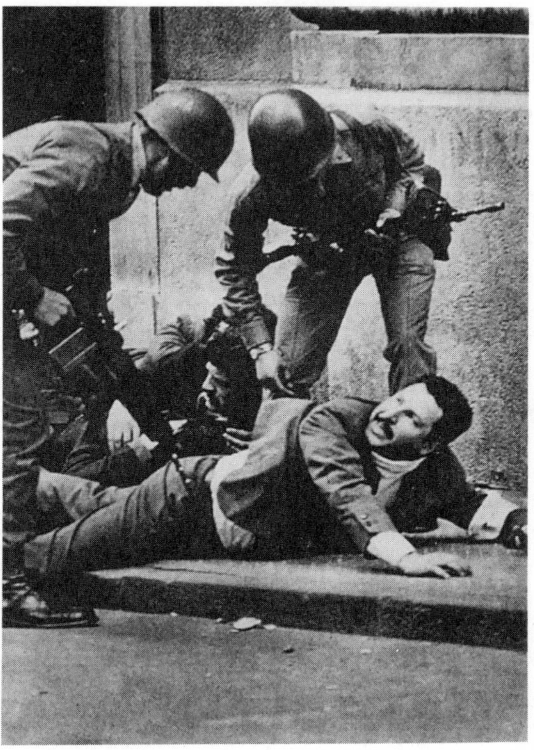

Figure 8–6. Prisoners at La Moneda Palace, Santiago, Chile, 1973. From *Memorias en blanco y negro. Imágenes fotográficas, 1970–1973* (Santiago: LOM Ediciones, 1993), photo 5. Courtesy of LOM Ediciones

sodes "were framed by application of military justice . . . and continuing military operations against the guerrillas."[27]

This description of the impact of security legislation and application of military codes and jurisdiction to civilians under an elected government reflects the general consequences of such legislation in most of Latin America. It also clearly identifies the apparent legal foundations for many of the actions later condemned as human rights violations. In military regimes such legislation was admittedly often expanded, but the basic provisions had long existed.[28] They were accreted over more than 150 years by numerous governments to protect the nation-state, the institutional order, internal security, and *la patria*. The military and police were to carry out their duty; indeed, they were ordered by civilian and military superiors to carry out their missions. How could fulfilling this historical, constitutional, legal, and organizational mission be called human rights violations?

In almost all of Latin America, military personnel are trained to obey superior orders unhesitatingly. Military codes expressly impose this obligation: "The first duty of all military personnel is to observe discipline and subordination, which consists of absolute and constant respect and obedience of subordinates to superiors; in the prompt and exact compliance with orders . . . without vacillation, without protest, and without any comments or observations, even when there might be cause for such, until after complying with [the orders]."[29] With few exceptions,[30] this obligation is not contingent on the legality of the orders issued, as it is in the United States, Britain, and much of continental Europe.[31] If superiors violate the law and exceed their authority, they are legally responsible, not the personnel who dutifully comply with orders. This is the principle of *obediencia debida*—a principle reaffirmed in Argentina and elsewhere in response to the dilemmas of human rights trials and liabilities. When individual soldiers and officers exceed their authority and commit crimes against other persons, they commit individual excesses, properly punishable, unlike actions taken in accord with *obediencia debida*. Those who exceed their authority or order others to act illegally should be brought to justice; those who obey illegal orders may claim this defense as a valid one. "Las órdenes se cumplen, no se discuten" (orders are to be obeyed, not debated).[32]

The Cold War and the New National Security Doctrine

Traditional military missions, constitutional obligations, defense and security legislation, and military law and ordinances provided firm moral, historical, and legal foundations for the armed forces' protection of *la patria*. The Cold War after World War II, the global struggle between communism and "freedom," and the incorporation of Latin American countries into the 1947 Rio Treaty for regional security introduced new threats to *la patria*. According to the precepts of Cold War national security doctrine, international communism denied the historical and sovereign "essence" of Latin American nations: it was godless, morally abominable, nefarious, resolute, and imperialistic. It recruited internal adherents from political parties, labor unions, university and community organizations, and the mass media. It sought to subvert patriotic values, even to penetrate and poison the armed forces.

The Cuban Revolution and its subsequent support for revolutionary political and guerrilla movements brought this threat directly and convincingly to the Western Hemisphere. Military leaders did not invent guerrilla *focos*, Communist parties, the shrill leftist media, and calls for revolution. They witnessed executions of Cuban officers after Fidel Castro's victory, attacks on the Catholic Church, Cuba's alignment with the Soviet Union, and radical transformation of the island's society. They heard clearly the Cubans' call for continental revolution, for overthrowing the old order and establishing revolutionary socialism. They saw Cuban support and training of local insurgents. They suffered losses in combat and through terrorist attacks. There was a real enemy—an enemy that had declared war on *la patria*, its institutions, and the military itself.

Borrowing from classic geopolitical formulations, from French counterinsurgency doctrines developed in Algeria, from Washington's Cold War doctrine, and from the original contributions of Peruvian, Brazilian, and other Latin American military theorists, the armed forces in each nation adopted variations on a new national security doctrine (NSD). This doctrine permeated the hemisphere's military institutions. Informed by national political and economic conditions, shaped by individual experiences with revolutionary movements and insurgency, and influenced by U.S. military assistance missions and training, the new NSD became, in its national variations, the dominant view of the Latin American military. Despite objections and reservations within all the military establishments, the basic premises of the NSD buttressed the armed forces' historical, constitutional, and legal mission.[33]

Many studies of the NSD and its influence have appeared since the 1960s.[34] In the present context a bare outline suffices. The NSD expanded greatly the concept of security, making it virtually synonymous with political, social, and economic development. It located the source of Latin American unrest and insurgency in internal socioeconomic and political conditions that made the poor and others vulnerable to subversive proposals; in the efforts of international (and Cuban) communism to take advantage of these conditions, importing

Figure 8–7. The Guatemalan Army in defense of *la patria*, public relations campaign in the 1990s.

exotic (Marxist, socialist, revolutionary) ideology and converting disciples and followers in Latin America; and in domestic revolutionaries, subversives, fellow travelers, and naive idealists, who furthered the Communist plan by deed and omission.

The NSD required a multifaceted national effort to overcome the internal conditions that blocked economic and social development and favored subversion and revolutionary movements; to defeat international communism's ideological and organizational thrusts into individual countries; and to direct military action against political movements, the media, student, labor, and other organizations, and groups engaged in armed struggle against the regime. This was essentially a call for a permanent and total war by the state against the enemies threatening *la patria* as well as a call for direct military involvement in the tasks of national development. The emphases and nuances given to the NSD depended on local circumstances. Where insurgent threats were minimal—for example, in Ecuador and Honduras in the 1970s and 1980s—more developmentalist and populist versions of the NSD tended to prevail, with the counterinsurgency theme muted. Where insurgent threats and high levels of political mobilization threatened political stability and "governability" of the country, more emphasis was given to the military, intelligence, and repressive aspects of the NSD, as in Uruguay, Chile, and Argentina.

But everywhere in the region the NSD focused on the lurking enemy: subversion and Marxism. This enemy—unscrupulous, devious, perverse, even satanic—was characterized as evil incarnate. Communism "seeks to implant the reign of materialism over the spiritual, rancor and fear instead of love, lies against truth, arbitrariness in place of justice . . . the return of slavery, the end of freedom."[35] And "communism is an intrinsically perverse doctrine, meaning that whatever springs forth from it, however salutary it appears, is rotted by the venom that corrodes its roots."[36] In Brazil, a military officer asked rhetorically, "Who were the Communists?" He responded: "Fanatics, patient in obtaining their final objectives [world conquest] . . . persistent in their subversion, vassals of the party, . . . radical, . . . cynical, . . . antireligious."[37] The enemy would use the uninformed, the well-intentioned, the naive (indeed, anyone) to achieve their objectives. Their tactical flexibility allowed temporary alliances, pacts, collaboration, and even professed adherence to "democratic" rules of the game. They would infiltrate the Catholic Church and invent "Christians for socialism." Their cynicism also allowed using terrorism while denouncing terrorists, and calling for a free press and respect for civil liberties while ultimately intending to abolish them. The enemy was flexible, but single-minded and untrustworthy. Those who lent themselves, however inadvertently, to the enemy's cause—whether anthropologists, environmentalists, or human rights activists—were also a danger to *la patria*. Such an enemy could only be defeated in a total war, a war without mercy, a war that addressed the underlying socioeconomic conditions that nurtured discontent, but also a war that extirpated the enemy and collaborators.

Communism threatened the "Western Christian way of life" and its Latin American versions; the entire civilization was at stake along with the survival of *la patria*. Even when not operating overtly, communism was actively plotting, conspiring, and planning its next move. Time was on its side; the enemy had a strategy without time limits for attaining victory. Communism sought "to weaken those societies that the Red sect does not control, to grasp them in its claws at the opportune moment, to convert them into new satellites of Soviet imperialism."[38] In Uruguay, the military *junta* told the Inter-American Human Rights Commission that "the declaration of war by Marxism-Leninism against the Western World is a state of 'permanent aggression,' as Karl Marx affirmed in 1848."[39]

Figure 8–8. Poster with pictures of military and police personnel who "died for God and *la patria*," Chile.

And were these ideas incorrect? Did not the Soviet Union and the Cubans openly proclaim their ultimate goals? Did not "peaceful coexistence" bring bloodshed, insurgency, and revolutionary war to Latin America? Was not *la patria* in grave danger? Ought not the armed forces be prepared to carry out their moral, historical, constitutional, and legal missions?

Conjunctures

Moral, historical, constitutional, legal, and strictly military rationales for saving *la patria* always exist. They become operational when a "crisis" arises. Only crisis (or in some cases, the imminent threat of one) justifies military action. The post-1964 military regimes all claimed to save their nations from a combined external and internal threat posed by international communism and its internal allies. As partners in the Cold War anti-Communist alliance and the inter-American security system designed after 1947, the Latin American military combined French, U.S., and their own new "national security doctrine" to legitimize expanded military political participation and, eventually, military government. The NSD provided new twists on old themes (particularly the anticommunism of the 1930s and 1940s), identified the "enemy," and gave immediacy to the military mission.

Conjunctural political and socioeconomic crises in individual Latin American countries provoked military responses, the installation of military or civil-military regimes, and fierce repression of the so-called enemy. Military regimes dominated South America and Central America from the 1960s to the 1980s; the armed forces in most civilian governments that engaged in counterinsurgency operations also adopted the strategies and methods associated with the NSD. Colombia, for example, endured more years of regimes of exception and the application of harsh national security laws and military jurisdiction over civilians, and experienced many more tortured and dead from the 1960s into the 1990s than some countries with military governments.[40]

In some cases these conflicts persisted into the late 1980s and 1990s (Colombia, El Salvador, Guatemala, Peru); in others the enemy was defeated, transformed, or pacified (Chile, Uruguay, Argentina). In most cases a legacy of this struggle is the demand for justice, for trials of human rights violators, for punishment of "criminals." (And in some cases a legacy of the struggle is continuing internal conflict, narcoterrorism, and organized crime.) The armed forces respond that they are heroes who saved *la patria,* in accord with their moral, historical, constitutional, legal, and conjunctural obligations. Are they wrong? Consider Argentina, Chile, and El Salvador, where individual excesses certainly occurred. And consider the official legal and political responses of the armed forces to their accusers.

Review, first, in Argentina, General Osiris G. Villegas's defense of General Ramón Camps, accused of homicide, illegal deprivation of liberty, and torture of prisoners:[41]

> 1. Colonel Camps participated in a war against subversion, a war in every sense. In war the enemy is attacked with whatever violence is necessary to destroy it. This war was the result of subversive attacks on the

political institutions of Argentina, which were virtually in collapse by the time of the 1976 military *pronunciamiento.*

2. In accord with the law, the armed forces participated in the war against subversion until its annihilation, as ordered by the constitutional government. This included declaration of a state of siege in 1975, outlawing of the ERP and Montoneros,[42] the prorogation of the state of siege, the laws adopted against subversion, sabotage, and the arms control law.

3. The police and security personnel supported the armed forces in this war.

4. Colonel (General) Camps, acting as police chief of Buenos Aires Province, acted in accord with existing laws and regulations, followed his superiors' orders, and conformed to the concept of *obediencia debida.*

5. In war, the laws of war apply, including the Geneva Conventions, if accepted by the belligerents—something the subversives were unwilling to do, as evidenced by their terrorist tactics. In this war, the armed forces reacted to the subversive enemies' terrorist methods in accord with international law, which allows "response in kind" when the parties do not abide by international conventions.

6. The Marxist subversives sought power by destroying the principles and values that constitute our national essence (*ser nacional*) to impose their atheist, materialist model. They intended to destroy the moral and legal foundations of the state. These objectives were clearly at odds with our "fundamental law."

7. The aggressor was international communism, directed by the Soviet Union, through Cuba, and its agents in Latin America, covert authors of the war suffered then by Argentina and now by El Salvador, Nicaragua, and Peru.

8. The [new] constitutional government [referring to President Alfonsín] has acknowledged that the fight against subversion was a war (Decree No. 157/83) declared by the previous de facto government. The conflict between the armed forces and the subversives was a *casus belli.* The decrees of the [Isabel] Perón government declared that "to combat the enemies of the people is converted into an imperative of the moment."

9. The participation of the defendant in this war was the result of operations that implied making decisions under extreme situations (*situación limite*), in full combat, on the front line, with the accompanying passion that combat generates in its inevitable atmosphere of destruction and death.

10. Colonel Camps operated openly, lawfully, and with the presumption of a state of war. He conformed to the natural chain of command and "obedience," ending with the Commander in Chief of the Army.

11. The real accused in this trial is the army, as an institution, in a political trial. Acts of war are not brought to trial; they are not justiciable. Camps and other officers who defended their *patria* and its institutions are being tried under the terms of ex-post-facto laws and in the glare of the

media. This allows the subversives who lost the war to determine their [the officers'] fate in collaboration with a government seeking revenge and political advantage rather than justice—all this with no effort by the same government to bring to justice the terrorists and subversives or to subject them to public exposure and repudiation, as has been done with military officers.

Why attack the army that had defended *la patria*? Why hold Colonel Camps accountable for fulfilling his duty, obeying orders, winning the war against terrorism and subversion? What if the terrorists had been victorious? Who would have defended human rights against godless, materialistic, satanic, Marxist-Leninist, Soviet imperialism and its Cuban satellite?[43]

Consider next the victory of the Chilean armed forces against the Popular Unity coalition, the Soviet menace, international communism, and Cuban intervention. Seventeen years after saving *la patria* from destruction and orchestrating economic recovery and institutional reform, including a new (1980) constitution that permitted a "transition to democracy," a truth commission (the Rettig Commission) accused the armed forces and police of human rights violations. The Chilean army answered as follows:[44]

1. The Allende government (1970–1973) acted illegitimately, destroyed national unity, fomented class struggle, drove the country toward fratricidal strife, broke the law, operated outside of constitutional norms. . . . [such that] anarchy prevailed, that the internal and external security of the country were in peril, that the very existence of Chile as an independent state was in jeopardy, and . . . in accord with our historic conceptions we deposed the illegitimate and immoral government, assuming the moral duty that *la patria* has imposed on us.[45]

2. The congressional majority and the supreme court previously called upon the military to restore order, the rule of law, and constitutional government.[46]

3. The Rettig Commission's report ignores the circumstances that provoked the 1973 *pronunciamiento* and the fact that only due to the energetic and drastic action taken by the armed forces was a bloody civil war avoided.

4. The report also ignores the existence of subversive war before and after the military government assumed control, and that once engaged in war a military institution can only seek total victory.

5. The report also failed to evaluate the magnitude and danger of the terrorist action and armed subversion, actual and imminent, from 1973 to 1990.

6. These were part of a planned strategy by international and domestic Marxists to regain the power they had lost in 1973, make the country ungovernable, and ultimately attempt the assassination of the president [General Pinochet] in 1986.

7. The armed forces and police acted legally to repress these threats and adopted constitutional and legal reforms as required. A new constitution

was approved in the plebiscite of 1980, with a transition to civilian government occurring as programmed in that constitution.

8. The institution [the army] insists that a state of war existed from the publication of Decree Law No. 5 (1973) and that the courts, which remained operative, did not challenge this decree.

9. The courts-martial that tried civilians operated under ordinances dating from 1839 that regulated the operations of *tribunales de tiempo de guerra*. These were not inventions of the military *junta* and acted in accord with Chilean law, including the Military Code of Justice.

10. The army with the other branches of the armed forces and police intervened in 1973 to overcome the moral, institutional, economic, and social crisis afflicting our country, in response to the clamor of the citizenry, that resulted precisely from the great trust the people of Chile have had throughout history in these institutions.

11. For this reason, it is unacceptable to link, even indirectly, supposed criminal activity committed by individuals with the historic role of the army in national life, and, moreover, when these supposed crimes (*delitos*) are founded in the declarations of persons who claim to be affected [by the action of members of the armed forces].

12. The army and the other armed forces and police were called upon to intervene in the worst institutional crisis in this century, as the ultimate recourse against a serious threat to national sovereignty and social peace (*bases mismas de la convivencia*). They completed their mission, defeating the totalitarian threat; they reconstructed and modernized the economy; they restored social peace and democracy; and returned political authority to civilians in a free country. . . .

13. The Chilean army certainly sees no reason to ask pardon from anyone for having taken part in this patriotic effort.

14. In particular the army rejects the [Rettig] Commission's conclusion that there was not a state of war [declared to suppress terrorism] in the country. This is an offense against those [soldiers] who died in this war.

15. The army also repudiates the campaign to besmirch its members in the press with accusations of torture and other crimes, instead of the appropriate procedures required in a state of law. It will not accept being put on trial in this fashion for having saved the liberty and sovereignty of *la patria* at the insistence of civil society. Still less is this acceptable when among the principal accusers are those responsible for the tragedy, as leaders of the Popular Unity [coalition].

16. The Chilean army reaffirms its decision to continue fulfilling its mission, guarding the institutional order of the Republic and respect for its external sovereignty.[47]

According to the army's official view, the armed forces fulfilled their mission. Individual "excesses" may have occurred, but these should be treated according to the rule of law by gathering evidence and bringing offenders to trial as appropriate (with the exception of most crimes committed before the self-amnesty decreed in 1978). This did not give the press, the former Allendistas, the subversives' families, or anyone else the license to excoriate the armed forces publicly, offend their honor, or deny the success of their patriotic mission. They had saved and reclaimed *la patria*—at civilian request. In the 1970s, former President Frei and current (1990–1994) President Patricio Aylwin had recognized the armed forces' victory over Marxism and the need for their intervention. Now that they had returned *la patria* intact to the civilians, to the politicians (even to those politicians who had participated in the 1970s debacle), what right did these civilians have to denigrate their accomplishments and to forget their sacrifice? Under such conditions they would be forced to maintain vigilance over *la patria* and prevent the return of subversion: "The survival of the incipient Latin American democracies depends, and will depend, with more emphasis in the future, on the action of Marxist subversion within each state. . . . if the democratic regimes are capable of defending themselves against subversion and totalitarian ideas they will be strengthened, and a new more promising political era will begin in this continent."[48]

Published just before the transition to civilian government in Chile, and full implementation of *perestroika* in the Soviet Union, these words might seem archaic in the late 1990s. Not so to Chilean and other Latin American officers still standing watch over their nations' destinies. War, conflict, and threat of conflict result from the unchangeable nature of human beings. There will always be "potentially threatening situations" and war. The armed forces are the last bulwark, for each nation, against the inevitable consequences of human nature itself. Again, how can the armed forces be faulted for carrying out their mission—a mission that F. A. Hayek, champion of human freedom and idol of the neoliberal hegemon sweeping Latin America and the globe, compared to organic survival: "When an external enemy threatens, when rebellion or lawless violence has broken out, or a natural catastrophe requires quick action by whatever means can be secured, powers of compulsory organization, which nobody normally possesses, must be granted to somebody. Like an animal in flight from mortal danger, society may in such

Figure 8–9. "There Was No War, Just Bloody Extermination of Defenseless People," demonstration of the Sebastian Acevedo Anti-Torture Group, Santiago, Chile, 1991. Photograph by Rosa Parissi M. Courtesy of Rosa Parissi M.

situations have to suspend temporarily even vital functions on which in the long run its existence depends if it is to escape destruction."[49]

To save *la patria* from destruction, the suspension of civil liberties and rights and the defeat of its enemies is essential. In war, human rights are suspended so long as the enemy attacks, resists, and remains an enemy that puts *la patria* in mortal danger. There can be no "rights" without survival, no survival without defense, defeat of the enemy, and eternal vigilance. The armed forces made survival possible—and not just survival, but renewal, economic growth, modernization, and hope for the future. For the *misión cumplida*, there should only be profound gratitude. Only with their victory over the mortal threat did discussion of human rights have meaning. Of course, the human rights organizations insisted that no "war" existed—just a bloody extermination campaign.

Consider, finally, El Salvador. There, the armed forces were unable to obtain "total victory," but with massive U.S. military assistance they prevented a repetition of the Sandinista defeat of the Somoza government in Nicaragua. In 1992 the Salvadoran military was forced to settle for peace accords, a political settlement after a prolonged civil war. As in Argentina and Chile after transition to civilian government, charges of human rights violations threatened the armed forces with trials, public criticism, and institutional reforms. No one could seriously contend that the Salvadoran military had not been at war. Casualties on both sides were extensive, although most wounded, "disappeared," and dead were civilians. The *Informe de la Comisión de la Verdad* (1993) identified human rights abuses perpetrated by both the Salvadoran armed forces and the guerrilla armies, but the vast majority were blamed on the military. Perhaps the most horrendous, the El Mozote Massacre, began on the anniversary of the signing of the Universal Declaration of Human Rights (December 10–13, 1981): "The Atlacatl Battalion, the first immediate-reaction infantry battalion in the Salvadoran army to be trained and equipped by the United States, massacred more than a thousand people in six hamlets located in the municipalities of Meanguera and Joateca, northern Morazán, El Salvador. As many as half of the victims were murdered in El Mozote on 11 December."[50] The victims, who included many women and small children, were not only killed; many had previously been viciously tortured, mutilated, and raped. All this occurred as part of Operation Rescue, a scorched-earth campaign to "rescue" the area from control by the FMLN guerrillas.

Much like their Chilean and Argentine comrades, the Salvadoran armed forces rejected the contextual and moral assertions of the Comisión de la Verdad. They responded publicly and vehemently:[51]

> 1. The Commission's conclusions falsify historical reality and formulate accusations totally lacking in foundation and objectivity, affecting thereby the process of pacification that is supported by all Salvadorans (*todos los sectores ciudadanos*).
>
> 2. Once again the armed forces reaffirm their faith and essential principles and values, those that have guided them in fulfilling their duties to society throughout their history.
>
> 3. Therefore, we remind the citizenry that we soldiers did not provoke the war, nor did we incite any of the civilian population to rise up in arms

against their brothers and against the laws of the Republic, nor did we assign ourselves the ignoble mission of destroying the infrastructure that sustains work and progress.

4. The armed forces act, and have always acted, in compliance with the orders of the highest state authorities and in support of the public administration. These actions were legitimated by the populace as demonstrated in multiple free and democratic elections.

5. The armed forces reaffirm their will to continue fulfilling their constitutional mission defending the sovereignty of the state, even when this implies the greatest of sacrifices.

6. The armed forces, as a permanent institution at the nation's service, will use the necessary legal recourses that they consider adequate to the legitimate right of defense against those who promote their destruction and that of the Republic.

7. The armed forces feel pride in having fulfilled their mission of defending society and the juridical-political system of the State. . . .

8. The armed forces, as the guarantor (*garante*) of the state's sovereignty, cannot accept that the report fails to recognize its constitutional authority to defend *la patria* against aggression in any of its forms.

9. In preparing its report, the Commission used sources and methods that ensured its reaching preconceived conclusions, with no other objective than staining (*mancillar*) the honor and dignity of the [military] institutions, thus causing the public to believe that the armed forces and its members systematically violated human rights.

10. The report does not mention the horror and suffering that communism's so-called "prolonged popular war" caused all strata of the population.

11. The FMLN used violence, destruction, kidnappings, assassinations, and systematic attacks on the citizenry in its effort to attain total power, obligating the country's legitimate government to use arms to repel the aggression that attacked it.

12. The armed forces are proud to have fulfilled the mission of defending the people (*pueblo*), . . . and contributed to the pacification and preservation of our republican, democratic system at the cost of blood and sacrifice, supported by our faith in God and our unending spirit of service to the nation.

La patria was threatened; extreme measures had to be taken. The armed forces fulfilled their duties, saved the nation from the Communist onslaught, and even received the approval of the citizenry in elections. The political party that had most consistently supported a hard line against the subversives won the presidency again after the peace accords. And now the Commission, the United Nations, and even some government politicians attacked the honor of the armed forces, purged officers who had defended *la patria*, and pushed for trials of so-called violators of human rights.

The armed forces were again betrayed by civilians who were unable to deliver the promised pensions, jobs, and land for retired veterans. Now they were accused of "crimes" for actions that had made possible the nation's survival. What recourse was left to the armed forces but to retrench and remind the citizenry of their missions to protect *la patria*'s permanent interests? And also to remind them that, like their Chilean comrades, should the civilians fail to protect these permanent interests, the armed forces might be forced to do so. This antipolitical perspective continues to frame Salvadoran and Latin American politics in the 1990s. But unlike their Chilean comrades, after 1993 high-ranking Salvadoran officers lost their careers and were subjected to public humiliation and social ostracism for human rights violations during the civil war. From the perspective of Salvadoran officers, the United Nations (and its peacekeeping mission) and changes in U.S. policy subverted their nation's sovereignty and military autonomy. Changes in military doctrine and a grudging acceptance of a new civilian-controlled police force were imposed on the Salvadoran military; they became the negative object lesson for other Latin American armed forces—the example of what happens when the war against subversion is not won and when national interests are subordinated to international public opinion and the caprice of U.S. foreign policy.

Epilogue

Perestroika and the end of the Cold War brought new threats to the armed forces and *la patria*. The United States lost interest in anticommunism and was discomfited by authoritarian allies and repressive policies. Past human rights abuses were viewed in a new light; support for "democratization" and a reduction in military expenditures replaced counterinsurgency and low-intensity conflict as buzzwords in Washington's official proclamations. Military nationalists saw U.S. support for human rights investigations, and even for introducing human rights courses in military curricula, as a deliberate effort to weaken or destroy the Latin American armed forces. Feigned concern for human rights by the world's strongest military power barely masked its intention to subordinate the region's security concerns and development to its own hemispheric and international agenda. In the view of Latin American military nationalists, arms control, limitations on technology transfers, pressures for reductions in military budgets, and a new emphasis on environmental problems and drug trafficking were all part of the strategic plan to impose U.S. hegemony in a unipolar "new world order."

A great plot existed to "annihilate the Latin American armed forces and the nations of IberoAmerica." This plot was denounced in a best-selling work, widely read by Latin American officers, edited by Argentina's Colonel Mohamed Alí Seineldín and the United States' self-styled "political prisoner" Lyndon H. LaRouche: "Ibero-American military history is, in every case, the vertebral column in the life of each of our peoples. For that reason the current masters of the world (new world order) have resolved to eliminate the armed and security forces of Ibero-America, the last barrier to these nations' total submission."[52] In two inflammatory volumes, officers from Brazil to Guatemala denounce the conspiracy to cripple the Latin American armed forces through budget cuts and the introduction of exotic doctrines into the military academies, and thereby to subvert Ibero-American sovereignty. These military nationalists claim that as part of this conspiracy, the discourse of human rights and the demand for trials are used to denigrate the armed forces and subordinate national law and security to international human rights agreements.

Perhaps the most blatant case of this strategy occurred in El Salvador, where the "Lying 'Truth Commission' " (*Mentirosa "Comisión de la Verdad"*) imposed international demands for constitutional change and purges of the armed forces:

> The most devastating, perhaps definitive, blow to El Salvador's sovereignty was the appearance of the United Nations' Truth Commission, 15 March 1993. The report not only treats the FMLN as a legitimate belligerent force, instead of considering it the narcoterrorist group that it is, but based on this redefines the war, initiated by the FMLN, as "state terrorism" and characterizes the casualties that occurred as "violations of human rights.". . . The report not only demands the immediate purge of the armed forces' command structure, but also the dismissal of all of El Salvador's Supreme Court. . . . Far from being impartial investigators of the truth, the "legal experts" integrating the Commission are old supporters of the Communist insurgents whom their report absolves of all important culpability.[53]

The Salvadoran Defense Ministry published a pamphlet in March 1993, *La amenaza a la soberanía nacional y la destrucción del estado*, which asked: Who could benefit by diffusing such lies and by maligning the armed forces? It answered: "Communism has not disappeared. Its immediate objective in El Salvador is the destruction of the armed forces to complete its assault on [the nation's governmental power]."[54] The Salvadorans, like Seineldín and his co-authors—Panama's General Manuel Noriega, Venezuela's General Francisco Visconti Osorio and Admiral Hernán Grüber Odremán, Brazil's General Ivan Moacyr da Frota, and Admiral Sérgio Tasso, among others—believed that international concerns for human rights and attacks on the armed forces were part of a continuing global conspiracy to erode Latin American sovereignty: "In the last years the [Brazilian] armed forces have been victims of permanent attacks, professionally elaborated and orchestrated by certain national and international mass media against their moral character. The strategic objective of this campaign is the systematic demoralization and maximum debilitation or the total destruction of the national military institutions. . . . Any pretext may be used for this purpose: drug trafficking, ecology, protection of Indian rights, etc."[55] General Frota's colleague, Admiral Tasso, added: "I believe firmly that just as the forces of the Devil cannot overcome the Church of Our God, while the armed forces exist, no one and nothing will limit Brazil's sovereignty or impede her struggle for peace, liberty, and justice."[56]

The armed forces did not want their victory over subversion and the defense of *la patria* to be undone by the creation of a new international order that destroys sovereignty. In General Frota's words, the armed forces are "the last bastion"; they must defend themselves and their nations from the international human rights conspiracy, whose victory would signify the demise of their nations. According to this vision, in the 1990s, the armed forces must prevent the ploy of human rights from destroying their institutions and their *patria*.

Figure 8–10. "Why Don't They Understand That, for *la Patria*, One Is Capable of Doing the Most Unpatriotic Things?" by Hervi. From *Diario La Epoca*, Santiago, Chile, January 27, 1996. Courtesy of Hernán Vidal

International and universal human rights are a fundamental challenge to the armed forces' traditional concepts of *patria*, sovereignty, patriotism, and nationalism. In times of crisis, they view calls to respect individual rights and civil liberties as a pretext for destroying all they hold dear. Yet somehow the Latin American officers forgot or suppressed their own oaths to uphold constitutions that forbade torture, and their criminal responsibility under military codes that outlawed torture and cruel punishment. In defending *la patria* they committed antipatriotic atrocities. The most recent constitutions in every case prohibited torture and usually the death penalty, and military codes and law did likewise. To defend *la patria* and its constitution, the members of the armed forces violated their own fundamental charters and constitutional oaths:

> *Argentina* The death sentence for political motives and all types of torture (*tormento*) and whipping are forever abolished. [Art. 18]
>
> *Bolivia* All types of torture, coercion, and physical and moral violence [against prisoners] are prohibited. [Art. 12]
>
> *Brazil* No one shall be subjected to torture or inhumane treatment. [Art. 5]
>
> *Chile* The Constitution guarantees the right to life and physical integrity; all illegitimate physical abuse is prohibited. [Art. 19]
>
> *Colombia* There shall be no death penalty. No one shall be subjected to forced disappearance, torture, or cruel treatment or criminal penalties. [Arts. 11–12]
>
> *Costa Rica* Human life is inviolable. [Art. 21] No one shall be subjected to cruel or degrading treatment, . . . any confession obtained by force shall be null. [Art. 40]

Dominican Republic In no case shall the death penalty, or torture, . . . be applied. [Art. 8]

Ecuador The State guarantees the inviolability of human life and physical integrity. There is no death penalty. All torture and all inhumane and degrading procedures are prohibited. [Art. 19]

El Salvador All persons have the right to life. [Art. 2] All types of torture are prohibited. [Art. 27]

Guatemala [Prisoners] should be treated as human beings, . . . and not subjected to cruel treatment or physical, moral, or psychological torture. [Art. 19]

Honduras The right to life is inviolable. [Art. 65] The death penalty is prohibited. [Art. 66] No one shall be subjected to torture, or cruel, inhumane, or degrading treatment. [Art. 68]

Mexico All mistreatment upon arrest or in the prisons . . . are abuses that shall be . . . repressed by the authorities. [Art. 19] Mutilation, whipping, mistreatment, beatings, and torture of all sorts are prohibited. [Art. 22]

Nicaragua The right to life is inviolable . . . in Nicaragua there is no capital punishment. [Art. 23] All persons have the right to have their physical, moral, and psychological integrity respected. No one shall be subjected to cruel, inhumane, or degrading treatment, or torture. . . . Violation of this constitutional right is a crime punishable by law. [Art. 36]

Panama There is no death penalty. [Art. 30]

Paraguay The death penalty is abolished. [Art. 4] No one shall be subjected to torture, inhumane, or degrading treatment. There is no statute of limitations for genocide and torture, or for "forced disappearance," kidnapping, or murder for political motives. [Art. 5]

Peru Confessions obtained through violence are null; those who obtain them incur criminal liability. [Art. 3 (j)] No one shall be subjected to torture or inhumane or humiliating treatment. [Art. 234]

Uruguay To no one shall be applied the death penalty. [Art. 26]

Venezuela No law shall establish a death penalty or shall any authority apply it. [Art. 58] No one shall be held incommunicado, or subjected to torture or other procedures that cause physical or moral suffering . . . [any such treatment] is punishable by law. [Art. 60 (3)]

In the salvation of *la patria* the armed forces went beyond the demons they sought to exorcise. What *patria,* what common good, what utopia could require a return to the Inquisition, with updated techniques of torment? Could professional officers really defend the application of electrical current to genitals, tongues, and breasts? Could they justify raping women with dogs and throwing living humans into the sea from airplanes? Could they excuse these horrors in the name of *"la patria"*? The demand to respect human rights when the very existence of *la patria* is in question cuts to the quick—not only in Latin America but around the globe. With this in mind, and the more general attack on the traditional international system of sovereign nations, the Latin

American armed forces looked to the twenty-first century with alarm and concern for the integrity of their *patrias* and their own institutions.[57]

Notes

1. Gen. Carlos Dellepiane, *Historia militar del Perú*, 6th ed. (Lima: Ministerio de Guerra, 1977), 2:448.

2. For an overview and discussion of the dilemmas of dealing with human rights violations see José Zalaquett, "Confronting Human Rights Violations Committed by Former Governments: Principles Applicable and Political Constraints," *Persona y Sociedad* 6(2–3) (1990): 51–80; *Nunca más: Informe de la Comisión Nacional sobre Desaparición de Personas* (Buenos Aires: Editorial Universitaria de Buenos Aires, 1985); Servicio Paz y Justicia (1989); *Informe de la Comisión Nacional de Verdad y Reconciliación* (1991); and *Informe de la Comisión de la Verdad para El Salvador; De la locura a la esperanza* (New York: United Nations, 1992–93).

3. In Paraguay, for example, the former chief of the secret police was tried and sentenced to prison; in Argentina, military leaders were tried and imprisoned, then pardoned; in Chile, police were tried in the case of the *degollados* (murder victims with slashed throats), and the former chief of the DINA was tried for the murder of Orlando Letelier in Washington, DC; in El Salvador, military personnel accused of killing nuns and Jesuit priests were also incarcerated, and others were later purged from the armed services. However, the victimizers of hundreds of thousands of abused, tortured, "disappeared," and murdered people in nonnotorious circumstances were rarely brought to trial.

4. Patrice McSherry, "Military Power, Impunity, and State-Society Change in Latin America," *Canadian Journal of Political Science* 25(3) (September 1992): 463–88.

5. For a list of such publications see *Human Rights Watch's* current publications catalogue and that of *Amnesty International*.

6. On the varied procedures and impacts of the truth commissions see Priscilla Hayner, "Fifteen Truth Commissions—1974 to 1994: A Comparative Study," *Human Rights Quarterly* 16 (November 1994): 597–655; A. Boraine and Ronel Scheffer, eds., *Dealing with the Past: Truth and Reconciliation in South Africa* (Cape Town: Institute for Democracy in South Africa, 1994).

7. See Col. José D. Ramos A., *Nunca será tarde, seguridad democrática* (Santiago: Gráfica Andes, 1988): 14.

8. A frontal assault on these premises is being made in El Salvador in the 1990s as a result of the "peace accords" ending the long civil war. See Ministerio de Defensa Nacional, El Salvador (1994). After 1985 in Argentina some efforts were made to redefine the internal role of the armed forces but less comprehensively than in El Salvador.

9. For a fascinating study of the "poetic system" (underlying myth and metaphor) in the Chilean General Staff's, *Historia del Ejército de Chile*, see Hernán Vidal, *Mitología militar chilena: Surrealismo desde el superego* (Minneapolis: Institute for the Study of Ideologies and Literature, 1989).

10. Rodríguez Solís, comp. (1964): 35.

11. "El Ser Militar," in *El Soldado* 94 (January–February 1984), cited in Perelli (1990): 97.

12. Rodríguez Solís (1964): 28. Emphasis in the original.

13. Molina Johnson (1987).

14. Benjamín Rattenbach, *El sistema social-militar en la sociedad moderna* (Buenos Aires: Editorial Pleamar, 1972).

15. Rodríguez Solís (1964): 40–41.

16. Fernando Landazábal Reyes, *El equilibrio del poder* (Bogotá: Plaza & Janes, 1993): 146.

17. Rodríguez Solís (1964): 45. Emphais added. Similar language can be found in military texts and *memorias* from Chile to Mexico. This Guatemalan example simply illustrates the "priest-warrior" self-image in relation to profession, morality, and *patria*. See also Nunn (1992) for a global comparison of militarylore.

18. *El Tiempo* (Bogotá), November 6, 1979: 1–A, 8–A, cited in Francisco Leal Buitrago, *El oficio de la guerra, La seguridad nacional en Colombia* (Bogotá: Tercer Mundo Editores, 1994): 55.

19. Molina Johnson (1987): 91–92.

20. Costa Rica is an obvious exception, with abolition of the army after 1948. In some other cases the armed forces are not created in the constitution, for example, in Argentina's 1853 Constitution.

21. Rodríguez Solís (1964): 121.

22. Ibid.: 142.

23. See Loveman (1993).

24. Cited in Donald C. Hodges, *Argentina's "Dirty War": An Intellectual Biography* (Austin: University of Texas Press, 1991): 125.

25. "Informe presentado ante el Consejo Nacional de Seguridad por el Comandante en Jefe de la Armada de Chile, Almirante Jorge Martínez Busch," March 27, 1991, published in *La Nación*, March 28, 1991. Emphasis in original. This was the navy's response to the Rettig Commission's report on human rights violations by the military government. Reprinted in "Respuestas de las fuerzas armadas y de orden al informe de la Comisión Nacional de Verdad y Reconciliación," *Estudios Públicos* 41 (Summer 1991), offprint.

26. Leal Buitrago (1994); Americas Watch, *Peru under Fire: Human Rights since the Return to Democracy* (New Haven: Yale University Press, 1992); Human Rights Watch, Americas, *State of War, Political Violence, and Counterinsurgency in Colombia* (New York, 1993); Americas Watch, *El Salvador's Decade of Terror: Human Rights since the Assassination of Archbishop Romero* (New Haven, CT: Yale University Press, 1991).

27. Leal Buitrago (1994): 54–55.

28. See, for example, Ministerio del Interior, *Orden público y seguridad del estado* (Santiago: Editorial Jurídica de Chile, 1993) for an updated compendium of such legislation.

29. *Código Militar de la República de Guatemala* (México: Talleres de El Libro Perfecto, 1951): 27.

30. El Salvador's 1934 military code had an ambiguous provision that has been interpreted, retrospectively, as an obligation, or at least authorization, to disobey illegal orders. Article 9 of the 1934 *Ordenanza del Ejército* read: "Las órdenes legales del superior deben cumplirse por los subordinados sin hacer observación ni reclamación alguna, sin vacilación y sin murmurar." However, the text continued: "pero podrán reclamar si hubiera lugar a ello, después de haberlas cumplido." Cited in *Doctrina militar* (1994): 58–59.

31. See *Doctrina militar* (1994): 53–57 for relevant language from military codes in the United States, England, Germany, France, Spain, and Italy. The section concludes with the observation that "the current doctrine in armies in Western democratic nations imposes the obligation of legitimate disobedience to those orders that imply illegal or criminal action" (p. 56).

32. In a major departure from this concept, Argentine army commander Lt. Gen. Martín Balza declared in April 1995 that "those who give or comply with immoral orders are criminals." If Balza's opinion were to become doctrine in Argentine military schools and courts, the longstanding tradition of *obediencia debida* would be seriously undermined.

33. The most important early versions of the NSD were Peruvian and Brazilian. Adaptations and revisions occurred throughout the hemisphere, were discussed among officers, and were published in military journals. See, for example, do Couto e Silva (1955); Gen. Fernando Landazábal Reyes, *Estrategia de la subversión y su desarrollo en América Latina* (Bogotá: Editorial Pax, 1969); Col. Osiris G. Villegas, *La guerra comunista* (Bogotá: Librería del Ejército, 1964); and Gen. Edgardo Mercado Jarrín, "La política y la estrategia militar en la guerra contrasubversiva en la América Latina," *Revista Militar del Perú* 701 (November–December 1967): 4–33.

34. A useful overview is found in Genaro Arriagada Herrera, *El pensamiento político de los militares* (Santiago: CISEC, Edición Privada, n.d.): 109–207; Comblin (1979); Margaret E. Crahan, "National Security Ideology and Human Rights," in Margaret E. Crahan, ed., *Human Rights and Basic Needs in the Americas* (Washington, DC: Georgetown University Press, 1982): 100–27; and Pion-Berlin (1989): 411–29.

35. Col. Osiris G. Villegas, *Guerra revolucionaria comunista* (Buenos Aires: Biblioteca del Oficial, 1962): 46.

36. Gen. Augusto Pinochet, "Discurso en el tercer aniversario del gobierno," Santiago, September 11, 1976.

37. A. De Lannes, "Conhecendo o inimigo interno. A ação revolucionaria," *Revista a Defesa Nacional* 675 (January–February 1978): 180.

38. Pinochet, "Discurso" (1976).

39. "Los derechos humanos en Uruguay. Respuesta del gobierno al informe de la Comisión Interamericana de Derechos Humanos, de fecha 24 de Mayo 1977" (Montevideo: Ministerio de Relaciones Exteriores, 1977).

40. For details see Leal Buitrago (1994).

41. This is a brief synopsis and paraphrase of parts of Osiris G. Villegas's *Testimonio de un alegato* (Buenos Aires: Compañía Impresora Argentina, 1990). The synopsis cannot do justice to the complex substantive and procedural arguments whereby Villegas argues for Camps's legal innocence. Villegas's brief, his appendices, and his mastery of the security legislation, military codes, and procedures are impressive. This schematic overview simply attempts to illustrate the overall "argument" and defense, not to replicate it in its nuance and technical ferocity.

42. The ERP (Ejército Revolucionario del Pueblo) and the Montoneros were two of the most important revolutionary organizations committed to armed struggle in Argentina. See Hodges (1991) for details.

43. The Argentine version of this view suffered a severe blow with the publication of former Lt. Comdr. Adolfo Scilingo's "confessions" of navy flights from which live prisoners were thrown into the ocean (Horacio Verbitsky, *El Vuelo* [Buenos Aires: Planeta, 1995]). Each of the armed forces' chiefs issued statements lamenting human rights abuses during the "dirty war." Thus, Lt. Gen. Martín Balza admitted that the army had used "illegitimate methods, including the

suppression of life"; and Adm. Enrique Molina Pico acknowledged that the navy used "mistaken methods which caused unacceptable horrors even in the context of a cruel war."

44. This is a synopsis and paraphrase of parts of the "Informe presentado ante el Consejo de Seguridad Nacional por el Comandante en Jefe del Ejército de Chile, General Augusto Pinochet Ugarte," March 27, 1991, reprinted from *La Nación*, March 28, 1991, and in *Estudios Públicos* 41 (Summer 1991), offprint.

45. "Bando No. 5 emitido por la Junta de Comandantes en Jefe de las FF. AA. y Director General de Carabineros de Chile el 11 de Septiembre de 1973."

46. The armed forces make reference here to the "Acuerdo de la Cámara de Diputados sobre el grave quebrantamiento del orden constitucional y legal de la República," Santiago, August 23, 1973; and the "Pronunciamiento de la Corte Suprema sobre la quiebra de la juridicidad en Chile," May 7, 1973.

47. This is a paraphrase of parts of the army's official response to the Rettig Commission's report. As with the Villegas defense of General Camps, this paraphrase does not do full justice to the army's document but seeks to capture the main thrusts and "spirit" of the response. "Informe presentado ante el Consejo de Seguridad Nacional por el Comandante en Jefe del Ejército, General Augusto Pinochet Ugarte," March 27, 1991.

48. Maj. Luis B. Olivares, *Subversión política y transición* (Santiago: Estado Mayor General de Ejército, 1988).

49. F. A. Hayek, *Law, Legislation, and Liberty* (Chicago: University of Chicago Press, 1979): 124.

50. Leigh Binford, *The El Mozote Massacre* (Tucson: University of Arizona Press, 1996): 3.

51. "La fuerza armada de El Salvador, Posición ante el informe de la Comisión de la Verdad," in "El Informe de la Comisión de la Verdad: Análisis, reflexiones y comentarios, San Salvador," *Estudios CentroAmericanos* 47 (April–May 1993): 484–86.

52. Gretchen Small and Dennis Small, *El complot para aniquilar a las fuerzas armadas y a las naciones de Iberoamérica*, 2 vols. (Mexico: Ejército Mexicano, Secretaría de la Defensa Nacional, 1994): 1:xiv.

53. *El complot* (1994): 1:169–72.

54. Ibid.: 1:188.

55. Brig. Gen. Ivan Moacyr da Frota, commander of the Brazilian Air Force, "Las fuerzas armadas, El último baluarte," *O Estado* (São Paulo), May 12, 1993, reprinted in *El complot* (1994): 2:390–96.

56. Adm. Sérgio Tasso Vasquez de Aquino, "Las fuerzas armadas de Brasil y la conyuntura nacional," in *El complot* (1994): 2:402.

57. As this book was going to press, toward the end of 1998, General Augusto Pinochet was arrested in England, at the request of a Spanish judge, for possible extradition to Spain in a case regarding the death and torture of Spanish citizens during his dictatorship in Chile. And in Argentina, General Jorge Videla was arrested on charges regarding children of the "disappeared" who had been "adopted" by military families. These cases illustrate once again the political significance of international human rights treaties and the profound impact of "globalization" for the Latin American armed forces.

9

La Patria and *Perestroika*

Toward the Twenty-first Century

> Hemispheric security partners, like dancing partners confronting unexpected music with a different rhythm, must confirm shared perceptions and review their complementary roles and agreements before trying out new dance steps.
>
> —Lt. Col. Richard Downes, USAF (ret.), 1995[1]

> The army that was born with *la patria* in May 1810 will finish its second century in a world whose uncertainty imposes unprecedented challenges on a society in a permanent process of change, demanding of its basic institutions systematic adaptation. . . . The army will more than fulfill [this mission] . . . always maintaining upright its traditions and the ethical values that are the foundations of the military profession.
>
> —Lt. Gen. Martín Balza, Argentina, 1995[2]

Latin American militarylore tells the same story from Mexico to Chile: the armed forces created new *patrias* in nineteenth-century wars, then defended their sovereignty and national values until the end of the twentieth century. When *la patria* is threatened, the armed forces rise to the challenge. The true military leader has a "gift," or *don de mando*, a vocation for the sacred duty of leadership and command. In times of crisis this *don* can be transferred from strictly military to political salvation of *la patria*.

La patria encapsulates all that the armed forces hold dear—family, religion, community, solidarity, territory, and honor. In a dangerous world, full of potential and actual threats (or SPOCs, using Argentine General Laiño's acronym),[3] it must be defended against the machinations of politicians, the subversion of "exotic" movements and ideologies, and the errors of transitory governments. And in the 1990s it must be defended against the internationalism that threatens its sovereignty. Despite tireless efforts at nation-building, within each Latin American state certain social, cultural, regional, and ideological differences block a universally shared patriotic vision and impede national development. Militarylore attributes the failure to overcome these impediments to national development mainly to generations of nefarious partisan politics and to civilian neglect—of *la patria* and of military institutions.

Military institutional doctrine from the 1880s to the 1990s wove antipolitical, antipartisan, and anticivilian threads into the fabric of military thinking. In part, this ethos was anti-Marxist, especially because of Marxism's appeal to internationalist (and therefore antinationalist and antipatriotic) values. This anti-Marxism and anticommunism repeatedly led to repression of anarchists, socialists, Communists, and so-called subversives from the beginning of the twentieth century. But military anti-Marxism was part of a broader emphasis on nationalism, sovereignty, and anti-internationalism that linked the military institutions to the modern nation-state. While Latin American national security laws and doctrine preceded the Cold War, post-World War II versions of national security doctrine that inspired the draconian repression of socialists and Communists from the 1950s to the 1990s also emphasized traditional themes of militarylore: the importance of strong governments, the directive role of the nation-state for social and economic development, and the connection between economic modernization, political order, and national security. These aspects of militarylore blended colonial traditions and legislation with the doctrines of European military missions in Latin America from the 1870s to World War II.

This concept of national security was associated with enhancing government capacity and with reinforcing sovereignty—both menaced by the linkages between internal subversion and international political movements, especially international communism after 1945. Threats to national security were threats to sovereignty, to autonomy, and to national independence, whether from internationalist doctrines, internal insurgencies, or U.S. hegemony. Neither Brazilian nor Peruvian versions of national security doctrine in the 1950s, and their adaptations elsewhere in the hemisphere, accepted U.S. hegemony or a dependent role for their nations or their armed forces. Nowhere in Latin America did the armed forces willingly accept the substitution of U.S. policy objectives for their own or willingly acquiesce in subordinating their own institutional and national interests to those of the United States. When guerrilla struggles broke out in the 1960s, the armed forces faced threats from self-declared revolutionary enemies. They accepted U.S. assistance and adapted U.S. training and doctrine to their own circumstances. But they sought to limit the "contamination" of this influence to the greatest extent possible, and they recognized that U.S. interests often diverged from their own. Latin American military institutions quietly resisted, as best they could, inconvenient "contributions" of U.S. advisers and objectionable policy constraints imposed by Washington.

Not surprisingly, as the armed forces battled revolutionary insurgencies (as they had deployed against workers' organizations and strikes since the nineteenth century), Marxists and other analysts of military political behavior identified the military as the armed instruments of certain class interests—first of the landowners, then of industrial, financial, and commercial elites, and then of the "middle class."[4] This class conflict-based interpretation of the military's political role is consistent with theories of politics and social change that emphasize the dependent and instrumental functions of military institutions and military elites. An updated and more complex version of this approach attributes coups and repressive military governments to linkages between transnational capital, U.S. foreign policy, domestic capital, and the armed forces.[5] Others attribute the iterated coups in Latin America to deep cultural and institutional contradictions between democracy, modernization, and the region's inherited Hispano-Catholic values and institutions. According to this view, political democracy and more egalitarian societies are incompatible with the Hispanic tradition. Whenever popular demands become too radical or threatening, the military restores political equilibrium—as it has in Spain and the Spanish American colonies since the 1780s.

The class-conflict and culturally based explanations of military behavior overlap. In both, the military is seen primarily as an instrument that exercises an assigned role as "enforcer" for the politically dominant groups. After World War II, still others pointed to the influence of Washington's Cold War policies and the impact of military assistance programs in supporting coups and military governments.[6] Again, the Latin American military was doing the bidding of others—in this version, acting as instruments of U.S. Cold War policies and defending the interests of transnational corporations. A variation on this explanation characterizes many of the region's armed forces as merely U.S. surrogates (and fails to identify the corporate, institutional, and political reasons for the military's repression of insurgencies while using U.S. assistance and public rationale to carry out their own objectives).

In the mid-1960s, Guillermo O'Donnell's influential work on "bureaucratic-authoritarian" regimes hypothesized that the 1960s coups that led to military dictatorships in the more industrialized Latin American countries resulted from their inability to contain popular demands and new forms of social mobilization. An acute social crisis threatened society and the military, making the armed forces "the last hope" and "also an organization which had acquired technical skill, training in 'social problems,' and sufficient internal unity to involve themselves directly and successfully on the socioeconomic battlefront."[7] Others emphasized the extent to which coups were precipitated by the military's perception that incumbent governments (or soon-to-take-office presidents, in the case of preemptive coups) threatened its institutional and professional interests.[8] A more recent interpretation asserts that factions within the armed forces often engineer coups to secure dominance over military institutions, making them an instrument for resolving internal factional battles even when effected in the name of patriotic and salvational motives.[9]

All these explanations for coups and military rule, as well as more idiosyncratic ones (deposing a drunkard president, for example), are useful for understanding particular military decisions to "save *la patria*." All coups involve personal decisions, factional behavior, immediate social, economic, and political circumstances, professional and institutional histories, national political structures and institutions, and international contexts. Depending on the level and detail of explanation sought, hundreds of potential explanations for coups, involving countless variables (whether "predispositional" or "triggering"), may be relevant. None of these explanations and variables applies to all coups, which occur for many reasons and under greatly differing circumstances. Social, economic, cultural, institutional, conjunctural, and personal variables contribute to military ousters of incumbent governments. Sometimes the interplay of these variables and the immediate motives for coups are fairly clear; at other times they are more confusing, even bizarre. In all cases they are embedded in a more enduring system of civil-military relations that routinely allows military influence and participation in policymaking.

Explaining why coups d'état occur in Latin American countries requires careful understanding of their political systems, since the coups are an integral part of political crisis resolution in most of the region. Understanding why a certain coup occurred requires the application of some theory of coup behavior to the immediate circumstances (the one in which General A ousted General B, for example, was the result of factional conflict within the armed forces), plus a detailed analysis of its idiosyncratic features (General A's faction had lost influence relative to General B's faction and sought to restore the balance). Most important, however, coups are a recurrent part of complex national systems of civil-military relations, more so in some countries than in others, but not the essence of civil-military relations or of the armed forces' influence and participation in politics and policymaking.

Civil-military relations consist of complex cultural, structural, and behavioral interactions among civilian government agencies, diverse social groups (religious, labor, business, landowner), mass media, political parties, and military institutions. And the particular patterns of civil-military relations that develop within each nation-state are framed by international and transnational systems. Explaining different aspects of these relations in particular cases, at particular historical moments, thus requires reference to an array of variables that encompass the broad cultural, institutional, and behavioral influences that create the contingencies from which emerge momentary political outcomes. Which variables exert the most influence at a specific historical moment it is not possible to predict; but the fact that changes in certain variables have tended to induce military coups or other sorts of changes in civil-military relations is clear from the historical record.

Military leaders and coup-makers often proclaim their revolutionary intentions, their determination to transform and thereby reconsecrate *la patria*. Coups have occurred not only to prevent change, to preempt the rise to power of certain parties or politicians, and to restore order but also to create new political regimes. This is seen clearly in the common use of such slogans as *Patria nueva* and *Gobierno revolucionario de las fuerzas armadas*, or even the less common "People-Army-Third Force" proclaimed in the 1950s by Gustavo Rojas Pinilla in Colombia, the worker-army alliance of Argentina's Peronismo, and Bolivia's mid-1960s "peasant-military pact."[10] Sometimes military governments have imposed their programs brutally, sometimes with restraint. They have responded to economic crisis, social unrest, political polarization, and public disorder. Military leaders have also toppled governments because of personal ambition, institutional malaise, and even "strikes" by enlisted personnel and noncommissioned officers (as in the "sergeants' movement" led by Fulgencio Batista in Cuba in 1933).[11]

Underlying all these motives for direct assumption of political power and also for the insistence on some participation in policymaking and virtual autonomy in certain defense and institutional matters is the military's belief in its supposed mystical connection to *la patria* and its historic mission as ultimate guardians. Whatever these officers did, whether seeking to defend the status quo or transform it, their action was justified publicly as political salvation, a return of the warrior-priest to protect, cleanse, and redeem *la patria*. They called on their sacred images, historical imperatives, and constitutional duties—on all the elements of militarylore—to legitimate their political decisions and actions. Even when such evocation of national symbols and patriotic catechism was cynical, it was still an essential ritual for sanctifying the military's political role. Importantly, this political role (that is, military guardianship) has been an integral element of Latin American constitutions and legislation since independence and is a premise widely shared by the general population and civilian political elites. Protected democracy and military guardianship evolved as part of Latin American political culture, with national variations in institutions and style. They were reinforced and further enhanced by the Cold War, the challenge of the Cuban Revolution and regional guerrilla movements, and several decades of counterinsurgency politics. And they were reaffirmed again by the transitions back to elected civilian governments and the "wave of democratization" from 1978 to 1993.

Thus, militarylore was a quasi-religious, catechistic foundation for military political action that was partly shared by popular political culture and was (is) embedded in constitutions, law, political rhetoric, and political practices. Ritual language justified recurrent crusades against multifarious threats to *la patria*. It framed military self-perception, was broadly shared, and changed slowly. Its transmittal in military schools and academies joined generation after generation of officers in the "priesthood of *la patria*";[12] it also pervaded civics textbooks for primary schools. In its national variations it outlasted in consistency and coherence all the major political ideologies and party programs proclaimed from the 1920s until the 1990s: *indigenismo*, social democracy, socialism, Marxism-Leninism, Aprismo, Peronismo, fascism, Christian democracy, Fidelismo, and many others. Militarylore informed a political subculture mythologizing and rationalizing the armed forces' role in society and national politics.[13]

Significantly, no modern political ideology or militarylore itself justified permanent military rule. The presumption always existed that eventually civilian government would be restored. While military institutions could be guardians of the national interests and paladins of *la patria*, they could never assert the historical and constitutional authority of a vanguard political party such as Cuba's Communist party, the Sandinistas in Nicaragua, and even a dominant revolutionary party such as Mexico's PRI. No legitimacy existed for permanent military government. Transition to civilian government was always a matter of circumstance and timing, even for the longest-lasting military regimes.

Historical and constitutional definitions of popular sovereignty, "democracy," and representative government were as much a part of militarylore as was patriotism. Of course, "democracy's" many meanings and interpretations were so contradictory that even most officers also favored some form of it, usually preferring Rousseauism and other versions emphasizing a "general will" and common good (*bien común*) to that based on the more individualistic ideas of John Locke, John Stuart Mill, and other liberal writers. Constitutions and statutes adopted by military governments in Brazil, Chile, Peru, Bolivia, El Salvador, and Guatemala in the 1970s and 1980s left no doubt. Military-imposed constitutions, decrees, and laws specified an eventual return to "democracy" and civilian rule while embedding new prerogatives for military institutions and legal limits on elected governments. Officers favored democracy with qualifications: "protected democracy," "limited democracy," "authoritarian democracy," or "true democracy."[14] (But so did many civilian political leaders.) To achieve this outcome they took additional precautions before transition back to civilian regimes, such as new laws to regulate political parties, elections, and the civil service, and legal guarantees of military professional autonomy.

While eventual transition to civilian government was always expected, the end of the Cold War and its challenges were not. Latin American armed forces had frequently returned formal government authority to civilians in the twentieth century after episodes of military rule. The post-1978 transitions were not, in this sense, unfamiliar. But they had never before confronted the complex regional and global threats to their institutions and nations that were unleashed in the 1980s and 1990s.[15]

La Patria and the New World Disorder

Militarylore and much of what the armed forces cherished were questioned with the end of the Cold War in the 1980s and 1990s. The disappearance of international communism as an internal threat, the international "democratization" fad, severe budget and debt crises, and pressures to reduce military expenditures forced the Latin American armed forces to retrench: to redefine their missions and to defend their political and economic prerogatives. Meanwhile, revolutions in communications, transportation, and military technology made traditional notions of sovereignty ever less viable—particularly in poor, less powerful, and less technologically advanced countries. Global production systems, investments, financial flows, and markets clouded the meaning of "national" enterprises. All nation-states were permeable and vulnerable as never before—to ideas, information, capital and commercial flows, immigration, disease, and environmental transformations. Global television and computer networks invaded sovereign spheres and imperiled national integrity. Nonstate actors, from bankers, multinational enterprises, nongovernmental organizations, and drug lords to religious prophets, sometimes exercised more influence than government officials in a postinternational world.[16]

Attacks on the concept of sovereignty and the increasing interdependence imposed by economic and technological globalization conflicted with military values and institutional interests. Disjunctures between the idea of sovereign authority and the reality of increasing international constraints on national policymaking made evident the further erosion of state autonomy. For most countries, sovereignty was a legal fiction and autonomy in making and implementing national policy an illusion. This was most obvious for small, less powerful countries, but even larger, more industrialized countries such as Brazil, Argentina, and Mexico chafed at the globalizing supranationalist impositions of the new world disorder. With the 1990s reconfiguration of international relations there emerged nastier, less containable external and internal threats to national identity and sovereignty:[17] ethnic and religious conflicts, economic sabotage, narcotics trafficking, private armies, weapons smuggling, money laundering, currency counterfeiting, political corruption, international terrorism, and sundry other dangers from nonstate actors. Nation-states (and the human race) faced security threats ranging from environmental deterioration to backyard scientists experimenting with biological and chemical agents.

For the armed forces, whose professional identity and worldview were coterminous with the nation-state, these developments were appalling. Worse still, even where they had retained considerable political influence, they could not expect to be spared the budget cleaver that hacked resources from the state. They had maintained their roles as guardians of *la patria*, but "democracy" slowly whittled away other prerogatives and economic privileges. To this were added attacks on their morality, probity, and professionalism from international and national human rights activists still unwilling to forget the recent past and to acknowledge the salvation of Latin America from international communism.

The Latin American militaries in the 1990s perceived themselves to be under siege. In response they sought to rejustify their historical missions and to identify new defense and security challenges that would make them even more indispensable. In particular, they focused on the multitudinous threats to sovereignty and national values—from traditional enemies and from more recent and exotic perils—the gamut of SPOCs identified by General Laiño. As usual, they reaffirmed their role as the last bastion of defense of *la patria*. They would uphold its values, defend its long-term objectives, its resources and patrimony. Indeed, they would guarantee its very existence in the new world disorder. Taking seriously the implications of globalization and the communications revolution, most of the region's armed forces presented their visions of the military role in national development in the post-*perestroika* world on elaborate Internet Web sites, replete with national symbols, histories of their institutions, and glorified descriptions of their contributions to *la patria*.

According to their views, the end of the Cold War and economic globalization did not mean the end of traditional military missions. To the contrary, the ultimate origin of warfare, human nature, remained the same; the sources of conflict within and among states were found in this immutable curse of humankind:

> The first thing that must be kept in mind is that the existence of the armed forces as an indispensable resource of societies that organize themselves to achieve the common good for their members is in the political nature of things (*es de naturaleza política*). . . . As long as situations of insecurity exist that affect directly or indirectly this objective, such as the severe poverty associated with critical levels of unemployment and external debt, corruption of the political and administrative systems, migration to seek ways to satisfy the necessities of life, drug production and trafficking, and violence . . . the sovereign expression of the popular will requires the presence of armed forces.[18]

The confusing and violent reshaping of the international system seemed to confirm this military assessment. Nation-states proliferated in the 1980s and 1990s. Some states self-destructed. Age-old ethnic, linguistic, and religious cleavages resurfaced as the putative boundaries of new nations.[19] Predictably, and paradoxically, these new nations asserted traditional sovereign authority in internal and external affairs. As interdependence in all domains intensified, the new states proclaimed their independence and autonomy on the model of post-1789 European nation-states. The myth of sovereignty prevailed. As in the past, its application resulted in bloodshed and mayhem. On every continent, subnationalists sought more political autonomy, if not outright independence. The resurgent ethnic, religious, cultural, agrarian, industrial, and regional conflicts compounded the legacies of the 1980s recession, the debt crisis, civil wars, and increased criminal violence. The armed forces sought to meet these threats to *la patria* and to their own institutional survival.

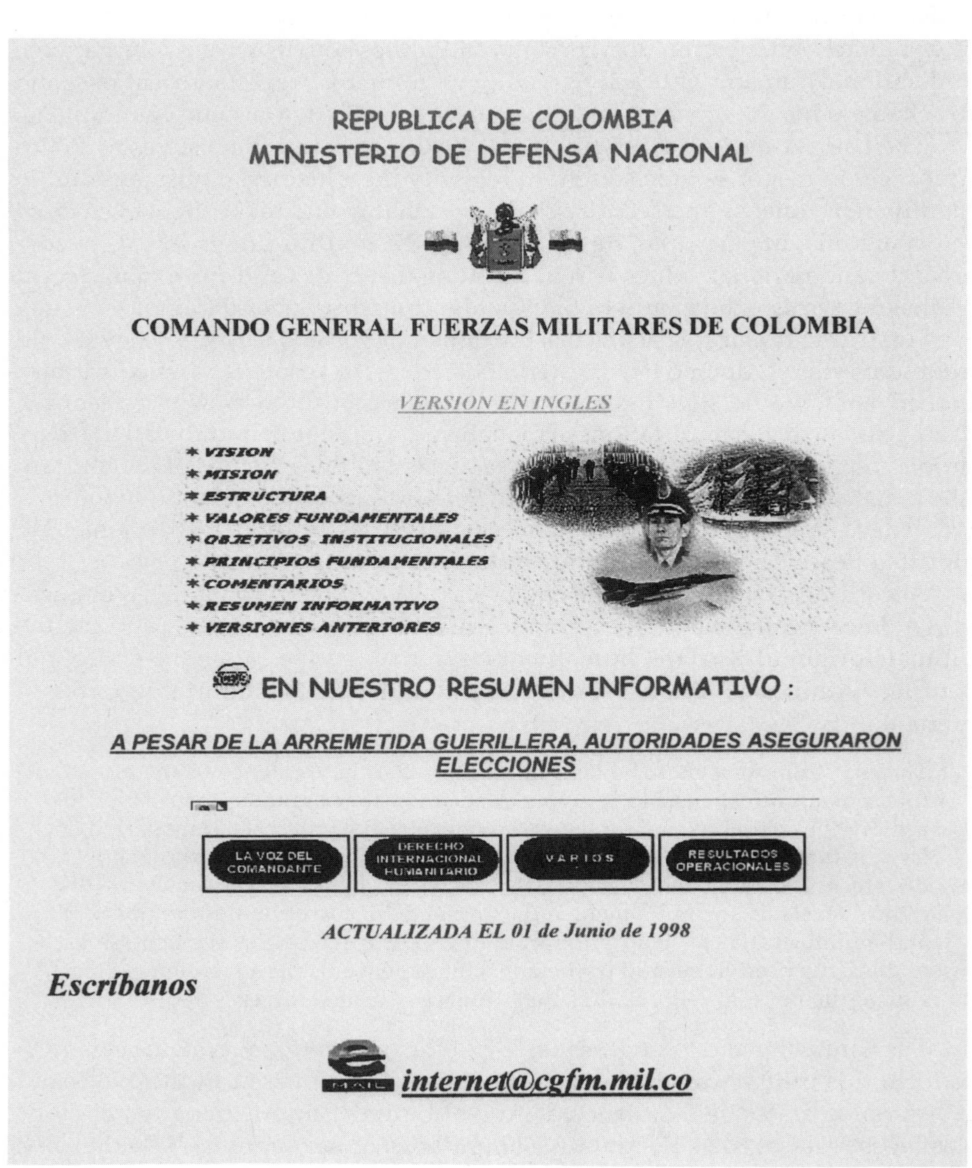

Figure 9–1. Colombian Ministry of Defense Web site, 1998.

Supranational Military Missions and National Sovereignty

One sign of the times was the ever more frequent deployment of supranational peacemaking and peacekeeping forces to trouble spots by the United Nations and regional security regimes, such as the Organization of American States/ Rio Treaty alliance. Military, political, electoral, and humanitarian intervention occurred around the globe.[20] Supranational observer delegations and the supervision of elections and plebiscites also became more common. Elections, the supposed expressions of popular sovereignty within various countries, came to resemble more those in the Caribbean and Central America from 1900 to the 1930s (supervised now by the United Nations rather than by the U.S. Marine Corps).

Peacemaking and peacekeeping missions by multilateral forces belied claims of sovereignty, as did renewed U.S. unilateralism. Would UN or regional armed forces impose environmental and human rights decisions on Latin American countries? Would foreign troops supervise trials by international tribunals of military officers charged with "crimes against humanity" (as in the former Yugoslavia)? Would Washington disregard territorial sovereignty (as it did in Mexico and Panama) to apprehend persons charged with crimes in the United States? Was U.S. unilateral military intervention in Panama a portent of the consequences of the end of the Cold War for Latin America? Could Latin Americans ignore the possibility that the United States, the OAS, and the United Nations would impose settlements in border disputes and internal political matters?[21]

Of course, no important military and economic powers allowed such missions. U.S., British, German, Japanese, Chinese, and Russian sovereignty were

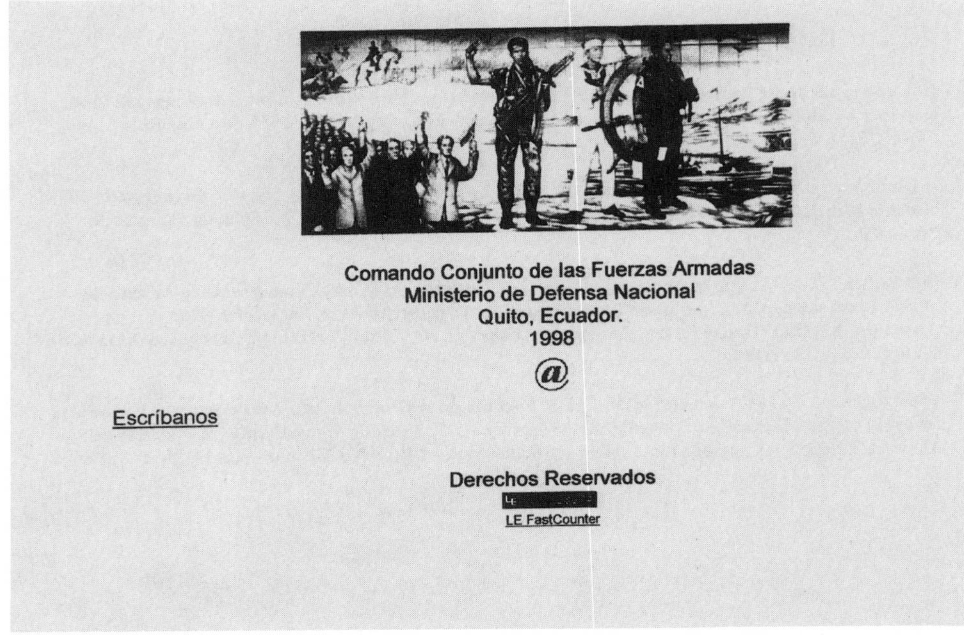

Figure 9–2. Joint Command, Ecuadorian Armed Forces Web site, 1998.

one thing; Haitian, Somalian, Angolan, Nicaraguan, and Salvadoran sovereignty were quite something else. What did the new world disorder imply for the various regional armed forces and their nations' sovereignty?

While Latin America faced fewer ethnic, linguistic, and religious demands for reconfiguring or dividing existing countries than did other regions, efforts by indigenous peoples (and their international supporters) to secure more political and cultural autonomy nonetheless challenged Brazil, the Andean na-

CENTRO DE ADIESTRAMIENTO Y OPERACIONES ESPECIALES

"KAIBIL"

BOSQUEJO HISTORICO

Con el propósito de Incrementar la mística de combate, compañerismo, iniciativa, agresividad, lealtad y disciplina en los miembros del Ejército, el 5 de diciembre de 1974, fue creada la "ESCUELA DE COMANDOS".

Inicialmente se le conoció como "ESCUELA DE COMANDOS" hasta que el 5 de marzo de 1975, el señor Ministro de la Defensa Nacional, ordenó que el nombre de dicha Escuela fuera el de "KAIBIL".

El nombre "KAIBIL" le correspondía a un Rey del Imperio Mam, quien gracias a su astucia nunca pudo ser capturado por las fuerzas invasoras conquistadoras Españolas de Pedro de Alvarado, KAIBIL BALAM era considerado como un verdadero estratega y recibía consultas de caciques de otras tribus.

El 12 de enero de 1989, fue el traslado de la Escuela de Adiestramiento y Operaciones Especiales "Kaibil", de las fincas denominadas El Infierno y La Pólvora en el municipio de Melchor de Mencos, Petén, a las antiguas instalaciones de la Zona Militar No. 23, con sede en Poptún, Petén.

"KAIBIL" significa:

HOMBRE ESTRATEGA,
EL QUE TIENE LA FUERZA Y LA ASTUCIA DE DOS TIGRES.

Figure 9–3. Guatemalan Special Forces, Kaibil Web site, 1998.

tions, and parts of Central America.[22] Even Mexico confronted rebellious ethnic insurgents in the 1990s. Other aspects of the new world disorder directly impinged on the Latin American nation-state: the reach of drug lords and narcoterrorism; the pressures to adhere to regional and global environmental treaties, trade agreements, and human rights standards; unregulated international migration (and extensive internal migration as a result of the economic dislocations induced by neoliberal reforms); the penetration of multinational capital, technology, information systems and mass media, and the challenges of innovation in military doctrine and technology.

For the armed forces, the external and internal attacks on the concept of sovereignty and traditional patriotism threatened their basic purpose, their *razón de ser*, while economic and budget crises brought demands for force reductions and mission redefinition.[23] Defense spending in the region declined from 3.7 percent to 1.6 percent of gross national product from 1987 to 1992. Latin America and the Caribbean had the lowest military budgets and fewest uniformed personnel per capita of any world region.[24] Military salaries declined generally, although periodic readjustments were obtained through behind-the-scenes and public discussion, particularly in Chile, Brazil, and Ecuador.

More and more military personnel, struggling to maintain the dignity that they associated with their service to *la patria*, took second and third jobs driving taxis, waiting on tables in restaurants, or operating small businesses in the informal economic sector. Officers' spouses entered technical and professional occupations, sometimes earning more than majors and colonels. The welcome addition to family income thus also complicated military careers and family life when duty assignments took officers to provincial garrisons and their spouses remained behind. Social modernization, changing gender roles, the job market, and economic necessity also threatened traditional military values at the brink of the twenty-first century.

If *la patria* began with the family, did transformation of the family (especially military families) mean reimagining *la patria*? Were feminism and the women's organizations that emerged in the 1980s and 1990s also a "security threat"? The answer, at least for some officers, was yes, for they believed that feminist movements threatened the very foundations of *la patria*: the idealized nuclear family. And the same held for abortion, divorce, and excessive birth control. Many countries gradually incorporated women into the armed forces in the 1970s and 1980s in conflict with fundamental precepts of militarylore. Demands for gender democratization also required modifying historic versions of *la patria*, but such changes were not easily digested.

Even as social and economic change menaced *la patria* and its traditional values, guerrillas, terrorists, drug-lord armies, and organized crime syndicates bloodied the region. Headlines from Mexico, Guatemala, El Salvador, Nicaragua, Colombia, and Brazil announced surging rates of violent crimes and waves of economically motivated kidnapping. Governments could not maintain law and order. Did "democracy" imply personal insecurity and pervasive criminal violence? Some military personnel derided civilian regimes for their complacency, while others contributed to the violence through death squads, kidnapping rings, smuggling, collaboration with drug producers and traffickers, and the most varied sorts of corruption. Naturally, such activities affected some military institutions more than others, but nowhere in Latin America were the armed forces completely immune from these nefarious influences.

Still, the armed forces' institutional myths and credos insisted that they protect *la patria* from traditional threats as well from such new afflictions, just as they had defended and conserved it for almost two centuries. In the 1980s and 1990s they organized more specialized, highly trained antiterrorist, antinarcotics, and intelligence units. After a disastrous 1985 attack on the Palace of Justice in Bogotá, occupied by members of the M-19 politico-guerrilla movement, Colombia created the Fuerzas Especiales Antiterroristas Urbanas (AFEAU).[25] A multiservice force, its missions ranged from hostage rescue and security for diplomats to attacks on targeted drug lords.[26] Guatemala's elite counterinsurgency force, the Kaibiles, posted signs at their training base: "If I advance, follow me; if I stop, grab me; if I retreat, kill me."[27] And in Mexico the Grupo Antiterrorista (GAT) combined Federal Judicial Police and army personnel "to perform a range of missions dealing with hostage-taking, terrorist and guerrilla violence and associated problems. . . . GAT members are also trained to infiltrate subversive or guerrilla groups such as the Revolutionary Workers Party and the Zapatista Liberation Army. . . . In a recent operation, elements of GAT were thought to be deployed to the Mexican states of Guerrero, Michoacán, Jalisco, and Chiapas."[28] In the past such specialized units played central roles in coup-making and military political initiatives in Bolivia, Argentina, Brazil, and Guatemala. The great autonomy that they required for intelligence gathering and "black" operations made subordination to civilian control and the rule of law unlikely.

The armed forces had learned from José de San Martín that everything was licit when *la patria* was threatened; it could not be allowed to perish. They had learned from Simón Bolívar that necessity recognizes no law. In the 1990s they were forced to ask again: What *patria*, and what necessity? How were they to fulfill their historic mission and keep their pact with *la patria* as they entered the twenty-first century? As in the past, some of the answers to these questions depended on changes in international politics and on U.S. hemispheric security policy, some on regional and domestic politics and political leadership in Latin America.

The U.S. Hemispheric Security Agenda in the 1990s

With the Sandinistas' electoral defeat in 1990 in Nicaragua, and the implosion of the Soviet Union after 1991, Washington's Latin American policy lost its Cold War rationale. Pieces of old policies and programs survived: a hard line against Fidel Castro's Cuban government, new initiatives to "promote democracy" concocted in the State Department and the Department of Defense, and a general return to the traditional focus on limiting European and other non-American influence in "our" hemisphere.[29] Other programs lost favor, such as the Inter-American Foundation's focus on grass-roots development and nongovernmental organizations. Overall, U.S. Latin American policy floundered because of underfinancing, excessive rhetoric, poor coordination among many government agencies, and minimal pragmatic initiatives. It returned to unilateralism, moral condescension, and a propensity to condition aid and favorable commercial treatment on compliance with declared U.S. objectives such as antinarcotics programs, trade liberalization, market-oriented economic reforms, and "democratization."[30]

Latin America took a back seat to European and Asian concerns, with special exceptions made for policies toward Mexico and Cuba. In the latter case, policymakers and military strategists speculated on the implications for the United States and the hemisphere of an eventual departure of Castro as head of the Havana government. Scenarios ranging from the assassination of Fidel and Raúl Castro by dissident military officers to Fidel's liberalization of Cuban politics and negotiations for his "possible retirement in exile" were published in U.S. military journals.[31] The lengthy list of possible activities in which the U.S. Army might participate after a Cuban political collapse could hardly have reassured Cuban nationalists (even anti-Fidelista nationalists) about the island's political future: reception, control, and processing of refugees; ecological cleanup; public health management; security of key installations, notably former military bases; prison management and inventory; control and recovery of small arms; inventory and disposition of major weapons systems; mapping support; formation or reformation of public forces; restoration of domestic order and police operations; establishment and enforcement of interim landlord-tenant rules; regularization of real property dispositions; provision of basic services; replacement of infrastructure; protection of U.S. citizens; resistance to criminal organizing (probable counterdrug emphasis); control of counterfeiting; self-protection security operations; temporary reinforcement of Guantánamo Bay's perimeter; peacekeeping, peace enforcement, conflict resolution, or war termination; counterguerrilla operations; registration of graves.[32]

While this scenario was not the official view of the U.S. Army, its publication in *Military Review* in 1994 gave new meaning to *déjà vu*. What could Latin American military readers of this article imagine? Did the Clinton administration intend to create a U.S.-led peacemaking and peacekeeping force to impose its own version of democracy on Cuba? Would it do the same elsewhere? Proposals in military publications for the creation of a new U.S. military force, specially trained, equipped, and solely dedicated to "expeditionary police service," added to the apprehension.[33]

Meanwhile, public and congressional support in the United States for military assistance to Latin America waned. U.S. and Latin American officers and key civilians struggled to secure continuing funding for the main inter-American military institutions: the Inter-American Defense Board; Inter-American Defense College (Fort McNair); Inter-American Air Forces Academy (Lackland Air Force Base); and the Naval Small Craft and Technical Training School (Panama). Reduced budgets also affected training and professional interchange programs at facilities such as the School of the Americas (Fort Benning), which, though with fewer instructors after 1993, still survived as a locus for officer-to-officer contacts despite critical journalism, revelations regarding a counterinsurgency manual that taught torture techniques to Latin American military personnel, and films labelling it a "school for dictators."[34]

The School of the Americas now included a mandatory course on human rights and required instructors to be certified in this area. Supposedly, Latin

American officers would return home and introduce such courses in their military curricula. The School also sought to respond to the new world disorder, "preparing the armed forces to confront the conditions of the post-Soviet world."[35] An expanded International Military Education and Training program (E-IMET) was partly justified by programs promoting greater respect for democracy and for civilian control of the military. These programs included civilians in courses related to defense and military matters. In theory, their inclusion would make civilian defense ministries and legislatures more able to communicate with, and exercise informed control over, the military.

Central to U.S. hemispheric defense and security policy after 1989 was a redefinition of roles for the Southern Command (SOUTHCOM) and for the military more generally, and also for Caribbean operations in a world without a Soviet threat.[36] This same challenge faced the Latin American armed forces, each in the unique way required by political and security circumstances in their own countries.[37] In December 1994 the leaders of every Western Hemisphere government except Cuba met in Miami for the Summit of the Americas. The United States claimed that this meeting was "impressive testimony to the progress of democracy in the region, bringing together 34 countries with democratically elected leaders."[38] Washington's policymakers were convinced that democratization would be assisted by promoting free trade, opening markets, encouraging private investment, and downsizing the Latin American states. Ironically, this approach sounded remarkably similar to President Dwight D. Eisenhower's policies for Latin America during the intensely Cold War 1950s.[39] Confusing democracy with capitalism, neoliberal economics with eternal economic truths, and the "end of history" with the global uncertainty and disorder after 1989 might appeal to U.S. policymakers, but it would not reassure many Latin American military officers and their civilian allies.[40]

Once again they saw the United States divert its attention and resources to other regions while peddling rhetoric on democracy and the advantages of market economies and capitalism to its southern neighbors.[41] If more liberal regimes promised overall economic growth and quicker modernization, they also brought unemployment, hunger, and displacement for millions in the short term. Poverty, internal migration, social dislocation, and increased concentration of income and wealth were juxtaposed to the return of electoral democracy. Many of the socioeconomic conditions that made the Cuban Revolution a hopeful alternative for millions in the 1960s (and that were to be improved with the Alliance for Progress) persisted. The post-1964 military regimes, defeat of most guerrilla movements, and implosion of communism had killed the utopian dream of socialist revolution—but had not overcome the socioeconomic and political origins of discontent. Indeed, in the 1980s and 1990s misery and despair increased in much of the hemisphere. What greater threat to *la patria* could exist?

In mid-1995 the Defense Ministerial of the Americas, "the first-ever gathering of the hemisphere's civilian and military leaders," reached a consensus agreement (at least according to William J. Perry, U.S. Secretary of Defense): "The bedrock foundation for our approach to the Americas is a shared commitment to democracy, the rule of law, conflict resolution, defense transparency, and mutual cooperation. To make this vision real, our vital security interests must be protected through diplomacy, peacetime engagement, rapid response capabilities, and close defense cooperation with our friends and allies in the region."[42] In September 1995 the Department of Defense (DoD) released *United States Security Strategy for the Americas*, which defined the "strategic challenge for the United States in its neighborhood."[43] The report proclaimed that democracy, peace, and prosperity in the region are the best guarantees of U.S. national security. DoD's regional strategy is to use the defense assets at its disposal to promote these goals."[44] It also identified three "threats to democracy, peace, and prosperity": 1) internal conflicts (such as guerrilla movements in Colombia, Peru, Guatemala, and Mexico); 2) border disputes (such as the brief Ecuador-Peru War in 1995); and 3) transnational threats (drug trafficking and terrorism). This statement was followed by two "opportunities for advancing global peace and security": 1) arms control (the Treaty of Tlatelolco on nuclear devices, the Mendoza Accord in which Chile, Argentina, and Brazil agreed to halt development, production, and purchase of biological and chemical weapons, and the 1992 OAS General Assembly resolution that endorsed various UN arms control and antiproliferation agreements); and 2) international peacekeeping.

Latin American Armed Forces and International Peacekeeping

While the DoD vision of regional security was only partly shared by Latin American military leaders, the new international disorder presented numerous "opportunities" for international peacemaking and peacekeeping operations. In June 1995, twenty American countries supported fifteen of the sixteen peace operations of the United Nations, contributing over 9,000 military and police personnel in missions from the former Yugoslavia to India, Pakistan, the Western Sahara, Angola, and Haiti. Some Latin American armed forces had limited experience in international peacekeeping efforts as military observers with the UN Truce Supervision Organization (UNTSO, 1948) in Lebanon and the India-Pakistan observer mission (1949). Colombia sent troops to Korea (1953–54); Brazil and Colombia, to the first UN Emergency Force (UNEF I) in the Suez (1956); Argentine pilots went to the Congo (1960); and Peru sent personnel to the Golan Heights (1974).[45] In the 1990s, Latin American participation in peacekeeping missions mushroomed. The number of Latin American countries deploying personnel in peacekeeping and observer missions increased from 1994 to 1997, as did the number of personnel and the variety of missions. Argentina, Uruguay, and Brazil played a particularly active role in such missions.

U.S. policymakers viewed these developments as encouraging. Latin American armed forces were participating in multilateral peacekeeping operations, upgrading their technical and professional skills, and cooperating with other military units in the region and with their international counterparts. All this activity would keep them out of domestic politics, serve as confidence-building measures with officers from neighboring countries in some cases, and commit them further to economic development and democracy.[46] It might even make young officers more cosmopolitan, less nationalistic, and more resistant to calls for military "salvation" via coup in times of crisis.

Table 9–1. Latin American Participation in UN Missions, September 1994 (including Troops, Military Observers, and Civilian Police)

UN Mission	*Country (number of personnel)*
UN Truce Supervision Organization (UNTSO)	Argentina (6), Chile (3)
UN Military Observer Group in India and Pakistan (UNMOGIP)	Chile (3), Uruguay (3)
UN Peacekeeping Forces in Cyprus (UNFICYP)	Argentina (391)
UN Angola Verification Mission (UNAVEM II)	Argentina (5), Brazil (24)
UN Iraq-Kuwait Observer Mission (UNIKOM)	Argentina (56), Uruguay (6), Venezuela (2)
UN Mission for the Referendum in Western Sahara (MINURSO)	Argentina (7), Honduras (16), Uruguay (19), Venezuela (8)
UN Observer Mission in El Salvador (ONUSAL)	Argentina (2), Brazil (43), Chile (15), Colombia (23), Mexico (29), Venezuela (3)
UN Protection Force in former Yugoslavia (UNPROFOR)	Argentina (890), Brazil (43), Colombia (12), Venezuela (3)
UN Mission in Mozambique (ONUMOZ)	Argentina (48), Bolivia (10), Brazil (264), Uruguay (874)
UN Observer Mission in Liberia (UNOMIL)	Uruguay (16)
UN Mission in Rwanda (UNAMIR)	Uruguay (27)
UN Mission in Haiti (UNOMIH)	Guatemala (2)
UN Mission in Georgia (former Soviet Union) (UNOMIG)	Uruguay (1)

Source: UN Military Staff Committee, September 30, 1994.[47]

Officers recognized some of the benefits of such missions, especially the opportunity to modernize doctrine, tactics, logistical capabilities, and weapons systems, and to collaborate with officers from around the world in warlike operations.[48] Argentine General Carlos María Zabala, former UN sector commander in Croatia, noted many advantages of peacekeeping for his nation's army: "On a professional level, it is an occasion to operate in a complex operational environment. You have the opportunity to work with other armies and appreciate their capabilities as well as your own. It provides firsthand knowledge of the effects of war, allowing our troops to appreciate the importance of the UN and its peace operations. On a personal level, it lends opportunity for travel to foreign locations and exposure to other cultures and customs. Additionally, it allows the troops to feel as representatives of their country in an important mission abroad."[49] In some cases, the United States facilitated weapons and matériel transfers to support Latin American peacekeeping, including sending surplus C-130 transport planes to Argentina and Uruguay, frigates to the Argentine navy, and helicopters and spare parts to Chile to support its role in Kuwait during the 1990 Persian Gulf War.[50] While these missions enhanced the experience and international prestige of Latin American armed forces, more fundamental questions remained regarding their domestic political role and that of their nations in the post-Cold War world. In these matters, much of the U.S. security agenda for the hemisphere was viewed with concern by Latin American officers.

Latin American Security Agendas and Civil-Military Relations

As always, the diversity of Latin American politics and military institutions makes it difficult to generalize about a shared security agenda in the late 1990s and beyond. Common concerns existed; each country also had a unique national security and defense agenda, and the armed forces confronted political conjunctures bequeathed by institutional histories and by the last decades of debt crisis and the end of the Cold War. In some cases, such as Argentina and El Salvador, the armed forces' political influence declined. In other cases, such as Mexico, Cuba, Ecuador, and Chile, their influence increased or remained very strong. Nowhere, however, did the armed forces' influence in politics evaporate. Nowhere could their subordination to civilian authority be taken for granted.

Overall, the performance of elected governments in the 1980s and 1990s did little to erase the military's historical conviction that political parties and elected politicians were corrupt, venal, and lacking in patriotism. International circumstances, particularly the apparent consensus on "democracy" (or at least on the desirability of elected governments), and the lack of internal support for renewed military government, kept the armed forces from direct intervention. Nevertheless, elected governments in the region were far from universally proving their probity, efficacy, or patriotism. In many cases they ruled by default rather than from deep public support for elections and democratic norms. Cynicism toward legislatures, courts, and public administration augured poorly for more than an instrumental commitment to democratic procedures and governance. The weakness and inefficacy of civilian governmental institutions, political parties, and nongovernmental organizations in most of Latin America remained an Achilles' heel for efforts to consolidate democracy.

Officers were left in a quandary. They neither regarded the moment propitious for direct intervention, nor favored a return to the presidential palace and the burden of administration. In any case, for professional, institutional, and political reasons, they generally preferred elected civilian governments. Yet they desired more material and symbolic support as well as greater commitment to military institutions, to the positive redefinition of missions and doctrine for the next century, and to modernization, professionalization, improved status, and prestige. They wanted defense and security issues to be treated seriously by competent policymakers.

How were they to wrest these commitments and resources away from the weak, economically hard-pressed elected governments that dotted the hemisphere in the mid-1990s? How could they create the political conditions to encourage legislative support for the military wish list? Almost no Latin American legislators lobbied for defense expenditures to appeal to the electorate's economic interests (as occurred in the United States, where the defense industry had constituents in almost every congressional district). How could they contend for scarce resources against the pent-up demands for social services, investment in infrastructure, and more politically attractive programs? What could they legitimately stake out as national defense and security objectives? How could they contribute to national development? And how could they avoid the pitfalls of the U.S. hemispheric security agenda that sought to make them gendarmes, road builders, and international peacekeepers rather than truly professional military officers?

Despite their diversity, the Latin American armed forces shared these concerns at the end of the twentieth century. They also had a common, if implicit, security and national defense agenda that involved several related policy priorities.[51] First, maintaining national sovereignty, their most traditional and legitimate role, in the new world disorder preoccupied Latin American military leaders. Attacks on sovereignty and national territory revalidated the need for professional, modern military establishments. Budget constraints and civilian intrusion into defense policymaking threatened the armed forces' ability to plan, organize, and implement military modernization. Thus, the post-Cold War milieu both justified their claims on resources for national defense and made it more difficult for them to obtain them. New threats to sovereignty, both internal and external, exacerbated this frustrating paradox in most of Latin America.

The Brazilian armed forces' security planning in the 1990s was typical in its concern for sovereignty, border defense, internal security, countersubversion, internal social and economic development, and inclusion of the military in policymaking and implementation. An important statement on the role of sovereignty in national security thinking in the 1990s was published by Brazil's Colonels Alvaro de Souza Pinheiro and Paulo Cesar Miranda de Azevedo.[52] Significantly, they emphasized threats to their nation's sovereignty from "international greed and attempts to interfere in the Brazilian Amazon area."[53]

• The Environmental Defense Fund and the National Wildlife Federation have pressed the Inter-American Development Bank to provide protection for the rain forest and the Indians. In December 1987 the Bank suspended the U.S. $58.5 million project loan because Brazil's Federal Government "had failed to create institutions to prevent unchecked devastation of the forest and the overrunning of Indian lands."

• In 1989 a subsidiary of Japan's Mitsubishi Corporation offered to buy Brazil's U.S. $115 billion foreign debt in exchange for mining rights over Amazon gold fields. Then-president José Sarney said that "Brazil's sovereignty cannot be swapped for anything."

• U.S. President George Bush, influenced by environmentalists, prevented Japan from financing construction of a road linking Brazil and Peru—the first road from the Pacific into the Amazon.

• French President François Mitterrand stressed a variety of social colonialist ideas, which he defended at the 1991 Conference on Ecology at the Hague. He urged the formation of a supranational body to evaluate the behavior of governments on environmental matters and raised the principle of *devoir d'ingérence* (duty to intervene).

The two colonels concluded, with wicked understatement: "Such statements suggest that international designs on the Amazon could directly affect Brazilian sovereignty."[54]

To counter such threats, the Brazilian armed forces took an active role in expanding military installations in the Amazon and in combating transborder smuggling, drug trafficking, illegal mining, and guerrilla operations on the Colombian and Venezuelan borders. They also redefined their mission, in accordance with the new constitution, to meet the challenges of the 1990s: 1) training men for jungle warfare (including upgrading the Jungle Warfare Training Center [CIGS] created in 1964, which also trains personnel from other Latin American countries, Portugal, and the United States); 2) operating where needed to safeguard Brazilian sovereignty and the national patrimony; 3) exercising surveillance of border areas; 4) establishing new settlements with civilian populations around remote military bases; 5) promoting education in all frontier units through high school; 6) providing health care to civilians and military personnel (80 to 85 percent of health care by military personnel was to civilians in the mid-1990s); and 7) improving transport throughout the Amazon.

The Brazilian armed forces' focus on the Amazon had parallel expressions of concern over "internal frontiers," countering paramilitary, insurgent, and guerrilla forces and promoting socioeconomic development in Mexico, Guatemala, Colombia, Venezuela, Peru, Ecuador, Bolivia, and Chile. Such concerns reemerged as part of the armed forces' efforts to clarify and reaffirm their importance to *la patria* after *perestroika*. Nation-building, development, "democracy," and protection of sovereignty all gave familiar rationales for conserving and protecting *la patria*.[55]

Second, every military establishment was primarily preoccupied with national geopolitical objectives, strategy, and doctrine as well as with the relationship of the armed forces to politics and development. Military leaders were absorbed with securing resources and respect for their institutions. They wished to conserve as many of their traditional prerogatives as possible without appearing openly to oppose democratization.[56] In any case they did not associate democratization with any erosion of professional autonomy or with the elimination of their historical and constitutional mission to defend *la patria*. This gave priority to traditional internal security, law and order, external defense, nation-building, and economic development missions. Possible threats from neighboring states remained a focus of military exercises, war games, and contingency planning in most of the hemisphere—although to these were added numerous multilateral exercises involving "military operations other than war," such as refugee evacuation, disaster relief, hostage rescue, urban insurgency, and peacekeeping.

To these missions the armed forces cautiously and selectively added from the agenda proposed by the United States. Most were particularly reticent to identify their institutions fully with the drug eradication and interdiction programs that alienated local populations and corrupted the Latin American armed forces. In contrast, many of the other "military operations other than war" incorporated into U.S. defense doctrine and taught at the School of the Americas in the mid-1990s coincided with the traditional subsidiary missions of the Latin American military. Disaster relief, public health services in remote areas, mapping and technical education, nation-building, and even international peacekeeping were part of the armed forces' historical experience.

Third, military leaders everywhere accepted some sort of developmentalist mission as a supplementary task, ranging from road building and communications to more exotic and comprehensive regional development projects as in Brazil, Ecuador, and Chile. Nowhere did officers accept economic development as their primary mission, although they readily agreed, as in the past, that poverty, despair, and backward economies threatened national security. They recognized the utility (and ambiguity) of the new U.S. doctrine introduced in the Army manual FM 100-5, *Operations*, regarding "military operations other than war" (MOOTW). Ironically, while this might be a new focus for U.S. officers, the Latin American officers at the School of the Americas found little that was innovative in such a doctrine. They fought few wars; most of their operations—from mapping, building roads and airports, maintaining internal order, breaking strikes, managing public enterprises, and operating internal political intelligence networks to occasionally ousting governments—had been "other than war" for most of the twentieth century.

Why not add "supporting democracy and promoting human rights" to the list? A Honduran general wrote in 1993: "The armed forces of this country, in addition to fulfilling their fundamental missions, must assume a new role: reinforcing the success of the process of democratization and supporting respect for human rights; supporting and stimulating economic development; impeding drug trafficking; protecting the environment to assure rational use of natural resources; actively joining in the Central American peace process; developing antiterrorist capabilities; and preventing a cholera epidemic."[57] Similarly, the Argentine Gendarmería commander, Juan Obdulio Saínz commented in 1994 that in deciding the numbers and composition of Latin America's armed forces, potential sources of regional and national instability had to be considered: "economic insecurity, the result of underdevelopment, of lack of productive capacity, of unjust social structures, of regressive distribution of income and lack of minimal subsistence conditions for much of the population; social insecurity, the result of unemployment and hunger, of the increase in crime and the absence of opportunity; political insecurity, that provokes frustration and grave social tensions that permanently threaten social peace."[58] To prepare the Latin American armed forces for the post-Cold War era, Saínz urged more emphasis on professional education, improved promotion and specialization procedures to ensure a lean and efficient officer corps, technological modernization with special attention to interservice operations and rapid deployment capabilities, and more flexible, collaborative, and decentralized leadership. In short, the armed forces needed to modernize and fully participate in national development—hardly a new theme for the region's military leaders.

According to this view, in many "operations other than war," the Latin American armed forces were still the vertebrae of *la patria*. They retained their external defense mission, contributed to internal security and development, and gained international prestige in peacemaking and peacekeeping missions around the globe. While some officers resisted these latter roles as diversions from their principal tasks, most "operations other than war" were as compatible with the Spanish Bourbon reforms of the 1780s as with the fads of "development" and "democratization" of the 1990s.

Fourth, despite the acceptance of subsidiary missions and the reluctant genuflection to "democracy" and human rights, none of the Latin American military establishments wished to be converted into quasi-police forces focused primarily on drug-eradication and -interdiction programs, immigration control, and environmental issues. The antidrug mission was particularly objectionable (as it was to many U.S. officers): it diverted professionals from conventional military tasks, corrupted military institutions and personnel, and turned officers into policemen.

U.S.-Latin American multiagency antidrug programs involving the region's military forces had negligible success from 1989 until the mid-1990s. Fancifully named operations such as Green Sweep, Green Merchant, Ghost Dancer, Ghost Zone, Grizzly, Wipeout, Badge, and Blast Furnace did almost nothing to reduce the supply of drugs reaching the United States while increasing levels of narco-terrorism, peasant resentment, corruption, and government frustration in Mexico, most of Central America, Colombia, Bolivia, and Peru. In testimony before the U.S. Congress in March 1995, SOUTHCOM's commander, General Barry R. McCaffrey, stated that in Bolivia "[coca leaf] cultivation has also increased to record levels despite U.S.-funded eradication programs."[59] Occasional "misunderstandings" between U.S. law enforcement and military teams and Latin American military units and police even led to violence. "Accidental" shootdowns of U.S. aircraft and the use for drug trafficking by Latin American military personnel of aircraft supplied to counter drug trafficking added to the nightmare.[60]

Officers recognized the security threat represented by the narco-terrorists. Some accepted fighting the drug industry as a legitimate task if the police and other security agencies could not contain threats to government authority and public order. Moreover, given changing U.S. priorities, antidrug operations financed training, matériel, and weapons acquisitions. They generally believed, however, that controlling the demand for drugs in the United States and Europe would be more effective than the militarized supply-suppression policies that bloodied their nations and cost them popular support. Why should Bolivian, Peruvian, and Guatemalan troops confront thousands of peasant producers of coca leaf and poppies? Protecting U.S. and European consumers seemed a poor excuse for the enmity gained in eradication programs. Perhaps pursuit of processors and traffickers made more sense. But wasn't this essentially a police function?

The political and professional ramifications of collaborating with the U.S.-declared war on drugs were frequently negative for Latin American military institutions. Some argued, referring to the prohibition of alcohol in the United States, that decriminalizing consumption would so reduce the price of drugs that the power and influence of the drug lords would be destroyed. Instead, the huge profits to be reaped in the international drug trade guaranteed that the traffickers and their sometimes guerrilla allies had larger budgets than most national armies. Such conditions brought to mind General Alvaro Obregón's cynical remark during the Mexican Revolution: "No general can resist a cannonade of pesos." It also angered Latin American military officers who were expected to protect their nations with decreasing budgetary resources and at the same time protect U.S. drug consumers from themselves.

Fifth, for these officers, "democracy" and "human rights" remained ambiguous terms—more instrumental rhetoric imposed by the United States and its temporary Latin American civilian allies than inviolable norms. Military institutions continued to press for amnesty decrees for earlier human rights abuses and to emphasize political stability and respect for law and order as the requisite conditions for development.

For the armed forces, democracy and subordination to civilian authority did not mean intrusion of politicians into military education, training, promotion and duty assignment decisions, or formulation of doctrine, strategy, and tactics. Until competent civilians could be found, defense policy was still considered a military bailiwick. In Chile, as in Brazil in the past, civilians were invited to study in military schools to obtain proper orientation toward defense issues and to understand the needs of military institutions. Elsewhere, research centers and universities provided new places for intellectual exchange and social contact between officers and civilians interested in defense and security issues. For the moment, however, a consensus existed that defense and security policies were too important to be left to civilians.

Sixth, whether implicitly or explicitly, commitment to the residual military guardianship role persisted, even when referred to less frequently in public due to international and regional trends that delegitimized direct military intervention in governance. Officers recognized that the United States had more than once exported the same democratic tonic in different bottles, only to "withdraw it from the market" under the stress of international or regional tensions. They worried that the U.S. security agenda for the 1990s had forgotten the real missions of the Latin American military: external defense, internal order, defense of *la patria*, and its transcendental national objectives.[61]

Even as the United States sought to invent a more economically integrated hemisphere at peace, with countries cooperating in regional security tasks such as fighting drug dealers and terrorists, preventing proliferation of weapons of mass destruction, impeding arms smuggling, protecting the environment, and monitoring illegal flows of immigrants, the Latin American militaries remembered historic border disputes and recent conflicts (see Map 9–1). They lived in increasingly violent societies. In Central America, governments failed to provide land, pensions, and economic opportunities to demobilized veterans and former guerrillas; armed bands engaged in political violence and crime-for-profit. In Bolivia, Mexico, Guatemala, Colombia, and Peru, armed forces and police engaged in guerrilla wars and destructive conflicts with drug lords. For officers, pressures to create leaner, more efficient, and tougher military institutions meant more sophisticated weapons; better communication and logistics systems; higher quality, more specialized personnel; more training and military exercises; and smarter intelligence operations—usually accompanied by

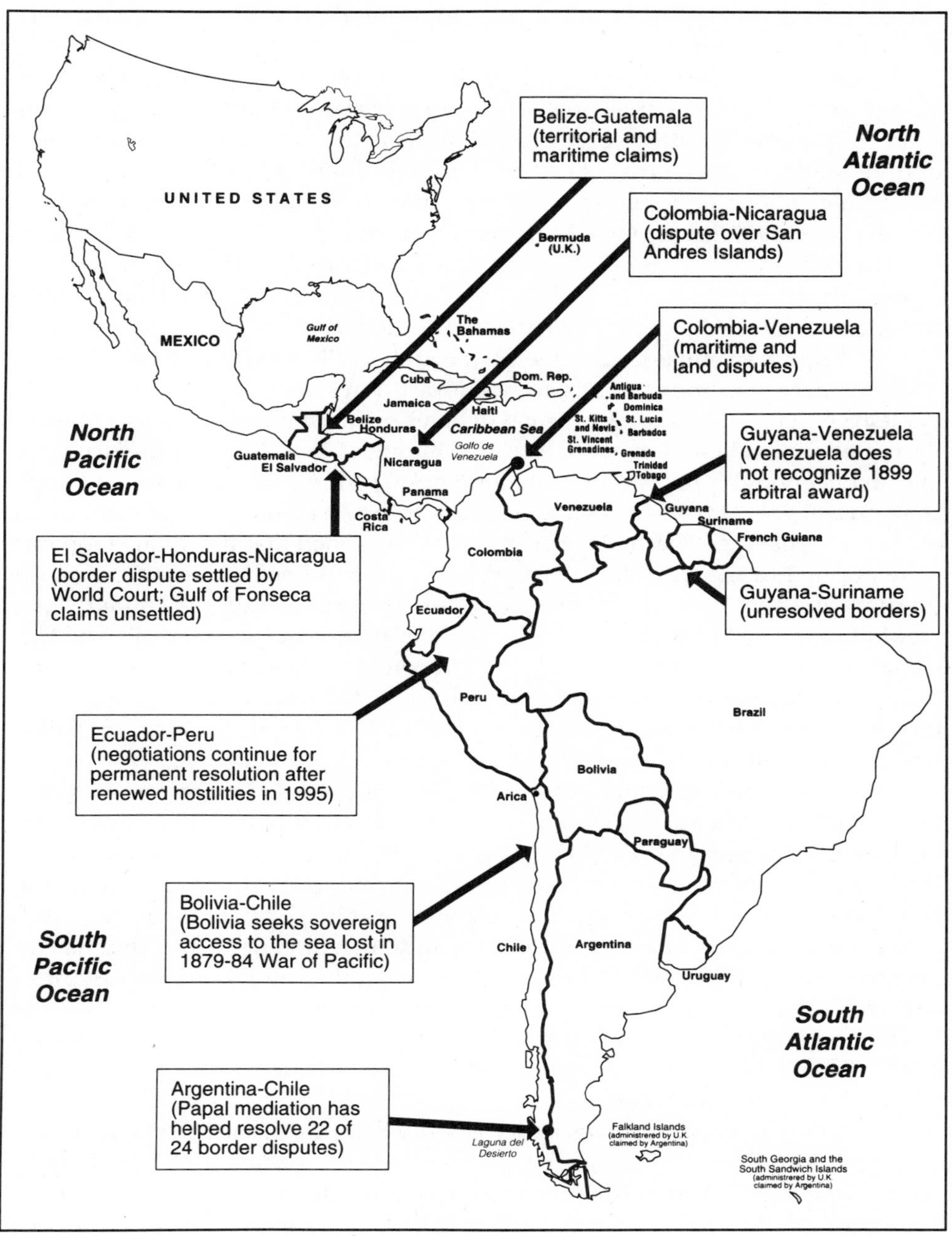

Map 9–1. Territorial Disputes. U.S. Department of Defense, Office of International Security Affairs, "United States Security Strategy for the Americas," September 1995: 13.

pressures to downsize. They wished to be patriotic, professional, technically modern, and respected. Moreover, they resented the second-rate role assigned to them in the U.S. scheme and were unable to ignore the fact that most Washington policymakers still had not learned much about Latin American military traditions and their historic contributions to *la patria.* (Of course, the progressive corruption of these armies by drug wars, smuggling, off-the-books businesses, and demoralization called into question all of militarylore's patriotic and virtuous discourse.)

Inconsistent efforts by the United States to withhold sophisticated technology and weapons, limit Latin American arms production and exports, relegate the region's armed forces to subsidiary and surrogate missions, and update the Monroe Doctrine's pretense of excluding foreign systems from the hemisphere alienated Latin American nationalists—among them most military officers. The 1989 invasion of Panama (Operation Just Cause, or "Operation Just Because," as cynics labeled it), with the subsequent destruction of the U.S.-trained Panama Defense Force, dramatically illustrated to Caribbean and Central American officers the U.S. disposition to unilateralism and disrespect for the sovereignty of small Latin American countries. The asymmetry of bilateral relations between Washington and most of the region's capitals was further evidenced in pompous congressional debates over whether Colombia, Mexico, Peru, Bolivia, and Guatemala had spilled enough blood fighting the drug cartels, made enough progress in protecting human rights, or implemented sufficient structural reforms in their economies to merit resumption of military or economic assistance. (Latin American officers reasoned that if similar standards were applied to the U.S. Customs Service, the Drug Enforcement Agency, the Immigration and Naturalization Service, and Congress itself, the United States would fail the test of probity and efficacy required of Latin America.) The U.S. Congress also sought in the early 1990s to condition assistance to the Nicaraguan government on its choice of an "appropriate" commander for its armed forces and to dictate the political behavior of Honduran, Dominican, Salvadoran, and even Argentine officers.

How were the last bastions of sovereignty, the Latin American armed forces, to react to such blatant hegemonic pretensions? What sort of democracy was the United States promoting? Why had the military institutions that buttressed U.S. Cold War strategy in the hemisphere become less valued, if not expendable, assets in the 1990s? And what could they do to reaffirm their value to *la patria*? Resuscitating old border disputes and ancient geopolitical threats was one obvious answer. Most Latin American states had pending disputes with neighbors over borders or redemptive claims from nineteenth- and twentieth-century wars. As described in Chapter 2, nationalism and independent military traditions in Latin America had originated to a great extent in nineteenth-century conflicts.

In 1995 war erupted in territory disputed by Peru and Ecuador in the Cenepa Basin. Elements of the dispute originated in claims that went back to Spanish colonial demarcations; the most recent juridical origins stemmed from ambiguity in the 1942 Rio Protocol that ended the June–August 1941 war between the two countries. The 1941 war not only resurrected historical animosities between Ecuador and Peru but also forged the reformist officer generation

Figure 9–4. "Armed Forces, True National Valor," Lima, Peru, 1997.

that had founded Peru's Centro de Altos Estudios Militares (CAEM). In Ecuador, which had lost territory in several wars since independence and sought to regain access to the Amazon Basin, the 1941 war contributed to its peoples' sense of victimization by larger, more powerful neighbors.

The basis for Peru's and Ecuador's competing claims were both historical and technical, ultimately involving questions regarding the topography and watershed between the Zamora and Santiago rivers.[62] More important than the details of the claims was the fact that two countries in South America governed by elected civilian presidents did not avoid armed conflict despite the high cost in lives and resources that such an engagement exacted, and despite Peru's ongoing battle against Sendero Luminoso, other guerrilla movements, and narco-terrorists.

The war involved high-performance aircraft, antiaircraft missiles, global-positioning satellites to pinpoint targets, and adaptation (by Ecuador) of "active defense" and "air-land battle" concepts from the Israeli and U.S. armed forces.[63] The motto, "Ecuador Is an Amazonian Country and Always Will Be," reflects the importance of traditional patriotism and national claims on civilian and military thinking. (A similar slogan in Bolivia exhorts its soldiers to regain access for *la patria* to the Pacific Ocean, lost to Chile in the 1879–1883 War of the Pacific.) Ecuador's defense minister, General José Gallardo, remarked in June 1995 that "the knowledge among the members of the armed forces of the immense territorial loss of our *patria* has created a sentiment of decisiveness that never again will the country be the victim of territorial plunder, of aggression against its dignity, its honor."[64]

In the 1990s, Ecuador's military was still generally respected and its budgets secret.[65] Military budgets increased significantly after the transition from military to civilian government, and the armed forces exercised considerable autonomy in defense policymaking and other areas defined as part of their extremely broad national security functions. Direct allocation of oil revenues to the armed forces and operation of numerous private enterprises contributed to this autonomy. Congressional oversight remained minimal. Peru's military, in contrast, had lost prestige after its direct rule of the country from 1968 to 1980. It had been engaged in gruesome combat against Sendero Luminoso and other guerrilla movements throughout the 1980s and was accused of massive human rights violations against civilian, especially peasant, populations. It was also riven with corruption and, along with the national police, tarnished by the penetration of drug cartels and organized crime.

Figure 9–5. "To Love Peru Is to Construct Its Development," Peruvian Army Web site, 1998.

Caught by surprise in the 1995 war, the Peruvian military sought to rearm, modernize, and regain its prestige in the next two years. Mobilization of public opinion against what was characterized as Ecuador's brazen violation of the 1942 Rio Protocol, and President Alberto Fujimori's support for enhanced military preparedness, renewed the Peruvian commitment to "appropriate" budgets and attention to the armed forces in their traditional patriotic role. Meanwhile, Chilean, Colombian, and Brazilian army, navy, and air force officers took note of the Ecuador-Peru conflict. New purchases of aircraft and naval armaments followed shortly. Regional spin-offs of the conflict created markets for arms dealers in Europe and the United States, even as the latter preached arms control.

Toward the Twenty-first Century

The resuscitation of dormant conflicts and the reality of border wars between ostensibly democratic states provided new political ammunition for the region's armed forces, even in the Southern Cone, where many historical disputes were being resolved diplomatically. Seeking to carve a suitable niche for themselves in the post-Cold War era, the military continued to insist on the importance of sovereignty, to concern themselves with internal security and external defense, to be the guardians of their nations' values and institutions, and to be the last bastion of defense for *la patria*'s transcendental interests. To do all this meant continued involvement in many different ways in politics: as guardians, as institutional interest groups, as potential allies for civilian movements and parties, as arbiters of political conflict among civilian politicians, as administrators and technocrats in numerous public agencies, and as symbols of national unity, patriotism, and destiny. On a day-to-day basis, the visibilty of military participation in politics varied considerably from country to country. Also, the influence of the Cold War national security doctrine ideology within some of the region's officer corps had declined. But whether quietly lobbying legislatures for funds, operating internal intelligence agencies, preparing for civil defense and disaster relief tasks, or publicly reminding civilian leaders of their responsibilities, the Latin American armed forces remained committed to their historical missions: internal and external security, public order, law enforcement, political intelligence, economic development, and defense of sovereignty. These missions were inherently political. The legal, institutional, and professional legacies of Spanish colonial militarism and the nineteenth-century European missions were still evident in the 1990s. The fusion of civil and military authority, the overlapping military and police functions, and the virtually mystical-religious identification of the armed forces with *la patria* persisted. Militarylore changed slowly despite the profound transformations wrought by technology, global economic interdependence, and the end of the Cold War.

The twenty-first century will bring new challenges from both domestic and international threats. The Latin American armed forces will likely continue to uphold their centuries-long traditions, perhaps redefined and repackaged for the era of "democratization" and globalization, but without abandoning reference to their ultimate justification and commitment: the *patrias* they had created, helped to shape and develop, ruled, and misruled since the 1820s. Whatever action taken would be in the name of *la patria*. In parts of Latin America such as Chile and Ecuador, the armed forces could count on substantial support if they were once again "forced" by circumstances to save their nations from subversion, civilian incompetence, and political corruption. Civilian corruption and political disorder in Colombia, Guatemala, Nicaragua, El Salvador, Peru, Venezuela, and Mexico could provoke a more overt military presence in government and policymaking, even without coups, with substantial popular approval. In other countries, such as Uruguay and Argentina, their lackluster performance as economic managers in the 1970s and 1980s and their horrendous human rights violations have inhibited broad support for more overt military participation in policymaking and governance.[66]

Nowhere did the armed forces lack some civilian social base if economic and political crises pushed countries to the brink. This social base was not usually majoritarian, but it was always politically and economically powerful. Everywhere, with the arguable exception of Costa Rica, the idea that the armed forces were ultimately responsible for preventing political chaos and for conserving the sovereignty and integrity of *la patria* was still a basic premise of politics in the late 1990s. This premise, shared by many civilians and military officers alike—glorified in historical traditions, public holidays, and school texts, sanctified in constitutions, codified in statutes and military regulations, reified in military oaths and national hymns—ensured a continuing political role for the Latin American armed forces in the post-Cold War era.

Paradoxically, political liberalization and erosion of military prerogatives in the 1990s did not alter the fundamental premises regarding the military's constitutional and political roles. Nevertheless, contestation over particular prerogatives, such as whether defense ministers should be officers or civilians, the extent of congressional review of military budgets and promotions, and the number of officers appointed as managers in public enterprises, went against the armed forces in many countries. The end of the Cold War and of insurgencies in most of the region brought reductions in military budgets and personnel. The mass media gradually risked more open coverage of security and defense issues. Obligatory military service, an article of faith for the armed forces since the early twentieth century, was eliminated in several countries and debated in others. Emphatic support for "democracy" (usually simply meaning elected governments) by U.S. policymakers, the European Community, and the Organization of American States made coups less acceptable. The threat of nonrecognition and economic sanctions discouraged military intervention even where civilian governments exceeded past levels of incompetence and corruption, as with the impeachments of presidents in Brazil and Venezuela in the early 1990s and the ouster of Ecuador's iconoclastic president in 1997. Support by Latin American civilian political leaders for their counterparts generally reinforced the "tide of democracy." With the exception of Haiti, no successful military coups occurred from the 1980s through 1998.

These changes altered the immediate balance in civil-military relations and allowed more effective exercise of civil liberties in much of the region. The military felt more constrained by hemispheric and global circumstances, inhibited from overt intervention against elected leaders. But none of this changed militarylore regarding guardianship of *la patria* or the military's basic constitutional and statutory missions, nor did it blank out the social memory of fear bequeathed by the 1970s and 1980s. Democracy was conditional; national security and antiterrorist legislation actually increased military jurisdiction over civilians in some countries, and human rights violations increased after transition to civilian rule in Peru, Guatemala, and Honduras. Military influence was also increasing in Mexico and Cuba.

Civil-military relations in Latin America thus varied greatly as the twenty-first century approached. Generally, military forces and budgets were being reduced, military prerogatives were under attack, and the armed forces struggled to adapt to the new world disorder. Yet nowhere had the normative and legal foundations for protected democracy and military guardianship been removed. Civilian leaders still lacked expertise in defense and security issues—a legacy of neglect, if not disdain, for military matters that had historically limited civilian oversight of the armed forces and reinforced their relative autonomy. For most civilians the military institutions, still partly totemic, inspired a combination of fear, reverence, and nationalistic pride. For their part, military leaders continued to doubt the politicians' sincerity, trustworthiness, and competency. These perceptions of the politicians and of the major political parties were shared by much of the civilian population. Transition to elected governments did not quickly overcome generations of mistrust and misunderstanding between civilians and military elites. And for many Latin Americans the memories of recent human rights violations remained open wounds.

If international economic and political conditions abruptly change, crises undermine elected civilian governments, or U.S. regional security policy veers (as it has so often in the past), the armed forces remain committed to protecting the permanent interests of their nations, as they define them. This commitment might not involve coups or direct rule by military *juntas*—or it might. In either case, Latin American nationalism and reactions to the supposed "end of history" will invariably involve the armed forces in their nations' political destinies.

As the twenty-first century nears, there is no foreseeable end to the Latin American armed forces' historical missions in defense of *la patria*. However, the persistence of militarylore and of these missions does not mean that no changes in attitudes have occurred within the armed forces and within civil society. To the contrary, the traumas of the last four decades have contributed to serious political rethinking by military officers and civilian politicians, labor leaders, and the broader civilian populations. But the post-1959 traumas have yet to be thoroughly "worked through" politically and socially. Reconciliation with the recent past is more a political slogan than reality. Civil-military relations are in flux as part of the more profound political and ideological transformations of the 1980s and 1990s.

The elected civilian governments that emerged after 1978 thus presided over traumatized and uncertain societies. Globalizing trends sparked reactive nationalism and widespread socioeconomic tensions. Despite the triumphalism of proponents of "market democracy" and of the neoliberal creed that temporarily dominated international politics in the 1990s, other voices proclaimed alternative futures and different political and economic visions. These quests for political and economic alternatives mean dissatisfaction with the present. Criminal and political violence have escalated; gaps between rich and poor within countries have widened. As Argentine General Laiño argued, a multitude of "potentially critical situations" threaten *la patria* at the advent of the twenty-first century. These threats reconfirm militarylore in its insistence on the need for eternal vigilance by the armed forces to protect the nation's security and its "destiny." If, and when, the armed forces in Latin America choose to counter such threats, they will claim to do so for *la patria*.

Notes

1. "New Security Relations in the Americas," *Strategic Forum* 47, National Defense University, Institute for National Strategic Studies (September 1995): 1.

2. *Memoria del Ejército Argentino, 1992–1995*, Ministerio de Defensa, Buenos Aires, 1995.

3. Laiño (1996). SPOCs is the acronym for *situaciones potencialmente críticas* (potentially critical situations).

4. José Nun, "The Middle-Class Military Coup Revisited," in Abraham F. Lowenthal and J. Samuel Fitch, eds., *Armies and Politics in Latin America*, rev. ed. (New York: Holmes and Meier, 1986): 59–65.

5. Pablo González Casanova, *Los militares y la política en América Latina* (México: Océano, 1988). "Los nuevos dictadores transnacionales son semejantes al subconjunto de un aparato estatal que echa sus principales raices en el capital monopólico, en el gobierno norteamericano y en las

fuerzas burguesas locales oligárquicas y neocoloniales. . . . en cada país y en cada región el aparato militar transnacional actúa según las circunstancias, con un sentido pragmático y flexible" (pp. 23–24).

6. For a discussion of the relationship between internal political motives for coups, military institutional concerns, and the role of the United States see Jan Knippers Black, *Sentinels of Empire: The United States and Latin American Militarism* (Westport, CT: Greenwood Press, 1986). A critical view of the U.S. role is Miles D. Wolpin, *Military Aid and Counterrevolution in the Third World* (Lexington, MA: D. C. Heath and Co., 1977).

7. Guillermo A. O'Donnell, "Modernization and Military Coups: Theory, Comparisons, and the Argentine Case," in Lowenthal and Fitch, eds. (1986): 105–6. See also the articles in David Collier, ed., *The New Authoritarianism in Latin America* (Princeton: Princeton University Press, 1979).

8. See Nunn (1983); and idem (1992).

9. Bruce W. Farcau, *The Transition to Democracy in Latin America: The Role of the Military* (Westport, CT: Praeger, 1996). Farcau adds: "Thus any theory of civil-military relations in Latin America must take into account the personal factor, the ambitions of the charismatic leader and his ability to form around himself a faction that could seize power. I still see the transition to democracy in Latin America as less of a transition than almost as another form of coup d'état, simply going in the other direction" (p. 160).

10. "Rojas marshalled the army, navy, and air force men in Bogotá's broad Plaza Bolívar. . . . Arranged on a platform at the foot of a statue of Liberator Simón Bolívar were a tall crucifix and eight urns containing the ashes of Colombian soldiers who fought in the Korean War and in the country's own backlands guerrilla war. Rojas then read off a solemn oath, swearing the servicemen, in the name of Jesus Christ and in the memory of Simón Bolívar, to 'fight for the domination of the Third Force until Colombians lay down their political hatreds before the national banner.' They took the oath. Next afternoon, at Bogotá's Campin stadium, Rojas likewise swore in a throng of youth, labor, farm, and women's groups." "Third Force," *Time* (June 25, 1956): 33, cited in Vernon Lee Fluharty, *Dance of the Millions: Military Rule and the Social Revolution in Colombia, 1930–1956* (Pittsburgh: University of Pittsburgh Press, 1957): 306.

11. See Pérez (1976).

12. Just as priests who stray from the path of righteousness do not undo the teachings of the Church, so individual military officers who violate their sacred patriotic duties do not decrease the moral and professional significance of militarylore.

13. The staying power of this aspect of militarylore is impressive. Almost on automatic pilot, officers use this sort of language in speeches and also in political and academic writing. To illustrate, Maj. Concepción Jiménez of Honduras wrote in 1996: "*Sacerdocio* es la devoción que toda persona siente por su profesión o carrera, y como nuestra carrera militar es una profesión, entonces todo militar o líder, no importa su jerarquía, debe consagrarse activa y celosamente al servicio de la patria y desempeñar sus funciones con eficiencia y probidad, porque ya sea en tiempo de paz o de guerra es quién ejerce la administración controlada de la violencia; de alli que nuestra profesión no es liberal sino un *sacerdocio* al servicio de la humanidad." "Contribución del Liderazgo a la Potencia de Combate," *Military Review* (Hispano-American edition, November–December 1996): 51.

14. For a recent version of "true democracy" according to Ecuadorian General Paco Moncayo, see "Las fuerzas armadas en la construcción de la democracia" on the army's World Wide Web site //www.ecuadoriannet.com/ccffaa/democracia.htm.

15. The voluminous literature on "transitions" from authoritarian regimes to elected government is replete with theories and case studies focused on the circumstances, variations in, and consequences of transition, and the dilemmas of "democratic consolidation." For an overview of the issues of "transitology" see Philippe C. Schmitter, "Transitology: The Science or the Art of Democratization," in Joseph S. Tulchin and Bernice Romero, eds., *The Consolidation of Democracy in Latin America* (Boulder, CO: Lynne Rienner, 1995): 11–44.

16. See Max C. Manwaring, ed., *Gray Area Phenomena: Confronting the New World Disorder* (Boulder, CO: Westview Press, 1993).

17. Kenneth Jowitt, "A World without Leninism," in Robert O. Slater, Barry M. Schutz, and Steven R. Dorr, eds., *Global Transformation and the Third World* (Boulder, CO: Lynne Rienner, 1993): 17.

18. "Fuerzas armadas y democracia en América," *Adelante*, Escuela de las Américas, Fort Benning, Georgia (Spring 1994): 47–48.

19. The implications of ethnic conflict for U.S. security quickly received attention in the early 1990s. See, for example, Thomas W. Couch, "Ethnicity, Ethnic Conflict, and Military Operations Other than War (MOOTW): A Paper Offering Terms, Presenting Information, and Annotating Related Holdings in the A–AF CLIC Resource and Research Collection (RRC) as of 1 November 1994," Army-Air Force Center for Low Intensity Conflict, Langley Air Force Base, Virginia, November 1994; and Timothy L. Sanz, "Ethno-National Conflicts: Research Sources," *European Security* 3(2) (Summer 1994): 359–81.

20. For an overview of the extensive peacemaking and peacekeeping operations after 1989 see Richard Jones, Tom Woodhouse, and Oliver Ramsbotham, eds. *International Peacekeeping News*, Farndon House Information Trust and Bradford School of Peace Studies (accessible on the Internet). A typical entry (issue 12, September/October 1995) reads: "The first 600 Brazilian peacekeepers arrived in Luanda to serve with UNAVEM III. The 100-strong advance guard, mainly military engineers, will be joined by 100 soldiers on September 12. A further 400 peacekeepers are expected at the end of the month. The Brazilian soldiers will be responsible for bridge-building and land-mine clearance."

21. In 1990 the OAS created the Unit for the Promotion of Democracy to "support the states in the consolidation of their democratic institutions." This unit participated in observing elections and extended its activities into other areas described in a document entitled "A New Vision of the OAS." In a working document prepared by the Office of the Secretary General, titled "The Law in a New Inter-American Order" (Washington, DC, January 1996), reference is made to the Santiago Commitment of 1991—"the inescapable commitment to the defense and promotion of representative democracy"—and called for "transparency in military budgets and expenditure, which is directly linked to other fundamental issues for the Hemisphere, such as strengthening democracy, integral development, and eradicating poverty *by reallocating military resources to these areas*" (emphasis added). All these intended intrusions into domestic policymaking begged the question of who would decide what was meant by "defending" representative democracy, and they ignored the traditional secretiveness surrounding national security budgets not only in Latin America but also in the United States, Europe, and elsewhere. Further initiatives for collective action against terrorism, corruption, and environmental degradation and for the protection of human rights also threatened traditional conceptions of national sovereignty. (See "Remarks by the Secretary General of the OAS, Dr. César Gaviria, at the Inter-American Specialized Conference on Terrorism," Lima, April 26, 1996.)

22. For an interesting exposition of the "threat to sovereignty" of indigenous rights in Venezuela see Friderike Seithe and Dirk Staehler, "Venezuela: Política indigenista," in *Boletín Comisión Andina de Juristas* 17 (February 1988): 37–46.

23. See Max G. Manwaring, "Latin American Security and Civil-Military Relations in the New World Disorder," *Low Intensity Conflict & Law Enforcement* 4(1) (Summer 1995): 29–43; and Carina Perelli and Juan Rial, "Changing Military World Views: The Armed Forces of South America in the 1990s," in Richard Millett and Michael Gold-Biss, eds., *Beyond Praetorianism: The Latin American Military in Transition* (Miami: North-South Center, University of Miami, 1996): 59–82.

24. U.S. Department of Defense, Office of International Security Affairs, *United States Security Strategy for the Americas* (September 1995): 16.

25. In November 1985 the M-19 occupied the Palace of Justice. Eventually the army commanders independently decided on an assault to retake the building. Over one hundred people died, including guerrillas, soldiers, government officials, judges, and visitors. The lack of training in urban tactics was apparent and led to the reassessment of training and the creation of new antiterrorism units. See Leal Buitrago (1994): 110–15.

26. *Special Warfare*, The Professional Bulletin of the John F. Kennedy Special Warfare Center and School, PB-93-1, 6(1) (February 1993).

27. Ibid., PB 93-2, 6(2) (May 1993). According to the Kaibil Web page (www.concyt.gob.gt/minist/mindef/kaibil.htm), the name of the group refers to a king of the Empire of Mam who, thanks to his astuteness, was never captured by the invading conquistadors led by Pedro de Alvarado: "KAIBIL BALAM was considered a true strategist and was consulted by the chiefs of other tribes." The Guatemalan special forces explain that "KAIBIL significa: Hombre estratega, el que tiene la fuerza y la astucia de dos tigres" (KAIBIL means: a strategist, one who has the force and the astuteness of two tigers). The Kaibiles' two main bases were called El Infierno (Hell) and La Pólvora (Gunpowder).

28. Ibid., PB 80-94-4, 7(4) (October 1994).

29. For an overview of U.S. policy in Latin America after 1989 see Joseph Tulchin, "Estados Unidos y América Latina en el mundo," in Francisco Rojas Aravena and William C. Smith, eds., *El Cono sur y las transformaciones globales* (Santiago: FLACSO, North-South Center, CLADDE, 1994): 151–89.

30. This unilateralism for some policies was accompanied by an increasing multilateralism in other areas such as trade, peacekeeping operations, and hemispheric "agenda setting" in so-called summits of the Americas. See Peter H. Smith, *Talons of the Eagle: Dynamics of U.S.-Latin American Relations* (New York: Oxford University Press, 1996).

31. Geoffrey B. Demarest (Lt. Col.), "The Cuba Contingency," *Military Review* 74 (January 1994): 58–66.

32. Ibid.: 59.

33. Geoffrey B. Demarest (Lt. Col.), "Expeditionary Police Service," United States Army, Foreign Military Studies Office, Fort Leavenworth, Kansas, 1996. An early version, "Beefing Up the Low End," appeared in *Military Review* (June 1993): 50–56.

34. See, for example, Douglas Waller, "Running a School for Dictators," *Newsweek* (August 9, 1993): 34–37; Calman McCarthy, "A U.S. Finishing School for Latin Thugs," *Washington Post*, May 10, 1994; and Kenneth Cooper, "Taking Aim at School for Assassins," *Washington Post*, May 19, 1994.

35. Geoffrey B. Demarest (Lt. Col.), "Una redefinición de la Escuela de las Américas," *Military Review* 74(6) (Spanish Edition) (November–December 1995): 35–45.

36. Demarest proposed the creation of a new constabulary-type force with special mobility and operational capabilities for peacemaking, peacekeeping, and other "foreign policy support" missions. This would create professional specialized capabilities and prevent the deflation of morale, military prestige, and warmaking capability in the regular army. See Demarest (1996). World Wide Web: http:/leav-www.army.mil/fmso.

37. For an early 1990s view on the role of the Latin America military in the post-Cold War era and U.S. security concerns see Gabriel Marcella, ed., *Warriors in Peacetime: The Military and Democracy in Latin America—New Directions for U.S. Policy* (London: Frank Cass, 1994).

38. *United States Security Strategy for the Americas* (1995): 1.

39. See Stephen G. Rabe, *Eisenhower and Latin America* (Chapel Hill: University of North Carolina Press, 1988) for details on the Eisenhower administration's emphasis on private foreign investment and freer trade as the model for Latin American economic development.

40. The "end of history" here refers to the thesis of F. Fukuyama that the U.S. victory over the Soviet Union in the Cold War meant that liberal capitalism would sweep across the globe as the dominant, if not exclusive, accepted political system. See F. Fukuyama, *The End of History and the Last Man* (New York: Free Press, 1992).

41. On the history of "exporting democracy" see Abraham F. Lowenthal, ed., *Exporting Democracy: The United States and Latin America* (Baltimore: Johns Hopkins University Press, 1991).

42. *United States Security Strategy for the Americas* (1995).

43. Ibid.: 3.

44. Ibid.: 4–5.

45. On the Argentina Congo mission see Carlos Eduardo Azcoitia, *La guerra olvidada: Argentina en la guerra del Congo* (Buenos Aires: Marymar Ediciones, 1992).

46. See Gabriel Marcella, "Warriors in Peacetime: Future Missions of the Latin American Armed Forces," *Small Wars and Insurgencies* 4(3) (Winter 1993): 1–33.

47. Cited in Antonio L. Palá (Major, USAF), "The Increased Role of Latin American Armed Forces in UN Peacekeeping: Opportunities and Challenges," *Air Power Journal* 9 (Special Edition, 1995): 17–28.

48. Palá (1995): 17–28.

49. Carlos María Zabala (Gen.), "Una oportunidad histórica," *Revista del Suboficial* 611 (March–April 1994): 24–25, cited in Palá (1995): note 13.

50. Palá (1995): 21.

51. For an overview and case studies of Latin American civil-military relations in the 1989–1995 period see Millett and Gold-Biss, eds. (1996).

52. Alvaro de Souza Pinheiro (Col.) and Paulo Cesar Miranda Azevedo (Col.), "A Vision of the Brazilian National Security Policy on the Amazon," *Low Intensity Conflict & Law Enforcement* 3(3) (Winter 1994): 387–409, reprinted by the Foreign Military Studies Office, Fort Leavenworth, Kansas.

53. The original list is here abbreviated and edited.

54. De Souza Pinheiro and Miranda Azevedo (1994): 11.

55. On the Brazilian military's views on development and the nation's destiny in the mid-1990s see Max G. Manwaring, "Brazilian Security in the New World Disorder: Implications for Civil-Military Relations," in Millett and Gold-Biss, eds. (1996): 223–40.

56. See David Pion-Berlin, "Military Autonomy and Emerging Democracies in South America," *Comparative Politics* 25 (October 1992): 83–102; and idem, "The Armed Forces and Politics: Gains and Snares in Recent Scholarship," *Latin American Research Review* 30(1) (1995): 147–62.

57. In *Adelante* (Winter 1993): 21, cited in Juan Obdulio Saínz (Comdr., Gendarmería Argentina), "El futuro de las fuerzas armadas en Centro América," *Adelante* (Spring 1994): 16.

58. Obdulio Saínz (1994): 18.

59. Prepared statement of Gen. Barry R. McCaffrey before the House National Security Committee, March 8, 1995, reprinted in *Defense Issues* 10(50), American Forces Information Service, Washington, DC.

60. For a detailed and somewhat more optimistic account see William W. Mendel (Col., U.S. Army, ret.), "Illusive Victory: From Blast Furnace to Green Sweep," *Military Review* 72 (December 1992): 74–87.

61. "Fuerzas armadas y democracia en América": 36.

62. See Gabriel Marcella, "War and Peace in the Amazon: Strategic Implications for the United States and Latin America of the 1995 Ecuador-Peru War," Strategic Studies Institute, U.S. Army War College, November 24, 1995.

63. Ibid.: 11.

64. "Los grandes combates: La epopeya del Cenepa," *Hoy* (Quito) (Special Edition, June 1995): 5, cited in Marcella (1995): 5–6.

65. According to J. Samuel Fitch, a 1991 survey conducted in Ecuador's two largest cities found that nearly 80 percent of respondents rated the armed forces and the Church as the country's most trusted institutions. Large majorities expressed distrust in the three branches of government, and almost 85 percent lacked confidence in the political parties. Over 75 percent agreed that "if national interests are in danger in times of crisis, the armed forces should intervene to change the government"; and 77 percent agreed that "if national security is threatened, the armed forces should take over the government." Some 85 percent agreed that the armed forces should avoid coups but should pressure the government when they see that things are not going well. Fitch remarked that "the results [of the survey] were so negative for the democratic regime that we agreed not to publish the results until after the installation of the new government." J. Samuel Fitch, "Military Role Beliefs in Latin American Democracies: Context, Ideology, and Doctrine in Argentina and Ecuador," Paper delivered at the 1995 meeting of the Latin American Studies Association, Washington, DC, September 28–30, 1995: 38.

66. For survey data on citizens' attitudes toward the military in Argentina, Chile, Brazil, and Uruguay in the mid-1990s see Juan Linz and Alfred Stepan, *Problems of Democratic Transition and Consolidation: Southern Europe, South America, and Post-Communist Europe* (Baltimore: Johns Hopkins University Press, 1996): 221–30.

Glossary

aguardiente — popular alcoholic beverage distilled from sugarcane or other plant, whose production and sale the Spanish colonial authorities attempted to regulate.

alcabala — sales tax.

alcalde mayor — district officer, comparable to a *corregidor.*

alférez — military rank of ensign or second lieutenant.

amparo — court order protecting arrested prisoners or restricting government action; historically related to writ of *socorro* in Guatemala.

armada real — royal navy; Spanish navy in the colonial period.

asiento — monopoly concession to import slaves into the Spanish empire; conceded to England after 1713.

audiencia — highest court and advisory body to the regional chief executive in the Spanish colonies; also the territorial jurisdiction of such courts; territories of the *audiencias* were one basis for determining boundaries of Spanish American countries after independence.

autogolpe — "self-coup" in which the incumbent government usurps authority and establishes an extraconstitutional regime; illegal closure of the congress by the president and imposition of a temporary emergency government.

banda oriental — territory across the Río de la Plata from Buenos Aires that became Uruguay.

bando — edict, proclamation, or decree; often refers to decrees issued to meet emergencies, rebellions, or crises.

bando militar — decree issued by military authorities.

cacique — Indian chieftain; *kuraka* in the Andes, *batab* in Mayan region; used also to refer to local political bosses.

castas — people of mixed racial background, including those with some Indian and African ancestry; term used to refer to Spanish American underclasses, neither strictly *mestizo* nor *mulatto.*

caudillismo — politics based on conflict among *caudillos;* refers often to 1820s–1880s period in Spanish America.

caudillo — leader whose authority is based on personal charisma.

cédula — decree issued by the Crown or its minister jointly with the Council of the Indies (Consejo de las Indias); a decree issued without the Council was a *real decreto.*

comarca — territorial jurisdiction in Brazil.

comuneros	members of a community sharing some land in common; supporters of a popular revolt; rebels in Paraguay in the 1720s and 1730s and in New Granada in 1780.
conquistadores	Spanish conquerors in the Western Hemisphere; refers usually to those of the sixteenth century.
consejo	council; Spain was governed under a conciliar form of government, including the Consejo de las Indias for the overseas colonies.
consejo de guerra	court-martial; military tribunal in wartime, or during periods of a regime of exception such as a state of siege or internal war.
continuismo	presidential "holding over" in office; establishment of long-term dictatorships with periodic fraudulent elections.
contras	members of the U.S.-supported guerrilla army opposing the Sandinistas in Nicaragua in the 1980s.
coronelismo	Brazilian version of *caudillismo*; domination of politics by local notables and landowners.
corregidor	magistrate and provinicial administrator in colonial Spanish America; *corregidor de indios* administered Indian communities; also refers to provincial administrator in colonial Brazil.
corregimiento	territorial jurisdiction of the *corregidor*.
coup d'état	unscheduled ouster of an incumbent government by a force that is predominantly military.
criollo	or Creole, person of pure Spanish ancestry born in the colonies.
derecho de gentes	literally, peoples' rights; an early version of human rights.
desaparecidos	those persons "disappeared" by dictatorial governments, with no bodies found and their fate unknown but presumed murdered.
dictablanda	"soft" dictatorship that usually refrains from the harsh measures of a *dictadura*.
donación	grant; cession of land.
escuelas de clase	specialized schools for noncommissioned officers.
estado de excepción	state of exception or regime of exception, *excepción* being a temporary suspension of civil liberties and rights with increased government authority; sometimes verges on constitutional dictatorship.
estado de sitio	state of siege; a common type of regime of exception, originating in France; has various legal and political consequences from country to country.
estado mayor	general staff; officers who have received specialized advanced training.
estado mayor general	general staff command.
facultades extraordinarias	extraordinary faculties, or special authority granted to presidents or others to meet crises; may include suspension of civil liberties and rights, emergency legislative authority, and constitutional dictatorship.

fijos	"fixed" Spanish military units sent from Spain to garrison the colonies.
focos	guerrilla cadres in the countryside; refers to Che Guevara's theory of guerrilla warfare
forjando patria	forging the nation, or nation-building.
fueros/foros	special legal and juridical privileges enjoyed by particular groups, for example, the clergy, military, and medieval towns.
fueros militares	special privileges extended to military personnel; refers also to the jurisdiction of military courts.
fuerza pública	public force, or the armed forces and police.
gamonal	rural landowner; manager of political party machine.
garantías	civil liberties and rights as guaranteed in constitutions.
golpe/golpistas	military coup/coup-makers.
hacendado	owner of large rural estate.
hacienda	large rural estate, usually with resident agricultural labor.
junta	small group of military officers, and sometimes civilians, formed to replace normal government institutions and to assume responsibilities for the management of the state.
junta de gobierno	executive committee directing the government; often a military *junta*.
latifundista	owner of large rural estate (*latifundio*); synonym for *hacendado*.
llanero	plainsman (Venezuela); similar to the *gaucho* in Argentina.
matanza	massacre; La Matanza refers to 1932 events in El Salvador.
mazombo	person of pure Portuguese ancestry born in Brazil.
mazorca	semi-official terrorist squad formed by Juan Manuel de Rosas in Argentina; an early instance of state terrorism in Latin America.
mestizo	person of first-generation mixture of Spanish and Indian.
mita/mitayos	Indian labor draft in Peru/Indians drafted to work in the mines.
montoneros	irregular armies or guerrillas; Peronist guerrillas in Argentina in the 1970s.
mulatto	person of first-generation mixture of Spanish and African.
papeles sediciosos	seditious writings and documents.
pardo	persons of mixture of Spanish (European) and African.
patria	nation, fatherland, or native land.
patria chica	subnational *patria* (farms, towns, province).
pena de azotes	punishment by whipping, common for infractions of military law and also as torture to extract information.
peninsular	person born in Spain or Portugal of pure European ancestry.
politiquería	politics, "dirty politics," populism, or demagoguery.

pragmática	royal ordinance or decree.
presidio	frontier garrison.
pronunciamiento	military proclamation; justification for military coup or rebellion against the government; also refers to the coup itself.
quinto	tax of one-fifth; the "royal fifth."
reconquista	reconquest; refers to the seven-hundred-year Christian war to retake the Iberian Peninsula from the Muslims that ended in 1492.
repartimiento	allocation of Indian labor to Spaniards by colonial authorities; forced labor system.
repartimiento de bienes	forced sale of merchandise by Spaniards to Indians.
republiqueta	mini-republic; subnational unit; guerrrilla enclave.
revanchismo	quest for revenge.
seguridad individual	personal civil liberties and rights in early Spanish American constitutions.
suma del poder	absolute or dictatorial power delegated by legislatures to presidents or chief executives to meet emergencies.
tenentes	junior officers, or lieutenants, in Brazil's army.
terço	one-third; refers to organizational unit of colonial militia.

Bibliography

Government Documents

"Acuerdo de la Cámara de Diputados sobre el grave quebrantamiento del orden constitucional y legal de la República," Santiago, August 23, 1973.

Applications of the Inter-American Treaty of Reciprocal Assistance, 1948–1956. Washington, DC: Pan-American Union, 1957.

"Bando No. 5 emitido por la Junta de Comandantes en Jefe de las FF. AA. y Director General de Carabineros de Chile el 11 de Septiembre de 1973," Santiago, 1973.

Código de Justicia Militar, September 27, 1890, as amended March 23, 1906. Madrid: Talleres del Depósito de la Guerra, 1906.

Código Militar de la República de Guatemala, Guatemala, August 1, 1878.

Código Militar de la República de Guatemala. México: Talleres de El Libro Perfecto, 1951.

Comisión Nacional sobre la Desaparición de Personas. Nunca Más: Informe de la Comisión Nacional sobre la Desaparición de Personas. Buenos Aires: Eudeba, 1984.

"Declaration of Punta del Este," 1961, Charter of the Alliance for Progress.

"Declaration of Solidarity for the Preservation of the Political Integrity of the American States against International Communist Intervention," Tenth Inter-American Conference, March 28, 1954, Caracas, Venezuela.

Los Derechos Humanos en Uruguay Respuesta del Gobierno al Informe de la Comisión Interamericana de Derechos Humanos, de fecha 24 de Mayo, 1977. Montevideo, Uruguay: Ministerio de Relaciones Exteriores, 1977.

"Discurso de Clausura" Seminario: Información, Comunicación y Ejército; Marco Conceptual de Relaciones," *Memorial del Ejército de Chile* No. 442/993, 1993.

"La fuerza armada de El Salvador, Posición ante el informe de la Comisión de la Verdad," in "El Informe de la Comisión de la Verdad: Análisis, reflexiones y comentarios, San Salvador," *Estudios CentroAmericanos* 47 (April–May 1993): 484–86.

Imprenta de la Escuela Militar, 1907–1957: 50 Años de la Escuela Militar, Bogotá, 1957.

Informe de la Comisión de la Verdad para El Salvador: De la locura a la esperanza. New York: United Nations, 1992–93.

Informe de la Comisión Nacional de Verdad y Reconciliación, 3 vols. Santiago: Ministerio Secretaría General de Gobierno, 1991.

"Informe presentado ante el Consejo de Seguridad Nacional por el Comandante en Jefe del Ejército de Chile, General Augusto Pinochet Ugarte," March 27, 1991, in *La Nación*, March 28, 1991, reprinted in "Respuestas de las fuerzas armadas y de orden al informe de la Comisión Nacional de Verdad y Reconciliación," *Estudios Públicos* 41 (Summer 1991), offprint.

"Informe presentado ante el Consejo Nacional de Seguridad por el Comandante en Jefe de la Armada de Chile, Almirante Jorge Martínez Busch," March 27, 1991, in *La Nación*, March 28, 1991, reprinted in "Respuestas de las fuerzas armadas y de orden al informe de la Comisión Nacional de Verdad y Reconciliación," *Estudios Públicos* 41 (Summer 1991), offprint.

McCaffrey, Barry R. (Gen.) before the House National Security Committee, March 8, 1995, reprinted in *Defense Issues* 10(50) (1995), American Forces Information Service, Washington, DC.

Memo for the Assistant Secretary of War, January 10, 1945, OPD 336 LA, Entry 418, Record Group 165, National Archives, Washington, DC.

Ministerio de Defensa, Buenos Aires, 1995. *Memoria del Ejército Argentino, 1992–1995*.

Ministerio de Defensa Nacional, El Salvador, *Doctrina militar y relaciones ejército/sociedad*. San Salvador: ONUSAL, 1994.

Ministerio del Interior, *Orden público y seguridad del estado*. Santiago: Editorial Jurídica de Chile, 1993.

NAVNC 2890, *Small Wars Manual*. Washington, DC: Government Printing Office, 1940: SWM 12-4.

Novísima recopilación de las Leyes de España, Madrid, 1805.

NSC-141 ("A Report to the National Security Council by the Secretaries of State and Defense and the Director for Mutual Security on Reexamination of United States Programs for National Security, 19 January 1953").

"Pronunciamiento de la Corte Suprema sobre la quiebra de la juridicidad en Chile," May 7, 1973.

Recopilación de Leyes de los Reynos de las Indias, 4 vols. Madrid, 1681; 1791, 3 vols. Madrid: Consejo de la Hispanidad, 1943.

The Report of the President's National Bipartisan Commission on Central America, Foreword by Henry Kissinger. New York: MacMillan, 1984.

The Rockefeller Report on the Americas: The Official Report of a United States Presidential Mission for the Western Hemisphere, by Nelson A. Rockefeller. Chicago: Quadrangle Books, 1969.

Secretaría de Guerra y Marina, México, *Reglamento de transportes militares por ferrocarril*, Talleres del Departamento de Estado Mayor, 1910.

"Texto de Acuerdo entre las Fuerzas Armadas y Políticos en el Que Se Acuerda el Nuevo Proceso Democrático," 1984; and "Ley de Caducidad de la Pretensión Punitiva del Estado por Delitos de Militares y Policías durante el Régimen de Facto," 1986 (Uruguay).

U.S. Arms Control and Disarmament Agency, Washington, DC, *World Military Expenditures and Arms Trade* (1963–1973; 1971–1980).

U.S. Congress, House Committee on Foreign Affairs, Communism in Latin America: Hearings before the Subcommittee on Inter-American Affairs, 89th Cong., 1st sess., February 9, 1965, p. 119. Washington, DC: Government Printing Office, 1965.

U.S. Department of Defense, Office of International Security Affairs, transmittal letter, *United States Security Strategy for the Americas*, September, 1995.

U.S. Department of State, "A New Concept for Hemispheric Defense and Development," January 15, 1961.

———. *Bulletin* (December 9, 1963): 903.

———. Bureau of Public Affairs, "Cuba's Renewed Support for Violence in Latin America," Special Report No. 90, December 14, 1981.

———. Serial Files on Bolivia, 1910–1929, Records relating to the Internal Affairs of Bolivia, National Archives, 824.20/31, Letter from Jesse S. Cottrell, June 1, 1925.

Books, Monographs, and Theses

Abente Brun, Diego, ed. *Paraguay en transición*. Caracas: Editorial Nueva Sociedad, 1993.

Abrahamsson, Bengt. *Military Professionalization and Political Power*. Beverly Hills, CA: Sage Publications, 1972.

Academia de Ciencias de la URSS. *El ejército y la sociedad*. Moscow, 1982.

Ackroyd, W. S. "Descendants of the Revolution: Civil-Military Relations in Mexico," Ph.D. dissertation, University of Arizona, 1988.

Acuña, Carlos, and Catalina Smulovtiz. *Ni olvido ni perdón. Derechos humanos y tensiones cívico-militares en la transición argentina*. Buenos Aires: CEDES, 1991.

Agüero, Felipe. *Soldiers, Civilians, and Democracy: Post-Franco Spain in Comparative Perspective*. Baltimore: Johns Hopkins University Press, 1995.

Aguilera Peralta, Gabriel. *Seguridad, función militar y democracia*. Guatemala: FLACSO, 1994.

———, coord. *Reconversión militar en América Latina*. Guatemala: FLACSO, 1994.

Alba, Víctor. *El militarismo*. México: UNAM, 1960.

Albi, Julio. *La defensa de las Indias (1764–1799)*. Madrid: ICI, Ediciones Cultura Hispánica, 1987.

Alonso, José Ramón. *Historia política del ejército español.* Madrid: Editora Nacional, 1974.
Americas Watch. *El Salvador's Decade of Terror: Human Rights Since the Assassination of Archbishop Romero.* New Haven, CT: Yale University Press, 1991.
———. *Peru under Fire: Human Rights since the Return to Democracy.* New Haven, CT: Yale University Press, 1992.
Amnesty International. *Honduras: Autoridad civil, poder militar, Violaciones de los derechos humanos en la década de 1980.* London: Publicaciones Amnistía Internacional, 1988.
Anderson, Benedict. *Imagined Communities: Reflections on the Origin and Spread of Nationalism.* London: Verso, 1983.
Anderson, Thomas P. *Matanza: El Salvador's Communist Revolt of 1932.* Lincoln: University of Nebraska Press, 1971.
Andrade, Víctor. *My Missions for Revolutionary Bolivia, 1944–1962.* Pittsburgh: University of Pittsburgh Press, 1976.
Archer, Christon I. *The Army in Bourbon Mexico, 1760–1810,* Albuquerque: University of New Mexico Press, 1977.
Ardao, Arturo. *Génesis de la idea y el nombre de América Latina.* Caracas: Centro de Estudios Rómulo Gallegos, 1980.
Arriagada Herrera, Genaro. *El pensamiento político de los militares. Estudios sobre Chile, Argentina, Brasil y Uruguay.* Santiago: CISEC, Edición Privada, n.d.
———. *Pinochet, The Politics of Power,* translated by Nancy Morris with Vincent Ercolano and Kristen A. Whitney. Boston: Unwin Hyman, 1988.
———. *Por la razón o la fuerza. Chile bajo Pinochet.* Santiago: Editorial Sudamericana, 1998.
Arruda, Antonio de. *A Escola Superior de Guerra.* 2d ed. São Paulo: Edições GRD, 1983.
Astrosa S., Renato. *Jurisdicción penal militar.* Santiago: Editorial Jurídica de Chile, 1973.
Atehortúa, Adolfo León, and Humberto Vélez Ramírez. *Estado y fuerzas armadas en Colombia.* Bogotá: Tercer Mundo Editores-Universidad Javeriana, Seccional Valle, 1994.
Atkins, G. Pope. *Arms and Politics in the Dominican Republic.* Boulder, CO: Westview Press, 1981.
Azcoitia, Carlos Eduardo. *La guerra olvidada: Argentina en la guerra del Congo.* Buenos Aires: Marymar Ediciones, 1992.
Bacchus, Wilfred A. *Mission in Mufti: Brazil's Military Regimes, 1964–1985.* Westport, CT: Greenwood Press, 1990.
Baily, Samuel L. *Nationalism in Latin America.* New York: Alfred A. Knopf, 1971.
Baloyra, Enrique. *El Salvador in Transition.* Chapel Hill: University of North Carolina Press, 1982.
Bañón Martínez, Rafael, and Thomas M. Barker, eds. *Armed Forces and Society in Spain Past and Present.* New York: Columbia University Press, 1988.
Barahona de Brito, Alexandra. *Human Rights and Democratization in Latin America: Uruguay and Chile.* New York: Oxford University Press, 1997.
Barber, Willard F., and C. Neale Ronning. *Internal Security and Military Power: Counterinsurgency and Civic Action in Latin America.* Columbus: Ohio State University Press, 1966.
Barman, Roderick J. *Brazil: The Forging of a Nation, 1798–1852.* Stanford, CA: Stanford University Press, 1988.
de la Barra, Felipe (Gen.). *Objetivo: Palacio del Gobierno.* Lima: Editorial Juana Mejía Baca, 1967.
del Barrio Reyna, Alvaro, and José Julio León Reyes. *Terrorismo, ley antiterrorista y derechos humanos.* Santiago: Programa de Derechos Humanos, Universidad Academia de Humanismo Cristiano, 1990.
Barrios, Raúl, and René Antonio Mayorga. *La cuestión militar en cuestión, Democracia y fuerzas armadas.* La Paz: Centro Boliviano de Estudios Multidisciplinarios (CEBEM), 1994.
Barros, Tobías (Capt.). *Vigilia de armas.* Santiago: 1920, reissued by Estado Mayor del Ejército in 1973 and in 1988.
Barros Arana, Diego. *Historia de la Guerra del Pacífico.* 2 vols. Santiago: Librería Central de Servat, 1880–81.
Basadre, Jorge. *Chile, Peru y Bolivia independientes.* Buenos Aires: Salvat Editores, 1948.
Basile, Clemente (Maj.). *Una guerra poca conocida.* 2 vols. Buenos Aires: Círculo Militar, Biblioteca del Oficial, 1943.

Batista, Juan. *La estrategia española en América durante el siglo de las luces*. Madrid: Editorial Mapfre, 1992.

Beirich, Heidi Ly. "The Birth of Spanish Militarism: The Bourbon Military Reforms (1766–1808)." Master's thesis, Department of Political Science, San Diego State University, 1994.

Beltrán, Virgilio Rafael, ed. *El papel político y social de las fuerzas armadas en América Latina*. Caracas: Monte Avila Editores, 1970.

Benítez Manut, Raúl. *La teoría militar y la guerra civil en El Salvador*. San Salvador: UCA, 1989.

Bergamini, John D. *The Spanish Bourbons: The History of a Tenacious Dynasty*. New York: G. P. Putnam's Sons, 1974.

Bergquist, Charles, Ricardo Peñaranda, and Gonzalo Sánchez, eds. *Violence in Colombia: The Contemporary Crisis in Historical Perspective*. Wilmington, DE: Scholarly Resources, 1992.

Bermúdez, Lilia. *Guerra de baja intensidad*. México: Siglo XXI Editores, 1988.

Best, Félix. *Historia de las guerras argentinas*. 2 vols. Buenos Aires: Peuser, 1960.

Bethell, Leslie, ed. *Cambridge History of Latin America*, 3 vols. London: Cambridge University Press, 1985–86.

———, and Ian Roxborough, eds. *Latin America between the Second World War and the Cold War, 1944–1948*. Cambridge, Eng.: Cambridge University Press, 1992.

Bienen, Henry, ed. *The Military Intervenes: Case Studies in Political Development*. New York: Russell Sage Foundation, 1968.

Binford, Leigh. *The El Mozote Massacre*. Tucson: University of Arizona Press, 1996.

Black, Jan Knippers. *Sentinels of Empire: The United States and Latin American Militarism*. Westport, CT: Greenwood Press, 1986.

Boils, Guillermo. *Los militares y la política en México 1915–1974*. México: Ediciones El Caballito, 1975.

Bolívar, Simón. *Obras Completas*. Vol. 1. Havana: Ed. Lex, 1947.

Booth, David, and Bernardo Sorji. *Military Reformism and Social Classes: The Peruvian Experience, 1968–1980*. New York: St. Martin's Press, 1983.

Boraine, A., and Ronel Scheffer, eds. *Dealing with the Past: Truth and Reconciliation in South Africa*. Cape Town: Institute for Democracy in South Africa, 1994.

Brading, D. A. *The First America: The Spanish Monarchy, Creole Patriots, and the Liberal State, 1492–1867*. Cambridge, Eng.: Cambridge University Press, 1991.

Browning, Reed. *The War of the Austrian Succession*. New York: St. Martin's Press, 1993.

Burggraaff, Winfield J. *The Venezuelan Armed Forces in Politics, 1935–1959*. Columbia: University of Missouri Press, 1972.

Burkholder, Mark A., and Lyman L. Johnson. *Colonial Latin America*. New York: Oxford University Press, 1990, 1994.

Burns, E. Bradford. *A History of Brazil*. New York: Columbia University Press, 1970.

Bushnell, David. *The Making of Modern Colombia: A Nation in Spite of Itself*. Berkeley: University of California Press, 1993.

———. *The Santander Regime in Gran Colombia*. Newark, DE: University of Delaware Press, 1954.

Bustamante, Fernando, et al., eds. *Democracia y fuerzas armadas en Sudamérica*. Quito: CORDES, 1988.

Cabrera, Luis, Ernesto Medina, Luis Bravo, and Julio Franzani. *Misión militar chilena en Ecuador*. Quito: Imprenta del Ejército, 1902.

Cáceres, Andrés A. *La Guerra del 79 sus campañas (memorias)*. Lima: Editorial Milla Batres, 1973 (lst ed., 1924).

Camp, Roderick A. *Generals in the Palacio: The Military in Modern Mexico*. New York: Oxford University Press, 1992.

Campbell, Leon. *The Military and Society in Colonial Peru, 1750–1810*. Philadelphia: American Philosophical Society, 1978.

Carneiro, Glauco. *O revolucionário Siqueiro Campos*. Rio de Janeiro: Gráfica Record Editora, 1966.

Carothers, Thomas. *In the Name of Democracy: U.S. Policy toward Latin America in the Reagan Years*. Berkeley: University of California Press, 1991.

Casey, Glenn Alton. "A Methodological Approach for Analyzing South American Arms Acquisition Behavior and U.S. Policy." Master's thesis, Naval Post-Graduate School, Monterey, CA, 1974.

Castañeda, Jorge G. *Utopia Unarmed: The Latin American Left after the Cold War*. New York: Alfred A. Knopf, 1993.

Castro Morán, Mariano (Lt. Col.). *Función política del ejército salvadoreño en el presente siglo*. El Salvador: UCA Editores, 1984.

Cavallo, Ascanio, Manuel Salazar, and Oscar Sepúlveda. *La historia oculta del régimen militar*. Santiago: Ediciones La Epoca, 1988; 1997.

Caviedes, César N. *The Southern Cone: Realities of the Authoritarian State*. Totowa, NJ: Rowman and Allanheld, 1984.

Cazeneuve, Jean, et al., eds. *Ejército y revolución industrial*. Buenos Aires: Jorge Alvarez Editor, 1964.

Cerda-Cruz, Rodolfo, Juan Rial, and Daniel Zovatto, eds. *Elecciones y democracia en América Latina, 1988–1991*. San José, Costa Rica: IIDH-CAPEL, 1992.

Ceresole, Norberto. *Crisis militar argentino*. Buenos Aires: Centro Editor de América Latina, 1983.

———. *El ejército y la crisis política argentina*. Buenos Aires: Editorial Política Internacional, 1970.

Chapman, Charles Edward. *Republican Hispanic America: A History*. New York: Macmillan, 1948.

Chasteen, John Charles. *Heroes on Horseback, A Life and Times of the Last Gaucho Caudillos*. Albuquerque: University of New Mexico Press, 1995.

Child, Jack. *Geopolitics and Conflict in South America: Quarrels among Neighbors*. Stanford, CA: Hoover Institution/Praeger Publishers, 1985.

———. *The Central American Peace Process, 1983–1991*. Boulder, CO: Lynne Rienner, 1992.

———. *Unequal Alliance: The Inter-American Military System, 1938–1978*. Boulder, CO: Westview Press, 1980.

Chirinos Arrieta, Carlos. *Terrorismo y delito*. Lima: Editorial Colmillo Blanco, 1990.

Christiansen, E. *The Origins of Military Power in Spain, 1800–1854*. London: Oxford University Press, 1967.

Ciancaglini, Sergio, and Martin Granovsky. *Nada más que la verdad, El juicio de las juntas*. Buenos Aires: Planeta, 1995

Clausewitz, Carl von. *On War*, edited by Anatol Rapoport. Baltimore: Penguin Books, 1968.

Cleaves, Peter S., and Martin J. Scurrah. *Agriculture, Bureaucracy, and Military Government in Peru*. Ithaca, NY: Cornell University Press, 1980.

Coatsworth, John H. *Central America and the United States: The Clients and the Colossus*. New York: Twayne, 1994.

Cobas, Efraín. *Fuerza armada, misiones militares y dependencia en el Perú*. Lima: Editorial Horizonte, 1982.

Colegio de Abogados de Chile. *Justicia militar en Chile*. Santiago: Imprenta Montegrande S.A., 1990.

Collier, David, ed. *The New Authoritarianism in Latin America*. Princeton: Princeton University Press, 1979.

Collier, Ruth B., and David Collier. *Shaping the Political Arena: Critical Junctures, the Labor Movement, and Regime Dynamics in Latin America*. Princeton: Princeton University Press, 1991.

Colón de Larriátegui, Félix. *Juzgados militares de España y sus Indias*. 5 vols. Paris: C. Farcy, 1828.

Comblin, José. *The Church and the National Security State*. Maryknoll, NY: Orbis Books, 1979.

Comisión Andina de Juristas. *Bolivia, neoliberalismo y derechos humanos*. Lima: Comisión Andina de Juristas, 1988.

———. *Derechos humanos en Ecuador: Problemas en democracia*. Lima: Comisión Andina de Juristas, 1988.

———. *Peru y Chile; Poder judicial y derechos humanos*. Lima: Comisión Andina de Juristas, 1988.

Committee of Santa Fe. *Santa Fe II: A Strategy for Latin America in the Nineties.* Washington, DC: Council for Inter-American Security, 1989.

Conaghan, Catherine M. *Restructuring Domination: Industrialists and the State in Ecuador.* Pittsburgh: University of Pittsburgh Press, 1988.

Constable, Pamela, and Arturo Valenzuela. *Chile under Pinochet: A Nation of Enemies.* New York, London: W. W. Norton and Co., 1991.

Corbett, Charles D. *The Latin American Military as a Socio-Political Force: Case Studies of Bolivia and Argentina.* Miami: Center for Advanced International Studies, University of Miami, 1972.

Corlazzoli, Pablo. *Los regímenes militares en América Latina: Estructuración e ideología: Los casos de Brasil, Chile y Uruguay.* Montevideo: Ediciones del Nuevo Mundo, 1987.

Corr, Edwin, and Stephen Sloan, eds. *Low Intensity Conflicts: Old Threats in a New World.* Boulder, CO: Westview Press, 1992.

Corradi, Juan E., Patricia Weiss Fagen, and Manuel Antonio Garretón, eds. *Fear at the Edge: State Terror and Resistance in Latin America.* Berkeley: University of California Press, 1992.

Cortada, James W., ed. *Spain in the Nineteenth-Century World: Essays on Spanish Diplomacy, 1789–1898.* Westport, CT: Greenwood Press, 1994.

Crahan, Margaret E., ed. *Human Rights and Basic Needs in the Americas.* Washington, DC: Georgetown University Press, 1982.

Crawford, W. Rex. *A Century of Latin American Thought.* Rev. ed. Cambridge, MA: Harvard University Press, 1944.

Crow, John A. *Spain: The Root and the Flower.* 3d ed. Berkeley: University of California Press, 1985.

Danopoulous, Constantine. ed. *The Decline of Military Regimes: The Civilian Influence.* Boulder, CO: Westview Press, 1988.

———. *From Military to Civilian Rule.* London: Routledge, 1982.

David, Steven R. *Third World Coups d'Etat and International Security.* Baltimore: Johns Hopkins University Press, 1987.

Davis, Sonny B. *A Brotherhood of Arms: Brazil-United States Relations, 1945–1977.* Niwot, CO: University of Colorado Press, 1996.

Debray, Regis. *Revolution in the Revolution?* New York: Grove Press, 1967.

Deleón Arriaga, Manuel L. (Gen.). *Lo que debe saber el soldado.* Quezaltenango: La Esfera, 1937.

Dellepiane, Carlos (Gen.). *Historia militar del Perú.* 6th ed., Vol. 2. Lima: Ministerio de Guerra, 1977.

DePalo, William A., Jr. *The Mexican National Army, 1822–1852.* College Station: Texas A & M University Press, 1997.

Diamond, Larry, and Mark F. Plattner, eds. *Civil-Military Relations and Democracy.* Baltimore: Johns Hopkins University Press, 1996.

Díaz A., Julio (Col.). *Historia del ejército de Bolivia, 1825–1932.* 2 vols. La Paz, n.d.

Díaz Bessone, Ramón Genaro (Gen.). *Guerra revolucionaria en la Argentina, 1959–1978.* 2d ed. Buenos Aires: Círculo Militar, Biblioteca del Oficial, 1988.

Díaz Cardona, Francia Elena. *Fuerzas armadas, militarismo y constitución nacional en América Latina.* México: UNAM, 1988.

Diffie, Bailey W., and George D. Winius. *Foundations of the Portuguese Empire, 1415–1580.* Minneapolis: University of Minnesota Press, 1977.

di Tella, Guido, and Cameron Watt, eds. *Argentina between the Great Powers, 1939–1946.* Pittsburgh: University of Pittsburgh Press, 1990.

Dix, Robert. *Colombia: The Political Dimensions of Change.* New Haven, CT: Yale University Press, 1967.

Dobyns, Henry, and Paul L. Doughty. *Peru, A Cultural History.* New York: Oxford University Press, 1976.

Donoso, Ricardo. *Alessandri, agitador y demoledor.* 2 vols. México: Fondo de Cultura Económica, 1952.

Dorfman, Ariel. *Widows,* trans. Stephen Kessler. New York: Pantheon Books, 1983.

Dosal, Paul J. *Doing Business with the Dictators: A Political History of United Fruit in Guatemala, 1899–1944.* Wilmington, DE: Scholarly Resources, 1993.

———. *Power in Transition: The Rise of Guatemala's Industrial Oligarchy, 1871–1994*. Westport, CT: Praeger, 1995.

Downing, Brian M. *The Military Revolution and Political Change: Origins of Democracy and Autocracy in Early Modern Europe*. Princeton: Princeton University Press, 1992.

Drake, Paul. *Labor Movements and Dictatorships; The Southern Cone in Comparative Perspective*. Baltimore: Johns Hopkins University Press, 1996.

———, and Eduardo Silva, eds. *Elections and Democratization in Latin America, 1980–1985*. San Diego: Center for Iberian and Latin American Studies, University of California, 1986.

———, and Iván Jaksić, eds. *The Struggle for Democracy in Chile, 1982–1994*. 2d ed. Lincoln: University of Nebraska Press, 1995.

Dunkerley, James. *The Long War: Dictatorship and Revolution in El Salvador*. London: Junction Books, 1982.

———. *The Pacification of Central America: Political Change in the Isthmus, 1987–1993*. London: Verso, 1994.

———. *Rebellion in the Veins: Political Struggle in Bolivia, 1952–1982*. London: Verso, 1984.

———. "The Politics of the Bolivian Army, Institutional Development to 1935." Doctoral thesis, Nuffield College, 1979.

Durch, William J., ed. *The Evolution of UN Peacekeeping: Case Studies and Comparative Analysis*. New York: St. Martin's Press, 1993.

Echeverría, Esteban. *Dogma socialista*. La Plata: Universidad Nacional de la Plata, 1940.

Einaudi, Luigi R., and Alfred C. Stepan. *Latin American Institutional Development: Changing Military Perspectives in Peru and Brazil*. Santa Monica, CA: Rand Corporation, April 1971, for the Office of External Research, U.S. Department of State, R-586-DOS.

Eisenhower, Dwight D. *The Eisenhower Diaries*, edited by Robert H. Ferrel. New York: W. W. Norton and Co., 1981.

Eley, Geoff, and Ronald Grigor Suny, eds. *Becoming National: A Reader*. New York: Oxford University Press, 1996.

Elliott, J. H. *Imperial Spain, 1469–1716*. New York: New American Library, 1963.

English, Adrian J. *Armed Forces of Latin America*. London: Jane's, 1984.

Epstein, Edward C., ed. *The New Argentine Democracy: The Search for a Successful Formula*. New York: Praeger, 1992.

Escola Superior de Guerra. *Manual basico*. Rio de Janeiro: ESG, 1983.

Estado Mayor del Ejército. *Historia del ejército de Chile*, multivolume. Santiago: EME, various publication dates.

Estep, Raymond. *United States Military Aid to Latin America*. Maxwell Air Force Base, AL: Aerospace Studies Institute, Air University, 1966.

Etchison, Don L. *The United States and Militarism in Central America*. New York: Praeger, 1975.

Ethier, D., ed. *Democratic Transition and Consolidation in Southern Europe, Latin America, and Asia*. Basingstoke, Eng.: MacMillan, 1990.

Fagg, John E. *Latin America: A General History*. New York: Macmillan, 1963.

Farcau, Bruce W. *The Transition to Democracy in Latin America: The Role of the Military*. Westport, CT: Praeger, 1996.

Feit, Edward. *The Armed Bureaucrats: Military Administrative Regimes and Political Development*. Boston: Houghton Mifflin, 1973.

Fermoselle, Rafael. *The Evolution of the Cuban Military, 1492–1986*. Miami: Ediciones Universal, 1987.

Fernández, Carlos. *Los militares en la transición política*. 2d ed. Barcelona: Editorial Argos Vergara, December 1982.

Fidel, Kenneth, ed. *Militarism in Developing Countries*. New Brunswick, NJ: Transaction Books, 1975.

Finer, Samuel. *The Man on Horseback: The Role of the Military in Politics*. 2d ed. Boulder, CO: Westview Press, 1988.

First, Ruth. *The Barrel of a Gun: Political Power in Africa and the Coup d'Etat*. London: Penguin Press, 1970.

Fisher, John R., Allan J. Kuethe, and Anthony McFarlane, eds. *Reform and Insurrection in Bourbon New Granada and Peru*. Baton Rouge: Louisiana State University Press, 1990.

Fisher, Lillian Estelle. *The Last Inca Revolt, 1780–1783*. Norman: University of Oklahoma Press, 1966.

Fitch, J. Samuel. *The Armed Forces and Democracy in Latin America*. Baltimore: Johns Hopkins University Press, 1998.

———. *The Military Coup d'Etat as a Political Process: Ecuador, 1948–1966*. Baltimore: Johns Hopkins University Press, 1977.

Flores, Mário César. *As Forças Armadas na Constituição*. São Paulo: Editora Convívio,1992.

———. *Bases para uma política militar*. Campinas, SP: Editora de UNICAMP, 1992.

Fluharty, Vernon Lee. *Dance of the Millions: Military Rule and the Social Revolution in Colombia, 1930–1956*. Pittsburgh: University of Pittsburgh Press, 1957.

Fontana, Andrés. *Fuerzas armadas, partidos políticos y transición a la democracia en la Argentina*. Buenos Aires: CEDES, 1984.

Fraga, Rosendo. *El ejército, Del escarnio al poder, 1973–1976*. Buenos Aires: Sudamericana, 1987.

Frühling, Hugo, Carlos Portales, and Augusto Varas, eds. *Estado y fuerzas armadas*. Santiago: Taller El Gráfico, 1982.

Fuentes, Jordi, Lia Cortes, Fernando Castillo Infante, and Arturo Valdés Phillips. *Diccionario histórico de Chile*. 7th ed. Santiago: Zig Zag, 1982.

Fukuyama, F. *The End of History and the Last Man*. New York: Free Press, 1992.

Gallón Giraldo, Gustavo. *Quince años de estado de sitio en Colombia, 1958–1978*. Bogotá: Editorial América Latina, 1979.

Gamarra, Eduardo. *The System of Justice in Bolivia: An Institutional Analysis*. Miami: Center for the Administration of Justice, Florida International University, 1991.

Gamio, Manuel. *Forjando patria*. 2d ed. México: Editorial Porrua, 1960.

García Aguilar, Adolfo (Lt. Col.). *Moral y educación militares*. 3d ed. Guatemala: Editorial del Ejército, 1988.

García Bauer, Carlos. *Los derechos humanos en América*. Guatemala: Tipografía Nacional, 1987.

García Durán, Mauricio. *De la Uribe a Tlaxcala, Procesos de Paz*. Bogotá: CINEP, 1992.

García-Gallo, Alfonso. *Los orígenes de la administración territorial de las Indias*. Madrid: Rivadeneyra, 1944.

———. *Los orígenes españoles de las instituciones americanas*. Estudios de Derecho Indiano. Madrid: Rivadeneyra, 1966.

García Martínez, Prudencio (Col.). *El drama de la autonomía militar, Argentina bajo las juntas Militares*. Madrid: Alianza Editorial, 1995.

García Méndez, Emilio. *Autoritarismo y control social, Argentina-Uruguay-Chile*. Buenos Aires: Editorial Hammurabi, 1987.

García-Sayán, Diego, ed. *Estados de emergencia en la región andina*. Lima: Comisión Andina de Juristas, 1987.

Garretón, Manuel Antonio. *Dictaduras y democratización*. Santiago: FLACSO, 1984.

———. *Hacia una nueva era política, Estudio sobre las democratizaciones*. México: Fondo de Cultura Económica, 1995.

Garst, Rachel. *Military Intelligence and Human Rights in Guatemala: The Archivo and the Case for Intelligence Reform*. Washington, DC: WOLA, 1995.

Gatti Cardozo, Gustavo. *El papel político de los militares en el Paraguay*. Asunción: Universidad Católica, Biblioteca de Estudios Paraguayos, 1990.

Genta, Jordán B. *Seguridad y desarrollo: Reflexiones sobre el terror en la Argentina*. Buenos Aires: Dictio, 1976.

Gibson, Charles. *Spain in America*. New York: Harper and Row, 1966.

Gillespie, Charles G. *Negotiating Democracy: Politicians and Generals in Uruguay*. Cambridge, Eng.: Cambridge University Press, 1991.

Gillespie, Richard. *Los soldados de Perón: Los montoneros*. Buenos Aires: Grijalbo, 1987.

Gilmore, Robert L. *Caudillism and Militarism in Venezuela, 1810–1910*. Athens: Ohio University Press, 1964.

Gleijeses, Piero. *Shattered Hope: The Guatemalan Revolution and the United States, 1944–1954*. Princeton: Princeton University Press, 1991.

Goldwert, Martin. *The Constabulary in the Dominican Republic and Nicaragua: Progeny and Legacy of U.S. Intervention*. Gainesville: University of Florida Press, 1962.

———. *Democracy, Militarism, and Nationalism in Argentina, 1930–1966*. Austin: University of Texas Press, 1972.

González, Marcela. *Las milicias; Origen y organización durante la colonia*. Córdoba: Centro de Estudios Históricos, 1995.

González Casanova, Pablo. *Los militares y la política en América Latina*. México: Océano, 1988.

González Morales, Felipe, Jorge Mera Figueroa, and Juan Enrique Vargas Viancos. *Protección democrática de la seguridad del estado, Estados de excepción y derecho penal político*. Santiago: Programa de Derechos Humanos, Universidad Academia de Humanismo Cristiano, 1991.

González Moya, Carlos A. *Ley Orgánica Constitucional de las Fuerzas Armadas (Ley No. 18948), Modificada por Ley No. 18967*. Santiago: Editora Jurídica Publiley, n.d.

Goodman, Louis W., Johanna S. R. Mendelson, and Juan Rial, eds. *The Military and Democracy: The Future of Civil-Military Relations in Latin America*. Lexington, MA: Lexington Books, 1990.

Gott, Richard. *Guerrilla Movements in Latin America*. New York: Anchor Books, 1972.

Graham, Lawrence S. *The Portuguese Military and the State: Rethinking Transitions in Europe and Latin America*. Boulder, CO: Westview Press, 1993.

Gramajo Morales, Héctor Alejandro (Gen. de Div.). *Tesis de la estabilidad nacional*. Guatemala: Editorial del Ejército, 1989.

Graves, Ernest, and Steven Hildreth. *U.S. Security Assistance: The Political Process*. Lexington, MA: Lexington Books, 1985.

Grecco, Jorge, and Gustavo González. *Argentina: El ejército que tenemos*. Buenos Aires: Editorial Sudamericana, 1990.

Greenfeld, Liah. *Nationalism: Five Roads to Modernity*. Cambridge, MA: Harvard University Press, 1992.

Grieb, Kenneth J. *Guatemalan Caudillo: The Regime of Jorge Ubico, 1931–1944*. Athens: University of Ohio Press, 1979.

Groisman, Enrique I., ed. *El derecho en la transición de la dictadura a la democracia: La experiencia en América Latina*. Buenos Aires: Centro Editor de América Latina, 1990.

Grüber Odremán, Hernán. *Antecedentes históricos de la insurrección militar del 27–N–1992*. Caracas: Centauro, 1993.

Guest, Iain. *Behind the Disappearances: Argentina's Dirty War against Human Rights and the United Nations*. Philadelphia: University of Pennsylvania Press, 1990.

Guidos Véjar, Rafael. *El ascenso del militarismo en El Salvador*. San Salvador: UCA Editores, 1980.

Gurtov, Melvin. *The United States against the Third World*. New York: Praeger, 1974.

Guzmán, Luis Humberto. *Políticos en uniforme, Un balance del poder del EPS*. Managua: Instituto Nicaragüense de Estudios Socio-Políticos, 1992.

Hahn, Walter F., ed. *Central America and the Reagan Doctrine*, introduction by Jeane J. Kirkpatrick. Lanham, MD: University Press of America, The Center for International Relations at Boston University in association with United States Strategic Institute, Washington, DC, 1987.

Hahner, June. *Civilian-Military Relations in Brazil, 1889–1898*. Columbia: University of South Carolina Press, 1969.

Halperín Donghi, Tulio. *The Aftermath of Revolution in Latin America*. New York: Harper and Row, 1973.

Hamill, Hugh M. *Caudillos: Dictators in Spanish America*. Norman: University of Oklahoma Press, 1992.

Handelman, Howard, and Thomas Sanders, eds. *Military Government and the Movement toward Democracy in South America*. Bloomington: Indiana University Press, 1981.

Harding, Richard. *Amphibious Warfare in the Eighteenth Century: The British Expeditions to the West Indies, 1740–1742*. Suffolk, Eng.: Royal Historical Society, Boydell Press, 1991.

Hargreaves-Mawdsley, W. N. *Eighteenth-Century Spain, 1700–1788: A Political, Diplomatic and Institutional History*. London: Macmillan, 1979.

Harries-Jenkins, Gwyn, and Jacques van Doorn, eds. *The Military and the Problem of Legitimacy*. Beverly Hills, CA: Sage Publications, 1976.

Hartlyn, Jonathan, Lars Schoultz, and Augusto Varas, eds. *The United States and Latin America in the 1990s*. Chapel Hill: University of North Carolina Press, 1992.

Hayek, F. A. *Law, Legislation, and Liberty*. Chicago: University of Chicago Press, 1979.

Hayes, Robert A. *The Armed Nation: The Brazilian Corporate Mystique*. Tempe: Arizona State University Press, 1989.

Herman, Edward S., and Frank Brodhead. *Demonstration Elections: U.S.-Staged Elections in the Dominican Republic, Vietnam, and El Salvador*. Boston: South End Press, 1984.

Hermet, Guy, Richard Rose, and Alain Rouquié, eds. *Elections without Choice*. New York: Wiley, 1978.

Herring, Hubert. *A History of Latin America: From the Beginnings to the Present*. New York: Alfred A. Knopf, 1961.

Hodges, Donald C. *Argentina's "Dirty War": An Intellectual Biography*. Austin: University of Texas Press, 1991.

———, and Abraham Guillén. *Revaloración de la guerrilla urbana*. México: Ediciones El Caballito, 1977.

Hoffman, Paul. *The Spanish Crown and the Defense of the Caribbean, 1535–1585*. Baton Rouge: Louisiana State University Press, 1980.

Horne, Alistair. *The French Army and Politics, 1870–1970*. London: Macmillan, 1984.

Hudson, Manley O. *The Verdict of the League: Colombia and Peru at Leticia*. Boston: World Peace Foundation, 1933.

Human Rights Watch. *State of War, Political Violence, and Counterinsurgency in Colombia*. New York: Human Rights Watch, 1993.

Hunter, Wendy. *Eroding Military Influence in Brazil: Politicians against Soldiers*. Chapel Hill: University of North Carolina Press, 1997.

Huntington, Samuel. *Political Order in Changing Societies*. New Haven, CT: Yale University Press, 1968.

———. *The Soldier and the State*. Cambridge, MA: Harvard University Press, 1957.

———. *The Soldier and the State: The Theory and Politics of Civil-Military Relations*. New York: Vantage Books, 1964.

———. *The Third Wave: Democratization in the Late Twentieth Century*. Norman: University of Oklahoma Press, 1991.

Hurtado, Osvaldo. *Political Power in Ecuador*, trans. Nick D. Mills. Albuquerque: University of New Mexico Press, 1980.

de Imaz, José Luis. *Los que Mandan* (Those Who Rule), trans. Carlos A. Astiz. Albany: State University of New York Press, 1970.

Immerman, Richard H. *The CIA in Guatemala*. Austin: University of Texas Press, 1982.

Instituto Centroamericano de Estudios Políticos. *Derechos humanos en Centroamérica 1986, Situación en El Salvador, Guatemala y Nicaragua*. Guatemala: INCEP, 1986.

Instituto de Investigaciones Jurídicas. *El constitucionalismo en las postrimerías del siglo XX, Constitucionalismo*, IV. México: UNAM, 1988–89.

International Commission of Jurists. *A Breach of Impunity: The Trial for the Murder of Jesuits in El Salvador*. New York: Fordham University Press, 1992.

International Institute for Strategic Studies. *The Military Balance, 1994–1995*. London: Brassey's, 1994.

Isaacs, Anita. *Military Rule and Transition in Ecuador*. Pittsburgh: University of Pittsburgh Press, 1993.

Janowitz, Morris. *The Military in the Political Development of New Nations*. Chicago: University of Chicago Press, 1964.

———. *The Professional Soldier: A Social and Political Portrait*. New York: Free Press, 1971.

———. *Military Institutions and Coercion in Developing Nations*. Chicago: University of Chicago Press, 1977.

———, and Jacques Van Doorn, eds. *On Military Ideology*. Rotterdam: Rotterdam University Press, 1971.

Jensen, Joan M. *Army Surveillance in America, 1775–1980*. New Haven, CT: Yale University Press, 1991.

Johnson, John J. *The Military and Society in Latin America*. Stanford, CA: Stanford University Press, 1964.

———, ed. *The Role of the Military in Underdeveloped Countries*. Princeton: Princeton University Press, 1962.

Jonas, Susanne. *The Battle for Guatemala: Rebels, Death Squads, and U.S. Power*. Boulder, CO: Westview Press, 1991.

Jones, Chester L. *Guatemala, Past and Present*. New York: Russell and Russell, 1966.

Joxe, Alain. *Las fuerzas armadas en el sistema político de Chile*. Santiago: Editorial Universitaria, 1970.

Kagan, Robert. *A Twilight Struggle: American Power and Nicaragua, 1977–1990*. New York: Free Press, 1996.

Kamen, Henry. *The War of Succession in Spain, 1700–1715*. Bloomington: Indiana University Press, 1969.

Karnes, Thomas. *The Failure of Union: Central America, 1824–1975*. Rev. ed. Tempe, AZ: Center for Latin American Studies, 1976.

Kaufman, Edy. *Uruguay in Transition: From Civilian to Military Rule*. New Brunswick, NJ: Transaction Books, 1979.

Keen, Benjamin, ed. *Readings in Latin American Civilization, 1492 to the Present*. Boston: Houghton-Mifflin, 1955.

Kicza, John E., ed. *The Indian in Latin American History: Resistance, Resilience, and Acculturation*. Wilmington, DE: Scholarly Resources, 1993.

Kieffer Guzmán, Fernando. *Ingavi, Batalla triunfal por la soberanía boliviana*. La Paz: "EDVIL," Edición Auspiciada por la H. Cámara de Diputados, 1991.

Kitchen, Martin. *The German Officer Corps, 1890–1914*. Oxford, Eng.: Clarendon Press, 1968.

Kjonnerod, L. Erik, ed. *Evolving U.S. Strategy for Latin America and the Caribbean*. Washington, DC: National Defense University Press, 1992.

Klare, Michael T., and Cynthia Arnson. *Supplying Repression: U.S. Support for Authoritarian Regimes Abroad*. Washington, DC: Institute for Policy Study, 1981.

Klare, Michael T., and Peter Kornbluh. *Low Intensity Warfare: Counterinsurgency, Proinsurgency, and Antiterrorism in the Eighties*. New York: Pantheon Books, 1988.

Klein, Herbert S. *Bolivia: The Evolution of a Multi-Ethnic Society*. New York: Oxford University Press, 1982.

———. *Parties and Political Change in Bolivia, 1880–1952*. London: Cambridge University Press, 1969.

Kolinski, Charles J. *Independence or Death! The Story of the Paraguayan War*. Gainesville: University of Florida Press, 1965.

Konetzke, Richard. *América Latina, II, La época colonial*. translated by Pedro Scaron, 4th ed. Madrid: Siglo XXI Editores, 1976.

———, ed. *Colecćion de documentos para la historia de la formación social de Hispanoamérica, 1493–1810*. Vol. 3. Madrid: Consejo Superior de Investigaciones Científicas, 1962.

Kruijt, Dirk. *La revolución por decreto; Perú durante el Gobierno Militar*. San José, Costa Rica: FLACSO/Mosca Azul, 1991.

———, and Edelberto Torres-Rivas, eds. *América Latina, Militares y sociedad*. 2 vols. San José, Costa Rica: FLACSO, 1991.

Kuethe, Allan J. *Cuba, 1753–1815: Crown, Military, and Society*. Knoxville: University of Tennessee Press, 1986.

———. *Military Reform and Society in New Granada, 1773–1808*. Gainesville: University Presses of Florida, 1978.

LaFrance, David G., and Errol D. Jones, eds. *Latin American Military History: An Annotated Bibliography*. New York: Garland, 1992.

Laguerre, Michel S. *The Military and Society in Haiti*. Knoxville: University of Tennessee Press, 1993.

Landazábal Reyes, Fernando (Gen.). *El equilibrio del poder*. Bogotá: Plaza & Janes, 1993.

———. *Estrategia de la subversión y su desarrollo en América Latina*. Bogotá: Editorial Pax, 1969.

Lanusse, Alejandro A. *Confesiones de un general*. Buenos Aires: Planeta, 1994.

Lázara, Simón. *Poder militar: Orígen, apogeo y transición*. Buenos Aires: Editorial Legasa, 1988.

Leal Buitrago, Francisco. *El oficio de la guerra, La seguridad nacional en Colombia*. Bogotá: Tercer Mundo Editores, 1994.

———. *Política e intervención militar en Colombia*. México: Ediciones de los Comuneros, n.d. [197?] (Companion article by John Saxe-Fernández, "Militarismo en América Latina".)

Lemus, José María (Lt. Col.). *Pueblo, ejército y doctrina revolucionaria*. San Salvador: Imprenta Nacional, 1952.

Levine, Robert M. *The Vargas Regime: The Critical Years*. New York: Columbia University Press, 1970.

Lewis, Paul H. *Paraguay under Stroessner*. Chapel Hill: University of North Carolina Press, 1980.

———. *Socialism, Liberalism, and Dictatorship in Paraguay*. New York: Praeger, 1982.

Lieuwen, Edwin. *Arms and Politics in Latin America*. New York: Frederick A. Praeger, 1960.

———. *Generals vs. Presidents: Neomilitarism in Latin America*. New York: Frederick A. Praeger, 1964.

———. *Mexican Militarism: The Political Rise and Fall of the Mexican Army*. Albuquerque: University of New Mexico Press, 1968.

Linz, Juan. *The Breakdown of Democratic Regimes: Latin America*. Baltimore: Johns Hopkins University Press, 1987.

———, and Alfred Stepan. *Problems of Democratic Transition and Consolidation: Southern Europe, South America, and Post-Communist Europe*. Baltimore: Johns Hopkins University Press, 1996.

Lira, Elizabeth, ed. *Psicología y violencia política en América Latina*. Santiago: ILAS, Ediciones ChileAmérica, CESOC, 1994.

———, and María Isabel Castillo. *Psicología de la amenaza política y del miedo*. Santiago: ILAS, 1991.

Liss, Peggy K. *Atlantic Empires: The Network of Trade and Revolution, 1713–1826*. Baltimore: Johns Hopkins University Press, 1983.

Littuma Arizaga, Alfonso (Col.). *La nación y su seguridad*. N.p.: Editorial Publitécnica, n.d.

Lockhart, James, and Stuart B. Schwartz. *Early Latin America: A History of Colonial Spanish America and Brazil*. New York: Cambridge University Press, 1983.

Looney, Robert E. *The Political Economy of Latin American Defense Expenditures: Case Studies of Venezuela and Argentina*. Lexington, MA: Lexington Books, 1986.

López, Ernesto. *Ni la ceniza ni la gloria: Actores, sistema político y cuestión militar en los años de Alfonsín*. Buenos Aires: Universidad Nacional de Quilmes, 1994.

———. *Seguridad nacional y sedición militar*. Buenos Aires: Ed. Legasa, 1987.

Love, Joseph. *Rio Grande do Sul and Brazilian Regionalism, 1882–1930*. Stanford, CA: Stanford University Press, 1971.

Loveman, Brian. *Chile: The Legacy of Hispanic Capitalism*. 2d ed. New York: Oxford University Press, 1988.

———. *The Constitution of Tyranny: Regimes of Exception in Spanish America*. Pittsburgh: University of Pittsburgh Press, 1993.

———. *Struggle in the Countryside: Politics and Rural Labor in Chile, 1919–1973*. Bloomington: Indiana University Press, 1976.

———, and Thomas M. Davies, Jr., eds. *Che Guevara, Guerrilla Warfare*. 3d ed. Wilmington, DE: Scholarly Resources, 1997.

———, and Thomas M. Davies, Jr., eds. *The Politics of Antipolitics: The Military in Latin America*. Lincoln: University of Nebraska Press, 1979; 1989.

———, and Thomas M. Davies, Jr., eds. *The Politics of Antipolitics: The Military in Latin America*. 3d ed. Wilmington, DE: Scholarly Resources, 1997.

Lowenthal, Abraham F., ed. *Armies and Politics in Latin America*. New York: Holmes and Meier, 1976.

———, ed. *Exporting Democracy: The United States and Latin America*. Baltimore: Johns Hopkins University Press, 1991.

———, ed. *The Peruvian Experiment Reconsidered*. Princeton: Princeton University Press, 1983.

———, and J. Samuel Fitch, eds. *Armies and Politics in Latin America*. Rev. ed. New York: Holmes and Meier, 1986.

Lozada, Salvador María. *Las fuerzas armadas en la política Hispanoamericana*. Buenos Aires: Colección Esquemas, 1967.

Lozada Uribe, Mario (Capt.). *Hacia un Perú mejor. El nuevo rol de los institutos armados y fuerzas auxiliares*. Lima: Imprenta LUX, 1957.

Luna, Félix. *Los caudillos*. Buenos Aires: Editorial Joge Alvarez, 1966.

Lynch, John. *Bourbon Spain, 1700–1808*. London: Basil Blackwell, 1989.

———. *Caudillos in Spanish America, 1800–1850*. New York: Oxford University Press,1992.

———. *The Hispanic World in Crisis and Change, 1598–1700*. Oxford: Blackwell, 1992.

———. *Spanish Colonial Administration: The Intendant System in the Viceroyalty of the Río de la Plata*. London: Athlone Press, 1958.

MacDonald, Austin F. *Latin American Politics and Government*. 2d ed. New York: Thomas Y. Crowell, 1954.

Machillanda Pinto, José (Col.). *Poder político y poder militar en Venezuela, 1958–1986*. 2d ed. Caracas: Ediciones Centauro, 1988.

MacLachlan, Colin. *Spain's Empire in the New World: The Role of Ideas in Institutional and Social Change*. Berkeley: University of California Press, 1988.

Maestre Alfonso, Juan. *Constituciones y Leyes Políticos de América Latina, Filipinas y Guinea Ecuatorial*, II, *Los Regímenes de Seguridad Nacional*, I, *Chile, Uruguay*, Seville: Escuela de Estudios Hispano-Americanos de Sevilla, 1989.

Mainwaring, Scott, Guillermo O'Donnell, and S. J. Valenzuela, eds. *The New Democracies in Latin America: Problems of Transition and Consolidation*. Notre Dame, IN: University of Notre Dame Press, 1991.

Maldifassi, José O., and Pier A. Abetti. *Defense Industries in Latin American Countries*. Westport, CT: Praeger, 1994.

Maldonado, Jaime Aníbal. *Con la espada y la luz*. Guatemala: Editorial del Ejército, 1974.

Maldonado Prieto, Carlos. *La milicia republicana, Historia de un ejército civil en Chile, 1932–1936*. Santiago: World University Services, 1988.

———, and Patricio Quiroga Zamora. *El prusianismo en las fuerzas armadas chilenas: Un estudio histórico, 1885–1945*. Santiago: Ediciones Documentas, 1988.

Mallon, Florencia E. *Peasant and Nation: The Making of Post-Colonial Mexico and Peru*. Berkeley: University of California Press, 1995.

Malloy, James, ed. *Authoritarianism and Corporatism in Latin America*. Pittsburgh: University of Pittsburgh Press, 1977.

———, and Eduardo Gamarra. *Revolution and Reaction: Bolivia*. Pittsburgh: University of Pittsburgh Press, 1988.

———, and Mitchell Seligson, eds. *Authoritarians and Democrats: Regime Transition in Latin America*. Pittsburgh: University of Pittsburgh Press, 1987.

Maniruzzaman, Talukder. *Military Withdrawal from Politics: A Comparative Study*. Cambridge, MA: Ballinger, 1987.

Manwaring, Max G., ed. *Gray Area Phenomena: Confronting the New World Disorder*. Boulder, CO: Westview Press, 1993.

———, and Court Prisk, eds. *El Salvador at War: An Oral History of Conflict from the 1979 Insurrection to the Present*. Washington, DC: National Defense University Press, 1988.

Marcella, Gabriel, ed. *Warriors in Peacetime: The Military and Democracy in Latin America—New Directions for U.S. Policy*. London: Frank Cass, 1994.

Marchena Fernández, Juan. *La institución militar en Cartagena de Indias, 1700–1810*. Seville: Escuela de Estudios Hispanoamericanos, 1982.

———. *Oficiales y soldados en el ejército de América*. Seville: Escuela de Estudios Hispanoamericanos, 1983.

Masterson, Daniel M. *Militarism and Politics in Latin America: Peru from Sánchez Cerro to Sendero Luminoso*. Westport, CT: Greenwood Press, 1991.

Maullin, R. *Soldiers, Guerrillas, and Politics in Colombia*. Lexington, MA: Lexington Books, 1973.

McAlister, Lyle N. *The "Fuero Militar" in New Spain, 1764–1800*. Gainesville: University of Florida Press, 1957.

———, et al., eds. *The Military in Latin American Socio-Political Evolution: Four Case Studies*. Washington, DC: Center for Research in Social Systems, 1970.

McFarlane, Anthony. *Colombia before Independence: Economy, Society, and Politics under Bourbon Rule*. New York: Cambridge University Press, 1993.

McSherry, J. Patrice. *Incomplete Transition: Military Power and Democracy in Argentina*. New York: St. Martin's Press, 1997.

Mecham, J. Lloyd. *A Survey of United States-Latin American Relations*. Boston: Houghton Mifflin Co., 1965.

Mena Sandoval, Francisco Emilio. *Del ejército nacional al ejército guerrillero*. San Salvador: Ediciones Arcoiris, 1991.

Méndez, Juan. *Truth and Partial Justice in Argentina*. New York: Americas Watch, 1988.

Mercado Jarrín, Edgardo. *Política y defensa nacional*. Lima: Comisión Nacional de Plan de Gobierno, 1982.
Meyer, Michael C., and William L. Sherman. *The Course of Mexican History*. 3d ed. New York: Oxford University Press, 1987.
Meza Gallont, Rafael. *El ejército de El Salvador (Breve boceto histórico)*. San Salvador: Imprenta Nacional, 1964.
Mignone, Emilio F. *Derechos humanos y sociedad: El caso argentino*. Buenos Aires: CELS, 1991.
———. *Witness to the Truth: The Complicity of Church and Dictatorship in Argentina, 1976–1983*. Maryknoll, NY: Orbis Books, 1988.
Milla Batres, Carlos, ed. *Memorias del Mariscal Andrés A. Cáceres*. 3 vols. Lima: Editorial Milla Batres, 1986.
Millett, Richard. *Guardians of the Dynasty*. Maryknoll, NY: Orbis, 1977.
———, and Michael Gold-Biss, eds. *Beyond Praetorianism: The Latin American Military in Transition*. Miami, FL: North-South Center, University of Miami, 1996.
Miranda, Carlos. *The Stroessner Era: Authoritarian Rule in Paraguay*. Boulder, CO: Westview Press, 1990.
Miró Quesada, Carlos. *Autopsia de los partidos políticos*. Lima: Ediciones "Paginas Peruanas," 1961.
Molina Johnson, Carlos (Lt. Col.). *Algunas de las razones del quiebre de la institucionalidad política*. Santiago: Estado Mayor del Ejército, 1987.
———. *Chile: Los militares y la política*. Santiago: Editorial Andrés Bello, 1989.
Moneta, C. J., and E. López. *La reforma militar*. Buenos Aires: Editorial Legasa, 1985.
Montagne Markholz, Ernesto. *Memorias del General de Brigada E. P. Ernesto Montagne Markholz*. Lima: N.p. 1962.
Montejo, Víctor. *Testimony: Death of a Guatemalan Village*, trans. Victor Perera. Willimantic, CT: Curbstone Press, 1987.
Montgomery, Tommie Sue. *Revolution in El Salvador: From Civil Strife to Civil Peace*. Boulder, CO: Westview Press, 1995.
———. *Revolution in El Salvador: Origin and Evolution*. Boulder, CO: Westview Press, 1982.
Moreira Alves, Maria Helena. *State and Opposition in Military Brazil*. Austin: University of Texas Press, 1985.
Morison, Samuel Eliot. *History of United States Naval Operations in World War II: The Battle of the Atlantic, September 1939–May 1943*. Vol. 1. Boston: Little, Brown and Co., 1947.
Morris, James. *Honduras: Caudillo Politics and Military Rulers*. Boulder, CO: Westview Press, 1984.
Muñoz, Heraldo, and Joseph S. Tulchin, eds. *Latin American Nations in World Politics*. 2d ed. Boulder, CO: Westview Press, 1996.
Muñoz Guillén, Mercedes. *El estado y la abolición del ejército, 1914–1949*. San José, Costa Rica: Editorial Porvenir, 1990.
Munro, Dana Gardner. *The Latin American Republics, A History*. 3d ed. New York: Appleton-Century Crofts, 1960.
Nohlen, Dieter. *Enciclopedia electoral latinoamericana y del Caribe*. San José, Costa Rica: Instituto InterAmericano de Derechos Humanos, 1993.
Norden, Deborah L. *Military Rebellion in Argentina: Between Coups and Consolidation*. Lincoln: University of Nebraska Press, 1996.
Nordlinger, Eric. *Soldiers in Politics: Military Coups and Governments*. Englewood Cliffs, NJ: Prentice-Hall, 1977.
North, Liisa. *Civil-Military Relations in Argentina, Chile, and Peru*. Berkeley: University of California, Institute of International Studies, 1966.
Nun, José. *Latin America: The Hegemonic Crisis and the Military Coup*. Berkeley: University of California, Institute of International Studies, 1969.
Nunn, Frederick M. *Chilean Politics, 1920–1931: The Honorable Mission of the Armed Forces*. Albuquerque: University of New Mexico Press, 1970.
———. *The Military in Chilean History: Essays on Civil-Military Relations, 1810–1973*. Albuquerque: University of New Mexico Press, 1976.
———. *The Time of the Generals: Latin American Professional Militarism in World Perspective*. Lincoln: University of Nebraska Press, 1992.
———. *Yesterday's Soldiers: European Military Professionalism in South America, 1890–1940*. Lincoln: University of Nebraska Press, 1983.

Obando Arbulu, Enrique. *Fuerzas armadas y constitución*. Lima: Centro Peruano de Estudios Internacionales, 1993.

———. *Industrias militares en América del Sur*. Lima: Centro Peruano de Estudios Internacionales, 1991.

O'Brien, Philip, and Paul Commack, ed. *Generals in Retreat: The Crisis of Military Rule in Latin America*. Manchester, Eng.: Manchester University Press, 1988.

O'Donnell, Guillermo. *Modernization and Bureaucratic Authoritarianism: Studies in South American Politics*. Berkeley: University of California, Institute of International Studies, 1973.

———, Philippe C. Schmitter, and Laurence Whitehead, eds. *Transitions from Authoritarian Rule: Comparative Perspectives*. Baltimore: Johns Hopkins University Press, 1986.

Oehling, Hermann. *La función política del ejército*. Santiago: Biblioteca del Oficial, Estado Mayor General del Ejército, 1977.

Olivares, Luis B. (Maj.). *Subversión política y transición*. Santiago: Estado Mayor General del Ejército, 1988.

ONUSAL. *Relaciones civiles-militares en el nuevo marco internacional*. San Salvador: Ministerio de Defensa Nacional, 1994.

O'Phelan Godoy, Scarlett. *Un siglo de rebeliones anticoloniales, Peru y Bolivia, 1700–1783*. Cusco: Centro de Estudios Rurales Andinos Bartolomé de las Casas, 1988.

Osanka, Frank M., ed. *Modern Guerrilla Warfare*. New York: Free Press of Glencoe, 1962.

de Otto Pardo, Ignacio. *Defensa de la constitución y partidos políticos*. Madrid: Centro de Estudios Constitucionales, 1985.

de Ouro Prêto, Visconde, and Alfonso Celso de Assis Figueiredo. *Advento da dictadura militar no Brasil*. Paris: F. Pichon, 1891.

Packenham, Nancy, and Annie Street, eds. *Honduras, Portrait of a Captive Nation*. New York: Praeger, 1985.

Palmer, Bruce (Gen.). *Intervention in the Caribbean: The Dominican Crisis of 1965*. Lexington: University Press of Kentucky, 1989.

Palmer, D. Scott. *Peru: The Authoritarian Tradition*. New York: Praeger, 1980.

———, ed. *The Shining Path of Peru*. New York: St. Martin's Press, 1992.

Paula Couto, Adolpho João de (Gen.). *Segurança interna: Guerra revolucionária*. Brasilia: Associação de Diplomados da Escola Superior de Guerra, 1971.

Payne, Stanley. *Politics and the Military in Modern Spain*. Stanford, CA: Stanford University Press, 1977.

Perelli, Carina. *Someter o convencer: El discurso militar*. Montevideo: Ediciones de la Banda Oriental, 1987.

Pérez, Louis A., Jr. *Army Politics in Cuba, 1898–1958*. Pittsburgh: University of Pittsburgh Press, 1976.

Pérez, María Angélica, ed. *Las fuerzas armadas en la sociedad civil*. Santiago: CISEC, 1978.

Pérez-Brignoli, Héctor. *A Brief History of Central America*, trans. Ricardo B. Sawrey and Susanne Settre de Sawrey. Berkeley: University of California Press, 1989.

Perina, Rubén M. *Onganía, Levingston, Lanusse, Los militares en la política argentina*. Buenos Aires: Editorial de Belgrano, 1983.

Perlmutter, Amos. *The Military and Politics in Modern Times*. New Haven, CT: Yale University Press, 1977.

———, and Valerie Bennett, eds. *The Political Influence of the Military*. New Haven, CT: Yale University Press, 1980.

Phelps, Gilbert. *Tragedy of Paraguay*. New York: St. Martin's Press, 1975.

Philip, George. *The Military in South American Politics*. London: Croom Helm, 1985.

———. *The Rise and Fall of the Peruvian Military Radicals, 1968–1976*. London: Aldene Press, 1978.

Pike, Frederick. *The Modern History of Peru*. New York: Praeger, 1969.

Piñeyro, J. L. *Ejército y sociedad en México: Pasado y presente*. Puebla: Universidad Autónoma de Puebla, 1985.

Pinkney, Robert. *Democracy in the Third World*. Boulder, CO: Lynne Rienner, 1994.

———. *Right-Wing Military Government*. Boston: Twayne,1990.

Pinochet Ugarte, Augusto. *Camino recorrido: Memorias de un soldado*. 3 vols. Santiago: Instituto Geográfico Militar de Chile, 1991.

———. *The Crucial Day*. Santiago: Editorial Renacimiento, 1982.

Pinzón de Lewin, Patrícia. *El ejército y las elecciones: Ensayo histórico*. Bogotá: Cerec, 1994.

Pion-Berlin, David. *The Ideology of State Terror: Economic Doctrine and Political Repression in Argentina and Peru*. Boulder, CO: Lynne Rienner, 1989.

———. *Through Corridors of Power: Institutions and Civil-Military Relations in Argentina*. University Park: Pennsylvania State University Press, 1997.

Piotti, Alberto Daniel, and Alberto Angel Fernández. *Defensa de la democracia, Nuevo enfoque sobre la represión de los delitos que atentan contra el orden Constitucional*. La Plata: Ediciones Torso, 1985.

Pomer, León. *La Guerra del Paraguay*. Buenos Aires: Centro Editor de América, 1971.

Porter, Bruce D. *War and the Rise of the State: The Military Foundations of Modern Politics*. New York: Free Press, 1994.

Posada-Carbó, Eduardo, ed. *Wars, Parties and Nationalism: Essays on the Politics and Society of Nineteenth-Century Latin America*. London: Institute of Latin American Studies, 1995.

Potash, Robert A. *The Army and Politics in Argentina, 1928–1945*. Stanford, CA: Stanford University Press, 1969.

———. *The Army and Politics in Argentina, 1945–1962: Perón to Frondizi*. Stanford, CA: Stanford University Press, 1980.

———. *The Army and Politics in Argentina, 1962–1973: From Frondizi's Fall to the Peronist Restoration*. Stanford, CA: Stanford University Press, 1996.

Prado, Caio, Jr. *The Colonial Background of Modern Brazil*, trans. Suzette Macedo. Berkeley: University of California Press, 1969.

Prado Salmon, Gary. *Poder y fuerzas armadas, 1949–1982*. La Paz: Editorial Los Amigos del Libro, 1984.

Primo de Rivera, José Antonio. *Obras completas*. Madrid: Delegación Nacional de la Sección Femenina de F.E.T. y de la J.O.N.S., 1954.

Quiroga, Patricio, and Carlos Maldonado. *El prusianismo en las fuerzas armadas chilenas: Un estudio histórico, 1885–1945*. Santiago: Ediciones Documentas, 1988.

Rabe, Stephen G. *Eisenhower and Latin America: The Foreign Policy of Anticommunism*. Chapel Hill: University of North Carolina Press, 1988.

Ramírez, Gabriel. *La cuestión militar, Democracia tutelada o democracia asociativa, el caso uruguayo*. Vol. 2. Montevideo: Arca, 1989.

Ramos A., José D. (Col.). *Nunca será tarde, Seguridad democrática*. Santiago: Gráfica Andes, 1988.

Rattenbach, Benjamín (Lt. Gen.). *El sistema social-militar en la sociedad moderna*. Buenos Aires: Editorial Pleamar, 1972.

———. *Sociología militar, Una contribución a su estudio*. Buenos Aires: Librería Perlado, 1958.

Rebolledo Paz, León. *La Guerra del Paraguay, Historia de una epopeya (1865–1965)*. Buenos Aires: Graf Lombardi & Cia., 1965.

Remmer, Karen. *Military Rule in Latin America*. Boulder, CO: Westview Press, 1991.

Renan, Ernest. *The Poetry of the Celtic Races and Other Studies*, trans. with an introduction and notes by William G. Hutchinson. London: W. Scott, 1896.

Requin, Francisco Isidoro (Gen.). *Datos históricos de la Guerra del Paraguay contra la Triple Alianza* (1875). Asunción: Imprenta Militar, 1971.

Reyes, D. F. *El ejército mexicano*. México: N.p., 1901.

Rial, Juan. *Estructura legal de las fuerzas armadas del Uruguay: Un análisis político*. Montevideo: Centro de Informes y Estudios del Uruguay, PEITHO, 1992.

———. *Las fuerzas armadas en los años 90, Una agenda de discusión*. Montevideo: PEITHO, 1990.

Ricci, Susan, and J. Samuel Fitch, ed. *The Military and Democracy: The Future of Civil-Military Relations in Latin America*. Boulder, CO: Westview Press, 1990.

Riquelme, Marcial Antonio. *Negotiating Democratic Corridors in Paraguay, The Report of the Latin American Studies Association Delegation to Observe the 1993 Paraguayan National Elections*. Pittsburgh: Latin American Studies Association, University of Pittsburgh Press, 1994.

———. *Stronismo: Golpe militar y apertura tutelada*. Asunción: Centro de Documentación y Estudios (CDE), QR Producciones, 1992.

Rivabella, Omar. *Requiem for a Woman's Soul*, trans. Paul Riviera and Omar Rivabella. New York: Random House, 1986.

Rivera Echenique, Silvia. *Militarismo en la Argentina, Golpe de Estado de junio de 1966.* México: UNAM, 1976.

Robertson, William Spence. *The Rise of the Spanish-American Republics.* New York: D. Appleton and Co., 1918.

Rocha V., Alberto. *La militarización del Estado; América Latina, 1960–1980.* Lima: IECOS-UNI, 1988.

Rock, David. *Argentina, 1516–1982: From the Spanish Colonization to the Falklands War.* Berkeley: University of California Press, 1985.

———. *Authoritarian Argentina: The Nationalist Movement, Its History, and its Impact.* Berkeley: University of California Press, 1993.

Rodman, Peter W. *More Precious than Peace: The Cold War and the Struggle for the Third World.* New York: Charles Scribner's Sons, 1994.

Rodó, José Enrique. *Obras completas.* 2d ed. Madrid: Aguilar, 1967.

Rodríguez, Linda Alexander, ed. *Rank and Privilege: The Military and Society in Latin America.* Wilmington, DE: Scholarly Resources, 1994.

Rodríguez Beruff, Jorge. *Los militares en el poder; Un ensayo sobre la doctrina militar en el Perú, 1948–1968.* Lima: Mosca Azul, 1983.

Rodríguez Solís, Manuel (Col.), comp. *Deontología militar; Tratado de los deberes militares.* Guatemala: Ministerio de la Defensa Nacional, 1964.

Roett, Riordan. *Brazil: Politics in a Patrimonial Society.* 3d ed. New York: Praeger, 1984.

Rojas Aravena, Francisco, ed. *Gasto militar en América Latina, Procesos de decisión y actores claves.* Santiago: CINDE/FLACSO, 1994.

———, and William C. Smith, eds. *El Cono Sur y las transformaciones globales.* Santiago: FLACSO, North-South Center, CLADDE, 1994.

Romero, José Luis. *A History of Argentine Political Thought,* trans. Thomas F. McCann. Stanford, CA: Stanford University Press, 1963.

Romero, Luis Alberto. *Los golpes militares, 1812–1955.* Buenos Aires: Carlos Pérez Editor, 1969.

Rosenberg, Tina. *Children of Cain: Violence and the Violent in Latin America.* New York: Penguin, 1991.

Rouquié, Alain. *El estado militar en América Latina.* México: Siglo Veintiuno Editores, 1984.

———. *The Military and the State in Latin America,* trans. Paul Sigmund. Berkeley: University of California Press, 1987.

Ruiz García, Enrique, ed. *Historial de la Escuela Politécnica.* Guatemala: Editorial del Ejército, 1973.

Salgado, Hernán, ed. *Las reformas constitucionales de 1986.* Quito: ILDIS, 1986.

Salomón, Leticia, ed. *Política y militares en Honduras.* Tegucigalpa: Centro de Documentación de Honduras, 1992.

———. *Los retos de la democracia.* Tegucigalpa: Centro de Documentación de Honduras, 1994.

Sánchez, Gonzalo. *Guerra y política en la sociedad colombiana.* Bogotá: El Âncora Editores, 1991.

Sanders, Ralph. *Arms Industries: New Suppliers and Regional Security.* Washington, DC: National Defense University, 1990.

Sanguinetti, Julio María. *El temor y la impaciencia, Ensayo sobre la transición democrática en América Latina.* Buenos Aires: Fondo de Cultura Económica, 1991.

Sater, William. *Chile and the War of the Pacific.* Lincoln: University of Nebraska Press, 1986.

Saxe-Fernández, John. *Proyecciones hemisféricas de la pax americana.* Lima: Instituto de Estudios Peruanos, 1971.

Schaposnik, Eduardo C. *Democratización de las fuerzas armadas venezolanas.* Caracas: Fundación Nacional Gonzalo Barrios, 1985.

Scheina, Robert L. *Latin America: A Naval History, 1810–1987.* Annapolis, MD: U.S. Naval Institute Press, 1987.

Schirmer, Jennifer. *The Guatemalan Military Project: A Violence Called Democracy.* Philadelphia: University of Pennsylvania Press, 1998.

Schlesinger, Stephen, and Stephen Kinzer. *Bitter Fruit: The Untold Story of the American Coup in Guatemala.* Garden City, NY: Doubleday, 1982.

Schmitter, Philippe C., ed. *Military Rule in Latin America: Function, Consequences, and Perspectives*. Beverly Hills, CA: Sage, 1973.

Schneider, Ronald M. *Communism in Guatemala*. New York: Octagon Books (reprint), 1979.

———. *"Order and Progress": A Political History of Brazil*. Boulder, CO: Westview Press, 1991.

Schodt, David W. *Ecuador, An Andean Enigma*. Boulder, CO: Westview Press, 1987.

Schoultz, Lars. *Human Rights and United States Policy toward Latin America*. Princeton: Princeton University Press, 1981.

———. *National Security and United States Policy toward Latin America*. Princeton: Princeton University Press, 1987.

———. *Beneath the United States: A History of U.S. Policy toward Latin America*. Cambridge, MA: Harvard University Press, 1998.

Schwarz, Benjamin. *American Counterinsurgency Doctrine and El Salvador: The Frustrations of Reforms and the Illusions of Nation Building*. Santa Monica, CA: Rand Corporation, 1991.

Schulz, Donald E., ed. *The Role of the Armed Forces in the Americas: Civil-Military Relations for the 21st Century*. Carlisle Barracks, PA: Strategic Studies Institute, 1998.

Serbin, Andrés, et al. *Venezuela: La democracia bajo presión*. Caracas: Instituto Venezolano de Estudios Sociales y Políticos (INVESP) and North-South Center, University of Miami, 1993.

Servicio Paz y Justicia. *Uruguay, Nunca Más, Human Rights Violations, 1972–1985*, trans. Elizabeth Hampsten with an introduction by Lawrence Weschler. Philadelphia: Temple University Press, 1989.

Shumway, Nicolas. *The Invention of Argentina*. Berkeley: University of California Press, 1991.

Sieder, Rachel, ed. *Impunity in Latin America*. London: Institute of Latin American Studies, 1995.

Silva, Golbery do Couto e (Gen.). *Conjuntura política nacional: O poder executivo e geopolítica do Brasil*. Rio de Janeiro: Livraria José Olympio, 1981.

———. *Planejamento estratégico*. Rio de Janeiro: Biblioteca do Exército, 1955.

da Silva Prado, Eduardo Paulo (pseud. Frederico de S.). *Fastos da dictadura militar no Brasil*. 3d ed. Lisbon: N.p., 1890.

Simmons, Charles W. *Marshal Deodoro and the Fall of Dom Pedro II*. Durham, NC: Duke University Press, 1966.

Sistemas electorales y representación política en Latinoamérica. 2 vols. Madrid: Fundación Friedrich Ebert/ICI, 1986.

Skidmore, Thomas E. *Politics in Brazil, 1930–1964: An Experiment in Democracy*. New York: Oxford University Press, 1967.

———. *The Politics of Military Rule in Brazil, 1964–1985*. New York: Oxford University Press, 1988.

Slater, Robert O., Barry M. Schutz, and Steven R. Dorr, eds. *Global Transformation and the Third World*. Boulder, CO: Lynne Rienner, 1993.

Small, Gretchen, and Dennis Small, eds. *El complot para aniquilar a las fuerzas armadas y a las naciones de iberoamérica*. 2 vols. México: Ejército Mexicano, Secretaría de la Defensa Nacional, 1994.

Smith, Peter H. *Talons of the Eagle: Dynamics of U.S.-Latin American Relations*. New York: Oxford University Press, 1996.

Solaún, Mauricio, and Michael A. Quinn. *Sinners and Heretics: The Politics of Military Intervention in Latin America*. Urbana: University of Illinois Press, 1973.

Solís Rivera, Luis Guillermo, and Francisco Rojas Aravena, eds. *De la guerra a la integración: La transición y la seguridad en Centroamérica*. San José, Costa Rica: FLACSO-Chile and Fundación Arias para la Paz y el Progreso Humano, 1994.

Stepan, Alfred. ed. *The Military in Politics: Changing Patterns in Brazil*. Princeton: Princeton University Press, 1971.

———. *Authoritarian Brazil: Origins, Policies, and Future*. New Haven, CT: Yale University Press, 1973.

———. *Rethinking Military Politics, Brazil and the Southern Cone*. Princeton: Princeton University Press, 1988.

Stevens, Donald F. *Origins of Instability in Early Republican Mexico*. Durham, NC: Duke University Press, 1991.

Stoan, Stephen K. *Pablo Morillo and Venezuela, 1811–1820*. Columbus: Ohio State University Press, 1974.

Stohl, Michael, and George A. López, eds. *Government Violence and Repression*. New York: Greenwood Press, 1986.

Stoll, David. *Between Two Armies in the Ixil Towns of Guatemala*. Berkeley: University of California Press, 1993.

Street, John. *Artigas and the Emancipation of Uruguay*. Cambridge, Eng.: Cambridge University Press, 1959.

Suárez, Santiago Gerardo. *Las fuerzas armadas venezolanas en la colonia*. Caracas: Biblioteca de la Academia Nacional de la Historia, 1979.

Suchliki, Jaime, ed. *The Cuban Military under Castro*, with an introduction by James A. Morris. Miami: University of Miami, North-South Center Publications for the Research Institute for Cuban Studies, 1989.

Tapia Valdés, Jorge. *Estrategocracia; El gobierno de los generales*. Santiago: Ediciones del Ornitorrinco, 1986.

Thompson, I. A. A. *War and Government in Habsburg Spain, 1560–1620*. London: Athlone Press, 1976.

Thompson, William R. *The Grievances of Military Coup-Makers*. London: Sage, 1973.

Tribunal Permanente de los Pueblos. *Proceso a la impunidad de crímenes de lesa humanidad en América Latina, 1989–1991*. Bogotá: N.p., 1991.

United Nations. *De la locura a la esperanza: Informe de la Comisión de la Verdad para El Salvador*. San Salvador, 1993.

Uricoechea, Fernando. *The Patrimonial Foundations of the Brazilian Bureaucratic State*. Berkeley: University of California Press, 1980.

Urrutia Suárez, Francisco (Col.). *Apuntes para la Historia: La agresión peruana*. Quito: Editorial Ecuatoriana, 1968.

Vagts, Alfred. *A History of Militarism*. Rev. ed. New York: Meridian Books, 1959.

Valadés, Diego. *La dictadura constitucional en América Latina*. México: UNAM, Instituto de Investigaciones Jurídicas, 1974.

Valencia Tovar, Alvaro (Gen.). *Armas e historia*. Bucaramanga: Imprenta del Departamento, 1970.

Valenzuela, J. Samuel, and Arturo Valenzuela, eds. *Military Rule in Chile*. Baltimore: Johns Hopkins University Press, 1986.

Vanger, Milton. *José Batlle y Ordóñez of Uruguay: The Creator of His Times, 1902–1907*. Cambridge, MA: Harvard University Press, 1963.

Varas, Augusto. *La política de las armas en América Latina*. Santiago: FLACSO, 1988.

———. *Los militares en el poder, Régimen y gobierno militar en Chile, 1973–1986*. Santiago: FLACSO, 1987.

———, ed. *Democracy under Siege: New Military Power in Latin America*. New York: Greenwood Press, 1989.

———, ed. *Hemispheric Security and U.S. Policy in Latin America*. Boulder, CO: Westview Press, 1989.

———, ed. *La autonomía militar en América Latina*. Venezuela: Editorial Nueva Sociedad, 1988.

———, ed. *Militarization and the International Arms Race in Latin America*. Boulder, CO: Westview Press, 1985.

———, and Felipe Agüero. *El desarrollo doctrinario de las fuerzas armadas chilenas*. Santiago: FLACSO, 1978.

———, and Felipe Agüero. *El proyecto político militar*. Santiago: FLACSO, 1984.

———, and Claudio Fuentes. *Defensa nacional, Chile, 1990–1994: Modernización y desarrollo*. Santiago: FLACSO, 1994.

Vélez Ramírez, Humberto, and Adolfo L. Atenortúa Cruz. *Militares, guerrilleros y autoridad civil*. Santiago de Cali: Editorial de la Facultad de Humanidades, 1993.

Verbitsky, Horacio. *El vuelo*. Buenos Aires: Planeta, 1995.

Vergara Quiroz, Sergio. *Historia social del ejército de Chile*. 2 vols. Santiago: Universidad de Chile, 1993.

Vidal, Hernán. *FPMR: El tabú del conflicto armado en Chile*. Santiago: Mosquito Editores, 1995.

———. *Mitología militar chilena: Surrealismo desde el superego*. Minneapolis: Institute for the Study of Ideologies and Literature, 1989.

Villanueva, Víctor. *Ejército peruano; Del caudillaje anárquico al militarismo reformista*. Lima: Editorial Juan Mejía Baca, 1973.

———. *El CAEM y la revolución de la fuerza armada*. Lima: Instituto de Estudios Peruanos, 1972.

Villavicencio, Felipe. *Delitos contra la seguridad pública, Delito de terrorismo*. 2d ed. Lima: Sesator, 1983.

Villegas, Osiris G. (Col.). *Testimonio de un alegato*. Buenos Aires: Compañía Impresora Argentina, 1990.

———. *Guerra revolucionaria comunista*. Buenos Aires: Biblioteca del Oficial, 1962.

Vittone, Luis. *Las fuerzas armadas paraguayas en sus distintas épocas*. Asunción: Editorial El Gráfico, 1969.

Volio Jiménez, Fernando. *El militarismo en Costa Rica y otros ensayos*. San José, Costa Rica: Libro Libre, 1985.

Waisman, Carlos. *Reversal of Development in Argentina: Postwar Counter-revolutionary Politics and Their Structural Consequences*. Princeton: Princeton University Press, 1987.

Warren, Harris Gaylord. *Paraguay and the Triple Alliance: The Postwar Decade, 1869–1878*. Austin: University of Texas Press, 1978.

Weinstein, Eugenia, Elizabeth Lira, and Eugenia Rojas. *Trauma, duelo y reparación*. Santiago: FASIC/Editorial InterAmericana, 1987.

Weinstein, Martin. *Democracy at the Crossroads*. Boulder, CO: Westview Press, 1988.

Weis, W. Michael. *Cold Warriors and Coups d'Etat: Brazilian-American Relations, 1945–1964*. Albuquerque: University of New Mexico Press, 1993.

Welch, Claude E., ed. *Civilian Control of the Military: Theory and Cases from Developing Countries*. New York: SUNY Press, 1976.

———, and Arthur K. Smith. *Military Role and Rule*. Belmont, CA: Duxbury Press, 1974.

Weschler, Lawrence. *A Miracle, A Universe: Settling Accounts with Torturers*. New York: Penguin Books, 1991.

Wesson, Robert, ed. *The Latin American Military Institution*. New York: Praeger, 1986.

———. *New Military Politics in Latin America*. New York: Praeger, 1982.

Wiarda, Howard. *Critical Elections and Critical Coups: State, Society, and the Military in the Process of Latin American Development*. Athens: Ohio University Center for International Studies, 1979.

Wickham-Crowley, Thomas P. *Guerrillas and Revolutionaries in Latin America: A Comparative Study of Insurgents and Regimes Since 1956*. Princeton: Princeton University Press, 1992.

Wilgus, A. Curtis, ed. *South American Dictators*. New York: Russell and Russell, 1937.

Wilkie, James W., and David Lorey, eds. *Statistical Abstract of Latin America*. Vol. 25. Los Angeles: UCLA Latin American Center Publications, 1987.

Williams, Philip J., and Knut Walter. *Militarization and Demilitarization in El Salvador's Transition to Democracy*. Pittsburgh: University of Pittsburgh Press, 1997.

Wolpin, Miles D. *Militarism and Social Revolution in the Third World*. Totowa, NJ: Allanheld, Osmun and Co., 1982.

———. *Military Aid and Counterrevolution in the Third World*. Lexington, MA: D. C. Heath and Co., 1977.

Wood, Bryce. *The United States and the Latin American Wars, 1932–1942*. New York: Columbia University Press, 1966.

Wood, David. *Armed Forces in Central and South America*. London: Adelphi Papers, 1967.

Woodward, Ralph Lee. *Central America: A Nation Divided*. 2d ed. New York: Oxford University Press, 1985.

Worcester, Donald E. *Brazil: From Colony to World Power*. New York: Charles Scribner's Sons, 1973.

Wright, Thomas C. *Latin America in the Era of the Cuban Revolution*. New York: Praeger, 1991.

Wyden, Peter. *Bay of Pigs: The Untold Story*. New York: Simon and Schuster, 1979.

Yelpo, José A. *Ejército, política, proyecto alternativo: 1920–1943*. Buenos Aires: Guardia Nacional, 1987.

Zagorski, Paul W. *Democracy vs. National Security: Civil-Military Relations in Latin America*. Boulder, CO: Lynne Rienner, 1992.

Zamora Castellanos, Pedro (Gen.). *Nuestros cuarteles*. Guatemala: Editorial del Ejército, 1972.

———. *Vida militar de Centro América*. 2 vols. 2d ed. Guatemala: Editorial del Ejército, 1966.

Zanabria Zamudio, Rómulo (Col.). *Luchas y victorias por la definición de una frontera*. Lima: Editorial Jurídica, 1969.

Zaverucha, Jorge. *Rumor de sabres, Tutela militar ou controle civil?* São Paulo: Editora Ática, 1994.

Ziems, Angel. *El gomecismo y la formación del ejército nacional*. Caracas: Editorial Ateneo de Caracas, 1979.

Zook, David, Jr. *Zarumilla-Marañón: The Ecuador-Peru Dispute*. New York: Bookman Associates, 1964.

Zum Felde, Alberto. *Proceso histórico del Uruguay: Esquema de una sociología nacional*. Montevideo: Máximo García, [1919].

Internet

"Expeditionary Police Service," United States Army, Foreign Military Studies Office, Fort Leavenworth, Kansas, 1996, URL: http:/leav-www.army.mil/fmso.

Jones, Richard, Tom Woodhouse, and Oliver Ramsbotham, eds. *International Peacekeeping News*, Farndon House Information Trust and Bradford School of Peace Studies, various issues.

Articles

Agüero, Felipe. "Debilitating Democracy: Political Elites and Military Rebels," in Louis W. Goodman et al., eds., *The Lessons of the Venezuelan Experience*, Baltimore: Woodrow Wilson Center and Johns Hopkins University Press, 1995: 136–62.

———. "The Military and the Limits to Democratization in South America," in Scott Mainwaring et al., eds., *Issues in Democratic Consolidation: The New South American Democracies in Comparative Perspective*, Notre Dame, IN: University of Notre Dame Press, 1992: 153–98.

Aguilera Peralta, Gabriel. "Las políticas de defensa en Guatemala," in Luis Guillermo Solís Rivera and Francisco Rojas Aravena, eds., *De la guerra a la integración: La transición y la seguridad en Centroamérica*, San José, Costa Rica: FLACSO-Chile and Fundación Arias para la Paz y el Progreso Humano, 1994: 99–126.

Alba, Víctor. "The Stages of Militarism in Latin America," in John J. Johnson, ed., *The Role of the Military in Underdeveloped Countries*, Princeton: Princeton University Press, 1962: 165–83.

Americas Watch. "The Trial of Responsibilities: The García Meza Tejada Trial," 5(6) (September 10, 1993).

———. "Truth and Partial Justice in Argentina, An Update" (April 1991).

Archer, Christon I. " '*La causa buena*': The Counterinsurgency Army of New Spain and the Ten Years' War," in Linda Alexander Rodríguez, ed., *Rank and Privilege: The Military and Society in Latin America*, Wilmington, DE: Scholarly Resources, 1994: 11–35.

Arriagada Herrera, Genaro. "National Security Doctrine in Latin America," *Peace and Change* 6(1–2) (1980): 49–60.

———, and Manuel Antonio Garretón. "América Latina a la hora de las doctrinas de la seguridad nacional," in María Angélica Pérez, ed., *Las fuerzas armadas en la sociedad civil*, Santiago: CISEC, 1978: 144–229.

Bacchus, Wilfried. "Long-Term Military Rulership in Brazil: Ideologic Consensus and Dissensus, 1963–1983," *Journal of Political and Military Sociology* 13 (Spring 1985): 99–123.

Bañales Guimaraens, Carlos. "Las fuerzas armadas en la crisis uruguaya," in Virgilio Rafael Beltrán, ed., *El papel político y social de las fuerzas armadas en América Latina*, Caracas: Monte Avila Editores, 1970: 287–329.

Baranyi, Stephen. "Ampliando los límites de lo posible: Misión de Paz de Naciones Unidas en América Central," in ONUSAL, *Relaciones civiles-militares en el nuevo marco internacional*, San Salvador: Ministerio de Defensa Nacional, 1994: 187–217.

Barros, Mario Van Buren. "Las fuerzas armadas como símbolo de la identidad nacional," *Política y Estrategia* 59 (May–August 1993): 39–60.

Beltrán, Virgilio Rafael. "Algunos problemas de la sociología militar en América Latina," in Virgilio Rafael Beltrán, ed., *El papel político y social de las fuerzas armadas en América Latina*, Caracas: Monte Avila Editores, 1970: 7–22.

———. "Estrategia, armas y cambio social en América Latina," in Virgilio Rafael Beltrán, ed., *El papel político y social de las fuerzas armadas en América Latina*, Caracas: Monte Avila Editores, 1970: 25–51.

Benavente Urbina, Andrés. "Acción Política Castrense, 1973–1988," in CEDENAC, *Comunidad Chilena y Defensa Nacional*, Santiago, 1988.

Bieber, León E. "La política militar alemana en Bolivia, 1900–1935," *Latin American Research Review* 29(1) (1994): 85–106.

Bigler, Gene. "Professional Soldiers and Restrained Politics in Venezuela," in Robert Wesson, ed., *New Military Politics in Latin America*, New York: Praeger, 1982: 175–96.

Black, Jan Knippers. "Almost Free, Almost Fair: Paraguay's Ambiguous Election," *NACLA Report on the Americas* 27(2) (September–October 1993): 26–28.

Boström, Mikael. "Political Waves in Latin America, 1940–1988," *Nordic Journal of Latin American Studies* 19(1) (1989): 3–19.

Boyer, Jefferson C. "Democratización y militarización en Honduras: Censecuencias de la Guerra de la 'Contra,' " in Carlos Vilas, coord., *Democracia emergente en Centroamérica*, México: UNAM, 1993: 217–45.

Brading, D. A. "Nationalism and State-Building in Latin American History," in Eduardo Posada-Carbó, ed., *Wars, Parties and Nationalism: Essays on the Politics and Society of Nineteenth-Century Latin America*, London: Institute of Latin American Studies, 1995: 89–107.

Buchanan, Paul. "U.S. Defense Policy for the Western Hemisphere: New Wine in Old Bottles, Old Wine in New Bottles, or Something Completely Different?" *Journal of Inter-American Studies and World Affairs* 38(1) (Spring 1996): 1–31.

Buenaventura, Manuel Sanmiguel. "Factores de perturbación de los derechos humanos en Colombia y el papel del gobierno y las fuerzas armadas para su defensa," *Military Review* 75 (Edición Hispanoaméricana) (March–April 1995): 60–82.

Bushnell, David. "Politics and Violence in Nineteenth-Century Colombia," in Charles Bergquist et al., eds., *Violence in Colombia: The Contemporary Crisis in Historical Perspective*, Wilmington, DE: Scholarly Resources, 1992: 11–30.

Camus, María Eugenia. "Las razones de un 'boinazo,' " *APSI* 451 (Santiago) (May 31–June 13, 1993): 14–16.

Castro, Rodolfo. "Nicaragua: El Ejército Popular Sandinista en la encrucijada (De la doctrina de la guerra popular de defensa a la doctrina de estabilidad nacional)," in Carlos Vilas, coord., *Democracia emergente en Centroamérica*, México: UNAM, 1993: 203–16.

"Caudillo de opereta," *Qué Pasa* 1307 (April 27, 1996): 32.

Central America UPDATE 2(3) (February 1–15, 1996).

CEPAL. "The Fight against Poverty in the Hemispheric Agenda," *CEPAL News* 14(12) (December 1994): 1.

Chapman, Charles. "The Age of the Caudillos: A Chapter in Hispanic American History," *Hispanic American Historical Review* 12 (1932): 281–300.

Child, Jack. "Geopolitical Thinking in Latin America," *Latin American Research Review* 14(2) (Summer 1979): 89–111.

———. "U.S. Policies toward Insurgencies in Latin America," in Georges Fauriol, ed., *Latin American Insurgencies*, Washington, DC: National Defense University, 1985: 132–60.

"The Chilean Plebiscite: A First Step Toward Redemocratization," Report by the International Commission of the Latin American Studies Association to Observe the Chilean Plebiscite, Pittsburgh, Pennsylvania, 1989.

Committee of Santa Fe, "A New Inter-American Policy for the Eighties," by L. Francis Bouchey, Roger Fontaine, David Jordan, Gordon Sumner, and Lewis Tambs (1980).

Cooper, Kenneth. "Taking Aim at School for Assassins," *Washington Post*, May 19, 1994.

Corradi, Juan E. "The Mode of Destruction: Terrorism in Argentina," *Telos* 54 (Winter 1982–83): 61–76.

Cortada, James W. "The United States," in James W. Cortada, ed., *Spain in the Nineteenth-Century World: Essays on Spanish Diplomacy, 1789–1898*, Westport, CT:

Greenwood Press, 1994: 131–47.
Couch, Thomas W. "Ethnicity, Ethnic Conflict, and Military Operations Other than War (MOOTW): A Paper Offering Terms, Presenting Information, and Annotating Related Holdings in the A-AF CLIC Resource and Research Collection (RRC) as of 1 November, 1994," Army-Air Force Center for Low Intensity Conflict, Langley Air Force Base, Virginia, November 1994.
Crahan, Margaret E. "The Evolution of the Military in Brazil, Chile, Peru, Venezuela, and Mexico: Implications for Human Rights," in Margaret E. Crahan, ed., *Human Rights and Basic Needs in the Americas*, Washington, DC: Georgetown University Press, 1982: 46–99.
———. "National Security Ideology and Human Rights," in Margaret E. Crahan, ed., *Human Rights and Basic Needs in the Americas*, Washington, DC: Georgetown University Press, 1982: 100–27.
Dean, Warren. "Latin American *Golpes* and Economic Fluctuations, 1823–1966," *Social Science Quarterly* 51 (June 1970): 70–80.
Demarest, Geoffrey B. (Lt. Col.). "The Cuba Contingency," *Military Review* 74 (January 1994): 58–66.
———. "Doctrina militar en el acontecer político de Sudamérica," *Military Review* 72 (Spanish edition) (November–December 1992): 3–15.
———. "Expeditionary Police Service," United States Army, Foreign Military Studies Office, Fort Leavenworth, Kansas, 1996. An early version, "Beefing Up the Low End," appeared in *Military Review* 73 (June 1993): 50–56.
———. "La Geopolítica y los conflictos urbanos en América Latina," *Military Review* 75 (Spanish edition) (January–February 1995): 65–87.
———. "Una redefinición de la Escuela de las Américas," *Military Review* 74(6) (Spanish Edition) (November–December 1995): 45–55.
Desch, Michael C. "Transitions to Democracy: The Role of the Militaries" [Third Draft, 12 July 1991], Center for International Studies, University of Southern California, Los Angeles.
Dix, Robert. "Military Coups and Military Rule in Latin America," *Armed Forces and Society* 20(3) (Spring 1994): 439–56.
Downes, Richard. "New Security Relations in the Americas," *Strategic Forum* 47, National Defense University, Institute for National Strategic Studies (September 1995): 1–4.
Dudley, William S. "Professionalization and the Brazilian Military in the Late Nineteenth Century," in Brian Loveman and Thomas M. Davies, Jr., eds., *The Politics of Antipolitics: The Military in Latin America*, Lincoln: University of Nebraska Press, 1979: 58–64.
Dunkerley, James, and Rachel Sieder. "The Military: The Challenge of Transition," in Rachel Sieder, ed., *Central America: Fragile Transition*, London: Institute of Latin American Studies, 1996: 55–101.
Elam, Robert V. "The Military and Politics in El Salvador, 1927–45," in Brian Loveman and Thomas M. Davies, Jr., eds., *The Politics of Antipolitics: The Military in Latin America*, 2d ed., Lincoln: University of Nebraska Press, 1989: 82–85.
Ensalaco, Marc. "Truth Commissions for Chile and El Salvador: A Report and Assessment," *Human Rights Quarterly* 16 (November 1994): 657–75.
Espadas Burgos, Manuel. "The Spanish Army during the Crisis of the Old Régime," in Rafael Bañón Martínez and Thomas M. Barker, eds., *Armed Forces and Society in Spain Past and Present*, New York: Columbia University Press, 1988: 81–103.
Feaver, Peter D. "The Civil-Military Problematique: Huntington, Janowitz, and the Question of Civilian Control," *Armed Forces and Society* 23(2) (Winter 1996): 149–78.
"Fiscal militar encargó reo por sedición el Abogado Héctor Salazar," *La Epoca* (April 15, 1994): 19.
Fitch, John Samuel. "Military Role Beliefs in Latin American Democracies: Context, Ideology, and Doctrine in Argentina and Ecuador," Paper delivered at the 1995 meeting of the Latin American Studies Association, Washington, DC, September 28–30, 1995.
———. "Democracy, Human Rights, and the Armed Forces in Latin America," in Jonathan Hartlyn et al., eds., *The United States and Latin America in the 1990s*, Chapel Hill: University of North Carolina Press, 1992: 181–213.

———. "The Decline of U.S. Military Influence in Latin America," *Journal of Inter-American Studies and World Affairs* 35(2) (Summer 1993): 1–41.

———. "The Political Impact of U.S. Military Aid to Latin America, Institutional and Individual Effects," *Armed Forces and Society* 5(3) (1979): 360–86.

Fitzgibbon, Russell H. "Argentina after Eva Perón," *Yale Review* 43 (Autumn 1952): 32–45.

Fix-Zamudio, Héctor. "La justicia constitucional en América Latina," in Instituto de Investigaciones Jurídicas, *El Constitucionalismo en las postrimerías del Siglo XX, Constitucionalismo, IV,* México: UNAM, 1988–89: 451–532.

Flatley, Thomas W. (Col.). "Latin American Armed Forces in the 1960s—A Review," *Military Review* 50 (April 1970): 10–20.

Foley, Michael W. "Laying the Groundwork: The Struggle for Civil Society in El Salvador," *Journal of Inter-American Studies and World Affairs* 38(1) (Spring 1996): 67–104.

Fossum, E. "Factors Influencing the Occurrence of Military Coups d'Etats in Latin America," *Journal of Peace Research* 4(3) (1967): 228–51.

Franko, Patrice. "The Economics of Security," *Hemisphere* 7(2) (1996): 14–19.

———. "*De facto* Demilitarization: Budget-Driven Downsizing in Latin America," *Journal of Inter-American Studies and World Affairs* 36(1) (Spring 1994): 37–74.

Frota, Ivan Moacyr da (Brig. Gen.). "Las fuerzas armadas, El último baluarte," *O Estado* (São Paulo), May 12, 1993, reprinted in Gretchen Small and Dennis Small, eds., *El complot para aniquilar a las fuerzas armadas y a las naciones de Iberoamérica,* 2 vols., México: Ejército Mexicano, Secretaría de la Defensa Nacional, 1994: 390–96.

"Fuerzas armadas y democracia en América." *Adelante,* Escuela de las Américas, Fort Benning, Georgia (Spring 1994): 47–48.

Gallardo Miranda, Juan M. (Lt. Col.), and Edmundo O'Kuinghttons Ocampo (Lt. Col.). "Doctrina militar en el acontecer político de Sudamérica," *Military Review* 72 (Spanish edition) (November–December 1992): 3–15.

Galtieri, Leopoldo Fortunato (Gen.), trans. and reprinted from *Clarín* (Buenos Aires), February 10, 1980. Speech reprinted in Brian Loveman and Thomas M. Davies, Jr., eds., *The Politics of Antipolitics: The Military in Latin America,* 2d ed., Lincoln: University of Nebraska Press, 1989: 201–4.

Gandásegui, Marco A., Jr. "The Military Regimes of Panama," *Journal of Inter-American Studies and World Affairs* 35 (Fall 1993): 1–17.

García, José Z. "The Tanda System and Institutional Autonomy of the Military," in Joseph S. Tulchin, ed., with Gary Bland, *Is There a Transition to Democracy in El Salvador?* Boulder, CO: Lynne Rienner, 1992: 95–104.

García-Sayán, Diego. "Perú: Estados de excepción y régimen jurídico," in Diego García-Sayán, ed., *Estados de emergencia en la región andina,* Lima: Comisión Andina de Juristas, 1987: 95–125.

Garro, Alejandro M. "Nine Years of Transition to Democracy in Argentina: Partial Failure or Qualified Success?" *Columbia Journal of Transnational Law* 31(1) 1993: 1–102.

Germani, Gino, and Kalman Silvert. "Politics, Social Structure and Military Intervention in Latin America," *European Journal of Sociology* 2 (1961): 62–81.

Gillespie, G. Charles. "Models of Democratic Transition in Southern America," in D. Ethier, ed., *Democratic Transition and Consolidation in Southern Europe, Latin America, and Asia,* Basingstoke, Eng.: MacMillan, 1990: 45–72.

Goldwert, Marvin. "The Rise of Modern Militarism in Argentina," *Hispanic American Historical Review* 48 (May 1968): 189–205.

González Morales, Felipe. "Modelos legislativos de seguridad interior, 1925–1989," *Revista Chilena de Derechos Humanos* 11 (November 1989): 18–24.

"Los grandes combates: La epopeya del Cenepa," *Hoy* (Quito) (Special edition, June 1995): 5.

Groisman, Enrique I. "La reconstrucción del Estado de Derecho en Argentina (1983–1989)," in Enrique I. Groisman, ed., *El derecho en la transición de la dictadura a la democracia: La experiencia en América Latina,* Buenos Aires: Centro Editor de América Latina, 1990: 40–53.

Guerrero, J. C. "La educación e instrucción de la raza indígena en las escuelas de tropa," *Boletín del Ministerio de Guerra y Marina* (Peru) (June 1910): 666–68.

Guevara, Ernesto "Che." "Guerrilla Warfare—A Method," in Brian Loveman and Thomas M. Davies, Jr., eds., *Che Guevara, Guerrilla Warfare*, Wilmington, DE: Scholarly Resources, 1997: 148–62.

———. "Message to the Tricontinental," Pamphlet published in English by the Executive Secretariat of the Organization of the Solidarity of the Peoples of Africa, Asia, and Latin America, Havana, April 16, 1967, reprinted in Brian Loveman and Thomas M. Davies, Jr., eds., *Che Guevara, Guerrilla Warfare*, Wilmington, DE: Scholarly Resources, 1997: 164–76.

Guillén, Pedro. "Militarismo y golpes de estado en América Latina," *Cuadernos Americanos* 140 (May–June 1965): 7–19.

Hakim, Peter, and Abraham F. Lowenthal. "Latin America's Fragile Democracies," in Larry Diamond and Marc F. Plattner, eds., *The Global Resurgence of Democracy*, Baltimore: Johns Hopkins University Press, 1993: 293–320.

Hamnett, Brian R. "Process and Pattern: A Re-examination of the Ibero-American Independence Movements, 1808–1826," *Journal of Latin American Studies* 29, part 2 (May 1997): 279–328.

Handelman, Howard. "The Military in Latin American Politics: Internal and External Determinants," *Latin American Research Review* 22(3) (1987): 185–95.

Handy, Jim. "Resurgent Democracy and the Guatemalan Military," *Journal of Latin American Studies* 18 (November 1986): 383–409.

Hayner, Priscilla. "Fifteen Truth Commissions—1974 to 1994: A Comparative Study," *Human Rights Quarterly* 16 (November 1994): 597–655.

Horowitz, Irving L. "The Military Elites," in Seymour M. Lipset and Aldo Solari, eds., *Elites in Latin America*, New York: Oxford University Press, 1967: 146–89.

Hunter, Wendy. "Politicians against Soldiers: Contesting the Military in Postauthoritarian Brazil," *Comparative Politics* 27(4) (July 1995): 425–43.

Huntington, Samuel. "Political Development and Political Decay," *World Politics* 17 (1965): 386–430.

J.E.A. "Consideraciones sobre la Ley de Amnistía," *Estudios Centroamericanos* (April–May 1993): 414–19.

de la Jara Basombrío, Ernesto. "El gobierno de la impunidad, 'Sólo falta que los muertos hablen,' " *Ideele* 5(59–60) (December 1993): 50–57.

Jowitt, Kenneth. "A World without Leninism," in Robert O. Slater et al., eds., *Global Transformation and the Third World*, Boulder, CO: Lynne Rienner, 1993: 9–27.

Karl, Terry. "Dilemmas of Democratization in Latin America," *Comparative Politics* 23(1) (1990): 1–21.

Kaye, Mike. "The Role of Truth Commissions in the Search for Justice, Reconciliation and Democratisation: The Salvadorean and Honduran Cases," *Journal of Latin American Studies* 29, part 3 (October 1997): 693–716.

Klette, Immanuel J. (Col.). "U.S. Assistance to Venezuela and Chile in Combatting Insurgency, 1963–1964—Two Cases," *Conflict* 3(4) (1982): 227–44.

Kling, Merle. "Towards a Theory of Power and Political Instability in Latin America," *Western Political Quarterly* 9 (March 1956): 21–35.

Ladd, Jonathan F. (Lt. Col.). "Some Reflections on Counterinsurgency," *Military Review* (October 1964): 72–78.

Lezcano, Carlos María. "El régimen militar de Alfredo Stroessner: Fuerzas armadas y política en el Paraguay (1954–1988)," *Revista Paraguaya de Sociología* 26(74) (January–April 1989): 117–47.

———. "Las fuerzas armadas en Paraguay," in Augusto Varas, ed., *La autonomía militar en América Latina*, Venezuela: Editorial Nueva Sociedad, 1988: 347–64.

López, George A. "National Security Ideology as an Impetus to State Violence and State Terror," in Michael Stohl and George A. López, eds., *Government Violence and Repression*, New York: Greenwood Press, 1986: 73–95.

Loveman, Brian. "Government and Regime Succession in Chile," *Third World Quarterly* 10(1) (January 1988): 260–80.

———. "*Misión Cumplida*? Civil-Military Relations and the Chilean Political Transition," *Journal of Inter-American Studies and World Affairs* 33(3) (Fall 1991): 35–74.

———. " 'Protected Democracies' and Military Guardianship: Political Transitions in Latin America, 1978–1993," *Journal of Inter-American Studies and World Affairs*, 36(2) (Summer 1994): 105–89.

———, and Thomas M. Davies, Jr. "*Guerrilla Warfare,* Revolutionary Theory, and Revolutionary Movements in Latin America," in Brian Loveman and Thomas M. Davies, Jr., eds., *Che Guevara, Guerrilla Warfare,* 3d ed. Wilmington, DE: Scholarly Resources, 1997: 3–37.

Lozano, Wilfredo, and Alejandra Liriano. "Estado, militares y sociedad en la República Dominicana," *Estudios Sociales Centroamericanos* 54 (September–December 1990): 59–84.

Manwaring, Max G. "Brazilian Security in the New World Disorder: Implications for Civil-Military Relations," in Richard Millett and Michael Gold-Biss, eds., *Beyond Praetorianism: The Latin American Military in Transition,* Miami, FL: North-South Center, University of Miami, 1996: 223–40.

———. "Latin American Security and Civil-Military Relations in the New World Disorder," *Low Intensity Conflict & Law Enforcement* 4(1) (Summer 1995): 29–43.

Marcella, Gabriel. "The Latin American Military, Low Intensity Conflict, and Democracy," *Journal of Inter-American Studies and World Affairs* 32(1) (Spring 1990): 45–82.

———. "War and Peace in the Amazon: Strategic Implications for the United States and Latin America of the 1995 Ecuador-Peru War," Strategic Studies Institute, U.S. Army War College, November 24, 1995.

———. "Warriors in Peacetime: Future Missions of the Latin American Armed Forces," *Small Wars and Insurgencies* 4(3) (Winter 1993): 1–33.

Marchena Fernández, Juan. "The Social World of the Military in Peru and New Granada: The Colonial Oligarchies in Conflict, 1750–1810," in John R. Fisher et al., eds., *Reform and Insurrection in Bourbon New Granada and Peru,* Baton Rouge: Louisiana State University Press, 1990: 54–95.

Margolis, Mac. "Alleged Coup Plot a Puzzling Piece of Political Theater," *Los Angeles Times,* January 15, 1994.

Marichal, Carlos, and Matilde Souto Mantecón. "Silver and Situados: New Spain and the Financing of the Spanish Empire in the Caribbean in the Eighteenth Century," *Hispanic American Historical Review* 74(4) (November 1994): 587–613.

Maríñez, Pablo A. "Las fuerzas armadas en la República Dominicana: Profesionalización y politización," *El Caribe Contemporáneo* 16 (January–June 1988): 107–32.

Martz, John. "The Military in Ecuador: Policies and Politics of Authoritarian Rule," Latin American Institute, University of New Mexico Occasional Papers Series, no. 3 (1988).

"Más elogios de Menem a militares y policías por ganar la 'guerra sucia,' " *Clarín,* (November 4, 1994).

Mayorga, René Antonio. "Sistema político, estado y fuerzas armadas: Problemas de la consolidación de la democracia en América Latina," in Raúl Berbal-Meza et al., *Integración solidaria: Reconstitución de los sistemas políticos latinoamericanos,* Caracas: Instituto de Altos Estudios de América Latina, 1993: 129–67.

McAlister, Lyle N. "Civil-Miliary Relations in Latin America," *Journal of Inter-American Studies* 3(4) (July 1961): 341–50.

———. "Recent Research and Writings on the Role of the Military in Latin America," *Latin American Research Review* 2 (Fall 1966): 5–36.

McCann, Frank, Jr. "The Brazilian Army and the Problem of Mission, 1939–1964," *Journal of Latin American Studies* 12(1) (1980): 107–216.

———. "The Brazilian General Staff and Brazil's Military Situation, 1900–1945," *Journal of Inter-American Studies and World Affairs* 25(3) (1983): 299–324.

———. "Origins of the 'New Professionalism' of the Brazilian Military," in Brian Loveman and Thomas M. Davies, Jr., eds., *The Politics of Antipolitics: The Military in Latin America,* 2d ed. Lincoln: University of Nebraska Press, 1989: 57–74.

McCarthy, Calman. "A U.S. Finishing School for Latin Thugs," *Washington Post,* May 10, 1994.

McDonald, Ronald. "The Rise of Military Politics in Uruguay," *Inter-American Economic Affairs* 28 (Spring 1975): 25–43.

McFarlane, Anthony. "The Rebellion of the *Barrios,*" in John R. Fisher et al., eds., *Reform and Insurrection in Bourbon New Granada and Peru,* Baton Rouge: Louisiana State University Press, 1990: 197–254.

McGann, Thomas F. "Introduction," in José Luis Romero, *A History of Argentine Political Thought,* trans. Thomas F. McGann, Stanford, CA: Stanford University Press, 1963: vii–xvi.

McSherry, J. Patrice. "Military Power, Impunity, and State-Society Change in Latin America," *Canadian Journal of Political Science* 25(3) (September 1992): 463–64.

Mendel, William W. (Col.). "Illusive Victory: From Blast Furnace to Green Sweep," *Military Review* 72 (December 1992): 74–87.

Mercado Jarrín, Edgardo (Gen.). "El ejército de hoy en su proyección en nuestra sociedad en período de transición," *Revista Militar del Perú* 685 (November–December 1964): 1–20.

———. "La política y la estrategia militar en la guerra contrasubversiva en la América Latina," *Revista Militar del Perú* 701 (November–December 1967): 4–33.

Molas Ribalta, Pere. "The Early Bourbons and the Military," in Rafael Bañón Martínez and Thomas M. Barker, eds., *Armed Forces and Society in Spain Past and Present*, New York: Columbia University Press, 1988: 51–80.

Molina Johnson, Carlos (Brig. Gen.). "Conflicto y cooperación: Un enforque conceptual," *Military Review* (Hispano-American edition) (January–February 1997): 30–41.

Morales Bermúdez, Francisco (Gen.). "Reflexiones sobre política nacional," *Defensa Nacional* (Revista del Centro de Altos Estudios Militares) 2(2) (1982): 32–48.

Munck, Gerardo. "Beyond Electoralism in El Salvador: Conflict Resolution through Negotiated Compromise," *Third World Quarterly* 14(1) (1993): 75–93.

Muñoz, Heraldo. "Collective Action for Democracy in the Americas," in Heraldo Muñoz and Joseph S. Tulchin, eds., *Latin American Nations in World Politics*, 2d ed., Boulder, CO: Westview Press, 1996: 17–34.

Needler, Martin. "Military Motivations in the Seizure of Power," *Latin American Research Review* 10(3) (1975): 63–80.

———. "Political Development and Military Intervention in Latin America," *American Political Science Review* 60 (September 1996): 616–26.

———. "The Latin American Military: Predatory Reactionaries or Modernizing Patriots?" *Journal of Inter-American Studies* 11 (April 1969): 237–44.

Neier, Aryeh. "Menem's Pardons and Purges," *New York Times*, October 2, 1989.

Nickson, R. Andrew. "Paraguay's Archivo del Terror," *Latin American Research Review* 30(1) (1995): 125–29.

Nun, José. "The Middle-Class Military Coup Revisited," in Abraham F. Lowenthal and J. Samuel Fitch, eds., *Armies and Politics in Latin America*, rev. ed., New York: Holmes and Meier, 1986: 59–95.

Obando, Enrique. "El poder de los militares," in Augusto Alvarez Rodrich, ed., *El poder en el Perú*, Lima: Editorial Apoyo, 1993: 75–85.

Obdulio Saínz, Juan (Comdr., Gendarmería Argentina). "El futuro de las fuerzas armadas en Centro América," *Adelante* (Spring 1994): 16.

Ochoa, Enrique C. "The Rapid Expansion of Voter Participation in Latin America: Presidential Elections, 1845–1986," in James W. Wilkie and David Lorey, eds., *Statistical Abstract of Latin America*, Vol. 25, Los Angeles: UCLA Latin American Center Publications, 1987: 862–910.

O'Donnell, Guillermo A. "Modernization and Military Coups: Theory, Comparisons, and the Argentine Case," in Abraham F. Lowenthal and J. Samuel Fitch, eds., *Armies and Politics in Latin America*, rev. ed., New York: Holmes and Meier, 1986: 96–133.

Palá, Antonio L. (Maj., USAF). "The Increased Role of Latin American Armed Forces in UN Peacekeeping: Opportunities and Challenges," *Air Power Journal* 9 (Special Edition, 1995): 17–28.

Parsons, Talcott. "Certain Primary Sources and Patterns of Aggression in the Social Structure of the Western World," in Talcott Parsons, ed., *Essays in Sociological Theory*, New York: Free Press, 1954: 298–322.

Pease García, Henry. "Perú: Del reformismo militar a la democracia tutelada," in Henry Pease García et al., eds., *América Latina 80: Democracia y movimiento popular*, Lima: DESCO, 1979: 439–73.

Pecaut, Daniel. "Guerrillas and Violence," in Charles Bergquist et al., eds., *Violence in Colombia: The Contemporary Crisis in Historical Perspective*, Wilmington, DE: Scholarly Resources, 1992: 217–39.

Perelli, Carina. "From Counterrevolutionary Warfare to Political Awakening: The Uruguayan and Argentine Armed Forces in the Seventies," *Armed Forces and Society* 20(1) (1993): 25–49.

———. "The Military's Perception of Threat in the Southern Cone of South America," in Louis W. Goodman et al., eds., *The Military and Democracy: The Future of Civil-Military Relations in Latin America*, Lexington, MA: Lexington Books, 1990: 93–105.
———, and Juan Rial. "Changing Military World Views: The Armed Forces of South America in the 1990s," in Richard Millett and Michael Gold-Biss, eds., *Beyond Praetorianism: The Latin American Military in Transition*, Miami, FL: North-South Center, University of Miami, 1996: 59–82.
Pérez Esquivel, Leonardo. "Marco jurídico de la defensa nacional, La seguridad interior y las fuerzas armadas en Argentina y Brasil" (Informe Preliminar), Buenos Aires: CEDES, 1992.
Perry, William, and Max Primorac. "The Inter-American Security Agenda," *Journal of Inter-American Studies and World Affairs* 36(3) (Fall 1994): 111–27.
"Peru's Premier Reportedly Quits over Rights Case," *Los Angeles Times*, February 17, 1994.
Philip, George. "The New Economic Liberalism and Democracy in Latin America: Friends or Enemies," *Third World Quarterly* 14(3) (1993): 551–71.
Pinochet Ugarte, Augusto (Gen.). "Discurso en el tercer aniversario del gobierno," Santiago, September 11, 1976.
Pion-Berlin, David. "The Armed Forces and Politics: Gains and Snares in Recent Scholarship," *Latin American Research Review* 30(1) (1995): 147–62.
———. "Latin American National Security Doctrines: Hard- and Soft-line Themes," *Armed Forces and Society* 15 (Spring 1989): 411–29.
———. "Military Autonomy and Emerging Democracies in South America," *Comparative Politics* 25 (October 1992): 83–102.
———. "To Prosecute or Pardon? Human Rights Decisions in the Latin American Southern Cone," *Human Rights Quarterly* 16 (February 1994): 205–30.
Pizarro, Eduardo. "Revolutionary Guerrilla Groups in Colombia," in Charles Bergquist et al., eds., *Violence in Colombia: The Contemporary Crisis in Historical Perspective*, Wilmington, DE: Scholarly Resources, 1992: 169–93.
Potash, Robert A. "Argentina," in Lyle N. McAlister et al., eds., *The Military in Latin American Socio-Political Evolution: Four Case Studies*, Washington, DC: Center for Research in Social Systems, 1970: 85–126.
Powell, John D. "Military Assistance and Militarism in Latin America," *Western Political Quarterly* 18 (1965): 382–92.
Przeworski, Adam. "The Neoliberal Fallacy," in Larry Diamond and Marc F. Plattner, eds., *Capitalism, Socialism, and Democracy Revisited*, Baltimore: Johns Hopkins University Press, 1993: 39–53.
Putnam, Robert D. "Toward Explaining Military Intervention in Latin American Politics," *World Politics* 20 (1967): 83–110.
Pye, Lucian. "Armies in the Process of Political Modernization," *European Journal of Sociology* 2 (1961): 82–92.
Rangel Rojas, Pedro R. "El papel de las fuerzas armadas: Renovación democrática, apertura económica y nuevas relaciones cívico-militares," in Andrés Serbín et al., eds., *Venezuela: La democracia bajo presión*, Caracas: Instituto Venezolano de Estudios Sociales y Políticos (INVESP) and North-South Center, University of Miami, 1993: 177–85.
Rankin, Richard C. "The Expanding Institutional Concerns of the Latin American Military Establishments," *Latin American Research Review* 9 (Spring 1974): 81–108.
Rawson, Arturo (Brig. Gen.). *Ejército y Armada* 3(30) (June 1943): 46.
Remmer, Karen. "Democratization in Latin America," in Robert O. Slater et al., eds., *Global Transformation and the Third World*, Boulder, CO: Lynne Rienner, 1993: 91–111.
———. "The Sustainability of Political Democracy: Lessons from South America," *Comparative Political Studies* 29 (1996): 611–34.
"Report of the Andean Commission of Jurists, Colombian Section, to the Committee against Torture," November 1995.
Rial, Juan. "The Armed Forces and Democracy: The Interests of Latin American Military Corporations in Sustaining Democratic Regimes," in Louis W. Goodman et al., eds., *The Military and Democracy: The Future of Civil-Military Relations in Latin America*, Lexington, MA: Lexington Books, 1990: 277–95.

———. "Los militares en tanto 'partido político sustituto' frente a la redemocratización en Uruguay," in Augusto Varas, ed., *La autonomía militar en América Latina*, Venezuela: Editorial Nueva Sociedad, 1988: 197–229.

Riquelme, Marcial Antonio. "Bases para la discusión de las relaciones Fuerzas Armadas/Sociedad Civil en el Paraguay," *Propuestas Democráticas* 1(3) (July–September 1994): 75–93.

———. "Desde el Stronismo hacia la transición a la democracia: El papel del actor militar," in Diego Abente Brun, ed., *Paraguay en transición*, Caracas: Editorial Nueva Sociedad, 1993: 189–215.

———. "Toward a Weberian Characterization of the Stroessner Regime in Paraguay (1954–1989)," *European Review of Latin American and Caribbean Studies* 57 (December 1994): 29–51.

Roa Bastos, Augusto. "Transiciones, política, poder y democracia en el Paraguay," *Revista Paraguaya de Sociología* 31(89) (January–April 1994): 23–30.

Rodó, José Enrique. "El concepto de la patria," *Almanaque Ilustrado del Uruguay* (1906), in José Enrique Rodó, *Obras Completas*, 2d ed., Madrid: Aguilar, 1967: 1184.

———. "Sobre América Latina," *Cartas y Caretas* (August 25, 1906), in José Enrique Rodó, *Obras completas*, 2d ed., Madrid: Aguilar, 1967: 1185.

Rodríguez, Laura. "The Spanish Riots of 1766," *Past and Present* 59 (1973): 117–46.

Roett, Riordan. "The Debt Crisis and Economic Development in Latin America," in Jonathan Hartlyn et al., eds., *The United States and Latin America in the 1990s*, Chapel Hill: University of North Carolina Press, 1992: 131–51.

Rojas Aravena, Francisco. "Esquipulas II: Un caso exitoso de negociación y cooperación para la paz," in *Cuadernos de Trabajo*, Centro para la Paz y Reconciliación, Costa Rica: Fundación Arias, 1992.

Ropp, Steven. "Explaining the Long-Term Maintenance of Military Regimes: Panama before the U.S. Invasion," *World Politics* 44(2) (January 1992): 210–34.

Rosenberg, Tina. "Overcoming the Legacies of Dictatorship," *Foreign Affairs* 74(3) (May–June 1995): 134–52.

Rostow, Walt W. "Countering Guerrilla Attack," in Frank M. Osanka, ed., *Modern Guerrilla Warfare*, New York: Free Press of Glencoe, 1962: 464–71.

Rouquié, Alain. "Demilitarization and the Institutionalization of Military-Dominated Polities in Latin America," in Guillermo O'Donnell et al., eds., *Transitions from Authoritarian Rule: Comparative Perspectives*, Baltimore: Johns Hopkins University Press, 1986: 108–36.

Rubio Correa, Marcial. "The Perception of the Subversive Threat in Peru," in Louis W. Goodman et al., eds., *The Military and Democracy: The Future of Civil-Military Relations in Latin America*, Lexington, MA: Lexington Books, 1990: 107–22.

Ruhl, J. Mark. "Redefining Civil-Military Relations in Honduras," *Journal of Inter-American Studies and World Affairs* 38(1) (Spring 1996): 33–66.

———. "Changing Civil-Military Relations in Latin America," *Latin American Research Review* 33(3) (1998): 257–69.

Safford, Frank. "Politics, Ideology, and Society in Post-Independence Spanish America," in Leslie Bethell, ed., *Cambridge History of Latin America*, vol. 3, London: Cambridge University Press, 1985–86: 347–421.

Salomón, Leticia. "Honduras: Las fuerzas armadas y retos de la consolidación democrática," in Leticia Salomón, ed., *Los retos de la democracia*, Tegucigalpa: Centro de Documentación de Honduras, 1994: 57–83.

———. "The National Security Doctrine in Honduras: Analysis of the Fall of General Gustavo Alvarez Martínez," in Nancy Packenham and Annie Street, eds., *Honduras, Portrait of a Captive Nation*, New York: Praeger, 1985: 197–207.

Sanz, Timothy L. "Ethno-National Conflicts: Research Sources," *European Security* 3(2) (Summer 1994): 359–81.

Schirmer, Jennifer. "Guatemala: Los militares y la tesis de estabilidad nacional," in Dirk Kruijt and Edelberto Torres-Rivas, eds., *América Latina: Militares y Sociedad*, vol. 1, San José, Costa Rica: FLACSO, 1991: 183–219.

Schmitter, Philippe C. "Transitology: The Science or the Art of Democratization," in Joseph S. Tulchin and Bernice Romero, eds., *The Consolidation of Democracy in Latin America*, Boulder, CO: Lynne Rienner, 1995: 11–44.

Seithe, Friderike, and Dirk Staehler. "Venezuela: Política indigenista," in *Boletín Comisión Andina de Juristas* 17 (February 1988): 37–46.

Serrano, Mónica. "The Armed Branch of the State: Civil-Military Relations in Mexico," *Journal of Latin American Studies* 27(2) (May 1995): 423–48.

Sieder, Rachel. "Honduras: The Politics of Exception and Military Reformism (1972–1978)," *Journal of Latin American Studies* 27(1) (February 1995): 99–127.

Slack, Keith. "Operation Condor and Human Rights: A Report from Paraguay's Archive of Terror," *Human Rights Quarterly* 18(2) (1996): 492–506.

Smallman, Shawn C. "Shady Business: Corruption in the Brazilian Army before 1954," *Latin American Research Review* 32(3) (1997): 39–62.

Smith, Anthony D. "The Origins of Nations," in Geoff Eley and Ronald Grigor Suny, eds., *Becoming National: A Reader*, New York: Oxford University Press, 1996: 106–8.

Sondrol, Paul. "The Paraguayan Military in Transition and the Evolution of Civil-Military Relations," *Armed Forces and Society* 19 (Fall 1992): 105–22.

de Souza Pinheiro, Alvaro (Col.). "Guerrilla in the Brazilian Amazon," Foreign Military Studies Office, Fort Leavenworth, Kansas, July 1995.

———, and Paulo César Miranda Azevedo (Col.). "A Vision of the Brazilian National Security Policy on the Amazon," *Low Intensity Conflict & Law Enforcement* 3(3) (Winter 1994): 387–409.

Special Warfare. The Professional Bulletin of the John F. Kennedy Special Warfare Center and School, PB 93-1, 6(1) (February 1993).

Special Warfare. PB 93-2, 6(2) (May 1993).

Special Warfare. PB 80-94-4, 7(4) (October 1994).

Special Warfare. PB 80-95-4, 8(4) (October 1995).

Special Warfare. "Guatemalan Military Forces Target Crime Wave," PB 80-96-1, 8(4) (January 1996).

Special Warfare. "Reorganization of Mexican Army Emphasizes 'Special Operation Forces,' " PB 80-96-1, 8(4) (January 1996).

Stepan, Alfred. "The New Professionalism of Internal Warfare and Military Role Expansion," in Alfred Stepan, ed., *Authoritarian Brazil: Origins, Policies, and Future*, New Haven: Yale University Press, 1973: 47–65.

Stokes, William S. "Violence as a Power Factor in Latin American Politics," *Western Political Quarterly* 5 (1952): 445–68.

Sznajder, Mario. "Legitimidad y poder político frente a las herencias autoritarias y consolidación democrática en América Latina," *Estudios Interdisciplinarios de América Latina y el Caribe* 5(1) (January–June 1993): 27–55.

Tasso Vasquez de Aquino, Sérgio (Adm.). "Las fuerzas armadas de Brasil y la conyuntura nacional," in Gretchen Small and Dennis Small, eds., *El complot para aniquilar a las fuerzas armadas y a las naciones de Iberoamérica*, 2 vols., México: Ejército Mexicano, Secretaría de la Defensa Nacional, 1994: 397–403.

Távora, Juárez do N. "A segurança nacional, A política e a estratégia," Lecture A-01-53, Escola Superior de Guerra (Brazil), March 14, 1953.

Taylor, William B. "Patterns and Variety in Mexican Village Uprisings," in John E. Kicza, ed., *The Indian in Latin American History: Resistance, Resilience, and Acculturation*, Wilmington, DE: Scholarly Resources, 1993: 109–40.

"Tensa situación en Uruguay por actuación de militares," *La Nación* (Santiago de Chile) (June 12, 1993): 8–9.

Thomson, Guy P. C. "Nineteenth-Century Latin American Caudillismo," in David G. LaFrance and Errol D. Jones, eds., *Latin American Military History: An Annotated Bibliography*, New York: Garland, 1992: 104–87.

Tolleson, Scott D. "Civil-Military Relations in Brazil: The Myth of Tutelary Democracy," Paper delivered at the 1995 meeting of the Latin American Studies Association, Washington, DC, September 28–30, 1995.

Tulchin, Joseph. "Estados Unidos y América Latina en el mundo," in Francisco Rojas Aravena and William C. Smith, eds., *El Cono Sur y las transformaciones globales*, Santiago: FLACSO, North-South Center, CLADDE, 1994: 151–89.

Unión Camilista-Ejército de Liberación Nacional. "Poder popular y nuevo gobierno," January 30, 1990.

Valenzuela, J. Samuel. "Democratic Consolidation in Post-Transitional Settings: Notions, Process, and Facilitating Conditions," in Scott Mainwaring et al., eds., *Issues in Democratic Consolidation: The New South American Democracies in Comparative Perspective*, Notre Dame, IN: University of Notre Dame Press, 1992: 57–104.

Varas, Augusto. "Fuerzas armadas y gobierno militar, Corporativización y politización castrense," *Revista Mexicana de Sociología* 44(2) (1982): 397–411.

Vicat, Luis (Col.). "El desarrollo industrial como empresa militar," in Jean Cazeneuve et al., eds., *Ejército y revolución industrial*, Buenos Aires: Jorge Alvarez Editor, 1964: 25–45.

Waksman, Guillermo. "Uruguay, consagración de la democracia tutelada," *Nueva Sociedad* 102 (July–August 1989): 13–19.

Waller, Douglas. "Running a School for Dictators," *Newsweek* (August 9, 1993): 34–37.

Walter, Knut, and Philip J. Williams. "The Military and Democratization in El Salvador," *Journal of Inter-American Studies and World Affairs* 35(1) (1993): 39–87.

Weinstein, Martin. "Uruguay: The Legislature and the Reconstitution of Democracy," in David Close, ed., *Legislatures and the New Democracies in Latin America*, Boulder, CO: Lynne Rienner, 1995: 137–50.

Welch, Claude E., Jr. "Military Disengagement from Politics: Paradigms, Processes, or Random Events," *Armed Forces and Society* 18(3) (Spring 1992): 323–42.

Wolf, Charles. "Political Effects of Military Programs: Some Indications from Latin America," *Orbis* 8 (1965): 871–89.

Wolf, Eric R., and Edward Hansen. "Caudillo Politics: A Structural Analysis," *Comparative Studies of Society and History* 9 (1967): 168–79.

Woodward, Margaret L. "The Spanish Army and the Loss of America, 1810–1824," *Hispanic American Historical Review* 48(4) (November 1968): 586–607.

"The World in a Funhouse Mirror." *NACLA Report* (November–December 1983): 2–34.

Wyckoff, Theodore. "The Role of the Military in Contemporary Latin American Politics," *Western Political Quarterly* 12 (September 1960): 745–63.

Yanes Quintero, Hernán. "El nacionalismo militar y la agenda cívico-militar en América del Sur en los años 90," *Cuadernos de Nuestra América* 11(21) (January–June 1994): 82–106.

Ycaza, Patricio. "Seguridad nacional y derechos humanos," in *Los derechos humanos: El caso ecuatoriano*, Quito: Editorial El Conejo, 1985: 259–79.

Youngers, Coletta. "Peru under Scrutiny: Human Rights and U.S. Drug Policy," Issue Brief #5, Washington Office on Latin America, Washington, DC (July 13, 1992): 24–29.

Yurrita, Alfonso. "The Transition from Military to Civilian Rule in Guatemala," in Louis W. Goodman et al., eds., *The Military and Democracy: The Future of Civil-Military Relations in Latin America*, Lexington, MA: Lexington Books, 1990: 75–90.

Zabala, Carlos María (Gen.). "Una oportunidad histórica," *Revista del Suboficial* 611 (March–April 1994): 24–25.

Zagorski, Paul. "Civil-Military Relations and Argentine Democracy: The Armed Forces under the Menem Government," *Armed Forces and Society* 20(3) (1994): 423–37.

Zalaquett, José. "Confronting Human Rights Violations Committed by Former Governments: Principles Applicable and Political Constraints," *Persona y Sociedad* 6(2–3) (1990): 51–80.

Zaverucha, Jorge. "The Degree of Military Political Autonomy during the Spanish, Argentine, and Brazilian Transitions," *Journal of Latin American Studies* 25 (1993): 283–99.

Zirker, Daniel. "Democracy and the Military in Brazil: Elite Accommodation in Cases of Torture," *Armed Forces and Society* 14 (Summer 1988): 587–605.

Index

Acción Democrática (AD, Venezuela), 101, 146, 173
Act of Bogotá (1948), 149
Act of Chapultepec (1945), 143
Adelantado, 1
Agency for International Development (AID), 171
Aguirre Cerda, Pedro, 128
Aguirre y Salinas, Osmín (Col.), 135
Alessandri, Arturo, 82–85, 126
Alianza Popular Revolucionaria Americana (APRA, Peru), 90–91, 173
Allende, Salvador, 130, 188, 241
Alliance for Progress, 162, 165–67, 168, 176, 177, 180, 199, 266
Altamirano, Luis (Gen.), 83
Alvear, Marcelo T., 117
Amnesty: use in Spain and colonies, 9, 19
Amnesty laws (Latin America, 1978–1993), 217
Antipolitics (and military governments): 186–92, 254; and labor organizations, 254–55; and "transition" to civilian governments (1978–1993), 213–21
Aragón, 2
Aramburu, Pedro (Gen.), 125
Arana, Francisco (Col.), 156
Aranda, Conde de, 9–11
Araujo, Arturo, 132
Arbenz, Jacobo, 155, 157, 158, 161
Areche, José Antonio de, 18
Arévalo, Juan José, 147, 155–56, 173
Argentina: antipolitics, 119–22; *caudillo* wars, 39–40, 50–51; civil-military relations, 115–25; Colegio Militar, 115; Conservative party, 115; constitutions, (1853) 188, (1949) 122; coups, (1930) 117, (1943) 120–21, (1944) 120, (1951–1955) 120, 122, (1966) 191; Ejército Revolucionario del Pueblo (ERP), 240; elections, 115–16, 118, 119; factions and interservice rivalries, 122–25; labor organizations and military, 122–25; Legión Cívica Argentina, 118; military professionalization, 115–16; Montoneros, 240; Palomar land scandal, 119; Peronismo, 121–25; Radical party, 115–17; rebellion (1905), 115; *semana trágica* (1919), 116; War of the Triple Alliance, 47, 48–52, 112; Yacimientos Petrolíferos Fiscales (YPF), 116
Argentine Anticommunist Alliance (AAA), 189
Arias, Oscar, 205
Army Special Forces School (U.S., Fort Bragg), 170
Army War College (U.S.), 177
Artigas, José, 34
Arze, José Antonio, 108
Atkins, G. Pope, 179
Audiencia, 7
Ayacucho: battle of (1824), 36
Ayala, Eusebio, 112
Aylwin, Patricio, 185, 243

Balaguer, Joaquín, 178
Ballivián, Hugo (Gen.), 110
Ballivián, José, 47
Balmaceda, José Manuel, 80
Banditry: in Spain, 11–12
Baquedano, Manuel, 55
Baron, Victor Allan, 95
Barquín, Ramón (Col.), 158
Barrios, Justo Rufino, 48
Barros Ortiz, Tobías, 74
Basadre, Jorge, 43, 58
Batista, Fulgencio, 71, 102, 158–60, 167, 195, 256
Bay of Pigs invasion (Cuba, 1961), 161, 165
Benavides, Oscar (Gen.), 86, 90–92, 102, 103
Bennett, Juan Pablo (Gen.), 83
Berger, Harry (a.k.a. Ewert, Arthur), 95
Berguño Meneses, Jorge (Brig. Gen.), 128
Billinghurst, Guillermo, 86, 90
Bismarck, Otto von, 70, 78–79
Blanche Espejo, Bartolomé (Lt. Col.), 83
Boer War, 77
Bogotá Conference (1948), 143, 149
Bolívar, Simón, 32–34, 35, 40, 41, 63
Bolivia: civil-military relations, 106–11; constitution (1938), 108, 111; coups, (1936–1939) 107–8, (1943) 109, (1964)

190; economic depression (1930), 106–7; Escuela de Guerra, 67; Escuela Militar, 106; guerrilla movements, 195; Indian Congress (1945), 109; Indian uprisings, 106, 110; International Tin Control Scheme (1931), 106; Jesús de Machaca uprising (1921), 106; military professionalization, 67–68; "military socialism," 108–10; Movimiento Nacionalista Revolucionario (MNR), 101, 109, 110, 145; Social Defense Law, 107; Uncía mine strike (1923), 106; War of the Pacific, 52–58; wars against Chile, 45, 47, 52–58; Yacimientos Petrolíferos Fiscales de Bolivia (YPFB), 108
Bosch, Juan, 175, 178
Bourbon reforms (Spain, Spanish America), 10, 17, chap. 2 passim
Bourbon rulers (Spain): and colonial rebellions, 16–20; consolidation of power, 7–13; enlightened despotism, 12; fusion of military and civil authority, 7–13
Boves, Tomás, 33
Braden, Spruille, 122
Brazil: Amnesty Law (1979), 217; civil-military relations, 92–96; Clube Militar, 93; Communist party, 95; constitution (1934), 95; coup (1964), 186–87, 190, 192; elections (1926, 1930), 94; Escuela Superior de Guerra (ESG), 151, 169, 177; Estado Nôvo (1937), 95; Febianos (FEB) in Italy, 186; French military mission, 92–94; guerrilla movements, 166; independence, 43; Lei do Ventre Livre (1871), 51; military professionalization, 92–97; military reforms (eighteenth century), 20–22; National Commission for the Repression of Communism, 95; National Security Tribunal (TSN), 95; Republic created (1889), 52; Rio Conference (1942), 119, 141; security agenda (1990s), 271; slavery, 51–52; torture, 95; Vargas government, 95–96; War of the Triple Alliance, 47, 48–52, 112
Bucaram, Abdalá, 216
Buenos Aires Peace Conference (1935), 108
Bulnes, Manuel, 47
Bulnes Pinto, Gonzalo, 82
Busch, Germán (Maj.), 102, 107, 108, 110
Bush, George, 271
Bushnell, David, 43

Cabañas, Lucio, 166
Cáceres, Andrés (Gen.), 58, 89
Cadiz Constitution (1812), 24
Calderón, Rafael, 147
Camacho, Eliodoro (Gen.), 57
Campero, Narciso (Gen.), 56
Camps, Ramón (Gen.), 239–41
Captaincies-general: in Spain, 7–8; replacing viceroyalties, 7
Caracas Company, 17
Caracas Declaration (1954), 157, 176
Cardenas, Lázaro, 108
Cardona, Edgardo (Col.), 149
Carías Andino, Tiburcio (Gen.), 102
"Caribbean Basin initiative," 203
Caribbean Legion, 147–49, 160
Carlos II of Spain, 4–6
Carlos III of Spain, 9–16; amnesties, 9; *reales ordenanzas*, 10–12
Carlos IV of Spain, 22–24
Carlos VI (Austrian Habsburg), 6
Carrera, José Miguel, 34
Cartagena: battle of (1741), 13–14
Carter, Jimmy, 168, 180, 192, 206
Carvalho, Leitão de, 92
Carvalho e Melo, Sebastião João de (Marqués de Pombal), 20–22
Castaneda Castro, Salvador (Gen.), 135
Castelo Branco, Humberto de Alencar, 95
Castilla, Ramón, 34
Castillo, Ramón (Gen.), 119–21
Castillo Armas, Carlos (Col.), 156
Castro, Fidel, 159, 161, 166, 167, 195, 264–65
Castro, Raúl, 265
Castro Morán, Mariano (Lt. Col.), xxi
Catavi workers' strife (1942), 109
Catholic Church: and Conquest, 2–3; in Cuba, 236; Inquisition, 2; subverted by Marxists, 238
Caubarrere, Sergio H. (Col.), xvii
Caudillos and *caudillismo*, 64; after independence, 33–43; definition, 39
Caxias, Luís, 50, 51
Central America: civil wars (1980s), 197–99
Central American Defense Council (CONDECA), 170
Central American Federation (1824–1838), 28
Central Intelligence Agency (CIA), 156–58, 165
Cevallos, Pedro de, 21
Chaco War (1932–1935), 68, 105–13
Chaves, Federico, 114
Chiang Kai-shek, 150
Child, Jack, 141
Chile: Academia de Guerra, 80; Amnesty Law (1978), 217; anticommunism, 127–31; Captaincy-General, 17;

carabineros, 84–85, 89; *chilenidad* campaign (1941), 128; civil-military relations, 56, 80–85, 125–31; civil war (1891), 81; Communist party, 129; Constitution (1925), 84; coups, (1924–25) 82, (1973) 188, 192; DINA (secret police), 214; elections, 84, and military, 82, 127–28; Escuela de Clases, 80; Escuela Militar, 80; foreign training missions, 72; labor organizations and military, 84; La Coruña strike (1925), 84; Law for the Permanent Defense of Democracy (1948), 129; Liga Militar, 82; military industries, 128; military professionalization, 80–85; militia, 126–27; naval mutiny (1931), 127; Popular Front government (1938–1941), 127; Popular Unity government (1970–1973), 241; Prussian influence in army, 80–85; Radical party, 129; Rettig Commission, 241–42; San Gregorio nitrate works strike, 82; War of the Pacific, 52–58; wars (1836–1841), 47

Civil-military relations, xii–xvii, 256–57; after independence in Latin America, 36–43; changes as result of counterinsurgency (after 1959), 180–86; civic action, 181; debt crisis (1980s), 196–97; definition, xiii; degrees of military autonomy, xiii; foreign missions in nineteenth century, 63–95; in 1990s, 221, 269–76; in colonial Brazil, 20–22; in Spanish American colonies, 13–20; key issues, xiii, 255–57; military reformism, 79; military subordination to civilian control, xiii; variations within Latin America, 105, 115 (*see also by country*)

Clément, Paul (Gen.), 86

Cold War, 155–58, 173, 175, 199, 266; beginnings in Latin America, 139; impact in Latin America, 236–37

Colombia: *caudillos*, 37–38; civil-military relations, 185, 234–35; Colombian Revolutionary Armed Forces (FARC), 204; guerrilla movements, 196, 203, 264; labor organizations and military, 256; Ministry of Defense (Internet Website), 260; National Liberation Army (ELN), 203; national security legislation, 234–35; war with Peru, 90

Colônia do Sacramento, 21

Colonial rebellions, 16–20

Columbus, Christopher, xix, 1–2

Comblin, José, 190

Committee of Santa Fe, 197, 200, 203; *Santa Fé II* Report, 204

CONDECA. *See* Central American Defense Council

Condorcanqui, José Gabriel. See Túpac Amaru II

Constabularies: U.S.-influenced in Caribbean, 70–72

Contadora Group, 200, 205

Contras (Nicaragua), 199, 204

Corregidores, 17

Costa e Silva, Artur da, 95

Costa Rica: civil-military relations, 147–49; Constitution (1949) and abolition of army, 148; Partido de Liberación Nacional, 173; Partido Vanguardia Popular (Communist party), 147

Cottrell, Jesse S., 67

Council for Inter-American Security, 203

Council of Castile, 9

Council of the Indies, 5

Counterinsurgency, 179–86

Coups d'état, 172, 175; causes, 173–75, 189; failed coups (1978–1993), 216; historical pattern in Latin America, 173–74. *See also by country*

Criollos: in colonial bureaucracy, 15; in colonial militia, 15–16

Croix, Teodoro de, 20

Cuba: British control of Havana, 14; Captaincy-General, 14; civil-military relations (before 1959), 158–59; colonial defense, 13–14; *foco* model of Revolution, 160, 167–68; military reforms (1765), 14; navy mutiny (1957), 158; Revolution (1956–1959), 111, 159–60, 184, 266; separation from Spain, xx; support for guerrilla movements in Latin America, 160–62

Cuban missile crisis (1962), 161

Daza, Hilarión (Gen.), 53, 56

Debray, Regis, 167

Declaration of Panama (1939), 140

Defense Ministerial of the Americas (1995), 266

Dellepiane, Luís (Gen.), 116–17

"Democratization": transitions to "democracy" and, 206–13

Desvoyes, Marcel (Gen.), 88

Díaz, Porfirio (Gen.), 59, 64, 76

Díaz de Medina, Francisco Tadeo, 19

Dios Vial, General Juan de, 68

"Disappearances": as policy in Spain, 10; under military governments in Latin America, 227, 229, 230

Documento de la grandeza (1676), 4

Dominican Republic: armed forces,178–79; civil-military relations, 178–79; coup (1963), 176; Partido Revolucionario Dominicano (PRD), 178; torture, 179; Trujillo regime, 178; U.S. intervention (1965), 178

Dorfman, Ariel, 192
Draper, William (Gen.), 169
Duarte, Napoleón, 200
Dulles, Allen, 156
Dulles, John Foster, 156, 157

Echeverría, Luis, 182
Economic Commission for Latin America, 196
Ecuador: Armed Forces Joint Command (Internet Website), 261; coups (1925–1937), 75; military regime (1972–1978), 189, 207; obligatory military service laws, 73; Quito tax protests (1765), 17–18; transition to civilian government, 202; war with Peru (1995), 276–78
Eisenhower, Dwight D., 156–58, 161, 169, 266
Eisenhower, Milton, 157
Ejército Revolucionario del Pueblo (ERP, Argentina), 240
Elections: presidential, by decade (Latin America), 174
El Mozote Massacre (El Salvador), 244
El Salvador: amnesty law (1987), 217; armed forces' response to UN Truth Commission, 247; Atlacatl Battalion, 244; Chilean military mission, 131; civil-military relations, 131–36; Communist influence, 132–35; constitutions, (1886) 134, (1938) 133, (1944) 134, (1948) 135, (1950) 135; coups, (1931) 102, 132, (1961) 172, (1979) 216; El Mozote Massacre, 244; Escuela Politécnica, 131; FMLN, 219, 220n. (d), 244–45, 247; guerrilla movements, 195; La Matanza Massacre (1932), 102, 132–33; military professionalization, 131–32; Partido Revolucionario de Unificación Democrático (PRUD), 135; Pro-Patria party, 133; war with Guatemala (1906), 73, 131
Enemark, W. A. (Brig. Gen.), 176
Enríquez, Alberto (Gen.), 102
Ensenada, Marqués de, 14
Eslava, Sebastián de (Lt. Gen.), 8
Espadas Burgos, Manuel, 22
Estigarribia, José Félix (Marshal), 102, 107, 112–13
Estrada Cabrera, Manuel, 65
Ewert, Arthur. *See* Berger, Harry

Facultades extraordinarias, 33
Farrell, Edelmiro (Gen.), 121
Faupel, Wilhelm (Gen.), 89
Febres Cordero, León, 216
Felipe V of Spain, 7–8
Ferdinand VI of Spain, 14
Ferdinand VII of Spain, 24, 32, 33
Figueres, José "Pepe," 147, 148, 173
Figueroa Larraín, Emiliano, 84
Fijo (garrison), 13–15
Filísola, Vicente, 44
Flores, Juan José, 28, 34, 38
Flores, Venancio (Gen.), 48, 50, 51
Foco theory. *See also* Guevara, Ernesto "Che"
Fonseca, Hermes da, 92
Forjando patria, 64
France: Commune (1871), 77; Ecole Supérieure de Guerre, 78; Franco-Prussian War, 77–78; military missions, (in Brazil) 78, 92–96, (in Guatemala) 65, 78, (in Peru) 78, 85–92; military sales to Latin America, 177; Revolution (1789), 9, and Spanish American independence, 22–24
Franco, Francisco, 101
Franco, Rafael (Col.), 102, 112–13
Franco-Prussian War, 76
Frei Montalva, Eduardo, 188, 231, 243
Frente Farabundo Martí para la Liberación Nacional (FMLN, El Salvador), 219, 220n. (d), 244–45, 247
Frota, Ivan Moacyr da (Gen.), 247
FSLN (Sandinista National Liberation Front), 167, 195
Fueros: definition, 1; in Brazil (*foros*), 21; in Spanish America, 14–15; military, 8
Fujimori, Alberto, 216

Gallardo, José (Gen.), 277
Galtieri, Leopoldo Fortunato (Gen.), xxiii, 216
Gamarra, Agustín, 33, 34, 47
Gamelin, Maurice (Gen.), 93
Gamio, Manuel, xix, 66
Garay, Eugenio Alejandro (Gen.), 81
García Meza, Luis (Gen.), 216
Giroldi, Moisés (Maj.), 216
Godoy, Manuel, 23–24
Góes Monteiro, Pedro Aurélio de, 94, 96
Goldwert, Marvin, 123
Goltz, Colmar von der, 68
Gomes, Eduardo, 95
Gómez, Juan Vicente, 72, 74
González Videla, Gabriel, 129
Good Neighbor Policy, 141, 142
Goulart, João, 186, 190
Graf Spee (German battleship), 140
Gramajo, Héctor A. (Gen.), 216
Gran Colombia, 28
Grenada, 192
Grove, Marmaduke (Maj.), 83
Grüber Odremán, Hernán (Adm.), 247
Guatemala: agrarian reform, 155–58; Amnesty Law (1985), 217; civil-

military relations, 65–67; constitutions (1965, 1983), 188; Escuela Politécnica, 65, 66; guerrilla movements, 180, 196; Kaibil special forces (Internet Website), 262; labor organizations and military, 155–58; Ley Constitutiva del Ejército (1936), 66; military professionalization, 65–67, 97; revolution (1944–1954), 155–58; U.S. intervention, 155–58; war with El Salvador, 73, 131
Güemes, Martín, 34
Guerrilla movements, 166–67, 179–86, 195, 267. *See also by country*
Guevara, Ernesto "Che," 111, 159, 166–67, 184, 191; *Guerrilla Warfare*, 160–61
Guise, Martin, 63
Gulf Oil Corporation, 170

Habsburg rulers (Spain), 3–9
Havana: loss to British (1762), 14
Haya de la Torre, Víctor Raúl, 90, 147
Hayek, F. A., 243–44
Hernández Martínez, Maximiliano (Gen.), 102, 132–34
Honduras: civil-military relations, 175; and *contras*, 204, 205; coups, 175, 176; military regime (1972–1982), 207
Human rights: in Argentina, 239–41; in Chile, 241–44; in Colombia, 239; in El Salvador, 244–46; U.S. policy, 168, 180, 198; violations by military governments, 227–50
Huntington, Samuel, 211

Ibáñez del Campo, Carlos, 80, 82–85, 126
Iglesias, Miguel, 58
Imaz, José Luis de, 120
Indian Congress (Bolivia, 1945), 109
Inquisition (Spain), 2, 22, 231
Inter-American Defense Board (IADB), 136, 161, 168; creation (1942), 119, 141; goals, 141–42, 144
Inter-American Defense College, 161
Inter-American Development Bank, 270
Inter-American Human Rights Commission, 238
Inter-American Military Cooperation Act (1946–1948), 142
Inter-American Police Academy (Canal Zone), 171
Inter-American Treaty of Reciprocal Assistance. *See* Rio Treaty
Internal Development and Security Act (1961), 162
International Military Education and Training (IMET), 171, 266
International Monetary Fund (IMF): role in Latin America, 196
International Petroleum Corporation, 170
International Tin Control Scheme, 106
Iturbide, Agustín de, 34

Jesuits: ejected from Spain, 9
Johnson, Lyndon, 168, 178
Juan José of Austria, 4–5
Justo, Agustín (Gen.), 101, 116–18

Kennedy, John F., 161, 165, 166, 168, 171, 176
Khrushchev, Nikita, 162
Kissinger, Henry, 192, 198
Kissinger Commission, 198
Klein, Herbert, 110
Klinger, Bertholdo, 92, 95
Korean War, 151, 155, 174
Körner, Emil, 80–85
Krupp armaments, 79
Kundt, Hans (Col.), 67–68, 107

Labor organizations and legislation, 103–4
Lacalle, Luis Alberto, 214–15
Laiño, Aníbal Ulises (Gen.), xi, xvii, xxii, 222, 253, 259, 281
La Mar, José de, 34
La Matanza Massacre (El Salvador, 1932), 102, 132–33
Landazábal Reyes, Fernando (Gen.), 231
LaRouche, Lyndon H., 246
Lavalleja, José Antonio, 47
League of Nations, 112
Leal Buitrago, Francisco, 234
Leguía, Augusto B., 89
Lei do Ventre Livre (Brazil, 1871), 51
Lemus, José María (Lt. Col.), 135
Lend-Lease program, 119, 140–41, 143
Leopold I of Austria, 6
Levine, Robert, 96
Lleras Camargo, Alberto, 144
Logias (secret societies within military), 72; General San Martín (Argentina), 116; GOS (Chile), 125; GOU (Argentina), 119–20, 121; Linea Recta (Chile), 125; PUMA (Chile), 125; RADEPA (Bolivia), 109; Sol de Mayo (Argentina), 123
Lonardi, Eduardo (Gen.), 125
López Contreras, Eleazar (Gen.), 102
López de Santa Anna, Antonio, 35
López Jordán, Ricardo, 51
López Reyes, Walter (Gen.), xxii
Louis XIV of France, 5, 6
Louis XVI of France, 15
Louis-Napoleon, 77
Lozada Uribe, Mario (Capt.), 169
Lucas García, B. (Gen.), 216
Luther, Martin, 3
Lynch, John, 17

M-19 (Colombia), 264
McAlister, Lyle N., 15
McCaffrey, Barry R. (Gen.), 273
McCarthy, Joseph, 155
McGill, Samuel (Col.), 74
Machado, Gerardo, 71
Maligne, A. (Lt. Col.), 68
Malvinas/Falkland Islands war (1982), 205
Mann, Thomas, 178
Mann Doctrine (1964), 168
Mao Tse-tung, 150
Marguerye, Paúl de, 86
Mariana of Austria, 4
Marie Louise of Orléans, 5
Marshall Plan, 151
Martí, Agustín Farabundo, 132
Martínez, Domingo (Gen.), 119
Martínez, Pedro Pablo (Gen.), 63, 90
Masterson, Daniel, 90
Mazorca (Argentine secret police), 39
Medina Franzani, Ernesto (Col.), 68
Mejía Víctores, Oscar H. (Gen.), 216
Melgar Castro, Juan A. (Gen.), 216
Melgarejo, Mariano, 52, 56
Menem, Carlos, 214
Menéndez, Andrés Ignacio (Gen.), 133, 134
Menéndez, José Ascencio (Col.), 133
Mexico: civil-military relations, 169; colonial rebellions, 17; debt crisis (1980s), 196; guerrilla movements, 166; independence, 32; military professionalization, 74; Revolution (1910), 182; Tlatelolco Massacre (1968), 182
Military Assistance Advisory Group (MAAG), 171
Military Assistance Program (MAP), 152, 171
Military jurisdiction over civilians: in Spain, 11–13; in Spanish colonies, 14–15
Militarylore, xii, xiv, 188, 228, 253, 257
Militia: *criollo cuerpos de patricios*, 19; and *fueros*, 14–15; in Brazil, 20–21, 92; in Peru, 19; in Spain, 8, 12–13; in Spanish colonies, 14–16
Minas Gerais revolt (1798), 21
Miranda, Francisco de, 35
Mita, 19
Mitre, Bartolomé, 40, 48–50
Mitterrand, François, 271
Molina, Juan Bautista (Gen.), 118
Moltke, Helmuth von, 76, 78
Monroe Doctrine, 156, 276
Montejo, Víctor, 192
Montoneros, 240
Morales Bermúdez, Francisco, xxii
Morillo, Pablo (Gen.), 32, 37
Morínigo, Higinio, 113
Mosconi, Enrique (Gen.), 116
Movimiento Nacionalista Revolucionario (MNR, Bolivia), 101, 109, 110, 145
Munro, Dana, 43
Mussolini, Benito, 101, 116

Napoleon, 16, 32, 207
Napoleonic Wars, 23–24
Narcotics (drug) trafficking, 202, 203, 267, 273
National Bipartisan Commission on Central America. *See* Kissinger Commission
National Endowment for Democracy, 198–99
National Liberation Army (ELN, Colombia), 203
National Security Doctrine (NSD): and broadening concept of "security," 183–84; and expansion of military intelligence functions, 184; and human rights, 236–39; in Brazil, 187–88; origins in foreign military missions, 69
Neff, Francisco (Adm.), 83
Nelson, Horatio (Adm.), 16
Neoliberal policies: impact in Latin America, 196–97
New Castile, 9–10
Nicaragua: *contras*, 199, 204; election (1990), 200, 203, 204; FSLN, 167, 195; guerrilla movements, 195; Rama Road, 140; revolution (1979), 195; U.S. policy toward, 204–5; World War II and, 140
Nixon, Richard, 169, 192
Nixon Doctrine, 168, 192
Noriega, Manuel (Gen.), 205–6, 247
North Atlantic Treaty Organization (NATO), 144, 154
Novoa Fuentes, Oscar (Gen.), 126
Nunn, Frederick, 83

Obando, José María, 35
Obediencia debida, 235–36
Obregón, Alvaro, 274
O'Donnell, Guillermo, 255
Odría, Manuel (Gen.), 146, 149, 159
Olate, Otilio, 147, 148
Onganía, Juan (Lt. Gen.), 214
Operation Just Cause, 276
Operation PBSUCCESS, 157
O'Phelan Godoy, Scarlet, 18
Ordenanza de Intendentes (1782, 1786, 1803), 9
Orellana, José María (Gen.), 65
Organization of American States (OAS), 138, 144, 261, 267, 280

Oribe, Manuel, 47
Ortiz, Roberto, 118
Osorio, Mariano (Gen.), 32
Osorio, Oscar (Lt. Col.), 135, 186
Ovando Candía, Alfredo (Gen.), 111

Páez, Federico, 102
Páez, José Antonio, 28, 33, 35, 41
Palleja, León (Col.), 42
Panama: Canal Treaty, 170; Canal Zone, 152, 170, 171; constitution (1972), 188; Contadora Group, 205; coup (1968), 168; military regimes (1968–1981), 186; Operation Just Cause, 276; Panama Defense Force, 206; U.S. invasion (1989), 205–6
Paraguay: Azules party, 113; Brazilian occupation, 50; civil-military relations, 111–14; Colorado party, 113–14; constitution (1940), 113; coups and rebellions, 113–14; elections, 113; Escuela Militar, 112; Escuela Superior de Guerra, 112; Febreristas, 113–14; labor and military, 113; military professionalization, 112–13; Nuevo Orden Nacionalista Revolucionario, 113
Paraguayan War. *See* War of the Triple Alliance
Pardo, José, 89
Patria y Libertad (Chile), 189
Patrón Costas, Robustiano, 119, 120
Paz Estenssoro, Víctor, 110, 175, 190
Paz García, Policarpio (Gen.), 216
Peacekeeping missions (U.S., UN), 267–69
Peace of Basle (1795), 23
Pearl Harbor: attack on, 119, 141
Peixoto, Floriano, 92
Peñaloza, Angel V., 40
Peñaranda, Enrique (Gen.), 107, 109
Pereira de Sousa, Washington Luis, 94–95
Pérez, Carlos Andrés, 216
Pérez, Louis, 71, 159
Pérez Jimenez, Marcos, 146, 148, 154
Perón, Juan Domingo, 118, 121, 122
Peronismo, 122–25, 257
Perry, William J., 266–67
Persian Gulf War, 269
Peru: Amnesty Law (1995), 217; APRA, 90–91, 173; army (Internet Website), 278; Centro de Altos Estudios Militares (CAEM), 147, 151, 169, 177; civil-military relations, 85–91; Código de Justicia Militar (1898), 86; constitutions, (1856) 213, (1920) 89, (1933) 91; coups, (1914) 86–87, (1919) 89, (1968), 190; Escuela Militar (Chorrillos), 86, 88, 146; Escuela Superior de Guerra, 86, 88; Guardia Civil, 89; guerrilla movements, 195; Internal Security Law (Odría), 146; Ley de Situación Militar, 88; military professionalization, 85–91; navy, 86, 89, 147; *oncenio*, 89–90; Sendero Luminoso, 170, 195; War of the Pacific, 52–58; wars, 47, 90, 277
Peru-Bolivia Confederation, 45, 50
Philip of Anjou (Felipe V), 5, 6
Piar, Manuel (Gen.), 33, 35
Picado, Teodoro, 148
Piérola, Nicolás, 57
Pinochet Ugarte, Augusto, 130, 205
Pombal, Marqués de, 20–22
Portales, Diego, 50
Portugal: Brazilian colony, 20–22; commercial policies, 21
Potosí: *mita* at, 19
Pragmática: on expulsion of Moors from Spain (1502), 1; on public order and *papeles sediciosos* (1774), 11–12
Prat, Arturo (Capt.), 55
Prestes, Luis Carlos, 93
Prieto Vial, Joaquín, 35
Primo de Rivera, Miguel (Gen.), 70, 101, 116
"Prolonged popular war," 167
Pronunciamiento, 4–5
"Protected democracy," xiv, 213–23
Protestant Reformation, 2
Pumacahua (*cacique*), 36

Quintanilla, Carlos (Gen.), 108
Quito uprising (1765), 17–18

Ramírez, Pedro (Gen.), 120
Rawson, Arturo (Brig. Gen.), 120
Reagan, Ronald, 192, 197–204
Reagan Doctrine, 198–99
Reconquista (reconquest), xxi, 1–2, 231
Regimes of exception ("emergency powers"), 38, 40, 215, 222, 225n.43, 232–33; martial law (El Salvador, 1932), 133; state of siege, 174–75, 185
Repartimiento, 19
Rettig Commission, 241–42
Revista Militar de Chile, 80
Ricla, Conde de, 14–15
Riego, Rafael (Col.), 32
Rio Conference (1942), 119, 141
Ríos Montt, José Efraín (Gen.), 216
Rio Treaty (1947), 136, 144, 146, 202, 236, 261; invocation by Costa Rica (1948), 148
Riots (in Spain): (1699–1700), 6; (1766), 9, 11; (1788–1791), 22
Riva-Agüero, José de la, 35
Rivabella, Omar, 192
Rivadavia, Bernardino, 35

Roca, Julio (Gen.), 59, 64, 115
Rockefeller, Nelson, 192
Rockefeller Report (1969), 168, 191
Rodó, José Enrique, xix, xx
Rodríguez, Andrés (Gen.), 219
Rojas Pinilla, Gustavo (Gen.), 139, 154, 158, 256
Romero, Arturo, 134–35
Romero Bosque, Pío, 131
Roosevelt, Franklin D., 119
Roosevelt, Theodore, 156
Rosas, Juan Manuel de, 39, 51, 207
Royal Dutch Shell Oil Co., 107
Rumi Maqui: revolt (1914), 88
Russo-Japanese War, 77

Saínz, Juan Obdulio (Gen.), 272
Salamanca, Daniel, 101, 106
Salaverry, Felipe Santiago, 33
Salazar, Oliveira, 96
Sánchez Cerro, Luis M. (Lt. Col.), 90, 102
Sandinista National Liberation Front (FSLN, Nicaragua), 167, 195
Sandino, Augusto César, 12
Sanguinetti, Julio María, 214
San Martín, José de, xviii, 32, 35, 38, 63, 185
Santa Cruz, Andrés, 28, 33, 45, 47
Santa María, Domingo, 80
Santander, Francisco de Paula, 39, 41
Sardá, José (Gen.), 39
Sarmiento, Domingo, 40
Sarney, José, 270
Savio, Manuel (Col.), 119
Seineldín, Mohamed Alí (Col.), 216, 246, 247
Sendero Luminoso (Peru), 170, 195
Seregni, Liber (Gen.), 215
Serrano, Jorge, 216
Seven Years War, 9, 14
Siles, Hernán, 106
Silva, Golbery do Couto e (Gen.), 187
Silva Bernardes, Artur da, 93
Situados, 15
Small Wars Manual (U.S. Marine Corps), 208–9
Social Democratic party (Germany), 78–80
Solano López, Carlos, 48–50, 51
Somoza García, Anastasio, 71, 102, 140, 147; Somoza dynasty, 167, 195
Sotomayor, Emilio (Col.), 80
Souza Pinheiro, Alvaro de (Col.), 166, 270
Sovereignty: and armed forces missions, xxii; definition, xxii; erosion of (1990s), 258–60
Soviet Union, 168, 169, 197, 199, 201, 203; collapse of, 199–200; policies in Latin America, 197–98; support for wars of national liberation, 170, 197–98, 240
Spain: administrative reforms, 5–13; *armada real*, 8; banditry, 9–13; civil-military relations, 6–13; colonies in Americas, 13–20; Constitution (1812), 230; Counter-Reformation and, 3; *documento de la grandeza* (1676), 4; *fueros*, 1, 2; guerrilla warfare, 24; Habsburgs and, 2–6; Inquisition, 2, 22, 231; navy and naval reforms, 8, 14; *ordenanzas* (1768), 10; participation in North American Revolution, 15; persecution of Jews, Muslims, gypsies, 2; political instability, 9–10; *reconquista* (reconquest), xxi, 1–2, 231; riots, 6, 9, 11, 22; royal instruction (1784), 12; war against French Convention (1793–1795), 16; "war of independence" against France (1808–1814), 24; warrior-priest tradition, 1
Spanish America: colonial defense system and policies, 13–16; independence movements (1810–1825), 32–39; militia, 13–16. *See also by country*
Spanish-American War (1898), 47
SPOCS (*situaciones potencialmente críticas*), xxii, 253, 259
Standard Oil Co., 107, 108
State of siege. *See* Regimes of exception
Stroessner, Alfredo (Gen.), 114
Sucre, José de, 33, 36, 43
Suffrage (Latin America): constitutional requirements, 208–9; female, 208; presidential elections, 174
Summit of the Americas (Miami, 1994), 266

Tabernillas, Francisco (Gen.), 158
Tamayo, Franz, 107
Tasso Vasquez de Aquino, Sérgio (Adm.), 247
Távora, Juarez, 94
Tejada Sorzano, José Luis, 107
Tenentes: in Brazil, 93
Terra, Gabriel, 102
Terrorism: state, 185
"Tordesillas line," 13
Toro, David (Col.), 101, 107
Torrelio Villa, Celso (Gen.), 216
Torture: constitutional prohibitions against, 248–49; in independence wars, 36–37; in military governments, 123, 185–86; in Spanish colonies, 19–20
Trafalgar: loss of Spanish fleet (1804), 16
Travasso, Mario (Col.), 187
Treaty of Ancón (1883), 55, 58
Treaty of Rastadt-Baden (1714), 7

Treaty of San Ildefonso (1796), 16
Treaty of Utrecht (1713), 7
Trujillo, Rafael, 71, 102, 159, 175, 178
Truman, Harry, 142, 150
Truman Doctrine, 143
Truth commissions: in Latin America, 227–28
Túpac Amaru II (Condorcanqui, José Gabriel), 18–20, 36
Turbay, Julio César, 231

Ubico, Jorge (Gen.), 65, 66, 102, 136
United Fruit Company, 65, 66, 155, 156
United Nations: creation, 144; peacekeeping missions, 261–62; Truth Commission in El Salvador, 244–46, 247
United States: antinarcotics policies, 202; civic action (military), 180–81; Color Plans for Latin America, 141; congressional opposition to military assistance, 180; containment doctrine, 156, 199; counterinsurgency programs, 167–72, 177, 179–84; Foreign Assistance Act (1961), 143; foreign military assistance programs, 180–84; human rights policies (Carter administration), 168, 180; Internal Security and Development Act (1961), 162; Military Assistance Advisory Group (MAAG), 171; Military Assistance Program (MAP), 152; military assistance and sales to Latin America, 152, 171–72; Mutual Defense Act (1949), 150; Mutual Defense Assistance Agreements (MDAAs), 151; Mutual Security Act (1951), 151; naval mission in Peru, 89, 141; NSC-68 (1950), 150; NSC-141 (1952), 151; policies toward military coups (1961–1964), 175–76; regional security policies, 197–202, 264–67; response to Cuban Revolution, 160–62, 165–70; rollback doctrine, 156, 199; School of the Americas, 170–71, 265; SOUTHCOM, 153, 170, 266; war on drugs, 273–75
Universal Declaration of Human Rights, 244
Urdanivia Ginés, José (Gen.), 88
Uriburu, José F. (Gen.), 80, 102, 116–18
Urquiza, Justo José de (Gen.), 48, 50, 51
Uruguay: Amnesty Law (1986), 217; civil-military relations, 174, 214–15; coup (1973), 192; Frente Amplio, 215; "Guerra Grande" (1838–1851), 44; guerrilla wars (nineteenth century), 47; independence, 47; military presidents, 51; military regime (1973–1984), 238; plebiscite (1989), 217; Servicio de Información del Ejército, 215

Valenzuela, Fernando, 4
Vandenberg, Arthur, 144
Vargas, Getúlio, 94–96, 102, 103, 187
Vargas Pazzos, Frank (Gen.), 216
Venezuela, 210: Captaincy-General, 17; *caudillos*, 35–36; guerrilla movements, 176, 180, 195; military professionalization, 74, 177
Vernon, Edward (Adm.), 13–14
Vial, Juan de Dios (Gen.), 68
Vicat, Luis (Col.), 69
Vietnam War, 168
Vilas, Adcel (Gen.), 233
Vildoso Calderón, Guido (Gen.), 216
Villa, Francisco (Pancho), 12
Villalba y Angulo, Juan de (Lt. Gen.), 14
Villanueva, Víctor, 214
Villarroel, Gualberto (Maj.), 109–10
Villegas, Osiris G. (Gen.), 239
Visconti Osorio, Francisco (Gen.), 247

War of Jenkins' Ear (1739–1748), 13
War of the Oranges (1799), 23
War of the Pacific (1879–1884), 52–58
War of the Spanish Succession (1701–1713), 4–7
War of the Triple Alliance (1865–1870), 47, 48–52, 112
Wars: Brazil-Río de la Plata Confederation, 47; Guatemala-El Salvador (1906), 73, 131; Peru-Bolivia Confederation and Chile (1836–1839), 47; Peru-Colombia (1933), 90; Peru-Ecuador (1940–1942), 277; Peru-Ecuador dispute (Cenepa Basin, 1995), 276–78; wars of independence (impact in Spanish America, 1810–1830), 32–39; wars of political consolidation and secession, 28, 44
William II of Germany, 78
Women: in armed forces, 263; female suffrage, 208
World Bank, 196
World War I: impact in Latin America, 72–73
World War II: impact in Latin America, 139–42

Yacimientos Petrolíferos Fiscales (YPF, Argentina), 116
Yacimientos Petrolíferos Fiscales de Bolivia (YPFB), 108
Yrigoyen, Hipólito, 115–17

Zabala, Carlos María (Gen.), 268
Zarumilla-Marañón boundary dispute, 105

Latin American Silhouettes
Studies in History and Culture

William H. Beezley and Judith Ewell
Editors

Volumes Published

William H. Beezley and Judith Ewell, eds., *The Human Tradition in Latin America: The Twentieth Century* (1987). Cloth ISBN 0-8420-2283-X Paper ISBN 0-8420-2284-8

Judith Ewell and William H. Beezley, eds., *The Human Tradition in Latin America: The Nineteenth Century* (1989). Cloth ISBN 0-8420-2331-3 Paper ISBN 0-8420-2332-1

David G. LaFrance, *The Mexican Revolution in Puebla, 1908–1913: The Maderista Movement and the Failure of Liberal Reform* (1989). ISBN 0-8420-2293-7

Mark A. Burkholder, *Politics of a Colonial Career: José Baquíjano and the Audiencia of Lima*, 2d ed. (1990). Cloth ISBN 0-8420-2353-4 Paper ISBN 0-8420-2352-6

Carlos B. Gil, ed., *Hope and Frustration: Interviews with Leaders of Mexico's Political Opposition* (1992). Cloth ISBN 0-8420-2395-X Paper ISBN 0-8420-2396-8

Heidi Zogbaum, *B. Traven: A Vision of Mexico* (1992). ISBN 0-8420-2392-5

Jaime E. Rodríguez O., ed., *Patterns of Contention in Mexican History* (1992). ISBN 0-8420-2399-2

Louis A. Pérez, Jr., ed., *Slaves, Sugar, and Colonial Society: Travel Accounts of Cuba, 1801–1899* (1992). Cloth ISBN 0-8420-2354-2 Paper ISBN 0-8420-2415-8

Peter Blanchard, *Slavery and Abolition in Early Republican Peru* (1992). Cloth ISBN 0-8420-2400-X Paper ISBN 0-8420-2429-8

Paul J. Vanderwood, *Disorder and Progress: Bandits, Police, and Mexican Development*, revised and enlarged edition (1992). Cloth ISBN 0-8420-2438-7 Paper ISBN 0-8420-2439-5

Sandra McGee Deutsch and Ronald H. Dolkart, eds., *The Argentine Right: Its History and Intellectual Origins, 1910 to the Present* (1993). Cloth ISBN 0-8420-2418-2 Paper ISBN 0-8420-2419-0

Steve Ellner, *Organized Labor in Venezuela, 1958–1991: Behavior and Concerns in a Democratic Setting* (1993). ISBN 0-8420-2443-3

Paul J. Dosal, *Doing Business with the Dictators: A Political History of United Fruit in Guatemala, 1899–1944* (1993). Cloth ISBN 0-8420-2475-1 Paper ISBN 0-8420-2590-1

Marquis James, *Merchant Adventurer: The Story of W. R. Grace* (1993). ISBN 0-8420-2444-1

John Charles Chasteen and Joseph S. Tulchin, eds., *Problems in Modern Latin American History: A Reader* (1994). Cloth ISBN 0-8420-2327-5 Paper ISBN 0-8420-2328-3

Marguerite Guzmán Bouvard, *Revolutionizing Motherhood: The Mothers of the Plaza de Mayo* (1994). Cloth ISBN 0-8420-2486-7 Paper ISBN 0-8420-2487-5

William H. Beezley, Cheryl English Martin, and William E. French, eds., *Rituals of Rule, Rituals of Resistance: Public Celebrations and Popular Culture in Mexico* (1994). Cloth ISBN 0-8420-2416-6 Paper ISBN 0-8420-2417-4

Stephen R. Niblo, *War, Diplomacy, and Development: The United States and Mexico, 1938–1954* (1995). ISBN 0-8420-2550-2

G. Harvey Summ, ed., *Brazilian Mosaic: Portraits of a Diverse People and Culture* (1995). Cloth ISBN 0-8420-2491-3 Paper ISBN 0-8420-2492-1

N. Patrick Peritore and Ana Karina Galve-Peritore, eds., *Biotechnology in Latin America: Politics, Impacts, and Risks*

(1995). Cloth ISBN 0-8420-2556-1 Paper ISBN 0-8420-2557-X

Silvia Marina Arrom and Servando Ortoll, eds., *Riots in the Cities: Popular Politics and the Urban Poor in Latin America, 1765–1910* (1996). Cloth ISBN 0-8420-2580-4 Paper ISBN 0-8420-2581-2

Roderic Ai Camp, ed., *Polling for Democracy: Public Opinion and Political Liberalization in Mexico* (1996). ISBN 0-8420-2583-9

Brian Loveman and Thomas M. Davies, Jr., eds., *The Politics of Antipolitics: The Military in Latin America*, 3d ed., revised and updated (1996). Cloth ISBN 0-8420-2609-6 Paper ISBN 0-8420-2611-8

Joseph S. Tulchin, Andrés Serbín, and Rafael Hernández, eds., *Cuba and the Caribbean: Regional Issues and Trends in the Post-Cold War Era* (1997). ISBN 0-8420-2652-5

Thomas W. Walker, ed., *Nicaragua without Illusions: Regime Transition and Structural Adjustment in the 1990s* (1997). Cloth ISBN 0-8420-2578-2 Paper ISBN 0-8420-2579-0

Dianne Walta Hart, *Undocumented in L.A.: An Immigrant's Story* (1997). Cloth ISBN 0-8420-2648-7 Paper ISBN 0-8420-2649-5

Jaime E. Rodríguez O. and Kathryn Vincent, eds., *Myths, Misdeeds, and Misunderstandings: The Roots of Conflict in U.S.-Mexican Relations* (1997). ISBN 0-8420-2662-2

Jaime E. Rodríguez O. and Kathryn Vincent, eds., *Common Border, Uncommon Paths: Race, Culture, and National Identity in U.S.-Mexican Relations* (1997). ISBN 0-8420-2673-8

William H. Beezley and Judith Ewell, eds., *The Human Tradition in Modern Latin America* (1997). Cloth ISBN 0-8420-2612-6 Paper ISBN 0-8420-2613-4

Donald F. Stevens, ed., *Based on a True Story: Latin American History at the Movies* (1997). ISBN 0-8420-2582-0

Jaime E. Rodríguez O., ed., *The Origins of Mexican National Politics, 1808–1847* (1997). Paper ISBN 0-8420-2723-8

Che Guevara, *Guerrilla Warfare*, with revised and updated introduction and case studies by Brian Loveman and Thomas M. Davies, Jr., 3d ed. (1997). Cloth ISBN 0-8420-2677-0 Paper ISBN 0-8420-2678-9

Adrian A. Bantjes, *As If Jesus Walked on Earth: Cardenismo, Sonora, and the Mexican Revolution* (1998). ISBN 0-8420-2653-3

Henry A. Dietz and Gil Shidlo, eds., *Urban Elections in Democratic Latin America* (1998). Cloth ISBN 0-8420-2627-4 Paper ISBN 0-8420-2628-2

A. Kim Clark, *The Redemptive Work: Railway and Nation in Ecuador, 1895–1930* (1998). ISBN 0-8420-2674-6

Joseph S. Tulchin, ed., with Allison M. Garland, *Argentina: The Challenges of Modernization* (1998). ISBN 0-8420-2721-1

Louis A. Pérez, Jr., ed., *Impressions of Cuba in the Nineteenth Century: The Travel Diary of Joseph J. Dimock* (1998). Cloth ISBN 0-8420-2657-6 Paper ISBN 0-8420-2658-4

June E. Hahner, ed., *Women through Women's Eyes: Latin American Women in Nineteenth-Century Travel Accounts* (1998). Cloth ISBN 0-8420-2633-9 Paper ISBN 0-8420-2634-7

James P. Brennan, ed., *Peronism and Argentina* (1998). ISBN 0-8420-2706-8

John Mason Hart, ed., *Border Crossings: Mexican and Mexican-American Workers* (1998). Cloth ISBN 0-8420-2716-5 Paper ISBN 0-8420-2717-3

Brian Loveman, *For* la Patria: *Politics and the Armed Forces in Latin America* (1999). Cloth ISBN 0-8420-2772-6 Paper ISBN 0-8420-2773-4

Guy P. C. Thomson, with David G. LaFrance, *Patriotism, Politics, and Popular Liberalism in Nineteenth-Century Mexico: Juan Francisco Lucas and the Puebla Sierra* (1999). ISBN 0-8420-2683-5

K. Lynn Stoner, ed./comp., with Luís Hipólito Serrano Pérez, *Cuban and Cuban-American Women: An Annotated Bibliography* (1999). ISBN 0-8420-2643-6

Robert Woodmansee Herr, in collaboration with Richard Herr, *An American Family in the Mexican Revolution* (1999). ISBN 0-8420-2724-6

Juan Pedro Viqueira Albán, trans. Sonya Lipsett-Rivera and Sergio Rivera Ayala, *Propriety and Permissiveness in Bourbon Mexico* (1999). Cloth ISBN 0-8420-2466-2 Paper ISBN 0-8420-2467-0

David E. Lorey, *The U.S.-Mexican Border in the Twentieth Century* (1999). Cloth ISBN 0-8420-2755-6 Paper ISBN 0-8420-2756-4

Mark T. Gilderhus, *The Second Century: U.S.-Latin American Relations since 1889* (2000). Cloth ISBN 0-8420-2413-1 Paper ISBN 0-8420-2414-X